Series V, No. 41

**Department of Economic
and Social Affairs**
Statistics Division

D0730304

World Statistics Pocketbook 2017 edition

United Nations, New York, 2017

The **Department of Economic and Social Affairs** of the United Nations Secretariat is a vital interface between global policies in the economic, social and environmental spheres and national action. The Department works in three main interlinked areas: (i) it compiles, generates and analyses a wide range of economic, social and environmental data and information on which Member States of the United Nations draw to review common problems and to take stock of policy options; (ii) it facilitates the negotiations of Member States in many intergovernmental bodies on joint courses of action to address ongoing or emerging global challenges; and (iii) it advises interested Governments on the ways and means of translating policy frameworks developed in United Nations conferences and summits into programmes at the country level and, through technical assistance, helps build national capacities.

Visit the United Nations World Wide Web site on the Internet:
For the Department of Economic and Social Affairs,
    http://www.un.org/esa/desa/
For statistics and statistical publications,
    http://unstats.un.org/unsd/
For UN publications, https://unp.un.org/

ST/ESA/STAT/SER.V/41
United Nations Publication
Sales No. E.17.XVII.14
ISBN-13: 978-92-1-161626-2
eISBN: 978-92-1-362704-4
Print ISSN: 2411-8915
Online ISSN: 2411-894X

Contents

World, Regional and Country profiles

Contents (*continued*)

Contents (*continued*)

Explanatory notes

The following symbols and abbreviations have been used in the *World Statistics Pocketbook*:

.	A point is used to indicate decimals.
...	Data are not available or not applicable.
~0.0	Not zero, but less than half of the unit employed.
−~0.0	Not zero, but negative and less than half of the unit employed.
%	Percentage
000	Thousands
CFA	African Financial Community
CFP	Change Franc Pacifique
CIF	Cost, Insurance and Freight
CO_2	Carbon dioxide
const.	Constant
CPI	Consumer price index
est.	Estimate
F	Females
FOB	Free on board
GDP	Gross domestic product
GNI	Gross national income
GVA	Gross value added
ISIC	International Standard Industrial Classification
ISO	International Organization for Standardization
Km^2	Square kilometres
M	Males
Nes	Not elsewhere specified
pop.	Population
SAR	Special Administrative Region
UN	United Nations
UNHCR	Office of the UN High Commissioner for Refugees
UNSD	United Nations Statistics Division
US$/USD	United States dollars

The metric system of weights and measures has been employed in the *World Statistics Pocketbook*. The equivalents of the basic British Imperial and United States weights and measures are as follows:

Area	1 square kilometre	= 0.386102 square mile
Weight or mass	1 ton	= 1.102311 short tons or
		= 0.987207 long ton
	1 kilogram	= 35.273962 avoirdupois ounces
		= 2.204623 avoirdupois pounds
Distance	1 kilometre	= 0.621371 mile
	1 millimetre	= 0.039 inch
Temperature	°C	= (°F - 32) × 5/9

The *World Statistics Pocketbook* is an annual compilation of key economic, social and environmental indicators, presented in one-page profiles. This edition includes profiles for the 30 world geographical regions and 232 countries or areas. Prepared by the United Nations Statistics Division of the Department of Economic and Social Affairs, it responds to General Assembly resolution 2626 (XXV), in which the Secretary-General is requested to supply basic national data that will increase international public awareness of countries' development efforts.

The indicators shown are selected from the wealth of international statistical information compiled regularly by the Statistics Division and the Population Division of the United Nations, the statistical services of the United Nations specialized agencies and other international organizations and institutions. Special recognition is gratefully given for their assistance in continually providing data.

Organization of the Pocketbook

The profiles are presented first with the world and its geographical regions and sub-regions, based on the M49 regional classification[1], and then countries and areas alphabetically according to their names in English. Each profile is organised into 5 sections, where relevant and/or available:

- *General information:* includes data on surface area, population and population density, sex ratio of the population, capital city and its population, currency and its exchange rate to the US dollar, location by geographical region and the date of admission to the United Nations.

- *Economic indicators:* includes data on national accounts Gross domestic product (GDP), GDP per capita, GDP growth rate, Gross Value Added (GVA) share by industry, employment share by industry, unemployment, labour force participation, consumer price index, production indices (industry, agriculture and food), the value of total exports, imports and the trade balance and balance of payments.

- *Major trading partners:* shows a country's main trading partners

- *Social indicators:* includes data on population (growth rates, including for the urban population), total fertility rate, life expectancy at birth, population age distribution, international migrant stock, refugees, infant mortality rate, health (expenditure and physicians), education (expenditure and gross enrolment ratios), intentional homicide rate and seats held by women in national parliaments.

- *Environmental and infrastructure indicators:* includes data on mobile-cellular telephone subscriptions, internet users, Research &

---

[1] See UNSD website: https://unstats.un.org/unsd/methodology/m49/

Introduction *(continued)*

Development expenditure, threatened species, forested area, CO2 emission estimates, energy production and energy supply per capita, tourist arrivals, important sites for terrestrial biodiversity protected, population using improved drinking water sources and improved sanitation facilities and Official Development Assistance received or disbursed.

The complete set of indicators, listed by category and in the order in which they appear in the profiles, is shown before the country profile section (see page ix). Not all indicators are shown for each country or area due to different degrees of data availability.

The technical notes section, which follows the country profile pages, contains brief descriptions of the concepts and methodologies used in the compilation of the indicators as well as information on the statistical sources for the indicators. Readers interested in longer time-series data or more detailed descriptions of the concepts or methodologies should consult the primary sources of the data and the references listed in the section following the technical notes.

For brevity the Pocketbook omits specific information on the source or methodology for individual data points, and when a data point is estimated no distinction is made between whether the estimation was done by the international or national organization. See the technical notes section for the primary source which may provide this information.

Time period

This issue of the *World Statistics Pocketbook* presents data for the economic, social, environmental and infrastructure sections for three reference years - 2005, 2010 and 2017 - when available or the most recent data previous to these years, back to 2000. These instances are footnoted in each profile. For the general information and major trading partners sections the reference year is 2017 and 2016 respectively, unless otherwise footnoted.

Acknowledgement

The *World Statistics Pocketbook* is prepared annually by the Statistical Services Branch of the Statistics Division, Department of Economic and Social Affairs of the United Nations Secretariat. The programme manager is Matthias Reister and the editor is Ian Rutherford. David Carter, Anuradha Chimata, and Mohamed Nabassoua provided production assistance and Eduardo Belinchon provided IT support. Comments on this publication are welcome and may be sent by e-mail to statistics@un.org.

Profile information and indicator list*

General information

Region
Population (000)
Population density (per km^2)
Capital city
Capital city pop. (000)

UN membership date
Surface area (km^2)
Sex ratio (males per 100 females)
National currency
Exchange rate (per US$)

Economic indicators

GDP: Gross domestic product (million current US$)
GDP growth rate (annual %, constant 2005 prices)
GDP per capita (current US$)
Economy: Agriculture, Industry and Services (% of Gross Value Added)
Employment: Agriculture, Industry and Services (% of employed)
Unemployment (% of labour force)
Labour force participation (% of female/male population)
CPI: Consumer price index (2010=100)
Agricultural production index (2004-2006=100)
Food production index (2004-2006=100)
Index of industrial production (2005=100)
International trade: Exports, Imports and Balance (million US$)
Balance of payments, current account (million US$)

Major trading partners (% of Exports and Imports)

Social indicators

Population growth rate (average annual %)
Urban population (% of total population)
Urban population growth rate (average annual %)
Fertility rate, total (live births per woman)
Life expectancy at birth (females/males, years)
Population age distribution (0-14 and 60+ years, %)
International migrant stock (000/% of total pop.)
Refugees and others of concern to UNHCR (000)
Infant mortality rate (per 1 000 live births)
Health: Total expenditure (% of GDP)
Health: Physicians (per 1 000 pop.)
Education: Government expenditure (% of GDP)
Education: Primary, Secondary and Tertiary gross enrolment ratio
(females/males per 100 population)
Intentional homicide rate (per 100 000 population)
Seats held by women in national parliaments (% of total seats)

Environment and infrastructure indicators

Mobile-cellular subscriptions (per 100 inhabitants)
Individuals using the Internet (per 100 inhabitants)
Research & Development expenditure (% of GDP)
Threatened species (number)
Forested area (% of land area)
CO$_2$ emission estimates (million tons/tons per capita)
Energy production, primary (Petajoules)
Energy supply per capita (Gigajoules)
Tourist/visitor arrivals at national borders (000)
Important sites for terrestrial biodiversity protected (%)
Population using improved drinking water sources (urban/rural, %)
Population using improved sanitation facilities (urban/rural, %)
Net Official Development Assistance disbursed (% of GNI of donor)
Net Official Development Assistance received (% of GNI of recipient)

* The complete set of information and indicators listed here may not be shown for
  each country or area depending upon data availability. The technical notes provide
  a brief description of each information item and indicator.

World, Regional and Country profiles

World

Population (000, 2017) 7 550 262[a]	Surface area (km2) 136 162 000[b]
Pop. density (per km2, 2017) 58.0[a]	Sex ratio (m per 100 f, 2017) 101.8[a]

Economic indicators	2005	2010	2017
GDP: Gross domestic product (million current US$)	47 539 451	65 911 732	74 176 854[b]
GDP growth rate (annual %, const. 2005 prices)	3.6	4.1	2.6[b]
GDP per capita (current US$)	7 293.3	9 513.7	10 095.0[b]
Employment: Agriculture (% of employed)[c]	36.0	32.4	28.8
Employment: Industry (% of employed)[c]	20.5	21.3	21.5
Employment: Services (% of employed)[c]	43.5	46.3	49.7
Unemployment (% of labour force)[c]	6.2	6.1	5.8
Labour force participation (female/male pop. %)[c]	51.9 / 77.6	50.0 / 76.5	49.4 / 76.1
Agricultural production index (2004-2006=100)	100	113	124[d]
Food production index (2004-2006=100)	100	113	124[d]
International trade: Exports (million US$)	10 372 753	15 097 799	15 840 182[e]
International trade: Imports (million US$)	10 576 337	15 258 942	15 931 970[e]
International trade: Balance (million US$)	- 203 584	- 161 143	- 91 788[e]

Social indicators	2005	2010	2017
Population growth rate (average annual %)[f]	1.3	1.2	1.2[b]
Urban population (% of total population)	49.1	51.6	54.0[b]
Urban population growth rate (average annual %)[f]	2.3	2.2	2.1[b]
Fertility rate, total (live births per woman)[f]	2.6	2.6	2.5[b]
Life expectancy at birth (females/males, years)[f]	69.5 / 65.0	71.3 / 66.9	73.1 / 68.6[b]
Population age distribution (0-14 and 60+ years, %)	28.0 / 10.3	26.8 / 11.1	25.9 / 12.7[a]
International migrant stock (000/% of total pop.)	191 269.1 / 2.9	221 714.2 / 3.2	243 700.2 / 3.3[b]
Refugees and others of concern to UNHCR (000)	...	...	57 959.7[b]
Infant mortality rate (per 1 000 live births)[f]	49.1	41.3	35.0[b]
Education: Primary gross enrol. ratio (f/m per 100 pop.)	99.7 / 104.6	103.9 / 106.6	104.1 / 104.5[b]
Education: Secondary gross enrol. ratio (f/m per 100 pop.)	62.0 / 65.5	69.5 / 72.0	76.0 / 76.9[b]
Education: Tertiary gross enrol. ratio (f/m per 100 pop.)	24.8 / 23.7	30.4 / 28.3	37.7 / 33.8[b]
Intentional homicide rate (per 100 000 pop.)	...	...	5.3[g,b]
Seats held by women in national parliaments (%)	15.9	19.0	23.4

Environment and infrastructure indicators	2005	2010	2017
Individuals using the Internet (per 100 inhabitants)	15.8	29.1	43.7[b]
Research & Development expenditure (% of GDP)	1.5	1.6	1.7[d]
Forested area (% of land area)	31.0	30.9	30.8[d]
CO2 emission estimates (million tons/tons per capita)	29 490.0 / 4.5	33 472.4 / 4.8	36 138.3 / 5.0[d]
Energy production, primary (Petajoules)	476 824	530 011	567 417[d]
Energy supply per capita (Gigajoules)	71	75	75[d]
Important sites for terrestrial biodiversity protected (%)	40.7	44.8	46.6
Pop. using improved drinking water (urban/rural, %)	95.8 / 75.7	96.1 / 80.2	96.4 / 84.5[b]
Pop. using improved sanitation facilities (urban/rural, %)	80.4 / 44.2	81.4 / 47.6	82.2 / 50.5[b]

a Projected estimate (medium fertility variant). b 2015. c Estimate. d 2014. e 2016. f Data refers to a 5-year period preceding the reference year. g Data is for 2015, or latest available data from 2010 onwards.

Africa

Region	World	Population (000, 2017)	1 256 268[a]
Surface area (km2)	30 311 000[b]	Pop. density (per km2, 2017)	42.4[a]
Sex ratio (m per 100 f, 2017)	99.8[a]		

Economic indicators	2005	2010	2017
GDP: Gross domestic product (million current US$)	1 116 958	1 942 476	2 267 610[b]
GDP growth rate (annual %, const. 2005 prices)	5.9	5.2	3.1[b]
GDP per capita (current US$)	1 215.6	1 863.2	1 914.4[b]
Employment: Agriculture (% of employed)[c]	53.3	52.3	50.9
Employment: Industry (% of employed)[c]	11.9	12.8	12.9
Employment: Services (% of employed)[c]	34.8	34.9	36.2
Unemployment (% of labour force)[c]	8.6	8.1	8.0
Labour force participation (female/male pop. %)[c]	53.8 / 75.4	54.5 / 75.4	55.6 / 75.8
Agricultural production index (2004-2006=100)	100	118	129[d]
Food production index (2004-2006=100)	100	118	129[d]
International trade: Exports (million US$)	306 656	496 304	401 945[e]
International trade: Imports (million US$)	246 228	467 978	475 287[e]
International trade: Balance (million US$)	60 428	28 325	- 73 342[e]

Social indicators	2005	2010	2017
Population growth rate (average annual %)[f]	2.5	2.5	2.6[b]
Urban population (% of total population)	36.3	38.3	40.4[b]
Urban population growth rate (average annual %)[f]	3.4	3.5	3.5[b]
Fertility rate, total (live births per woman)[f]	5.1	4.9	4.7[b]
Life expectancy at birth (females/males, years)[f]	55.2 / 52.2	58.4 / 55.5	61.9 / 58.6[b]
Population age distribution (0-14 and 60+ years, %)	41.8 / 5.2	41.4 / 5.2	40.8 / 5.5[a]
International migrant stock (000/% of total pop.)	15 191.1 / 1.7	16 840.0 / 1.6	20 649.6 / 1.7[b]
Refugees and others of concern to UNHCR (000)	...	...	17 067.3[b]
Infant mortality rate (per 1 000 live births)[f]	80.7	68.1	57.2[b]
Education: Primary gross enrol. ratio (f/m per 100 pop.)	89.1 / 99.5	94.7 / 101.3	96.5 / 102.2[c,b]
Education: Secondary gross enrol. ratio (f/m per 100 pop.)	35.7 / 42.2	41.8 / 48.4	45.2 / 50.2[c,b]
Education: Tertiary gross enrol. ratio (f/m per 100 pop.)	8.6 / 10.8	10.4 / 12.4	11.8 / 13.7[c,b]

Environment and infrastructure indicators	2005	2010	2017
Forested area (% of land area)	22.1	21.5	21.1[d]
Energy production, primary (Petajoules)	44 944	47 607	45 612[d]
Energy supply per capita (Gigajoules)	27	27	27[d]

a Projected estimate (medium fertility variant). b 2015. c Estimate. d 2014. e 2016. f Data refers to a 5-year period preceding the reference year.

Northern Africa

Region	Africa	Population (000, 2017)	233 604[a]
Surface area (km2)	7 880 000[b]	Pop. density (per km2, 2017)	30.1[a]
Sex ratio (m per 100 f, 2017)	100.9[a]		

Economic indicators	2005	2010	2017
GDP: Gross domestic product (million current US$)	373 106	647 993	736 257[b]
GDP growth rate (annual %, const. 2005 prices)	5.7	4.4	3.3[b]
GDP per capita (current US$)	1 917.4	3 188.9	3 296.9[b]
Employment: Agriculture (% of employed)[c]	30.2	27.0	24.5
Employment: Industry (% of employed)[c]	22.1	25.7	25.5
Employment: Services (% of employed)[c]	47.7	47.4	50.0
Unemployment (% of labour force)[c]	12.7	10.3	12.0
Labour force participation (female/male pop. %)[c]	21.4 / 74.3	22.0 / 73.8	22.9 / 74.1
Agricultural production index (2004-2006=100)	99	111	123[d]
Food production index (2004-2006=100)	99	112	124[d]
International trade: Exports (million US$)	114 104	165 544	95 253[e]
International trade: Imports (million US$)	87 571	181 147	182 830[e]
International trade: Balance (million US$)	26 533	- 15 603	- 87 577[e]

Social indicators	2005	2010	2017
Population growth rate (average annual %)[f]	1.7	1.7	1.9[b]
Urban population (% of total population)	49.4	50.5	51.6[b]
Urban population growth rate (average annual %)[f]	2.0	2.1	2.1[b]
Fertility rate, total (live births per woman)[f]	3.2	3.1	3.3[b]
Life expectancy at birth (females/males, years)[f]	69.9 / 66.0	71.6 / 67.7	72.8 / 69.4[b]
Population age distribution (0-14 and 60+ years, %)	33.3 / 7.0	31.9 / 7.4	32.5 / 8.3[a]
International migrant stock (000/% of total pop.)[g]	1 782.1 / 1.0	1 921.6 / 0.9	2 159.0 / 1.0[b]
Infant mortality rate (per 1 000 live births)[f]	39.3	33.3	28.1[b]
Education: Primary gross enrol. ratio (f/m per 100 pop.)[g]	100.2 / 107.1	107.3 / 112.0	107.5 / 110.3[c,b]
Education: Secondary gross enrol. ratio (f/m per 100 pop.)[g]	73.7 / 74.3[c]	77.7 / 78.5	86.3 / 86.8[c,b]
Education: Tertiary gross enrol. ratio (f/m per 100 pop.)[g]	24.9 / 26.2	30.0 / 28.1	37.4 / 33.7[b]
Seats held by women in national parliaments (%)	8.7	10.9	23.8

Environment and infrastructure indicators	2005	2010	2017
Individuals using the Internet (per 100 inhabitants)	9.1	24.1	38.9[b]
Research & Development expenditure (% of GDP)	0.3	0.4	0.5[d]
Forested area (% of land area)	4.4	4.4	3.5[d]
Important sites for terrestrial biodiversity protected (%)[g]	22.1	25.3	38.6
Pop. using improved drinking water (urban/rural, %)	92.6 / 76.8	91.5 / 76.8	94.9 / 90.2[b]
Pop. using improved sanitation facilities (urban/rural, %)	86.0 / 59.3	85.8 / 62.9	92.2 / 86.1[b]

a Projected estimate (medium fertility variant). b 2015. c Estimate. d 2014. e 2016. f Data refers to a 5-year period preceding the reference year. g Excluding Sudan.

Sub-Saharan Africa

Region	Africa	Population (000, 2017)	1 022 664 [a]	
Surface area (km2)	22 431 000 [b,c]	Pop. density (per km2, 2017)	46.7 [a]	
Sex ratio (m per 100 f, 2017)	99.5 [a]			

Economic indicators	2005	2010	2017
Employment: Agriculture (% of employed) [d]	57.9	57.4	55.6
Employment: Industry (% of employed) [d]	9.9	10.2	10.7
Employment: Services (% of employed) [d]	32.2	32.4	33.7
Unemployment (% of labour force) [d]	7.8	7.6	7.2
Labour force participation (female/male pop. %) [d]	63.7 / 75.8	64.1 / 75.8	64.6 / 76.3
International trade: Exports (million US$)	192 552	330 760	306 692 [e]
International trade: Imports (million US$)	158 657	286 832	292 458 [e]
International trade: Balance (million US$)	33 895	43 928	14 234 [e]

Social indicators	2005	2010	2017
Population growth rate (average annual %) [f]	2.7	2.7	2.7 [c]
Urban population (% of total population)	33.0	35.4	37.9 [c]
Urban population growth rate (average annual %) [f]	4.0	4.1	4.0 [c]
Fertility rate, total (live births per woman) [f]	5.6	5.4	5.1 [c]
Life expectancy at birth (females/males, years) [f]	52.1 / 49.3	55.7 / 52.9	59.5 / 56.2 [c]
Population age distribution (0-14 and 60+ years, %)	44.0 / 4.7	43.7 / 4.7	42.7 / 4.8 [a]
International migrant stock (000/% of total pop.) [g]	13 951.1 / 1.9	15 496.8 / 1.8	18 994.0 / 2.0 [c]
Infant mortality rate (per 1 000 live births) [f]	87.3	73.7	62.1 [c]
Education: Primary gross enrol. ratio (f/m per 100 pop.) [g]	87.4 / 98.3	93.2 / 100.0	95.2 / 101.3 [d,c]
Education: Secondary gross enrol. ratio (f/m per 100 pop.) [g]	28.2 / 35.6	35.7 / 43.2	39.6 / 45.0 [d,c]
Education: Tertiary gross enrol. ratio (f/m per 100 pop.) [g]	5.0 / 7.2	6.4 / 9.0	7.4 / 10.2 [d,c]
Intentional homicide rate (per 100 000 pop.)	...	...	9.6 [h,c]
Seats held by women in national parliaments (%)	14.4	18.4	23.7

Environment and infrastructure indicators	2005	2010	2017
Individuals using the Internet (per 100 inhabitants)	2.1	9.3	22.2 [c]
Research & Development expenditure (% of GDP)	0.4	0.4	0.4 [i]
Forested area (% of land area) [b]	29.0	28.3	28.1 [i]
Important sites for terrestrial biodiversity protected (%)	41.5	45.7	47.4
Pop. using improved drinking water (urban/rural, %)	85.1 / 46.0	86.1 / 51.0	86.8 / 56.1 [c]
Pop. using improved sanitation facilities (urban/rural, %)	40.0 / 20.6	40.4 / 22.1	40.3 / 23.3 [c]

a Projected estimate (medium fertility variant). **b** Calculated by the United Nations Statistics Division. **c** 2015. **d** Estimate. **e** 2016. **f** Data refers to a 5-year period preceding the reference year. **g** Including Sudan. **h** Data is for 2015, or latest available data from 2010 onwards. **i** 2014.

Region	Sub-Saharan Africa	Population (000, 2017)	422 036[a]
Surface area (km2)	7 005 000[b]	Pop. density (per km2, 2017)	63.3[a]
Sex ratio (m per 100 f, 2017)	98.5[a]		

Economic indicators	2005	2010	2017
GDP: Gross domestic product (million current US$)	110 318	212 886	307 528[b]
GDP growth rate (annual %, const. 2005 prices)	6.3	7.7	5.5[b]
GDP per capita (current US$)	382.3	623.0	781.8[b]
Employment: Agriculture (% of employed)[c]	66.3	70.6	69.4
Employment: Industry (% of employed)[c]	7.7	7.1	7.5
Employment: Services (% of employed)[c]	26.0	22.3	23.1
Unemployment (% of labour force)[c]	6.9	6.8	6.5
Labour force participation (female/male pop. %)[c]	77.0 / 84.8	76.5 / 84.1	75.1 / 83.5
Agricultural production index (2004-2006=100)	100	126	140[d]
Food production index (2004-2006=100)	100	127	141[d]
International trade: Exports (million US$)	16 297	31 282	37 487[e]
International trade: Imports (million US$)	31 243	62 505	81 096[e]
International trade: Balance (million US$)	- 14 945	- 31 223	- 43 609[e]

Social indicators	2005	2010	2017
Population growth rate (average annual %)[f]	2.8	2.9	2.8[b]
Urban population (% of total population)	21.8	23.5	25.6[b]
Urban population growth rate (average annual %)[f]	3.9	4.3	4.5[b]
Fertility rate, total (live births per woman)[f]	5.8	5.3	4.9[b]
Life expectancy at birth (females/males, years)[f]	53.5 / 50.4	58.5 / 55.5	63.4 / 59.5[b]
Population age distribution (0-14 and 60+ years, %)	45.5 / 4.5	44.8 / 4.5	42.8 / 4.7[a]
International migrant stock (000/% of total pop.)	4 745.8 / 1.6	4 657.1 / 1.4	6 129.1 / 1.6[b]
Infant mortality rate (per 1 000 live births)[f]	77.4	62.8	52.2[b]
Seats held by women in national parliaments (%)	16.6	21.6	29.7

Environment and infrastructure indicators	2005	2010	2017
Individuals using the Internet (per 100 inhabitants)	1.3	5.4	15.3[b]
Forested area (% of land area)	33.6	32.4	32.8[d]
Pop. using improved drinking water (urban/rural, %)	84.7 / 43.6	85.3 / 49.3	85.7 / 55.9[b]
Pop. using improved sanitation facilities (urban/rural, %)	34.8 / 18.5	35.6 / 21.5	35.3 / 24.0[b]

a Projected estimate (medium fertility variant). **b** 2015. **c** Estimate. **d** 2014. **e** 2016. **f** Data refers to a 5-year period preceding the reference year.

Middle Africa

Region: Sub-Saharan Africa
Surface area (km2): 6 613 000[b]
Sex ratio (m per 100 f, 2017): 99.3[a]
Population (000, 2017): 163 495[a]
Pop. density (per km2, 2017): 25.2[a]

Economic indicators	2005	2010	2017
GDP: Gross domestic product (million current US$)	97 928	182 587	231 955[b]
GDP growth rate (annual %, const. 2005 prices)	8.5	4.4	3.4[b]
GDP per capita (current US$)	875.0	1 398.1	1 526.5[b]
Employment: Agriculture (% of employed)[c]	58.1	57.5	55.4
Employment: Industry (% of employed)[c]	11.5	11.5	11.4
Employment: Services (% of employed)[c]	30.4	31.0	33.1
Unemployment (% of labour force)[c]	5.2	5.1	5.0
Labour force participation (female/male pop. %)[c]	67.8 / 75.7	67.7 / 75.5	67.8 / 75.3
Agricultural production index (2004-2006=100)	102	133	137[d]
Food production index (2004-2006=100)	102	135	139[d]
International trade: Exports (million US$)	48 958	90 869	43 292[e]
International trade: Imports (million US$)	18 680	43 639	39 432[e]
International trade: Balance (million US$)	30 278	47 231	3 860[e]

Social indicators	2005	2010	2017
Population growth rate (average annual %)[f]	3.1	3.2	3.1[b]
Urban population (% of total population)	39.1	41.5	44.0[b]
Urban population growth rate (average annual %)[f]	4.1	4.1	3.9[b]
Fertility rate, total (live births per woman)[f]	6.4	6.2	5.9[b]
Life expectancy at birth (females/males, years)[f]	52.2 / 49.3	55.9 / 52.9	59.1 / 55.8[b]
Population age distribution (0-14 and 60+ years, %)	45.6 / 4.6	45.7 / 4.5	45.5 / 4.6[a]
International migrant stock (000/% of total pop.)	1 928.8 / 1.7	2 140.0 / 1.6	2 307.7 / 1.5[b]
Infant mortality rate (per 1 000 live births)[f]	100.1	84.6	72.2[b]
Seats held by women in national parliaments (%)	11.2	13.5	17.4

Environment and infrastructure indicators	2005	2010	2017
Individuals using the Internet (per 100 inhabitants)	0.7	2.0	8.3[b]
Forested area (% of land area)	47.8	47.2	46.8[d]
Pop. using improved drinking water (urban/rural, %)	82.2 / 34.6	83.4 / 35.7	83.8 / 36.5[b]
Pop. using improved sanitation facilities (urban/rural, %)	43.1 / 19.4	44.7 / 21.6	45.7 / 23.6[b]

a Projected estimate (medium fertility variant). b 2015. c Estimate. d 2014. e 2016. f Data refers to a 5-year period preceding the reference year.

Region	Sub-Saharan Africa	Population (000, 2017)	65 143[a]
Surface area (km2)	2 675 000[b]	Pop. density (per km2, 2017)	24.6[a]
Sex ratio (m per 100 f, 2017)	96.2[a]		

Economic indicators	2005	2010	2017
GDP: Gross domestic product (million current US$)	279 299	406 135	346 595[b]
GDP growth rate (annual %, const. 2005 prices)	5.2	3.3	1.3[b]
GDP per capita (current US$)	5 053.0	6 875.9	5 533.7[b]
Employment: Agriculture (% of employed)[c]	10.9	8.7	9.7
Employment: Industry (% of employed)[c]	23.2	22.1	24.7
Employment: Services (% of employed)[c]	66.0	69.2	65.7
Unemployment (% of labour force)[c]	24.2	24.3	25.6
Labour force participation (female/male pop. %)[c]	48.0 / 62.9	45.5 / 60.9	48.0 / 62.5
Agricultural production index (2004-2006=100)	102	116	123[d]
Food production index (2004-2006=100)	102	117	124[d]
International trade: Exports (million US$)	56 076	95 227	88 777[e]
International trade: Imports (million US$)	63 786	97 572	90 027[e]
International trade: Balance (million US$)	- 7 711	- 2 345	- 1 251[e]

Social indicators	2005	2010	2017
Population growth rate (average annual %)[f]	1.3	1.1	1.4[b]
Urban population (% of total population)	56.5	59.1	61.6[b]
Urban population growth rate (average annual %)[f]	2.4	2.2	1.7[b]
Fertility rate, total (live births per woman)[f]	2.9	2.7	2.6[b]
Life expectancy at birth (females/males, years)[f]	55.8 / 50.7	55.4 / 50.6	62.7 / 56.0[b]
Population age distribution (0-14 and 60+ years, %)	32.6 / 6.6	31.2 / 7.0	29.8 / 8.1[a]
International migrant stock (000/% of total pop.)	1 439.4 / 2.6	2 203.3 / 3.7	3 435.2 / 5.5[b]
Infant mortality rate (per 1 000 live births)[f]	62.4	53.7	38.0[b]
Seats held by women in national parliaments (%)	24.6	33.4	33.4

Environment and infrastructure indicators	2005	2010	2017
Individuals using the Internet (per 100 inhabitants)	7.0	22.0	48.3[b]
Forested area (% of land area)	11.1	10.7	10.5[d]
Pop. using improved drinking water (urban/rural, %)	98.7 / 74.1	99.1 / 77.8	99.4 / 81.1[b]
Pop. using improved sanitation facilities (urban/rural, %)	66.6 / 46.4	67.8 / 51.0	68.9 / 55.1[b]

a Projected estimate (medium fertility variant). **b** 2015. **c** Estimate. **d** 2014. **e** 2016. **f** Data refers to a 5-year period preceding the reference year.

Western Africa

Region	Sub-Saharan Africa	Population (000, 2017)	371 990[a]
Surface area (km2)	6 138 000[b]	Pop. density (per km2, 2017)	61.3[a]
Sex ratio (m per 100 f, 2017)	101.3[a,c]		

Economic indicators	2005	2010	2017
GDP: Gross domestic product (million current US$)	256 307	492 876	645 275[b]
GDP growth rate (annual %, const. 2005 prices)	6.1	7.3	3.3[b]
GDP per capita (current US$)	954.6	1 600.4	1 826.8[b]
Employment: Agriculture (% of employed)[d]	54.8	47.1	43.7
Employment: Industry (% of employed)[d]	9.8	12.0	12.6
Employment: Services (% of employed)[d]	35.4	40.9	43.7
Unemployment (% of labour force)[d]	6.6	6.5	5.8
Labour force participation (female/male pop. %)[d]	51.9 / 69.5	53.7 / 70.8	55.1 / 71.9
Agricultural production index (2004-2006=100)	100	113	125[e]
Food production index (2004-2006=100)	100	115	126[e]
International trade: Exports (million US$)	71 221	113 381	137 136[f]
International trade: Imports (million US$)	44 948	83 116	81 902[f]
International trade: Balance (million US$)	26 273	30 265	55 234[f]

Social indicators	2005	2010	2017
Population growth rate (average annual %)[g]	2.6	2.7	2.7[b]
Urban population (% of total population)	38.1	41.6	45.1[b]
Urban population growth rate (average annual %)[g]	4.4	4.5	4.3[b]
Fertility rate, total (live births per woman)[c,g]	6.0	5.8	5.5[b]
Life expectancy at birth (females/males, years)[c,g]	50.2 / 48.4	53.2 / 51.5	55.6 / 53.9[b]
Population age distribution (0-14 and 60+ years, %)[c]	44.0 / 4.6	44.1 / 4.6	43.7 / 4.6[a]
International migrant stock (000/% of total pop.)	5 295.0 / 2.0	5 918.1 / 1.9	6 618.5 / 1.9[b]
Infant mortality rate (per 1 000 live births)[c,g]	95.7	82.7	70.5[b]
Seats held by women in national parliaments (%)	10.2	11.6	14.9

Environment and infrastructure indicators	2005	2010	2017
Individuals using the Internet (per 100 inhabitants)	2.5	14.3	31.1[b]
Forested area (% of land area)	12.2	11.6	11.2[e]
Pop. using improved drinking water (urban/rural, %)	82.3 / 49.8	84.1 / 56.0	85.7 / 61.5[b]
Pop. using improved sanitation facilities (urban/rural, %)	33.8 / 20.3	34.2 / 19.3	34.3 / 18.3[b]

a Projected estimate (medium fertility variant). **b** 2015. **c** Including Saint Helena. **d** Estimate. **e** 2014. **f** 2016. **g** Data refers to a 5-year period preceding the reference year.

Americas

Region	World	Population (000, 2017)	1 006 801 [a,b]
Surface area (km2)	42 322 000 [b,c]	Pop. density (per km2, 2017)	26.0 [a,b]
Sex ratio (m per 100 f, 2017)	97.8 [a,b]		

Economic indicators	2005	2010	2017
GDP: Gross domestic product (million current US$)	17 115 581	21 917 163	25 000 541 [c]
GDP growth rate (annual %, const. 2005 prices)	3.5	3.1	2.0 [c]
GDP per capita (current US$)	19 205.5	23 248.6	25 228.8 [c]
Employment: Agriculture (% of employed) [d]	10.8	10.9	10.3
Employment: Industry (% of employed) [d]	21.4	20.4	20.0
Employment: Services (% of employed) [d]	67.8	68.8	69.8
Unemployment (% of labour force) [d]	7.6	8.3	7.2
Labour force participation (female/male pop. %) [d]	54.3 / 77.1	54.4 / 75.9	54.0 / 74.5
Agricultural production index (2004-2006=100)	100	111	120 [e]
Food production index (2004-2006=100)	100	112	120 [e]
International trade: Exports (million US$)	1 835 325	2 550 359	2 711 385 [f]
International trade: Imports (million US$)	2 557 148	3 228 875	3 558 310 [f]
International trade: Balance (million US$)	- 721 823	- 678 516	- 846 925 [f]

Social indicators	2005	2010	2017
Population age distribution (0-14 and 60+ years, %) [b]	26.5 / 11.8	24.8 / 13.0	22.6 / 15.3 [a]

Environment and infrastructure indicators	2005	2010	2017
Forested area (% of land area)	41.7	41.3	41.1 [e]

a Projected estimate (medium fertility variant). **b** Calculated by the United Nations Statistics Division. **c** 2015. **d** Estimate. **e** 2014. **f** 2016.

Northern America

Region	Americas	Population (000, 2017)	361 208[a]
Surface area (km2)	21 776 000[b]	Pop. density (per km2, 2017)	19.4[a]
Sex ratio (m per 100 f, 2017)	98.1[a,c]		

Economic indicators	2005	2010	2017
GDP: Gross domestic product (million current US$)	14 269 637	16 585 978	19 597 386[b]
GDP growth rate (annual %, const. 2005 prices)	3.3	2.6	2.5[b]
GDP per capita (current US$)	43 436.4	48 197.8	54 767.0[b]
Employment: Agriculture (% of employed)[d]	1.7	1.7	1.5
Employment: Industry (% of employed)[d]	20.4	18.0	17.5
Employment: Services (% of employed)[d]	77.9	80.3	81.0
Unemployment (% of labour force)[d]	5.3	9.4	5.1
Labour force participation (female/male pop. %)[d]	58.5 / 72.2	58.0 / 70.2	56.2 / 68.3
Agricultural production index (2004-2006=100)	100	105	111[e]
Food production index (2004-2006=100)	100	106	112[e]
International trade: Exports (million US$)	1 265 374	1 665 222	1 843 292[f]
International trade: Imports (million US$)	2 048 668	2 362 939	2 656 839[f]
International trade: Balance (million US$)	- 783 295	- 697 718	- 813 547[f]

Social indicators	2005	2010	2017
Population growth rate (average annual %)[g]	0.9	0.9	0.7[b]
Urban population (% of total population)	80.0	80.8	81.6[b]
Urban population growth rate (average annual %)[g]	1.2	1.2	1.0[b]
Fertility rate, total (live births per woman)[c,g]	2.0	2.0	1.9[b]
Life expectancy at birth (females/males, years)[c,g]	80.0 / 74.8	80.9 / 75.9	81.5 / 76.8[b]
Population age distribution (0-14 and 60+ years, %)[c]	20.6 / 16.8	19.8 / 18.5	18.6 / 21.7[a]
International migrant stock (000/% of total pop.)	45 363.4 / 13.8	51 221.0 / 14.9	54 488.7 / 15.2[b]
Refugees and others of concern to UNHCR (000)	...	...	655.4[b]
Infant mortality rate (per 1 000 live births)[c,g]	6.9	6.7	5.9[b]
Seats held by women in national parliaments (%)	17.5	19.0	22.2

Environment and infrastructure indicators	2005	2010	2017
Individuals using the Internet (per 100 inhabitants)	68.7	75.2	79.2[b]
Research & Development expenditure (% of GDP)	2.5	2.7	2.6[e]
Forested area (% of land area)	34.9	35.2	35.2[e]
Pop. using improved drinking water (urban/rural, %)	99.6 / 96.9	99.5 / 97.8	99.5 / 98.2[b]
Pop. using improved sanitation facilities (urban/rural, %)	99.9 / 99.5	100.0 / 99.8	100.0 / 99.9[b]

a Projected estimate (medium fertility variant). b 2015. c Including Bermuda, Greenland, and Saint Pierre and Miquelon. d Estimate. e 2014. f 2016. g Data refers to a 5-year period preceding the reference year.

Latin America and the Caribbean

Region	Americas	Population (000, 2017)	645 593 [a]
Surface area (km2)	20 546 000 [b]	Pop. density (per km2, 2017)	32.1 [a]
Sex ratio (m per 100 f, 2017)	97.7 [a]		

Economic indicators	2005	2010	2017
GDP: Gross domestic product (million current US$)	2 845 944	5 331 185	5 403 154 [b]
GDP growth rate (annual %, const. 2005 prices)	4.3	5.7	0.1 [b]
GDP per capita (current US$)	5 058.0	8 906.0	8 534.2 [b]
Employment: Agriculture (% of employed) [c]	17.0	16.5	15.6
Employment: Industry (% of employed) [c]	22.1	21.8	21.5
Employment: Services (% of employed) [c]	60.9	61.7	63.0
Unemployment (% of labour force) [c]	9.2	7.7	8.4
Labour force participation (female/male pop. %) [c]	51.4 / 80.4	52.1 / 79.6	52.7 / 78.3
International trade: Exports (million US$)	569 951	885 137	868 093 [d]
International trade: Imports (million US$)	508 480	865 935	901 471 [d]
International trade: Balance (million US$)	61 471	19 202	- 33 378 [d]

Social indicators	2005	2010	2017
Population growth rate (average annual %) [e]	1.3	1.2	1.1 [b]
Urban population (% of total population)	76.9	78.4	79.8 [b]
Urban population growth rate (average annual %) [e]	1.8	1.5	1.4 [b]
Fertility rate, total (live births per woman) [e]	2.5	2.3	2.1 [b]
Life expectancy at birth (females/males, years) [e]	75.5 / 68.8	76.8 / 70.1	78.0 / 71.4 [b]
Population age distribution (0-14 and 60+ years, %)	29.9 / 8.8	27.6 / 9.8	24.9 / 11.8 [a]
International migrant stock (000/% of total pop.)	7 233.1 / 1.3	8 238.8 / 1.4	9 234.0 / 1.5 [b]
Refugees and others of concern to UNHCR (000)	...	...	7 071.2 [b]
Infant mortality rate (per 1 000 live births) [e]	25.4	21.4	18.7 [b]
Education: Primary gross enrol. ratio (f/m per 100 pop.)	114.0 / 117.5	110.6 / 114.1	108.3 / 110.3 [b]
Education: Secondary gross enrol. ratio (f/m per 100 pop.)	90.3 / 83.5	93.4 / 86.2	95.3 / 90.5 [b]
Education: Tertiary gross enrol. ratio (f/m per 100 pop.)	33.7 / 27.9	45.8 / 35.4	53.0 / 40.3 [c,b]
Intentional homicide rate (per 100 000 pop.)	...	...	22.3 [f,b]
Seats held by women in national parliaments (%)	19.0	22.7	29.4

Environment and infrastructure indicators	2005	2010	2017
Individuals using the Internet (per 100 inhabitants)	16.6	34.7	54.6 [b]
Research & Development expenditure (% of GDP)	0.6	0.6	0.7 [g]
Forested area (% of land area) [h]	47.9	47.0	46.6 [g]
Important sites for terrestrial biodiversity protected (%)	32.7	36.3	38.0
Pop. using improved drinking water (urban/rural, %)	96.3 / 75.7	96.9 / 80.2	97.4 / 83.9 [b]
Pop. using improved sanitation facilities (urban/rural, %)	85.1 / 53.6	86.7 / 59.4	87.9 / 64.1 [b]

a Projected estimate (medium fertility variant). **b** 2015. **c** Estimate. **d** 2016. **e** Data refers to a 5-year period preceding the reference year. **f** Data is for 2015, or latest available data from 2010 onwards. **g** 2014. **h** Calculated by the United Nations Statistics Division.

Caribbean

Region	Latin America & Caribbean	Population (000, 2017)	43 883[a]
Surface area (km2)	234 000[b]	Pop. density (per km2, 2017)	194.2[a]
Sex ratio (m per 100 f, 2017)	97.9[a,c]		

Economic indicators	2005	2010	2017
GDP: Gross domestic product (million current US$)	219 320	286 653	337 854[b]
GDP growth rate (annual %, const. 2005 prices)	3.7	1.7	2.7[b]
GDP per capita (current US$)	5 613.1	7 053.1	8 005.4[b]
Employment: Agriculture (% of employed)[d]	22.6	22.8	20.6
Employment: Industry (% of employed)[d]	18.5	16.4	14.8
Employment: Services (% of employed)[d]	58.8	60.8	64.7
Unemployment (% of labour force)[d]	10.7	10.1	10.3
Labour force participation (female/male pop. %)[d]	47.4 / 71.2	49.0 / 70.6	50.5 / 70.7
Agricultural production index (2004-2006=100)	98	107	118[e]
Food production index (2004-2006=100)	98	107	119[e]
International trade: Exports (million US$)	21 331	24 192	29 845[f]
International trade: Imports (million US$)	36 923	51 256	50 576[f]
International trade: Balance (million US$)	- 15 592	- 27 064	- 20 731[f]

Social indicators	2005	2010	2017
Population growth rate (average annual %)[g]	0.9	0.8	0.7[b]
Urban population (% of total population)	64.3	67.5	70.4[b]
Urban population growth rate (average annual %)[g]	1.9	1.7	1.5[b]
Fertility rate, total (live births per woman)[c,g]	2.5	2.4	2.3[b]
Life expectancy at birth (females/males, years)[c,g]	72.6 / 67.4	74.0 / 68.7	75.2 / 69.8[b]
Population age distribution (0-14 and 60+ years, %)[c]	28.2 / 11.1	26.5 / 12.0	24.5 / 13.8[a]
International migrant stock (000/% of total pop.)	1 328.7 / 3.3	1 345.7 / 3.2	1 367.4 / 3.2[b]
Infant mortality rate (per 1 000 live births)[c,g]	33.0	30.4	27.0[b]
Seats held by women in national parliaments (%)	26.0	29.4	33.8

Environment and infrastructure indicators	2005	2010	2017
Individuals using the Internet (per 100 inhabitants)	12.6	23.8	41.5[b]
Forested area (% of land area)	28.1	29.8	31.8[e]
Pop. using improved drinking water (urban/rural, %)	90.5 / 71.5	88.2 / 73.0	85.8 / 74.5[b]
Pop. using improved sanitation facilities (urban/rural, %)	81.1 / 57.0	80.2 / 60.0	79.1 / 62.3[b]

a Projected estimate (medium fertility variant). **b** 2015. **c** Including Anguilla, Bonaire, St. Eustatius & Saba, British Virgin Islands, Cayman Islands, Dominica, Montserrat, Saint Kitts and Nevis, Sint Maarten (Dutch part) and Turks and Caicos Islands. **d** Estimate. **e** 2014. **f** 2016. **g** Data refers to a 5-year period preceding the reference year.

Central America

Region   Latin America & Caribbean   Population (000, 2017)   177 316[a]
Surface area (km2)   2 480 000[b]   Pop. density (per km2, 2017) 72.3[a]
Sex ratio (m per 100 f, 2017) 98.5[a]

Economic indicators	2005	2010	2017
GDP: Gross domestic product (million current US$)	961 724	1 204 845	1 370 237[b]
GDP growth rate (annual %, const. 2005 prices)	3.2	5.0	2.7[b]
GDP per capita (current US$)	6 455.0	7 478.1	7 932.4[b]
Employment: Agriculture (% of employed)[c]	18.4	17.1	16.3
Employment: Industry (% of employed)[c]	24.5	23.8	23.6
Employment: Services (% of employed)[c]	57.1	59.1	60.1
Unemployment (% of labour force)[c]	4.0	5.5	4.3
Labour force participation (female/male pop. %)[c]	41.7 / 81.4	44.0 / 81.1	45.8 / 80.1
Agricultural production index (2004-2006=100)	98	111	123[d]
Food production index (2004-2006=100)	98	110	123[d]
International trade: Exports (million US$)	233 506	336 529	406 463[e]
International trade: Imports (million US$)	259 847	366 171	456 251[e]
International trade: Balance (million US$)	- 26 340	- 29 642	- 49 789[e]

Social indicators	2005	2010	2017
Population growth rate (average annual %)[f]	1.4	1.6	1.5[b]
Urban population (% of total population)	70.6	72.2	73.8[b]
Urban population growth rate (average annual %)[f]	1.9	1.9	1.8[b]
Fertility rate, total (live births per woman)[f]	2.8	2.5	2.4[b]
Life expectancy at birth (females/males, years)[f]	76.5 / 71.3	77.4 / 72.3	78.4 / 73.2[b]
Population age distribution (0-14 and 60+ years, %)	33.6 / 7.5	31.0 / 8.2	27.7 / 9.7[a]
International migrant stock (000/% of total pop.)	1 385.7 / 0.9	1 749.9 / 1.1	2 040.2 / 1.2[b]
Infant mortality rate (per 1 000 live births)[f]	23.3	21.8	20.0[b]
Seats held by women in national parliaments (%)	17.4	21.6	33.1

Environment and infrastructure indicators	2005	2010	2017
Forested area (% of land area)	36.4	35.7	35.3[d]
Pop. using improved drinking water (urban/rural, %)	95.3 / 78.5	96.5 / 84.3	97.4 / 88.9[b]
Pop. using improved sanitation facilities (urban/rural, %)	83.5 / 56.6	85.4 / 63.4	86.8 / 68.6[b]

a Projected estimate (medium fertility variant). b 2015. c Estimate. d 2014. e 2016. f Data refers to a 5-year period preceding the reference year.

South America

Region	Latin America & Caribbean	Population (000, 2017)	424 394[a]
Surface area (km2)	17 832 000[b]	Pop. density (per km2, 2017)	24.3[a]
Sex ratio (m per 100 f, 2017)	97.4[a,c]		

Economic indicators	2005	2010	2017
GDP: Gross domestic product (million current US$)	1 664 900	3 839 687	3 695 063[b]
GDP growth rate (annual %, const. 2005 prices)	5.0	6.5	- 1.5[b]
GDP per capita (current US$)	4 444.4	9 675.5	8 836.1[b]
Employment: Agriculture (% of employed)[d]	16.0	15.7	14.8
Employment: Industry (% of employed)[d]	21.6	21.6	21.2
Employment: Services (% of employed)[d]	62.4	62.7	64.0
Unemployment (% of labour force)[d]	10.8	8.2	9.8
Labour force participation (female/male pop. %)[d]	55.4 / 80.9	55.5 / 80.0	55.6 / 78.4
Agricultural production index (2004-2006=100)	100	118	129[e]
Food production index (2004-2006=100)	100	119	130[e]
International trade: Exports (million US$)	315 113	524 416	431 786[f]
International trade: Imports (million US$)	211 710	448 508	394 644[f]
International trade: Balance (million US$)	103 404	75 908	37 142[f]

Social indicators	2005	2010	2017
Population growth rate (average annual %)[g]	1.3	1.1	1.0[b]
Urban population (% of total population)	80.9	82.1	83.3[b]
Urban population growth rate (average annual %)[g]	1.7	1.4	1.3[b]
Fertility rate, total (live births per woman)[c,g]	2.4	2.1	2.0[b]
Life expectancy at birth (females/males, years)[c,g]	75.5 / 68.1	76.9 / 69.6	78.1 / 71.0[b]
Population age distribution (0-14 and 60+ years, %)[c]	28.6 / 9.1	26.4 / 10.2	23.7 / 12.4[a]
International migrant stock (000/% of total pop.)	4 518.6 / 1.2	5 143.1 / 1.3	5 826.4 / 1.4[b]
Infant mortality rate (per 1 000 live births)[c,g]	25.5	20.3	17.1[b]
Education: Primary gross enrol. ratio (f/m per 100 pop.)	120.4 / 124.6	112.9 / 117.4	108.9 / 111.2[b]
Education: Secondary gross enrol. ratio (f/m per 100 pop.)	97.0 / 89.5	100.0 / 92.1	101.2 / 96.4[b]
Education: Tertiary gross enrol. ratio (f/m per 100 pop.)	37.3 / 30.5	53.2 / 39.9	65.1 / 47.4[b]
Seats held by women in national parliaments (%)	15.8	19.2	24.5

Environment and infrastructure indicators	2005	2010	2017
Forested area (% of land area)	49.7	48.8	48.3[e]
Energy production, primary (Petajoules)	26 630	29 391	31 217[e]
Energy supply per capita (Gigajoules)	51	56	59[e]
Pop. using improved drinking water (urban/rural, %)	97.0 / 74.7	97.7 / 78.9	98.2 / 82.3[b]
Pop. using improved sanitation facilities (urban/rural, %)	86.0 / 51.0	87.7 / 56.7	89.1 / 61.5[b]

a Projected estimate (medium fertility variant). **b** 2015. **c** Including Falkland Islands (Malvinas). **d** Estimate. **e** 2014. **f** 2016. **g** Data refers to a 5-year period preceding the reference year.

Asia

Region	World	Population (000, 2017)	4 504 428[a]
Surface area (km2)	31 915 000[b]	Pop. density (per km2, 2017)	145.1[a]
Sex ratio (m per 100 f, 2017)	104.8[a]		

Economic indicators	2005	2010	2017
GDP: Gross domestic product (million current US$)	12 321 485	20 769 947	26 514 784[b]
GDP growth rate (annual %, const. 2005 prices)	5.3	7.2	4.0[b]
GDP per capita (current US$)	3 123.8	4 981.4	6 035.6[b]
Agricultural production index (2004-2006=100)	100	118	132[c]
Food production index (2004-2006=100)	100	119	132[c]
International trade: Exports (million US$)	3 569 166	5 893 524	6 430 832[d]
International trade: Imports (million US$)	3 171 536	5 445 416	5 889 037[d]
International trade: Balance (million US$)	397 630	448 108	541 795[d]

Social indicators	2005	2010	2017
Population growth rate (average annual %)[e]	1.2	1.1	1.0[b]
Urban population (% of total population)	41.1	44.8	48.2[b]
Urban population growth rate (average annual %)[e]	3.0	2.8	2.5[b]
Fertility rate, total (live births per woman)[e]	2.4	2.3	2.2[b]
Life expectancy at birth (females/males, years)[e]	70.3 / 67.0	72.2 / 68.6	73.8 / 69.9[b]
Population age distribution (0-14 and 60+ years, %)	27.4 / 9.3	25.6 / 10.1	24.2 / 12.2[a]
International migrant stock (000/% of total pop.)	53 371.2 / 1.4	65 914.3 / 1.6	75 081.1 / 1.7[b]
Refugees and others of concern to UNHCR (000)	...	...	28 420.7[b]
Infant mortality rate (per 1 000 live births)[e]	45.6	37.2	30.5[b]
Education: Primary gross enrol. ratio (f/m per 100 pop.)	101.4 / 105.0[f]	107.3 / 108.5	107.6 / 105.2[b]
Education: Secondary gross enrol. ratio (f/m per 100 pop.)	57.8 / 62.6[f]	68.8 / 71.6	78.3 / 78.5[b]
Education: Tertiary gross enrol. ratio (f/m per 100 pop.)	16.3 / 18.9	22.5 / 24.3	34.2 / 32.6[b]
Seats held by women in national parliaments (%)	13.4	16.8	18.4

Environment and infrastructure indicators	2005	2010	2017
Forested area (% of land area)	18.7	19.0	19.1[c]
Energy production, primary (Petajoules)	192 217	235 722	259 583[c]
Energy supply per capita (Gigajoules)	46	56	61[c]

a Projected estimate (medium fertility variant). b 2015. c 2014. d 2016. e Data refers to a 5-year period preceding the reference year. f Estimate.

Central Asia

Region	Asia	Population (000, 2017)	70 840 [a]
Surface area (km2)	4 103 000 [b,c]	Pop. density (per km2, 2017)	18.0 [a]
Sex ratio (m per 100 f, 2017)	97.9 [a]		

Economic indicators	2005	2010	2017
GDP: Gross domestic product (million current US$)	90 474	220 593	302 780 [c]
GDP growth rate (annual %, const. 2005 prices)	9.4	7.6	3.4 [c]
GDP per capita (current US$)	1 558.7	3 550.0	4 498.0 [c]
Employment: Agriculture (% of employed) [d]	37.6	32.3	28.3
Employment: Industry (% of employed) [d]	20.3	22.2	22.4
Employment: Services (% of employed) [d]	42.1	45.5	49.3
Unemployment (% of labour force) [d]	9.1	8.4	8.1
Labour force participation (female/male pop. %) [d]	53.9 / 73.8	54.1 / 75.3	54.6 / 77.2
Agricultural production index (2004-2006=100)	100	115	136 [e]
Food production index (2004-2006=100)	100	119	143 [e]
International trade: Exports (million US$)	36 890	74 850	70 785 [f]
International trade: Imports (million US$)	25 644	40 684	60 317 [f]
International trade: Balance (million US$)	11 246	34 166	10 468 [f]

Social indicators	2005	2010	2017
Population growth rate (average annual %) [g]	1.1	1.5	1.7 [c]
Urban population (% of total population)	40.9	40.4	40.5 [c]
Urban population growth rate (average annual %) [g]	0.6	1.1	1.4 [c]
Fertility rate, total (live births per woman) [g]	2.5	2.7	2.7 [c]
Life expectancy at birth (females/males, years) [g]	70.1 / 61.7	71.6 / 63.5	73.3 / 66.3 [c]
Population age distribution (0-14 and 60+ years, %)	31.0 / 7.3	28.7 / 7.0	29.5 / 8.3 [a]
International migrant stock (000/% of total pop.) [g]	5 238.7 / 9.0	5 262.4 / 8.5	5 393.5 / 8.0 [c]
Infant mortality rate (per 1 000 live births)	48.0	38.0	28.5 [c]
Seats held by women in national parliaments (%)	13.4	20.0	21.3

Environment and infrastructure indicators	2005	2010	2017
Individuals using the Internet (per 100 inhabitants)	3.3	18.4	43.5 [c]
Research & Development expenditure (% of GDP)	0.2	0.2	0.2 [e]
Forested area (% of land area)	3.1	3.0	3.0 [e]
Pop. using improved drinking water (urban/rural, %)	96.9 / 74.8	98.0 / 78.8	98.1 / 79.0 [c]
Pop. using improved sanitation facilities (urban/rural, %)	95.1 / 92.1	97.4 / 98.0	97.4 / 98.4 [c]

a Projected estimate (medium fertility variant). **b** Calculated by the United Nations Statistics Division. **c** 2015. **d** Estimate. **e** 2014. **f** 2016. **g** Data refers to a 5-year period preceding the reference year.

Region	Asia	Population (000, 2017)	1 648 165[a]
Surface area (km2)	11 799 000[b]	Pop. density (per km2, 2017)	142.6[a]
Sex ratio (m per 100 f, 2017)	104.8[a]		

Economic indicators	2005	2010	2017
GDP: Gross domestic product (million current US$)	8 547 753	13 584 987	17 826 442[b]
GDP growth rate (annual %, const. 2005 prices)	4.7	7.1	3.8[b]
GDP per capita (current US$)	5 562.8	8 624.0	11 056.3[b]
Employment: Agriculture (% of employed)[c]	38.5	31.1	24.8
Employment: Industry (% of employed)[c]	22.5	24.2	24.1
Employment: Services (% of employed)[c]	39.0	44.7	51.0
Unemployment (% of labour force)[c]	4.2	4.3	4.5
Labour force participation (female/male pop. %)[c]	64.4 / 78.9	61.9 / 77.0	61.3 / 76.8
Agricultural production index (2004-2006=100)	100	118	129[d]
Food production index (2004-2006=100)	100	119	130[d]
International trade: Exports (million US$)	1 937 757	3 219 262	3 783 102[e]
International trade: Imports (million US$)	1 744 378	2 967 502	3 163 966[e]
International trade: Balance (million US$)	193 379	251 759	619 136[e]

Social indicators	2005	2010	2017
Population growth rate (average annual %)[f]	0.6	0.5	0.5[b]
Urban population (% of total population)	48.3	54.3	60.0[b]
Urban population growth rate (average annual %)[f]	3.3	2.9	2.5[b]
Fertility rate, total (live births per woman)[f]	1.5	1.6	1.6[b]
Life expectancy at birth (females/males, years)[f]	76.2 / 72.3	77.8 / 73.8	78.7 / 74.9[b]
Population age distribution (0-14 and 60+ years, %)	19.4 / 12.4	17.5 / 14.1	17.2 / 17.7[a]
International migrant stock (000/% of total pop.)	6 229.5 / 0.4	7 061.8 / 0.4	7 596.7 / 0.5[b]
Infant mortality rate (per 1 000 live births)[f]	23.2	15.7	11.0[b]
Education: Primary gross enrol. ratio (f/m per 100 pop.)[g]	102.3 / 102.7[c]	110.9 / 112.6	103.6 / 103.4[b]
Education: Secondary gross enrol. ratio (f/m per 100 pop.)[g]	66.7 / 67.5[c]	85.5 / 85.7	95.7 / 93.4[b]
Education: Tertiary gross enrol. ratio (f/m per 100 pop.)[g]	20.2 / 23.5	26.4 / 25.8	48.1 / 42.1[b]
Seats held by women in national parliaments (%)	18.1	18.7	20.5

Environment and infrastructure indicators	2005	2010	2017
Individuals using the Internet (per 100 inhabitants)	16.1	39.5	54.4[b]
Research & Development expenditure (% of GDP)	2.1	2.2	2.5[d]
Forested area (% of land area)	20.9	21.7	22.1[d]
Important sites for terrestrial biodiversity protected (%)[g]	44.9	45.9	46.7
Pop. using improved drinking water (urban/rural, %)	97.8 / 79.0	97.9 / 86.0	97.9 / 93.1[b]
Pop. using improved sanitation facilities (urban/rural, %)	83.3 / 55.9	86.0 / 60.3	88.8 / 64.8[b]

a Projected estimate (medium fertility variant). **b** 2015. **c** Estimate. **d** 2014. **e** 2016. **f** Data refers to a 5-year period preceding the reference year. **g** Excludes Japan.

Southern Asia

Region | Asia
Surface area (km2) | 6 688 000[b,c]
Sex ratio (m per 100 f, 2017) | 106.1[a]
Population (000, 2017) | 1 868 985[a]
Pop. density (per km2, 2017) | 292.0[a]

Economic indicators	2005	2010	2017
GDP: Gross domestic product (million current US$)	1 251 993	2 500 434	3 104 480[c]
GDP growth rate (annual %, const. 2005 prices)	7.9	8.6	6.3[c]
GDP per capita (current US$)	791.8	1 468.3	1 703.0[c]
Employment: Agriculture (% of employed)[d]	53.2	49.5	43.4
Employment: Industry (% of employed)[d]	18.9	21.6	23.3
Employment: Services (% of employed)[d]	27.9	28.9	33.3
Unemployment (% of labour force)[d]	5.0	4.3	4.1
Labour force participation (female/male pop. %)[d]	35.8 / 82.8	29.5 / 80.5	28.6 / 79.4
Agricultural production index (2004-2006=100)	100	121	138[e]
Food production index (2004-2006=100)	100	121	138[e]
International trade: Exports (million US$)	193 182	354 892	375 981[f]
International trade: Imports (million US$)	229 179	497 340	523 794[f]
International trade: Balance (million US$)	- 35 997	- 142 448	- 147 813[f]

Social indicators	2005	2010	2017
Population growth rate (average annual %)[g]	1.7	1.5	1.3[c]
Urban population (% of total population)	30.8	32.7	34.8[c]
Urban population growth rate (average annual %)[g]	2.8	2.6	2.5[c]
Fertility rate, total (live births per woman)[g]	3.2	2.9	2.5[c]
Life expectancy at birth (females/males, years)[g]	65.0 / 63.1	67.0 / 64.9	69.4 / 66.5[c]
Population age distribution (0-14 and 60+ years, %)	33.4 / 7.1	31.5 / 7.5	28.7 / 8.8[a]
International migrant stock (000/% of total pop.)	13 722.0 / 0.9	14 326.6 / 0.8	14 103.7 / 0.8[c]
Infant mortality rate (per 1 000 live births)[g]	61.4	51.9	44.1[c]
Education: Primary gross enrol. ratio (f/m per 100 pop.)	100.7 / 106.2[d]	107.2 / 107.7	111.8 / 105.0[c]
Education: Secondary gross enrol. ratio (f/m per 100 pop.)	46.9 / 55.3	57.4 / 62.0	69.7 / 70.1[c]
Education: Tertiary gross enrol. ratio (f/m per 100 pop.)	8.7 / 11.8	14.9 / 19.5	24.3 / 25.5[c]
Seats held by women in national parliaments (%)	8.8	18.2	18.0

Environment and infrastructure indicators	2005	2010	2017
Individuals using the Internet (per 100 inhabitants)	2.8	7.6	24.6[c]
Research & Development expenditure (% of GDP)	0.7	0.7	0.7[e]
Forested area (% of land area)	14.3	14.6	14.7[e]
Important sites for terrestrial biodiversity protected (%)	29.5	30.6	33.1
Pop. using improved drinking water (urban/rural, %)	93.4 / 81.3	94.6 / 86.6	95.5 / 91.0[c]
Pop. using improved sanitation facilities (urban/rural, %)	62.0 / 25.8	65.0 / 31.3	67.2 / 36.0[c]

a Projected estimate (medium fertility variant). **b** Calculated by the United Nations Statistics Division. **c** 2015. **d** Estimate. **e** 2014. **f** 2016. **g** Data refers to a 5-year period preceding the reference year.

South-eastern Asia

Region	Asia	Population (000, 2017)	648 780 [a]
Surface area (km2)	4 495 000 [b]	Pop. density (per km2, 2017)	149.5 [a]
Sex ratio (m per 100 f, 2017)	99.7 [a]		

Economic indicators	2005	2010	2017
GDP: Gross domestic product (million current US$)	958 699	1 980 390	2 440 849 [b]
GDP growth rate (annual %, const. 2005 prices)	5.7	8.0	4.4 [b]
GDP per capita (current US$)	1 702.4	3 318.9	3 853.0 [b]
Employment: Agriculture (% of employed) [c]	43.8	39.3	31.9
Employment: Industry (% of employed) [c]	17.7	18.5	20.8
Employment: Services (% of employed) [c]	38.5	42.2	47.2
Unemployment (% of labour force) [c]	6.2	4.6	3.7
Labour force participation (female/male pop. %) [c]	58.5 / 82.7	59.1 / 82.1	58.7 / 81.8
Agricultural production index (2004-2006=100)	99	120	133 [d]
Food production index (2004-2006=100)	99	121	133 [d]
International trade: Exports (million US$)	654 380	1 051 658	1 142 558 [e]
International trade: Imports (million US$)	583 336	951 476	1 081 570 [e]
International trade: Balance (million US$)	71 044	100 182	60 988 [e]

Social indicators	2005	2010	2017
Population growth rate (average annual %) [f]	1.4	1.2	1.2 [b]
Urban population (% of total population)	41.3	44.5	47.6 [b]
Urban population growth rate (average annual %) [f]	3.0	2.7	2.5 [b]
Fertility rate, total (live births per woman) [f]	2.5	2.4	2.3 [b]
Life expectancy at birth (females/males, years) [f]	70.9 / 65.4	72.3 / 66.5	73.4 / 67.7 [b]
Population age distribution (0-14 and 60+ years, %)	30.0 / 7.6	28.0 / 8.1	26.2 / 9.9 [a]
International migrant stock (000/% of total pop.)	6 522.3 / 1.2	8 661.9 / 1.5	9 867.7 / 1.6 [b]
Infant mortality rate (per 1 000 live births) [f]	34.1	28.6	24.0 [b]
Education: Primary gross enrol. ratio (f/m per 100 pop.)	103.4 / 106.4	107.1 / 106.7	106.6 / 109.1 [b]
Education: Secondary gross enrol. ratio (f/m per 100 pop.)	61.4 / 61.7	70.7 / 70.0	80.2 / 80.0 [c,b]
Education: Tertiary gross enrol. ratio (f/m per 100 pop.)	20.7 / 20.7 [c]	27.7 / 26.0	30.2 / 25.3 [b]
Seats held by women in national parliaments (%)	15.5	19.3	19.3

Environment and infrastructure indicators	2005	2010	2017
Individuals using the Internet (per 100 inhabitants)	8.7	18.8	34.2 [b]
Research & Development expenditure (% of GDP)	0.6	0.8	0.8 [d]
Forested area (% of land area)	50.0	49.4	48.7 [d]
Important sites for terrestrial biodiversity protected (%)	31.4	33.6	35.2
Pop. using improved drinking water (urban/rural, %)	93.1 / 76.7	94.4 / 81.4	95.5 / 85.6 [b]
Pop. using improved sanitation facilities (urban/rural, %)	76.2 / 54.9	78.8 / 60.0	80.8 / 64.3 [b]

a Projected estimate (medium fertility variant). b 2015. c Estimate. d 2014. e 2016. f Data refers to a 5-year period preceding the reference year.

Western Asia

Region	Asia	Population (000, 2017)	267 660[a]
Surface area (km2)	4 831 000[b]	Pop. density (per km2, 2017)	55.7[a]
Sex ratio (m per 100 f, 2017)	109.5[a]		

Economic indicators	2005	2010	2017
GDP: Gross domestic product (million current US$)	1 472 566	2 483 544	2 840 232[b]
GDP growth rate (annual %, const. 2005 prices)	6.7	6.1	2.8[b]
GDP per capita (current US$)	7 165.3	10 685.2	11 053.3[b]
Employment: Agriculture (% of employed)[c,d]	14.6	11.0	12.6
Employment: Industry (% of employed)[c,d]	22.8	24.3	25.1
Employment: Services (% of employed)[c,d]	62.7	64.8	62.3
Unemployment (% of labour force)[c,d]	10.9	9.8	10.6
Labour force participation (female/male pop. %)[c,d]	18.7 / 74.5	20.0 / 75.6	21.2 / 76.4
Agricultural production index (2004-2006=100)	101	106	111[e]
Food production index (2004-2006=100)	101	107	113[e]
International trade: Exports (million US$)	557 564	919 156	777 927[f]
International trade: Imports (million US$)	407 407	737 099	828 459[f]
International trade: Balance (million US$)	150 158	182 058	- 50 532[f]

Social indicators	2005	2010	2017
Population growth rate (average annual %)[g]	2.1	2.5	2.1[b]
Urban population (% of total population)	65.9	68.1	69.9[b]
Urban population growth rate (average annual %)[g]	2.9	3.1	2.4[b]
Fertility rate, total (live births per woman)[g]	3.2	3.0	2.9[b]
Life expectancy at birth (females/males, years)[g]	73.5 / 68.4	74.8 / 69.5	75.7 / 70.1[b]
Population age distribution (0-14 and 60+ years, %)	33.4 / 7.2	31.0 / 7.3	29.4 / 8.3[a]
International migrant stock (000/% of total pop.)	21 658.6 / 10.5	30 601.6 / 13.2	38 119.5 / 14.8[b]
Infant mortality rate (per 1 000 live births)[g]	30.9	25.0	22.8[b]
Education: Primary gross enrol. ratio (f/m per 100 pop.)[c]	95.6 / 105.7	98.1 / 105.8	97.4 / 104.4[d,b]
Education: Secondary gross enrol. ratio (f/m per 100 pop.)[c]	66.1 / 78.3	70.1 / 78.7	76.6 / 84.4[d,b]
Education: Tertiary gross enrol. ratio (f/m per 100 pop.)[c]	22.9 / 27.1	32.7 / 35.8	49.9 / 52.6[b]
Seats held by women in national parliaments (%)	5.7	9.3	13.8

Environment and infrastructure indicators	2005	2010	2017
Individuals using the Internet (per 100 inhabitants)	11.1	32.5	50.3[b]
Research & Development expenditure (% of GDP)	0.5	0.5	0.6[e]
Forested area (% of land area)	3.8	4.0	4.1[e]
Important sites for terrestrial biodiversity protected (%)[c]	6.3	8.0	9.3
Pop. using improved drinking water (urban/rural, %)	95.5 / 75.7	95.7 / 78.7	96.7 / 89.9[b]
Pop. using improved sanitation facilities (urban/rural, %)	94.6 / 69.6	95.4 / 74.3	95.9 / 88.6[b]

a Projected estimate (medium fertility variant). **b** 2015. **c** Data excludes Armenia, Azerbaijan, Cyprus, Georgia, Israel and Turkey. **d** Estimate. **e** 2014. **f** 2016. **g** Data refers to a 5-year period preceding the reference year.

Europe

Region	World	Population (000, 2017)	742 074 [a]
Surface area (km2)	23 049 000 [b]	Pop. density (per km2, 2017)	33.5 [a]
Sex ratio (m per 100 f, 2017)	93.5 [a]		

Economic indicators	2005	2010	2017
GDP: Gross domestic product (million current US$)	16 084 260	19 805 957	18 945 444 [b]
GDP growth rate (annual %, const. 2005 prices)	2.3	2.3	1.8 [b]
GDP per capita (current US$)	22 011.7	26 866.6	25 590.1 [b]
Agricultural production index (2004-2006=100)	99	99	108 [c]
Food production index (2004-2006=100)	99	99	108 [c]
International trade: Exports (million US$)	4 527 059	5 904 713	6 059 004 [d]
International trade: Imports (million US$)	4 439 990	5 869 522	5 761 863 [d]
International trade: Balance (million US$)	87 068	35 191	297 141 [d]

Social indicators	2005	2010	2017
Population growth rate (average annual %) [e]	0.1	0.2	0.1 [b]
Urban population (% of total population)	71.7	72.7	73.6 [b]
Urban population growth rate (average annual %) [e]	0.3	0.5	0.3 [b]
Fertility rate, total (live births per woman) [e]	1.4	1.5	1.6 [b]
Life expectancy at birth (females/males, years) [e]	78.1 / 69.6	79.3 / 71.3	80.7 / 73.7 [b]
Population age distribution (0-14 and 60+ years, %)	15.9 / 20.6	15.5 / 22.0	15.9 / 24.7 [a]
International migrant stock (000/% of total pop.)	64 086.8 / 8.8	72 374.8 / 9.8	76 146.0 / 10.3 [b]
Refugees and others of concern to UNHCR (000)	...	...	4 673.8 [b]
Infant mortality rate (per 1 000 live births) [e]	8.4	6.5	5.3 [b]
Education: Primary gross enrol. ratio (f/m per 100 pop.)	101.9 / 102.6	102.8 / 103.4	102.5 / 102.5 [b]
Education: Secondary gross enrol. ratio (f/m per 100 pop.)	97.3 / 97.8	100.2 / 101.5	109.2 / 109.7 [b]
Education: Tertiary gross enrol. ratio (f/m per 100 pop.)	70.9 / 55.3	77.3 / 60.1	77.6 / 63.5 [b]
Seats held by women in national parliaments (%)	20.5	23.2	28.0

Environment and infrastructure indicators	2005	2010	2017
Individuals using the Internet (per 100 inhabitants)	35.3	57.7	73.1 [b]
Research & Development expenditure (% of GDP)	1.6	1.7	1.8 [c]
Forested area (% of land area)	45.4	45.8	45.9 [c]
Energy production, primary (Petajoules)	102 532	102 460	100 312 [c]
Energy supply per capita (Gigajoules)	154	152	142 [c]
Pop. using improved drinking water (urban/rural, %)	99.4 / 95.4	99.5 / 96.7	99.5 / 97.6 [b]
Pop. using improved sanitation facilities (urban/rural, %)	93.9 / 86.5	94.1 / 87.4	94.2 / 88.1 [b]

a Projected estimate (medium fertility variant). b 2015. c 2014. d 2016. e Data refers to a 5-year period preceding the reference year.

Eastern Europe

Region	Europe	Population (000, 2017)	292 454[a]
Surface area (km2)	18 814 000[b]	Pop. density (per km2, 2017)	16.2[a]
Sex ratio (m per 100 f, 2017)	88.9[a]		

Economic indicators	2005	2010	2017
GDP: Gross domestic product (million current US$)	1 619 644	2 851 190	2 575 830[b]
GDP growth rate (annual %, const. 2005 prices)	5.4	3.6	- 0.6[b]
GDP per capita (current US$)	5 444.5	9 678.5	8 792.9[b]
Employment: Agriculture (% of employed)[c]	15.1	11.7	9.8
Employment: Industry (% of employed)[c]	29.6	28.7	28.0
Employment: Services (% of employed)[c]	55.4	59.5	62.3
Unemployment (% of labour force)[c]	8.5	7.8	6.1
Labour force participation (female/male pop. %)[c]	52.7 / 65.8	52.9 / 67.3	53.0 / 68.1
Agricultural production index (2004-2006=100)	99	97	118[d]
Food production index (2004-2006=100)	99	97	118[d]
International trade: Exports (million US$)	594 285	993 297	975 327[e]
International trade: Imports (million US$)	490 657	867 387	852 440[e]
International trade: Balance (million US$)	103 628	125 910	122 888[e]

Social indicators	2005	2010	2017
Population growth rate (average annual %)[f]	- 0.4	- 0.2	- 0.1[b]
Urban population (% of total population)	68.5	68.9	69.4[b]
Urban population growth rate (average annual %)[f]	- 0.3	---0.0	- 0.1[b]
Fertility rate, total (live births per woman)[f]	1.3	1.4	1.6[b]
Life expectancy at birth (females/males, years)[f]	73.8 / 62.4	75.1 / 64.1	77.1 / 67.3[b]
Population age distribution (0-14 and 60+ years, %)	15.4 / 18.2	14.8 / 19.3	16.4 / 22.5[a]
International migrant stock (000/% of total pop.)	19 747.4 / 6.6	19 116.9 / 6.5	19 684.4 / 6.7[b]
Infant mortality rate (per 1 000 live births)[f]	13.8	9.8	7.6[b]
Seats held by women in national parliaments (%)	14.1	15.2	19.4

Environment and infrastructure indicators	2005	2010	2017
Forested area (% of land area)	47.2	47.6	47.7[d]
Pop. using improved drinking water (urban/rural, %)	98.7 / 90.5	98.7 / 93.2	98.6 / 95.1[b]
Pop. using improved sanitation facilities (urban/rural, %)	86.0 / 73.0	86.1 / 74.7	86.2 / 76.0[b]

a Projected estimate (medium fertility variant). b 2015. c Estimate. d 2014. e 2016. f Data refers to a 5-year period preceding the reference year.

Region	Europe	Population (000, 2017)	104 200[a]
Surface area (km2)	1 810 000[b]	Pop. density (per km2, 2017)	61.2[a]
Sex ratio (m per 100 f, 2017)	97.3[a,c]		

Economic indicators	2005	2010	2017
GDP: Gross domestic product (million current US$)	3 960 212	4 231 377	4 664 906[b]
GDP growth rate (annual %, const. 2005 prices)	3.1	2.2	3.5[b]
GDP per capita (current US$)	41 271.3	42 573.6	45 708.3[b]
Employment: Agriculture (% of employed)[d]	2.8	2.1	2.0
Employment: Industry (% of employed)[d]	23.1	20.0	19.0
Employment: Services (% of employed)[d]	74.1	77.8	78.9
Unemployment (% of labour force)[d]	5.5	8.6	5.8
Labour force participation (female/male pop. %)[d]	55.6 / 69.0	56.4 / 68.3	57.1 / 67.9
Agricultural production index (2004-2006=100)	101	101	107[e]
Food production index (2004-2006=100)	101	101	107[e]
International trade: Exports (million US$)	913 599	1 043 670	981 599[f]
International trade: Imports (million US$)	937 990	1 118 189	1 135 048[f]
International trade: Balance (million US$)	- 24 391	- 74 519	- 153 449[f]

Social indicators	2005	2010	2017
Population growth rate (average annual %)[g]	0.4	0.8	0.5[b]
Urban population (% of total population)	78.9	80.1	81.2[b]
Urban population growth rate (average annual %)[g]	0.6	0.8	0.8[b]
Fertility rate, total (live births per woman)[c,g]	1.7	1.9	1.8[b]
Life expectancy at birth (females/males, years)[c,g]	80.5 / 75.2	81.6 / 76.6	82.7 / 78.3[b]
Population age distribution (0-14 and 60+ years, %)[c]	18.0 / 21.1	17.4 / 22.6	17.6 / 24.2[a]
International migrant stock (000/% of total pop.)	9 588.8 / 10.0	11 858.4 / 11.9	13 331.4 / 13.0[b]
Infant mortality rate (per 1 000 live births)[c,g]	5.0	4.4	3.7[b]
Seats held by women in national parliaments (%)	28.0	29.6	33.3

Environment and infrastructure indicators	2005	2010	2017
Forested area (% of land area)	43.7	43.8	44.0[e]
Pop. using improved drinking water (urban/rural, %)	99.8 / 98.7	99.9 / 99.0	99.9 / 99.2[b]
Pop. using improved sanitation facilities (urban/rural, %)	98.4 / 96.2	98.5 / 96.5	98.6 / 96.8[b]

a Projected estimate (medium fertility variant). **b** 2015. **c** Including the Faroe Islands and the Isle of Man. **d** Estimate. **e** 2014. **f** 2016. **g** Data refers to a 5-year period preceding the reference year.

Southern Europe

Region	Europe	Population (000, 2017)	151 989[a]
Surface area (km2)	1 317 000[b]	Pop. density (per km2, 2017)	117.4[a]
Sex ratio (m per 100 f, 2017)	95.5[a,c]		

Economic indicators	2005	2010	2017
GDP: Gross domestic product (million current US$)	3 606 117	4 304 152	3 599 558[b]
GDP growth rate (annual %, const. 2005 prices)	1.9	0.6	1.6[b]
GDP per capita (current US$)	24 088.1	28 071.4	23 632.4[b]
Employment: Agriculture (% of employed)[d]	8.6	7.7	6.8
Employment: Industry (% of employed)[d]	29.2	25.8	23.3
Employment: Services (% of employed)[d]	62.1	66.5	69.9
Unemployment (% of labour force)[d]	10.1	14.3	15.3
Labour force participation (female/male pop. %)[d]	42.7 / 64.4	44.4 / 62.9	45.0 / 60.7
Agricultural production index (2004-2006=100)	98	98	95[e]
Food production index (2004-2006=100)	98	99	95[e]
International trade: Exports (million US$)	660 817	830 354	899 660[f]
International trade: Imports (million US$)	861 881	1 039 442	921 887[f]
International trade: Balance (million US$)	- 201 064	- 209 088	- 22 227[f]

Social indicators	2005	2010	2017
Population growth rate (average annual %)[g]	0.6	0.5	- 0.2[b]
Urban population (% of total population)	67.6	68.9	70.1[b]
Urban population growth rate (average annual %)[g]	1.0	1.0	0.5[b]
Fertility rate, total (live births per woman)[c,g]	1.4	1.4	1.4[b]
Life expectancy at birth (females/males, years)[c,g]	81.8 / 75.6	82.9 / 77.1	83.7 / 78.4[b]
Population age distribution (0-14 and 60+ years, %)[c]	15.1 / 22.5	14.8 / 24.1	14.3 / 26.9[a]
International migrant stock (000/% of total pop.)	11 974.3 / 8.0	16 154.1 / 10.5	15 747.7 / 10.3[b]
Infant mortality rate (per 1 000 live births)[c,g]	5.8	4.7	4.0[b]
Seats held by women in national parliaments (%)	17.1	23.0	29.4

Environment and infrastructure indicators	2005	2010	2017
Forested area (% of land area)	33.4	34.8	35.1[e]
Pop. using improved drinking water (urban/rural, %)	99.9 / 99.2	99.9 / 99.5	99.9 / 99.7[b]
Pop. using improved sanitation facilities (urban/rural, %)	99.2 / 97.2	99.3 / 97.8	99.4 / 98.0[b]

a Projected estimate (medium fertility variant). b 2015. c Including Andorra, Gibraltar, Holy See, and San Marino. d Estimate. e 2014. f 2016. g Data refers to a 5-year period preceding the reference year.

Region	Europe	Population (000, 2017)	193 431 [a]
Surface area (km2)	1 108 000 [b]	Pop. density (per km2, 2017)	178.3 [a]
Sex ratio (m per 100 f, 2017)	97.1 [a,c]		

Economic indicators	2005	2010	2017
GDP: Gross domestic product (million current US$)	6 898 287	8 419 238	8 105 149 [b]
GDP growth rate (annual %, const. 2005 prices)	1.4	2.9	1.5 [b]
GDP per capita (current US$)	36 776.6	44 338.4	41 989.4 [b]
Employment: Agriculture (% of employed) [d]	3.0	2.4	2.1
Employment: Industry (% of employed) [d]	26.3	24.6	23.4
Employment: Services (% of employed) [d]	70.7	73.0	74.5
Unemployment (% of labour force) [d]	9.2	7.3	6.4
Labour force participation (female/male pop. %) [d]	51.0 / 65.8	52.7 / 65.3	53.3 / 64.1
Agricultural production index (2004-2006=100)	100	101	108 [e]
Food production index (2004-2006=100)	100	101	108 [e]
International trade: Exports (million US$)	2 358 357	3 037 392	3 202 418 [f]
International trade: Imports (million US$)	2 149 462	2 844 504	2 852 488 [f]
International trade: Balance (million US$)	208 895	192 888	349 929 [f]

Social indicators	2005	2010	2017
Population growth rate (average annual %) [g]	0.3	0.3	0.4 [b]
Urban population (% of total population)	76.4	77.7	78.9 [b]
Urban population growth rate (average annual %) [g]	0.7	0.6	0.6 [b]
Fertility rate, total (live births per woman) [c,g]	1.6	1.6	1.7 [b]
Life expectancy at birth (females/males, years) [c,g]	82.0 / 75.8	83.0 / 77.3	83.7 / 78.4 [b]
Population age distribution (0-14 and 60+ years, %) [c]	16.4 / 22.6	15.9 / 24.3	15.4 / 26.4 [a]
International migrant stock (000/% of total pop.)	22 776.3 / 12.3	25 245.3 / 13.4	27 382.5 / 14.4 [b]
Infant mortality rate (per 1 000 live births) [c,g]	4.3	3.7	3.4 [b]
Seats held by women in national parliaments (%)	25.8	28.4	32.1

Environment and infrastructure indicators	2005	2010	2017
Forested area (% of land area)	30.8	31.4	31.8 [e]
Pop. using improved drinking water (urban/rural, %)	100.0 / 100.0	100.0 / 100.0	100.0 / 100.0 [b]
Pop. using improved sanitation facilities (urban/rural, %)	99.0 / 99.1	98.9 / 99.1	98.9 / 99.1 [b]

a Projected estimate (medium fertility variant). **b** 2015. **c** Including Liechtenstein, and Monaco. **d** Estimate. **e** 2014. **f** 2016. **g** Data refers to a 5-year period preceding the reference year.

Oceania

Region	World	Population (000, 2017)	40 691[a]
Surface area (km2)	8 564 000[b]	Pop. density (per km2, 2017)	4.8[a]
Sex ratio (m per 100 f, 2017)	100.1[a]		

Economic indicators	2005	2010	2017
GDP: Gross domestic product (million current US$)	901 167	1 476 189	1 448 476[b]
GDP growth rate (annual %, const. 2005 prices)	3.0	2.3	2.6[b]
GDP per capita (current US$)	27 249.9	40 862.8	37 107.5[b]
Employment: Agriculture (% of employed)[c]	17.0	16.9	16.3
Employment: Industry (% of employed)[c]	18.0	17.6	17.8
Employment: Services (% of employed)[c]	65.0	65.5	65.9
Unemployment (% of labour force)[c]	4.9	5.3	5.5
Labour force participation (female/male pop. %)[c]	58.9 / 72.9	60.1 / 72.7	59.9 / 71.0
Agricultural production index (2004-2006=100)	105	102	111[d]
Food production index (2004-2006=100)	105	103	111[d]
International trade: Exports (million US$)	134 548	252 899	237 017[e]
International trade: Imports (million US$)	161 435	247 151	247 473[e]
International trade: Balance (million US$)	- 26 888	5 748	- 10 457[e]

Social indicators	2005	2010	2017
Population growth rate (average annual %)[f]	1.4	1.7	1.5[b]
Urban population (% of total population)	70.5	70.7	70.8[b]
Urban population growth rate (average annual %)[f]	1.5	1.8	1.4[b]
Fertility rate, total (live births per woman)[f]	2.4	2.5	2.4[b]
Life expectancy at birth (females/males, years)[f]	78.2 / 73.1	79.4 / 74.6	80.2 / 75.7[b]
Population age distribution (0-14 and 60+ years, %)	24.9 / 14.1	24.0 / 15.3	23.5 / 17.0[a]
International migrant stock (000/% of total pop.)	6 023.4 / 18.1	7 125.4 / 19.6	8 100.9 / 20.6[b]
Refugees and others of concern to UNHCR (000)	...	...	71.3[b]
Infant mortality rate (per 1 000 live births)[f]	25.2	22.4	20.8[b]
Education: Primary gross enrol. ratio (f/m per 100 pop.)	90.0 / 91.9	99.1 / 101.8	104.6 / 108.2[b]
Education: Secondary gross enrol. ratio (f/m per 100 pop.)	107.0 / 110.2	98.2 / 102.3	97.7 / 103.5[c,b]
Education: Tertiary gross enrol. ratio (f/m per 100 pop.)	58.6 / 45.6	67.1 / 48.9	72.2 / 52.2[c,b]
Seats held by women in national parliaments (%)	11.2	13.2	15.0

Environment and infrastructure indicators	2005	2010	2017
Individuals using the Internet (per 100 inhabitants)	47.6	58.2	66.5[b]
Research & Development expenditure (% of GDP)	1.9	2.2	2.0[d]
Forested area (% of land area)	20.8	20.3	20.4[d]
Energy production, primary (Petajoules)	12 213	14 500	16 196[d]
Energy supply per capita (Gigajoules)	171	179	167[d]
Important sites for terrestrial biodiversity protected (%)	10.7	20.6	21.5
Pop. using improved drinking water (urban/rural, %)	99.4 / 60.0	99.5 / 60.1	99.5 / 59.4[b]
Pop. using improved sanitation facilities (urban/rural, %)	97.5 / 43.7	97.5 / 42.8	97.4 / 41.1[b]

a Projected estimate (medium fertility variant). b 2015. c Estimate. d 2014. e 2016. f Data refers to a 5-year period preceding the reference year.

Australia and New Zealand

Region	Oceania	Population (000, 2017)	29 156[a]
Surface area (km2)	8 012 000[b]	Pop. density (per km2, 2017)	3.7[a]
Sex ratio (m per 100 f, 2017)	98.9[a]		

Economic indicators	2005	2010	2017
GDP: Gross domestic product (million current US$)	876 503	1 439 785	1 404 276[b]
GDP growth rate (annual %, const. 2005 prices)	3.0	2.2	2.5[b]
GDP per capita (current US$)	35 909.1	54 266.2	49 277.2[b]
Agricultural production index (2004-2006=100)	105	101	113[c]
Food production index (2004-2006=100)	105	103	113[c]
International trade: Exports (million US$)	127 740	243 041	223 463[d]
International trade: Imports (million US$)	151 453	231 861	225 829[d]
International trade: Balance (million US$)	- 23 714	11 179	- 2 365[d]

Social indicators	2005	2010	2017
Population growth rate (average annual %)[e]	1.2	1.7	1.4[b]
Urban population (% of total population)	87.7	88.3	88.9[b]
Urban population growth rate (average annual %)[e]	1.5	1.8	1.4[b]
Fertility rate, total (live births per woman)[e]	1.8	2.0	1.9[b]
Life expectancy at birth (females/males, years)[e]	82.6 / 77.6	83.5 / 79.0	84.2 / 80.1[b]
Population age distribution (0-14 and 60+ years, %)	20.1 / 17.3	19.3 / 18.8	19.1 / 20.9[a]
International migrant stock (000/% of total pop.)	5 718.0 / 23.4	6 830.4 / 25.7	7 803.4 / 27.4[b]
Infant mortality rate (per 1 000 live births)[e]	5.0	4.5	4.0[b]
Intentional homicide rate (per 100 000 pop.)	...	...	1.0[f,b]
Seats held by women in national parliaments (%)	26.3	30.1	31.1

Environment and infrastructure indicators	2005	2010	2017
Individuals using the Internet (per 100 inhabitants)	63.0	76.7	85.2[b]
Research & Development expenditure (% of GDP)	1.9	2.2	2.1[c]
Forested area (% of land area)	17.3	16.8	16.9[c]
Important sites for terrestrial biodiversity protected (%)	46.6	51.3	53.1
Pop. using improved drinking water (urban/rural, %)	100.0 / 100.0	100.0 / 100.0	100.0 / 100.0[b]
Pop. using improved sanitation facilities (urban/rural, %)	100.0 / 100.0	100.0 / 100.0	100.0 / 100.0[b]

a Projected estimate (medium fertility variant). **b** 2015. **c** 2014. **d** 2016. **e** Data refers to a 5-year period preceding the reference year. **f** Data is for 2015, or latest available data from 2010 onwards.

Melanesia

Region	Oceania	Population (000, 2017)	10 320[a]
Surface area (km2)	541 000[b]	Pop. density (per km2, 2017)	19.5[a]
Sex ratio (m per 100 f, 2017)	103.4[a]		

Economic indicators	2005	2010	2017
GDP: Gross domestic product (million current US$)	17 354	28 121	36 455[b]
GDP growth rate (annual %, const. 2005 prices)	3.5	8.2	4.8[b]
GDP per capita (current US$)	2 220.2	3 226.3	3 788.4[b]
Agricultural production index (2004-2006=100)	99	110	86[c]
Food production index (2004-2006=100)	99	110	86[c]
International trade: Exports (million US$)	5 199	8 112	11 517[d]
International trade: Imports (million US$)	5 397	9 665	14 483[d]
International trade: Balance (million US$)	- 197	- 1 553	- 2 966[d]

Social indicators	2005	2010	2017
Population growth rate (average annual %)[e]	2.2	2.2	2.0[b]
Urban population (% of total population)	19.0	19.1	19.3[b]
Urban population growth rate (average annual %)[e]	2.2	2.3	2.1[b]
Fertility rate, total (live births per woman)[e]	4.2	3.9	3.7[b]
Life expectancy at birth (females/males, years)[e]	66.1 / 61.4	67.7 / 62.9	68.7 / 63.8[b]
Population age distribution (0-14 and 60+ years, %)	38.1 / 5.4	37.1 / 5.8	35.1 / 6.6[a]
International migrant stock (000/% of total pop.)	103.9 / 1.3	105.7 / 1.2	109.6 / 1.1[b]
Infant mortality rate (per 1 000 live births)[e]	51.0	47.3	44.3[b]
Seats held by women in national parliaments (%)	3.2	1.4	4.6

Environment and infrastructure indicators	2005	2010	2017
Forested area (% of land area)	71.9	71.9	71.8[c]
Pop. using improved drinking water (urban/rural, %)	91.9 / 38.3	92.6 / 40.1	92.8 / 40.6[b]
Pop. using improved sanitation facilities (urban/rural, %)	72.8 / 19.2	72.7 / 19.7	72.4 / 19.3[b]

a Projected estimate (medium fertility variant). b 2015. c 2014. d 2016. e Data refers to a 5-year period preceding the reference year.

Micronesia

Region	Oceania	Population (000, 2017)	528[a]
Surface area (km2)	3 000[b]	Pop. density (per km2, 2017)	166.4[a]
Sex ratio (m per 100 f, 2017)	101.5[a,c]		

Economic indicators	2005	2010	2017
GDP: Gross domestic product (million current US$)	707	863	1 107[b]
GDP growth rate (annual %, const. 2005 prices)	2.9	1.6	5.1[b]
GDP per capita (current US$)	2 518.7	2 982.7	3 673.1[b]
Agricultural production index (2004-2006=100)	97	77	79[d]
Food production index (2004-2006=100)	97	77	79[d]
International trade: Exports (million US$)	1 295	1 508	1 778[e]
International trade: Imports (million US$)	2 379	3 292	4 948[e]
International trade: Balance (million US$)	- 1 084	- 1 783	- 3 170[e]

Social indicators	2005	2010	2017
Population growth rate (average annual %)[f]	0.2	~0.0	0.6[b]
Urban population (% of total population)	66.0	66.0	66.8[b]
Urban population growth rate (average annual %)[f]	0.4	- 0.2	1.1[b]
Fertility rate, total (live births per woman)[c,f]	3.2	3.0	3.0[b]
Life expectancy at birth (females/males, years)[c,f]	73.1 / 68.9	74.3 / 69.7	75.3 / 70.5[b]
Population age distribution (0-14 and 60+ years, %)[c]	33.3 / 6.5	32.1 / 7.8	29.2 / 10.4[a]
International migrant stock (000/% of total pop.)	128.4 / 25.5	116.2 / 23.1	115.8 / 22.0[b]
Infant mortality rate (per 1 000 live births)[c,f]	31.0	29.1	27.9[b]
Seats held by women in national parliaments (%)	2.4	2.4	7.8

Environment and infrastructure indicators	2005	2010	2017
Forested area (% of land area)	58.4	58.2	58.0[d]
Pop. using improved drinking water (urban/rural, %)	95.7 / 77.2	96.1 / 77.0	96.4 / 76.6[b]

a Projected estimate (medium fertility variant). **b** 2015. **c** Including Marshall Islands, Nauru, Northern Mariana Islands, and Palau. **d** 2014. **e** 2016. **f** Data refers to a 5-year period preceding the reference year.

Polynesia

Region	Oceania	Population (000, 2017)	686 [a,b]
Surface area (km2)	8 000 [c]	Pop. density (per km2, 2017)	84.8 [a,b]
Sex ratio (m per 100 f, 2017)	103.4 [b,d]		

Economic indicators	2005	2010	2017
GDP: Gross domestic product (million current US$)	6 603	7 421	6 639 [c]
GDP growth rate (annual %, const. 2005 prices)	1.6	- 1.8	1.9 [c]
GDP per capita (current US$)	11 691.7	12 617.2	10 831.3 [c]
Agricultural production index (2004-2006=100)	101	111	111 [e]
Food production index (2004-2006=100)	101	111	111 [e]
International trade: Exports (million US$)	314	238	258 [f]
International trade: Imports (million US$)	2 206	2 333	2 214 [f]
International trade: Balance (million US$)	- 1 893	- 2 095	- 1 956 [f]

Social indicators	2005	2010	2017
Population growth rate (average annual %) [a,g]	0.9	0.5	0.5 [c]
Urban population (% of total population)	43.2	42.8	42.5 [c]
Urban population growth rate (average annual %) [g]	1.1	0.4	0.6 [c]
Fertility rate, total (live births per woman) [d,g]	3.3	3.2	3.0 [c]
Life expectancy at birth (females/males, years) [d,g]	74.6 / 68.9	76.1 / 70.6	77.4 / 72.0 [c]
Population age distribution (0-14 and 60+ years, %) [d]	33.9 / 7.7	31.9 / 8.4	29.8 / 10.2 [b]
International migrant stock (000/% of total pop.)	73.2 / 11.4	73.0 / 11.1	72.1 / 10.5 [c]
Infant mortality rate (per 1 000 live births) [d,g]	19.9	17.6	15.2 [c]
Seats held by women in national parliaments (%)	3.2	5.2	7.7

Environment and infrastructure indicators	2005	2010	2017
Forested area (% of land area)	45.8	48.8	48.7 [e]
Pop. using improved drinking water (urban/rural, %)	99.3 / 97.7	99.5 / 98.9	99.6 / 99.6 [c]
Pop. using improved sanitation facilities (urban/rural, %)	89.7 / 92.8	89.7 / 92.7	89.5 / 92.9 [c]

a Including Pitcairn. b Projected estimate (medium fertility variant). c 2015. d Including American Samoa, Cook Islands, Niue, Pitcairn, Tokelau, Tuvalu, and Wallis and Futuna Islands. e 2014. f 2016. g Data refers to a 5-year period preceding the reference year.

Afghanistan

Region	Southern Asia	UN membership date	19 November 1946
Population (000, 2017)	35 530 [a]	Surface area (km2)	652 864 [b]
Pop. density (per km2, 2017)	54.4 [a]	Sex ratio (m per 100 f, 2017)	106.3 [a]
Capital city	Kabul	National currency	Afghani (AFN)
Capital city pop. (000)	4 634.9 [b]	Exchange rate (per US$)	66.8 [c]

Economic indicators

	2005	2010	2017
GDP: Gross domestic product (million current US$)	6 622	16 078	20 270 [b]
GDP growth rate (annual %, const. 2005 prices)	9.9	3.2	- 2.4 [b]
GDP per capita (current US$)	271.4	575.0	623.2 [b]
Economy: Agriculture (% of GVA)	36.6	29.6	23.3 [b]
Economy: Industry (% of GVA)	26.9	21.9	23.3 [b]
Economy: Services and other activity (% of GVA)	36.5	48.5	53.3 [b]
Employment: Agriculture (% of employed) [d]	65.3	64.2	61.6
Employment: Industry (% of employed) [d]	11.2	9.4	10.0
Employment: Services (% of employed) [d]	23.5	26.4	28.5
Unemployment (% of labour force)	8.5	8.2 [d]	8.6 [d]
Labour force participation (female/male pop. %) [d]	16.4 / 84.3	16.5 / 84.0	19.3 / 83.6
Agricultural production index (2004-2006=100)	107	117	125 [e]
Food production index (2004-2006=100)	107	117	125 [e]
International trade: Exports (million US$)	...	388	1 458 [c]
International trade: Imports (million US$)	...	5 154	3 568 [c]
International trade: Balance (million US$)	...	- 4 766	- 2 110 [c]
Balance of payments, current account (million US$)	...	- 1 673	- 5 121 [b]

Major trading partners

						2016
Export partners (% of exports)	Pakistan	39.7	India	33.1	Iran (Islamic Rep.)	5.1
Import partners (% of imports)	Iran (Islamic Rep.)	23.4	Pakistan	17.4	China	13.5

Social indicators

	2005	2010	2017
Population growth rate (average annual %) [f]	4.4	2.8	3.2 [b]
Urban population (% of total population)	22.9	24.7	26.7 [b]
Urban population growth rate (average annual %) [f]	5.2	4.2	4.0 [b]
Fertility rate, total (live births per woman) [f]	7.2	6.4	5.3 [b]
Life expectancy at birth (females/males, years) [f]	58.1 / 55.8	61.3 / 58.9	63.5 / 61.0 [b]
Population age distribution (0-14 and 60+ years, %)	47.6 / 3.6	47.8 / 3.9	43.2 / 4.1 [a]
International migrant stock (000/% of total pop.)	87.3 / 0.4	102.2 / 0.4	382.4 / 1.2 [b]
Refugees and others of concern to UNHCR (000)	159.6 [g]	1 200.0 [g]	1 513.1 [c]
Infant mortality rate (per 1 000 live births) [f]	89.4	76.7	68.6 [b]
Health: Total expenditure (% of GDP) [h,i,j]	8.1	9.2	8.2 [e]
Health: Physicians (per 1 000 pop.)	0.2 [k]	0.2	0.3 [e]
Education: Government expenditure (% of GDP)	...	3.5	3.3 [b]
Education: Primary gross enrol. ratio (f/m per 100 pop.)	76.5 / 130.4	85.3 / 124.6	91.1 / 131.6 [b]
Education: Secondary gross enrol. ratio (f/m per 100 pop.)	9.6 / 29.3	35.1 / 70.3	39.7 / 70.7 [b]
Education: Tertiary gross enrol. ratio (f/m per 100 pop.)	0.5 / 1.9 [l]	1.5 / 6.2 [m]	3.7 / 13.3 [e]
Intentional homicide rate (per 100 000 pop.)	...	3.5	6.6 [n]
Seats held by women in national parliaments (%)	...	27.3	27.7

Environment and infrastructure indicators

	2005	2010	2017
Mobile-cellular subscriptions (per 100 inhabitants)	4.8	36.0 [d]	61.6 [o,p,b]
Individuals using the Internet (per 100 inhabitants)	1.2	4.0 [d]	8.3 [d,b]
Threatened species (number)	33 [l]	34	42
Forested area (% of land area) [d]	2.1	2.1	2.1 [e]
CO2 emission estimates (million tons/tons per capita)	1.3 / ~0.0	8.5 / 0.3	9.8 / 0.3 [e]
Energy production, primary (Petajoules)	23	41	63 [e]
Energy supply per capita (Gigajoules)	1	5	5 [d,e]
Important sites for terrestrial biodiversity protected (%)	~0.0	6.1	6.1
Pop. using improved drinking water (urban/rural, %)	61.5 / 32.4	70.7 / 40.5	78.2 / 47.0 [b]
Pop. using improved sanitation facilities (urban/rural, %)	36.1 / 23.3	41.1 / 25.4	45.1 / 27.0 [b]
Net Official Development Assist. received (% of GNI)	45.15	40.45	21.43 [b]

a Projected estimate (medium fertility variant). **b** 2015. **c** 2016. **d** Estimate. **e** 2014. **f** Data refers to a 5-year period preceding the reference year. **g** Data as at the end of December. **h** Data revision. **i** Government expenditures include external assistance (external budget). **j** Non-profit institutions (such as NGOs) serving households are accounted for in "external assistance" and recorded under government expenditure. GDP includes both licit and illicit GDPs (for example, opium). **k** 2001. **l** 2004. **m** 2009. **n** 2012. **o** Data refers to active subscriptions only. **p** Break in the time series.

Albania

Region	Southern Europe	UN membership date	14 December 1955
Population (000, 2017)	2 930 [a]	Surface area (km2)	28 748 [b]
Pop. density (per km2, 2017)	106.9 [a]	Sex ratio (m per 100 f, 2017)	101.9 [a]
Capital city	Tirana	National currency	Lek (ALL)
Capital city pop. (000)	453.5 [b]	Exchange rate (per US$)	128.2 [c]

Economic indicators

	2005	2010	2017
GDP: Gross domestic product (million current US$)	8 052	11 927	11 541 [b]
GDP growth rate (annual %, const. 2005 prices)	5.5	3.7	2.6 [b]
GDP per capita (current US$)	2 612.5	4 110.1	3 984.2 [b]
Economy: Agriculture (% of GVA) [d]	21.5	20.7	22.4 [b]
Economy: Industry (% of GVA) [d]	28.7	28.7	26.0 [b]
Economy: Services and other activity (% of GVA) [d]	49.8	50.7	51.7 [b]
Employment: Agriculture (% of employed) [e]	49.3	42.6	41.4
Employment: Industry (% of employed) [e]	17.8	19.9	18.3
Employment: Services (% of employed) [e]	32.9	37.5	40.3
Unemployment (% of labour force)	13.8 [e]	14.2	15.8 [e]
Labour force participation (female/male pop. %) [e]	47.6 / 68.5	44.1 / 63.6	40.2 / 61.0
CPI: Consumer Price Index (2000=100)	117	135	147 [f]
Agricultural production index (2004-2006=100)	98	119	134 [f]
Food production index (2004-2006=100)	98	119	134 [f]
Index of industrial production (2005=100)	100	200	355 [f]
International trade: Exports (million US$)	658	1 550	1 962 [c]
International trade: Imports (million US$)	2 614	4 603	4 669 [c]
International trade: Balance (million US$)	- 1 956	- 3 053	- 2 707 [c]
Balance of payments, current account (million US$)	- 571	- 1 354	- 1 222 [b]

Major trading partners

						2016
Export partners (% of exports)	Italy	54.6	Serbia	8.7	Greece	4.6
Import partners (% of imports)	Italy	29.3	Germany	9.5	China	8.8

Social indicators

	2005	2010	2017
Population growth rate (average annual %) [g]	- 0.3	- 0.9	- 0.1 [b]
Urban population (% of total population)	46.7	52.2	57.4 [b]
Urban population growth rate (average annual %) [g]	1.6	1.9	2.2 [b]
Fertility rate, total (live births per woman) [g]	1.9	1.6	1.7 [b]
Life expectancy at birth (females/males, years) [g]	77.8 / 72.2	78.5 / 73.2	79.9 / 75.6 [b]
Population age distribution (0-14 and 60+ years, %)	26.5 / 12.3	22.5 / 15.0	17.4 / 19.0 [a]
International migrant stock (000/% of total pop.)	64.7 / 2.1	52.8 / 1.8	57.6 / 2.0 [b]
Refugees and others of concern to UNHCR (000)	0.1 [h]	0.1 [h]	8.8 [c]
Infant mortality rate (per 1 000 live births) [g]	21.1	16.8	14.6 [b]
Health: Total expenditure (% of GDP)	6.1	5.3	5.9 [f]
Health: Physicians (per 1 000 pop.)	...	1.3	1.3 [i]
Education: Government expenditure (% of GDP)	3.2	3.3 [j]	3.5 [i]
Education: Primary gross enrol. ratio (f/m per 100 pop.)	101.0 / 101.9	97.7 / 100.2	111.7 / 115.5 [b]
Education: Secondary gross enrol. ratio (f/m per 100 pop.)	75.0 / 78.7	88.0 / 88.8	92.5 / 98.8 [b]
Education: Tertiary gross enrol. ratio (f/m per 100 pop.)	27.3 / 19.1	52.4 / 37.5	68.1 / 48.7 [b]
Intentional homicide rate (per 100 000 pop.)	5.0	4.4	2.3 [b]
Seats held by women in national parliaments (%)	6.4	16.4	22.9

Environment and infrastructure indicators

	2005	2010	2017
Mobile-cellular subscriptions (per 100 inhabitants)	47.9	85.5 [e]	106.4 [b]
Individuals using the Internet (per 100 inhabitants)	6.0	45.0	63.3 [e,b]
Research & Development expenditure (% of GDP)	...	0.2 [k,l]	...
Threatened species (number)	37 [m]	100	130
Forested area (% of land area) [e]	28.6	28.3	28.2 [f]
CO2 emission estimates (million tons/tons per capita)	4.3 / 1.4	4.6 / 1.6	5.7 / 2.0 [f]
Energy production, primary (Petajoules)	48	69	84 [f]
Energy supply per capita (Gigajoules)	29	31	36 [f]
Tourist/visitor arrivals at national borders (000) [n]	...	2 191	3 784 [b]
Important sites for terrestrial biodiversity protected (%)	44.0	58.8	68.5
Pop. using improved drinking water (urban/rural, %)	98.4 / 94.0	96.5 / 94.7	94.9 / 95.2 [b]
Pop. using improved sanitation facilities (urban/rural, %)	95.0 / 80.7	95.3 / 86.1	95.5 / 90.2 [b]
Net Official Development Assist. received (% of GNI)	3.79	3.09	2.96 [b]

a Projected estimate (medium fertility variant). **b** 2015. **c** 2016. **d** Data classified according to ISIC Rev. 4. **e** Estimate. **f** 2014. **g** Data refers to a 5-year period preceding the reference year. **h** Data as at the end of December. **i** 2013. **j** 2007. **k** Partial data. **l** 2008. **m** 2004. **n** Excluding nationals residing abroad.

Algeria

Region	Northern Africa	UN membership date	08 October 1962
Population (000, 2017)	41 318[a]	Surface area (km2)	2 381 741[b]
Pop. density (per km2, 2017)	17.3[a]	Sex ratio (m per 100 f, 2017)	102.0[a]
Capital city	Algiers	National currency	Algerian Dinar (DZD)
Capital city pop. (000)	2 594.1[c,b]	Exchange rate (per US$)	110.5[d]

Economic indicators

	2005	2010	2017
GDP: Gross domestic product (million current US$)	103 198	161 207	164 779[b]
GDP growth rate (annual %, const. 2005 prices)	5.9	3.6	3.8[b]
GDP per capita (current US$)	3 102.0	4 473.5	4 154.1[b]
Economy: Agriculture (% of GVA)	8.0	8.6	12.2[b]
Economy: Industry (% of GVA)	59.7	51.4	37.3[b]
Economy: Services and other activity (% of GVA)	32.3	40.0	50.5[b]
Employment: Agriculture (% of employed)[e]	17.2	12.5	10.8
Employment: Industry (% of employed)[e]	27.1	33.9	34.5
Employment: Services (% of employed)[e]	55.7	53.6	54.7
Unemployment (% of labour force)	15.3	10.0	11.4[e]
Labour force participation (female/male pop. %)[e]	12.8 / 71.8	14.4 / 70.0	17.0 / 70.7
CPI: Consumer Price Index (2000=100)	117	146	183[f]
Agricultural production index (2004-2006=100)	99	125	160[f]
Food production index (2004-2006=100)	99	125	161[f]
Index of industrial production (2005=100)[g]	100	97	104[f]
International trade: Exports (million US$)	46 002	57 051	29 992[d]
International trade: Imports (million US$)	20 357	41 000	47 091[d]
International trade: Balance (million US$)	25 645	16 051	- 17 099[d]
Balance of payments, current account (million US$)	21 180	12 220[h]	- 27 229[b]

Major trading partners

							2016
Export partners (% of exports)	Italy	17.4	Spain	12.9	United States	12.9
Import partners (% of imports)	China	17.9	France	10.1	Italy	9.9

Social indicators

	2005	2010	2017
Population growth rate (average annual %)[i]	1.3	1.6	2.0[b]
Urban population (% of total population)	63.8	67.5	70.7[b]
Urban population growth rate (average annual %)[i]	2.6	2.9	2.8[b]
Fertility rate, total (live births per woman)[i]	2.4	2.7	3.0[b]
Life expectancy at birth (females/males, years)[i]	72.9 / 70.1	75.2 / 72.6	76.5 / 74.1[b]
Population age distribution (0-14 and 60+ years, %)	29.1 / 7.0	27.2 / 7.8	29.3 / 9.4[a]
International migrant stock (000/% of total pop.)[j,k]	247.5 / 0.7	245.0 / 0.7	242.4 / 0.6[b]
Refugees and others of concern to UNHCR (000)	94.4[l]	94.4[l]	99.8[d]
Infant mortality rate (per 1 000 live births)[i]	37.3	32.6	27.7[b]
Health: Total expenditure (% of GDP)	3.2	5.1	7.2[f]
Health: Physicians (per 1 000 pop.)	1.0	1.2[m]	...
Education: Government expenditure (% of GDP)	...	4.4[n]	...
Education: Primary gross enrol. ratio (f/m per 100 pop.)	103.4 / 111.9	111.3 / 119.4	112.7 / 119.5[b]
Education: Secondary gross enrol. ratio (f/m per 100 pop.)	82.5 / 75.3	98.9 / 95.6	101.7 / 98.1[o]
Education: Tertiary gross enrol. ratio (f/m per 100 pop.)	23.3 / 18.3	35.3 / 24.5	45.1 / 28.9[b]
Intentional homicide rate (per 100 000 pop.)	0.6	0.7	1.4[b]
Seats held by women in national parliaments (%)	6.2	7.7	31.6

Environment and infrastructure indicators

	2005	2010	2017
Mobile-cellular subscriptions (per 100 inhabitants)	40.2	88.4	113.0[b]
Individuals using the Internet (per 100 inhabitants)	5.8	12.5	38.2[e,b]
Research & Development expenditure (% of GDP)	0.1[p]	...	...
Threatened species (number)	50[q]	105	135
Forested area (% of land area)	0.6	0.8	0.8[e,f]
CO2 emission estimates (million tons/tons per capita)	107.3 / 3.3	119.2 / 3.3	145.4 / 3.7[f]
Energy production, primary (Petajoules)	7 534	6 200	5 900[f]
Energy supply per capita (Gigajoules)	48	46	55[f]
Tourist/visitor arrivals at national borders (000)[r]	1 443	2 070	1 710[b]
Important sites for terrestrial biodiversity protected (%)	38.4	38.4	38.8
Pop. using improved drinking water (urban/rural, %)	90.3 / 83.3	87.3 / 82.5	84.3 / 81.8[b]
Pop. using improved sanitation facilities (urban/rural, %)	90.7 / 75.6	90.3 / 78.9	89.8 / 82.2[b]
Net Official Development Assist. received (% of GNI)	0.35	0.13	0.05[b]

a Projected estimate (medium fertility variant). **b** 2015. **c** Refers to the Governorate of Grand Algiers. **d** 2016. **e** Estimate. **f** 2014. **g** Data classified according to ISIC Rev. 3. **h** Break in the time series. **i** Data refers to a 5-year period preceding the reference year. **j** Including refugees. **k** Refers to foreign citizens. **l** Data as at the end of December. **m** 2007. **n** 2008. **o** 2011. **p** Partial data. **q** 2004. **r** Including nationals residing abroad.

American Samoa

Region	Polynesia	Population (000, 2017)	56[a]	
Surface area (km2)	199[b]	Pop. density (per km2, 2017)	278.2[a]	
Sex ratio (m per 100 f, 2017)	103.6[c,d]	Capital city	Pago Pago	
National currency	US Dollar (USD)	Capital city pop. (000)	48.3[e]	

Economic indicators	2005	2010	2017
Employment: Agriculture (% of employed)[f,g]	3.1[h]	3.0[c]	...
Employment: Industry (% of employed)[f,g]	41.7[h]	23.2[c]	...
Employment: Services (% of employed)[f,g]	51.9[h]	73.8[c]	...
Unemployment (% of labour force)[g]	5.1[h]	9.2[c]	...
Labour force participation (female/male pop. %)	41.2 / 58.8[g,h]	... / ...	... / ...
CPI: Consumer Price Index (2000=100)[i]	122	156	168[j]
Agricultural production index (2004-2006=100)	100	110	112[e]
Food production index (2004-2006=100)	100	110	112[e]

Social indicators	2005	2010	2017
Population growth rate (average annual %)[k]	0.5	- 1.2	~-0.0[b]
Urban population (% of total population)	88.1	87.6	87.2[b]
Urban population growth rate (average annual %)[k]	0.4	- 1.3	- 0.1[b]
Fertility rate, total (live births per woman)	...	...	2.6[l]
Life expectancy at birth (females/males, years)	... / ...	76.2 / 68.5[m]	77.8 / 71.1[i]
Population age distribution (0-14 and 60+ years, %)	38.8 / 5.4[n,o,h]	35.0 / 6.7[n,o]	33.3 / 9.0[c,d]
International migrant stock (000/% of total pop.)	24.2 / 41.0	23.6 / 42.3	23.2 / 41.8[b]
Infant mortality rate (per 1 000 live births)	...	...	9.6[p,q]

Environment and infrastructure indicators	2005	2010	2017
Mobile-cellular subscriptions (per 100 inhabitants)	3.5[h]	...	...
Threatened species (number)	24[r]	79	92
Forested area (% of land area)[s]	89.4	88.6	87.9[e]
Tourist/visitor arrivals at national borders (000)	24	23	20[b]
Important sites for terrestrial biodiversity protected (%)	61.5	61.5	61.5
Pop. using improved drinking water (urban/rural, %)	99.9 / 99.9	100.0 / 100.0	100.0 / 100.0[b]
Pop. using improved sanitation facilities (urban/rural, %)	61.9 / 61.9	62.3 / 62.3	62.5 / 62.5[b]

a Projected estimate (medium fertility variant). b 2015. c Break in the time series. d 2016. e 2014. f Data classified according to ISIC Rev. 3. g Population aged 16 years and over. h 2000. i Excluding "Rent". j 2011. k Data refers to a 5-year period preceding the reference year. l 2013. m 2006. n De jure population. o Including armed forces stationed in the area. p Data refers to a 2-year period up to and including the reference year. q 2012. r 2004. s Estimate.

Region	Southern Europe	UN membership date	28 July 1993	
Population (000, 2017)	77[a]	Surface area (km2)	468[b]	
Pop. density (per km2, 2017)	163.8[a]	Sex ratio (m per 100 f, 2017)	102.3[c,d,e]	
Capital city	Andorra la Vella	National currency	Euro (EUR)	
Capital city pop. (000)	23.4[f]	Exchange rate (per US$)	0.9[e]	

Economic indicators

	2005	2010	2017
GDP: Gross domestic product (million current US$)	3 256	3 355	2 812[b]
GDP growth rate (annual %, const. 2005 prices)	7.4	- 5.4	0.8[b]
GDP per capita (current US$)	40 083.6	39 748.1	39 896.4[b]
Economy: Agriculture (% of GVA)[g]	0.4	0.5	0.5[b]
Economy: Industry (% of GVA)[g]	17.3	14.6	10.8[b]
Economy: Services and other activity (% of GVA)[g]	82.3	84.8	88.6[b]
CPI: Consumer Price Index (2000=100)[h]	113	126	132[f]
International trade: Exports (million US$)	143	92	100[e]
International trade: Imports (million US$)	1 796	1 541	1 355[e]
International trade: Balance (million US$)	- 1 653	- 1 448	- 1 255[e]

Major trading partners

					2016
Export partners (% of exports)	Spain	59.0	France	17.9	Norway	5.5
Import partners (% of imports)	Spain	61.7	France	15.5	China	4.1

Social indicators

	2005	2010	2017
Population growth rate (average annual %)[i]	3.7	1.4	- 1.6[b]
Urban population (% of total population)	90.3	87.8	85.1[b]
Urban population growth rate (average annual %)[i]	3.9	- 1.4	0.1[b]
Fertility rate, total (live births per woman)	1.2	1.2	1.2[j]
Population age distribution (0-14 and 60+ years, %)[d,c]	15.1 / 16.1	14.0 / 18.6	14.4 / 19.0[e]
International migrant stock (000/% of total pop.)[k]	50.3 / 61.9	52.1 / 61.7	42.1 / 59.7[b]
Health: Total expenditure (% of GDP)	5.2	8.0	8.1[f]
Health: Physicians (per 1 000 pop.)	3.3[l]	3.1[m]	3.7[b]
Education: Government expenditure (% of GDP)	1.6	3.1	3.3[b]
Intentional homicide rate (per 100 000 pop.)	1.3[n]	1.2	1.2[o]
Seats held by women in national parliaments (%)	14.3	35.7	32.1

Environment and infrastructure indicators

	2005	2010	2017
Mobile-cellular subscriptions (per 100 inhabitants)	79.5	84.1	88.1[b]
Individuals using the Internet (per 100 inhabitants)	37.6	81.0	96.9[p,b]
Threatened species (number)	5[n]	8	13
Forested area (% of land area)[p]	34.0	34.0	34.0[f]
CO2 emission estimates (million tons/tons per capita)	0.6 / 7.4	0.5 / 6.2	0.5 / 6.4[f]
Energy production, primary (Petajoules)	0	1	1[f]
Energy supply per capita (Gigajoules)	130	114	119[f]
Tourist/visitor arrivals at national borders (000)	2 418	1 808[q]	2 670[b]
Important sites for terrestrial biodiversity protected (%)	5.7	5.7	19.4
Pop. using improved drinking water (urban/rural, %)	100.0 / 100.0	100.0 / 100.0	100.0 / 100.0[b]
Pop. using improved sanitation facilities (urban/rural, %)	100.0 / 100.0	100.0 / 100.0	100.0 / 100.0[b]

a Projected estimate (medium fertility variant). b 2015. c Population statistics are compiled from registers. d De jure population. e 2016. f 2014. g Data classified according to ISIC Rev. 4. h Index base: 2001=100. i Data refers to a 5-year period preceding the reference year. j 2012. k Refers to foreign citizens. l 2003. m 2009. n 2004. o 2011. p Estimate. q Break in the time series.

Angola

Region	Middle Africa	UN membership date	01 December 1976
Population (000, 2017)	29 784[a]	Surface area (km2)	1 246 700[b]
Pop. density (per km2, 2017)	23.9[a]	Sex ratio (m per 100 f, 2017)	96.2[a]
Capital city	Luanda	National currency	Kwanza (AOA)
Capital city pop. (000)	5 506.0[b]	Exchange rate (per US$)	165.9[c]

Economic indicators	2005	2010	2017
GDP: Gross domestic product (million current US$)	36 971	83 799	117 955[b]
GDP growth rate (annual %, const. 2005 prices)	15.0	4.7	3.0[b]
GDP per capita (current US$)	2 063.9	3 949.1	4 714.1[b]
Economy: Agriculture (% of GVA)	5.0	6.2	6.8[b]
Economy: Industry (% of GVA)	59.8	52.1	51.2[b]
Economy: Services and other activity (% of GVA)	35.2	41.7	42.0[b]
Employment: Agriculture (% of employed)[d]	7.1	4.9	4.2
Employment: Industry (% of employed)[d]	38.0	37.9	37.6
Employment: Services (% of employed)[d]	54.9	57.2	58.2
Unemployment (% of labour force)[d]	7.0	6.8	6.6
Labour force participation (female/male pop. %)[d]	61.4 / 76.9	59.3 / 77.4	59.8 / 77.1
CPI: Consumer Price Index (2000=100)[e]	1 846	3 438[f]	4 680[g]
Agricultural production index (2004-2006=100)	102	167	175[h]
Food production index (2004-2006=100)	102	168	176[h]
International trade: Exports (million US$)[i]	23 835	52 612	21 011[c]
International trade: Imports (million US$)[i]	8 321	18 143	8 790[c]
International trade: Balance (million US$)[i]	15 514	34 469	12 221[c]
Balance of payments, current account (million US$)	5 138	7 506	- 10 273[b]

Major trading partners						2016
Export partners (% of exports)	China	43.2	India	8.1	Spain	6.8
Import partners (% of imports)	China	16.9	Portugal	14.6	Republic of Korea	8.6

Social indicators	2005	2010	2017
Population growth rate (average annual %)[j]	3.5	3.6	3.5[b]
Urban population (% of total population)	36.2	40.1	44.1[b]
Urban population growth rate (average annual %)[j]	5.6	5.4	5.0[b]
Fertility rate, total (live births per woman)[j]	6.6	6.4	6.0[b]
Life expectancy at birth (females/males, years)[j]	52.5 / 47.5	58.2 / 53.0	63.0 / 57.4[b]
Population age distribution (0-14 and 60+ years, %)	47.2 / 3.7	47.3 / 3.6	46.8 / 4.0[a]
International migrant stock (000/% of total pop.)[k]	61.3 / 0.3	76.5 / 0.4	106.8 / 0.4[b]
Refugees and others of concern to UNHCR (000)	14.9[l]	19.4[l]	45.7[m,c]
Infant mortality rate (per 1 000 live births)[j]	108.3	83.8	65.4[b]
Health: Total expenditure (% of GDP)	4.1	3.4	3.3[h]
Health: Physicians (per 1 000 pop.)	0.1[n]	0.1[o]	...
Education: Government expenditure (% of GDP)	2.8	3.5	...
Education: Primary gross enrol. ratio (f/m per 100 pop.)	... / ...	101.8 / 125.2	100.4 / 156.9[p]
Education: Secondary gross enrol. ratio (f/m per 100 pop.)	15.2 / 18.4[d,q]	23.4 / 34.2	22.7 / 35.1[p]
Education: Tertiary gross enrol. ratio (f/m per 100 pop.)	0.6 / 1.0[d,q]	... / ...	8.2 / 10.4[b]
Intentional homicide rate (per 100 000 pop.)	11.5	10.5	9.6[b]
Seats held by women in national parliaments (%)	15.0	38.6	38.2

Environment and infrastructure indicators	2005	2010	2017
Mobile-cellular subscriptions (per 100 inhabitants)	9.7	48.1[d]	60.8[b]
Individuals using the Internet (per 100 inhabitants)	1.1	2.8[d]	12.4[d,b]
Threatened species (number)	76[n]	117	146
Forested area (% of land area)	47.4	46.9	46.5[d,h]
CO2 emission estimates (million tons/tons per capita)	19.2 / 1.2	29.1 / 1.4	34.8 / 1.4[h]
Energy production, primary (Petajoules)	2 934	4 057	3 902[h]
Energy supply per capita (Gigajoules)	22	24	25[h]
Tourist/visitor arrivals at national borders (000)	210	425	592[b]
Important sites for terrestrial biodiversity protected (%)	28.4	28.4	28.4
Pop. using improved drinking water (urban/rural, %)	66.1 / 34.6	71.9 / 30.6	75.4 / 28.2[b]
Pop. using improved sanitation facilities (urban/rural, %)	79.0 / 16.3	85.0 / 20.2	88.6 / 22.5[b]
Net Official Development Assist. received (% of GNI)	1.71	0.32	0.42[b]

a Projected estimate (medium fertility variant). **b** 2015. **c** 2016. **d** Estimate. **e** Luanda **f** Series linked to former series. **g** 2013. **h** 2014. **i** Imports FOB. **j** Data refers to a 5-year period preceding the reference year. **k** Including refugees. **l** Data as at the end of December. **m** Data relates to the end of 2015. **n** 2004. **o** 2009. **p** 2011. **q** 2002.

Anguilla

Region	Caribbean	Population (000, 2017)	15[a]
Surface area (km2)	91[b]	Pop. density (per km2, 2017)	165.7[a]
Sex ratio (m per 100 f, 2017)	97.6[c,d]	Capital city	The Valley
National currency	E. Caribbean Dollar (XCD)[e]	Capital city pop. (000)	1.0[f]
Exchange rate (per US$)	2.7[g]		

Economic indicators

	2005	2010	2017
GDP: Gross domestic product (million current US$)	229	268	320[b]
GDP growth rate (annual %, const. 2005 prices)	13.1	- 4.5	2.9[b]
GDP per capita (current US$)	18 130.5	19 460.3	21 879.6[b]
Economy: Agriculture (% of GVA)	2.7	2.0	2.3[b]
Economy: Industry (% of GVA)	19.3	15.8	15.7[b]
Economy: Services and other activity (% of GVA)	78.0	82.2	82.0[b]
Employment: Agriculture (% of employed)	2.9[h,i,j]	...	...
Employment: Industry (% of employed)	18.9[h,i,j]	...	...
Employment: Services (% of employed)	76.7[h,i,j]	...	...
Unemployment (% of labour force)	7.8[k]	...	...
Labour force participation (female/male pop. %)	67.2 / 77.2[k]	... / ...	... / ...
CPI: Consumer Price Index (2000=100)[l]	114	138	148[f]
International trade: Exports (million US$)	7	12	2[g]
International trade: Imports (million US$)	133	157	154[g]
International trade: Balance (million US$)	- 126	- 145	- 153[g]
Balance of payments, current account (million US$)	- 52	- 51	- 48[m]

Major trading partners

						2016
Export partners (% of exports)	United States	51.9	Saint Lucia	8.1	Israel	5.4
Import partners (% of imports)	United States	65.6	Japan	4.6	United Kingdom	3.8

Social indicators

	2005	2010	2017
Population growth rate (average annual %)[n]	2.6	1.7	1.2[b]
Urban population (% of total population)	100.0	100.0	100.0[b]
Urban population growth rate (average annual %)[n]	2.6	1.7	1.2[b]
Fertility rate, total (live births per woman)	1.8	2.0[o]	...
Life expectancy at birth (females/males, years)	81.1 / 76.5[p,q]	... / ...	... / ...
Population age distribution (0-14 and 60+ years, %)	27.7 / 10.2[j]	... / ...	23.3 / 7.6[c,d,r]
International migrant stock (000/% of total pop.)	4.7 / 37.1	5.1 / 37.1	5.5 / 37.4[b]
Refugees and others of concern to UNHCR (000)	...	...	~0.0[g]
Education: Government expenditure (% of GDP)	...	2.8[s]	...
Intentional homicide rate (per 100 000 pop.)	16.2[q]	7.4[t]	27.7[f]

Environment and infrastructure indicators

	2005	2010	2017
Mobile-cellular subscriptions (per 100 inhabitants)	103.4	186.6	177.9[u,b]
Individuals using the Internet (per 100 inhabitants)[u]	29.0	49.6	76.0[b]
Threatened species (number)	18[q]	33	52
Forested area (% of land area)[u]	61.1	61.1	61.1[f]
CO2 emission estimates (million tons/tons per capita)	0.1 / 9.5	0.2 / 10.9	0.1 / 9.8[f]
Energy production, primary (Petajoules)[u]	0	0	0[f]
Energy supply per capita (Gigajoules)[u]	132	155	136[f]
Tourist/visitor arrivals at national borders (000)[v]	62	62	73[b]
Important sites for terrestrial biodiversity protected (%)	6.3	6.3	6.3
Pop. using improved drinking water (urban/rural, %)	94.0 / ...	94.5 / ...	94.6 / ...[b]
Pop. using improved sanitation facilities (urban/rural, %)	94.7 / ...	97.3 / ...	97.9 / ...[b]

a Projected estimate (medium fertility variant). **b** 2015. **c** Provisional data. **d** 2011. **e** East Caribbean Dollar. **f** 2014. **g** 2016. **h** Break in the time series. **i** Data classified according to ISIC Rev. 3. **j** 2001. **k** 2002. **l** Index base: 2001=100. **m** 2013. **n** Data refers to a 5-year period preceding the reference year. **o** 2006. **p** Data refers to a 3-year period up to and including the reference year. **q** 2004. **r** Population aged 65 years and over. **s** 2008. **t** 2009. **u** Estimate. **v** Excluding nationals residing abroad.

Antigua and Barbuda

Region	Caribbean	UN membership date	11 November 1981
Population (000, 2017)	102 [a]	Surface area (km2)	442 [b]
Pop. density (per km2, 2017)	231.8 [a]	Sex ratio (m per 100 f, 2017)	92.3 [a]
Capital city	Saint John's	National currency	E. Caribbean Dollar (XCD) [c]
Capital city pop. (000)	22.0 [d]	Exchange rate (per US$)	2.7 [e]

Economic indicators	2005	2010	2017
GDP: Gross domestic product (million current US$)	1 015	1 148	1 356 [b]
GDP growth rate (annual %, const. 2005 prices)	6.3	- 7.0	4.1 [b]
GDP per capita (current US$)	12 293.1	13 159.5	14 764.5 [b]
Economy: Agriculture (% of GVA)	2.0	1.8	1.9 [b]
Economy: Industry (% of GVA)	16.5	18.3	18.3 [b]
Economy: Services and other activity (% of GVA)	81.5	79.9	79.8 [b]
Employment: Agriculture (% of employed) [f]	2.8	2.8 [g]	...
Employment: Industry (% of employed) [f]	15.6	15.6 [g]	...
Employment: Services (% of employed) [f]	81.6	81.6 [g]	...
Unemployment (% of labour force)	8.4 [h]	...	...
Labour force participation (female/male pop. %)	65.9 / 78.4 [h]	... / ...	... / ...
CPI: Consumer Price Index (2000=100)	110	123	133 [i]
Agricultural production index (2004-2006=100)	95	87	88 [d]
Food production index (2004-2006=100)	95	87	88 [d]
International trade: Exports (million US$)	121	35	61 [e]
International trade: Imports (million US$)	525	501	491 [e]
International trade: Balance (million US$)	- 405	- 466	- 429 [e]
Balance of payments, current account (million US$)	- 171	- 167	- 204 [i]

Major trading partners						2016
Export partners (% of exports)	United Kingdom	52.5	United States	16.2	Spain	12.8
Import partners (% of imports)	United States	53.5	China	6.3	Japan	4.7

Social indicators	2005	2010	2017
Population growth rate (average annual %) [j]	1.3	1.2	1.1 [b]
Urban population (% of total population)	29.2	26.2	23.8 [b]
Urban population growth rate (average annual %) [j]	- 0.7	- 1.1	- 0.9 [b]
Fertility rate, total (live births per woman) [j]	2.3	2.2	2.1 [b]
Life expectancy at birth (females/males, years) [j]	76.4 / 71.5	77.4 / 72.6	78.2 / 73.3 [b]
Population age distribution (0-14 and 60+ years, %)	28.4 / 9.3	26.6 / 8.9	23.9 / 10.9 [a]
International migrant stock (000/% of total pop.)	24.7 / 30.0	26.4 / 30.3	28.1 / 30.6 [b]
Refugees and others of concern to UNHCR (000)	...	...	~0.0 [e]
Infant mortality rate (per 1 000 live births) [j]	12.2	10.0	9.1 [b]
Health: Total expenditure (%·of GDP) [k]	4.4	5.6	5.5 [d]
Education: Government expenditure (% of GDP)	3.4 [l]	2.6 [m]	...
Education: Primary gross enrol. ratio (f/m per 100 pop.)	... / ...	98.8 / 107.9	94.1 / 100.0 [b]
Education: Secondary gross enrol. ratio (f/m per 100 pop.)	73.6 / 82.8 [n,o]	106.7 / 105.7	103.8 / 101.6 [b]
Education: Tertiary gross enrol. ratio (f/m per 100 pop.)	... / ...	22.7 / 9.1	31.1 / 15.1 [p]
Intentional homicide rate (per 100 000 pop.)	3.6	6.9	11.2 [p]
Seats held by women in national parliaments (%)	10.5	10.5	11.1

Environment and infrastructure indicators	2005	2010	2017
Mobile-cellular subscriptions (per 100 inhabitants)	104.2	192.6	137.2 [n,b]
Individuals using the Internet (per 100 inhabitants) [n]	27.0	47.0	65.2 [b]
Threatened species (number)	22 [q]	38	55
Forested area (% of land area) [n]	22.3	22.3	22.3 [d]
CO2 emission estimates (million tons/tons per capita)	0.4 / 5.1	0.5 / 6.0	0.5 / 5.8 [d]
Energy supply per capita (Gigajoules) [n]	75	86	84 [d]
Tourist/visitor arrivals at national borders (000) [r]	245 [s]	230 [s]	250 [b]
Important sites for terrestrial biodiversity protected (%)	19.0	19.0	19.0
Pop. using improved drinking water (urban/rural, %)	97.8 / 97.8	97.9 / 97.9	97.9 / 97.9 [b]
Pop. using improved sanitation facilities (urban/rural, %)	89.5 / 89.5	91.4 / 91.4	91.4 / 91.4 [t]
Net Official Development Assist. received (% of GNI)	0.84	1.78	0.12 [b]

a Projected estimate (medium fertility variant). **b** 2015. **c** East Caribbean Dollar. **d** 2014. **e** 2016. **f** Data classified according to ISIC Rev. 3. **g** 2008. **h** 2001. **i** 2013. **j** Data refers to a 5-year period preceding the reference year. **k** Data revision. **l** 2002. **m** 2009. **n** Estimate. **o** 2000. **p** 2012. **q** 2004. **r** Excluding nationals residing abroad. **s** Arrivals by air. **t** 2011.

Argentina

Region	South America	UN membership date	24 October 1945	
Population (000, 2017)	44 271 [a]	Surface area (km2)	2 780 400 [b]	
Pop. density (per km2, 2017)	16.2 [a]	Sex ratio (m per 100 f, 2017)	95.9 [a]	
Capital city	Buenos Aires	National currency	Argentine Peso (ARS)	
Capital city pop. (000)	15 180.2 [c,b]	Exchange rate (per US$)	15.9 [d]	

Economic indicators	2005	2010	2017
GDP: Gross domestic product (million current US$)	201 388	428 792	632 343 [b]
GDP growth rate (annual %, const. 2005 prices)	8.9	10.4	2.4 [b]
GDP per capita (current US$)	5 144.6	10 401.8	14 564.5 [b]
Economy: Agriculture (% of GVA)	9.3	8.4	6.0 [b]
Economy: Industry (% of GVA)	33.5	29.9	27.8 [b]
Economy: Services and other activity (% of GVA)	57.2	61.7	66.2 [b]
Employment: Agriculture (% of employed) [e]	1.1	1.3	2.0
Employment: Industry (% of employed) [e]	23.5	23.3	24.8
Employment: Services (% of employed) [e]	75.4	75.4	73.1
Unemployment (% of labour force)	11.5	7.7	6.5 [e]
Labour force participation (female/male pop. %) [e]	48.8 / 76.6	47.0 / 74.9	48.6 / 74.4
CPI: Consumer Price Index (2000=100) [f,g]	162	249	332 [h]
Agricultural production index (2004-2006=100)	105	112	119 [i]
Food production index (2004-2006=100)	105	112	119 [i]
International trade: Exports (million US$)	40 106	68 174	57 733 [d]
International trade: Imports (million US$)	28 689	56 792	55 610 [d]
International trade: Balance (million US$)	11 418	11 382	2 124 [d]
Balance of payments, current account (million US$)	5 274	- 1 516	- 15 944 [b]

Major trading partners						2016
Export partners (% of exports)	Brazil	15.6	United States	8.4	China	7.7
Import partners (% of imports)	Brazil	24.5	China	18.8	United States	13.1

Social indicators	2005	2010	2017
Population growth rate (average annual %) [j]	1.1	1.0	1.0 [b]
Urban population (% of total population)	90.1	91.0	91.8 [b]
Urban population growth rate (average annual %) [j]	1.1	1.1	1.0 [b]
Fertility rate, total (live births per woman) [j]	2.5	2.4	2.3 [b]
Life expectancy at birth (females/males, years) [j]	78.1 / 70.6	79.0 / 71.3	79.8 / 72.2 [b]
Population age distribution (0-14 and 60+ years, %)	26.9 / 13.8	25.9 / 14.4	24.9 / 15.4 [a]
International migrant stock (000/% of total pop.)	1 673.1 / 4.3	1 806.0 / 4.4	2 086.3 / 4.8 [b]
Refugees and others of concern to UNHCR (000)	3.9 [k]	4.2 [k]	5.0 [d]
Infant mortality rate (per 1 000 live births) [j]	15.0	14.6	13.7 [b]
Health: Total expenditure (% of GDP) [l]	6.8	6.6	4.8 [i]
Health: Physicians (per 1 000 pop.)	3.2 [m]	...	3.8 [h]
Education: Government expenditure (% of GDP)	3.8	5.0	5.3 [i]
Education: Primary gross enrol. ratio (f/m per 100 pop.)	116.6 / 117.7	115.9 / 117.5	109.8 / 110.2 [i]
Education: Secondary gross enrol. ratio (f/m per 100 pop.)	98.4 / 89.8	106.6 / 97.1	110.3 / 103.4 [i]
Education: Tertiary gross enrol. ratio (f/m per 100 pop.)	75.8 / 52.1	89.2 / 59.1	102.9 / 63.5 [i]
Intentional homicide rate (per 100 000 pop.)	...	...	6.5 [b]
Seats held by women in national parliaments (%)	33.7	38.5	38.9

Environment and infrastructure indicators	2005	2010	2017
Mobile-cellular subscriptions (per 100 inhabitants)	57.3	141.4	143.9 [n,b]
Individuals using the Internet (per 100 inhabitants)	17.7	45.0 [e]	69.4 [e,b]
Research & Development expenditure (% of GDP)	0.4	0.5	0.6 [i]
Threatened species (number)	186 [m]	213	256
Forested area (% of land area) [e]	11.0	10.4	10.0 [i]
CO2 emission estimates (million tons/tons per capita)	162.1 / 4.2	187.9 / 4.5	204.0 / 4.7 [i]
Energy production, primary (Petajoules)	3 609	3 343	3 167 [i]
Energy supply per capita (Gigajoules)	75	80	85 [i]
Tourist/visitor arrivals at national borders (000)	3 823	5 325	5 736 [b]
Important sites for terrestrial biodiversity protected (%)	29.7	32.0	33.2
Pop. using improved drinking water (urban/rural, %)	98.4 / 87.5	98.7 / 93.7	99.0 / 100.0 [b]
Pop. using improved sanitation facilities (urban/rural, %)	93.7 / 87.9	95.0 / 93.9	96.2 / 98.3 [b]
Net Official Development Assist. received (% of GNI)	0.04	0.03	0.01 [i]

a Projected estimate (medium fertility variant). b 2015. c Refers to Gran Buenos Aires. d 2016. e Estimate. f Buenos Aires g Metropolitan areas. h 2013. i 2014. j Data refers to a 5-year period preceding the reference year. k Data as at the end of December. l Data revision. m 2004. n Provisional data.

Armenia

Region	Western Asia	
Population (000, 2017)	2 930[a]	
Pop. density (per km2, 2017)	102.9[a]	
Capital city	Yerevan	
Capital city pop. (000)	1 044.4[b]	

UN membership date	02 March 1992
Surface area (km2)	29 743[b]
Sex ratio (m per 100 f, 2017)	88.8[a]
National currency	Armenian Dram (AMD)
Exchange rate (per US$)	483.9[c]

Economic indicators	2005	2010	2017
GDP: Gross domestic product (million current US$)	5 226	9 875	10 529[b]
GDP growth rate (annual %, const. 2005 prices)	13.9	2.2	3.0[b]
GDP per capita (current US$)	1 733.4	3 332.3	3 489.1[b]
Economy: Agriculture (% of GVA)[d]	20.0	18.0	19.0[b]
Economy: Industry (% of GVA)[d]	44.0	35.1	28.3[b]
Economy: Services and other activity (% of GVA)[d]	36.0	46.9	52.8[b]
Employment: Agriculture (% of employed)[e]	38.7	38.6	35.0
Employment: Industry (% of employed)[e]	18.3	17.3	15.7
Employment: Services (% of employed)[e]	43.0	44.0	49.3
Unemployment (% of labour force)	17.2[e]	19.0	16.6[e]
Labour force participation (female/male pop. %)[e]	48.5 / 67.7	50.9 / 72.3	55.3 / 74.2
CPI: Consumer Price Index (2000=100)	117	154	185[f]
Agricultural production index (2004-2006=100)	103	102	135[f]
Food production index (2004-2006=100)	103	102	135[f]
Index of industrial production (2005=100)[g]	100	105	...
International trade: Exports (million US$)	937	1 011	1 776[c]
International trade: Imports (million US$)	1 692	3 782	3 230[c]
International trade: Balance (million US$)	- 755	- 2 770	- 1 455[c]
Balance of payments, current account (million US$)	- 124	- 1 261	- 279[b]

Major trading partners						2016
Export partners (% of exports)	Russian Federation	20.9	Bulgaria	8.6	Georgia	8.0
Import partners (% of imports)	Russian Federation	30.8	China	11.0	Iran (Islamic Rep.)	5.1

Social indicators	2005	2010	2017
Population growth rate (average annual %)[h]	- 0.6	- 0.7	0.3[b]
Urban population (% of total population)	64.2	63.6	62.7[b]
Urban population growth rate (average annual %)[h]	- 0.6	- 0.5	- 0.1[b]
Fertility rate, total (live births per woman)[h]	1.6	1.7	1.6[b]
Life expectancy at birth (females/males, years)[h]	75.3 / 69.1	75.8 / 69.4	77.0 / 70.6[b]
Population age distribution (0-14 and 60+ years, %)	21.5 / 14.4	19.5 / 14.8	20.0 / 16.9[a]
International migrant stock (000/% of total pop.)[i]	469.1 / 15.6	221.6 / 7.5	191.2 / 6.3[b]
Refugees and others of concern to UNHCR (000)	219.6[j]	85.8[j]	19.3[c]
Infant mortality rate (per 1 000 live births)[h]	27.0	21.0	13.2[b]
Health: Total expenditure (% of GDP)	5.3	4.6	4.5[f]
Health: Physicians (per 1 000 pop.)	...	2.8	2.8[f]
Education: Government expenditure (% of GDP)	2.7	3.2	2.8[b]
Education: Primary gross enrol. ratio (f/m per 100 pop.)	98.2 / 91.0	111.2 / 95.8[k]	98.5 / 98.5[b]
Education: Secondary gross enrol. ratio (f/m per 100 pop.)	94.5 / 87.0[l]	105.1 / 89.9[k]	89.0 / 88.1[b]
Education: Tertiary gross enrol. ratio (f/m per 100 pop.)	46.7 / 30.4	63.1 / 40.3	46.9 / 41.6[b]
Intentional homicide rate (per 100 000 pop.)	1.9	1.9	2.4[b]
Seats held by women in national parliaments (%)	5.3	9.2	9.9

Environment and infrastructure indicators	2005	2010	2017
Mobile-cellular subscriptions (per 100 inhabitants)	10.6	130.4	115.2[b]
Individuals using the Internet (per 100 inhabitants)	5.3	25.0[e]	58.2[e,b]
Research & Development expenditure (% of GDP)	0.3[m]	0.2[m]	0.2[n,f]
Threatened species (number)	35[o]	36	114
Forested area (% of land area)	11.7	11.6	11.7[e,f]
CO2 emission estimates (million tons/tons per capita)	4.4 / 1.4	4.2 / 1.4	5.5 / 1.8[f]
Energy production, primary (Petajoules)	36	52	48[f]
Energy supply per capita (Gigajoules)	34	40[e]	46[f]
Tourist/visitor arrivals at national borders (000)	319	684	1 192[b]
Important sites for terrestrial biodiversity protected (%)	24.8	30.5	30.5
Pop. using improved drinking water (urban/rural, %)	99.1 / 89.1	99.6 / 96.5	100.0 / 100.0[b]
Pop. using improved sanitation facilities (urban/rural, %)	95.7 / 78.3	95.9 / 78.2	96.2 / 78.2[b]
Net Official Development Assist. received (% of GNI)	3.38	3.52	3.17[b]

a Projected estimate (medium fertility variant). **b** 2015. **c** 2016. **d** Data classified according to ISIC Rev. 4. **e** Estimate. **f** 2014. **g** Data classified according to ISIC Rev. 3. **h** Data refers to a 5-year period preceding the reference year. **i** Including refugees. **j** Data as at the end of December. **k** 2009. **l** 2000. **m** Partial data. **n** Excluding business enterprise. **o** 2004.

Aruba

Region	Caribbean	Population (000, 2017)	105[a]
Surface area (km2)	180[b]	Pop. density (per km2, 2017)	584.8[a]
Sex ratio (m per 100 f, 2017)	90.4[a]	Capital city	Oranjestad
National currency	Aruban Florin (AWG)	Capital city pop. (000)	29.0[c]
Exchange rate (per US$)	1.8[d]		

Economic indicators	2005	2010	2017
GDP: Gross domestic product (million current US$)	2 331	2 391	2 702[b]
GDP growth rate (annual %, const. 2005 prices)	1.2	- 3.4	0.1[b]
GDP per capita (current US$)	23 302.8	23 529.3	26 005.4[b]
Economy: Agriculture (% of GVA)[e]	0.4	0.5	0.5[b]
Economy: Industry (% of GVA)[f]	19.6	15.4	15.4[b]
Economy: Services and other activity (% of GVA)	80.0	84.2	84.1[b]
Employment: Agriculture (% of employed)[g,h]	0.5[i]	0.6[j]	0.6[k]
Employment: Industry (% of employed)[g,h]	16.4[i]	14.5[j]	14.0[k]
Employment: Services (% of employed)[g,h]	82.3[i]	84.4[j]	85.1[k]
Unemployment (% of labour force)	6.9[l]	10.6[g,i]	...
Labour force participation (female/male pop. %)[g]	... / ...	59.5 / 68.9[j,m]	58.8 / 69.6[k]
CPI: Consumer Price Index (2000=100)	117	139	143[c]
International trade: Exports (million US$)	106	125	95[d]
International trade: Imports (million US$)	1 030	1 071	1 117[d]
International trade: Balance (million US$)	- 924	- 947	- 1 022[d]
Balance of payments, current account (million US$)	105	- 460	96[b]

Major trading partners						2016
Export partners (% of exports)	Colombia	24.3	United States	19.4	Netherlands	16.6
Import partners (% of imports)	United States	55.1	Netherlands	12.8	Areas nes[n]	12.0

Social indicators	2005	2010	2017
Population growth rate (average annual %)[o]	1.9	0.3	0.5[b]
Urban population (% of total population)	44.9	43.1	41.5[b]
Urban population growth rate (average annual %)[o]	1.1	- 0.5	- 0.3[b]
Fertility rate, total (live births per woman)[o]	1.8	1.8	1.8[b]
Life expectancy at birth (females/males, years)[o]	76.4 / 71.5	77.1 / 72.2	77.8 / 72.9[b]
Population age distribution (0-14 and 60+ years, %)	21.5 / 12.6	20.9 / 15.5	17.9 / 19.7[a]
International migrant stock (000/% of total pop.)	32.5 / 32.5	34.3 / 33.8	36.1 / 34.8[b]
Refugees and others of concern to UNHCR (000)	...	~0.0[p]	~0.0[d]
Infant mortality rate (per 1 000 live births)[o]	17.8	16.2	14.8[b]
Education: Government expenditure (% of GDP)	4.7	6.7	6.2[c]
Education: Primary gross enrol. ratio (f/m per 100 pop.)	107.8 / 115.0	113.0 / 114.5	115.4 / 119.1[c]
Education: Secondary gross enrol. ratio (f/m per 100 pop.)	96.1 / 95.7	98.3 / 93.5	112.1 / 110.3[q]
Education: Tertiary gross enrol. ratio (f/m per 100 pop.)	37.3 / 25.9	43.9 / 31.1	21.4 / 9.4[b]
Intentional homicide rate (per 100 000 pop.)	12.0	3.9	...

Environment and infrastructure indicators	2005	2010	2017
Mobile-cellular subscriptions (per 100 inhabitants)	103.4	129.7[r]	135.7[r,b]
Individuals using the Internet (per 100 inhabitants)[r]	25.4	62.0	88.7[b]
Threatened species (number)	18[s]	22	32
Forested area (% of land area)[r]	2.3	2.3	2.3[c]
CO2 emission estimates (million tons/tons per capita)	2.7 / 26.9	2.5 / 24.7	0.9 / 8.4[c]
Energy production, primary (Petajoules)[r]	5	5	1[c]
Energy supply per capita (Gigajoules)	299	273[r]	120[r,c]
Tourist/visitor arrivals at national borders (000)	733	824	1 225[b]
Important sites for terrestrial biodiversity protected (%)	0.0	0.0	0.0
Pop. using improved drinking water (urban/rural, %)	95.8 / 95.8	97.4 / 97.4	98.1 / 98.1[b]
Pop. using improved sanitation facilities (urban/rural, %)	98.0 / 98.0	97.7 / 97.7	97.7 / 97.7[b]

a Projected estimate (medium fertility variant). b 2015. c 2014. d 2016. e Includes mining and quarrying. f Excludes mining and quarrying. g Break in the time series. h Data classified according to ISIC Rev. 3. i 2000. j Population aged 14 years and over. k 2011. l 2001. m Resident population (de jure). n Areas not elsewhere specified. o Data refers to a 5-year period preceding the reference year. p Data as at the end of December. q 2012. r Estimate. s 2004.

Australia

Region	Oceania	UN membership date	01 November 1945
Population (000, 2017)	24 451 [a,b]	Surface area (km2)	7 692 060 [c,d]
Pop. density (per km2, 2017)	3.2 [a,b]	Sex ratio (m per 100 f, 2017)	99.3 [a,b]
Capital city	Canberra	National currency	Australian Dollar (AUD)
Capital city pop. (000)	422.7 [d]	Exchange rate (per US$)	1.4 [e]

Economic indicators

	2005	2010	2017
GDP: Gross domestic product (million current US$)	761 783	1 293 201	1 230 859 [d]
GDP growth rate (annual %, const. 2005 prices)	3.0	2.4	2.4 [d]
GDP per capita (current US$)	37 573.8	58 349.9	51 352.2 [d]
Economy: Agriculture (% of GVA) [f]	3.0	2.5	2.5 [d]
Economy: Industry (% of GVA) [f]	27.9	28.5	26.5 [d]
Economy: Services and other activity (% of GVA) [f]	69.1	69.0	71.1 [d]
Employment: Agriculture (% of employed) [g]	3.5	3.3	2.7
Employment: Industry (% of employed) [g]	21.4	20.9	21.2
Employment: Services (% of employed) [g]	75.1	75.7	76.1
Unemployment (% of labour force)	5.0	5.2	5.5 [g]
Labour force participation (female/male pop. %) [g]	57.0 / 72.2	58.7 / 72.5	58.4 / 70.7
CPI: Consumer Price Index (2000=100)	116	134	148 [h]
Agricultural production index (2004-2006=100)	108	100	111 [h]
Food production index (2004-2006=100)	108	102	111 [h]
Index of industrial production (2005=100) [i]	100	111	123 [h]
International trade: Exports (million US$) [j]	106 011	212 109	189 630 [e]
International trade: Imports (million US$) [j]	125 221	201 703	189 406 [e]
International trade: Balance (million US$) [j]	- 19 210	10 405	224 [e]
Balance of payments, current account (million US$)	- 43 342	- 44 714	- 57 746 [d]

Major trading partners

						2016
Export partners (% of exports)	China	31.6	Japan	13.9	Republic of Korea	6.7
Import partners (% of imports)	China	23.4	United States	11.5	Japan	7.7

Social indicators

	2005	2010	2017
Population growth rate (average annual %) [b,k]	1.2	1.8	1.5 [d]
Urban population (% of total population) [b]	88.0	88.7	89.4 [d]
Urban population growth rate (average annual %) [b,k]	1.5	1.9	1.5 [d]
Fertility rate, total (live births per woman) [b,k]	1.8	2.0	1.9 [d]
Life expectancy at birth (females/males, years) [b,k]	82.8 / 77.8	83.8 / 79.2	84.4 / 80.2 [d]
Population age distribution (0-14 and 60+ years, %) [b]	19.8 / 17.4	19.0 / 18.9	19.0 / 21.0 [a]
International migrant stock (000/% of total pop.) [b]	4 878.0 / 24.1	5 883.0 / 26.5	6 763.7 / 28.2 [d]
Refugees and others of concern to UNHCR (000)	66.8 [l]	25.6 [l]	58.2 [e]
Infant mortality rate (per 1 000 live births) [b,k]	4.9	4.4	3.9 [d]
Health: Total expenditure (% of GDP)	8.5	9.0	9.4 [h]
Health: Physicians (per 1 000 pop.)	2.5 [m]	2.9 [n]	3.4 [o]
Education: Government expenditure (% of GDP)	4.9	5.6	5.2 [h]
Education: Primary gross enrol. ratio (f/m per 100 pop.)	103.2 / 101.6	105.6 / 105.8	102.1 / 102.3 [d]
Education: Secondary gross enrol. ratio (f/m per 100 pop.)	146.5 / 150.1	130.3 / 134.4	133.6 / 141.3 [h]
Education: Tertiary gross enrol. ratio (f/m per 100 pop.)	80.8 / 64.2	94.5 / 68.4	106.3 / 75.4 [h]
Intentional homicide rate (per 100 000 pop.)	1.3	1.0	1.0 [d]
Seats held by women in national parliaments (%)	24.7	27.3	28.7

Environment and infrastructure indicators

	2005	2010	2017
Mobile-cellular subscriptions (per 100 inhabitants)	89.8	100.4	132.8 [p,d]
Individuals using the Internet (per 100 inhabitants)	63.0 [q]	76.0 [g]	84.6 [q,d]
Research & Development expenditure (% of GDP)	1.9 [r]	2.4 [g]	2.2 [g,o]
Threatened species (number) [s]	621 [r]	853	948
Forested area (% of land area)	16.6	16.0	16.2 [g,h]
CO2 emission estimates (million tons/tons per capita)	350.2 / 17.2	390.9 / 17.6	361.3 / 15.3 [h]
Energy production, primary (Petajoules) [s]	11 451	13 620	15 282 [h]
Energy supply per capita (Gigajoules) [s]	233	245	222 [h]
Tourist/visitor arrivals at national borders (000) [t]	5 499	5 790	7 444 [d]
Important sites for terrestrial biodiversity protected (%)	46.3	51.3	53.2
Pop. using improved drinking water (urban/rural, %)	100.0 / 100.0	100.0 / 100.0	100.0 / 100.0 [d]
Pop. using improved sanitation facilities (urban/rural, %)	100.0 / 100.0	100.0 / 100.0	100.0 / 100.0 [d]
Net Official Development Assist. disbursed (% of GNI) [u]	0.25	0.32	0.25 [v,e]

a Projected estimate (medium fertility variant). b Including Christmas Island, Cocos (Keeling) Islands and Norfolk Island. c Including Norfolk Island. d 2015. e 2016. f Data classified according to ISIC Rev. 4. g Estimate. h 2014. i Twelve months ending 30 June of the year stated. j Imports FOB. k Data refers to a 5-year period preceding the reference year. l Data as at the end of December. m 2001. n 2009. o 2013. p Data as at the end of June. q Population aged 15 years and over. r 2004. s Excluding overseas territories. t Excluding nationals residing abroad and crew members. u Development Assistance Committee member (OECD) v Provisional data.

Austria

Region	Western Europe	UN membership date	14 December 1955
Population (000, 2017)	8 736 [a]	Surface area (km2)	83 871 [b]
Pop. density (per km2, 2017)	106.0 [a]	Sex ratio (m per 100 f, 2017)	96.2 [a]
Capital city	Vienna	National currency	Euro (EUR)
Capital city pop. (000)	1 752.8 [b]	Exchange rate (per US$)	0.9 [c]

Economic indicators

	2005	2010	2017
GDP: Gross domestic product (million current US$)	314 641	390 212	376 967 [b]
GDP growth rate (annual %, const. 2005 prices)	2.1	1.9	1.0 [b]
GDP per capita (current US$)	38 208.4	46 498.2	44 117.7 [b]
Economy: Agriculture (% of GVA) [d]	1.4	1.4	1.3 [b]
Economy: Industry (% of GVA) [d]	30.4	28.7	28.3 [b]
Economy: Services and other activity (% of GVA) [d]	68.2	69.9	70.4 [b]
Employment: Agriculture (% of employed) [e]	5.3	5.2	4.7
Employment: Industry (% of employed) [e]	27.6	24.8	25.6
Employment: Services (% of employed) [e]	67.2	70.0	69.7
Unemployment (% of labour force)	5.6	4.8	6.2 [e]
Labour force participation (female/male pop. %) [e]	51.2 / 67.3	53.9 / 67.6	54.6 / 65.8
CPI: Consumer Price Index (2000=100)	111	121	133 [f]
Agricultural production index (2004-2006=100)	100	105	108 [f]
Food production index (2004-2006=100)	100	105	108 [f]
Index of industrial production (2005=100)	100	110	119 [f]
International trade: Exports (million US$)	117 722	144 882	145 503 [c]
International trade: Imports (million US$)	119 950	150 593	149 299 [c]
International trade: Balance (million US$)	- 2 228	- 5 711	- 3 795 [c]
Balance of payments, current account (million US$)	6 245	11 480	7 020 [b]

Major trading partners

						2016
Export partners (% of exports)	Germany	29.5	United States	6.7	Italy	6.2
Import partners (% of imports)	Germany	36.4	Italy	6.0	China	5.9

Social indicators

	2005	2010	2017
Population growth rate (average annual %) [g]	0.5	0.4	0.6 [b]
Urban population (% of total population)	65.8	65.9	66.0 [b]
Urban population growth rate (average annual %) [g]	0.5	0.4	0.4 [b]
Fertility rate, total (live births per woman) [g]	1.4	1.4	1.4 [b]
Life expectancy at birth (females/males, years) [g]	81.7 / 75.9	82.8 / 77.3	83.5 / 78.4 [b]
Population age distribution (0-14 and 60+ years, %)	16.0 / 22.1	14.7 / 23.3	14.1 / 25.1 [a]
International migrant stock (000/% of total pop.)	1 136.3 / 13.8	1 276.0 / 15.2	1 492.4 / 17.5 [b]
Refugees and others of concern to UNHCR (000)	62.8 [h]	68.7 [h]	166.4 [c]
Infant mortality rate (per 1 000 live births) [g]	4.5	3.8	3.3 [b]
Health: Total expenditure (% of GDP)	10.5	11.2	11.2 [f]
Health: Physicians (per 1 000 pop.)	...	4.8	5.2 [b]
Education: Government expenditure (% of GDP)	5.3	5.7	5.5 [f]
Education: Primary gross enrol. ratio (f/m per 100 pop.)	100.9 / 101.1	99.1 / 100.5	102.2 / 103.7 [b]
Education: Secondary gross enrol. ratio (f/m per 100 pop.)	98.0 / 102.9	96.8 / 100.8	97.6 / 102.4 [b]
Education: Tertiary gross enrol. ratio (f/m per 100 pop.)	52.2 / 43.5	74.2 / 63.4	89.2 / 74.3 [b]
Intentional homicide rate (per 100 000 pop.)	0.7	0.7	0.5 [b]
Seats held by women in national parliaments (%)	33.9	27.9	30.6

Environment and infrastructure indicators

	2005	2010	2017
Mobile-cellular subscriptions (per 100 inhabitants)	105.2	145.7	157.4 [b]
Individuals using the Internet (per 100 inhabitants) [i]	58.0	75.2	83.9 [b]
Research & Development expenditure (% of GDP) [e]	2.4	2.7	3.0 [f]
Threatened species (number)	67 [j]	82	118
Forested area (% of land area)	46.6 [e]	46.7	46.9 [e,f]
CO2 emission estimates (million tons/tons per capita)	74.2 / 9.0	67.5 / 8.0	58.7 / 6.9 [f]
Energy production, primary (Petajoules)	418	503	505 [f]
Energy supply per capita (Gigajoules)	173	170	158 [f]
Tourist/visitor arrivals at national borders (000) [k]	19 952	22 004	26 719 [b]
Important sites for terrestrial biodiversity protected (%)	62.6	64.9	65.0
Pop. using improved drinking water (urban/rural, %)	100.0 / 100.0	100.0 / 100.0	100.0 / 100.0 [b]
Pop. using improved sanitation facilities (urban/rural, %)	100.0 / 100.0	100.0 / 100.0	100.0 / 100.0 [b]
Net Official Development Assist. disbursed (% of GNI) [l]	0.52	0.32	0.41 [m,c]

a Projected estimate (medium fertility variant). **b** 2015. **c** 2016. **d** Data classified according to ISIC Rev. 4. **e** Estimate. **f** 2014. **g** Data refers to a 5-year period preceding the reference year. **h** Data as at the end of December. **i** Population aged 16 to 74 years. **j** 2004. **k** Including leisure and business trips abroad with at least one overnight stay. **l** Development Assistance Committee member (OECD) **m** Provisional data.

Azerbaijan

Region	Western Asia	UN membership date	02 March 1992
Population (000, 2017)	9 828[a,b]	Surface area (km2)	86 600[c]
Pop. density (per km2, 2017)	118.9[a,b]	Sex ratio (m per 100 f, 2017)	99.3[a,b]
Capital city	Baku	National currency	Azerbaijan manat (AZN)
Capital city pop. (000)	2 373.6[d,c]	Exchange rate (per US$)	1.8[e]

Economic indicators	2005	2010	2017
GDP: Gross domestic product (million current US$)	13 245	52 906	53 049[c]
GDP growth rate (annual %, const. 2005 prices)	28.0	4.6	0.7[c]
GDP per capita (current US$)	1 546.7	5 813.9	5 438.7[c]
Economy: Agriculture (% of GVA)[f]	9.8	5.9	6.7[c]
Economy: Industry (% of GVA)[f]	63.2	64.0	49.9[c]
Economy: Services and other activity (% of GVA)[f]	27.0	30.1	43.4[c]
Employment: Agriculture (% of employed)[g]	39.3	38.2	36.7
Employment: Industry (% of employed)[g]	12.0	13.7	14.2
Employment: Services (% of employed)[g]	48.6	48.1	49.1
Unemployment (% of labour force)	7.3	5.6	5.2[g]
Labour force participation (female/male pop. %)[g]	60.5 / 66.3	61.8 / 67.4	62.0 / 68.8
CPI: Consumer Price Index (2000=100)	125	204	...
Agricultural production index (2004-2006=100)	104	118	131[h]
Food production index (2004-2006=100)	103	122	136[h]
Index of industrial production (2005=100)	100	200	188[h]
International trade: Exports (million US$)	4 347	21 278	9 143[e]
International trade: Imports (million US$)	4 211	6 597	8 532[e]
International trade: Balance (million US$)	136	14 682	611[e]
Balance of payments, current account (million US$)	167	15 040	- 222[c]

Major trading partners						2016
Export partners (% of exports)	Italy	21.3	Germany	10.8	Spain	9.6
Import partners (% of imports)	Russian Federation	15.6	Turkey	12.7	United States	9.2

Social indicators	2005	2010	2017
Population growth rate (average annual %)[b,i]	1.0	1.1	1.3[c]
Urban population (% of total population)[b]	52.4	53.4	54.6[c]
Urban population growth rate (average annual %)[b,i]	1.5	1.6	1.6[c]
Fertility rate, total (live births per woman)[b,i]	1.9	1.8	2.1[c]
Life expectancy at birth (females/males, years)[b,i]	70.3 / 64.6	73.4 / 66.9	74.6 / 68.6[c]
Population age distribution (0-14 and 60+ years, %)[b]	26.2 / 8.5	22.8 / 8.1	23.3 / 10.1[a]
International migrant stock (000/% of total pop.)[b,i]	302.2 / 3.5	276.9 / 3.0	264.2 / 2.7[c]
Refugees and others of concern to UNHCR (000)	584.3[k]	596.9[k]	623.3[e]
Infant mortality rate (per 1 000 live births)[b,i]	54.2	40.7	31.4[c]
Health: Total expenditure (% of GDP)[l]	7.9	5.3	6.0[h]
Health: Physicians (per 1 000 pop.)	...	3.6	3.4[h]
Education: Government expenditure (% of GDP)	3.0	2.8	2.6[h]
Education: Primary gross enrol. ratio (f/m per 100 pop.)[g]	92.8 / 98.2	93.2 / 94.2	105.6 / 107.4[c]
Education: Tertiary gross enrol. ratio (f/m per 100 pop.)[g]	... / ...	19.2 / 19.4	27.5 / 23.6[c]
Intentional homicide rate (per 100 000 pop.)	2.2	2.1	2.4[h]
Seats held by women in national parliaments (%)	10.5	11.4	16.8

Environment and infrastructure indicators	2005	2010	2017
Mobile-cellular subscriptions (per 100 inhabitants)	26.2	100.1	111.3[c]
Individuals using the Internet (per 100 inhabitants)	8.0	46.0[m]	77.0[m,c]
Research & Development expenditure (% of GDP)	0.2[n]	0.2	0.2[h]
Threatened species (number)	38[o]	45	97
Forested area (% of land area)[g]	10.6	12.2	13.5[h]
CO2 emission estimates (million tons/tons per capita)	34.3 / 4.0	30.7 / 3.4	37.5 / 3.9[h]
Energy production, primary (Petajoules)	1 155	2 759	2 459[h]
Energy supply per capita (Gigajoules)	67	53	61[h]
Tourist/visitor arrivals at national borders (000)	693	1 280	1 922[c]
Important sites for terrestrial biodiversity protected (%)	33.3	39.4	39.4
Pop. using improved drinking water (urban/rural, %)	90.5 / 65.3	92.6 / 71.5	94.7 / 77.8[c]
Pop. using improved sanitation facilities (urban/rural, %)	81.9 / 64.6	86.8 / 75.6	91.6 / 86.6[c]
Net Official Development Assist. disbursed (% of GNI)	...	...	0.02[c]
Net Official Development Assist. received (% of GNI)	1.82	0.33	0.14[c]

a Projected estimate (medium fertility variant). **b** Including Nagorno-Karabakh. **c** 2015. **d** Including communities under the authority of the Town Council. **e** 2016. **f** Data classified according to ISIC Rev. 4. **g** Estimate. **h** 2014. **i** Data refers to a 5-year period preceding the reference year. **j** Including refugees. **k** Data as at the end of December. **l** Adjustments for currency change (from old to new manat) were made for the entire Azerbaijan series starting from World Health Statistics 2008. **m** Population aged 7 years and over. **n** Data have been converted from the former national currency using the appropriate conversion rate. **o** 2004.

Bahamas

Region	Caribbean	UN membership date	18 September 1973
Population (000, 2017)	395[a]	Surface area (km2)	13 940[b]
Pop. density (per km2, 2017)	39.5[a]	Sex ratio (m per 100 f, 2017)	95.9[a]
Capital city	Nassau	National currency	Bahamian Dollar (BSD)
Capital city pop. (000)	266.8[c]	Exchange rate (per US$)	1.0[d]

Economic indicators

	2005	2010	2017
GDP: Gross domestic product (million current US$)	7 706	7 910	8 854[b]
GDP growth rate (annual %, const. 2005 prices)	3.4	1.5	- 1.7[b]
GDP per capita (current US$)	23 405.9	21 920.5	22 817.2[b]
Economy: Agriculture (% of GVA)[e,f]	2.1	2.2	1.6[b]
Economy: Industry (% of GVA)[e,f]	14.6	15.2	12.7[b]
Economy: Services and other activity (% of GVA)[e,f]	83.4	82.6	85.7[b]
Employment: Agriculture (% of employed)[g]	3.5	3.3	3.9
Employment: Industry (% of employed)[g]	17.8	14.4	14.2
Employment: Services (% of employed)[g]	78.7	82.2	81.9
Unemployment (% of labour force)	10.2	14.3[g]	14.7[g]
Labour force participation (female/male pop. %)[g]	67.7 / 77.8	69.5 / 79.2	69.4 / 79.1[g]
CPI: Consumer Price Index (2000=100)	110[h]	125	133[c]
Agricultural production index (2004-2006=100)	99	124	132[c]
Food production index (2004-2006=100)	99	124	132[c]
International trade: Exports (million US$)[i]	271	620	365[d]
International trade: Imports (million US$)[i]	2 567	2 862	2 904[d]
International trade: Balance (million US$)[i]	- 2 296	- 2 242	- 2 539[d]
Balance of payments, current account (million US$)	- 701	- 814	- 1 409[b]

Major trading partners

						2016
Export partners (% of exports)	United States	83.1	France	4.4	Finland	3.2
Import partners (% of imports)	United States	81.9	Areas nes[j]	3.0	Dominica	1.5

Social indicators

	2005	2010	2017
Population growth rate (average annual %)[k]	2.0	1.8	1.4[b]
Urban population (% of total population)	82.3	82.5	82.9[b]
Urban population growth rate (average annual %)[k]	2.1	1.9	1.5[b]
Fertility rate, total (live births per woman)[k]	1.9	1.9	1.8[b]
Life expectancy at birth (females/males, years)[k]	76.2 / 70.0	77.3 / 71.2	78.1 / 72.0[b]
Population age distribution (0-14 and 60+ years, %)	25.6 / 9.4	22.5 / 10.5	20.5 / 13.5[a]
International migrant stock (000/% of total pop.)	45.6 / 13.8	54.7 / 15.2	59.3 / 15.3[b]
Refugees and others of concern to UNHCR (000)	...	~0.0[l]	0.1[d]
Infant mortality rate (per 1 000 live births)[k]	11.6	10.0	9.1[b]
Health: Total expenditure (% of GDP)	6.0	7.4	7.7[c]
Health: Physicians (per 1 000 pop.)	...	2.7[m]	...
Education: Government expenditure (% of GDP)	2.8[g,n]	...	...
Education: Primary gross enrol. ratio (f/m per 100 pop.)	108.4 / 109.9	108.9 / 106.9	... / ...
Education: Secondary gross enrol. ratio (f/m per 100 pop.)	89.1 / 89.5	95.1 / 90.2	... / ...
Intentional homicide rate (per 100 000 pop.)	15.8	26.0	29.8[o]
Seats held by women in national parliaments (%)	20.0	12.2	13.2

Environment and infrastructure indicators

	2005	2010	2017
Mobile-cellular subscriptions (per 100 inhabitants)	69.2	118.8	80.3[b]
Individuals using the Internet (per 100 inhabitants)[g]	25.0	43.0	78.0[b]
Threatened species (number)	42[p]	62	86
Forested area (% of land area)[g]	51.4	51.4	51.4[c]
CO2 emission estimates (million tons/tons per capita)	1.7 / 5.5	1.7 / 4.6	2.4 / 6.3[c]
Energy production, primary (Petajoules)	0	0	0[c]
Energy supply per capita (Gigajoules)	79[g]	67	90[c]
Tourist/visitor arrivals at national borders (000)	1 608	1 370	1 484[b]
Important sites for terrestrial biodiversity protected (%)	9.7	9.8	9.8
Pop. using improved drinking water (urban/rural, %)	97.3 / 97.3	98.1 / 98.1	98.4 / 98.4[b]
Pop. using improved sanitation facilities (urban/rural, %)	90.0 / 90.0	91.4 / 91.4	92.0 / 92.0[b]

a Projected estimate (medium fertility variant). **b** 2015. **c** 2014. **d** 2016. **e** Data classified according to ISIC Rev. 4. **f** At producers' prices. **g** Estimate. **h** Break in the time series. **i** Trade statistics exclude certain oil and chemical products. **j** Areas not elsewhere specified. **k** Data refers to a 5-year period preceding the reference year. **l** Data as at the end of December. **m** 2008. **n** 2000. **o** 2012. **p** 2004.

Bahrain

Region	Western Asia	
Population (000, 2017)	1 493[a]	
Pop. density (per km2, 2017)	1 963.9[a]	
Capital city	Manama	
Capital city pop. (000)	411.2[c,b]	

UN membership date	21 September 1971	
Surface area (km2)	771[b]	
Sex ratio (m per 100 f, 2017)	168.3[a]	
National currency	Bahraini Dinar (BHD)	
Exchange rate (per US$)	0.4[d]	

Economic indicators	2005	2010	2017
GDP: Gross domestic product (million current US$)	15 969	25 713	31 126[b]
GDP growth rate (annual %, const. 2005 prices)	6.8	4.3	2.9[b]
GDP per capita (current US$)	18 418.1	20 386.0	22 600.2[b]
Economy: Agriculture (% of GVA)[e]	0.3	0.3	0.3[b]
Economy: Industry (% of GVA)[e]	42.8	45.5	40.7[b]
Economy: Services and other activity (% of GVA)[e]	56.9	54.2	59.0[b]
Employment: Agriculture (% of employed)[f]	1.4	1.1	1.0
Employment: Industry (% of employed)[f]	30.2	35.7	33.4
Employment: Services (% of employed)[f]	68.4	63.2	65.6
Unemployment (% of labour force)	1.3[f]	1.1	1.3[f]
Labour force participation (female/male pop. %)[f]	36.2 / 84.5	41.3 / 87.0	38.5 / 84.9
CPI: Consumer Price Index (2000=100)	105[g]	120	130[h]
Agricultural production index (2004-2006=100)	91	113	167[h]
Food production index (2004-2006=100)	91	113	167[h]
Index of industrial production (2005=100)[i]	100	117	134[h]
International trade: Exports (million US$)	10 239	16 059	12 892[d]
International trade: Imports (million US$)	9 339	16 002	14 749[d]
International trade: Balance (million US$)	899	58	- 1 856[d]
Balance of payments, current account (million US$)	1 474	770	1 124[h]

Major trading partners						2016
Export partners (% of exports)	Saudi Arabia	18.1	United Arab Emirates	17.3	United States	11.5
Import partners (% of imports)	Areas nes[j]	21.4	China	9.7	United States	8.6

Social indicators	2005	2010	2017
Population growth rate (average annual %)[k]	5.8	6.7	2.0[b]
Urban population (% of total population)	88.4	88.5	88.8[b]
Urban population growth rate (average annual %)[k]	5.5	7.1	1.7[b]
Fertility rate, total (live births per woman)[k]	2.6	2.2	2.1[b]
Life expectancy at birth (females/males, years)[k]	75.8 / 74.2	76.7 / 74.9	77.5 / 75.6[b]
Population age distribution (0-14 and 60+ years, %)	25.7 / 3.4	20.3 / 3.5	19.7 / 4.6[a]
International migrant stock (000/% of total pop.)[l]	404.0 / 46.6	657.9 / 52.2	704.1 / 51.1[b]
Refugees and others of concern to UNHCR (000)	~0.0[m]	0.2[h]	0.4[d]
Infant mortality rate (per 1 000 live births)[k]	9.8	8.0	6.9[b]
Health: Total expenditure (% of GDP)[n]	3.2	3.6	5.0[h]
Health: Physicians (per 1 000 pop.)	1.1	0.9	0.9[h]
Education: Government expenditure (% of GDP)	...	2.5[o]	2.7[b]
Education: Primary gross enrol. ratio (f/m per 100 pop.)	97.5 / 94.1	101.0 / 96.1[p]	101.8 / 100.6[b]
Education: Secondary gross enrol. ratio (f/m per 100 pop.)	101.5 / 91.5	93.5 / 92.2	101.9 / 102.4[b]
Education: Tertiary gross enrol. ratio (f/m per 100 pop.)	39.9 / 13.0	38.3 / 12.2[p]	59.4 / 30.9[b]
Intentional homicide rate (per 100 000 pop.)	0.5	0.9	0.5[q]
Seats held by women in national parliaments (%)	0.0	2.5	7.5

Environment and infrastructure indicators	2005	2010	2017
Mobile-cellular subscriptions (per 100 inhabitants)	87.2	125.2	185.3[b]
Individuals using the Internet (per 100 inhabitants)	21.3	55.0	93.5[r,b]
Research & Development expenditure (% of GDP)	...	...	0.1[h]
Threatened species (number)	18[s]	32	36
Forested area (% of land area)[f]	0.6	0.7	0.8[h]
CO2 emission estimates (million tons/tons per capita)	19.2 / 26.5	29.3 / 23.2	31.3 / 23.0[h]
Energy production, primary (Petajoules)	672	849	961[h]
Energy supply per capita (Gigajoules)	446	410	413[h]
Tourist/visitor arrivals at national borders (000)	6 313	11 952	11 621[b]
Important sites for terrestrial biodiversity protected (%)	19.6	27.5	27.5
Pop. using improved drinking water (urban/rural, %)	100.0 / 100.0	100.0 / 100.0	100.0 / 100.0[b]
Pop. using improved sanitation facilities (urban/rural, %)	99.2 / 99.2	99.2 / 99.2	99.2 / 99.2[b]

a Projected estimate (medium fertility variant). **b** 2015. **c** Refers to the urban area of the municipality of Al-Manamah. **d** 2016. **e** At producers' prices. **f** Estimate. **g** Break in the time series. **h** 2014. **i** Data classified according to ISIC Rev. 3. **j** Areas not elsewhere specified. **k** Data refers to a 5-year period preceding the reference year. **l** Refers to foreign citizens. **m** Data as at the end of December. **n** Data revision. **o** 2008. **p** 2006. **q** 2011. **r** Population aged 15 years and over. **s** 2004.

Bangladesh

Region	Southern Asia	UN membership date	17 September 1974
Population (000, 2017)	164 670[a]	Surface area (km2)	147 570[b]
Pop. density (per km2, 2017)	1 265.0[a]	Sex ratio (m per 100 f, 2017)	101.7[a]
Capital city	Dhaka	National currency	Taka (BDT)
Capital city pop. (000)	17 598.2[c,b]	Exchange rate (per US$)	78.7[d]

Economic indicators

	2005	2010	2017
GDP: Gross domestic product (million current US$)	57 628	114 508	194 466[b]
GDP growth rate (annual %, const. 2005 prices)	6.0	5.6	6.6[b]
GDP per capita (current US$)	403.2	755.2	1 207.9[b]
Economy: Agriculture (% of GVA)	20.1	17.8	15.5[b]
Economy: Industry (% of GVA)	27.2	26.1	28.1[b]
Economy: Services and other activity (% of GVA)	52.6	56.0	56.3[b]
Employment: Agriculture (% of employed)[e]	48.1	47.3	40.6
Employment: Industry (% of employed)[e]	14.5	17.6	19.1
Employment: Services (% of employed)[e]	37.5	35.1	40.3
Unemployment (% of labour force)	4.3	4.5	4.0[e]
Labour force participation (female/male pop. %)[e]	48.1 / 84.1	42.0 / 82.3	43.2 / 81.1
CPI: Consumer Price Index (2000=100)[f]	127	183	264[g]
Agricultural production index (2004-2006=100)	103	129	141[g]
Food production index (2004-2006=100)	103	130	140[g]
Index of industrial production (2005=100)[h,i]	100	148	206[j]
International trade: Exports (million US$)	9 332	19 231	36 031[d]
International trade: Imports (million US$)	12 631	30 504	52 624[d]
International trade: Balance (million US$)	- 3 299	- 11 273	- 16 593[d]
Balance of payments, current account (million US$)	508[k]	2 109	2 687[b]

Major trading partners

							2016
Export partners (% of exports)	United States	19.3	Germany	14.7	United Kingdom	11.0
Import partners (% of imports)	China	21.5	India	12.2	Singapore	9.2

Social indicators

	2005	2010	2017
Population growth rate (average annual %)[l]	1.7	1.2	1.2[b]
Urban population (% of total population)	26.8	30.5	34.3[b]
Urban population growth rate (average annual %)[l]	4.1	3.6	3.6[b]
Fertility rate, total (live births per woman)[l]	2.9	2.5	2.2[b]
Life expectancy at birth (females/males, years)[l]	67.3 / 66.2	70.0 / 68.2	72.9 / 69.8[b]
Population age distribution (0-14 and 60+ years, %)	34.4 / 6.6	32.1 / 6.9	28.4 / 7.3[a]
International migrant stock (000/% of total pop.)[m]	1 166.7 / 0.8	1 345.5 / 0.9	1 422.8 / 0.9[b]
Refugees and others of concern to UNHCR (000)	271.2[n]	229.3[n]	233.0[b]
Infant mortality rate (per 1 000 live births)[l]	56.0	43.3	33.3[b]
Health: Total expenditure (% of GDP)[o]	2.7	3.1	2.8[g]
Health: Physicians (per 1 000 pop.)	0.3	0.4	0.4[p]
Education: Government expenditure (% of GDP)	1.9[q]	1.9[r]	1.9[d]
Education: Primary gross enrol. ratio (f/m per 100 pop.)	100.9 / 96.5	105.9 / 99.6[e]	125.1 / 116.0[b]
Education: Secondary gross enrol. ratio (f/m per 100 pop.)	47.0 / 44.1	53.1 / 47.3	67.4 / 59.8[b]
Education: Tertiary gross enrol. ratio (f/m per 100 pop.)	4.2 / 8.2	7.9 / 13.1[r]	11.4 / 15.4[g]
Intentional homicide rate (per 100 000 pop.)	2.5	2.6	2.5[b]
Seats held by women in national parliaments (%)	2.0	18.6	20.3

Environment and infrastructure indicators

	2005	2010	2017
Mobile-cellular subscriptions (per 100 inhabitants)	6.3	45.0	83.4[n,b]
Individuals using the Internet (per 100 inhabitants)[e]	0.2	3.7	14.4[b]
Threatened species (number)	85[q]	122	151
Forested area (% of land area)	11.2	11.1[e]	11.0[e,g]
CO2 emission estimates (million tons/tons per capita)	39.5 / 0.3	59.9 / 0.4	73.2 / 0.5[g]
Energy production, primary (Petajoules)	1 027	1 300	1 438[g]
Energy supply per capita (Gigajoules)	8	10	11[g]
Tourist/visitor arrivals at national borders (000)	208	303	125[g]
Important sites for terrestrial biodiversity protected (%)	37.9	48.0	48.0
Pop. using improved drinking water (urban/rural, %)	84.3 / 78.2	85.4 / 82.6	86.5 / 87.0[b]
Pop. using improved sanitation facilities (urban/rural, %)	53.3 / 49.8	55.5 / 55.9	57.7 / 62.1[b]
Net Official Development Assist. received (% of GNI)	1.82	1.13	1.24[b]

a Projected estimate (medium fertility variant). **b** 2015. **c** Mega city. **d** 2016. **e** Estimate. **f** Government officials. **g** 2014. **h** Data classified according to ISIC Rev. 3. **i** Twelve months ending 30 June of the year stated. **j** 2013. **k** Break in the time series. **l** Data refers to a 5-year period preceding the reference year. **m** Including refugees. **n** Data as at the end of December. **o** Data revision. **p** 2012. **q** 2004. **r** 2009.

Barbados

Region	Caribbean	UN membership date	09 December 1966
Population (000, 2017)	286[a]	Surface area (km2)	431[b]
Pop. density (per km2, 2017)	664.5[a]	Sex ratio (m per 100 f, 2017)	91.9[a]
Capital city	Bridgetown	National currency	Barbados Dollar (BBD)
Capital city pop. (000)	90.3[c]	Exchange rate (per US$)	2.0[d]

Economic indicators

	2005	2010	2017
GDP: Gross domestic product (million current US$)	3 897	4 447	4 385[b]
GDP growth rate (annual %, const. 2005 prices)	4.0	0.3	0.9[b]
GDP per capita (current US$)	14 223.0	15 905.7	15 429.4[b]
Economy: Agriculture (% of GVA)	1.8	1.5	1.7[b]
Economy: Industry (% of GVA)	16.9	14.4	12.1[b]
Economy: Services and other activity (% of GVA)	81.3	84.0	86.2[b]
Employment: Agriculture (% of employed)[e]	3.1	3.0	2.8
Employment: Industry (% of employed)[e]	16.5	19.3	19.3
Employment: Services (% of employed)[e]	80.3	77.7	77.9
Unemployment (% of labour force)	9.1	10.7	11.3[e]
Labour force participation (female/male pop. %)[e]	64.2 / 75.4	63.5 / 73.1	61.8 / 70.0
CPI: Consumer Price Index (2000=100)	113	149	177[c]
Agricultural production index (2004-2006=100)	106	91	88[c]
Food production index (2004-2006=100)	106	91	88[c]
Index of industrial production (2005=100)[f]	100	88	80[c]
International trade: Exports (million US$)	361	314	517[d]
International trade: Imports (million US$)	1 672	1 196	1 621[d]
International trade: Balance (million US$)	- 1 311	- 883	- 1 104[d]
Balance of payments, current account (million US$)	- 467	- 236	- 248[g]

Major trading partners

							2016
Export partners (% of exports)	United States	34.4	Jamaica	9.4	Trinidad and Tobago	7.8
Import partners (% of imports)	United States	39.1	Trinidad and Tobago	13.4	China	7.3

Social indicators

	2005	2010	2017
Population growth rate (average annual %)[h]	0.3	0.4	0.3[b]
Urban population (% of total population)	32.9	32.1	31.5[b]
Urban population growth rate (average annual %)[h]	- 0.1	-0.0	0.1[b]
Fertility rate, total (live births per woman)[h]	1.8	1.8	1.8[b]
Life expectancy at birth (females/males, years)[h]	76.0 / 71.4	76.9 / 72.1	77.7 / 72.9[b]
Population age distribution (0-14 and 60+ years, %)	20.7 / 15.5	19.9 / 17.3	19.1 / 21.0[a]
International migrant stock (000/% of total pop.)	30.6 / 11.2	32.8 / 11.7	34.5 / 12.1[b]
Refugees and others of concern to UNHCR (000)	...	...	~0.0[b]
Infant mortality rate (per 1 000 live births)[h]	12.4	11.0	9.6[b]
Health: Total expenditure (% of GDP)	5.4	6.2	7.5[c]
Health: Physicians (per 1 000 pop.)	1.8	...	...
Education: Government expenditure (% of GDP)	5.6	5.9	6.6[c]
Education: Primary gross enrol. ratio (f/m per 100 pop.)	95.9 / 96.3	100.6 / 98.9[e]	94.2 / 93.1[c]
Education: Secondary gross enrol. ratio (f/m per 100 pop.)	108.0 / 109.1	102.2 / 101.7[e]	110.7 / 107.9[c]
Education: Tertiary gross enrol. ratio (f/m per 100 pop.)	57.0 / 23.1[i]	95.9 / 43.9	90.6 / 40.3[j]
Intentional homicide rate (per 100 000 pop.)	10.6	11.1	10.9[b]
Seats held by women in national parliaments (%)	13.3	10.0	16.7

Environment and infrastructure indicators

	2005	2010	2017
Mobile-cellular subscriptions (per 100 inhabitants)	75.4	124.8	116.5[b]
Individuals using the Internet (per 100 inhabitants)[e]	52.5	65.1	76.1[b]
Threatened species (number)	20[k]	36	56
Forested area (% of land area)	14.7	14.7	14.7[e,c]
CO2 emission estimates (million tons/tons per capita)	1.4 / 5.0	1.5 / 5.3	1.3 / 4.5[c]
Energy production, primary (Petajoules)	5	4	2[c]
Energy supply per capita (Gigajoules)	66	73	59[c]
Tourist/visitor arrivals at national borders (000)	548	532	592[b]
Important sites for terrestrial biodiversity protected (%)	2.1	2.1	2.1
Pop. using improved drinking water (urban/rural, %)	98.4 / 98.4	99.1 / 99.1	99.7 / 99.7[b]
Pop. using improved sanitation facilities (urban/rural, %)	90.1 / 90.1	93.5 / 93.5	96.2 / 96.2[b]
Net Official Development Assist. received (% of GNI)	- 0.06	0.37	...

a Projected estimate (medium fertility variant). **b** 2015. **c** 2014. **d** 2016. **e** Estimate. **f** Data classified according to ISIC Rev. 3. **g** 2013. **h** Data refers to a 5-year period preceding the reference year. **i** 2001. **j** 2011. **k** 2004.

Belarus

Region	Eastern Europe	UN membership date	24 October 1945
Population (000, 2017)	9 468 [a]	Surface area (km2)	207 600 [b]
Pop. density (per km2, 2017)	46.7 [a]	Sex ratio (m per 100 f, 2017)	87.0 [a]
Capital city	Minsk	National currency	Belarusian Ruble (BYR)
Capital city pop. (000)	1 915.4 [c,b]	Exchange rate (per US$)	2.0 [d]

Economic indicators

	2005	2010	2017
GDP: Gross domestic product (million current US$)	30 210	55 221	54 609 [b]
GDP growth rate (annual %, const. 2005 prices)	9.4	7.7	-3.9 [b]
GDP per capita (current US$)	3 133.6	5 817.6	5 750.8 [b]
Economy: Agriculture (% of GVA)	9.8	10.2	7.5 [b]
Economy: Industry (% of GVA)	43.4	40.8	38.9 [b]
Economy: Services and other activity (% of GVA)	46.8	49.0	53.6 [b]
Employment: Agriculture (% of employed) [e]	12.1	11.1	9.6
Employment: Industry (% of employed) [e]	35.1	33.8	32.0
Employment: Services (% of employed) [e]	52.8	55.1	58.4
Unemployment (% of labour force)	0.7 [e]	0.7	0.5 [e]
Labour force participation (female/male pop. %) [e]	53.8 / 66.6	54.5 / 67.7	54.0 / 67.8
CPI: Consumer Price Index (2000=100)	- 384 [f]	623 [g]	...
Agricultural production index (2004-2006=100)	98	117	122 [h]
Food production index (2004-2006=100)	98	117	122 [h]
Index of industrial production (2005=100) [i]	100	146	163 [h]
International trade: Exports (million US$)	15 977	25 283	23 414 [d]
International trade: Imports (million US$)	16 699	34 884	27 464 [d]
International trade: Balance (million US$)	- 722	- 9 601	- 4 050 [d]
Balance of payments, current account (million US$)	459	- 8 280	- 2 037 [b]

Major trading partners

							2016
Export partners (% of exports)	Russian Federation	45.8	Ukraine	12.0	United Kingdom	4.7
Import partners (% of imports)	Russian Federation	56.3	China	7.6	Germany	4.9

Social indicators

	2005	2010	2017
Population growth rate (average annual %) [j]	- 0.6	- 0.3	-0.0 [b]
Urban population (% of total population)	72.4	74.6	76.7 [b]
Urban population growth rate (average annual %) [j]	-0.0	0.3	-0.0 [b]
Fertility rate, total (live births per woman) [j]	1.3	1.4	1.6 [b]
Life expectancy at birth (females/males, years) [j]	73.6 / 62.3	75.2 / 63.6	77.7 / 66.5 [b]
Population age distribution (0-14 and 60+ years, %)	15.6 / 18.6	14.8 / 19.1	16.7 / 21.3 [a]
International migrant stock (000/% of total pop.)	1 107.0 / 11.5	1 090.4 / 11.5	1 082.9 / 11.4 [b]
Refugees and others of concern to UNHCR (000)	13.2 [k]	8.4 [k]	7.9 [d]
Infant mortality rate (per 1 000 live births) [j]	9.6	6.3	3.6 [b]
Health: Total expenditure (% of GDP)	6.9	5.6	5.7 [h]
Health: Physicians (per 1 000 pop.)	...	3.5	4.1 [h]
Education: Government expenditure (% of GDP)	5.9	5.4	4.9 [b]
Education: Primary gross enrol. ratio (f/m per 100 pop.)	95.6 / 98.9	103.4 / 103.5	101.3 / 101.4 [b]
Education: Secondary gross enrol. ratio (f/m per 100 pop.)	... / ...	105.3 / 108.7	106.4 / 107.8 [b]
Education: Tertiary gross enrol. ratio (f/m per 100 pop.)	77.8 / 56.8	94.4 / 65.2 [e]	100.7 / 75.9 [b]
Intentional homicide rate (per 100 000 pop.)	8.6	5.1	3.6 [b]
Seats held by women in national parliaments (%)	29.4	31.8	34.5

Environment and infrastructure indicators

	2005	2010	2017
Mobile-cellular subscriptions (per 100 inhabitants)	42.4	108.9	123.6 [b]
Individuals using the Internet (per 100 inhabitants)	1.9 [l]	31.8 [m]	62.2 [n,b]
Research & Development expenditure (% of GDP)	0.7	0.7	0.7 [o]
Threatened species (number)	18 [p]	16	25
Forested area (% of land area)	41.6	42.1	42.5 [e,h]
CO2 emission estimates (million tons/tons per capita)	59.2 / 6.0	63.0 / 6.6	63.5 / 6.7 [h]
Energy production, primary (Petajoules)	159	166	155 [h]
Energy supply per capita (Gigajoules)	115	122	122 [h]
Tourist/visitor arrivals at national borders (000) [q]	91	119	102 [b]
Important sites for terrestrial biodiversity protected (%)	37.0	37.3	47.1
Pop. using improved drinking water (urban/rural, %)	99.7 / 99.1	99.8 / 99.1	99.9 / 99.1 [b]
Pop. using improved sanitation facilities (urban/rural, %)	94.0 / 96.4	94.0 / 95.8	94.1 / 95.2 [b]
Net Official Development Assist. received (% of GNI)	0.19	0.25	0.20 [b]

a Projected estimate (medium fertility variant). b 2015. c Including communities under the authority of the Town Council. d 2016. e Estimate. f Annual average is weighted mean of monthly data. g Series linked to former series. h 2014. i Data classified according to ISIC Rev. 3. j Data refers to a 5-year period preceding the reference year. k Data as at the end of December. l 2000. m Population aged 16 years and over. n Population aged 6 years and over. o 2013. p 2004. q Package tour only.

Belgium

Region	Western Europe	UN membership date	27 December 1945
Population (000, 2017)	11 429 a	Surface area (km2)	30 528 b
Pop. density (per km2, 2017)	377.5 a	Sex ratio (m per 100 f, 2017)	97.3 a
Capital city	Brussels	National currency	Euro (EUR)
Capital city pop. (000)	2 045.0 c,b	Exchange rate (per US$)	0.9 d

Economic indicators

	2005	2010	2017
GDP: Gross domestic product (million current US$)	387 356	483 549	455 107 b
GDP growth rate (annual %, const. 2005 prices)	2.1	2.7	1.5 b
GDP per capita (current US$)	36 676.5	44 240.6	40 277.8 b
Economy: Agriculture (% of GVA) e	0.9	0.9	0.7 b
Economy: Industry (% of GVA) e	25.1	23.2	22.2 b
Economy: Services and other activity (% of GVA) e	74.0	76.0	77.1 b
Employment: Agriculture (% of employed) f	2.0	1.4	1.2
Employment: Industry (% of employed) f	24.7	23.4	21.2
Employment: Services (% of employed) f	73.3	75.2	77.6
Unemployment (% of labour force)	8.4	8.3	8.3 f
Labour force participation (female/male pop. %) f	45.8 / 61.4	47.8 / 60.8	48.1 / 58.9
CPI: Consumer Price Index (2000=100)	111	123	139 g,h
Agricultural production index (2004-2006=100)	100	100	108 h
Food production index (2004-2006=100)	100	99	107 h
Index of industrial production (2005=100)	100	117	121 h
International trade: Exports (million US$)	335 692 i	407 596	398 033 d
International trade: Imports (million US$)	319 085 i	391 256	372 713 d
International trade: Balance (million US$)	16 606 i	16 340	25 321 d
Balance of payments, current account (million US$)	7 703	7 973	1 936 b

Major trading partners

							2016
Export partners (% of exports)	Germany	16.7	France	15.4	Netherlands	11.2
Import partners (% of imports)	Netherlands	16.1	Germany	13.6	France	9.5

Social indicators

	2005	2010	2017
Population growth rate (average annual %) j	0.5	0.7	0.6 b
Urban population (% of total population)	97.4	97.6	97.9 b
Urban population growth rate (average annual %) j	0.5	0.9	0.5 b
Fertility rate, total (live births per woman) j	1.7	1.8	1.8 b
Life expectancy at birth (females/males, years) j	81.4 / 75.3	82.3 / 76.8	83.0 / 78.0 b
Population age distribution (0-14 and 60+ years, %)	17.2 / 22.1	16.9 / 23.2	17.1 / 24.6 a
International migrant stock (000/% of total pop.) k	870.9 / 8.2	1 052.8 / 9.6	1 387.9 / 12.3 b
Refugees and others of concern to UNHCR (000)	34.6 l	36.9 l	63.8 d
Infant mortality rate (per 1 000 live births) j	4.2	3.8	3.5 b
Health: Total expenditure (% of GDP)	9.2	10.2	10.6 h
Health: Physicians (per 1 000 pop.)	2.0	2.9	3.0 h
Education: Government expenditure (% of GDP)	5.8	6.4	6.6 h
Education: Primary gross enrol. ratio (f/m per 100 pop.)	101.0 / 101.4	103.2 / 103.3	104.2 / 104.2 b
Education: Secondary gross enrol. ratio (f/m per 100 pop.)	106.5 / 110.1	104.2 / 107.3	177.7 / 156.4 b
Education: Tertiary gross enrol. ratio (f/m per 100 pop.)	67.7 / 55.2	75.8 / 59.9	85.4 / 65.0 b
Intentional homicide rate (per 100 000 pop.) m	2.1	1.7	2.0 b
Seats held by women in national parliaments (%)	34.7	38.0	38.0

Environment and infrastructure indicators

	2005	2010	2017
Mobile-cellular subscriptions (per 100 inhabitants)	91.4	111.1	115.7 b
Individuals using the Internet (per 100 inhabitants)	55.8 f	75.0	85.1 n,b
Research & Development expenditure (% of GDP)	1.8	2.1	2.5 f,h
Threatened species (number)	36 o	27	37
Forested area (% of land area)	22.3	22.5	22.6 f,h
CO2 emission estimates (million tons/tons per capita)	108.5 / 10.4	110.8 / 10.2	93.4 / 8.3 h
Energy production, primary (Petajoules)	577	644	520 h
Energy supply per capita (Gigajoules)	234	231	196 h
Tourist/visitor arrivals at national borders (000)	6 747	7 186	8 355 p,b
Important sites for terrestrial biodiversity protected (%)	79.4	79.4	79.4
Pop. using improved drinking water (urban/rural, %)	100.0 / 100.0	100.0 / 100.0	100.0 / 100.0 b
Pop. using improved sanitation facilities (urban/rural, %)	99.5 / 99.5	99.5 / 99.4	99.5 / 99.4 b
Net Official Development Assist. disbursed (% of GNI) q	0.53	0.64	0.49 r,d

a Projected estimate (medium fertility variant). b 2015. c Refers to the population of Brussels-Capital Region and "communes" of the agglomeration and suburbs. d 2016. e Data classified according to ISIC Rev. 4. f Estimate. g Series linked to former series. h 2014. i Prior to 1997, the data refer to the Economic Union of Belgium and Luxembourg and intertrade between the two countries is excluded. Beginning January 1997, data refer to Belgium only and include trade between Belgium and Luxembourg. j Data refers to a 5-year period preceding the reference year. k Refers to foreign citizens. l Data as at the end of December. m Data refer to offences, not victims, of intentional homicide. n Population aged 16 to 74 years. o 2004. p Break in the time series. q Development Assistance Committee member (OECD) r Provisional data.

Belize

Region	Central America	UN membership date	25 September 1981
Population (000, 2017)	375[a]	Surface area (km2)	22 966[b]
Pop. density (per km2, 2017)	16.4[a]	Sex ratio (m per 100 f, 2017)	99.2[a]
Capital city	Belmopan	National currency	Belize Dollar (BZD)
Capital city pop. (000)	16.9[c]	Exchange rate (per US$)	2.0[d]

Economic indicators	2005	2010	2017
GDP: Gross domestic product (million current US$)	1 114	1 397	1 721[b]
GDP growth rate (annual %, const. 2005 prices)	3.0	3.3	1.2[b]
GDP per capita (current US$)	3 933.3	4 344.1	4 789.4[b]
Economy: Agriculture (% of GVA)	14.7	12.6	14.6[b]
Economy: Industry (% of GVA)	16.5	20.7	18.5[b]
Economy: Services and other activity (% of GVA)	68.8	66.7	66.9[b]
Employment: Agriculture (% of employed)[e]	19.5	17.3	16.1
Employment: Industry (% of employed)[e]	17.8	17.6	15.9
Employment: Services (% of employed)[e]	62.7	65.1	67.9
Unemployment (% of labour force)	11.0	13.2[e]	11.5[e]
Labour force participation (female/male pop. %)[e]	45.7 / 81.8	51.9 / 82.6	56.7 / 83.8
CPI: Consumer Price Index (2000=100)	113	128	134[c]
Agricultural production index (2004-2006=100)	97	93	97[c]
Food production index (2004-2006=100)	97	93	97[c]
Index of industrial production (2005=100)	100[f]	...	...
International trade: Exports (million US$)	208	282	246[d]
International trade: Imports (million US$)	439	700	952[d]
International trade: Balance (million US$)	- 231	- 418	- 706[d]
Balance of payments, current account (million US$)	- 151	- 46	- 175[b]

Major trading partners					2016
Export partners (% of exports)	United States	33.2	United Kingdom	28.4	Jamaica	5.6
Import partners (% of imports)	United States	37.4	China	11.7	Mexico	10.8

Social indicators	2005	2010	2017
Population growth rate (average annual %)[g]	2.7	2.5	2.2[b]
Urban population (% of total population)	46.3	45.0	44.0[b]
Urban population growth rate (average annual %)[g]	2.0	1.9	1.9[b]
Fertility rate, total (live births per woman)[g]	3.4	2.8	2.6[b]
Life expectancy at birth (females/males, years)[g]	71.6 / 65.7	72.4 / 67.0	72.7 / 67.2[b]
Population age distribution (0-14 and 60+ years, %)	39.0 / 4.7	35.7 / 5.7	31.4 / 6.2[a]
International migrant stock (000/% of total pop.)[h]	41.4 / 14.6	46.4 / 14.4	53.9 / 15.0[b]
Refugees and others of concern to UNHCR (000)	0.6[i]	0.2[i]	3.1[d]
Infant mortality rate (per 1 000 live births)[g]	19.7	17.0	14.3[b]
Health: Total expenditure (% of GDP)[j]	4.5	5.8	5.8[c]
Health: Physicians (per 1 000 pop.)	1.0[k]	0.8[l]	...
Education: Government expenditure (% of GDP)	5.3[m]	6.6	6.4[c]
Education: Primary gross enrol. ratio (f/m per 100 pop.)	110.8 / 115.8	110.3 / 114.8	110.4 / 115.8[b]
Education: Secondary gross enrol. ratio (f/m per 100 pop.)	77.7 / 75.3	78.2 / 72.5	81.8 / 79.8[b]
Education: Tertiary gross enrol. ratio (f/m per 100 pop.)	19.7 / 12.5	26.9 / 16.8	28.7 / 17.9[b]
Intentional homicide rate (per 100 000 pop.)	28.6	40.1	34.4[c]
Seats held by women in national parliaments (%)	6.7	0.0	9.4

Environment and infrastructure indicators	2005	2010	2017
Mobile-cellular subscriptions (per 100 inhabitants)	35.3[e]	62.9[n]	48.9[e,b]
Individuals using the Internet (per 100 inhabitants)	17.0[e]	28.2[o]	41.6[e,b]
Threatened species (number)	67[m]	92	117
Forested area (% of land area)[e]	62.1	61.0	60.1[c]
CO2 emission estimates (million tons/tons per capita)	0.4 / 1.5	0.5 / 1.7	0.5 / 1.4[c]
Energy production, primary (Petajoules)	4	14	9[c]
Energy supply per capita (Gigajoules)	39	40	36[c]
Tourist/visitor arrivals at national borders (000)	237	242	341[b]
Important sites for terrestrial biodiversity protected (%)	45.8	45.8	46.0
Pop. using improved drinking water (urban/rural, %)	94.9 / 87.8	97.4 / 97.1	98.9 / 100.0[b]
Pop. using improved sanitation facilities (urban/rural, %)	88.8 / 83.5	92.6 / 86.5	93.5 / 88.2[b]
Net Official Development Assist. received (% of GNI)	1.20	1.99	1.68[b]

a Projected estimate (medium fertility variant). **b** 2015. **c** 2014. **d** 2016. **e** Estimate. **f** Data classified according to ISIC Rev. 3. **g** Data refers to a 5-year period preceding the reference year. **h** Including refugees. **i** Data as at the end of December. **j** Data revision. **k** 2000. **l** 2009. **m** 2004. **n** Includes mobile GSM mobile base. **o** Population aged 5 years and over.

Benin

Region	Western Africa	UN membership date	20 September 1960
Population (000, 2017)	11 176[a]	Surface area (km2)	114 763[b]
Pop. density (per km2, 2017)	99.1[a]	Sex ratio (m per 100 f, 2017)	99.5[a]
Capital city	Porto-Novo[c]	National currency	CFA Franc (XOF)
Capital city pop. (000)	268.1[d]	Exchange rate (per US$)	622.3[e]

Economic indicators	2005	2010	2017
GDP: Gross domestic product (million current US$)	4 804	6 970	8 476[b]
GDP growth rate (annual %, const. 2005 prices)	1.7	2.1	5.2[b]
GDP per capita (current US$)	587.1	733.0	779.1[b]
Economy: Agriculture (% of GVA)	27.1	25.4	23.2[b]
Economy: Industry (% of GVA)	30.3	24.7	24.9[b]
Economy: Services and other activity (% of GVA)	42.5	49.9	51.9[b]
Employment: Agriculture (% of employed)[f]	46.1	45.3	43.2
Employment: Industry (% of employed)[f]	9.9	10.5	10.2
Employment: Services (% of employed)[f]	44.0	44.2	46.6
Unemployment (% of labour force)	0.9[f]	1.0	1.0[f]
Labour force participation (female/male pop. %)[f]	67.4 / 77.0	69.3 / 73.7	70.0 / 73.4
CPI: Consumer Price Index (2000=100)[g]	115	134[h]	146[d]
Agricultural production index (2004-2006=100)	102	116	152[d]
Food production index (2004-2006=100)	102	123	158[d]
Index of industrial production (2005=100)[i,j]	100	129	148[k]
International trade: Exports (million US$)	288	534	410[e]
International trade: Imports (million US$)	899	2 134	2 630[e]
International trade: Balance (million US$)	- 611	- 1 600	- 2 220[e]
Balance of payments, current account (million US$)	- 270	- 618	- 885[d]

Major trading partners						2016
Export partners (% of exports)	India	15.4	Malaysia	13.2	Bangladesh	10.2
Import partners (% of imports)	India	14.9	Thailand	12.4	France	10.1

Social indicators	2005	2010	2017
Population growth rate (average annual %)[l]	3.0	2.8	2.8[b]
Urban population (% of total population)	40.0	41.9	44.0[b]
Urban population growth rate (average annual %)[l]	4.1	3.9	3.7[b]
Fertility rate, total (live births per woman)[l]	5.8	5.5	5.2[b]
Life expectancy at birth (females/males, years)[l]	57.7 / 54.6	60.0 / 57.1	61.4 / 58.5[b]
Population age distribution (0-14 and 60+ years, %)	44.4 / 5.0	43.8 / 4.9	42.7 / 5.0[a]
International migrant stock (000/% of total pop.)[m,n]	171.5 / 2.1	209.3 / 2.2	245.4 / 2.3[b]
Refugees and others of concern to UNHCR (000)	32.1[o]	7.3[o]	0.8[e]
Infant mortality rate (per 1 000 live births)[l]	84.1	74.5	67.7[b]
Health: Total expenditure (% of GDP)	4.7	4.9	4.6[d]
Health: Physicians (per 1 000 pop.)	~0.0[p]	0.1[q]	0.1[k]
Education: Government expenditure (% of GDP)	3.6	5.0	4.4[b]
Education: Primary gross enrol. ratio (f/m per 100 pop.)	85.8 / 111.3	108.6 / 123.9	123.7 / 134.2[b]
Education: Secondary gross enrol. ratio (f/m per 100 pop.)	17.9 / 38.9[p]	... / ...	46.8 / 66.7[b]
Education: Tertiary gross enrol. ratio (f/m per 100 pop.)	1.7 / 7.3[f,r]	6.9 / 19.6	8.4 / 22.4[k]
Intentional homicide rate (per 100 000 pop.)	7.0	6.4	6.0[b]
Seats held by women in national parliaments (%)	7.2	10.8	7.2

Environment and infrastructure indicators	2005	2010	2017
Mobile-cellular subscriptions (per 100 inhabitants)	7.3	74.4	85.6[b]
Individuals using the Internet (per 100 inhabitants)	1.3	3.1	6.8[f,b]
Threatened species (number)	31[p]	62	88
Forested area (% of land area)[f]	42.7	40.4	38.7[d]
CO2 emission estimates (million tons/tons per capita)	2.4 / 0.3	5.1 / 0.6	6.3 / 0.6[d]
Energy production, primary (Petajoules)	70	86	96[d]
Energy supply per capita (Gigajoules)	14	16	17[d]
Tourist/visitor arrivals at national borders (000)	176	199	255[b]
Important sites for terrestrial biodiversity protected (%)	77.4	77.4	77.4
Pop. using improved drinking water (urban/rural, %)	80.6 / 63.4	83.2 / 68.3	85.2 / 72.1[b]
Pop. using improved sanitation facilities (urban/rural, %)	29.0 / 4.9	32.7 / 6.2	35.6 / 7.3[b]
Net Official Development Assist. received (% of GNI)	7.29	9.96	5.09[b]

a Projected estimate (medium fertility variant). **b** 2015. **c** Porto-Novo is the constitutional capital and Cotonou is the economic capital. **d** 2014. **e** 2016. **f** Estimate. **g** Cotonou **h** Series linked to former series. **i** Data classified according to ISIC Rev. 3. **j** Country data supplemented with data from the Observatoire Economique et Statistique d'Afrique Subsaharienne (Afristat). **k** 2013. **l** Data refers to a 5-year period preceding the reference year. **m** Including refugees. **n** Refers to foreign citizens. **o** Data as at the end of December. **p** 2004. **q** 2008. **r** 2001.

Bermuda

Region	Northern America	Population (000, 2017)	61[a]
Surface area (km2)	53[b]	Pop. density (per km2, 2017)	1 227.0[a]
Sex ratio (m per 100 f, 2017)	91.4[c,d]	Capital city	Hamilton
National currency	Bermudian Dollar (BMD)	Capital city pop. (000)	10.3[e]
Exchange rate (per US$)	1.0[f]		

Economic indicators	2005	2010	2017
GDP: Gross domestic product (million current US$)	4 868	5 855	5 853[b]
GDP growth rate (annual %, const. 2005 prices)	1.7	- 2.5	0.4[b]
GDP per capita (current US$)	74 752.9	91 555.4	94 399.9[b]
Economy: Agriculture (% of GVA)	0.8	0.7	0.7[b]
Economy: Industry (% of GVA)	9.7	7.1	5.3[b]
Economy: Services and other activity (% of GVA)	89.5	92.2	94.0[b]
Employment: Agriculture (% of employed)	1.7[g,h]	1.4[i,j,k]	1.6[i,j,k,l,m]
Employment: Industry (% of employed)	12.1[g,h]	12.9[i,j,k]	10.3[i,j,k,l,m]
Employment: Services (% of employed)	86.2[g,h]	85.7[i,j,k]	87.6[i,j,k,l,m]
Unemployment (% of labour force)[i]	2.7[n]	4.5[j,o]	6.7[l,m]
Labour force participation (female/male pop. %)	67.4 / 79.2[n]	81.0 / 87.0[i]	72.6 / 80.0[i,l,p]
CPI: Consumer Price Index (2000=100)	116	136	148[e]
Agricultural production index (2004-2006=100)	100	111	115[e]
Food production index (2004-2006=100)	100	111	115[e]
International trade: Exports (million US$)	49	15	8[f]
International trade: Imports (million US$)	988	970	971[f]
International trade: Balance (million US$)	- 939	- 955	- 963[f]
Balance of payments, current account (million US$)	...	696	817[b]

Major trading partners						2016
Export partners (% of exports)	United States	90.0	United Kingdom	5.2	Canada	2.7
Import partners (% of imports)	United States	70.0	Canada	11.3	United Kingdom	3.2

Social indicators	2005	2010	2017
Population growth rate (average annual %)[q]	0.3	- 0.4	- 0.6[b]
Urban population (% of total population)	100.0	100.0	100.0[b]
Urban population growth rate (average annual %)[q]	0.4	0.3	0.2[b]
Fertility rate, total (live births per woman)	1.8	1.7	1.5[f]
Life expectancy at birth (females/males, years)	... / ...	82.3 / 76.9	85.1 / 77.5[f]
Population age distribution (0-14 and 60+ years, %)[d]	18.4 / 16.4	17.4 / 18.7	14.8 / 24.9[c]
International migrant stock (000/% of total pop.)	18.3 / 28.1	18.9 / 29.5	19.1 / 30.8[b]
Education: Government expenditure (% of GDP)	2.0	2.6	1.7[b]
Education: Primary gross enrol. ratio (f/m per 100 pop.)	101.5 / 96.8	100.7 / 93.7[r]	89.4 / 91.3[b]
Education: Secondary gross enrol. ratio (f/m per 100 pop.)	85.9 / 76.0	85.4 / 72.3	75.5 / 67.7[b]
Education: Tertiary gross enrol. ratio (f/m per 100 pop.)	... / ...	40.6 / 19.3	34.1 / 14.7[b]
Intentional homicide rate (per 100 000 pop.)	3.1	11.0	6.4[b]

Environment and infrastructure indicators	2005	2010	2017
Mobile-cellular subscriptions (per 100 inhabitants)	82.2	135.8[s]	58.0[s,b]
Individuals using the Internet (per 100 inhabitants)	65.4	84.2[s]	98.3[s,b]
Research & Development expenditure (% of GDP)[u]	...	0.2[f]	0.2[e]
Threatened species (number)	47[h]	50	72
Forested area (% of land area)[s]	20.0	20.0	20.0[e]
CO2 emission estimates (million tons/tons per capita)	0.6 / 9.1	0.6 / 9.5	0.6 / 9.2[e]
Energy production, primary (Petajoules)[s]	...	1	1[e]
Energy supply per capita (Gigajoules)	124[s]	138[s]	136[e]
Tourist/visitor arrivals at national borders (000)[v]	270	232	220[b]
Important sites for terrestrial biodiversity protected (%)	57.7	57.7	57.7

a Projected estimate (medium fertility variant). b 2015. c Data refer to projections based on the 2010 Population Census. d De jure population. e 2014. f 2016. g Data classified according to ISIC Rev. 2. h 2004. i Population aged 16 years and over. j Break in the time series. k Data classified according to ISIC Rev. 3. l Excluding the institutional population. m 2013. n 2000. o 2009. p 2012. q Data refers to a 5-year period preceding the reference year. r 2006. s Estimate. t Excluding most or all capital expenditures. u Overestimated or based on overestimated data. v Arrivals by air.

Bhutan

Region	Southern Asia	
Population (000, 2017)	808 [a]	
Pop. density (per km2, 2017)	21.2 [a]	
Capital city	Thimphu	
Capital city pop. (000)	152.4 [c]	

UN membership date	21 September 1971	
Surface area (km2)	38 394 [b]	
Sex ratio (m per 100 f, 2017)	113.1 [a]	
National currency	Ngultrum (BTN)	
Exchange rate (per US$)	68.0 [d]	

Economic indicators

	2005	2010	2017
GDP: Gross domestic product (million current US$)	819	1 585	2 074 [b]
GDP growth rate (annual %, const. 2005 prices)	7.1	11.7	5.2 [b]
GDP per capita (current US$)	1 257.5	2 201.3	2 677.1 [b]
Economy: Agriculture (% of GVA)	23.2	17.5	17.2 [b]
Economy: Industry (% of GVA)	37.3	44.6	43.9 [b]
Economy: Services and other activity (% of GVA)	39.5	37.9	38.8 [b]
Employment: Agriculture (% of employed) [e]	49.7	59.4	56.6
Employment: Industry (% of employed) [e]	19.5	6.8	9.7
Employment: Services (% of employed) [e]	30.8	33.8	33.7
Unemployment (% of labour force)	3.1	3.3	2.4 [e]
Labour force participation (female/male pop. %) [e]	65.2 / 77.7	63.8 / 74.5	59.4 / 73.5
CPI: Consumer Price Index (2000=100)	117	156	222 [c]
Agricultural production index (2004-2006=100)	106	94	98 [c]
Food production index (2004-2006=100)	106	94	98 [c]
International trade: Exports (million US$)	258	413	616 [d]
International trade: Imports (million US$)	387	854	1 688 [d]
International trade: Balance (million US$)	- 129	- 440	- 1 072 [d]
Balance of payments, current account (million US$)	...	- 323	- 579 [b]

Major trading partners

							2016
Export partners (% of exports)	India	68.3	Bangladesh	23.5	United States	2.3	
Import partners (% of imports)	India	82.9	Singapore	3.1	Thailand	2.6	

Social indicators

	2005	2010	2017
Population growth rate (average annual %) [f]	2.7	2.1	1.6 [b]
Urban population (% of total population)	31.0	34.8	38.6 [b]
Urban population growth rate (average annual %) [f]	6.8	4.3	3.7 [b]
Fertility rate, total (live births per woman) [f]	3.1	2.6	2.2 [b]
Life expectancy at birth (females/males, years) [f]	63.1 / 62.7	66.7 / 66.3	68.9 / 68.6 [b]
Population age distribution (0-14 and 60+ years, %)	34.9 / 5.7	30.6 / 6.2	26.5 / 7.3 [a]
International migrant stock (000/% of total pop.)	40.3 / 6.2	48.4 / 6.7	51.1 / 6.6 [b]
Infant mortality rate (per 1 000 live births) [f]	51.9	39.5	30.5 [b]
Health: Total expenditure (% of GDP) [g]	5.3	5.2	3.6 [c]
Health: Physicians (per 1 000 pop.)	0.2 [h]	0.2 [i]	0.3 [c]
Education: Government expenditure (% of GDP)	7.1	4.0	7.4 [b]
Education: Primary gross enrol. ratio (f/m per 100 pop.)	93.4 / 95.7	110.7 / 108.2	96.9 / 96.6 [d]
Education: Secondary gross enrol. ratio (f/m per 100 pop.)	43.0 / 48.5	66.7 / 65.6	87.1 / 81.4 [c]
Education: Tertiary gross enrol. ratio (f/m per 100 pop.)	3.7 / 5.6	5.3 / 8.6	9.2 / 12.6 [j]
Intentional homicide rate (per 100 000 pop.)	...	1.9	2.8 [c]
Seats held by women in national parliaments (%)	9.3	8.5	8.5

Environment and infrastructure indicators

	2005	2010	2017
Mobile-cellular subscriptions (per 100 inhabitants)	5.5	55.0 [k]	87.1 [k,b]
Individuals using the Internet (per 100 inhabitants)	3.8	13.6 [e]	39.8 [e,b]
Threatened species (number)	48 [h]	59	71
Forested area (% of land area)	69.7	71.0	72.0 [e,c]
CO2 emission estimates (million tons/tons per capita)	0.4 / 0.6	0.5 / 0.7	1.0 / 1.3 [c]
Energy production, primary (Petajoules)	53	73	75 [c]
Energy supply per capita (Gigajoules)	73	81	82 [c]
Tourist/visitor arrivals at national borders (000)	14	41 [l]	155 [b]
Important sites for terrestrial biodiversity protected (%)	38.6	41.2	42.9
Pop. using improved drinking water (urban/rural, %)	98.9 / 86.6	99.5 / 94.1	100.0 / 100.0 [b]
Pop. using improved sanitation facilities (urban/rural, %)	67.2 / 26.4	76.0 / 31.2	77.9 / 33.1 [b]
Net Official Development Assist. received (% of GNI)	11.16	8.78	5.26 [b]

a Projected estimate (medium fertility variant). **b** 2015. **c** 2014. **d** 2016. **e** Estimate. **f** Data refers to a 5-year period preceding the reference year. **g** Data revision. **h** 2004. **i** 2008. **j** 2013. **k** Both Bhutan Telecom and Tashi Cell provide mobile-cellular services. **l** Break in the time series.

Bolivia (Plurinational State of)

Region	South America	
Population (000, 2017)	11 052 [a]	
Pop. density (per km2, 2017)	10.2 [a]	
Capital city	Sucre [d]	
Capital city pop. (000)	371.9 [c]	

UN membership date	14 November 1945	
Surface area (km2)	1 098 581 [b,c]	
Sex ratio (m per 100 f, 2017)	100.2 [a]	
National currency	Boliviano (BOB)	
Exchange rate (per US$)	6.9 [e]	

Economic indicators

	2005	2010	2017
GDP: Gross domestic product (million current US$)	9 549	19 650	32 998 [c]
GDP growth rate (annual %, const. 2005 prices)	4.4	4.1	4.8 [c]
GDP per capita (current US$)	1 046.4	1 981.2	3 076.8 [c]
Economy: Agriculture (% of GVA)	13.9	12.4	12.6 [c]
Economy: Industry (% of GVA)	30.9	35.8	31.0 [c]
Economy: Services and other activity (% of GVA)	55.2	51.8	56.5 [c]
Employment: Agriculture (% of employed) [f]	34.9	31.1	29.5
Employment: Industry (% of employed) [f]	20.2	21.9	21.1
Employment: Services (% of employed) [f]	44.9	47.1	49.4
Unemployment (% of labour force)	5.4	6.0	3.8 [f]
Labour force participation (female/male pop. %) [f]	60.7 / 81.4	62.5 / 82.3	64.1 / 82.6
CPI: Consumer Price Index (2000=100) [g]	117	160	205 [h]
Agricultural production index (2004-2006=100)	100	119	142 [h]
Food production index (2004-2006=100)	100	120	143 [h]
International trade: Exports (million US$)	2 797	6 965	6 969 [e]
International trade: Imports (million US$)	2 343	5 604	8 374 [e]
International trade: Balance (million US$)	454	1 361	- 1 405 [e]
Balance of payments, current account (million US$)	622	874	- 1 854 [c]

Major trading partners

							2016
Export partners (% of exports)	Brazil	28.0	Argentina	16.9	United States	12.1
Import partners (% of imports)	China	17.9	Brazil	16.5	Argentina	11.8

Social indicators

	2005	2010	2017
Population growth rate (average annual %) [i]	1.8	1.7	1.6 [c]
Urban population (% of total population)	64.2	66.4	68.5 [c]
Urban population growth rate (average annual %) [i]	2.7	2.3	2.3 [c]
Fertility rate, total (live births per woman) [i]	3.8	3.4	3.0 [c]
Life expectancy at birth (females/males, years) [i]	64.3 / 60.0	67.3 / 62.7	70.2 / 65.3 [c]
Population age distribution (0-14 and 60+ years, %)	36.6 / 7.8	34.7 / 8.3	31.6 / 9.5 [a]
International migrant stock (000/% of total pop.)	107.7 / 1.2	122.8 / 1.2	143.0 / 1.3 [c]
Refugees and others of concern to UNHCR (000)	0.5 [j]	0.7 [j]	0.8 [e]
Infant mortality rate (per 1 000 live births) [i]	61.2	51.0	42.9 [c]
Health: Total expenditure (% of GDP) [k,l]	5.7	5.4	6.3 [h]
Health: Physicians (per 1 000 pop.)	1.2 [m]	0.4	0.5 [n]
Education: Government expenditure (% of GDP)	6.4 [o]	7.6	7.3 [h]
Education: Primary gross enrol. ratio (f/m per 100 pop.)	114.4 / 115.5	103.6 / 105.7	95.7 / 98.5 [c]
Education: Secondary gross enrol. ratio (f/m per 100 pop.)	84.3 / 89.6	82.6 / 83.6	85.7 / 87.1 [c]
Education: Tertiary gross enrol. ratio (f/m per 100 pop.)	... / ...	34.9 / 41.8 [f,p]	... / ...
Intentional homicide rate (per 100 000 pop.)	7.2	10.6	12.4 [q]
Seats held by women in national parliaments (%)	19.2	22.3	53.1

Environment and infrastructure indicators

	2005	2010	2017
Mobile-cellular subscriptions (per 100 inhabitants)	25.9	70.7	92.2 [c]
Individuals using the Internet (per 100 inhabitants)	5.2	22.4 [f]	45.1 [f,c]
Research & Development expenditure (% of GDP)	0.3 [r]	0.2 [s,t]	...
Threatened species (number)	150 [u]	163	231
Forested area (% of land area)	54.2	51.9 [f]	50.8 [f,h]
CO2 emission estimates (million tons/tons per capita)	12.2 / 1.3	15.2 / 1.5	20.4 / 1.9 [h]
Energy production, primary (Petajoules)	586	659	962 [h]
Energy supply per capita (Gigajoules)	24	27	32 [h]
Tourist/visitor arrivals at national borders (000)	524	679	882 [c]
Important sites for terrestrial biodiversity protected (%)	53.5	55.4	57.0
Pop. using improved drinking water (urban/rural, %)	94.4 / 62.4	95.6 / 69.7	96.7 / 75.6 [c]
Pop. using improved sanitation facilities (urban/rural, %)	53.8 / 21.4	57.7 / 24.8	60.8 / 27.5 [c]
Net Official Development Assist. received (% of GNI)	7.01	3.82	2.38 [c]

a Projected estimate (medium fertility variant). b Data updated according to "Superintendencia Agraria". Interior waters correspond to natural or artificial bodies of water or snow. c 2015. d La Paz is the seat of government and Sucre is the constitutional capital. e 2016. f Estimate. g Urban areas. h 2014. i Data refers to a 5-year period preceding the reference year. j Data as at the end of December. k Data revision. l Funds previously included in social security were reclassified. m 2001. n 2011. o 2003. p 2007. q 2012. r 2002. s Break in the time series. t 2009. u 2004.

Bonaire, Sint Eustatius and Saba

Region	Caribbean	Population (000, 2017)	25[a]
Pop. density (per km2, 2017)	77.4[a]	Capital city	Kralendijk
National currency	US Dollar (USD)	Capital city pop. (000)	14.6[b,c]

Social indicators	2005	2010	2017
Population growth rate (average annual %)[d]	~0.0	7.5	3.2[e]
Urban population (% of total population)	74.8	74.7	74.7[e]
Urban population growth rate (average annual %)[d]	~-0.0	4.0	2.4[e]
International migrant stock (000/% of total pop.)	... / ...	11.4 / 54.7	13.0 / 52.3[e]
Refugees and others of concern to UNHCR (000)	...	~0.0[f,g]	...

Environment and infrastructure indicators	2005	2010	2017
Threatened species (number)	...	...	56
CO2 emission estimates (million tons/tons per capita)	... / ...	... / ...	0.3 / 13.3[c]
Energy production, primary (Petajoules)	...	...	0[c]
Energy supply per capita (Gigajoules)	...	...	208[h,c]
Important sites for terrestrial biodiversity protected (%)	41.9	41.9	41.9

a Projected estimate (medium fertility variant). **b** Refers to the island of Bonaire. **c** 2014. **d** Data refers to a 5-year period preceding the reference year. **e** 2015. **f** Bonaire only. **g** Data as at the end of December. **h** Estimate.

Bosnia and Herzegovina

Region	Southern Europe	UN membership date	22 May 1992
Population (000, 2017)	3 507[a]	Surface area (km2)	51 209[b]
Pop. density (per km2, 2017)	68.8[a]	Sex ratio (m per 100 f, 2017)	96.4[a]
Capital city	Sarajevo	National currency	Convertible Mark (BAM)
Capital city pop. (000)	318.4[b]	Exchange rate (per US$)	1.9[c]

Economic indicators

	2005	2010	2017
GDP: Gross domestic product (million current US$)	11 225	17 164	16 251[b]
GDP growth rate (annual %, const. 2005 prices)	3.9	0.8	3.1[b]
GDP per capita (current US$)	2 928.2	4 475.3	4 265.0[b]
Economy: Agriculture (% of GVA)[d]	9.8	8.0	7.3[b]
Economy: Industry (% of GVA)[d]	25.3	26.4	26.5[b]
Economy: Services and other activity (% of GVA)[d]	64.9	65.6	66.2[b]
Employment: Agriculture (% of employed)[e]	26.9	20.2	18.0
Employment: Industry (% of employed)[e]	27.0	28.7	30.4
Employment: Services (% of employed)[e]	46.1	51.2	51.7
Unemployment (% of labour force)	21.6[e]	27.2	25.4[e]
Labour force participation (female/male pop. %)[e]	31.8 / 58.3	34.6 / 59.6	34.3 / 57.5
CPI: Consumer Price Index (2000=100)[f]	100	118	123[g]
Agricultural production index (2004-2006=100)	98	107	96[g]
Food production index (2004-2006=100)	98	108	97[g]
Index of industrial production (2005=100)[h]	100	135	143[i]
International trade: Exports (million US$)	2 388	4 803	5 327[c]
International trade: Imports (million US$)	7 054	9 223	9 130[c]
International trade: Balance (million US$)	- 4 665	- 4 420	- 3 803[c]
Balance of payments, current account (million US$)	- 1 844	- 1 031	- 923[b]

Major trading partners

						2016
Export partners (% of exports)	Germany	16.4	Italy	12.2	Serbia	10.7
Import partners (% of imports)	Germany	12.3	Italy	11.7	Serbia	11.3

Social indicators

	2005	2010	2017
Population growth rate (average annual %)[j]	0.1	- 0.3	- 1.0[b]
Urban population (% of total population)	39.2	39.2	39.8[b]
Urban population growth rate (average annual %)[j]	0.2	- 0.2	0.1[b]
Fertility rate, total (live births per woman)[j]	1.3	1.3	1.3[b]
Life expectancy at birth (females/males, years)[j]	77.5 / 72.0	78.1 / 72.9	78.8 / 73.7[b]
Population age distribution (0-14 and 60+ years, %)	17.7 / 17.4	15.7 / 19.2	14.1 / 23.4[a]
International migrant stock (000/% of total pop.)[e,k]	47.3 / 1.2	38.8 / 1.0	34.8 / 0.9[b]
Refugees and others of concern to UNHCR (000)	199.5[l]	179.0[l]	157.6[c]
Infant mortality rate (per 1 000 live births)[j]	9.9	9.0	7.6[b]
Health: Total expenditure (% of GDP)	8.5	9.6	9.6[g]
Health: Physicians (per 1 000 pop.)	...	1.7	1.9[m]
Intentional homicide rate (per 100 000 pop.)	...	1.5	1.5[b]
Seats held by women in national parliaments (%)	16.7	19.0	21.4

Environment and infrastructure indicators

	2005	2010	2017
Mobile-cellular subscriptions (per 100 inhabitants)	41.1	80.9	90.2[b]
Individuals using the Internet (per 100 inhabitants)	21.3	42.8[e]	65.1[e,b]
Research & Development expenditure (% of GDP)	~0.0[n]	~0.0[n,o]	0.3[g]
Threatened species (number)	40[p]	67	91
Forested area (% of land area)[e]	42.7	42.7	42.7[g]
CO2 emission estimates (million tons/tons per capita)	16.2 / 4.3	21.3 / 5.5	22.2 / 5.8[g]
Energy production, primary (Petajoules)	152	182	252[g]
Energy supply per capita (Gigajoules)	54	70	85[g]
Tourist/visitor arrivals at national borders (000)	217	365	678[b]
Important sites for terrestrial biodiversity protected (%)	~0.0	12.5	12.5
Pop. using improved drinking water (urban/rural, %)	99.5 / 97.6	99.6 / 98.9	99.7 / 100.0[b]
Pop. using improved sanitation facilities (urban/rural, %)	98.6 / 92.5	98.8 / 92.2	98.9 / 92.0[b]
Net Official Development Assist. received (% of GNI)	4.62	2.93	2.20[b]

a Projected estimate (medium fertility variant). b 2015. c 2016. d Data classified according to ISIC Rev. 4. e Estimate. f Index base: 2005=100. g 2014. h Data classified according to ISIC Rev. 3. i 2011. j Data refers to a 5-year period preceding the reference year. k Including refugees. l Data as at the end of December. m 2013. n Partial data. o 2009. p 2004.

Botswana

Region	Southern Africa	
Population (000, 2017)	2 292[a]	
Pop. density (per km2, 2017)	4.0[a]	
Capital city	Gaborone	
Capital city pop. (000)	246.6[c]	

UN membership date	17 October 1966
Surface area (km2)	582 000[b]
Sex ratio (m per 100 f, 2017)	97.7[a]
National currency	Pula (BWP)
Exchange rate (per US$)	10.6[d]

Economic indicators	2005	2010	2017
GDP: Gross domestic product (million current US$)	9 931	12 790	14 391[b]
GDP growth rate (annual %, const. 2005 prices)	4.6	8.6	- 0.3[b]
GDP per capita (current US$)	5 327.9	6 245.8	6 360.6[b]
Economy: Agriculture (% of GVA)	2.0	2.8	2.4[b]
Economy: Industry (% of GVA)	47.6	35.6	33.4[b]
Economy: Services and other activity (% of GVA)	50.3	61.6	64.2[b]
Employment: Agriculture (% of employed)[e]	26.4	28.8	25.7
Employment: Industry (% of employed)[e]	17.4	15.3	14.9
Employment: Services (% of employed)[e]	56.2	55.9	59.4
Unemployment (% of labour force)	20.5[e]	17.9	18.6[e]
Labour force participation (female/male pop. %)[e]	71.4 / 80.9	72.7 / 81.0	73.6 / 81.6
CPI: Consumer Price Index (2000=100)	146	227	293[c]
Agricultural production index (2004-2006=100)	102	125	110[c]
Food production index (2004-2006=100)	102	125	110[c]
International trade: Exports (million US$)	4 431	4 693	7 321[d]
International trade: Imports (million US$)	3 162	5 657	6 103[d]
International trade: Balance (million US$)	1 268	- 964	1 218[d]
Balance of payments, current account (million US$)	1 598	- 352	1 120[b]

Major trading partners						2016
Export partners (% of exports)	Belgium	18.9	India	15.1	South Africa	13.6
Import partners (% of imports)	South Africa	64.6	Namibia	10.5	Canada	5.6

Social indicators	2005	2010	2017
Population growth rate (average annual %)[f]	1.4	1.6	1.8[b]
Urban population (% of total population)	55.1	56.2	57.4[b]
Urban population growth rate (average annual %)[f]	2.0	1.4	1.3[b]
Fertility rate, total (live births per woman)[f]	3.2	2.9	2.9[b]
Life expectancy at birth (females/males, years)[f]	51.0 / 47.3	58.5 / 54.4	66.1 / 59.8[b]
Population age distribution (0-14 and 60+ years, %)	35.1 / 5.0	33.0 / 5.3	31.4 / 6.4[a]
International migrant stock (000/% of total pop.)[g]	88.8 / 4.8	120.9 / 5.9	160.6 / 7.1[b]
Refugees and others of concern to UNHCR (000)	3.7[h]	3.3[h]	2.8[d]
Infant mortality rate (per 1 000 live births)[f]	65.4	46.5	35.2[b]
Health: Total expenditure (% of GDP)	5.6	5.6	5.4[c]
Health: Physicians (per 1 000 pop.)	0.2	0.3[i]	0.4[i]
Education: Government expenditure (% of GDP)	10.7	9.6[i]	...
Education: Primary gross enrol. ratio (f/m per 100 pop.)	106.5 / 107.9	105.7 / 109.3[i]	105.8 / 109.4[c]
Education: Secondary gross enrol. ratio (f/m per 100 pop.)	79.7 / 77.3	80.3 / 73.5[k]	... / ...
Education: Tertiary gross enrol. ratio (f/m per 100 pop.)	8.6 / 9.7	9.0 / 11.0[l]	27.7 / 19.2[d]
Intentional homicide rate (per 100 000 pop.)	15.6	14.8	10.5[m]
Seats held by women in national parliaments (%)	11.1	7.9	9.5

Environment and infrastructure indicators	2005	2010	2017
Mobile-cellular subscriptions (per 100 inhabitants)	30.1	120.0	169.0[b]
Individuals using the Internet (per 100 inhabitants)	3.3[e]	6.0	27.5[e,b]
Research & Development expenditure (% of GDP)	0.5	...	0.3[n,j]
Threatened species (number)	15[o]	18	28
Forested area (% of land area)[e]	21.1	20.0	19.3[c]
CO2 emission estimates (million tons/tons per capita)	4.1 / 2.2	4.7 / 2.3	7.0 / 3.2[c]
Energy production, primary (Petajoules)	29	30	47[c]
Energy supply per capita (Gigajoules)	35	37	44[c]
Tourist/visitor arrivals at national borders (000)	1 474	1 973	1 528[b]
Important sites for terrestrial biodiversity protected (%)	47.1	47.1	47.1
Pop. using improved drinking water (urban/rural, %)	99.4 / 90.4	99.2 / 91.6	99.2 / 92.3[b]
Pop. using improved sanitation facilities (urban/rural, %)	72.8 / 36.1	76.4 / 40.4	78.5 / 43.1[b]
Net Official Development Assist. received (% of GNI)	0.53	1.26	0.46[b]

a Projected estimate (medium fertility variant). **b** 2015. **c** 2014. **d** 2016. **e** Estimate. **f** Data refers to a 5-year period preceding the reference year. **g** Refers to foreign citizens. **h** Data as at the end of December. **i** 2009. **j** 2012. **k** 2008. **l** 2006. **m** 2011. **n** Break in the time series. **o** 2004.

Brazil

Region	South America	UN membership date	24 October 1945
Population (000, 2017)	209 288[a]	Surface area (km2)	8 515 767[b]
Pop. density (per km2, 2017)	25.0[a]	Sex ratio (m per 100 f, 2017)	96.6[a]
Capital city	Brasilia	National currency	Brazilian Real (BRL)
Capital city pop. (000)	4 155.5[c,b]	Exchange rate (per US$)	3.3[d]

Economic indicators

	2005	2010	2017
GDP: Gross domestic product (million current US$)	891 634	2 208 838	1 772 591[b]
GDP growth rate (annual %, const. 2005 prices)	3.2	7.5	- 3.8[b]
GDP per capita (current US$)	4 730.7	11 121.2	8 528.3[b]
Economy: Agriculture (% of GVA)[e]	5.5	4.8	5.2[b]
Economy: Industry (% of GVA)[e]	28.5	27.4	22.7[b]
Economy: Services and other activity (% of GVA)[e]	66.0	67.8	72.0[b]
Employment: Agriculture (% of employed)[f]	20.4	16.1	15.2
Employment: Industry (% of employed)[f]	21.4	22.4	21.5
Employment: Services (% of employed)[f]	58.1	61.6	63.2
Unemployment (% of labour force)[f]	11.4	8.5	12.4
Labour force participation (female/male pop. %)[f]	59.1 / 82.4	57.6 / 80.7	56.0 / 78.2
CPI: Consumer Price Index (2000=100)	151	190	242[g]
Agricultural production index (2004-2006=100)	99	122	135[g]
Food production index (2004-2006=100)	99	123	136[g]
Index of industrial production (2005=100)	100	115	111[g]
International trade: Exports (million US$)	118 529	201 915	185 235[d]
International trade: Imports (million US$)	73 600	181 768	137 552[d]
International trade: Balance (million US$)	44 928	20 147	47 683[d]
Balance of payments, current account (million US$)	13 984	- 75 760[h]	- 58 882[b]

Major trading partners

						2016
Export partners (% of exports)	China	19.0	United States	13.3	Argentina	7.2
Import partners (% of imports)	United States	17.5	China	17.0	Germany	6.6

Social indicators

	2005	2010	2017
Population growth rate (average annual %)[i]	1.3	1.0	0.9[b]
Urban population (% of total population)	82.8	84.3	85.7[b]
Urban population growth rate (average annual %)[i]	1.7	1.3	1.2[b]
Fertility rate, total (live births per woman)[i]	2.1	1.9	1.8[b]
Life expectancy at birth (females/males, years)[i]	75.0 / 67.3	76.7 / 69.2	78.4 / 71.0[b]
Population age distribution (0-14 and 60+ years, %)	27.4 / 8.7	24.9 / 10.0	21.7 / 12.6[a]
International migrant stock (000/% of total pop.)	638.6 / 0.3	592.6 / 0.3	713.6 / 0.3[b]
Refugees and others of concern to UNHCR (000)	7.7[j]	5.2[j]	41.1[d]
Infant mortality rate (per 1 000 live births)[i]	28.2	20.4	15.8[b]
Health: Total expenditure (% of GDP)	8.3	8.3	8.3[g]
Health: Physicians (per 1 000 pop.)	1.6	1.8	1.9[k]
Education: Government expenditure (% of GDP)	4.5	5.6	6.0[k]
Education: Primary gross enrol. ratio (f/m per 100 pop.)[f]	129.2 / 137.2	128.2 / 133.9[l]	113.8 / 116.8[b]
Education: Secondary gross enrol. ratio (f/m per 100 pop.)[f]	106.2 / 96.5	102.1 / 91.5[l]	102.2 / 97.2[b]
Education: Tertiary gross enrol. ratio (f/m per 100 pop.)[f]	29.3 / 22.8	42.2 / 31.9[l]	59.3 / 42.4[b]
Intentional homicide rate (per 100 000 pop.)	...	21.8	26.7[b]
Seats held by women in national parliaments (%)	8.6	8.8	10.7

Environment and infrastructure indicators

	2005	2010	2017
Mobile-cellular subscriptions (per 100 inhabitants)	46.3	100.9	126.6[b]
Individuals using the Internet (per 100 inhabitants)	21.0[m,n]	40.6[m,n]	59.1[f,b]
Research & Development expenditure (% of GDP)	1.0	1.2	1.2[k]
Threatened species (number)	697[o]	773	990
Forested area (% of land area)[f]	60.6	59.6	59.2[g]
CO2 emission estimates (million tons/tons per capita)	347.3 / 1.9	419.8 / 2.1	529.8 / 2.6[g]
Energy production, primary (Petajoules)	8 344	10 050	10 948[g]
Energy supply per capita (Gigajoules)	50	55	61[g]
Tourist/visitor arrivals at national borders (000)	5 358	5 161	6 306[b]
Important sites for terrestrial biodiversity protected (%)	42.1	47.2	47.4
Pop. using improved drinking water (urban/rural, %)	98.4 / 79.7	99.3 / 83.8	100.0 / 87.0[b]
Pop. using improved sanitation facilities (urban/rural, %)	84.7 / 43.8	86.5 / 48.1	88.0 / 51.5[b]
Net Official Development Assist. received (% of GNI)	0.02	0.02	0.06[b]

a. Projected estimate (medium fertility variant). b. 2015. c. Refers to the "Região Integrada de Desenvolvimento do Distrito Federal e Entorno". d. 2016. e. Data classified according to ISIC Rev. 4. f. Estimate. g. 2014. h. Break in the time series. i. Data refers to a 5-year period preceding the reference year. j. Data as at the end of December. k. 2013. l. 2009. m. Population aged 10 years and over. n. Users in the last 3 months. o. 2004.

British Virgin Islands

Region	Caribbean	Population (000, 2017)	31 [a]
Surface area (km2)	151 [b]	Pop. density (per km2, 2017)	208.0 [a]
Sex ratio (m per 100 f, 2017)	97.1 [c]	Capital city	Road Town
National currency	US Dollar (USD)	Capital city pop. (000)	13.1 [d]

Economic indicators

	2005	2010	2017
GDP: Gross domestic product (million current US$)	870	894	908 [b]
GDP growth rate (annual %, const. 2005 prices)	14.3	1.3	- 1.1 [b]
GDP per capita (current US$)	37 550.2	32 839.9	30 144.5 [b]
Economy: Agriculture (% of GVA)	1.1	1.0	1.0 [b]
Economy: Industry (% of GVA)	11.9	10.0	11.1 [b]
Economy: Services and other activity (% of GVA)	87.1	89.0	87.8 [b]
Employment: Agriculture (% of employed)	...	0.5 [e]	...
Employment: Industry (% of employed)	...	11.1 [e]	...
Employment: Services (% of employed)	...	87.4 [e]	...
CPI: Consumer Price Index (2000=100)	110	...	...
Agricultural production index (2004-2006=100)	100	102	103 [d]
Food production index (2004-2006=100)	100	102	103 [d]
International trade: Exports (million US$)	~0	~0	~0 [f]
International trade: Imports (million US$)	227	313	444 [f]
International trade: Balance (million US$)	- 226	- 313	- 444 [f]

Major trading partners   2016

Export partners (% of exports)	United States	26.0	Mexico	12.3	United Kingdom	6.3
Import partners (% of imports)	United States	41.1	Switzerland	11.2	Italy	6.7

Social indicators

	2005	2010	2017
Population growth rate (average annual %) [g]	2.3	3.2	2.0 [b]
Urban population (% of total population)	43.2	44.6	46.2 [b]
Urban population growth rate (average annual %) [g]	3.0	3.9	1.8 [b]
Fertility rate, total (live births per woman)	2.0 [h]	...	...
Life expectancy at birth (females/males, years)	78.5 / 69.9 [h]	... / ...	... / ...
Population age distribution (0-14 and 60+ years, %)	26.3 / 7.4 [i]	22.3 / 9.7	... / ...
International migrant stock (000/% of total pop.)	13.8 / 59.6	15.6 / 57.2	17.3 / 57.5 [b]
Refugees and others of concern to UNHCR (000)	...	~0.0 [j]	...
Education: Government expenditure (% of GDP)	...	4.4	6.6 [b]
Intentional homicide rate (per 100 000 pop.)	17.8 [h]	8.4 [k]	...

Environment and infrastructure indicators

	2005	2010	2017
Mobile-cellular subscriptions (per 100 inhabitants)	...	174.6	145.8 [l,b]
Individuals using the Internet (per 100 inhabitants)	...	37.0	37.6 [m]
Threatened species (number)	30 [h]	43	67
Forested area (% of land area) [l]	24.4	24.3	24.1 [d]
CO2 emission estimates (million tons/tons per capita)	0.1 / 6.0	0.2 / 6.3	0.2 / 6.0 [d]
Energy production, primary (Petajoules)	0	0	0 [d]
Energy supply per capita (Gigajoules) [l]	85	89	85 [d]
Tourist/visitor arrivals at national borders (000)	337	330	393 [b]
Important sites for terrestrial biodiversity protected (%)	7.0	7.0	7.0
Pop. using improved drinking water (urban/rural, %)	94.9 / 94.9	... / ...	... / ...
Pop. using improved sanitation facilities (urban/rural, %)	97.5 / 97.5	97.5 / 97.5	97.5 / 97.5 [b]

a Projected estimate (medium fertility variant). **b** 2015. **c** 2010. **d** 2014. **e** Data classified according to ISIC Rev. 3. **f** 2016. **g** Data refers to a 5-year period preceding the reference year. **h** 2004. **i** 2001. **j** Data as at the end of December. **k** 2006. **l** Estimate. **m** 2012.

Brunei Darussalam

Region	South-eastern Asia	UN membership date	21 September 1984
Population (000, 2017)	429[a]	Surface area (km2)	5 765[b]
Pop. density (per km2, 2017)	81.3[a]	Sex ratio (m per 100 f, 2017)	106.0[a]
Capital city	Bandar Seri Begawan	National currency	Brunei Dollar (BND)
Capital city pop. (000)	14.0[c]	Exchange rate (per US$)	1.4[d]

Economic indicators

	2005	2010	2017
GDP: Gross domestic product (million current US$)	10 561	13 707	12 930[b]
GDP growth rate (annual %, const. 2005 prices)	0.4	2.6	- 0.6[b]
GDP per capita (current US$)	29 183.8	34 851.4	30 552.7[b]
Economy: Agriculture (% of GVA)[e]	0.9	0.7	1.1[b]
Economy: Industry (% of GVA)[e]	72.0	67.4	60.2[b]
Economy: Services and other activity (% of GVA)[e]	27.1	31.9	38.7[b]
Employment: Agriculture (% of employed)[f]	1.0	0.8	0.6
Employment: Industry (% of employed)[f]	21.0	20.2	19.4
Employment: Services (% of employed)[f]	78.0	79.1	80.1
Unemployment (% of labour force)[f]	2.4	1.7	2.1
Labour force participation (female/male pop. %)[f]	55.2 / 78.1	54.1 / 76.9	50.6 / 75.0
CPI: Consumer Price Index (2000=100)	101	105[g]	105[c]
Agricultural production index (2004-2006=100)	75	139	157[c]
Food production index (2004-2006=100)	75	140	157[c]
Index of industrial production (2005=100)[h]	100	88	79[c]
International trade: Exports (million US$)	6 242	9 172	4 875[d]
International trade: Imports (million US$)	1 447	3 364	2 679[d]
International trade: Balance (million US$)	4 794	5 809	2 197[d]
Balance of payments, current account (million US$)	4 033	5 016[i]	2 071[b]

Major trading partners

						2016
Export partners (% of exports)	Japan	34.7	Republic of Korea	14.3	India	9.4
Import partners (% of imports)	Malaysia	21.1	Singapore	19.2	China	13.0

Social indicators

	2005	2010	2017
Population growth rate (average annual %)[j]	1.8	1.2	1.4[b]
Urban population (% of total population)	73.5	75.5	77.2[b]
Urban population growth rate (average annual %)[j]	2.7	2.2	1.8[b]
Fertility rate, total (live births per woman)[j]	2.0	1.8	1.9[b]
Life expectancy at birth (females/males, years)[j]	77.4 / 74.2	78.4 / 75.1	78.4 / 75.1[b]
Population age distribution (0-14 and 60+ years, %)	27.8 / 4.8	26.0 / 5.4	23.0 / 8.0[a]
International migrant stock (000/% of total pop.)	98.4 / 27.2	100.6 / 25.6	102.7 / 24.3[b]
Refugees and others of concern to UNHCR (000)	...	21.0[k]	20.5[d]
Infant mortality rate (per 1 000 live births)[j]	8.2	6.5	6.5[b]
Health: Total expenditure (% of GDP)	2.6	2.7	2.6[c]
Health: Physicians (per 1 000 pop.)	1.1	1.4	1.5[l]
Education: Government expenditure (% of GDP)	3.7[m]	2.0	4.4[d]
Education: Primary gross enrol. ratio (f/m per 100 pop.)	111.0 / 113.1	106.9 / 107.3	108.2 / 108.1[b]
Education: Secondary gross enrol. ratio (f/m per 100 pop.)	98.0 / 97.2	99.7 / 98.9	96.3 / 95.9[b]
Education: Tertiary gross enrol. ratio (f/m per 100 pop.)	19.7 / 9.9	20.6 / 11.1	38.6 / 23.5[b]
Intentional homicide rate (per 100 000 pop.)	0.6	0.2	0.5[n]
Seats held by women in national parliaments (%)	...	...	9.1

Environment and infrastructure indicators

	2005	2010	2017
Mobile-cellular subscriptions (per 100 inhabitants)	63.3	108.6	108.1[b]
Individuals using the Internet (per 100 inhabitants)	36.5	53.0[f]	71.2[f,b]
Research & Development expenditure (% of GDP)	~0.0[i,o,p]	...	...
Threatened species (number)	148[p]	170	193
Forested area (% of land area)[f]	73.8	72.1	72.1[c]
CO2 emission estimates (million tons/tons per capita)	5.0 / 13.8	8.2 / 20.9	9.1 / 21.8[c]
Energy production, primary (Petajoules)	848	775	679[c]
Energy supply per capita (Gigajoules)	210	345	357[c]
Tourist/visitor arrivals at national borders (000)[q]	126	214	218[b]
Important sites for terrestrial biodiversity protected (%)	62.9	62.9	62.9

a Projected estimate (medium fertility variant). **b** 2015. **c** 2014. **d** 2016. **e** Data classified according to ISIC Rev. 4. **f** Estimate. **g** Series linked to former series. **h** Data classified according to ISIC Rev. 3. **i** Break in the time series. **j** Data refers to a 5-year period preceding the reference year. **k** Data as at the end of December. **l** 2012. **m** 2000. **n** 2013. **o** Partial data. **p** 2004. **q** Arrivals by air.

Bulgaria

Region	Eastern Europe	UN membership date	14 December 1955
Population (000, 2017)	7 085[a]	Surface area (km2)	111 002[b]
Pop. density (per km2, 2017)	65.3[a]	Sex ratio (m per 100 f, 2017)	94.6[a]
Capital city	Sofia	National currency	Bulgarian Lev (BGN)
Capital city pop. (000)	1 226.2[b]	Exchange rate (per US$)	1.9[c]

Economic indicators

	2005	2010	2017
GDP: Gross domestic product (million current US$)	29 821	49 939	48 953[b]
GDP growth rate (annual %, const. 2005 prices)	7.2	0.1	3.0[b]
GDP per capita (current US$)	3 881.6	6 741.9	6 846.8[b]
Economy: Agriculture (% of GVA)[d]	8.5	4.9	5.1[b]
Economy: Industry (% of GVA)[d]	28.2	27.5	27.6[b]
Economy: Services and other activity (% of GVA)[d]	63.3	67.6	67.2[b]
Employment: Agriculture (% of employed)[e]	8.9	6.8	6.5
Employment: Industry (% of employed)[e]	34.2	33.4	29.4
Employment: Services (% of employed)[e]	56.8	59.8	64.1
Unemployment (% of labour force)	10.1	10.3	8.1[e]
Labour force participation (female/male pop. %)[e]	44.6 / 56.3	47.5 / 59.5	48.5 / 60.1
CPI: Consumer Price Index (2000=100)	130	178	190[f]
Agricultural production index (2004-2006=100)	91	106	117[f]
Food production index (2004-2006=100)	91	107	119[f]
Index of industrial production (2005=100)	100	98[g]	105[g,f]
International trade: Exports (million US$)	11 739	20 608	26 088[c]
International trade: Imports (million US$)	18 162	25 360	28 875[c]
International trade: Balance (million US$)	- 6 423	- 4 752	- 2 787[c]
Balance of payments, current account (million US$)	- 3 347	- 965[h]	196[b]

Major trading partners

							2016
Export partners (% of exports)	Germany	15.4	Romania	9.9	Italy	9.2
Import partners (% of imports)	Germany	13.1	Russian Federation	8.9	Italy	7.9

Social indicators

	2005	2010	2017
Population growth rate (average annual %)[i]	- 0.8	- 0.7	- 0.6[b]
Urban population (% of total population)	70.6	72.3	73.9[b]
Urban population growth rate (average annual %)[i]	- 0.3	- 0.3	- 0.3[b]
Fertility rate, total (live births per woman)[i]	1.2	1.4	1.5[b]
Life expectancy at birth (females/males, years)[i]	75.8 / 68.8	76.7 / 69.7	77.8 / 70.8[b]
Population age distribution (0-14 and 60+ years, %)	13.6 / 23.1	13.3 / 25.3	14.2 / 27.7[a]
International migrant stock (000/% of total pop.)	61.1 / 0.8	76.3 / 1.0	102.1 / 1.4[b]
Refugees and others of concern to UNHCR (000)	5.2[j]	6.9[i]	33.7[c]
Infant mortality rate (per 1 000 live births)[i]	12.7	9.5	8.3[b]
Health: Total expenditure (% of GDP)	7.1	7.2	8.4[f]
Health: Physicians (per 1 000 pop.)	...	3.8	4.0[f]
Education: Government expenditure (% of GDP)	4.1	3.9	4.1[k]
Education: Primary gross enrol. ratio (f/m per 100 pop.)	100.6 / 101.8	103.7 / 103.6	96.7 / 97.7[b]
Education: Secondary gross enrol. ratio (f/m per 100 pop.)	88.4 / 92.4	88.3 / 92.4	97.4 / 100.5[b]
Education: Tertiary gross enrol. ratio (f/m per 100 pop.)	47.6 / 41.1	66.4 / 50.1	82.9 / 65.4[b]
Intentional homicide rate (per 100 000 pop.)	2.6	2.0	1.8[b]
Seats held by women in national parliaments (%)	26.3	20.8	19.2

Environment and infrastructure indicators

	2005	2010	2017
Mobile-cellular subscriptions (per 100 inhabitants)	81.3	138.0	129.3[l,b]
Individuals using the Internet (per 100 inhabitants)[m]	20.0	46.2	56.7[b]
Research & Development expenditure (% of GDP)	0.4	0.6	0.8[f]
Threatened species (number)	44[n]	66	104
Forested area (% of land area)	33.6	34.4[e]	35.1[e,f]
CO2 emission estimates (million tons/tons per capita)	47.9 / 6.2	44.1 / 5.9	42.4 / 5.9[f]
Energy production, primary (Petajoules)	444	442	474[f]
Energy supply per capita (Gigajoules)	107	100	103[f]
Tourist/visitor arrivals at national borders (000)	4 837	6 047	7 099[b]
Important sites for terrestrial biodiversity protected (%)	40.9	95.6	95.6
Pop. using improved drinking water (urban/rural, %)	99.8 / 99.3	99.7 / 99.1	99.6 / 99.0[b]
Pop. using improved sanitation facilities (urban/rural, %)	86.8 / 83.6	86.8 / 83.7	86.8 / 83.7[b]
Net Official Development Assist. disbursed (% of GNI)	...	0.09	0.09[b]

a Projected estimate (medium fertility variant). **b** 2015. **c** 2016. **d** Data classified according to ISIC Rev. 4. **e** Estimate. **f** 2014. **g** Excluding water and waste management. **h** Break in the time series. **i** Data refers to a 5-year period preceding the reference year. **j** Data as at the end of December. **k** 2013. **l** Provisional data. **m** Population aged 16 to 74 years. **n** 2004.

Burkina Faso

Region	Western Africa	UN membership date	20 September 1960
Population (000, 2017)	19 193[a]	Surface area (km2)	272 967[b]
Pop. density (per km2, 2017)	70.2[a]	Sex ratio (m per 100 f, 2017)	99.5[a]
Capital city	Ouagadougou	National currency	CFA Franc (XOF)
Capital city pop. (000)	2 741.1[b]	Exchange rate (per US$)	622.3[c]

Economic indicators

	2005	2010	2017
GDP: Gross domestic product (million current US$)	5 463	8 980	11 065[b]
GDP growth rate (annual %, const. 2005 prices)	8.7	8.4	4.1[b]
GDP per capita (current US$)	407.0	574.5	611.1[b]
Economy: Agriculture (% of GVA)	38.5	35.1	34.5[b]
Economy: Industry (% of GVA)	17.7	20.2	21.8[b]
Economy: Services and other activity (% of GVA)	43.8	44.7	43.7[b]
Employment: Agriculture (% of employed)[d]	84.7	80.8	80.0
Employment: Industry (% of employed)[d]	3.1	5.1	4.9
Employment: Services (% of employed)[d]	12.2	14.1	15.1
Unemployment (% of labour force)	4.0	3.3[d]	2.9[d]
Labour force participation (female/male pop. %)[d]	76.5 / 91.0	76.6 / 91.0	76.5 / 90.5
CPI: Consumer Price Index (2000=100)[e]	116	131[f]	141[g]
Agricultural production index (2004-2006=100)	104	118	131[g]
Food production index (2004-2006=100)	104	125	134[g]
International trade: Exports (million US$)	332	1 288	2 019[c]
International trade: Imports (million US$)	1 161	2 048	3 699[c]
International trade: Balance (million US$)	- 828	- 760	- 1 680[c]
Balance of payments, current account (million US$)	- 819	- 549	- 998[g]

Major trading partners

						2016
Export partners (% of exports)	Switzerland	50.6	India	10.3	Singapore	10.0
Import partners (% of imports)	China	11.1	France	9.0	Côte d'Ivoire	8.4

Social indicators

	2005	2010	2017
Population growth rate (average annual %)[h]	2.9	3.0	3.0[b]
Urban population (% of total population)	21.5	25.7	29.9[b]
Urban population growth rate (average annual %)[h]	6.7	6.4	5.9[b]
Fertility rate, total (live births per woman)[h]	6.4	6.1	5.6[b]
Life expectancy at birth (females/males, years)[h]	52.6 / 50.5	55.8 / 54.6	59.3 / 58.0[b]
Population age distribution (0-14 and 60+ years, %)	46.5 / 4.1	46.2 / 3.9	45.2 / 3.9[a]
International migrant stock (000/% of total pop.)[i]	597.0 / 4.4	673.9 / 4.3	704.7 / 3.9[b]
Refugees and others of concern to UNHCR (000)	1.3[j]	1.1[j]	32.7[c]
Infant mortality rate (per 1 000 live births)[h]	90.0	77.6	64.8[b]
Health: Total expenditure (% of GDP)	6.9	7.2	5.0[g]
Health: Physicians (per 1 000 pop.)	0.1[k]	~0.0	~0.0[l]
Education: Government expenditure (% of GDP)	4.4	3.9	4.1[b]
Education: Primary gross enrol. ratio (f/m per 100 pop.)	51.8 / 64.7	73.9 / 81.6	86.1 / 89.9[b]
Education: Secondary gross enrol. ratio (f/m per 100 pop.)	11.8 / 16.7	18.9 / 24.8	32.2 / 35.1[b]
Education: Tertiary gross enrol. ratio (f/m per 100 pop.)	1.4 / 3.2	2.3 / 4.8	3.8 / 7.3[c]
Intentional homicide rate (per 100 000 pop.)	0.6	0.6	0.7[l]
Seats held by women in national parliaments (%)	11.7	15.3	11.0

Environment and infrastructure indicators

	2005	2010	2017
Mobile-cellular subscriptions (per 100 inhabitants)	4.7	36.7	80.6[b]
Individuals using the Internet (per 100 inhabitants)	0.5	2.4[d]	11.4[d,b]
Research & Development expenditure (% of GDP)	0.2[m]	0.2[n]	...
Threatened species (number)	11[k]	24	31
Forested area (% of land area)[d]	21.7	20.6	19.8[g]
CO2 emission estimates (million tons/tons per capita)	1.1 / 0.1	2.0 / 0.1	2.8 / 0.1[g]
Energy production, primary (Petajoules)	98	118	123[g]
Energy supply per capita (Gigajoules)	8	9	9[g]
Tourist/visitor arrivals at national borders (000)	245	274	163[b]
Important sites for terrestrial biodiversity protected (%)	66.7	71.8	71.8
Pop. using improved drinking water (urban/rural, %)	90.0 / 63.4	95.3 / 72.3	97.5 / 75.8[b]
Pop. using improved sanitation facilities (urban/rural, %)	48.3 / 5.1	49.8 / 6.2	50.4 / 6.7[b]
Net Official Development Assist. received (% of GNI)	12.83	11.35	9.11[b]

a Projected estimate (medium fertility variant). **b** 2015. **c** 2016. **d** Estimate. **e** Ouagadougou **f** Series linked to former series. **g** 2014. **h** Data refers to a 5-year period preceding the reference year. **i** Including refugees. **j** Data as at the end of December. **k** 2004. **l** 2012. **m** Partial data. **n** 2009.

Burundi

Region	Eastern Africa	UN membership date	18 September 1962
Population (000, 2017)	10 864[a]	Surface area (km2)	27 830[b]
Pop. density (per km2, 2017)	423.1[a]	Sex ratio (m per 100 f, 2017)	96.9[a]
Capital city	Bujumbura	National currency	Burundi Franc (BIF)
Capital city pop. (000)	750.9[b]	Exchange rate (per US$)	1 688.6[c]

Economic indicators	2005	2010	2017
GDP: Gross domestic product (million current US$)	1 117	2 032	2 735[b]
GDP growth rate (annual %, const. 2005 prices)	0.9	5.1	- 4.1[b]
GDP per capita (current US$)	140.8	214.8	244.6[b]
Economy: Agriculture (% of GVA)	43.0	40.7	36.3[b]
Economy: Industry (% of GVA)	17.8	16.3	13.9[b]
Economy: Services and other activity (% of GVA)	39.1	43.0	49.8[b]
Employment: Agriculture (% of employed)[d]	91.1	90.8	91.1
Employment: Industry (% of employed)[d]	2.8	2.6	2.6
Employment: Services (% of employed)[d]	6.1	6.5	6.3
Unemployment (% of labour force)[d]	1.7	1.6	1.7
Labour force participation (female/male pop. %)[d]	84.0 / 81.8	84.0 / 81.6	84.6 / 82.7
CPI: Consumer Price Index (2000=100)[e]	145	236	344[f,g]
Agricultural production index (2004-2006=100)	92	108	109[g]
Food production index (2004-2006=100)	100	114	122[g]
International trade: Exports (million US$)	114	118	123[c]
International trade: Imports (million US$)	258	404	625[c]
International trade: Balance (million US$)	- 144	- 286	- 502[c]
Balance of payments, current account (million US$)	- 222[h]	- 301	- 375[b]

Major trading partners						2016
Export partners (% of exports)	Dem. Rep. of Congo	22.3	Switzerland	17.9	United Arab Emirates	13.1
Import partners (% of imports)	China	16.6	India	14.1	United Rep. Tanzania	8.2

Social indicators	2005	2010	2017
Population growth rate (average annual %)[i]	3.0	3.3	3.0[b]
Urban population (% of total population)	9.4	10.6	12.1[b]
Urban population growth rate (average annual %)[i]	5.6	6.0	5.7[b]
Fertility rate, total (live births per woman)[i]	6.8	6.5	6.0[b]
Life expectancy at birth (females/males, years)[i]	53.7 / 50.3	55.4 / 52.0	58.0 / 54.2[b]
Population age distribution (0-14 and 60+ years, %)	45.7 / 4.2	44.1 / 4.0	45.0 / 4.4[a]
International migrant stock (000/% of total pop.)[j]	172.9 / 2.2	235.3 / 2.5	286.8 / 2.6[b]
Refugees and others of concern to UNHCR (000)	53.6[k]	200.8[k]	103.2[c]
Infant mortality rate (per 1 000 live births)[i]	94.6	86.2	77.8[b]
Health: Total expenditure (% of GDP)[l,m]	9.8	8.8	7.5[g]
Health: Physicians (per 1 000 pop.)	~0.0[n]	...	...
Education: Government expenditure (% of GDP)	3.6	6.8	5.4[o]
Education: Primary gross enrol. ratio (f/m per 100 pop.)	72.4 / 85.8	129.2 / 133.7	124.5 / 123.1[b]
Education: Secondary gross enrol. ratio (f/m per 100 pop.)	10.7 / 14.8[d]	18.7 / 27.2	40.5 / 44.5[b]
Education: Tertiary gross enrol. ratio (f/m per 100 pop.)	1.3 / 3.4[d]	2.2 / 4.2	2.4 / 7.7[g]
Intentional homicide rate (per 100 000 pop.)	...	3.7	4.0[g]
Seats held by women in national parliaments (%)	18.4	31.4	36.4

Environment and infrastructure indicators	2005	2010	2017
Mobile-cellular subscriptions (per 100 inhabitants)	2.0	18.2[d]	46.2[b]
Individuals using the Internet (per 100 inhabitants)	0.5	1.0[d]	4.9[d,b]
Research & Development expenditure (% of GDP)[p]	...	0.1	0.1[q]
Threatened species (number)	28[n]	52	61
Forested area (% of land area)[d]	7.0	9.9	10.6[g]
CO2 emission estimates (million tons/tons per capita)	0.2 / ~0.0	0.2 / ~0.0	0.4 / ~0.0[g]
Energy production, primary (Petajoules)	79	86	56[g]
Energy supply per capita (Gigajoules)	11	9	6[g]
Tourist/visitor arrivals at national borders (000)[r]	148	142[h]	131[b]
Important sites for terrestrial biodiversity protected (%)	45.5	45.5	51.2
Pop. using improved drinking water (urban/rural, %)	92.9 / 71.2	91.9 / 72.6	91.1 / 73.8[b]
Pop. using improved sanitation facilities (urban/rural, %)	39.1 / 46.3	41.7 / 47.6	43.8 / 48.6[b]
Net Official Development Assist. received (% of GNI)	33.23	31.16	11.91[b]

a Projected estimate (medium fertility variant). **b** 2015. **c** 2016. **d** Estimate. **e** Bujumbura **f** Series linked to former series. **g** 2014. **h** Break in the time series. **i** Data refers to a 5-year period preceding the reference year. **j** Including refugees. **k** Data as at the end of December. **l** Estimates should be viewed with caution as these are derived from scarce data. **m** Data revision. **n** 2004. **o** 2013. **p** Partial data. **q** 2011. **r** Including nationals residing abroad.

Cabo Verde

Region	Western Africa	UN membership date	16 September 1975	
Population (000, 2017)	546[a]	Surface area (km2)	4 033[b]	
Pop. density (per km2, 2017)	135.6[a]	Sex ratio (m per 100 f, 2017)	99.3[a]	
Capital city	Praia	National currency	Cabo Verde Escudo (CVE)	
Capital city pop. (000)	144.6[c]	Exchange rate (per US$)	104.6[d]	

Economic indicators	2005	2010	2017
GDP: Gross domestic product (million current US$)	1 105	1 664	1 603[b]
GDP growth rate (annual %, const. 2005 prices)	6.5	1.5	1.5[b]
GDP per capita (current US$)	2 331.0	3 393.9	3 080.2[b]
Economy: Agriculture (% of GVA)	11.7	9.2	9.5[b]
Economy: Industry (% of GVA)	22.8	20.8	19.8[b]
Economy: Services and other activity (% of GVA)	65.5	70.1	70.7[b]
Employment: Agriculture (% of employed)[e]	35.3	30.2	27.2
Employment: Industry (% of employed)[e]	9.9	11.3	11.5
Employment: Services (% of employed)[e]	54.9	58.5	61.3
Unemployment (% of labour force)	11.1[e]	10.7	10.5[e]
Labour force participation (female/male pop. %)[e]	48.0 / 82.2	50.9 / 82.8	53.7 / 84.6
CPI: Consumer Price Index (2000=100)	105	127	138[c]
Agricultural production index (2004-2006=100)	99	103	98[c]
Food production index (2004-2006=100)	99	103	98[c]
International trade: Exports (million US$)	89	220	29[d]
International trade: Imports (million US$)	438	731	485[d]
International trade: Balance (million US$)	- 349	- 511	- 455[d]
Balance of payments, current account (million US$)	- 41	- 223	- 73[b]

Major trading partners						2016
Export partners (% of exports)	Areas nes[f]	27.5	Portugal	25.4	Spain	24.7
Import partners (% of imports)	Portugal	43.5	Netherlands	12.3	Spain	7.3

Social indicators	2005	2010	2017
Population growth rate (average annual %)[g]	1.7	1.1	1.2[b]
Urban population (% of total population)	57.7	61.8	65.5[b]
Urban population growth rate (average annual %)[g]	3.1	1.8	2.0[b]
Fertility rate, total (live births per woman)[g]	3.4	2.9	2.5[b]
Life expectancy at birth (females/males, years)[g]	72.8 / 69.5	73.4 / 69.9	74.0 / 70.1[b]
Population age distribution (0-14 and 60+ years, %)	38.1 / 7.2	34.0 / 6.7	30.2 / 6.9[a]
International migrant stock (000/% of total pop.)	12.7 / 2.7	14.4 / 2.9	14.9 / 2.9[a]
Refugees and others of concern to UNHCR (000)	~0.0[h]	...	0.1[d]
Infant mortality rate (per 1 000 live births)[g]	25.0	23.5	22.5[b]
Health: Total expenditure (% of GDP)	4.9	4.8	4.8[c]
Health: Physicians (per 1 000 pop.)	0.5[i]	0.3	0.3[i]
Education: Government expenditure (% of GDP)	7.5[i]	5.6	5.0[k]
Education: Primary gross enrol. ratio (f/m per 100 pop.)	108.0 / 112.4	108.6 / 114.7	106.9 / 112.8[b]
Education: Secondary gross enrol. ratio (f/m per 100 pop.)	73.0 / 64.5	93.4 / 79.5	98.3 / 87.7[b]
Education: Tertiary gross enrol. ratio (f/m per 100 pop.)	7.7 / 7.2	19.4 / 15.3	25.2 / 18.1[b]
Intentional homicide rate (per 100 000 pop.)	...	8.0	8.8[b]
Seats held by women in national parliaments (%)	11.1	18.1	23.6

Environment and infrastructure indicators	2005	2010	2017
Mobile-cellular subscriptions (per 100 inhabitants)	17.1	76.3	127.2[b]
Individuals using the Internet (per 100 inhabitants)	6.1	30.0[e]	43.0[e,b]
Research & Development expenditure (% of GDP)	...	...	0.1[l,m,j]
Threatened species (number)	23[i]	31	65
Forested area (% of land area)	20.7	21.1	22.1[a,c]
CO2 emission estimates (million tons/tons per capita)	0.4 / 0.9	0.6 / 1.1	0.5 / 1.0[c]
Energy production, primary (Petajoules)	2	1	2[c]
Energy supply per capita (Gigajoules)	16	19	17[c]
Tourist/visitor arrivals at national borders (000)[n]	198	336	520[b]
Important sites for terrestrial biodiversity protected (%)	0.0	0.0	7.1
Pop. using improved drinking water (urban/rural, %)	87.5 / 83.1	91.1 / 85.4	94.0 / 87.3[b]
Pop. using improved sanitation facilities (urban/rural, %)	67.8 / 35.2	75.5 / 45.8	81.6 / 54.3[b]
Net Official Development Assist. received (% of GNI)	17.36	20.55	9.81[b]

a Projected estimate (medium fertility variant). **b** 2015. **c** 2014. **d** 2016. **e** Estimate. **f** Areas not elsewhere specified. **g** Data refers to a 5-year period preceding the reference year. **h** Data as at the end of December. **i** 2004. **j** 2011. **k** 2013. **l** Higher Education only. **m** Partial data. **n** Arrivals of non-resident tourists in hotels and similar establishments.

Cambodia

Region	South-eastern Asia	
Population (000, 2017)	16 005 [a]	
Pop. density (per km2, 2017)	90.7 [a]	
Capital city	Phnom Penh	
Capital city pop. (000)	1 731.3 [c,b]	

UN membership date	14 December 1955	
Surface area (km2)	181 035 [b]	
Sex ratio (m per 100 f, 2017)	95.3 [a]	
National currency	Riel (KHR)	
Exchange rate (per US$)	4 044.5 [d]	

Economic indicators	2005	2010	2017
GDP: Gross domestic product (million current US$)	6 293	11 242	18 050 [b]
GDP growth rate (annual %, const. 2005 prices)	13.2	6.0	7.0 [b]
GDP per capita (current US$)	472.4	782.7	1 158.7 [b]
Economy: Agriculture (% of GVA)	32.4	36.0	28.2 [b]
Economy: Industry (% of GVA)	26.4	23.3	29.4 [b]
Economy: Services and other activity (% of GVA)	41.2	40.7	42.3 [b]
Employment: Agriculture (% of employed) [e]	59.8	54.2	42.4
Employment: Industry (% of employed) [e]	14.6	16.2	19.6
Employment: Services (% of employed) [e]	25.7	29.6	38.0
Unemployment (% of labour force)	1.8 [e]	0.4	0.3 [e]
Labour force participation (female/male pop. %) [e]	75.9 / 86.6	81.6 / 88.6	75.6 / 87.0
CPI: Consumer Price Index (2000=100) [f]	114	165	185 [g]
Agricultural production index (2004-2006=100)	105	149	175 [h]
Food production index (2004-2006=100)	105	148	177 [h]
International trade: Exports (million US$)	3 019	5 590	13 204 [d]
International trade: Imports (million US$)	2 552	4 903	15 313 [d]
International trade: Balance (million US$)	467	688	- 2 109 [d]
Balance of payments, current account (million US$)	- 321 [i]	- 410	- 1 657 [h]

Major trading partners						2016
Export partners (% of exports)	United States	25.0	United Kingdom	10.2	Germany	8.8
Import partners (% of imports)	China	36.8	Thailand	14.6	Viet Nam	8.7

Social indicators	2005	2010	2017
Population growth rate (average annual %) [j]	1.8	1.5	1.6 [b]
Urban population (% of total population)	19.2	19.8	20.7 [b]
Urban population growth rate (average annual %) [j]	2.4	2.1	2.6 [b]
Fertility rate, total (live births per woman) [j]	3.4	3.1	2.7 [b]
Life expectancy at birth (females/males, years) [j]	63.0 / 58.5	67.4 / 62.7	69.6 / 65.5 [b]
Population age distribution (0-14 and 60+ years, %)	37.1 / 5.3	33.3 / 5.9	31.3 / 7.1 [a]
International migrant stock (000/% of total pop.)	114.0 / 0.9	82.0 / 0.6	74.0 / 0.5 [b]
Refugees and others of concern to UNHCR (000)	0.4 [k]	0.2 [k]	0.3 [d]
Infant mortality rate (per 1 000 live births) [j]	65.9	45.0	29.9 [b]
Health: Total expenditure (% of GDP) [l]	5.8	6.0	5.7 [h]
Health: Physicians (per 1 000 pop.)	0.2 [m]	0.2	0.2 [g]
Education: Government expenditure (% of GDP)	1.7 [n]	1.5	1.9 [h]
Education: Primary gross enrol. ratio (f/m per 100 pop.)	125.6 / 135.1	119.8 / 126.9	116.2 / 117.1 [b]
Education: Secondary gross enrol. ratio (f/m per 100 pop.)	25.6 / 36.6 [e,n]	41.4 / 48.5 [e,o]	... / ...
Education: Tertiary gross enrol. ratio (f/m per 100 pop.)	2.1 / 4.6	10.5 / 17.6	11.8 / 14.3 [b]
Intentional homicide rate (per 100 000 pop.)	3.4	2.3	1.8 [p]
Seats held by women in national parliaments (%)	9.8	21.1	20.3

Environment and infrastructure indicators	2005	2010	2017
Mobile-cellular subscriptions (per 100 inhabitants)	8.0	56.7	133.0 [b]
Individuals using the Internet (per 100 inhabitants)	0.3	1.3	19.0 [e,b]
Research & Development expenditure (% of GDP)	~0.0 [q,r]	...	...
Threatened species (number)	103 [n]	204	255
Forested area (% of land area)	60.8	57.2 [e]	54.3 [e,h]
CO2 emission estimates (million tons/tons per capita)	2.8 / 0.2	5.0 / 0.4	6.7 / 0.4 [h]
Energy production, primary (Petajoules)	105	152	178 [h]
Energy supply per capita (Gigajoules)	11	15	17 [h]
Tourist/visitor arrivals at national borders (000) [s]	1 422	2 508	4 775 [b]
Important sites for terrestrial biodiversity protected (%)	38.1	39.5	39.5
Pop. using improved drinking water (urban/rural, %)	71.6 / 48.4	86.1 / 58.8	100.0 / 69.1 [b]
Pop. using improved sanitation facilities (urban/rural, %)	58.6 / 16.9	73.8 / 23.7	88.1 / 30.5 [b]
Net Official Development Assist. received (% of GNI)	8.97	6.84	3.97 [b]

a Projected estimate (medium fertility variant). **b** 2015. **c** Refers to the municipality of Phnom Penh including suburban areas. **d** 2016. **e** Estimate. **f** Phnom Penh **g** 2013. **h** 2014. **i** Break in the time series. **j** Data refers to a 5-year period preceding the reference year. **k** Data as at the end of December. **l** 2012 data are based on a health accounts study based on SHA2011. Numbers were converted to SHA 1.0 format for comparability. **m** 2000. **n** 2004. **o** 2008. **p** 2011. **q** Partial data. **r** 2002. **s** Arrivals by all means of transport.

Cameroon

Region	Middle Africa	UN membership date	20 September 1960
Population (000, 2017)	24 054 [a]	Surface area (km2)	475 650 [b]
Pop. density (per km2, 2017)	50.9 [a]	Sex ratio (m per 100 f, 2017)	100.2 [a]
Capital city	Yaoundé	National currency	CFA Franc (XAF)
Capital city pop. (000)	3 065.7 [b]	Exchange rate (per US$)	622.3 [c]

Economic indicators

	2005	2010	2017
GDP: Gross domestic product (million current US$)	16 588	23 622	28 416 [b]
GDP growth rate (annual %, const. 2005 prices)	2.3	3.3	5.8 [b]
GDP per capita (current US$)	915.1	1 147.2	1 217.3 [b]
Economy: Agriculture (% of GVA)	20.4	23.3	22.7 [b]
Economy: Industry (% of GVA)	31.8	29.7	28.3 [b]
Economy: Services and other activity (% of GVA)	47.8	47.0	49.1 [b]
Employment: Agriculture (% of employed) [d]	64.1	63.7	61.8
Employment: Industry (% of employed) [d]	8.8	8.8	8.7
Employment: Services (% of employed) [d]	27.2	27.4	29.5
Unemployment (% of labour force)	4.4	4.1	4.6 [d]
Labour force participation (female/male pop. %) [d]	67.1 / 79.5	70.5 / 81.2	71.1 / 81.2
CPI: Consumer Price Index (2000=100)	111	129	141 [e]
Agricultural production index (2004-2006=100)	103	140	155 [e]
Food production index (2004-2006=100)	102	144	160 [e]
Index of industrial production (2005=100) [f]	100 [g]	102 [h]	112 [h,i]
International trade: Exports (million US$)	2 849	3 878	2 130 [c]
International trade: Imports (million US$)	2 800	5 133	4 899 [c]
International trade: Balance (million US$)	49	- 1 255	- 2 768 [c]
Balance of payments, current account (million US$)	- 495	- 856	- 1 173 [b]

Major trading partners

						2016
Export partners (% of exports)	Netherlands	21.4	Belgium	9.3	Italy	7.8
Import partners (% of imports)	China	21.4	France	12.0	Nigeria	4.6

Social indicators

	2005	2010	2017
Population growth rate (average annual %) [j]	2.6	2.7	2.7 [b]
Urban population (% of total population)	48.5	51.5	54.4 [b]
Urban population growth rate (average annual %) [j]	3.9	3.8	3.6 [b]
Fertility rate, total (live births per woman) [j]	5.4	5.2	5.0 [b]
Life expectancy at birth (females/males, years) [j]	52.3 / 50.6	55.4 / 53.4	57.7 / 55.1 [b]
Population age distribution (0-14 and 60+ years, %)	44.0 / 5.0	43.5 / 4.9	42.7 / 4.8 [a]
International migrant stock (000/% of total pop.)	258.7 / 1.4	289.1 / 1.4	382.0 / 1.6 [b]
Refugees and others of concern to UNHCR (000)	66.3 [k]	106.7 [k]	544.9 [c]
Infant mortality rate (per 1 000 live births) [j]	88.5	77.2	67.5 [b]
Health: Total expenditure (% of GDP) [l]	4.8	5.3	4.1 [e]
Health: Physicians (per 1 000 pop.)	0.1	0.1	...
Education: Government expenditure (% of GDP)	3.1	3.3	3.0 [m]
Education: Primary gross enrol. ratio (f/m per 100 pop.)	91.4 / 109.2 [d]	98.4 / 113.9	110.7 / 123.5 [b]
Education: Secondary gross enrol. ratio (f/m per 100 pop.)	23.5 / 29.8	36.0 / 43.2 [n]	53.5 / 62.6 [b]
Education: Tertiary gross enrol. ratio (f/m per 100 pop.)	4.6 / 7.0 [d]	9.9 / 12.2	15.2 / 19.7 [b]
Intentional homicide rate (per 100 000 pop.)	...	4.8	5.9 [b]
Seats held by women in national parliaments (%)	8.9	13.9	31.1

Environment and infrastructure indicators

	2005	2010	2017
Mobile-cellular subscriptions (per 100 inhabitants)	12.4	41.9	71.8 [o,b]
Individuals using the Internet (per 100 inhabitants)	1.4	4.3 [d]	20.7 [d,b]
Threatened species (number)	484 [p]	624	775
Forested area (% of land area)	44.5	42.1 [d]	40.3 [d,e]
CO2 emission estimates (million tons/tons per capita)	3.7 / 0.2	6.8 / 0.3	7.0 / 0.3 [e]
Energy production, primary (Petajoules)	442	351	408 [e]
Energy supply per capita (Gigajoules)	17	14	14 [e]
Tourist/visitor arrivals at national borders (000)	...	573	822 [e]
Important sites for terrestrial biodiversity protected (%)	30.5	33.0	36.3
Pop. using improved drinking water (urban/rural, %)	89.1 / 46.0	92.6 / 50.2	94.8 / 52.7 [b]
Pop. using improved sanitation facilities (urban/rural, %)	61.1 / 26.7	61.5 / 26.7	61.8 / 26.8 [b]
Net Official Development Assist. received (% of GNI)	2.59	2.31	2.31 [b]

a Projected estimate (medium fertility variant). **b** 2015. **c** 2016. **d** Estimate. **e** 2014. **f** Data classified according to ISIC Rev. 3. **g** Country data supplemented with data from the Observatoire Economique et Statistique d'Afrique Subsaharienne (Afristat). **h** Data refers to manufacturing and utilities only. **i** 2012. **j** Data refers to a 5-year period preceding the reference year. **k** Data as at the end of December. **l** Data revision. **m** 2013. **n** 2009. **o** Data as at the end of September. **p** 2004.

Canada

Region	Northern America	UN membership date	09 November 1945
Population (000, 2017)	36 624[a]	Surface area (km2)	9 984 670[b]
Pop. density (per km2, 2017)	4.0[a]	Sex ratio (m per 100 f, 2017)	98.5[a]
Capital city	Ottawa	National currency	Canadian Dollar (CAD)
Capital city pop. (000)	1 325.8[c,b]	Exchange rate (per US$)	1.3[d]

Economic indicators

	2005	2010	2017
GDP: Gross domestic product (million current US$)	1 169 393	1 613 463	1 552 808[b]
GDP growth rate (annual %, const. 2005 prices)	3.2	3.1	0.9[b]
GDP per capita (current US$)	36 253.1	47 279.4	43 205.6[b]
Economy: Agriculture (% of GVA)	1.8	1.4[e]	1.8[e,b]
Economy: Industry (% of GVA)	32.4	28.6[e]	28.6[e,b]
Economy: Services and other activity (% of GVA)	65.8	70.0[e]	69.6[e,b]
Employment: Agriculture (% of employed)[f]	2.7	2.2	2.1
Employment: Industry (% of employed)[f]	22.1	20.2	19.5
Employment: Services (% of employed)[f]	75.2	77.6	78.4
Unemployment (% of labour force)	6.8	8.1	7.1[f]
Labour force participation (female/male pop. %)[f]	60.9 / 72.6	61.8 / 71.5	60.7 / 69.9
CPI: Consumer Price Index (2000=100)	112	122	131[g]
Agricultural production index (2004-2006=100)	102	102	109[g]
Food production index (2004-2006=100)	102	103	109[g]
Index of industrial production (2005=100)[h]	100	88	92[i]
International trade: Exports (million US$)[j]	360 552	386 580	388 911[d]
International trade: Imports (million US$)[j]	314 444	392 109	402 954[d]
International trade: Balance (million US$)[j]	46 108	- 5 529	- 14 043[d]
Balance of payments, current account (million US$)	21 931	- 58 160	- 53 083[b]

Major trading partners

						2016
Export partners (% of exports)	United States	76.2	China	4.1	United Kingdom	3.3
Import partners (% of imports)	United States	52.2	China	12.1	Mexico	6.2

Social indicators

	2005	2010	2017
Population growth rate (average annual %)[k]	1.0	1.1	1.0[b]
Urban population (% of total population)	80.1	80.9	81.8[b]
Urban population growth rate (average annual %)[k]	1.2	1.3	1.2[b]
Fertility rate, total (live births per woman)[k]	1.5	1.6	1.6[b]
Life expectancy at birth (females/males, years)[k]	82.1 / 77.2	83.0 / 78.4	83.8 / 79.7[b]
Population age distribution (0-14 and 60+ years, %)	17.7 / 17.9	16.5 / 20.0	16.0 / 23.5[a]
International migrant stock (000/% of total pop.)	6 079.0 / 18.8	7 011.2 / 20.5	7 835.5 / 21.8[b]
Refugees and others of concern to UNHCR (000)	167.7[l]	216.6[l]	155.8[d]
Infant mortality rate (per 1 000 live births)[k]	5.3	5.1	4.7[b]
Health: Total expenditure (% of GDP)	9.6	11.2	10.4[g]
Health: Physicians (per 1 000 pop.)	1.9[m]	2.0	2.5[n]
Education: Government expenditure (% of GDP)	4.8	5.4	5.3[i]
Education: Primary gross enrol. ratio (f/m per 100 pop.)	96.6 / 97.5	98.9 / 98.5	101.1 / 100.1[o]
Education: Secondary gross enrol. ratio (f/m per 100 pop.)	99.9 / 102.2	101.1 / 103.6	110.0 / 109.8[o]
Education: Tertiary gross enrol. ratio (f/m per 100 pop.)	67.7 / 50.5[p]	... / ...	... / ...
Intentional homicide rate (per 100 000 pop.)	2.1	1.6	1.7[b]
Seats held by women in national parliaments (%)	21.1	22.1	26.3

Environment and infrastructure indicators

	2005	2010	2017
Mobile-cellular subscriptions (per 100 inhabitants)	52.8	75.7	81.9[f,b]
Individuals using the Internet (per 100 inhabitants)	71.7[q]	80.3[q,r]	88.5[f,b]
Research & Development expenditure (% of GDP)	2.0	1.8	1.6[s,g]
Threatened species (number)	74[m]	77	122
Forested area (% of land area)	38.2	38.2	38.2[f,g]
CO2 emission estimates (million tons/tons per capita)	557.4 / 17.3	534.7 / 15.7	537.2 / 15.1[g]
Energy production, primary (Petajoules)	16 756	16 450	19 276[g]
Energy supply per capita (Gigajoules)	348	319	324[g]
Tourist/visitor arrivals at national borders (000)	18 771	16 219	17 971[b]
Important sites for terrestrial biodiversity protected (%)	21.2	25.4	25.7
Pop. using improved drinking water (urban/rural, %)	100.0 / 99.0	100.0 / 99.0	100.0 / 99.0[b]
Pop. using improved sanitation facilities (urban/rural, %)	100.0 / 99.0	100.0 / 99.0	100.0 / 99.0[b]
Net Official Development Assist. disbursed (% of GNI)[t]	0.34	0.34	0.26[s,d]

a Projected estimate (medium fertility variant). b 2015. c Refers to Ottawa-Gatineau, the Census Metropolitan Area. d 2016. e Data classified according to ISIC Rev. 4. f Estimate. g 2014. h Data classified according to ISIC Rev. 3. i 2011. j Imports FOB. k Data refers to a 5-year period preceding the reference year. l Data as at the end of December. m 2004. n 2012. o 2013. p 2000. q Population aged 16 years and over. r Break in the time series. s Provisional data. t Development Assistance Committee member (OECD)

Cayman Islands

Region	Caribbean	Population (000, 2017)	62[a]
Surface area (km2)	264[b]	Pop. density (per km2, 2017)	256.5[a]
Sex ratio (m per 100 f, 2017)	100.4[c,b]	Capital city	George Town
National currency	Cayman Islands Dollar (KYD)	Capital city pop. (000)	30.6[d]
Exchange rate (per US$)	0.8[e,f]		

Economic indicators	2005	2010	2017
GDP: Gross domestic product (million current US$)	3 042	3 267	3 726[b]
GDP growth rate (annual %, const. 2005 prices)	6.5	- 2.7	0.7[b]
GDP per capita (current US$)	62 558.1	58 856.7	62 132.0[b]
Economy: Agriculture (% of GVA)[g]	0.2	0.3	0.3[b]
Economy: Industry (% of GVA)[g]	9.1	7.7	7.5[b]
Economy: Services and other activity (% of GVA)[g]	90.6	92.0	92.2[b]
Employment: Agriculture (% of employed)	1.7[h]	0.6[i]	0.8[i,j]
Employment: Industry (% of employed)	22.2[h]	14.9[i]	15.5[i,j]
Employment: Services (% of employed)	75.5[h]	84.2[i]	83.6[i,j]
Unemployment (% of labour force)	3.5	6.7	6.3[i]
Labour force participation (female/male pop. %)	... / ...	80.6 / 88.0[i,k,l]	80.6 / 85.6[i]
CPI: Consumer Price Index (2000=100)	117	125	132[d]
Agricultural production index (2004-2006=100)	100	100	104[d]
Food production index (2004-2006=100)	100	100	104[d]
International trade: Exports (million US$)	52	13	18[f]
International trade: Imports (million US$)	1 191	828	991[f]
International trade: Balance (million US$)	- 1 138	- 815	- 972[f]

Major trading partners						2016
Export partners (% of exports)	United States	62.2	Guatemala	16.4	France	4.5
Import partners (% of imports)	United States	78.4	Bahamas	4.9	Brazil	2.4

Social indicators	2005	2010	2017
Population growth rate (average annual %)[m]	3.1	2.6	1.5[b]
Urban population (% of total population)	100.0	100.0	100.0[b]
Urban population growth rate (average annual %)[m]	3.1	2.6	1.5[b]
Fertility rate, total (live births per woman)	...	1.6[n]	...
Life expectancy at birth (females/males, years)	... / ...	83.8 / 76.3[o,p]	... / ...
Population age distribution (0-14 and 60+ years, %)[c]	... / ...	18.1 / 8.6[q]	18.3 / 6.7[b,r]
International migrant stock (000/% of total pop.)[s]	21.7 / 44.5	24.1 / 43.3	23.7 / 39.6[b]
Refugees and others of concern to UNHCR (000)	...	~0.0[t]	0.1[f]
Intentional homicide rate (per 100 000 pop.)	12.3[u]	14.7[l]	...

Environment and infrastructure indicators	2005	2010	2017
Mobile-cellular subscriptions (per 100 inhabitants)[v]	166.5	181.2	155.5[b]
Individuals using the Internet (per 100 inhabitants)	38.0	66.0[w]	77.0[w,b]
Threatened species (number)	19[u]	34	74
Forested area (% of land area)[w]	52.9	52.9	52.9[d]
CO2 emission estimates (million tons/tons per capita)	0.5 / 9.1	0.6 / 10.1	0.5 / 9.2[d]
Energy supply per capita (Gigajoules)	130	144	130[d]
Tourist/visitor arrivals at national borders (000)[x]	168	288	385[b]
Important sites for terrestrial biodiversity protected (%)	31.6	31.7	32.5
Pop. using improved drinking water (urban/rural, %)	95.0 / ...	96.7 / ...	97.4 / ...[b]
Pop. using improved sanitation facilities (urban/rural, %)	95.5 / ...	95.6 / ...	95.6 / ...[b]

a Projected estimate (medium fertility variant). b 2015. c De jure population. d 2014. e UN operational exchange rate. f 2016. g Data classified according to ISIC Rev. 4. h Data classified according to ISIC Rev. 3. i Break in the time series. j 2013. k Resident population (de jure). l 2009. m Data refers to a 5-year period preceding the reference year. n 2007. o Data are based on a small number of deaths. p 2006. q Excluding the institutional population. r Population aged 65 years and over. s Refers to foreign citizens. t Data as at the end of December. u 2004. v Data refers to number of mobile handsets in operation. w Estimate. x Arrivals by air.

Central African Republic

Region	Middle Africa	UN membership date	20 September 1960
Population (000, 2017)	4 659[a]	Surface area (km2)	622 984[b]
Pop. density (per km2, 2017)	7.5[a]	Sex ratio (m per 100 f, 2017)	97.3[a]
Capital city	Bangui	National currency	CFA Franc (XAF)
Capital city pop. (000)	794.0[b]	Exchange rate (per US$)	622.3[c]

Economic indicators	2005	2010	2017
GDP: Gross domestic product (million current US$)	1 413	2 034	1 633[b]
GDP growth rate (annual %, const. 2005 prices)	2.4	3.6	4.8[b]
GDP per capita (current US$)	348.4	457.6	333.2[b]
Economy: Agriculture (% of GVA)	45.0	41.2	34.9[b]
Economy: Industry (% of GVA)	18.6	24.0	24.8[b]
Economy: Services and other activity (% of GVA)	36.5	34.8	40.4[b]
Employment: Agriculture (% of employed)[d]	69.9	69.6	72.2
Employment: Industry (% of employed)[d]	4.5	4.6	4.3
Employment: Services (% of employed)[d]	25.6	25.8	23.4
Unemployment (% of labour force)[d]	6.8	6.8	6.9
Labour force participation (female/male pop. %)[d]	69.9 / 85.7	69.8 / 85.2	71.9 / 84.6
CPI: Consumer Price Index (2000=100)[e,f]	112	138	150[g]
Agricultural production index (2004-2006=100)	101	116	114[h]
Food production index (2004-2006=100)	101	115	113[h]
Index of industrial production (2005=100)[i,j]	100	126	86[g]
International trade: Exports (million US$)	111	90	213[c]
International trade: Imports (million US$)	185	210	147[c]
International trade: Balance (million US$)	- 75	- 120	66[c]

Major trading partners						2016
Export partners (% of exports)	France	63.6	Chad	11.5	Cameroon	8.8
Import partners (% of imports)	France	21.1	United States	12.2	Zambia	9.6

Social indicators	2005	2010	2017
Population growth rate (average annual %)[k]	1.9	1.5	0.4[b]
Urban population (% of total population)	38.1	38.8	40.0[b]
Urban population growth rate (average annual %)[k]	1.9	2.3	2.6[b]
Fertility rate, total (live births per woman)[k]	5.4	5.3	5.1[b]
Life expectancy at birth (females/males, years)[k]	44.9 / 42.5	47.4 / 44.6	51.0 / 47.8[b]
Population age distribution (0-14 and 60+ years, %)	42.2 / 5.7	42.5 / 5.5	43.2 / 5.5[a]
International migrant stock (000/% of total pop.)[l]	94.4 / 2.3	93.5 / 2.1	81.6 / 1.7[b]
Refugees and others of concern to UNHCR (000)	28.7[m]	215.3[m]	470.5[c]
Infant mortality rate (per 1 000 live births)[k]	113.4	105.9	93.5[b]
Health: Total expenditure (% of GDP)[n]	4.3	3.9	4.2[h]
Health: Physicians (per 1 000 pop.)	0.1[o]	~0.0[p]	...
Education: Government expenditure (% of GDP)	1.6	1.2	1.2[q]
Education: Primary gross enrol. ratio (f/m per 100 pop.)	53.1 / 77.1	76.4 / 107.4	79.8 / 107.3[r]
Education: Secondary gross enrol. ratio (f/m per 100 pop.)	8.1 / 15.6[d,s]	9.8 / 17.7[p]	11.8 / 23.0[r]
Education: Tertiary gross enrol. ratio (f/m per 100 pop.)	0.6 / 3.2[t]	1.2 / 3.9	1.5 / 4.1[r]
Intentional homicide rate (per 100 000 pop.)	14.9	13.6	13.1[b]
Seats held by women in national parliaments (%)	7.3[t]	9.6	8.6

Environment and infrastructure indicators	2005	2010	2017
Mobile-cellular subscriptions (per 100 inhabitants)	2.5	22.5[u]	20.4[d,b]
Individuals using the Internet (per 100 inhabitants)[d]	0.3	2.0	4.6[b]
Threatened species (number)	30[o]	36	60
Forested area (% of land area)	35.8	35.7	35.6[d,h]
CO2 emission estimates (million tons/tons per capita)	0.2 / 0.1	0.3 / 0.1	0.3 / 0.1[h]
Energy production, primary (Petajoules)	19	19	19[h]
Energy supply per capita (Gigajoules)	5	5	5[h]
Tourist/visitor arrivals at national borders (000)[v]	12	54	120[b]
Important sites for terrestrial biodiversity protected (%)	74.2	74.4	74.4
Pop. using improved drinking water (urban/rural, %)	86.2 / 51.6	88.6 / 53.6	89.6 / 54.4[b]
Pop. using improved sanitation facilities (urban/rural, %)	35.3 / 8.8	41.2 / 7.7	43.6 / 7.2[b]
Net Official Development Assist. received (% of GNI)	6.64	13.08	32.25[b]

a Projected estimate (medium fertility variant). b 2015. c 2016. d Estimate. e Bangui f Excluding "Rent". g 2013. h 2014. i Data classified according to ISIC Rev. 3. j Country data supplemented with data from the Observatoire Économique et Statistique d'Afrique Subsaharienne (Afristat). k Data refers to a 5-year period preceding the reference year. l Refers to foreign citizens. m Data as at the end of December. n Estimates should be viewed with caution as these are derived from scarce data. o 2004. p 2009. q 2011. r 2012. s 2001. t 2000. u Data refers to active subscriptions only. v Arrivals by air at Bangui only.

Chad

Region	Middle Africa	UN membership date	20 September 1960	
Population (000, 2017)	14 900[a]	Surface area (km2)	1 284 000[b]	
Pop. density (per km2, 2017)	11.8[a]	Sex ratio (m per 100 f, 2017)	100.2[a]	
Capital city	N'Djamena	National currency	CFA Franc (XAF)	
Capital city pop. (000)	1 260.1[b]	Exchange rate (per US$)	622.3[c]	

Economic indicators	2005	2010	2017
GDP: Gross domestic product (million current US$)	6 681	9 791	10 009[b]
GDP growth rate (annual %, const. 2005 prices)	7.9	13.4	6.6[b]
GDP per capita (current US$)	663.6	823.0	713.0[b]
Economy: Agriculture (% of GVA)	26.1	35.9	25.4[b]
Economy: Industry (% of GVA)	34.9	36.7	39.0[b]
Economy: Services and other activity (% of GVA)	39.0	27.4	35.6[b]
Employment: Agriculture (% of employed)[d]	76.7	78.0	76.6
Employment: Industry (% of employed)[d]	1.8	1.9	2.0
Employment: Services (% of employed)[d]	21.5	20.0	21.4
Unemployment (% of labour force)[d]	5.8	5.8	5.8
Labour force participation (female/male pop. %)[d]	64.2 / 79.5	64.1 / 79.3	64.0 / 79.3
CPI: Consumer Price Index (2000=100)[e]	126	147	161[f]
Agricultural production index (2004-2006=100)	107	154	146[g]
Food production index (2004-2006=100)	107	163	151[g]
Index of industrial production (2005=100)[h,j]	100	79	65[f]
International trade: Exports (million US$)	3 095	3 410	1 990[c]
International trade: Imports (million US$)	953	2 507	1 371[c]
International trade: Balance (million US$)	2 142	904	619[c]

Major trading partners						2016
Export partners (% of exports)	United States	61.1	India	9.0	China	6.7
Import partners (% of imports)	France	16.8	China	13.3	Cameroon	12.7

Social indicators	2005	2010	2017
Population growth rate (average annual %)[j]	3.8	3.3	3.3[b]
Urban population (% of total population)	21.8	22.0	22.5[b]
Urban population growth rate (average annual %)[j]	3.9	3.3	3.4[b]
Fertility rate, total (live births per woman)[j]	7.2	6.9	6.3[b]
Life expectancy at birth (females/males, years)[j]	48.5 / 46.8	49.7 / 48.0	52.8 / 50.5[b]
Population age distribution (0-14 and 60+ years, %)	49.1 / 4.2	48.6 / 4.0	47.1 / 4.0[a]
International migrant stock (000/% of total pop.)[k]	352.1 / 3.5	416.9 / 3.5	517.0 / 3.7[b]
Refugees and others of concern to UNHCR (000)	275.5[l]	533.0[l]	512.3[c]
Infant mortality rate (per 1 000 live births)[j]	110.8	105.2	91.2[b]
Health: Total expenditure (% of GDP)[m]	3.9	2.9	3.6[g]
Health: Physicians (per 1 000 pop.)	~0.0[n]	~0.0[o]	~0.0[f]
Education: Government expenditure (% of GDP)	1.7	2.0	2.8[f]
Education: Primary gross enrol. ratio (f/m per 100 pop.)	58.0 / 85.6	69.9 / 95.1	88.0 / 114.6[f]
Education: Secondary gross enrol. ratio (f/m per 100 pop.)	8.1 / 23.2[d]	13.4 / 31.8	14.0 / 30.7[p]
Education: Tertiary gross enrol. ratio (f/m per 100 pop.)	0.2 / 2.7	0.6 / 3.6[d]	1.1 / 5.7[d,g]
Intentional homicide rate (per 100 000 pop.)	10.7	9.7	9.0[b]
Seats held by women in national parliaments (%)	6.5	5.2	12.8

Environment and infrastructure indicators	2005	2010	2017
Mobile-cellular subscriptions (per 100 inhabitants)	2.1	24.5	40.2[b]
Individuals using the Internet (per 100 inhabitants)	0.4	1.7[d]	2.7[d,b]
Threatened species (number)	21[n]	30	43
Forested area (% of land area)	4.9	4.4	4.0[d,g]
CO2 emission estimates (million tons/tons per capita)	0.4 / ~0.0	0.5 / ~0.0	0.7 / ~0.0[g]
Energy production, primary (Petajoules)	433	324	288[g]
Energy supply per capita (Gigajoules)	7	6	6[g]
Tourist/visitor arrivals at national borders (000)	...	71	120[b]
Important sites for terrestrial biodiversity protected (%)	70.6	70.6	70.6
Pop. using improved drinking water (urban/rural, %)	64.7 / 42.4	69.8 / 44.1	71.8 / 44.8[b]
Pop. using improved sanitation facilities (urban/rural, %)	28.1 / 5.8	30.5 / 6.3	31.4 / 6.5[b]
Net Official Development Assist. received (% of GNI)	6.87	4.76	5.74[b]

a Projected estimate (medium fertility variant). b 2015. c 2016. d Estimate. e N'Djamena f 2013. g 2014. h Data classified according to ISIC Rev. 3. i Country data supplemented with data from the Observatoire Economique et Statistique d'Afrique Subsaharienne (Afristat). j Data refers to a 5-year period preceding the reference year. k Including refugees. l Data as at the end of December. m Estimates should be viewed with caution as these are derived from scarce data. n 2004. o 2006. p 2012.

Channel Islands

Region	Northern Europe	Population (000, 2017)	165 [a,b]	
Surface area (km2)	180 [a,c]	Pop. density (per km2, 2017)	870.1 [a,b]	
Sex ratio (m per 100 f, 2017)	98.4 [a,b]	Capital city	Saint Helier	
National currency	Pound Sterling (GBP)	Capital city pop. (000)	35.1 [d,e]	
Exchange rate (per US$)	0.8 [f]			

Economic indicators	2005	2010	2017
Employment: Agriculture (% of employed) [g]	5.3	5.2	5.0
Employment: Industry (% of employed) [g]	25.1	24.8	24.5
Employment: Services (% of employed) [g]	69.6	70.0	70.5
Unemployment (% of labour force) [g]	8.6	8.9	8.7
Labour force participation (female/male pop. %) [g]	51.1 / 68.8	52.2 / 67.0	49.9 / 65.4

Social indicators	2005	2010	2017
Population growth rate (average annual %) [a,h]	0.7	0.7	0.5 [c]
Urban population (% of total population) [a]	30.7	31.1	31.5 [c]
Urban population growth rate (average annual %) [a,h]	0.9	0.9	0.8 [c]
Fertility rate, total (live births per woman) [a,h]	1.4	1.4	1.5 [c]
Life expectancy at birth (females/males, years) [a,h]	80.5 / 76.0	81.7 / 77.5	82.4 / 78.7 [c]
Population age distribution (0-14 and 60+ years, %) [a]	16.3 / 20.4	15.3 / 21.7	14.5 / 24.5 [b]
International migrant stock (000/% of total pop.) [a]	70.9 / 46.0	77.6 / 48.6	82.3 / 50.3 [c]
Infant mortality rate (per 1 000 live births) [a,h]	10.3	8.7	7.9 [c]

Environment and infrastructure indicators	2005	2010	2017
Forested area (% of land area) [g]	4.2	4.2	4.2 [e]

a Refers to Guernsey and Jersey. **b** Projected estimate (medium fertility variant). **c** 2015. **d** Data refer to the parish of St. Helier, the capital of the Bailiwick of Jersey. **e** 2014. **f** 2016. **g** Estimate. **h** Data refers to a 5-year period preceding the reference year.

Chile

Region	South America	UN membership date	24 October 1945
Population (000, 2017)	18 055[a]	Surface area (km2)	756 102[b]
Pop. density (per km2, 2017)	24.3[a]	Sex ratio (m per 100 f, 2017)	98.2[a]
Capital city	Santiago	National currency	Chilean Peso (CLP)
Capital city pop. (000)	6 507.4[b]	Exchange rate (per US$)	667.3[c]

Economic indicators	2005	2010	2017
GDP: Gross domestic product (million current US$)	123 056	217 538	240 796[b]
GDP growth rate (annual %, const. 2005 prices)	6.2	5.8	2.3[b]
GDP per capita (current US$)	7 644.9	12 785.1	13 416.2[b]
Economy: Agriculture (% of GVA)[d]	4.1	3.5	3.9[b]
Economy: Industry (% of GVA)[d]	40.3	39.6	32.8[b]
Economy: Services and other activity (% of GVA)[d]	55.6	57.0	63.3[b]
Employment: Agriculture (% of employed)[e]	13.1	10.9	9.6
Employment: Industry (% of employed)[e]	22.8	23.5	22.9
Employment: Services (% of employed)[e]	64.1	65.6	67.5
Unemployment (% of labour force)	8.0	8.1	6.8[e]
Labour force participation (female/male pop. %)[e]	38.2 / 73.1	46.8 / 74.7	50.7 / 74.7
CPI: Consumer Price Index (2000=100)	114[f]	101[g,h]	115[g,i,j]
Agricultural production index (2004-2006=100)	100	108	111[j]
Food production index (2004-2006=100)	100	108	111[j]
International trade: Exports (million US$)	41 973	71 106	59 884[c]
International trade: Imports (million US$)	32 926	59 207	58 804[c]
International trade: Balance (million US$)	9 047	11 899	1 080[c]
Balance of payments, current account (million US$)	1 449	3 581	- 4 761[b]

Major trading partners						2016
Export partners (% of exports)	China	28.5	United States	14.1	Japan	8.6
Import partners (% of imports)	China	24.1	United States	17.4	Brazil	8.0

Social indicators	2005	2010	2017
Population growth rate (average annual %)[k]	1.1	1.0	0.9[b]
Urban population (% of total population)	87.4	88.6	89.5[b]
Urban population growth rate (average annual %)[k]	1.4	1.2	1.1[b]
Fertility rate, total (live births per woman)[k]	2.0	1.9	1.8[b]
Life expectancy at birth (females/males, years)[k]	80.3 / 74.3	80.8 / 75.3	81.3 / 76.2[b]
Population age distribution (0-14 and 60+ years, %)	24.6 / 11.8	22.5 / 13.2	20.3 / 16.0[a]
International migrant stock (000/% of total pop.)	273.4 / 1.7	369.4 / 2.2	469.4 / 2.6[b]
Refugees and others of concern to UNHCR (000)	0.9[l]	1.9[f]	3.7[c]
Infant mortality rate (per 1 000 live births)[k]	8.4	7.8	7.4[b]
Health: Total expenditure (% of GDP)	6.7	7.0	7.8[j]
Health: Physicians (per 1 000 pop.)	1.0	1.0[m]	...
Education: Government expenditure (% of GDP)	3.2	4.2	4.9[b]
Education: Primary gross enrol. ratio (f/m per 100 pop.)	106.6 / 112.3	101.6 / 104.9	100.0 / 103.3[b]
Education: Secondary gross enrol. ratio (f/m per 100 pop.)	97.8 / 97.5	96.0 / 93.2	101.3 / 100.0[b]
Education: Tertiary gross enrol. ratio (f/m per 100 pop.)	48.6 / 51.3	72.3 / 67.1	94.4 / 83.0[b]
Intentional homicide rate (per 100 000 pop.)	3.6	3.2	3.6[j]
Seats held by women in national parliaments (%)	12.5	14.2	15.8

Environment and infrastructure indicators	2005	2010	2017
Mobile-cellular subscriptions (per 100 inhabitants)	64.7	115.8	129.5[b]
Individuals using the Internet (per 100 inhabitants)[e]	31.2[n]	45.0[n]	64.3[b]
Research & Development expenditure (% of GDP)	...	0.3	0.4[o,j]
Threatened species (number)	123[p]	145	197
Forested area (% of land area)	21.6	21.8	23.4[a,e,j]
CO2 emission estimates (million tons/tons per capita)	61.8 / 3.8	72.3 / 4.3	82.6 / 4.7[j]
Energy production, primary (Petajoules)	390	384	540[j]
Energy supply per capita (Gigajoules)	72	75	85[j]
Tourist/visitor arrivals at national borders (000)	2 027	2 801[q]	4 478[a,b]
Important sites for terrestrial biodiversity protected (%)	33.4	35.2	35.7
Pop. using improved drinking water (urban/rural, %)	99.4 / 77.6	99.6 / 87.4	99.7 / 93.3[b]
Pop. using improved sanitation facilities (urban/rural, %)	97.3 / 77.6	99.2 / 85.9	100.0 / 90.9[b]
Net Official Development Assist. received (% of GNI)	0.15	0.09	0.02[b]

a Projected estimate (medium fertility variant). **b** 2015. **c** 2016. **d** At producers' prices. **e** Estimate. **f** Santiago **g** Index base: 2009=100. **h** Break in the time series. **i** Series linked to former series. **j** 2014. **k** Data refers to a 5-year period preceding the reference year. **l** Data as at the end of December. **m** 2009. **n** Population aged 5 years and over. **o** Provisional data. **p** 2004. **q** Including nationals residing abroad.

China

Region	Eastern Asia
Population (000, 2017)	1 409 517 [a,b]
Pop. density (per km2, 2017)	150.1 [a,b]
Capital city	Beijing
Capital city pop. (000)	20 384.0 [c]

UN membership date	24 October 1945
Surface area (km2)	9 600 000 [c]
Sex ratio (m per 100 f, 2017)	106.3 [a,b]
National currency	Yuan Renminbi (CNY)
Exchange rate (per US$)	6.9 [d]

Economic indicators	2005	2010	2017
GDP: Gross domestic product (million current US$) [b]	2 308 800	6 066 351	11 158 457 [c]
GDP growth rate (annual %, const. 2005 prices) [b]	11.4	10.6	6.9 [c]
GDP per capita (current US$) [b]	1 768.4	4 523.9	8 109.1 [c]
Economy: Agriculture (% of GVA) [b,e]	12.0	9.8	9.2 [c]
Economy: Industry (% of GVA) [b,e]	47.2	46.6	41.1 [c]
Economy: Services and other activity (% of GVA) [b,e]	40.9	43.6	49.7 [c]
Employment: Agriculture (% of employed) [b,f]	42.6	34.1	27.0
Employment: Industry (% of employed) [b,f]	21.8	24.0	23.9
Employment: Services (% of employed) [b,f]	35.6	41.9	49.1
Unemployment (% of labour force) [b,f]	4.1	4.2	4.6
Labour force participation (female/male pop. %) [b,f]	66.9 / 79.8	63.7 / 77.8	63.0 / 77.7
CPI: Consumer Price Index (2000=100) [b,g]	107	124	140 [h]
Agricultural production index (2004-2006=100) [b]	100	120	132 [h]
Food production index (2004-2006=100) [b]	100	120	133 [h]
International trade: Exports (million US$) [b]	761 953	1 577 764	2 118 981 [d]
International trade: Imports (million US$) [b]	659 953	1 396 002	1 588 696 [d]
International trade: Balance (million US$) [b]	102 001	181 762	530 285 [d]
Balance of payments, current account (million US$) [b]	132 378 [i]	237 810	330 602 [c]

Major trading partners						2016
Export partners (% of exports)	United States	18.3	China, Hong Kong SAR	13.8	Japan	6.1
Import partners (% of imports)	Republic of Korea	10.0	Japan	9.2	Asia nes [j]	8.8

Social indicators	2005	2010	2017
Population growth rate (average annual %) [b,k]	0.6	0.6	0.5 [c]
Urban population (% of total population) [b]	42.5	49.2	55.6 [c]
Urban population growth rate (average annual %) [b,k]	4.0	3.6	3.0 [c]
Fertility rate, total (live births per woman) [b,k]	1.6	1.6	1.6 [c]
Life expectancy at birth (females/males, years) [b,k]	74.7 / 71.7	76.3 / 73.2	77.2 / 74.2 [c]
Population age distribution (0-14 and 60+ years, %) [b]	19.9 / 11.0	17.8 / 12.6	17.7 / 16.2 [a]
International migrant stock (000/% of total pop.) [b,l]	678.9 / 0.1	849.9 / 0.1	978.0 / 0.1 [c]
Refugees and others of concern to UNHCR (000) [b]	301.1 [m]	301.1 [m]	301.7 [d]
Infant mortality rate (per 1 000 live births) [b,k]	25.3	16.7	11.6 [c]
Health: Total expenditure (% of GDP) [n]	4.7	4.9	5.5 [h]
Health: Physicians (per 1 000 pop.)	1.1 [o]	1.5	1.5 [p]
Education: Primary gross enrol. ratio (f/m per 100 pop.) [b]	113.2 / 113.7 [q]	111.6 / 113.3	104.3 / 104.0 [c]
Education: Secondary gross enrol. ratio (f/m per 100 pop.) [b]	60.7 / 63.7 [q]	84.8 / 85.0	95.6 / 93.2 [c]
Education: Tertiary gross enrol. ratio (f/m per 100 pop.) [b]	18.3 / 20.3	24.8 / 23.1	47.3 / 39.9 [c]
Intentional homicide rate (per 100 000 pop.) [b]	1.6	1.0	0.7 [c]
Seats held by women in national parliaments (%)	20.2	21.3	23.7

Environment and infrastructure indicators	2005	2010	2017
Mobile-cellular subscriptions (per 100 inhabitants) [b]	29.8	63.2	93.2 [c]
Individuals using the Internet (per 100 inhabitants) [b]	8.5	34.3	50.3 [f,r,s,c]
Research & Development expenditure (% of GDP) [b]	1.3	1.7	2.0 [h]
Threatened species (number) [b]	773 [t]	859	1 080
Forested area (% of land area) [f,b]	20.6	21.4	22.0 [h]
CO2 emission estimates (million tons/tons per capita) [b]	5 897.0 / 4.5	8 776.0 / 6.5	10 291.9 / 7.5 [h]
Energy production, primary (Petajoules) [b]	63 831	88 553	101 394 [h]
Energy supply per capita (Gigajoules) [b]	53	76	87 [h]
Tourist/visitor arrivals at national borders (000) [b]	46 809	55 664	56 886 [c]
Important sites for terrestrial biodiversity protected (%) [b]	51.2	51.4	52.0
Pop. using improved drinking water (urban/rural, %) [b]	97.3 / 78.2	97.4 / 85.6	97.5 / 93.0 [c]
Pop. using improved sanitation facilities (urban/rural, %) [b]	79.1 / 54.3	82.9 / 59.0	86.6 / 63.7 [c]
Net Official Development Assist. received (% of GNI) [b]	0.08	0.01	0.00 [c]

a Projected estimate (medium fertility variant). b For statistical purposes, the data for China do not include those for the Hong Kong Special Administrative Region (Hong Kong SAR), Macao Special Administrative Region (Macao SAR) and Taiwan Province of China. c 2015. d 2016. e At producers' prices. f Estimate. g Index base period: the same month of 2000=100. h 2014. i Break in the time series. j Asia not elsewhere specified. k Data refers to a 5-year period preceding the reference year. l Refers to foreign citizens. m Data as at the end of December. n General government expenditure series was revised using the one provided by the IMF. As a result, some ratios may have changed from last year. o 2002. p 2011. q 2003. r Users in the last 6 months. s Population aged 6 years and over. t 2004.

China, Hong Kong SAR

Region	Eastern Asia	Population (000, 2017)	7 365[a]
Surface area (km2)	1 106[b]	Pop. density (per km2, 2017)	7 014.2[a]
Sex ratio (m per 100 f, 2017)	85.1[a]	Capital city	Hong Kong
National currency	Hong Kong Dollar (HKD)	Capital city pop. (000)	7 313.6[c,b]
Exchange rate (per US$)	7.8[d]		

Economic indicators	2005	2010	2017
GDP: Gross domestic product (million current US$)	181 569	228 639	309 236[b]
GDP growth rate (annual %, const. 2005 prices)	7.4	6.8	2.4[b]
GDP per capita (current US$)	26 535.7	32 692.7	42 431.0[b]
Economy: Agriculture (% of GVA)[e]	0.1	0.1	0.1[b]
Economy: Industry (% of GVA)	8.7	7.0	7.2[b]
Economy: Services and other activity (% of GVA)[f]	91.3	93.0	92.7[b]
Employment: Agriculture (% of employed)[g]	0.3	0.2	0.2
Employment: Industry (% of employed)[g]	20.1	16.5	14.9
Employment: Services (% of employed)[g]	79.5	83.3	84.9
Unemployment (% of labour force)	5.6	4.3	3.5[g]
Labour force participation (female/male pop. %)[g]	51.7 / 71.3	51.8 / 68.5	52.6 / 67.8
CPI: Consumer Price Index (2000=100)	94[h]	104	119[i]
Agricultural production index (2004-2006=100)	99	55	34[j]
Food production index (2004-2006=100)	99	55	34[j]
International trade: Exports (million US$)	292 119	400 692	516 588[d]
International trade: Imports (million US$)	300 160	441 369	547 124[d]
International trade: Balance (million US$)	- 8 042	- 40 677	- 30 536[d]
Balance of payments, current account (million US$)	21 575	16 012	10 101[b]

Major trading partners						2016
Export partners (% of exports)	China	55.3	United States	8.1	India	3.0
Import partners (% of imports)	China	44.7	Asia nes	8.9	Japan	6.3

Social indicators	2005	2010	2017
Population growth rate (average annual %)[k]	0.5	0.6	0.6[b]
Urban population (% of total population)	100.0	100.0	100.0[b]
Urban population growth rate (average annual %)[k]	0.2	0.4	0.7[b]
Fertility rate, total (live births per woman)[k]	1.0	1.0	1.2[b]
Life expectancy at birth (females/males, years)[k]	84.4 / 78.5	85.5 / 79.5	86.4 / 80.5[b]
Population age distribution (0-14 and 60+ years, %)	14.4 / 15.6	11.9 / 18.4	11.5 / 23.5[a]
International migrant stock (000/% of total pop.)	2 721.2 / 39.8	2 780.0 / 39.8	2 838.7 / 38.9[b]
Refugees and others of concern to UNHCR (000)	3.0[l]	0.6[l]	2.5[d]
Infant mortality rate (per 1 000 live births)[k]	2.5	1.9	1.6[b]
Education: Government expenditure (% of GDP)	4.1	3.5	3.3[b]
Education: Secondary gross enrol. ratio (f/m per 100 pop.)	80.3 / 80.5	87.6 / 88.4	98.8 / 102.8[b]
Education: Tertiary gross enrol. ratio (f/m per 100 pop.)	31.9 / 32.7	58.1 / 58.9[g]	73.7 / 63.5[b]
Intentional homicide rate (per 100 000 pop.)	0.5	0.5	0.3[b]

Environment and infrastructure indicators	2005	2010	2017
Mobile-cellular subscriptions (per 100 inhabitants)	123.9	195.7	228.8[b]
Individuals using the Internet (per 100 inhabitants)[m]	56.9	72.0	84.9[b]
Research & Development expenditure (% of GDP)	0.8	0.7	0.7[i]
Threatened species (number)	39[n]	49	64
CO2 emission estimates (million tons/tons per capita)	43.9 / 6.5	40.7 / 5.8	46.2 / 6.4[i]
Energy supply per capita (Gigajoules)	85	79	83[i]
Tourist/visitor arrivals at national borders (000)	14 773	20 085	26 686[b]
Important sites for terrestrial biodiversity protected (%)	56.7	56.7	56.7

a Projected estimate (medium fertility variant). b 2015. c Consists of the population of Hong Kong Island, New Kowloon the new towns in New Territories and the marine areas. d 2016. e Excludes hunting and forestry. f Excludes waste management. g Estimate. h Break in the time series. i 2013. j 2014. k Data refers to a 5-year period preceding the reference year. l Data as at the end of December. m Population aged 10 years and over. n 2004.

China, Macao SAR

Region	Eastern Asia	Population (000, 2017)	623[a]	
Surface area (km2)	30[b,c]	Pop. density (per km2, 2017)	20 821.6[a]	
Sex ratio (m per 100 f, 2017)	92.3[a]	Capital city	Macao	
National currency	Pataca (MOP)	Capital city pop. (000)	584.4[c]	
Exchange rate (per US$)	8.0[d]			

Economic indicators	2005	2010	2017
GDP: Gross domestic product (million current US$)	12 092	28 124	46 178[c]
GDP growth rate (annual %, const. 2005 prices)	8.1	25.3	- 20.3[c]
GDP per capita (current US$)	25 830.0	52 604.2	78 586.4[c]
Economy: Industry (% of GVA)	14.9	7.4	6.6[c]
Economy: Services and other activity (% of GVA)	85.1	92.6	93.4[c]
Employment: Agriculture (% of employed)[e]	0.1	0.2	0.3
Employment: Industry (% of employed)[e]	26.8	15.6	17.7
Employment: Services (% of employed)[e]	73.1	84.2	82.1
Unemployment (% of labour force)	4.2	2.8	3.2[e]
Labour force participation (female/male pop. %)[e]	59.0 / 74.3	65.5 / 77.1	65.6 / 76.4
CPI: Consumer Price Index (2000=100)	99[f]	124	156[g,h]
Agricultural production index (2004-2006=100)	100	95	86[h]
Food production index (2004-2006=100)	100	95	86[h]
Index of industrial production (2005=100)[i]	100	45[j]	42[j,k]
International trade: Exports (million US$)	2 474	870	1 257[d]
International trade: Imports (million US$)	4 514	5 629	8 924[d]
International trade: Balance (million US$)	- 2 040	- 4 760	- 7 668[d]
Balance of payments, current account (million US$)	2 902	11 089	11 557[c]

Major trading partners					2016
Export partners (% of exports)	Areas nes[l]	58.7	China, Hong Kong SAR 31.6	China	6.8
Import partners (% of imports)	China	35.1	China, Hong Kong SAR 8.9	France	8.0

Social indicators	2005	2010	2017
Population growth rate (average annual %)[m]	2.4	2.1	2.3[c]
Urban population (% of total population)	100.0	100.0	100.0[c]
Urban population growth rate (average annual %)[m]	1.6	2.7	1.8[c]
Fertility rate, total (live births per woman)[m]	0.8	0.9	1.2[c]
Life expectancy at birth (females/males, years)[m]	83.6 / 78.2	84.9 / 79.1	86.2 / 80.3[c]
Population age distribution (0-14 and 60+ years, %)	16.9 / 9.6	12.7 / 11.0	13.3 / 16.1[a]
International migrant stock (000/% of total pop.)	279.3 / 59.7	318.5 / 59.6	342.7 / 58.3[c]
Refugees and others of concern to UNHCR (000)	...	~0.0[n]	~0.0[d]
Infant mortality rate (per 1 000 live births)[m]	4.9	3.8	3.0[c]
Education: Government expenditure (% of GDP)	2.3	2.6	2.0[h]
Education: Primary gross enrol. ratio (f/m per 100 pop.)	101.4 / 107.5	93.3 / 95.3	99.7 / 101.1[c]
Education: Secondary gross enrol. ratio (f/m per 100 pop.)	106.7 / 103.8	93.3 / 94.2	95.9 / 97.0[c]
Education: Tertiary gross enrol. ratio (f/m per 100 pop.)	50.4 / 79.0	60.9 / 62.7	86.3 / 65.2[c]
Intentional homicide rate (per 100 000 pop.)	1.5	0.4	0.2[c]

Environment and infrastructure indicators	2005	2010	2017
Mobile-cellular subscriptions (per 100 inhabitants)	113.8	209.9	324.4[c]
Individuals using the Internet (per 100 inhabitants)	34.9[e]	55.2[o]	77.6[o,c]
Research & Development expenditure (% of GDP)[p]	0.1	~0.0	0.1[h]
Threatened species (number)	5[q]	9	11
CO2 emission estimates (million tons/tons per capita)	1.8 / 3.8	1.4 / 2.6	1.3 / 2.2[h]
Energy production, primary (Petajoules)[e]	2	2	2[h]
Energy supply per capita (Gigajoules)	58	62	62[h]
Tourist/visitor arrivals at national borders (000)[e]	9 014	11 926[r]	14 308[r,c]
Important sites for terrestrial biodiversity protected (%)	0.0	0.0	0.0

a Projected estimate (medium fertility variant). **b** Inland waters include the reservoirs. **c** 2015. **d** 2016. **e** Estimate. **f** Break in the time series. **g** Series linked to former series. **h** 2014. **i** Data classified according to ISIC Rev. 3. **j** Data refers to manufacturing and utilities only. **k** 2012. **l** Areas not elsewhere specified. **m** Data refers to a 5-year period preceding the reference year. **n** Data as at the end of December. **o** Population aged 3 years and over. **p** Partial data. **q** 2004. **r** Does not include other non-residents namely workers, students, etc.

Colombia

Region	South America	UN membership date	05 November 1945
Population (000, 2017)	49 066[a]	Surface area (km2)	1 141 748[b]
Pop. density (per km2, 2017)	44.2[a]	Sex ratio (m per 100 f, 2017)	96.8[a]
Capital city	Bogota	National currency	Colombian Peso (COP)
Capital city pop. (000)	9 764.8[c,b]	Exchange rate (per US$)	3 000.7[d]

Economic indicators	2005	2010	2017
GDP: Gross domestic product (million current US$)	146 566	287 018	292 080[b]
GDP growth rate (annual %, const. 2005 prices)	4.7	4.0	3.1[b]
GDP per capita (current US$)	3 386.0	6 250.7	6 056.1[b]
Economy: Agriculture (% of GVA)	8.4	7.1	6.8[b]
Economy: Industry (% of GVA)	32.8	35.0	34.0[b]
Economy: Services and other activity (% of GVA)	58.8	57.9	59.2[b]
Employment: Agriculture (% of employed)[e]	18.5	16.0	13.5
Employment: Industry (% of employed)[e]	16.4	17.1	16.6
Employment: Services (% of employed)[e]	65.2	66.9	69.9
Unemployment (% of labour force)	11.9	11.8	10.5[e]
Labour force participation (female/male pop. %)[e]	53.0 / 81.2	55.5 / 80.3	58.0 / 79.8
CPI: Consumer Price Index (2000=100)[f]	140	177	200[g]
Agricultural production index (2004-2006=100)	99	101	114[g]
Food production index (2004-2006=100)	99	102	115[g]
International trade: Exports (million US$)	21 190	39 820	31 045[d]
International trade: Imports (million US$)	21 204	40 683	44 831[d]
International trade: Balance (million US$)	- 14	- 863	- 13 786[d]
Balance of payments, current account (million US$)	- 1 892	- 8 663	- 18 922[b]

Major trading partners						2016
Export partners (% of exports)	United States	32.9	Panama	6.2	Netherlands	3.9
Import partners (% of imports)	United States	26.7	China	19.3	Mexico	7.6

Social indicators	2005	2010	2017
Population growth rate (average annual %)[h]	1.4	1.2	1.0[b]
Urban population (% of total population)	73.6	75.0	76.4[b]
Urban population growth rate (average annual %)[h]	2.0	1.8	1.7[b]
Fertility rate, total (live births per woman)[h]	2.3	2.1	1.9[b]
Life expectancy at birth (females/males, years)[h]	75.4 / 68.0	76.6 / 69.2	77.4 / 70.2[b]
Population age distribution (0-14 and 60+ years, %)	28.9 / 7.6	26.4 / 9.0	23.5 / 11.6[a]
International migrant stock (000/% of total pop.)	107.6 / 0.2	124.3 / 0.3	133.1 / 0.3[b]
Refugees and others of concern to UNHCR (000)	2 000.2[i]	3 672.4[i]	7 127.0[d]
Infant mortality rate (per 1 000 live births)[h]	20.5	19.0	17.9[b]
Health: Total expenditure (% of GDP)[j]	5.8	6.8	7.2[g]
Health: Physicians (per 1 000 pop.)	1.5	1.6	...
Education: Government expenditure (% of GDP)	4.0	4.8	4.5[b]
Education: Primary gross enrol. ratio (f/m per 100 pop.)	126.2 / 128.7	123.1 / 125.4	111.6 / 115.4[b]
Education: Secondary gross enrol. ratio (f/m per 100 pop.)	87.7 / 79.3	106.9 / 97.3	101.5 / 94.8[b]
Education: Tertiary gross enrol. ratio (f/m per 100 pop.)	30.4 / 28.0	41.3 / 37.6	59.9 / 51.5[b]
Intentional homicide rate (per 100 000 pop.)	39.5	32.7	26.5[b]
Seats held by women in national parliaments (%)	12.0	8.4	18.7

Environment and infrastructure indicators	2005	2010	2017
Mobile-cellular subscriptions (per 100 inhabitants)	50.6	95.8	115.7[b]
Individuals using the Internet (per 100 inhabitants)	11.0	36.5[k]	55.9[k,b]
Research & Development expenditure (% of GDP)	0.2	0.2	0.2[g]
Threatened species (number)	593[l]	681	835
Forested area (% of land area)	54.3	52.8	52.8[e,g]
CO2 emission estimates (million tons/tons per capita)	60.9 / 1.4	76.2 / 1.7	84.1 / 1.8[g]
Energy production, primary (Petajoules)	3 335	4 486	5 380[g]
Energy supply per capita (Gigajoules)	27	30	31[g]
Tourist/visitor arrivals at national borders (000)	933[m]	1 405	2 978[b]
Important sites for terrestrial biodiversity protected (%)	25.6	30.9	38.6
Pop. using improved drinking water (urban/rural, %)	97.1 / 72.1	96.9 / 73.2	96.8 / 73.8[b]
Pop. using improved sanitation facilities (urban/rural, %)	84.0 / 57.8	84.6 / 63.4	85.2 / 67.9[b]
Net Official Development Assist. received (% of GNI)	0.44	0.24	0.47[b]

a Projected estimate (medium fertility variant). b 2015. c Refers to the nuclei of Santa Fe de Bogotá, Soacha, Chia and Funza. d 2016. e Estimate. f Low income group. g 2014. h Data refers to a 5-year period preceding the reference year. i Data as at the end of December. j Data revision. k Population aged 5 years and over. l 2004. m Break in the time series.

Comoros

Region	Eastern Africa	UN membership date	12 November 1975
Population (000, 2017)	814[a]	Surface area (km2)	2 235[b]
Pop. density (per km2, 2017)	437.4[a]	Sex ratio (m per 100 f, 2017)	101.8[a]
Capital city	Moroni	National currency	Comorian Franc (KMF)
Capital city pop. (000)	55.9[c]	Exchange rate (per US$)	466.7[d]

Economic indicators	2005	2010	2017
GDP: Gross domestic product (million current US$)	782	995	1 079[b]
GDP growth rate (annual %, const. 2005 prices)	2.8	- 0.7	4.8[b]
GDP per capita (current US$)	1 264.2	1 424.5	1 368.9[b]
Economy: Agriculture (% of GVA)	34.4	32.5	30.7[b]
Economy: Industry (% of GVA)	4.0	4.2	4.0[b]
Economy: Services and other activity (% of GVA)	61.7	63.3	65.3[b]
Employment: Agriculture (% of employed)[e]	61.8	62.2	62.0
Employment: Industry (% of employed)[e]	5.5	5.3	5.2
Employment: Services (% of employed)[e]	32.7	32.5	32.8
Unemployment (% of labour force)[e]	20.3	19.9	20.0
Labour force participation (female/male pop. %)[e]	32.2 / 78.7	34.1 / 79.0	35.7 / 79.5
Agricultural production index (2004-2006=100)	96	107	107[c]
Food production index (2004-2006=100)	96	107	107[c]
International trade: Exports (million US$)	4	14	20[d]
International trade: Imports (million US$)	85	181	193[d]
International trade: Balance (million US$)	- 81	- 167	- 173[d]
Balance of payments, current account (million US$)	- 29	- 91	...

Major trading partners						2016
Export partners (% of exports)	India	30.0	France	12.2	United Arab Emirates	11.3
Import partners (% of imports)	United Rep. Tanzania	41.7	China	12.2	France	10.9

Social indicators	2005	2010	2017
Population growth rate (average annual %)[f]	2.4	2.4	2.4[b]
Urban population (% of total population)	27.9	27.9	28.3[b]
Urban population growth rate (average annual %)[f]	2.4	2.6	2.7[b]
Fertility rate, total (live births per woman)[f]	5.2	4.9	4.6[b]
Life expectancy at birth (females/males, years)[f]	61.2 / 58.0	62.5 / 59.3	64.5 / 61.2[b]
Population age distribution (0-14 and 60+ years, %)	42.3 / 4.6	41.0 / 4.5	39.8 / 4.9[a]
International migrant stock (000/% of total pop.)	13.2 / 2.1	12.6 / 1.8	12.6 / 1.6[b]
Refugees and others of concern to UNHCR (000)	~0.0[g]	...	...
Infant mortality rate (per 1 000 live births)[f]	72.6	66.7	58.1[b]
Health: Total expenditure (% of GDP)	4.3	5.8	6.7[c]
Health: Physicians (per 1 000 pop.)	0.2[h]	...	...
Education: Government expenditure (% of GDP)	3.9[i]	7.7[i]	4.3[b]
Education: Primary gross enrol. ratio (f/m per 100 pop.)	100.9 / 113.7[h]	102.8 / 111.6[j]	99.5 / 106.8[c]
Education: Secondary gross enrol. ratio (f/m per 100 pop.)	37.5 / 49.1[h]	... / ...	62.4 / 58.4[c]
Education: Tertiary gross enrol. ratio (f/m per 100 pop.)	2.6 / 3.4[k]	4.9 / 6.5	8.0 / 9.8[c]
Intentional homicide rate (per 100 000 pop.)	9.4	8.4	7.6[b]
Seats held by women in national parliaments (%)	3.0	3.0	6.1

Environment and infrastructure indicators	2005	2010	2017
Mobile-cellular subscriptions (per 100 inhabitants)	2.6	24.2	54.8[e,b]
Individuals using the Internet (per 100 inhabitants)[e]	2.0	5.1	7.5[b]
Threatened species (number)	27[h]	89	114
Forested area (% of land area)[e]	22.6	21.0	20.1[c]
CO2 emission estimates (million tons/tons per capita)	0.1 / 0.2	0.2 / 0.2	0.2 / 0.2[c]
Energy production, primary (Petajoules)	2	2	3[c]
Energy supply per capita (Gigajoules)	6[e]	7[e]	6[c]
Tourist/visitor arrivals at national borders (000)	26	15	24[b]
Important sites for terrestrial biodiversity protected (%)	0.0	14.8	14.8
Pop. using improved drinking water (urban/rural, %)	93.8 / 88.6	93.1 / 88.9	92.6 / 89.1[b]
Pop. using improved sanitation facilities (urban/rural, %)	41.7 / 23.9	45.4 / 27.8	48.3 / 30.9[b]
Net Official Development Assist. received (% of GNI)	6.11	13.24	12.05[c]

a Projected estimate (medium fertility variant). **b** 2015. **c** 2014. **d** 2016. **e** Estimate. **f** Data refers to a 5-year period preceding the reference year. **g** Data as at the end of December. **h** 2004. **i** 2002. **j** 2008. **k** 2003.

Congo

Region	Middle Africa	UN membership date	20 September 1960
Population (000, 2017)	5 261[a]	Surface area (km2)	342 000[b]
Pop. density (per km2, 2017)	15.4[a]	Sex ratio (m per 100 f, 2017)	100.1[a]
Capital city	Brazzaville	National currency	CFA Franc (XAF)
Capital city pop. (000)	1 887.6[b]	Exchange rate (per US$)	622.3[c]

Economic indicators	2005	2010	2017
GDP: Gross domestic product (million current US$)	6 087	12 281	8 493[b]
GDP growth rate (annual %, const. 2005 prices)	7.6	8.7	1.2[b]
GDP per capita (current US$)	1 737.6	3 020.4	1 838.1[b]
Economy: Agriculture (% of GVA)	4.6	3.7	4.7[b]
Economy: Industry (% of GVA)	73.4	78.1	70.0[b]
Economy: Services and other activity (% of GVA)	22.0	18.2	25.3[b]
Employment: Agriculture (% of employed)[d]	43.2	41.7	40.7
Employment: Industry (% of employed)[d]	25.9	25.2	25.8
Employment: Services (% of employed)[d]	31.0	33.0	33.5
Unemployment (% of labour force)[d]	15.9	14.6	11.5
Labour force participation (female/male pop. %)[d]	67.4 / 71.5	67.5 / 72.3	67.1 / 72.6
CPI: Consumer Price Index (2000=100)[e,f]	110	139[g]	154[h]
Agricultural production index (2004-2006=100)	100	124	106[i]
Food production index (2004-2006=100)	100	125	106[i]
Index of industrial production (2005=100)[j,k]	100	159[l,m]	...
International trade: Exports (million US$)	4 744	6 918	2 540[c]
International trade: Imports (million US$)	1 342	4 369	9 793[c]
International trade: Balance (million US$)	3 402	2 548	- 7 253[c]
Balance of payments, current account (million US$)	696	...	...

Major trading partners						2016
Export partners (% of exports)	China	34.9	Australia	9.0	Gabon	8.3
Import partners (% of imports)	France	17.2	China	15.4	Belgium	13.5

Social indicators	2005	2010	2017
Population growth rate (average annual %)[n]	2.8	3.3	2.6[b]
Urban population (% of total population)	61.0	63.2	65.4[b]
Urban population growth rate (average annual %)[n]	3.3	3.7	3.2[b]
Fertility rate, total (live births per woman)[n]	5.1	5.0	4.9[b]
Life expectancy at birth (females/males, years)[n]	53.1 / 51.1	59.2 / 56.7	64.1 / 61.0[b]
Population age distribution (0-14 and 60+ years, %)	41.6 / 5.2	41.7 / 5.0	42.3 / 5.2[a]
International migrant stock (000/% of total pop.)	315.2 / 9.0	419.6 / 10.3	393.0 / 8.5[b]
Refugees and others of concern to UNHCR (000)	77.6[o]	138.7[o]	54.9[c]
Infant mortality rate (per 1 000 live births)[n]	81.1	61.0	46.5[b]
Health: Total expenditure (% of GDP)	2.4	2.3	5.2[i]
Health: Physicians (per 1 000 pop.)	0.2[p]	0.1[q]	...
Education: Government expenditure (% of GDP)	1.8	6.2	...
Education: Primary gross enrol. ratio (f/m per 100 pop.)	107.8 / 115.9	109.8 / 116.3	114.8 / 107.0[r]
Education: Secondary gross enrol. ratio (f/m per 100 pop.)	42.0 / 49.7[d,p]	... / ...	50.6 / 58.4[r]
Education: Tertiary gross enrol. ratio (f/m per 100 pop.)	2.2 / 5.5[d,s]	2.3 / 10.8[m]	8.3 / 11.1[h]
Intentional homicide rate (per 100 000 pop.)	11.3	10.6	10.1[b]
Seats held by women in national parliaments (%)	8.5	7.3	7.4

Environment and infrastructure indicators	2005	2010	2017
Mobile-cellular subscriptions (per 100 inhabitants)	15.8	90.4	111.7[d,b]
Individuals using the Internet (per 100 inhabitants)[d]	1.5	5.0	7.6[b]
Threatened species (number)	65[p]	103	134
Forested area (% of land area)[d]	65.8	65.6	65.4[i]
CO2 emission estimates (million tons/tons per capita)	1.0 / 0.3	2.0 / 0.5	3.1 / 0.7[i]
Energy production, primary (Petajoules)	563	724	648[i]
Energy supply per capita (Gigajoules)	13	17	24[i]
Tourist/visitor arrivals at national borders (000)	35	194[t]	227[t,i]
Important sites for terrestrial biodiversity protected (%)	51.5	61.2	72.1
Pop. using improved drinking water (urban/rural, %)	95.5 / 34.6	95.6 / 37.6	95.8 / 40.0[b]
Pop. using improved sanitation facilities (urban/rural, %)	18.4 / 5.6	19.3 / 5.6	20.0 / 5.6[b]
Net Official Development Assist. received (% of GNI)	35.36	14.57	1.05[b]

a Projected estimate (medium fertility variant). b 2015. c 2016. d Estimate. e African population. f Brazzaville g Series linked to former series. h 2013. i 2014. j Data classified according to ISIC Rev. 3. k Country data supplemented with data from the Observatoire Economique et Statistique d'Afrique Subsaharienne (Afristat). l Data refers to manufacturing and utilities only. m 2009. n Data refers to a 5-year period preceding the reference year. o Data as at the end of December. p 2004. q 2007. r 2012. s 2003. t Including nationals residing abroad.

Cook Islands

Region	Polynesia	Population (000, 2017)	17[a]
Surface area (km2)	236[b]	Pop. density (per km2, 2017)	72.4[a]
Sex ratio (m per 100 f, 2017)	97.4[c,d]	Capital city	Avarua
National currency	New Zealand Dollar (NZD)	Capital city pop. (000)	5.0[e]
Exchange rate (per US$)	1.4[d]		

Economic indicators

	2005	2010	2017
GDP: Gross domestic product (million current US$)	183	255	294[b]
GDP growth rate (annual %, const. 2005 prices)	- 1.1	- 3.0	5.5[b]
GDP per capita (current US$)	9 410.7	12 578.7	14 118.7[b]
Economy: Agriculture (% of GVA)[f]	6.9	4.9	8.1[b]
Economy: Industry (% of GVA)[f]	9.6	8.5	9.0[b]
Economy: Services and other activity (% of GVA)[f]	83.5	86.6	82.9[b]
Employment: Agriculture (% of employed)	...	...	4.3[g,e]
Employment: Industry (% of employed)	...	...	11.7[g,e]
Employment: Services (% of employed)	...	...	84.0[g,e]
Unemployment (% of labour force)	13.1[h]	6.9[c,g,i]	8.2[g,e]
Labour force participation (female/male pop. %)	63.0 / 75.5[j,h]	64.2 / 76.1[c,g,i]	65.4 / 76.6[g,e]
CPI: Consumer Price Index (2000=100)[k]	118	144	158[l]
Agricultural production index (2004-2006=100)	100	93	91[l]
Food production index (2004-2006=100)	100	92	91[l]
International trade: Exports (million US$)	5	5	14[d]
International trade: Imports (million US$)	81	91	98[d]
International trade: Balance (million US$)	- 76	- 85	- 84[d]

Major trading partners

						2016
Export partners (% of exports)	Japan	39.0	Germany	11.7	France	7.0
Import partners (% of imports)	New Zealand	46.7	Italy	16.0	Fiji	8.2

Social indicators

	2005	2010	2017
Population growth rate (average annual %)[m]	1.7	- 1.2	- 1.2[b]
Urban population (% of total population)	71.0	73.3	74.5[b]
Urban population growth rate (average annual %)[m]	3.4	1.5	0.9[b]
Fertility rate, total (live births per woman)	...	...	2.6[e]
Life expectancy at birth (females/males, years)	74.0 / 68.0[h]	76.2 / 69.5[j]	79.6 / 71.7[c,n,o]
Population age distribution (0-14 and 60+ years, %)	30.0 / 10.6[h]	26.1 / 11.9[p,j]	26.9 / 14.2[c,d]
International migrant stock (000/% of total pop.)	3.3 / 16.9	3.8 / 18.6	4.2 / 19.9[b]
Infant mortality rate (per 1 000 live births)	...	...	3.6[n,o]
Health: Total expenditure (% of GDP)	4.7	3.6	3.4[l]
Health: Physicians (per 1 000 pop.)	1.0[q]	1.2[r]	...
Education: Government expenditure (% of GDP)	...	...	3.9[b]
Education: Primary gross enrol. ratio (f/m per 100 pop.)[s]	113.0 / 110.2	103.6 / 104.6	99.3 / 106.0[b]
Education: Secondary gross enrol. ratio (f/m per 100 pop.)[s]	84.9 / 75.1	88.1 / 80.7	90.1 / 83.0[b]
Education: Tertiary gross enrol. ratio (f/m per 100 pop.)	... / ...	... / ...	49.5 / 40.1[s,t]
Intentional homicide rate (per 100 000 pop.)	...	...	3.1[t]

Environment and infrastructure indicators

	2005	2010	2017
Threatened species (number)	23[q]	53	75
Forested area (% of land area)	62.9	62.9	62.9[s,l]
CO2 emission estimates (million tons/tons per capita)	0.1 / 3.2	0.1 / 3.5	0.1 / 3.4[l]
Energy supply per capita (Gigajoules)	45	49[s]	48[s,l]
Tourist/visitor arrivals at national borders (000)	88	104	125[b]
Important sites for terrestrial biodiversity protected (%)	16.8	16.8	16.8
Pop. using improved drinking water (urban/rural, %)	99.9 / 99.9	99.9 / 99.9	99.9 / 99.9[b]
Pop. using improved sanitation facilities (urban/rural, %)	94.2 / 94.2	96.4 / 96.4	97.6 / 97.6[b]

a Projected estimate (medium fertility variant). b 2015. c Break in the time series. d 2016. e 2011. f At producers' prices. g Resident population (de jure). h 2001. i 2006. j Population aged 15 to 69 years. k Rarotonga l 2014. m Data refers to a 5-year period preceding the reference year. n Data refers to a 5-year period up to and including the reference year. o 2013. p Provisional data. q 2004. r 2009. s Estimate. t 2012.

Costa Rica

Region	Central America	
Population (000, 2017)	4 906[a]	
Pop. density (per km2, 2017)	96.1[a]	
Capital city	San José	
Capital city pop. (000)	1 170.2[c,b]	

UN membership date	02 November 1945
Surface area (km2)	51 100[b]
Sex ratio (m per 100 f, 2017)	100.1[a]
National currency	Costa Rican Colon (CRC)
Exchange rate (per US$)	554.6[d]

Economic indicators

	2005	2010	2017
GDP: Gross domestic product (million current US$)	19 952	37 269	52 958[b]
GDP growth rate (annual %, const. 2005 prices)	3.9	5.0	3.7[b]
GDP per capita (current US$)	4 697.0	8 199.4	11 015.0[b]
Economy: Agriculture (% of GVA)[e]	9.6	7.2	5.1[b]
Economy: Industry (% of GVA)[e]	26.9	25.4	21.5[b]
Economy: Services and other activity (% of GVA)[e]	63.6	67.4	73.4[b]
Employment: Agriculture (% of employed)[f]	15.2	15.1	11.6
Employment: Industry (% of employed)[f]	21.7	19.6	19.1
Employment: Services (% of employed)[f]	63.1	65.3	69.3
Unemployment (% of labour force)	6.6	8.9	8.6[f]
Labour force participation (female/male pop. %)[f]	43.6 / 80.2	44.1 / 77.1	46.9 / 76.5
CPI: Consumer Price Index (2000=100)[g]	170	268	323[h]
Agricultural production index (2004-2006=100)	98	114	127[h]
Food production index (2004-2006=100)	98	115	129[h]
International trade: Exports (million US$)	7 151	9 045	9 908[d]
International trade: Imports (million US$)	9 173	13 920	15 322[d]
International trade: Balance (million US$)	- 2 023	- 4 875	- 5 414[d]
Balance of payments, current account (million US$)	- 860	- 1 214	- 2 493[b]

Major trading partners

						2016
Export partners (% of exports)	United States	41.0	Netherlands	5.8	Panama	5.7
Import partners (% of imports)	United States	37.3	China	13.6	Mexico	7.0

Social indicators

	2005	2010	2017
Population growth rate (average annual %)[i]	1.6	1.4	1.1[b]
Urban population (% of total population)	65.7	71.7	76.8[b]
Urban population growth rate (average annual %)[i]	4.0	3.3	2.7[b]
Fertility rate, total (live births per woman)[i]	2.2	2.0	1.9[b]
Life expectancy at birth (females/males, years)[i]	80.2 / 75.5	80.8 / 76.1	81.7 / 76.7[b]
Population age distribution (0-14 and 60+ years, %)	27.4 / 9.4	24.6 / 11.1	21.6 / 13.6[a]
International migrant stock (000/% of total pop.)[i]	358.2 / 8.4	405.4 / 8.9	421.7 / 8.8[b]
Refugees and others of concern to UNHCR (000)	11.5[k]	19.9[k]	10.1[d]
Infant mortality rate (per 1 000 live births)[i]	10.9	10.0	9.3[b]
Health: Total expenditure (% of GDP)[i]	7.7	9.7	9.3[h]
Health: Physicians (per 1 000 pop.)	1.3[m]	...	1.2[n]
Education: Government expenditure (% of GDP)	4.9[o]	6.6	7.2[b]
Education: Primary gross enrol. ratio (f/m per 100 pop.)	111.5 / 114.4	115.8 / 118.1	109.5 / 110.1[b]
Education: Secondary gross enrol. ratio (f/m per 100 pop.)	86.2 / 82.6	104.3 / 100.1	125.6 / 120.7[b]
Education: Tertiary gross enrol. ratio (f/m per 100 pop.)	30.2 / 24.5[o]	... / ...	60.9 / 46.6[b]
Intentional homicide rate (per 100 000 pop.)	7.9	11.6	11.8[b]
Seats held by women in national parliaments (%)	35.1	36.8	35.1

Environment and infrastructure indicators

	2005	2010	2017
Mobile-cellular subscriptions (per 100 inhabitants)	25.5	67.0	150.7[p,b]
Individuals using the Internet (per 100 inhabitants)[q]	22.1	36.5[r]	59.8[r,b]
Research & Development expenditure (% of GDP)	0.4[o]	0.5	0.6[n]
Threatened species (number)	231[o]	285	340
Forested area (% of land area)[f]	48.8	51.0	53.4[b]
CO2 emission estimates (million tons/tons per capita)	6.9 / 1.6	7.6 / 1.7	7.8 / 1.6[h]
Energy production, primary (Petajoules)	93	104	110[h]
Energy supply per capita (Gigajoules)	41	45	44[h]
Tourist/visitor arrivals at national borders (000)	1 679	2 100	2 660[b]
Important sites for terrestrial biodiversity protected (%)	44.8	45.3	45.3
Pop. using improved drinking water (urban/rural, %)	99.4 / 90.0	99.5 / 91.2	99.6 / 91.9[b]
Pop. using improved sanitation facilities (urban/rural, %)	94.8 / 88.9	95.1 / 91.0	95.2 / 92.3[b]
Net Official Development Assist. received (% of GNI)	0.13	0.27	0.22[b]

a Projected estimate (medium fertility variant). **b** 2015. **c** Refers to the urban population of cantons. **d** 2016. **e** Data classified according to ISIC Rev. 4. **f** Estimate. **g** Central area, **h** 2014. **i** Data refers to a 5-year period preceding the reference year. **j** Including refugees. **k** Data as at the end of December. **l** Data revision. **m** 2000. **n** 2013. **o** 2004. **p** Provisional data. **q** Population aged 5 years and over. **r** Users in the last 3 months.

Côte d'Ivoire

Region	Western Africa	UN membership date	20 September 1960
Population (000, 2017)	24 295[a]	Surface area (km2)	322 463[b]
Pop. density (per km2, 2017)	76.4[a]	Sex ratio (m per 100 f, 2017)	102.7[a]
Capital city	Yamoussoukro[c]	National currency	CFA Franc (XOF)
Capital city pop. (000)	259.0[d]	Exchange rate (per US$)	622.3[e]

Economic indicators

	2005	2010	2017
GDP: Gross domestic product (million current US$)	17 085	24 884	32 076[b]
GDP growth rate (annual %, const. 2005 prices)	1.7	2.0	9.5[b]
GDP per capita (current US$)	942.2	1 236.1	1 412.9[b]
Economy: Agriculture (% of GVA)	25.2	27.0	23.7[b]
Economy: Industry (% of GVA)	25.5	24.7	28.3[b]
Economy: Services and other activity (% of GVA)	49.3	48.3	48.1[b]
Employment: Agriculture (% of employed)[f]	60.9	60.3	56.0
Employment: Industry (% of employed)[f]	5.0	5.1	5.7
Employment: Services (% of employed)[f]	34.0	34.6	38.4
Unemployment (% of labour force)[f]	9.2	9.2	9.3
Labour force participation (female/male pop. %)[f]	50.5 / 82.0	51.8 / 81.4	52.6 / 80.9
CPI: Consumer Price Index (2000=100)[g,h]	117[i]	133[i]	145[k]
Agricultural production index (2004-2006=100)	100	107	122[d]
Food production index (2004-2006=100)	98	109	123[d]
Index of industrial production (2005=100)[i,m]	100	103	140[d]
International trade: Exports (million US$)	7 248	10 284	10 661[e]
International trade: Imports (million US$)	5 865	7 849	8 380[e]
International trade: Balance (million US$)	1 383	2 434	2 281[e]
Balance of payments, current account (million US$)	40	465	- 633[k]

Major trading partners

						2016
Export partners (% of exports)	Netherlands	12.1	United States	8.1	Belgium	6.5
Import partners (% of imports)	Nigeria	15.2	France	13.8	China	11.7

Social indicators

	2005	2010	2017
Population growth rate (average annual %)[n]	1.9	2.1	2.5[b]
Urban population (% of total population)	46.8	50.6	54.2[b]
Urban population growth rate (average annual %)[n]	3.0	3.3	3.7[b]
Fertility rate, total (live births per woman)[n]	5.7	5.4	5.1[b]
Life expectancy at birth (females/males, years)[n]	47.6 / 45.9	50.0 / 48.5	53.2 / 50.4[b]
Population age distribution (0-14 and 60+ years, %)	44.1 / 4.6	43.7 / 4.7	42.4 / 4.8[a]
International migrant stock (000/% of total pop.)[o]	2 010.8 / 11.1	2 095.2 / 10.4	2 175.4 / 9.6[b]
Refugees and others of concern to UNHCR (000)	115.1[p]	564.5[p]	1 023.0[e]
Infant mortality rate (per 1 000 live births)[n]	91.6	84.6	71.6[b]
Health: Total expenditure (% of GDP)	5.4	6.3	5.7[d]
Health: Physicians (per 1 000 pop.)	0.1	0.1[q]	...
Education: Government expenditure (% of GDP)	4.1	4.6	5.0[f,b]
Education: Primary gross enrol. ratio (f/m per 100 pop.)	64.4 / 80.4[f,r]	65.6 / 80.3[s]	88.0 / 99.2[b]
Education: Secondary gross enrol. ratio (f/m per 100 pop.)	... / ...	... / ...	36.6 / 51.0[b]
Education: Tertiary gross enrol. ratio (f/m per 100 pop.)	... / ...	5.5 / 10.6	7.3 / 11.0[b]
Intentional homicide rate (per 100 000 pop.)	14.9	12.8	11.8[b]
Seats held by women in national parliaments (%)	8.5	8.9	11.5

Environment and infrastructure indicators

	2005	2010	2017
Mobile-cellular subscriptions (per 100 inhabitants)	13.5	82.2	119.3[b]
Individuals using the Internet (per 100 inhabitants)	1.0	2.7[f]	21.0[f,b]
Threatened species (number)	167[t]	210	249
Forested area (% of land area)[f]	32.7	32.7	32.7[d]
CO2 emission estimates (million tons/tons per capita)	7.8 / 0.4	7.0 / 0.3	11.0 / 0.5[d]
Energy production, primary (Petajoules)	451	467	540[d]
Energy supply per capita (Gigajoules)	23	21	26[d]
Tourist/visitor arrivals at national borders (000)	...	252	1 441[i,b]
Important sites for terrestrial biodiversity protected (%)	77.7	77.7	77.7
Pop. using improved drinking water (urban/rural, %)	92.0 / 68.0	92.6 / 68.4	93.1 / 68.8[b]
Pop. using improved sanitation facilities (urban/rural, %)	30.9 / 8.9	32.0 / 9.7	32.8 / 10.3[b]
Net Official Development Assist. received (% of GNI)	0.56	3.52	2.22[b]

a Projected estimate (medium fertility variant). **b** 2015. **c** Yamoussoukro is the capital and Abidjan is the administrative capital. **d** 2014. **e** 2016. **f** Estimate. **g** African population. **h** Abidjan **i** Break in the time series. **j** Series linked to former series. **k** 2013. **l** Data classified according to ISIC Rev. 3. **m** Country data supplemented with data from the Observatoire Economique et Statistique d'Afrique Subsaharienne (Afristat). **n** Data refers to a 5-year period preceding the reference year. **o** Refers to foreign citizens. **p** Data as at the end of December. **q** 2008. **r** 2003. **s** 2009. **t** 2004.

Croatia

Region	Southern Europe	UN membership date	22 May 1992	
Population (000, 2017)	4 189[a]	Surface area (km2)	56 594[b]	
Pop. density (per km2, 2017)	74.9[a]	Sex ratio (m per 100 f, 2017)	93.1[a]	
Capital city	Zagreb	National currency	Kuna (HRK)	
Capital city pop. (000)	686.9[c,b]	Exchange rate (per US$)	7.2[d]	

Economic indicators

	2005	2010	2017
GDP: Gross domestic product (million current US$)	45 416	59 665	48 676[b]
GDP growth rate (annual %, const. 2005 prices)	4.2	- 1.7	1.6[b]
GDP per capita (current US$)	10 373.6	13 822.9	11 479.4[b]
Economy: Agriculture (% of GVA)[e]	5.0	4.9	4.1[b]
Economy: Industry (% of GVA)[e]	29.0	27.1	26.6[b]
Economy: Services and other activity (% of GVA)[e]	66.0	68.1	69.3[b]
Employment: Agriculture (% of employed)[f]	17.3	14.3	9.2
Employment: Industry (% of employed)[f]	28.6	27.6	26.8
Employment: Services (% of employed)[f]	54.1	58.1	64.0
Unemployment (% of labour force)	12.6	11.6	11.7[f]
Labour force participation (female/male pop. %)[f]	46.2 / 61.1	45.8 / 59.2	46.3 / 58.4
CPI: Consumer Price Index (2000=100)	114	133	143[g]
Agricultural production index (2004-2006=100)	98	100	91[g]
Food production index (2004-2006=100)	98	100	91[g]
Index of industrial production (2005=100)	100	99[h]	92[h,g]
International trade: Exports (million US$)	8 773	11 811	13 648[d]
International trade: Imports (million US$)	18 560	20 067	21 830[d]
International trade: Balance (million US$)	- 9 788	- 8 256	- 8 182[d]
Balance of payments, current account (million US$)	- 2 479	- 894	2 492[b]

Major trading partners

					2016
Export partners (% of exports)	Italy	13.7	Slovenia	12.5	Germany	11.8
Import partners (% of imports)	Germany	16.1	Italy	12.6	Slovenia	10.9

Social indicators

	2005	2010	2017
Population growth rate (average annual %)[i]	- 0.2	- 0.2	- 0.4[b]
Urban population (% of total population)	56.4	57.5	59.0[b]
Urban population growth rate (average annual %)[i]	- 0.1	0.2	0.1[b]
Fertility rate, total (live births per woman)[i]	1.4	1.5	1.5[b]
Life expectancy at birth (females/males, years)[i]	78.4 / 71.4	79.5 / 72.6	80.4 / 73.6[b]
Population age distribution (0-14 and 60+ years, %)	15.7 / 21.9	15.4 / 23.8	14.7 / 26.8[a]
International migrant stock (000/% of total pop.)	579.3 / 13.2	573.2 / 13.3	576.9 / 13.6[b]
Refugees and others of concern to UNHCR (000)	10.9[k]	25.5[k]	15.5[d]
Infant mortality rate (per 1 000 live births)[i]	6.5	5.7	3.9[b]
Health: Total expenditure (% of GDP)	6.9	8.2	7.8[g]
Health: Physicians (per 1 000 pop.)	...	2.9	3.1[g]
Education: Government expenditure (% of GDP)	3.8[l]	4.3	4.6[m]
Education: Primary gross enrol. ratio (f/m per 100 pop.)	103.3 / 103.3	91.9 / 91.7	98.1 / 97.8[b]
Education: Secondary gross enrol. ratio (f/m per 100 pop.)	94.7 / 91.6	104.2 / 97.3	100.6 / 95.9[b]
Education: Tertiary gross enrol. ratio (f/m per 100 pop.)	49.2 / 40.5	62.8 / 46.8	79.8 / 58.8[b]
Intentional homicide rate (per 100 000 pop.)	1.5	1.4	0.9[b]
Seats held by women in national parliaments (%)	21.7	23.5	19.9

Environment and infrastructure indicators

	2005	2010	2017
Mobile-cellular subscriptions (per 100 inhabitants)	83.2	113.6[f,n]	103.8[b]
Individuals using the Internet (per 100 inhabitants)[o]	33.1	56.6	69.8[b]
Research & Development expenditure (% of GDP)	0.9[l]	0.7	0.8[g]
Threatened species (number)	57[l]	101	176
Forested area (% of land area)	34.0	34.3	34.3[f,g]
CO2 emission estimates (million tons/tons per capita)	22.6 / 5.1	20.2 / 4.7	16.8 / 4.0[g]
Energy production, primary (Petajoules)	199	215	182[g]
Energy supply per capita (Gigajoules)	92	90	79[g]
Tourist/visitor arrivals at national borders (000)	7 743[p,q]	9 111	12 683[b]
Important sites for terrestrial biodiversity protected (%)	20.5	22.3	65.2
Pop. using improved drinking water (urban/rural, %)	99.8 / 97.4	99.7 / 98.6	99.6 / 99.7[b]
Pop. using improved sanitation facilities (urban/rural, %)	98.1 / 96.1	98.0 / 95.9	97.8 / 95.8[b]
Net Official Development Assist. disbursed (% of GNI)	...	...	0.07[r,d]
Net Official Development Assist. received (% of GNI)	0.28	0.23	

a Projected estimate (medium fertility variant). **b** 2015. **c** Refers to the settlement of Zagreb. **d** 2016. **e** Data classified according to ISIC Rev. 4. **f** Estimate. **g** 2014. **h** Excluding water and waste management. **i** Data refers to a 5-year period preceding the reference year. **j** Including refugees. **k** Data as at the end of December. **l** 2004. **m** 2013. **n** Includes data-only subscriptions. **o** Population aged 16 to 74 years. **p** Break in the time series. **q** Data from 2005 to 2009 were revised so they can be comparable to 2010 (nautical ports were excluded). **r** Provisional data.

Cuba

Region	Caribbean	UN membership date	24 October 1945
Population (000, 2017)	11 485[a]	Surface area (km2)	109 884[b]
Pop. density (per km2, 2017)	107.9[a]	Sex ratio (m per 100 f, 2017)	100.1[a]
Capital city	Havana	National currency	Cuban Peso (CUP)[c]
Capital city pop. (000)	2 137.1[b]	Exchange rate (per US$)	1.0[d,e]

Economic indicators	2005	2010	2017
GDP: Gross domestic product (million current US$)	42 644	64 328	87 206[b]
GDP growth rate (annual %, const. 2005 prices)	11.2	2.4	4.4[b]
GDP per capita (current US$)	3 786.8	5 688.6	7 656.6[b]
Economy: Agriculture (% of GVA)	5.6	5.0	5.0[b]
Economy: Industry (% of GVA)	19.4	20.5	20.5[b]
Economy: Services and other activity (% of GVA)	75.0	74.5	74.5[b]
Employment: Agriculture (% of employed)[f]	20.1	18.6	12.9
Employment: Industry (% of employed)[f]	19.1	17.1	11.7
Employment: Services (% of employed)[f]	60.9	64.3	75.3
Unemployment (% of labour force)	1.9	2.5	3.0[f]
Labour force participation (female/male pop. %)[f]	38.2 / 67.3	42.4 / 68.9	42.1 / 68.3
CPI: Consumer Price Index (2000=100)	109	125[g]	...
Agricultural production index (2004-2006=100)	97	88	100[h]
Food production index (2004-2006=100)	97	88	101[h]
International trade: Exports (million US$)	2 319	4 945	18 000[e]
International trade: Imports (million US$)	8 084	10 913	4 911[e]
International trade: Balance (million US$)	- 5 766	- 5 968	13 089[e]

Major trading partners						2016
Export partners (% of exports)	Canada	17.2	China	16.0	Netherlands	9.4
Import partners (% of imports)	China	27.2	Spain	15.3	Italy	5.3

Social indicators	2005	2010	2017
Population growth rate (average annual %)[i]	0.2	0.1	0.2[b]
Urban population (% of total population)	76.1	76.6	77.1[b]
Urban population growth rate (average annual %)[i]	0.5	0.1	0.1[b]
Fertility rate, total (live births per woman)[i]	1.6	1.6	1.7[b]
Life expectancy at birth (females/males, years)[i]	79.1 / 75.3	80.7 / 76.6	81.3 / 77.1[b]
Population age distribution (0-14 and 60+ years, %)	19.4 / 15.2	17.4 / 17.0	16.0 / 20.1[a]
International migrant stock (000/% of total pop.)	17.0 / 0.2	14.8 / 0.1	13.3 / 0.1[b]
Refugees and others of concern to UNHCR (000)	0.7[j]	0.4[j]	0.4[e]
Infant mortality rate (per 1 000 live births)[i]	6.1	5.7	5.5[b]
Health: Total expenditure (% of GDP)	9.4	10.2	11.1[h]
Health: Physicians (per 1 000 pop.)	6.3	6.8	7.5[h]
Education: Government expenditure (% of GDP)	10.6	12.8	...
Education: Primary gross enrol. ratio (f/m per 100 pop.)	97.5 / 100.1	101.8 / 103.0	94.9 / 100.1[b]
Education: Secondary gross enrol. ratio (f/m per 100 pop.)	93.6 / 91.8	92.5 / 91.3	102.7 / 98.2[b]
Education: Tertiary gross enrol. ratio (f/m per 100 pop.)	79.6 / 46.8[f]	122.1 / 73.5	43.0 / 30.1[b]
Intentional homicide rate (per 100 000 pop.)	6.1	4.5	4.7[k]
Seats held by women in national parliaments (%)	36.0	43.2	48.9

Environment and infrastructure indicators	2005	2010	2017
Mobile-cellular subscriptions (per 100 inhabitants)	1.2	8.9	29.6[b]
Individuals using the Internet (per 100 inhabitants)	9.7[l]	15.9[l]	31.1[f,b]
Research & Development expenditure (% of GDP)	0.5	0.6	0.4[h]
Threatened species (number)	272[m]	304	339
Forested area (% of land area)	25.3	27.5[f]	30.2[f,h]
CO2 emission estimates (million tons/tons per capita)	26.0 / 2.3	38.4 / 3.4	34.8 / 3.0[h]
Energy production, primary (Petajoules)	205	200	212[h]
Energy supply per capita (Gigajoules)	37	50	47[h]
Tourist/visitor arrivals at national borders (000)[n]	2 261	2 507	3 491[b]
Important sites for terrestrial biodiversity protected (%)	44.1	69.4	74.3
Pop. using improved drinking water (urban/rural, %)	95.4 / 81.5	95.9 / 85.6	96.4 / 89.8[b]
Pop. using improved sanitation facilities (urban/rural, %)	91.5 / 81.9	93.3 / 86.4	94.4 / 89.1[b]
Net Official Development Assist. received (% of GNI)	0.22	0.21	...

a Projected estimate (medium fertility variant). b 2015. c The national currency of Cuba is the Cuban Peso (CUP). The convertible peso (CUC) is used by foreigners and tourists in Cuba. d UN operational exchange rate. e 2016. f Estimate. g 2008. h 2014. i Data refers to a 5-year period preceding the reference year. j Data as at the end of December. k 2011. l Including users of the international network and also those having access only to the Cuban network. m 2004. n Arrivals by air.

Curaçao

Region	Caribbean	Population (000, 2017)	160[a]
Surface area (km2)	444[b]	Pop. density (per km2, 2017)	361.6[a]
Sex ratio (m per 100 f, 2017)	84.6[a]	Capital city	Willemstad
National currency	Neth. Ant. Guilder (ANG)[c]	Capital city pop. (000)	144.7[d,e]
Exchange rate (per US$)	1.8[f]		

Economic indicators	2005	2010	2017
GDP: Gross domestic product (million current US$)	2 345	2 951	3 152[b]
GDP growth rate (annual %, const. 2005 prices)	...	0.1	0.3[b]
GDP per capita (current US$)	18 119.6	19 994.9	20 049.9[b]
Economy: Agriculture (% of GVA)[g]	0.6	0.5	0.5[b]
Economy: Industry (% of GVA)	16.4	16.0	19.8[b]
Economy: Services and other activity (% of GVA)	83.0	83.5	79.8[b]
Employment: Agriculture (% of employed)[h]	0.9	1.1[i]	...
Employment: Industry (% of employed)[h]	15.3	17.6[i]	...
Employment: Services (% of employed)[h]	83.8	81.3[i]	...
Unemployment (% of labour force)	18.2	9.6[j,k,l]	13.0[i,m]
Labour force participation (female/male pop. %)	54.8 / 65.4	53.2 / 66.5[i]	... / ...
CPI: Consumer Price Index (2000=100)	110	130	141[e]
Balance of payments, current account (million US$)	...	...	- 517[b]

Social indicators	2005	2010	2017
Population growth rate (average annual %)[n]	- 0.4	2.6	1.4[b]
Urban population (% of total population)	90.5	89.9	89.3[b]
Urban population growth rate (average annual %)[n]	- 0.5	2.5	2.0[b]
Fertility rate, total (live births per woman)[n]	2.1	2.0	2.1[b]
Life expectancy at birth (females/males, years)[n]	78.6 / 71.2	79.4 / 72.6	80.7 / 74.5[b]
Population age distribution (0-14 and 60+ years, %)	21.1 / 17.2	19.9 / 18.8	18.7 / 22.9[a]
International migrant stock (000/% of total pop.)	... / ...	34.6 / 23.5	37.6 / 23.9[b]
Refugees and others of concern to UNHCR (000)	...	~0.0[o]	0.1[f]
Infant mortality rate (per 1 000 live births)[n]	14.7	13.0	10.3[b]
Education: Government expenditure (% of GDP)	...	...	4.9[m]
Education: Primary gross enrol. ratio (f/m per 100 pop.)	... / ...	... / ...	171.3 / 179.1[m]
Education: Secondary gross enrol. ratio (f/m per 100 pop.)	... / ...	... / ...	90.6 / 86.1[m]
Education: Tertiary gross enrol. ratio (f/m per 100 pop.)	... / ...	... / ...	28.4 / 12.2[m]

Environment and infrastructure indicators	2005	2010	2017
Threatened species (number)	...	...	51
CO2 emission estimates (million tons/tons per capita)	... / ...	... / ...	5.9 / 37.8[e]
Energy production, primary (Petajoules)	...	...	0[e] .
Energy supply per capita (Gigajoules)	...	...	545[e]
Tourist/visitor arrivals at national borders (000)[p]	222	342	468[b]
Important sites for terrestrial biodiversity protected (%)	6.1	6.1	40.4

a Projected estimate (medium fertility variant). **b** 2015. **c** Netherlands Antillean Guilder. **d** Total population of Curaçao excluding some neighborhoods (see source). **e** 2014. **f** 2016. **g** Includes mining and quarrying. **h** Data classified according to ISIC Rev. 3. **i** 2008. **j** Excluding the institutional population. **k** Break in the time series. **l** 2009. **m** 2013. **n** Data refers to a 5-year period preceding the reference year. **o** Data as at the end of December. **p** Arrivals by air.

Cyprus

Region	Western Asia	UN membership date	20 September 1960
Population (000, 2017)	1 180 [a,b]	Surface area (km2)	9 251 [c]
Pop. density (per km2, 2017)	127.7 [a,b]	Sex ratio (m per 100 f, 2017)	100.2 [a,b]
Capital city	Nicosia	National currency	Euro (EUR)
Capital city pop. (000)	251.1 [d]	Exchange rate (per US$)	0.9 [e]

Economic indicators	2005	2010	2017
GDP: Gross domestic product (million current US$) [f]	18 694	25 561	19 561 [c]
GDP growth rate (annual %, const. 2005 prices) [f]	3.7	1.3	1.7 [c]
GDP per capita (current US$) [f]	25 311.4	30 816.6	21 941.9 [c]
Economy: Agriculture (% of GVA) [f,g]	3.1	2.4	2.3 [c]
Economy: Industry (% of GVA) [f,g]	20.5	16.7	10.6 [c]
Economy: Services and other activity (% of GVA) [f,g]	76.4	80.9	87.2 [c]
Employment: Agriculture (% of employed) [h]	4.7	3.8	4.1
Employment: Industry (% of employed) [h]	24.0	20.4	16.7
Employment: Services (% of employed) [h]	71.2	75.8	79.2
Unemployment (% of labour force)	5.3	6.3	10.3 [h]
Labour force participation (female/male pop. %) [h]	53.6 / 73.1	57.1 / 71.3	57.8 / 70.4
CPI: Consumer Price Index (2000=100)	115	129	134 [d]
Agricultural production index (2004-2006=100)	98	83	80 [d]
Food production index (2004-2006=100)	98	84	80 [d]
Index of industrial production (2005=100) [i]	100	100	72 [d]
International trade: Exports (million US$)	1 546	1 506	1 920 [e]
International trade: Imports (million US$)	6 382	8 645	6 604 [e]
International trade: Balance (million US$)	- 4 836	- 7 138	- 4 684 [e]
Balance of payments, current account (million US$)	- 971	- 2 906	- 576 [c]

Major trading partners						2016
Export partners (% of exports)	Greece	12.3	United Kingdom	7.6	Libya	7.5
Import partners (% of imports)	Greece	21.3	Germany	16.3	Italy	6.6

Social indicators	2005	2010	2017
Population growth rate (average annual %) [b,j]	1.7	1.6	0.9 [c]
Urban population (% of total population)	68.3	67.6	66.9 [c]
Urban population growth rate (average annual %) [j]	1.7	1.1	0.9 [c]
Fertility rate, total (live births per woman) [b,j]	1.6	1.5	1.4 [c]
Life expectancy at birth (females/males, years) [b,j]	80.4 / 76.2	81.1 / 76.8	82.2 / 77.7 [c]
Population age distribution (0-14 and 60+ years, %) [b]	20.0 / 14.9	17.8 / 16.1	16.8 / 18.5 [a]
International migrant stock (000/% of total pop.) [k]	117.2 / 11.3	187.9 / 17.0	196.2 / 16.8 [c]
Refugees and others of concern to UNHCR (000)	13.8 [l]	8.8 [l]	16.2 [e]
Infant mortality rate (per 1 000 live births) [b,j]	5.6	4.4	4.2 [c]
Health: Total expenditure (% of GDP) [m]	6.4	7.2 [n]	7.4 [n,d]
Health: Physicians (per 1 000 pop.)	...	2.2	2.5 [d]
Education: Government expenditure (% of GDP)	6.2	6.6	6.1 [d]
Education: Primary gross enrol. ratio (f/m per 100 pop.) [h]	100.8 / 100.9	101.6 / 101.6	99.3 / 99.3 [c]
Education: Secondary gross enrol. ratio (f/m per 100 pop.) [h]	97.5 / 95.7	92.0 / 90.9	99.4 / 100.1 [c]
Education: Tertiary gross enrol. ratio (f/m per 100 pop.) [h]	35.3 / 31.2	45.6 / 50.9	69.4 / 51.1 [c]
Intentional homicide rate (per 100 000 pop.)	1.9	0.7	1.3 [c]
Seats held by women in national parliaments (%)	16.1	12.5	17.9

Environment and infrastructure indicators	2005	2010	2017
Mobile-cellular subscriptions (per 100 inhabitants)	75.8	93.7	95.4 [c]
Individuals using the Internet (per 100 inhabitants) [o]	32.8	53.0	71.7 [c]
Research & Development expenditure (% of GDP)	0.4	0.5	0.5 [p,d]
Threatened species (number)	25 [q]	43	72
Forested area (% of land area)	18.7	18.7	18.7 [h,d]
CO2 emission estimates (million tons/tons per capita)	7.5 / 7.3	7.7 / 7.0	6.1 / 5.2 [d]
Energy production, primary (Petajoules)	0	4	5 [d]
Energy supply per capita (Gigajoules)	89	94	72 [d]
Tourist/visitor arrivals at national borders (000)	2 470	2 173	2 659 [c]
Important sites for terrestrial biodiversity protected (%)	36.1	54.5	57.8
Pop. using improved drinking water (urban/rural, %)	100.0 / 100.0	100.0 / 100.0	100.0 / 100.0 [c]
Pop. using improved sanitation facilities (urban/rural, %)	100.0 / 100.0	100.0 / 100.0	100.0 / 100.0 [c]
Net Official Development Assist. disbursed (% of GNI) [j]	0.09	0.23	0.09 [c]

a Projected estimate (medium fertility variant). b Refers to the whole country. c 2015. d 2014. e 2016. f Excluding northern Cyprus. g Data classified according to ISIC Rev. 4. h Estimate. i Data refer to government controlled areas. j Data refers to a 5-year period preceding the reference year. k Including northern Cyprus. l Data as at the end of December. m Data is converted from SHA 2011. n Break in the time series. o Population aged 16 to 74 years. p Provisional data. q 2004.

Czechia

Region	Eastern Europe	UN membership date	19 January 1993
Population (000, 2017)	10 618[a]	Surface area (km2)	78 868[b]
Pop. density (per km2, 2017)	137.5[a]	Sex ratio (m per 100 f, 2017)	96.7[a]
Capital city	Prague	National currency	Czech Koruna (CZK)
Capital city pop. (000)	1 313.6[b]	Exchange rate (per US$)	25.6[c]

Economic indicators

	2005	2010	2017
GDP: Gross domestic product (million current US$)	135 990	207 016	185 156[b]
GDP growth rate (annual %, const. 2005 prices)	6.4	2.3	4.5[b]
GDP per capita (current US$)	13 292.1	19 703.4	17 561.7[b]
Economy: Agriculture (% of GVA)[d]	2.4	1.7	2.5[b]
Economy: Industry (% of GVA)[d]	37.7	36.8	37.8[b]
Economy: Services and other activity (% of GVA)[d]	59.8	61.5	59.7[b]
Employment: Agriculture (% of employed)[e]	4.0	3.1	2.5
Employment: Industry (% of employed)[e]	39.5	38.0	37.0
Employment: Services (% of employed)[e]	56.5	58.9	60.5
Unemployment (% of labour force)	7.9	7.3	3.9[e]
Labour force participation (female/male pop. %)[e]	50.8 / 68.9	49.3 / 68.0	51.3 / 67.8
CPI: Consumer Price Index (2000=100)	112	129	138[f]
Agricultural production index (2004-2006=100)	100	91	102[f]
Food production index (2004-2006=100)	100	91	102[f]
Index of industrial production (2005=100)	100	110[g]	122[g,f]
International trade: Exports (million US$)	78 209	132 141	161 248[c]
International trade: Imports (million US$)	76 527	125 691	140 316[c]
International trade: Balance (million US$)	1 681	6 450	20 932[c]
Balance of payments, current account (million US$)	- 2 810	- 7 351	1 683[b]

Major trading partners

					2016
Export partners (% of exports)	Germany	32.5	Slovakia	8.4	Poland	5.7
Import partners (% of imports)	Germany	26.7	China	12.7	Poland	8.3

Social indicators

	2005	2010	2017
Population growth rate (average annual %)[h]	- 0.1	0.5	0.1[b]
Urban population (% of total population)	73.6	73.3	73.0[b]
Urban population growth rate (average annual %)[h]	- 0.1	0.5	0.3[b]
Fertility rate, total (live births per woman)[h]	1.2	1.4	1.5[b]
Life expectancy at birth (females/males, years)[h]	78.8 / 72.2	80.1 / 73.8	81.2 / 75.1[b]
Population age distribution (0-14 and 60+ years, %)	14.7 / 19.8	14.2 / 22.4	15.4 / 25.6[a]
International migrant stock (000/% of total pop.)[i]	322.5 / 3.2	397.8 / 3.8	405.1 / 3.8[b]
Refugees and others of concern to UNHCR (000)	2.7[j]	3.5[j]	6.0[c]
Infant mortality rate (per 1 000 live births)[h]	3.9	3.1	2.5[b]
Health: Total expenditure (% of GDP)	6.9	7.4	7.4[f]
Health: Physicians (per 1 000 pop.)	...	3.6	3.7[k]
Education: Government expenditure (% of GDP)	3.9	4.1	4.1[k]
Education: Primary gross enrol. ratio (f/m per 100 pop.)	98.7 / 100.1	103.8 / 104.2	99.9 / 99.6[b]
Education: Secondary gross enrol. ratio (f/m per 100 pop.)	96.7 / 95.0	95.1 / 94.6	106.1 / 105.1[b]
Education: Tertiary gross enrol. ratio (f/m per 100 pop.)	52.1 / 44.9	75.0 / 53.7	76.3 / 54.2[b]
Intentional homicide rate (per 100 000 pop.)	1.1	1.0	0.8[b]
Seats held by women in national parliaments (%)	17.0	15.5	20.0

Environment and infrastructure indicators

	2005	2010	2017
Mobile-cellular subscriptions (per 100 inhabitants)	115.1	122.6	129.2[e,b]
Individuals using the Internet (per 100 inhabitants)[f]	35.3	68.8	81.3[b]
Research & Development expenditure (% of GDP)	1.2	1.3	2.0[m,f]
Threatened species (number)	45[n]	33	53
Forested area (% of land area)	34.3	34.4	34.5[e,f]
CO2 emission estimates (million tons/tons per capita)	120.1 / 11.7	111.6 / 10.6	96.5 / 9.2[f]
Energy production, primary (Petajoules)	1 374	1 321	1 221[f]
Energy supply per capita (Gigajoules)	184	177	164[f]
Tourist/visitor arrivals at national borders (000)	9 404	8 629	11 148[b]
Important sites for terrestrial biodiversity protected (%)	89.2	93.8	93.8
Pop. using improved drinking water (urban/rural, %)	99.9 / 99.7	100.0 / 99.9	100.0 / 100.0[b]
Pop. using improved sanitation facilities (urban/rural, %)	99.1 / 99.2	99.1 / 99.2	99.1 / 99.2[b]
Net Official Development Assist. disbursed (% of GNI)[o]	0.11	0.13	0.14[m,c]

a Projected estimate (medium fertility variant). **b** 2015. **c** 2016. **d** Data classified according to ISIC Rev. 4. **e** Estimate. **f** 2014. **g** Excluding water and waste management. **h** Data refers to a 5-year period preceding the reference year. **i** Refers to foreign citizens. **j** Data as at the end of December. **k** 2013. **l** Population aged 16 to 74 years. **m** Provisional data. **n** 2004. **o** Development Assistance Committee member (OECD)

Democratic People's Republic of Korea

Region	Eastern Asia	UN membership date	17 September 1991
Population (000, 2017)	25 491 [a]	Surface area (km2)	120 538 [b]
Pop. density (per km2, 2017)	211.7 [a]	Sex ratio (m per 100 f, 2017)	95.7 [a]
Capital city	Pyongyang	National currency	North Korean Won (KPW)
Capital city pop. (000)	2 862.9 [b]	Exchange rate (per US$)	110.9 [c,d]

Economic indicators

	2005	2010	2017
GDP: Gross domestic product (million current US$)	13 031	13 945	16 283 [b]
GDP growth rate (annual %, const. 2005 prices)	3.8	- 0.5	- 1.1 [b]
GDP per capita (current US$)	547.9	569.8	648.0 [b]
Economy: Agriculture (% of GVA)	25.0	20.8	21.6 [b]
Economy: Industry (% of GVA)	42.8	48.2	46.2 [b]
Economy: Services and other activity (% of GVA)	32.2	31.0	32.2 [b]
Employment: Agriculture (% of employed) [e]	59.7	58.9	58.9
Employment: Industry (% of employed) [e]	18.5	19.6	19.3
Employment: Services (% of employed) [e]	21.9	21.4	21.8
Unemployment (% of labour force) [e]	4.5	4.4	4.3
Labour force participation (female/male pop. %) [e]	74.5 / 88.6	73.9 / 86.9	73.6 / 85.9
Agricultural production index (2004-2006=100)	101	98	104 [f]
Food production index (2004-2006=100)	101	97	103 [f]
International trade: Exports (million US$)	787	882	1 010 [d]
International trade: Imports (million US$)	1 466	1 957	2 757 [d]
International trade: Balance (million US$)	- 679	- 1 075	- 1 748 [d]

Major trading partners

						2016
Export partners (% of exports)	China	84.0	India	2.8	Philippines	1.7
Import partners (% of imports)	China	88.4	Thailand	2.3	Russian Federation	2.1

Social indicators

	2005	2010	2017
Population growth rate (average annual %) [g]	0.8	0.6	0.5 [b]
Urban population (% of total population)	59.8	60.2	60.9 [b]
Urban population growth rate (average annual %) [g]	1.0	0.7	0.7 [b]
Fertility rate, total (live births per woman) [g]	2.0	2.0	2.0 [b]
Life expectancy at birth (females/males, years) [g]	71.5 / 64.2	71.8 / 64.8	74.1 / 67.2 [b]
Population age distribution (0-14 and 60+ years, %)	24.7 / 11.9	22.8 / 12.9	20.6 / 13.5 [a]
International migrant stock (000/% of total pop.) [e]	40.1 / 0.2	44.0 / 0.2	48.5 / 0.2 [b]
Infant mortality rate (per 1 000 live births) [g]	28.5	27.3	18.5 [b]
Health: Physicians (per 1 000 pop.)	3.2 [h]	...	2.8 [i]
Education: Primary gross enrol. ratio (f/m per 100 pop.)	... / ...	99.8 / 99.8 [i]	76.9 / 76.7 [b]
Education: Secondary gross enrol. ratio (f/m per 100 pop.)	... / ...	102.0 / 102.1 [i]	93.9 / 92.9 [b]
Education: Tertiary gross enrol. ratio (f/m per 100 pop.)	... / ...	20.6 / 40.8 [i]	19.8 / 36.0 [b]
Intentional homicide rate (per 100 000 pop.)	5.1	4.8	4.4 [b]
Seats held by women in national parliaments (%)	20.1	15.6	16.3

Environment and infrastructure indicators

	2005	2010	2017
Mobile-cellular subscriptions (per 100 inhabitants)	0.0	1.8	12.9 [e,b]
Individuals using the Internet (per 100 inhabitants)	0.0 [k]	0.0 [e]	0.0 [e,l]
Threatened species (number)	44 [m]	52	78
Forested area (% of land area) [e]	52.3	47.1	42.8 [f]
CO2 emission estimates (million tons/tons per capita)	75.6 / 3.2	66.5 / 2.7	40.5 / 1.6 [f]
Energy production, primary (Petajoules)	923	872	871 [f]
Energy supply per capita (Gigajoules)	38	32	20 [f]
Important sites for terrestrial biodiversity protected (%)	10.2	10.2	10.2
Pop. using improved drinking water (urban/rural, %)	99.9 / 99.6	99.9 / 99.4	99.9 / 99.4 [b]
Pop. using improved sanitation facilities (urban/rural, %)	75.5 / 62.8	85.9 / 70.9	87.9 / 72.5 [b]

a Projected estimate (medium fertility variant). **b** 2015. **c** UN operational exchange rate. **d** 2016. **e** Estimate. **f** 2014. **g** Data refers to a 5-year period preceding the reference year. **h** 2003. **i** 2011. **j** 2009. **k** Commercially not available. Local Intranet available in country. **l** 2012. **m** 2004.

Democratic Republic of the Congo

Region	Middle Africa	UN membership date	20 September 1960
Population (000, 2017)	81 340 a	Surface area (km2)	2 344 858 b
Pop. density (per km2, 2017)	35.9 a	Sex ratio (m per 100 f, 2017)	99.6 a
Capital city	Kinshasa	National currency	Congolese Franc (CDF)
Capital city pop. (000)	11 586.9 b	Exchange rate (per US$)	1 215.6 c

Economic indicators	2005	2010	2017
GDP: Gross domestic product (million current US$)	11 965	21 672	37 569 b
GDP growth rate (annual %, const. 2005 prices)	6.1	7.1	7.0 b
GDP per capita (current US$)	213.3	328.7	486.2 b
Economy: Agriculture (% of GVA)	22.3	22.4	19.9 b
Economy: Industry (% of GVA)	32.9	40.5	44.2 b
Economy: Services and other activity (% of GVA)	44.9	37.0	35.9 b
Employment: Agriculture (% of employed) d	68.7	68.1	65.3
Employment: Industry (% of employed) d	6.1	6.0	5.9
Employment: Services (% of employed) d	25.2	25.9	28.9
Unemployment (% of labour force)	3.7	3.7 d	3.6 d
Labour force participation (female/male pop. %) d	70.9 / 73.0	70.7 / 72.2	70.4 / 71.8
Agricultural production index (2004-2006=100)	100	106	104 e
Food production index (2004-2006=100)	100	106	104 e
International trade: Exports (million US$)	2 190	5 300	5 103 c
International trade: Imports (million US$)	2 268	4 500	5 906 c
International trade: Balance (million US$)	- 78	800	- 803 c
Balance of payments, current account (million US$)	- 389	- 2 174	- 1 546 b

Major trading partners						2016
Export partners (% of exports)	China	37.4	Zambia	15.0	Saudi Arabia	9.0
Import partners (% of imports)	China	20.3	South Africa	15.9	Zambia	9.9

Social indicators	2005	2010	2017
Population growth rate (average annual %) f	3.0	3.3	3.3 b
Urban population (% of total population)	37.5	39.9	42.5 b
Urban population growth rate (average annual %) f	4.1	4.1	4.0 b
Fertility rate, total (live births per woman) f	6.7	6.6	6.4 b
Life expectancy at birth (females/males, years) f	53.3 / 50.4	56.9 / 54.0	59.5 / 56.7 b
Population age distribution (0-14 and 60+ years, %)	45.8 / 4.7	46.1 / 4.7	46.3 / 4.7 a
International migrant stock (000/% of total pop.) g	622.9 / 1.1	589.0 / 0.9	545.7 / 0.7 b
Refugees and others of concern to UNHCR (000)	251.9 h	2 363.9 h	2 163.3 c
Infant mortality rate (per 1 000 live births) f	99.5	83.9	73.2 b
Health: Total expenditure (% of GDP) i	3.1	4.0	4.3 e
Health: Physicians (per 1 000 pop.)	...	0.1 j	...
Education: Government expenditure (% of GDP)	...	1.6	2.2 k
Education: Primary gross enrol. ratio (f/m per 100 pop.)	56.5 / 71.6 l	89.1 / 102.3	101.8 / 112.0 e
Education: Secondary gross enrol. ratio (f/m per 100 pop.)	... / ...	28.8 / 49.9	33.3 / 53.6 e
Education: Tertiary gross enrol. ratio (f/m per 100 pop.)	... / ...	3.1 / 9.9 j	4.2 / 9.1 k
Intentional homicide rate (per 100 000 pop.)	14.3	14.0	13.4 b
Seats held by women in national parliaments (%)	12.0	8.4	8.9

Environment and infrastructure indicators	2005	2010	2017
Mobile-cellular subscriptions (per 100 inhabitants)	5.1 m	19.0	53.0 b
Individuals using the Internet (per 100 inhabitants) d	0.2	0.7	3.8 b
Research & Development expenditure (% of GDP) o,p	0.1 n	0.1 j	...
Threatened species (number)	171 q	296	349
Forested area (% of land area) d	68.7	68.0	67.4 e
CO2 emission estimates (million tons/tons per capita)	1.5 / ~0.0	2.0 / ~0.0	4.7 / 0.1 e
Energy production, primary (Petajoules)	866	855	1 179 e
Energy supply per capita (Gigajoules)	14	13	16 e
Tourist/visitor arrivals at national borders (000)	61	81 r	191 s,k
Important sites for terrestrial biodiversity protected (%)	34.7	36.7	36.7
Pop. using improved drinking water (urban/rural, %)	83.5 / 28.2	82.3 / 29.7	81.1 / 31.2 b
Pop. using improved sanitation facilities (urban/rural, %)	29.2 / 22.2	28.9 / 25.5	28.5 / 28.7 b
Net Official Development Assist. received (% of GNI)	16.43	17.76	8.01 b

a Projected estimate (medium fertility variant). b 2015. c 2016. d Estimate. e 2014. f Data refers to a 5-year period preceding the reference year. g Including refugees. h Data as at the end of December. i Data revision. j 2009. k 2013. l 2002. m Includes inactive subscriptions. n Break in the time series. o Government only. p S&T budget instead of R&D expenditure. q 2004. r Arrivals by air. s The arrivals data relate only to three border posts (N'Djili airport in Kinshasa, the Luano airport in Lubumbashi, and the land border-crossing of Kasumbalesa in Katanga province).

Denmark

Region	Northern Europe	UN membership date	24 October 1945
Population (000, 2017)	5 734[a]	Surface area (km2)	42 921[b]
Pop. density (per km2, 2017)	135.1[a]	Sex ratio (m per 100 f, 2017)	99.0[a]
Capital city	Copenhagen	National currency	Danish Krone (DKK)
Capital city pop. (000)	1 268.1[c,b]	Exchange rate (per US$)	7.1[d]

Economic indicators

	2005	2010	2017
GDP: Gross domestic product (million current US$)	264 467	321 995	301 308[b]
GDP growth rate (annual %, const. 2005 prices)	2.3	1.9	1.6[b]
GDP per capita (current US$)	48 815.4	58 007.2	53 149.3[b]
Economy: Agriculture (% of GVA)[e]	1.3	1.4	1.2[b]
Economy: Industry (% of GVA)[e]	26.2	22.8	22.9[b]
Economy: Services and other activity (% of GVA)[e]	72.5	75.8	75.8[b]
Employment: Agriculture (% of employed)[f]	3.2	2.4	2.4
Employment: Industry (% of employed)[f]	23.9	19.6	19.2
Employment: Services (% of employed)[f]	72.9	78.0	78.4
Unemployment (% of labour force)	4.8	7.5	6.0[f]
Labour force participation (female/male pop. %)[f]	60.5 / 71.4	59.8 / 69.1	58.1 / 66.0
CPI: Consumer Price Index (2000=100)	110	122	131[g]
Agricultural production index (2004-2006=100)	101	101	105[g]
Food production index (2004-2006=100)	101	101	105[g]
Index of industrial production (2005=100)	100	86[h]	89[h,g]
International trade: Exports (million US$)	82 278	96 217	94 355[d]
International trade: Imports (million US$)	72 716	82 724	85 133[d]
International trade: Balance (million US$)	9 562	13 492	9 222[d]
Balance of payments, current account (million US$)	11 104	18 183	27 582[b]

Major trading partners

						2016
Export partners (% of exports)	Germany	20.3	Sweden	14.1	Norway	6.2
Import partners (% of imports)	Germany	21.6	Sweden	12.1	Netherlands	8.0

Social indicators

	2005	2010	2017
Population growth rate (average annual %)[i]	0.3	0.5	0.5[b]
Urban population (% of total population)	85.9	86.8	87.7[b]
Urban population growth rate (average annual %)[i]	0.5	0.7	0.6[b]
Fertility rate, total (live births per woman)[i]	1.8	1.9	1.7[b]
Life expectancy at birth (females/males, years)[i]	79.6 / 75.0	80.8 / 76.4	82.2 / 78.1[b]
Population age distribution (0-14 and 60+ years, %)	18.7 / 21.2	17.9 / 23.3	16.5 / 25.3[a]
International migrant stock (000/% of total pop.)	440.4 / 8.1	509.7 / 9.2	572.5 / 10.1[b]
Refugees and others of concern to UNHCR (000)	45.5[j]	24.5[j]	48.2[d]
Infant mortality rate (per 1 000 live births)[i]	4.5	3.7	3.5[b]
Health: Total expenditure (% of GDP)	9.8	11.1	10.8[g]
Health: Physicians (per 1 000 pop.)	3.2	3.6	3.6[k]
Education: Government expenditure (% of GDP)	8.1	8.6	8.6[k]
Education: Primary gross enrol. ratio (f/m per 100 pop.)	98.7 / 98.9	99.7 / 99.5	100.7 / 102.3[b]
Education: Secondary gross enrol. ratio (f/m per 100 pop.)	126.5 / 122.0	120.1 / 119.0	133.4 / 128.3[b]
Education: Tertiary gross enrol. ratio (f/m per 100 pop.)	93.4 / 67.7	87.5 / 60.4	96.3 / 69.7[b]
Intentional homicide rate (per 100 000 pop.)	1.0	0.8	1.0[b]
Seats held by women in national parliaments (%)	38.0	38.0	37.4

Environment and infrastructure indicators

	2005	2010	2017
Mobile-cellular subscriptions (per 100 inhabitants)	100.6	115.7[l,m]	128.3[b]
Individuals using the Internet (per 100 inhabitants)[n]	82.7	88.7	96.3[b]
Research & Development expenditure (% of GDP)	2.4	2.9	3.1[f,g]
Threatened species (number)	35[o]	33	47
Forested area (% of land area)	13.1	13.8	14.4[f,g]
CO2 emission estimates (million tons/tons per capita)	47.1 / 8.7	46.6 / 8.4	33.5 / 5.9[g]
Energy production, primary (Petajoules)[p]	1 298	968	666[g]
Energy supply per capita (Gigajoules)[p]	145	146	119[g]
Tourist/visitor arrivals at national borders (000)	9 587	9 425	10 424[b]
Important sites for terrestrial biodiversity protected (%)	89.8	90.3	90.3
Pop. using improved drinking water (urban/rural, %)	100.0 / 100.0	100.0 / 100.0	100.0 / 100.0[b]
Pop. using improved sanitation facilities (urban/rural, %)	99.6 / 99.6	99.6 / 99.6	99.6 / 99.6[b]
Net Official Development Assist. disbursed (% of GNI)[q]	0.81	0.91	0.75[r,d]

a Projected estimate (medium fertility variant). b 2015. c Refers to the Greater Copenhagen Region, consisting of (parts of) 16 municipalities. d 2016. e Data classified according to ISIC Rev. 4. f Estimate. g 2014. h Excluding water and waste management. i Data refers to a 5-year period preceding the reference year. j Data as at the end of December. k 2013. l Excludes telemetry subscriptions. m Break in the time series. n Population aged 16 to 74 years. o 2004. p Excluding the Faroe Islands and Greenland. q Development Assistance Committee member (OECD) r Provisional data.

Djibouti

Region	Eastern Africa	UN membership date	20 September 1977
Population (000, 2017)	957[a]	Surface area (km2)	23 200[b]
Pop. density (per km2, 2017)	41.3[a]	Sex ratio (m per 100 f, 2017)	100.7[a]
Capital city	Djibouti	National currency	Djibouti Franc (DJF)
Capital city pop. (000)	528.6[c,b]	Exchange rate (per US$)	177.7[d]

Economic indicators	2005	2010	2017
GDP: Gross domestic product (million current US$)	709	1 067	1 737[b]
GDP growth rate (annual %, const. 2005 prices)	3.2	3.5	6.5[b]
GDP per capita (current US$)	910.4	1 284.3	1 956.3[b]
Economy: Agriculture (% of GVA)	3.6	3.6	3.3[b]
Economy: Industry (% of GVA)	16.2	19.0	21.4[b]
Economy: Services and other activity (% of GVA)	80.2	77.4	75.3[b]
Employment: Agriculture (% of employed)[e]	27.0	25.5	22.8
Employment: Industry (% of employed)[e]	21.2	22.9	23.9
Employment: Services (% of employed)[e]	51.8	51.5	53.2
Unemployment (% of labour force)[e]	6.8	6.7	6.6
Labour force participation (female/male pop. %)[e]	33.0 / 66.2	35.6 / 66.8	36.5 / 68.5
Agricultural production index (2004-2006=100)	95	116	133[f]
Food production index (2004-2006=100)	95	116	133[f]
International trade: Exports (million US$)	39	100	134[d]
International trade: Imports (million US$)	277	420	987[d]
International trade: Balance (million US$)	- 238	- 320	- 852[d]
Balance of payments, current account (million US$)	20	50	- 548[b]

Major trading partners							2016
Export partners (% of exports)	United States	23.3	Saudi Arabia	21.3	United Arab Emirates	15.1
Import partners (% of imports)	China	49.2	India	6.1	Indonesia	4.7

Social indicators	2005	2010	2017
Population growth rate (average annual %)[g]	1.8	1.7	1.7[b]
Urban population (% of total population)	76.8	77.0	77.3[b]
Urban population growth rate (average annual %)[g]	1.5	1.5	1.6[b]
Fertility rate, total (live births per woman)[g]	4.2	3.6	3.1[b]
Life expectancy at birth (females/males, years)[g]	58.8 / 55.8	60.5 / 57.6	63.2 / 60.0[b]
Population age distribution (0-14 and 60+ years, %)	37.9 / 5.2	34.8 / 5.8	31.1 / 6.4[a]
International migrant stock (000/% of total pop.)[h]	92.1 / 11.8	101.6 / 12.2	112.4 / 12.7[b]
Refugees and others of concern to UNHCR (000)	18.1[i]	15.8[i]	19.9[d]
Infant mortality rate (per 1 000 live births)[g]	68.1	63.4	55.3[b]
Health: Total expenditure (% of GDP)	7.2	8.8	10.6[f]
Health: Physicians (per 1 000 pop.)	0.2	0.2[j]	0.2[f]
Education: Government expenditure (% of GDP)	8.4	4.5	...
Education: Primary gross enrol. ratio (f/m per 100 pop.)	39.2 / 47.6	56.6 / 62.8[k]	60.9 / 68.6[d]
Education: Secondary gross enrol. ratio (f/m per 100 pop.)	18.0 / 26.9	28.4 / 38.5[k]	43.5 / 52.9[d]
Education: Tertiary gross enrol. ratio (f/m per 100 pop.)	2.0 / 2.7	2.8 / 4.1	4.0 / 5.9[l]
Intentional homicide rate (per 100 000 pop.)	8.2	7.6	6.8[b]
Seats held by women in national parliaments (%)	10.8	13.8	10.8

Environment and infrastructure indicators	2005	2010	2017
Mobile-cellular subscriptions (per 100 inhabitants)	5.7	19.9	34.7[e,b]
Individuals using the Internet (per 100 inhabitants)	1.0	6.5[e]	11.9[e,b]
Threatened species (number)	21[m]	81	98
Forested area (% of land area)[e]	0.2	0.2	0.2[f]
CO2 emission estimates (million tons/tons per capita)	0.4 / 0.5	0.5 / 0.6	0.7 / 0.8[f]
Energy production, primary (Petajoules)	3	3	3[f]
Energy supply per capita (Gigajoules)	11[e]	13	13[e,f]
Tourist/visitor arrivals at national borders (000)	30	51	63[n]
Important sites for terrestrial biodiversity protected (%)	0.0	0.0	0.9
Pop. using improved drinking water (urban/rural, %)	92.5 / 63.3	96.6 / 64.5	97.4 / 64.7[b]
Pop. using improved sanitation facilities (urban/rural, %)	64.5 / 18.9	60.6 / 7.4	59.8 / 5.1[b]
Net Official Development Assist. received (% of GNI)	9.56	...	...

a Projected estimate (medium fertility variant). b 2015. c Refers to the population of the "cercle". d 2016. e Estimate. f 2014. g Data refers to a 5-year period preceding the reference year. h Including refugees. i Data as at the end of December. j 2006. k 2009. l 2011. m 2004. n 2013.

Dominica

Region	Caribbean	UN membership date	18 December 1978
Population (000, 2017)	74[a]	Surface area (km2)	750[b]
Pop. density (per km2, 2017)	98.6[a]	Sex ratio (m per 100 f, 2017)	103.0[c]
Capital city	Roseau	National currency	E. Caribbean Dollar (XCD)[d]
Capital city pop. (000)	15.0[c]	Exchange rate (per US$)	2.7[e]

Economic indicators

	2005	2010	2017
GDP: Gross domestic product (million current US$)	370	494	512[b]
GDP growth rate (annual %, const. 2005 prices)	- 0.3	1.2	- 1.8[b]
GDP per capita (current US$)	5 251.0	6 939.0	7 051.1[b]
Economy: Agriculture (% of GVA)	13.2	13.8	15.4[b]
Economy: Industry (% of GVA)	15.0	14.4	13.2[b]
Economy: Services and other activity (% of GVA)	71.9	71.8	71.5[b]
Employment: Agriculture (% of employed)	21.0[f,g,h]	...	...
Employment: Industry (% of employed)	20.0[f,g,h]	...	...
Employment: Services (% of employed)	58.8[f,g,h]	...	...
Unemployment (% of labour force)	11.0[h]	...	...
Labour force participation (female/male pop. %)	45.0 / 70.2[h]	... / ...	... / ...
CPI: Consumer Price Index (2000=100)[i]	106[f]	122[j]	126[k]
Agricultural production index (2004-2006=100)	99	108	110[c]
Food production index (2004-2006=100)	99	108	111[c]
International trade: Exports (million US$)	42	34	23[e]
International trade: Imports (million US$)	165	225	214[e]
International trade: Balance (million US$)	- 124	- 190	- 191[e]
Balance of payments, current account (million US$)	- 76	- 80	- 72[k]

Major trading partners

						2016
Export partners (% of exports)	Bahamas	43.0	Poland	20.5	Saudi Arabia	6.9
Import partners (% of imports)	United States	24.4	China	16.8	United Kingdom	5.7

Social indicators

	2005	2010	2017
Population growth rate (average annual %)[l]	0.3	0.2	0.5[b]
Urban population (% of total population)	66.6	68.1	69.5[b]
Urban population growth rate (average annual %)[l]	0.7	0.6	0.8[b]
Fertility rate, total (live births per woman)	3.0[h]	...	...
Life expectancy at birth (females/males, years)	... / ...	78.2 / 73.8[m]	... / ...
Population age distribution (0-14 and 60+ years, %)	29.0 / 13.2[n,h]	29.5 / 13.3[o]	... / ...
International migrant stock (000/% of total pop.)	4.7 / 6.7	5.8 / 8.1	6.7 / 9.2[b]
Health: Total expenditure (% of GDP)	4.6	5.7	5.5[c]
Health: Physicians (per 1 000 pop.)	1.8[h]		
Education: Primary gross enrol. ratio (f/m per 100 pop.)	99.4 / 99.4	107.6 / 110.0	114.8 / 117.2[b]
Education: Secondary gross enrol. ratio (f/m per 100 pop.)	111.7 / 103.3	101.4 / 92.8	99.8 / 101.2[b]
Intentional homicide rate (per 100 000 pop.)	11.3	21.1	8.4[p]
Seats held by women in national parliaments (%)	19.4	14.3	25.0

Environment and infrastructure indicators

	2005	2010	2017
Mobile-cellular subscriptions (per 100 inhabitants)	73.7	148.3[q]	106.3[b]
Individuals using the Internet (per 100 inhabitants)	38.5[q]	47.4	67.6[q,b]
Threatened species (number)	33[r]	48	66
Forested area (% of land area)[q]	61.3	59.5	58.1[c]
CO2 emission estimates (million tons/tons per capita)	0.1 / 1.7	0.1 / 1.9	0.1 / 1.9[c]
Energy production, primary (Petajoules)	0	0	0[c]
Energy supply per capita (Gigajoules)	26	29[q]	29[q,c]
Tourist/visitor arrivals at national borders (000)	79	77	75[b]
Important sites for terrestrial biodiversity protected (%)	44.3	44.3	44.3
Pop. using improved drinking water (urban/rural, %)	95.7 / 91.8	95.7 / ...	95.7 / ...[b]
Pop. using improved sanitation facilities (urban/rural, %)	79.6 / 84.3	... / ...	... / ...
Net Official Development Assist. received (% of GNI)	6.19	6.71	2.36[b]

a Projected estimate (medium fertility variant). **b** 2015. **c** 2014. **d** East Caribbean Dollar. **e** 2016. **f** Break in the time series. **g** Data classified according to ISIC Rev. 2. **h** 2001. **i** Index base: 2001=100. **j** Series linked to former series. **k** 2013. **l** Data refers to a 5-year period preceding the reference year. **m** 2008. **n** Data have not been adjusted for underenumeration, estimated at 1.4 per cent. **o** 2006. **p** 2011. **q** Estimate. **r** 2004.

Dominican Republic

Region	Caribbean	UN membership date	24 October 1945
Population (000, 2017)	10 767[a]	Surface area (km2)	48 671[b]
Pop. density (per km2, 2017)	222.8[a]	Sex ratio (m per 100 f, 2017)	99.2[a]
Capital city	Santo Domingo	National currency	Dominican Peso (DOP)
Capital city pop. (000)	2 945.4[b]	Exchange rate (per US$)	46.7[c]

Economic indicators	2005	2010	2017
GDP: Gross domestic product (million current US$)	35 510	53 043	67 103[b]
GDP growth rate (annual %, const. 2005 prices)	9.3	8.3	7.0[b]
GDP per capita (current US$)	3 844.1	5 359.0	6 373.6[b]
Economy: Agriculture (% of GVA)[d]	7.7	6.5	6.6[b]
Economy: Industry (% of GVA)[d]	32.5	30.1	28.0[b]
Economy: Services and other activity (% of GVA)[d]	59.8	63.4	65.4[b]
Employment: Agriculture (% of employed)[e]	14.5	14.6	13.1
Employment: Industry (% of employed)[e]	22.3	18.1	16.9
Employment: Services (% of employed)[e]	63.3	67.3	70.0
Unemployment (% of labour force)	18.0	12.4	14.4[e]
Labour force participation (female/male pop. %)[e]	48.8 / 80.7	49.3 / 78.7	52.3 / 78.6
CPI: Consumer Price Index (2000=100)	230	314	381[f]
Agricultural production index (2004-2006=100)	99	127	136[f]
Food production index (2004-2006=100)	99	129	138[f]
Index of industrial production (2005=100)[g]	100	114	129[h]
International trade: Exports (million US$)[i,j]	6 183	4 767	3 747[c]
International trade: Imports (million US$)[i,j]	6 804	15 138	22 725[c]
International trade: Balance (million US$)[i,j]	- 621	- 10 371	- 18 978[c]
Balance of payments, current account (million US$)	- 473	- 4 024[k]	- 1 335[b]

Major trading partners						2016
Export partners (% of exports)	United States	53.6	Haiti	12.1	Canada	8.4
Import partners (% of imports)	United States	41.3	China	13.4	Mexico	4.6

Social indicators	2005	2010	2017
Population growth rate (average annual %)[l]	1.5	1.4	1.2[b]
Urban population (% of total population)	67.4	73.8	79.0[b]
Urban population growth rate (average annual %)[l]	3.3	3.2	2.6[b]
Fertility rate, total (live births per woman)[l]	2.8	2.7	2.5[b]
Life expectancy at birth (females/males, years)[l]	74.4 / 68.1	75.4 / 69.2	76.4 / 70.2[b]
Population age distribution (0-14 and 60+ years, %)	33.2 / 8.0	31.4 / 8.7	29.3 / 10.2[a]
International migrant stock (000/% of total pop.)	376.0 / 4.1	393.7 / 4.0	415.6 / 3.9[b]
Refugees and others of concern to UNHCR (000)	...	2.4[m]	1.3[c]
Infant mortality rate (per 1 000 live births)[l]	34.9	29.6	25.1[b]
Health: Total expenditure (% of GDP)[n]	4.3	4.1	4.4[f]
Health: Physicians (per 1 000 pop.)	1.8[o]	1.1[p]	1.5[q]
Education: Government expenditure (% of GDP)	1.9[e,r]	2.0[s]	...
Education: Primary gross enrol. ratio (f/m per 100 pop.)	103.3 / 108.6	100.5 / 114.1	98.7 / 108.1[b]
Education: Secondary gross enrol. ratio (f/m per 100 pop.)	76.0 / 63.6	80.6 / 71.5	81.7 / 74.1[b]
Education: Tertiary gross enrol. ratio (f/m per 100 pop.)	40.7 / 25.9[r]	... / ...	65.0 / 35.4[b]
Intentional homicide rate (per 100 000 pop.)	25.9	25.0	17.4[f]
Seats held by women in national parliaments (%)	17.3	19.7	26.8

Environment and infrastructure indicators	2005	2010	2017
Mobile-cellular subscriptions (per 100 inhabitants)	38.8	88.8	82.6[b]
Individuals using the Internet (per 100 inhabitants)	11.5	31.4[e]	51.9[t,b]
Threatened species (number)	104[u]	126	184
Forested area (% of land area)	34.2	37.6	40.4[e,f]
CO2 emission estimates (million tons/tons per capita)	18.6 / 2.0	21.0 / 2.1	21.5 / 2.1[f]
Energy production, primary (Petajoules)	28	27	28[f]
Energy supply per capita (Gigajoules)	29	30	28[f]
Tourist/visitor arrivals at national borders (000)[v]	3 691	4 125	5 600[b]
Important sites for terrestrial biodiversity protected (%)	71.4	71.4	74.6
Pop. using improved drinking water (urban/rural, %)	89.9 / 79.4	87.7 / 80.7	85.4 / 81.9[b]
Pop. using improved sanitation facilities (urban/rural, %)	84.6 / 70.0	85.4 / 72.9	86.2 / 75.7[b]
Net Official Development Assist. received (% of GNI)	0.24	0.34	0.43[b]

a Projected estimate (medium fertility variant). **b** 2015. **c** 2016. **d** Data classified according to ISIC Rev. 4. **e** Estimate. **f** 2014. **g** Data classified according to ISIC Rev. 3. **h** 2013. **i** Export and import values exclude trade in the processing zone. **j** Imports FOB. **k** Break in the time series. **l** Data refers to a 5-year period preceding the reference year. **m** Data as at the end of December. **n** Data revision. **o** 2000. **p** 2008. **q** 2011. **r** 2003. **s** 2007. **t** Population aged 12 years and over. **u** 2004. **v** Arrivals by air only; including nationals residing abroad.

Ecuador

Region	South America	UN membership date	21 December 1945
Population (000, 2017)	16 625[a]	Surface area (km2)	257 217[b]
Pop. density (per km2, 2017)	66.9[a]	Sex ratio (m per 100 f, 2017)	99.9[a]
Capital city	Quito	National currency	US Dollar (USD)
Capital city pop. (000)	1 726.1[b]		

Economic indicators	2005	2010	2017
GDP: Gross domestic product (million current US$)	41 507	69 555	100 177[b]
GDP growth rate (annual %, const. 2005 prices)	5.3	3.5	0.2[b]
GDP per capita (current US$)	3 021.9	4 657.3	6 205.1[b]
Economy: Agriculture (% of GVA)[c]	10.0	10.2	10.1[b]
Economy: Industry (% of GVA)[c]	33.4	36.3	34.1[b]
Economy: Services and other activity (% of GVA)[c]	56.6	53.5	55.8[b]
Employment: Agriculture (% of employed)[d]	8.3	27.3	25.7
Employment: Industry (% of employed)[d]	21.2	18.1	19.2
Employment: Services (% of employed)[d]	70.5	54.6	55.1
Unemployment (% of labour force)	7.7	5.0	5.8[d]
Labour force participation (female/male pop. %)[d]	55.3 / 84.6	49.9 / 80.6	49.1 / 79.9
CPI: Consumer Price Index (2000=100)	175[e]	219	256[f]
Agricultural production index (2004-2006=100)	99	122	118[f]
Food production index (2004-2006=100)	98	123	119[f]
International trade: Exports (million US$)	9 869	17 490	16 798[g]
International trade: Imports (million US$)	9 609	20 591	16 189[g]
International trade: Balance (million US$)	261	- 3 101	609[g]
Balance of payments, current account (million US$)	474	- 1 586	- 2 201[b]

Major trading partners						2016
Export partners (% of exports)	United States	32.4	Chile	6.8	Viet Nam	6.6
Import partners (% of imports)	United States	23.2	China	19.1	Colombia	8.1

Social indicators	2005	2010	2017
Population growth rate (average annual %)[h]	1.7	1.7	1.6[b]
Urban population (% of total population)	61.7	62.7	63.7[b]
Urban population growth rate (average annual %)[h]	2.4	2.0	1.9[b]
Fertility rate, total (live births per woman)[h]	2.9	2.7	2.6[b]
Life expectancy at birth (females/males, years)[h]	76.8 / 70.6	77.5 / 71.7	78.4 / 72.8[b]
Population age distribution (0-14 and 60+ years, %)	32.7 / 8.0	30.7 / 8.7	28.4 / 10.5[a]
International migrant stock (000/% of total pop.)[i]	187.4 / 1.4	325.4 / 2.2	387.5 / 2.4[b]
Refugees and others of concern to UNHCR (000)	262.6[j]	171.1[i]	133.1[k,g]
Infant mortality rate (per 1 000 live births)[h]	27.1	23.4	21.1[b]
Health: Total expenditure (% of GDP)[l]	5.9	5.9	9.2[f]
Health: Physicians (per 1 000 pop.)	1.5[m]	1.6[n]	1.7[o]
Education: Government expenditure (% of GDP)	1.2[p]	4.5	5.0[b]
Education: Primary gross enrol. ratio (f/m per 100 pop.)	111.5 / 112.0	116.0 / 115.7	107.9 / 107.4[g]
Education: Secondary gross enrol. ratio (f/m per 100 pop.)	62.2 / 61.5	91.0 / 86.6	109.2 / 105.3[g]
Education: Tertiary gross enrol. ratio (f/m per 100 pop.)	... / ...	41.5 / 36.0[q]	45.3 / 34.6[r]
Intentional homicide rate (per 100 000 pop.)	15.4	17.7	8.2[f]
Seats held by women in national parliaments (%)	16.0	32.3	41.6

Environment and infrastructure indicators	2005	2010	2017
Mobile-cellular subscriptions (per 100 inhabitants)	45.3	98.5	79.4[s,b]
Individuals using the Internet (per 100 inhabitants)	6.0[d]	29.0[t]	48.9[t,b]
Research & Development expenditure (% of GDP)	0.1[m]	0.4	0.3[o]
Threatened species (number)	2 151[u]	2 255	2 358
Forested area (% of land area)	53.7	52.1	50.8[d,f]
CO2 emission estimates (million tons/tons per capita)	30.3 / 2.2	36.5 / 2.5	43.9 / 2.8[f]
Energy production, primary (Petajoules)	1 251	1 077	1 247[f]
Energy supply per capita (Gigajoules)	35	38	42[f]
Tourist/visitor arrivals at national borders (000)[v]	860	1 047	1 543[b]
Important sites for terrestrial biodiversity protected (%)	25.7	28.0	29.1
Pop. using improved drinking water (urban/rural, %)	89.8 / 70.2	91.8 / 73.2	93.4 / 75.5[b]
Pop. using improved sanitation facilities (urban/rural, %)	82.2 / 64.1	85.0 / 73.3	87.0 / 80.7[b]
Net Official Development Assist. received (% of GNI)	0.59	0.22	0.31[b]

a Projected estimate (medium fertility variant). **b** 2015. **c** Data classified according to ISIC Rev. 4. **d** Estimate. **e** Series linked to former series. **f** 2014. **g** 2016. **h** Data refers to a 5-year period preceding the reference year. **i** Including refugees. **j** Data as at the end of December. **k** Data relates to the end of 2015. **l** Data revision. **m** 2003. **n** 2009. **o** 2011. **p** 2000. **q** 2008. **r** 2012. **s** Decrease due to operator updating their records to exclude inactive subscriptions. **t** Population aged 5 years and over. **u** 2004. **v** Excluding nationals residing abroad.

Egypt

Region	Northern Africa	UN membership date	24 October 1945
Population (000, 2017)	97 553 [a]	Surface area (km2)	1 002 000 [b]
Pop. density (per km2, 2017)	98.0 [a]	Sex ratio (m per 100 f, 2017)	102.3 [a]
Capital city	Cairo	National currency	Egyptian Pound (EGP)
Capital city pop. (000)	18 771.8 [b]	Exchange rate (per US$)	18.1 [c]

Economic indicators	2005	2010	2017
GDP: Gross domestic product (million current US$)	94 456	214 630	315 917 [b]
GDP growth rate (annual %, const. 2005 prices)	4.5	5.1	4.2 [b]
GDP per capita (current US$)	1 260.4	2 616.1	3 452.3 [b]
Economy: Agriculture (% of GVA) [d]	14.4	14.0	11.2 [b]
Economy: Industry (% of GVA) [d]	36.9	37.5	36.3 [b]
Economy: Services and other activity (% of GVA) [d]	48.8	48.5	52.5 [b]
Employment: Agriculture (% of employed) [e]	30.9	28.8	25.4
Employment: Industry (% of employed) [e]	21.4	25.9	25.3
Employment: Services (% of employed) [e]	47.6	45.3	49.3
Unemployment (% of labour force)	11.2	9.0	11.5 [e]
Labour force participation (female/male pop. %) [e]	20.5 / 75.3	22.7 / 75.6	23.1 / 76.2
CPI: Consumer Price Index (2000=100)	134	232 [f]	329 [g]
Agricultural production index (2004-2006=100)	99	109	120 [g]
Food production index (2004-2006=100)	99	110	122 [g]
International trade: Exports (million US$) [h,i]	10 646	26 332	22 507 [c]
International trade: Imports (million US$) [h,i]	19 812	53 003	58 053 [c]
International trade: Balance (million US$) [h,i]	- 9 166	- 26 672	- 35 545 [c]
Balance of payments, current account (million US$)	2 103	- 4 504	- 16 786 [b]

Major trading partners					2016
Export partners (% of exports)	United Arab Emirates 12.6	Saudi Arabia	7.8	Italy	6.5
Import partners (% of imports)	China. 13.0	Germany	8.7	United States	5.3

Social indicators	2005	2010	2017
Population growth rate (average annual %) [j]	1.9	1.8	2.2 [b]
Urban population (% of total population)	43.0	43.0	43.1 [b]
Urban population growth rate (average annual %) [j]	1.7	1.7	1.7 [b]
Fertility rate, total (live births per woman) [j]	3.2	3.0	3.4 [b]
Life expectancy at birth (females/males, years) [j]	71.4 / 66.6	72.2 / 67.6	73.0 / 68.7 [b]
Population age distribution (0-14 and 60+ years, %)	33.3 / 7.1	32.1 / 7.5	33.5 / 7.9 [a]
International migrant stock (000/% of total pop.) [k]	274.0 / 0.4	295.7 / 0.4	491.6 / 0.5 [b]
Refugees and others of concern to UNHCR (000)	100.2 [l]	109.9 [l]	256.5 [c]
Infant mortality rate (per 1 000 live births) [j]	29.4	23.5	18.9 [b]
Health: Total expenditure (% of GDP)	5.1	4.8	5.6 [g]
Health: Physicians (per 1 000 pop.)	2.4	2.8 [m]	0.8 [g]
Education: Government expenditure (% of GDP)	4.8	3.8 [n]	...
Education: Primary gross enrol. ratio (f/m per 100 pop.)	97.5 / 102.9	105.5 / 108.6	103.8 / 104.1 [g]
Education: Secondary gross enrol. ratio (f/m per 100 pop.)	78.6 / 82.9 [e,o]	70.5 / 72.5	85.9 / 86.3 [g]
Education: Tertiary gross enrol. ratio (f/m per 100 pop.)	27.1 / 32.2	29.5 / 32.2	35.6 / 36.9 [b]
Intentional homicide rate (per 100 000 pop.)	0.7	2.2	3.2 [p]
Seats held by women in national parliaments (%)	2.0	1.8	14.9

Environment and infrastructure indicators	2005	2010	2017
Mobile-cellular subscriptions (per 100 inhabitants)	19.0	90.5	111.0 [b]
Individuals using the Internet (per 100 inhabitants)	12.8	21.6 [q]	35.9 [b]
Research & Development expenditure (% of GDP)	0.2 [r,s]	0.4 [t,u]	0.7 [g]
Threatened species (number)	46 [o]	121	156
Forested area (% of land area)	0.1	0.1 [e]	0.1 [e,g]
CO2 emission estimates (million tons/tons per capita)	167.2 / 2.2	202.7 / 2.5	201.9 / 2.2 [g]
Energy production, primary (Petajoules)	3 383	3 692	3 509 [g]
Energy supply per capita (Gigajoules)	37	40	36 [g]
Tourist/visitor arrivals at national borders (000)	8 244	14 051	9 139 [b]
Important sites for terrestrial biodiversity protected (%)	37.9	39.6	39.6
Pop. using improved drinking water (urban/rural, %)	98.9 / 95.8	99.6 / 97.4	100.0 / 99.0 [b]
Pop. using improved sanitation facilities (urban/rural, %)	95.8 / 85.5	96.8 / 93.1	96.8 / 93.1 [b]
Net Official Development Assist. received (% of GNI)	1.17	0.28	0.78 [b]

a Projected estimate (medium fertility variant). **b** 2015. **c** 2016. **d** At factor cost. **e** Estimate. **f** Series linked to former series. **g** 2014. **h** Prior to 2008, special trade. **i** Imports exclude petroleum imported without stated value. Exports cover domestic exports. **j** Data refers to a 5-year period preceding the reference year. **k** Including refugees. **l** Data as at the end of December. **m** 2009. **n** 2008. **o** 2004. **p** 2011. **q** Population aged 6 years and over. **r** Government only. **s** Partial data. **t** Excluding business enterprise. **u** Excluding private non-profit.

El Salvador

Region	Central America	UN membership date	24 October 1945
Population (000, 2017)	6 378 [a]	Surface area (km2)	21 041 [b,c]
Pop. density (per km2, 2017)	307.8 [a]	Sex ratio (m per 100 f, 2017)	88.5 [a]
Capital city	San Salvador	National currency	El Salvador Colon (SVC) [d]
Capital city pop. (000)	1 098.5 [e,c]	Exchange rate (per US$)	8.8 [f]

Economic indicators	2005	2010	2017
GDP: Gross domestic product (million current US$)	17 094	21 418	25 850 [c]
GDP growth rate (annual %, const. 2005 prices)	3.6	1.4	2.5 [c]
GDP per capita (current US$)	2 874.3	3 547.1	4 219.4 [c]
Economy: Agriculture (% of GVA) [g]	10.2	12.1	10.8 [c]
Economy: Industry (% of GVA) [g]	28.7	25.9	25.8 [c]
Economy: Services and other activity (% of GVA) [g]	61.1	62.1	63.3 [c]
Employment: Agriculture (% of employed) [h]	20.0	20.8	18.6
Employment: Industry (% of employed) [h]	22.3	21.5	20.2
Employment: Services (% of employed) [h]	57.7	57.7	61.2
Unemployment (% of labour force)	7.2	7.1	6.4 [h]
Labour force participation (female/male pop. %) [h]	45.2 / 78.5	46.4 / 78.9	49.5 / 79.5
CPI: Consumer Price Index (2000=100) [i]	118	140 [j]	152 [k]
Agricultural production index (2004-2006=100)	99	107	111 [k]
Food production index (2004-2006=100)	99	105	117 [k]
Index of industrial production (2005=100) [l]	100	106	116 [k]
International trade: Exports (million US$)	3 436	4 499	5 335 [f]
International trade: Imports (million US$)	6 809	8 416	9 855 [f]
International trade: Balance (million US$)	- 3 373	- 3 917	- 4 519 [f]
Balance of payments, current account (million US$)	- 622	- 533	- 920 [c]

Major trading partners						2016
Export partners (% of exports)	United States	48.2	Honduras	14.1	Guatemala	13.5
Import partners (% of imports)	United States	37.3	Guatemala	10.0	China	8.7

Social indicators	2005	2010	2017
Population growth rate (average annual %) [m]	0.5	0.4	0.5 [c]
Urban population (% of total population)	61.6	64.3	66.7 [c]
Urban population growth rate (average annual %) [m]	1.3	1.3	1.4 [c]
Fertility rate, total (live births per woman) [m]	2.7	2.4	2.2 [c]
Life expectancy at birth (females/males, years) [m]	74.1 / 65.0	75.6 / 66.4	77.1 / 67.9 [c]
Population age distribution (0-14 and 60+ years, %)	34.8 / 9.1	31.6 / 10.0	27.4 / 11.6 [a]
International migrant stock (000/% of total pop.) [n]	36.0 / 0.6	40.3 / 0.7	42.0 / 0.7 [c]
Refugees and others of concern to UNHCR (000)	0.1 [o]	0.1 [o]	4.7 [f]
Infant mortality rate (per 1 000 live births) [m]	23.6	20.7	17.0 [c]
Health: Total expenditure (% of GDP) [p]	7.2	6.9	6.8 [k]
Health: Physicians (per 1 000 pop.)	1.7	1.9 [q]	...
Education: Government expenditure (% of GDP)	2.7 [h]	3.5	3.5 [c]
Education: Primary gross enrol. ratio (f/m per 100 pop.)	121.2 / 125.4	118.0 / 123.6	106.8 / 111.4 [c]
Education: Secondary gross enrol. ratio (f/m per 100 pop.)	68.5 / 68.5	71.8 / 72.3	79.7 / 79.2 [c]
Education: Tertiary gross enrol. ratio (f/m per 100 pop.)	24.3 / 21.7	27.6 / 25.0	30.5 / 27.7 [c]
Intentional homicide rate (per 100 000 pop.)	63.5	66.0	108.6 [c]
Seats held by women in national parliaments (%)	10.7	19.0	32.1

Environment and infrastructure indicators	2005	2010	2017
Mobile-cellular subscriptions (per 100 inhabitants)	39.7	123.8 [h,r]	145.3 [c]
Individuals using the Internet (per 100 inhabitants)	4.2 [h,s]	15.9 [s]	26.9 [h,c]
Research & Development expenditure (% of GDP)	...	0.1	0.1 [k]
Threatened species (number)	49 [t]	72	86
Forested area (% of land area) [h]	14.9	13.9	13.0 [k]
CO2 emission estimates (million tons/tons per capita)	6.5 / 1.1	6.5 / 1.1	6.3 / 1.0 [k]
Energy production, primary (Petajoules)	104	95	86 [k]
Energy supply per capita (Gigajoules)	31	29	28 [k]
Tourist/visitor arrivals at national borders (000)	1 127	1 150	1 402 [c]
Important sites for terrestrial biodiversity protected (%)	9.9	22.4	26.6
Pop. using improved drinking water (urban/rural, %)	94.7 / 72.2	96.1 / 79.4	97.5 / 86.5 [c]
Pop. using improved sanitation facilities (urban/rural, %)	78.4 / 48.3	80.4 / 54.2	82.4 / 60.0 [c]
Net Official Development Assist. received (% of GNI)	1.20	1.35	0.36 [c]

a Projected estimate (medium fertility variant). **b** The total surface is 21 040.79 square kilometres, without taking into account the last ruling of The Hague. **c** 2015. **d** The Colon is still legal tender as banks in El Salvador accept Colons in small quantities. However, nearly all transactions are settled in US Dollars since 95 per cent of the Colons are no longer in circulation. **e** Refers to the urban parts of the municipalities San Salvador, Mejicanos, Soyapango, Delgado, Ilopango, Cuscatancingo, Ayutuxtepeque and San Marcos. **f** 2016. **g** At producers' prices. **h** Estimate. **i** Urban areas. **j** Series linked to former series. **k** 2014. **l** Data classified according to ISIC Rev. 3. **m** Data refers to a 5-year period preceding the reference year. **n** Including refugees. **o** Data as at the end of December. **p** Data revision. **q** 2008. **r** Data as at the end of June. **s** Population aged 10 years and over. **t** 2004.

Equatorial Guinea

Region	Middle Africa	UN membership date	12 November 1968
Population (000, 2017)	1 268[a]	Surface area (km2)	28 052[b]
Pop. density (per km2, 2017)	45.2[a]	Sex ratio (m per 100 f, 2017)	124.0[a]
Capital city	Malabo	National currency	CFA Franc (XAF)
Capital city pop. (000)	145.1[c]	Exchange rate (per US$)	622.3[d]

Economic indicators	2005	2010	2017
GDP: Gross domestic product (million current US$)	8 520	16 299	13 812[b]
GDP growth rate (annual %, const. 2005 prices)	8.9	- 8.9	- 7.4[b]
GDP per capita (current US$)	13 612.6	22 366.3	16 344.1[b]
Economy: Agriculture (% of GVA)	1.5	1.1	1.2[b]
Economy: Industry (% of GVA)	81.3	74.3	73.1[b]
Economy: Services and other activity (% of GVA)	17.2	24.6	25.7[b]
Employment: Agriculture (% of employed)[e]	16.8	16.9	18.8
Employment: Industry (% of employed)[e]	17.3	20.4	18.0
Employment: Services (% of employed)[e]	65.9	62.7	63.2
Unemployment (% of labour force)[e]	6.7	6.6	7.7
Labour force participation (female/male pop. %)[e]	69.3 / 92.6	70.4 / 92.3	71.5 / 91.8
Agricultural production index (2004-2006=100)	101	110	117[c]
Food production index (2004-2006=100)	101	111	118[c]
International trade: Exports (million US$)	7 062	9 964	7 443[d]
International trade: Imports (million US$)	1 309	5 679	5 456[d]
International trade: Balance (million US$)	5 753	4 285	1 987[d]

Major trading partners					2016
Export partners (% of exports)	India	19.7	China	13.7	Republic of Korea	13.4
Import partners (% of imports)	Netherlands	21.4	United States	18.0	Spain	16.9

Social indicators	2005	2010	2017
Population growth rate (average annual %)[f]	4.2	4.6	4.2[b]
Urban population (% of total population)	38.9	39.2	39.9[b]
Urban population growth rate (average annual %)[f]	3.1	3.0	3.1[b]
Fertility rate, total (live births per woman)[f]	5.7	5.4	5.0[b]
Life expectancy at birth (females/males, years)[f]	54.9 / 52.3	56.2 / 53.8	58.4 / 55.5[b]
Population age distribution (0-14 and 60+ years, %)	39.5 / 5.3	38.4 / 4.8	37.2 / 4.4[a]
International migrant stock (000/% of total pop.)[g]	6.6 / 1.1	8.7 / 1.2	10.8 / 1.3[b]
Infant mortality rate (per 1 000 live births)[f]	89.7	80.4	70.0[b]
Health: Total expenditure (% of GDP)[h]	1.6	3.8	3.8[c]
Health: Physicians (per 1 000 pop.)	0.3[i]	...	...
Education: Primary gross enrol. ratio (f/m per 100 pop.)	94.0 / 98.3	80.6 / 82.6	78.2 / 80.0[b]
Education: Secondary gross enrol. ratio (f/m per 100 pop.)	22.9 / 31.8	... / ...	... / ...
Education: Tertiary gross enrol. ratio (f/m per 100 pop.)	2.0 / 4.4[j]	... / ...	... / ...
Intentional homicide rate (per 100 000 pop.)	3.5	3.4	3.2[b]
Seats held by women in national parliaments (%)	18.0	10.0	24.0

Environment and infrastructure indicators	2005	2010	2017
Mobile-cellular subscriptions (per 100 inhabitants)	16.0	57.4	66.7[b]
Individuals using the Internet (per 100 inhabitants)	1.1	6.0	21.3[e,b]
Threatened species (number)	101[i]	130	177
Forested area (% of land area)	60.1	58.0	56.3[e,c]
CO2 emission estimates (million tons/tons per capita)	4.7 / 7.7	4.7 / 6.4	5.3 / 6.5[c]
Energy production, primary (Petajoules)	823	813	841[c]
Energy supply per capita (Gigajoules)	86	94	87[c]
Important sites for terrestrial biodiversity protected (%)	100.0	100.0	100.0
Pop. using improved drinking water (urban/rural, %)	64.1 / 36.7	69.3 / 33.5	72.5 / 31.5[b]
Pop. using improved sanitation facilities (urban/rural, %)	80.4 / 76.4	80.1 / 73.0	79.9 / 71.0[b]
Net Official Development Assist. received (% of GNI)	0.91	1.42	0.15[b]

a Projected estimate (medium fertility variant). **b** 2015. **c** 2014. **d** 2016. **e** Estimate. **f** Data refers to a 5-year period preceding the reference year. **g** Refers to foreign citizens. **h** Estimates should be viewed with caution as these are derived from scarce data. **i** 2004. **j** 2000.

Eritrea

Region	Eastern Africa	UN membership date		28 May 1993
Population (000, 2017)	5 069[a]	Surface area (km2)		117 600[b]
Pop. density (per km2, 2017)	50.2[a]	Sex ratio (m per 100 f, 2017)		100.4[a]
Capital city	Asmara	National currency		Nakfa (ERN)
Capital city pop. (000)	803.8[b]	Exchange rate (per US$)		15.4[c]

Economic indicators

	2005	2010	2017
GDP: Gross domestic product (million current US$)	1 098	2 117	4 783[b]
GDP growth rate (annual %, const. 2005 prices)	1.5	2.2	4.8[b]
GDP per capita (current US$)	262.1	451.4	914.9[b]
Economy: Agriculture (% of GVA)	24.2	19.1	17.2[b]
Economy: Industry (% of GVA)	21.9	23.1	23.5[b]
Economy: Services and other activity (% of GVA)	53.9	57.8	59.3[b]
Employment: Agriculture (% of employed)[d]	61.1	61.2	57.0
Employment: Industry (% of employed)[d]	6.5	6.6	7.6
Employment: Services (% of employed)[d]	32.4	32.2	35.4
Unemployment (% of labour force)[d]	7.5	7.2	7.3
Labour force participation (female/male pop. %)[d]	76.5 / 89.2	77.6 / 89.8	77.8 / 90.1
Agricultural production index (2004-2006=100)	108	105	109[c]
Food production index (2004-2006=100)	108	105	109[c]
International trade: Exports (million US$)	11	13	16[e]
International trade: Imports (million US$)	503	1 187	3 325[e]
International trade: Balance (million US$)	- 493	- 1 175	- 3 310[e]

Major trading partners

							2016
Export partners (% of exports)	China	55.3	India		20.4	United Arab Emirates	4.7
Import partners (% of imports)	China	21.8	Egypt		21.6	United Arab Emirates	9.8

Social indicators

	2005	2010	2017
Population growth rate (average annual %)[f]	3.1	2.0	2.0[b]
Urban population (% of total population)	18.9	20.6	22.6[b]
Urban population growth rate (average annual %)[f]	5.6	5.1	5.1[b]
Fertility rate, total (live births per woman)[f]	5.1	4.8	4.4[b]
Life expectancy at birth (females/males, years)[f]	58.8 / 54.7	62.7 / 58.7	65.6 / 61.4[b]
Population age distribution (0-14 and 60+ years, %)	41.0 / 5.5	41.6 / 5.5	41.8 / 5.3[a]
International migrant stock (000/% of total pop.)[d]	14.3 / 0.3	15.7 / 0.3	15.9 / 0.3[b]
Refugees and others of concern to UNHCR (000)	6.0[g]	5.0[g]	2.3[e]
Infant mortality rate (per 1 000 live births)[f]	59.4	51.7	45.0[b]
Health: Total expenditure (% of GDP)[h]	3.0	3.2	3.3[c]
Health: Physicians (per 1 000 pop.)	0.1[i]	...	...
Education: Government expenditure (% of GDP)	3.1[i]	2.1[j]	...
Education: Primary gross enrol. ratio (f/m per 100 pop.)	63.6 / 77.5	45.1 / 52.6	45.9 / 53.2[b]
Education: Secondary gross enrol. ratio (f/m per 100 pop.)	21.4 / 35.4	29.7 / 38.4	28.1 / 32.9[b]
Education: Tertiary gross enrol. ratio (f/m per 100 pop.)	0.3 / 1.8[i]	1.3 / 3.4	1.7 / 3.4[c]
Intentional homicide rate (per 100 000 pop.)	9.1	8.3	7.5[b]
Seats held by women in national parliaments (%)	22.0	22.0	22.0

Environment and infrastructure indicators

	2005	2010	2017
Mobile-cellular subscriptions (per 100 inhabitants)	0.8	3.2	7.0[d,b]
Individuals using the Internet (per 100 inhabitants)	0.1[k]	0.6[d]	1.1[d,b]
Threatened species (number)	34[i]	97	122
Forested area (% of land area)[d]	15.4	15.2	15.0[c]
CO2 emission estimates (million tons/tons per capita)	0.8 / 0.2	0.5 / 0.1	0.7 / 0.1[c]
Energy production, primary (Petajoules)	21	24	27[c]
Energy supply per capita (Gigajoules)	7	7	7[c]
Tourist/visitor arrivals at national borders (000)[l]	83	84	...
Important sites for terrestrial biodiversity protected (%)	13.3	13.3	13.3
Pop. using improved drinking water (urban/rural, %)	70.2 / 49.8	72.3 / 52.3	73.2 / 53.3[b]
Pop. using improved sanitation facilities (urban/rural, %)	49.8 / 4.4	46.0 / 6.5	44.6 / 7.3[b]
Net Official Development Assist. received (% of GNI)	32.12	7.74	

a Projected estimate (medium fertility variant). **b** 2015. **c** 2014. **d** Estimate. **e** 2016. **f** Data refers to a 5-year period preceding the reference year. **g** Data as at the end of December. **h** Estimates should be viewed with caution as these are derived from scarce data. **i** 2004. **j** 2006. **k** 2000. **l** Including nationals residing abroad.

Estonia

Region	Northern Europe	UN membership date	17 September 1991
Population (000, 2017)	1 310 a	Surface area (km2)	45 227 b
Pop. density (per km2, 2017)	30.9 a	Sex ratio (m per 100 f, 2017)	88.2 a
Capital city	Tallinn	National currency	Euro (EUR)
Capital city pop. (000)	391.1 b	Exchange rate (per US$)	0.9 c

Economic indicators	2005	2010	2017
GDP: Gross domestic product (million current US$)	14 003	19 503	22 460 b
GDP growth rate (annual %, const. 2005 prices)	9.4	2.4	1.4 b
GDP per capita (current US$)	10 329.6	14 640.5	17 112.0 b
Economy: Agriculture (% of GVA) d	3.5	3.2	3.4 b
Economy: Industry (% of GVA) d	29.8	28.0	27.4 b
Economy: Services and other activity (% of GVA) d	66.7	68.8	69.2 b
Employment: Agriculture (% of employed) e	5.2	4.2	3.8
Employment: Industry (% of employed) e	34.1	30.6	29.0
Employment: Services (% of employed) e	60.7	65.2	67.3
Unemployment (% of labour force)	8.0	16.7	7.2 e
Labour force participation (female/male pop. %) e	53.4 / 65.6	56.0 / 67.7	55.4 / 69.4
CPI: Consumer Price Index (2000=100)	119 f	151	169 g
Agricultural production index (2004-2006=100)	103	110	136 g
Food production index (2004-2006=100)	103	110	136 g
Index of industrial production (2005=100)	100	104 h	134 h,g
International trade: Exports (million US$)	8 247	12 811	13 952 c
International trade: Imports (million US$)	11 018	13 197	15 759 c
International trade: Balance (million US$)	- 2 770	- 385	- 1 807 c
Balance of payments, current account (million US$)	- 1 386	344	493 b

Major trading partners						2016
Export partners (% of exports)	Sweden	16.8	Finland	15.0	Russian Federation	9.3
Import partners (% of imports)	Germany	10.7	Finland	9.6	China	8.0

Social indicators	2005	2010	2017
Population growth rate (average annual %) i	- 0.6	- 0.4	- 0.3 b
Urban population (% of total population)	68.7	68.1	67.5 b
Urban population growth rate (average annual %) i	- 0.8	- 0.6	- 0.4 b
Fertility rate, total (live births per woman) i	1.4	1.7	1.6 b
Life expectancy at birth (females/males, years) i	77.1 / 66.0	79.0 / 68.3	81.2 / 71.8 b
Population age distribution (0-14 and 60+ years, %)	15.2 / 21.9	15.1 / 23.2	16.4 / 25.9 a
International migrant stock (000/% of total pop.)	233.7 / 17.2	217.9 / 16.4	202.3 / 15.4 b
Refugees and others of concern to UNHCR (000)	136.0 j	101.0 j	84.2 c
Infant mortality rate (per 1 000 live births) i	7.3	4.7	3.2 b
Health: Total expenditure (% of GDP)	5.0	6.2	6.4 g
Health: Physicians (per 1 000 pop.)	4.4 k	3.2	3.3 g
Education: Government expenditure (% of GDP)	4.8	5.5	5.5 g
Education: Primary gross enrol. ratio (f/m per 100 pop.)	97.6 / 100.2	102.2 / 103.8	98.5 / 98.3 b
Education: Secondary gross enrol. ratio (f/m per 100 pop.)	104.7 / 101.0	105.3 / 105.3	114.7 / 115.6 b
Education: Tertiary gross enrol. ratio (f/m per 100 pop.)	85.8 / 50.9	85.8 / 51.6	84.8 / 55.4 b
Intentional homicide rate (per 100 000 pop.)	8.3	5.2	3.2 b
Seats held by women in national parliaments (%)	18.8	22.8	26.7

Environment and infrastructure indicators	2005	2010	2017
Mobile-cellular subscriptions (per 100 inhabitants)	109.1	127.3 l	148.7 l,b
Individuals using the Internet (per 100 inhabitants) m	61.4	74.1 n	88.4 b
Research & Development expenditure (% of GDP)	0.9	1.6	1.4 g
Threatened species (number)	12 o	11	23
Forested area (% of land area)	53.1	52.7	52.7 e,g
CO2 emission estimates (million tons/tons per capita)	16.8 / 12.4	18.1 / 13.6	19.5 / 14.8 g
Energy production, primary (Petajoules)	163	205	242 g
Energy supply per capita (Gigajoules)	164	177	193 g
Tourist/visitor arrivals at national borders (000)	1 917 f,p	2 372 f,q	2 989 q,b
Important sites for terrestrial biodiversity protected (%)	94.7	94.8	94.9
Pop. using improved drinking water (urban/rural, %)	99.8 / 97.9	99.9 / 98.5	100.0 / 99.0 b
Pop. using improved sanitation facilities (urban/rural, %)	97.5 / 96.1	97.5 / 96.4	97.5 / 96.6 b
Net Official Development Assist. disbursed (% of GNI)	0.08	0.10	0.19 r,c

a Projected estimate (medium fertility variant). b 2015. c 2016. d Data classified according to ISIC Rev. 4. e Estimate. f Break in the time series. g 2014. h Excluding water and waste management. i Data refers to a 5-year period preceding the reference year. j Data as at the end of December. k 2000. l Excludes prepaid cards that are used to provide Travel SIM/WorldMobile service. m Population aged 16 to 74 years. n Users in the last 3 months. o 2004. p Calculated on the basis of accommodation statistics and "Foreign Visitor Survey" carried out by the Statistical Office of Estonia. Starting from 2004, border statistics are not collected any more. q Based on mobile positioning data by the Bank of Estonia and Positium LBS. r Provisional data.

Ethiopia

Region	Eastern Africa	UN membership date	13 November 1945
Population (000, 2017)	104 957[a]	Surface area (km2)	1 104 300[b]
Pop. density (per km2, 2017)	105.0[a]	Sex ratio (m per 100 f, 2017)	99.7[a]
Capital city	Addis Ababa	National currency	Ethiopian Birr (ETB)
Capital city pop. (000)	3 237.5[b]	Exchange rate (per US$)	22.6[c,d]

Economic indicators

	2005	2010	2017
GDP: Gross domestic product (million current US$)	12 164	26 311	59 917[b]
GDP growth rate (annual %, const. 2005 prices)	11.8	12.6	9.6[b]
GDP per capita (current US$)	158.8	300.5	602.8[b]
Economy: Agriculture (% of GVA)	45.2	45.3	40.5[b]
Economy: Industry (% of GVA)	13.1	10.4	16.0[b]
Economy: Services and other activity (% of GVA)	41.7	44.3	43.5[b]
Employment: Agriculture (% of employed)[e]	46.7	66.8	70.5
Employment: Industry (% of employed)[e]	13.6	9.1	8.4
Employment: Services (% of employed)[e]	39.8	24.1	21.1
Unemployment (% of labour force)	5.4	5.2[e]	5.7[e]
Labour force participation (female/male pop. %)[e]	78.4 / 90.8	77.5 / 90.0	77.1 / 89.1
CPI: Consumer Price Index (2000=100)[f]	138[g]	313	601[h]
Agricultural production index (2004-2006=100)	102	137	158[h]
Food production index (2004-2006=100)	103	137	157[h]
Index of industrial production (2005=100)[i,j]	100	159	242[k]
International trade: Exports (million US$)	926	2 330	1 724[d]
International trade: Imports (million US$)	4 095	8 602	19 121[d]
International trade: Balance (million US$)	- 3 169	- 6 272	- 17 397[d]
Balance of payments, current account (million US$)	- 1 568	- 425	...

Major trading partners

						2016
Export partners (% of exports)	United States	9.8	Saudi Arabia	9.7	Germany	8.6
Import partners (% of imports)	China	31.9	United States	8.8	India	7.5

Social indicators

	2005	2010	2017
Population growth rate (average annual %)[l]	2.8	2.7	2.6[b]
Urban population (% of total population)	15.7	17.3	19.5[b]
Urban population growth rate (average annual %)[l]	4.1	4.6	4.9[b]
Fertility rate, total (live births per woman)[l]	6.1	5.3	4.6[b]
Life expectancy at birth (females/males, years)[l]	55.0 / 52.3	60.6 / 57.6	65.5 / 61.9[b]
Population age distribution (0-14 and 60+ years, %)	46.2 / 4.9	44.5 / 5.1	40.6 / 5.3[a]
International migrant stock (000/% of total pop.)[m]	514.2 / 0.7	567.7 / 0.6	1 072.9 / 1.1[b]
Refugees and others of concern to UNHCR (000)	105.1[n]	155.4[n]	745.7[b]
Infant mortality rate (per 1 000 live births)[l]	78.0	59.9	45.8[b]
Health: Total expenditure (% of GDP)	4.2	6.9	4.9[h]
Health: Physicians (per 1 000 pop.)	~0.0	~0.0[o]	...
Education: Government expenditure (% of GDP)	3.6[e,p]	4.5	4.5[k]
Education: Primary gross enrol. ratio (f/m per 100 pop.)	71.9 / 86.1	88.3 / 95.6	97.2 / 106.9[b]
Education: Secondary gross enrol. ratio (f/m per 100 pop.)	18.6 / 30.8	31.6 / 38.0	34.4 / 35.9[b]
Education: Tertiary gross enrol. ratio (f/m per 100 pop.)	1.3 / 4.2	4.4 / 10.2	5.3 / 10.9[h]
Intentional homicide rate (per 100 000 pop.)	9.4	8.5	7.6[b]
Seats held by women in national parliaments (%)	7.7	21.9	38.8

Environment and infrastructure indicators

	2005	2010	2017
Mobile-cellular subscriptions (per 100 inhabitants)	0.5	7.9	42.8[q,b]
Individuals using the Internet (per 100 inhabitants)	0.2	0.8[e]	11.6[e,b]
Research & Development expenditure (% of GDP)	0.2[r]	0.2[q]	0.6[k]
Threatened species (number)	93[s]	120	148
Forested area (% of land area)[e]	13.0	12.3	12.5[h]
CO2 emission estimates (million tons/tons per capita)	5.1 / 0.1	6.6 / 0.1	11.6 / 0.1[h]
Energy production, primary (Petajoules)	1 070	1 212	1 308[h]
Energy supply per capita (Gigajoules)	15	15	15[h]
Tourist/visitor arrivals at national borders (000)[t,u]	227	468	864[b]
Important sites for terrestrial biodiversity protected (%)	18.6	19.8	19.8
Pop. using improved drinking water (urban/rural, %)	89.1 / 28.8	91.1 / 38.7	93.1 / 48.6[b]
Pop. using improved sanitation facilities (urban/rural, %)	24.3 / 13.5	25.7 / 20.9	27.2 / 28.2[b]
Net Official Development Assist. received (% of GNI)	15.60	11.58	5.28[b]

a Projected estimate (medium fertility variant). b 2015. c UN operational exchange rate. d 2016. e Estimate. f Index base: 2001=100. g Break in the time series. h 2014. i Data classified according to ISIC Rev. 3. j Twelve months ending 30 June of the year stated. k 2013. l Data refers to a 5-year period preceding the reference year. m Including refugees. n Data as at the end of December. o 2009. p 2002. q There is an ongoing Telecom Expansion Project (TEP), which resulted in about 12 Million new subscriber than the previous year. r Partial data. s 2004. t Arrivals through all ports of entry. u Including nationals residing abroad.

Falkland Islands (Malvinas)

Region	South America	Population (000, 2017)	3[a,b]
Surface area (km2)	12 173[b,c]	Pop. density (per km2, 2017)	0.2[a,b]
Sex ratio (m per 100 f, 2017)	110.5[b,d,e]		

Economic indicators	2005	2010	2017
Unemployment (% of labour force)	...	...	1.2[f,g]
Labour force participation (female/male pop. %)	... / ...	... / ...	77.2 / 86.0[f,h,g]
Agricultural production index (2004-2006=100)	103	96	96[i]
Food production index (2004-2006=100)	100	105	105[i]
International trade: Exports (million US$)	11	9	4[j]
International trade: Imports (million US$)	8	50	17[j]
International trade: Balance (million US$)	2	- 41	- 13[j]

Major trading partners						2016
Export partners (% of exports)	Spain	71.7	Namibia	9.5	United States	7.7
Import partners (% of imports)	United Kingdom	73.1	Greece	9.0	Spain	5.9

Social indicators	2005	2010	2017
Population growth rate (average annual %)[k]	0.4	- 0.6	0.3[c]
Urban population (% of total population)	70.8	73.7	76.2[c]
Urban population growth rate (average annual %)[k]	1.4	1.2	1.0[c]
Population age distribution (0-14 and 60+ years, %)[b]	15.0 / 12.0[l]	15.9 / 14.0[m]	16.4 / 15.7[d,e]
International migrant stock (000/% of total pop.)	1.2 / 39.6	1.4 / 50.3	1.6 / 54.1[c]

Environment and infrastructure indicators	2005	2010	2017
Mobile-cellular subscriptions (per 100 inhabitants)	25.9[n]	107.9	163.5[o,c]
Individuals using the Internet (per 100 inhabitants)	84.0[o]	95.8	98.3[o,c]
Threatened species (number)	26[p]	23	23
Forested area (% of land area)[o]	0.0	0.0	0.0[i]
CO2 emission estimates (million tons/tons per capita)	0.1 / 17.5	0.1 / 19.1	0.1 / 18.9[i]
Energy production, primary (Petajoules)[o]	0	0	0[i]
Energy supply per capita (Gigajoules)[o]	235	261	257[i]
Important sites for terrestrial biodiversity protected (%)	10.9	10.9	10.9

a Projected estimate (medium fertility variant). b A dispute exists between the governments of Argentina and the United Kingdom of Great Britain and Northern Ireland concerning sovereignty over the Falkland Islands (Malvinas). c 2015. d Excluding military personnel and their families, visitors and transients. e 2012. f Population aged 16 to 65 years. g 2013. h Break in the time series. i 2014. j 2016. k Data refers to a 5-year period preceding the reference year. l 2001. m 2006. n GSM mobile was only launched on 12 December 2005. o Estimate. p 2004.

Faroe Islands

Region	Northern Europe	Population (000, 2017)	49[a]
Surface area (km2)	1 393[b]	Pop. density (per km2, 2017)	35.3[a]
Sex ratio (m per 100 f, 2017)	107.2[c,b]	Capital city	Tórshavn
National currency	Danish Krone (DKK)	Capital city pop. (000)	20.6[d]
Exchange rate (per US$)	7.1[e]		

Economic indicators	2005	2010	2017
Employment: Agriculture (% of employed)	11.1[f,g]	...	...
Employment: Industry (% of employed)	22.2[f,g]	...	...
Employment: Services (% of employed)	66.7[f,g]	...	...
Unemployment (% of labour force)	3.2[f]	6.4[h,i,j]	4.0[h,i,k]
Labour force participation (female/male pop. %)[h,i]	... / ...	77.5 / 85.3	79.4 / 86.0[k]
CPI: Consumer Price Index (2000=100)	109	121	125[d]
Agricultural production index (2004-2006=100)	100	100	102[d]
Food production index (2004-2006=100)	100	100	102[d]
International trade: Exports (million US$)	602	839	1 192[e]
International trade: Imports (million US$)	747	780	976[e]
International trade: Balance (million US$)	- 145	59	216[e]
Balance of payments, current account (million US$)	31	144	...

Major trading partners						2016
Export partners (% of exports)	United Kingdom	20.9	Russian Federation	19.1	Denmark	13.7
Import partners (% of imports)	Denmark	51.2	Germany	11.0	Norway	8.8

Social indicators	2005	2010	2017
Population growth rate (average annual %)[l]	0.4	0.1	0.2[b]
Urban population (% of total population)	39.8	40.9	42.0[b]
Urban population growth rate (average annual %)[l]	2.9	0.7	0.5[b]
Fertility rate, total (live births per woman)	2.6	2.5	2.4[b]
Life expectancy at birth (females/males, years)	... / ...	82.3 / 76.8[m]	84.5 / 78.3[n,e]
Population age distribution (0-14 and 60+ years, %)[c]	... / ...	22.0 / 19.3[m]	21.0 / 22.5[b]
International migrant stock (000/% of total pop.)	4.6 / 9.5	5.1 / 10.5	5.5 / 11.4[b]

Environment and infrastructure indicators	2005	2010	2017
Mobile-cellular subscriptions (per 100 inhabitants)	85.5	119.9	127.3[o,b]
Individuals using the Internet (per 100 inhabitants)	67.9[o]	75.2	94.2[o,b]
Threatened species (number)	11[p]	13	21
Forested area (% of land area)[o]	0.1	0.1	0.1[d]
CO2 emission estimates (million tons/tons per capita)	0.7 / 15.0	0.6 / 12.9	0.6 / 12.4[d]
Energy production, primary (Petajoules)	0	0	1[d]
Energy supply per capita (Gigajoules)[o]	216	184	182[d]
Important sites for terrestrial biodiversity protected (%)	0.0	0.0	6.7

a Projected estimate (medium fertility variant). b 2015. c De jure population. d 2014. e 2016. f Population aged 16 years and over. g Data classified according to ISIC Rev. 2. h Population aged 15 to 74 years. i Excluding the institutional population. j Break in the time series. k 2013. l Data refers to a 5-year period preceding the reference year. m 2008. n Data refers to a 2-year period up to and including the reference year. o Estimate. p 2004.

Fiji

Region	Melanesia	UN membership date	13 October 1970
Population (000, 2017)	906[a]	Surface area (km2)	18 272[b]
Pop. density (per km2, 2017)	49.6[a]	Sex ratio (m per 100 f, 2017)	103.1[a]
Capital city	Suva	National currency	Fiji Dollar (FJD)
Capital city pop. (000)	176.4[c]	Exchange rate (per US$)	2.1[d]

Economic indicators

	2005	2010	2017
GDP: Gross domestic product (million current US$)	2 981	3 141	4 391[b]
GDP growth rate (annual %, const. 2005 prices)	0.7	3.1	3.6[b]
GDP per capita (current US$)	3 626.9	3 652.1	4 921.9[b]
Economy: Agriculture (% of GVA)[e]	12.8	10.2	11.3[b]
Economy: Industry (% of GVA)[e]	17.9	19.9	18.1[b]
Economy: Services and other activity (% of GVA)[e]	69.2	69.9	70.7[b]
Employment: Agriculture (% of employed)[f]	23.3	23.0	21.3
Employment: Industry (% of employed)[f]	3.0	3.0	2.9
Employment: Services (% of employed)[f]	73.7	74.0	75.8
Unemployment (% of labour force)	4.6	8.9	7.7[f]
Labour force participation (female/male pop. %)[f]	38.1 / 73.8	37.4 / 71.8	37.0 / 71.2
CPI: Consumer Price Index (2000=100)[j]	115	146	164[g,c]
Agricultural production index (2004-2006=100)	99	82	88[c]
Food production index (2004-2006=100)	99	82	88[c]
Index of industrial production (2005=100)[h]	100	101	104[i]
International trade: Exports (million US$)	702	841	926[d]
International trade: Imports (million US$)	1 607	1 808	2 316[d]
International trade: Balance (million US$)	- 906	- 967	- 1 391[d]
Balance of payments, current account (million US$)	- 206[j]	- 149	- 72[b]

Major trading partners

						2016
Export partners (% of exports)	United States	15.7	Australia	15.1	Areas nes[k]	6.5
Import partners (% of imports)	Singapore	19.0	Australia	15.4	China	14.6

Social indicators

	2005	2010	2017
Population growth rate (average annual %)[l]	0.3	0.9	0.7[b]
Urban population (% of total population)	49.9	51.8	53.7[b]
Urban population growth rate (average annual %)[l]	1.1	1.7	1.5[b]
Fertility rate, total (live births per woman)[l]	3.0	2.8	2.6[b]
Life expectancy at birth (females/males, years)[l]	70.7 / 65.5	71.9 / 66.1	72.9 / 66.9[b]
Population age distribution (0-14 and 60+ years, %)	30.5 / 6.9	29.0 / 7.9	28.5 / 9.9[a]
International migrant stock (000/% of total pop.)	12.4 / 1.5	13.4 / 1.6	13.8 / 1.5[b]
Refugees and others of concern to UNHCR (000)	...	~0.0[m]	~0.0[d]
Infant mortality rate (per 1 000 live births)[l]	19.0	17.9	16.0[b]
Health: Total expenditure (% of GDP)[n]	3.6	4.2	4.5[c]
Health: Physicians (per 1 000 pop.)	0.5[o]	0.4[p]	...
Education: Government expenditure (% of GDP)	5.1	4.5[p]	3.9[q]
Education: Primary gross enrol. ratio (f/m per 100 pop.)	111.8 / 113.4[r]	104.3 / 105.9[p]	105.1 / 106.0[b]
Education: Secondary gross enrol. ratio (f/m per 100 pop.)	93.9 / 88.0[r]	90.9 / 83.1[p]	93.4 / 84.3[s]
Education: Tertiary gross enrol. ratio (f/m per 100 pop.)	17.6 / 14.7[f]	... / ...	... / ...
Intentional homicide rate (per 100 000 pop.)	...	2.8	3.0[s]
Seats held by women in national parliaments (%)	8.5	8.5[t]	16.0

Environment and infrastructure indicators

	2005	2010	2017
Mobile-cellular subscriptions (per 100 inhabitants)	24.9[u]	81.1[v]	108.2[b]
Individuals using the Internet (per 100 inhabitants)	8.5	20.0[f]	46.3[f,b]
Threatened species (number)	101[r]	192	291
Forested area (% of land area)[f]	54.6	54.3	55.4[c]
CO2 emission estimates (million tons/tons per capita)	1.1 / 1.3	1.2 / 1.4	1.2 / 1.3[c]
Energy production, primary (Petajoules)	9	6	8[c]
Energy supply per capita (Gigajoules)	29	26	26[f,c]
Tourist/visitor arrivals at national borders (000)[w]	545	632	755[b]
Important sites for terrestrial biodiversity protected (%)	3.8	7.2	7.2
Pop. using improved drinking water (urban/rural, %)	98.0 / 87.9	99.3 / 90.7	99.5 / 91.2[b]
Pop. using improved sanitation facilities (urban/rural, %)	91.1 / 73.6	93.0 / 86.0	93.4 / 88.4[b]
Net Official Development Assist. received (% of GNI)	2.17	2.49	2.46[b]

a Projected estimate (medium fertility variant). **b** 2015. **c** 2014. **d** 2016. **e** Data classified according to ISIC Rev. 4. **f** Estimate. **g** Series linked to former series. **h** Data classified according to ISIC Rev. 3. **i** 2011. **j** Break in the time series. **k** Areas not elsewhere specified. **l** Data refers to a 5-year period preceding the reference year. **m** Data as at the end of December. **n** Data revision. **o** 2003. **p** 2009. **q** 2013. **r** 2004. **s** 2012. **t** 2006. **u** Year ending 31 March of the following year. **v** Data as at the end of June. **w** Excluding nationals residing abroad.

Finland

Region	Northern Europe	UN membership date	14 December 1955
Population (000, 2017)	5 523[a,b]	Surface area (km2)	338 440[b,c]
Pop. density (per km2, 2017)	18.2[a,b]	Sex ratio (m per 100 f, 2017)	97.2[a,b]
Capital city	Helsinki	National currency	Euro (EUR)
Capital city pop. (000)	1 179.9[c]	Exchange rate (per US$)	0.9[d]

Economic indicators	2005	2010	2017
GDP: Gross domestic product (million current US$)	204 431	247 800	231 960[c]
GDP growth rate (annual %, const. 2005 prices)	2.8	3.0	0.2[c]
GDP per capita (current US$)	38 966.2	46 165.0	42 148.1[c]
Economy: Agriculture (% of GVA)[e]	2.6	2.7	2.5[c]
Economy: Industry (% of GVA)[e]	33.5	30.0	26.8[c]
Economy: Services and other activity (% of GVA)[e]	63.8	67.3	70.6[c]
Employment: Agriculture (% of employed)[f]	4.8	4.4	4.2
Employment: Industry (% of employed)[f]	25.8	23.3	22.0
Employment: Services (% of employed)[f]	69.4	72.3	73.8
Unemployment (% of labour force)	8.4	8.4	8.9[f]
Labour force participation (female/male pop. %)[f]	56.8 / 65.4	56.2 / 64.6	54.5 / 61.7
CPI: Consumer Price Index (2000=100)	106[g]	116	127[h]
Agricultural production index (2004-2006=100)	102	94	101[h]
Food production index (2004-2006=100)	102	94	101[h]
Index of industrial production (2005=100)	100	100	94[h]
International trade: Exports (million US$)	65 238	70 117	57 326[d]
International trade: Imports (million US$)	58 473	68 767	60 502[d]
International trade: Balance (million US$)	6 766	1 349	- 3 176[d]
Balance of payments, current account (million US$)	7 788[i]	3 168	- 979[c]

Major trading partners						2016
Export partners (% of exports)	Germany	12.8	Sweden	10.6	United States	7.2
Import partners (% of imports)	Germany	14.6	Sweden	11.2	Russian Federation	11.1

Social indicators	2005	2010	2017
Population growth rate (average annual %)[b,j]	0.3	0.4	0.4[c]
Urban population (% of total population)[b]	82.9	83.6	84.2[c]
Urban population growth rate (average annual %)[b,j]	0.4	0.6	0.5[c]
Fertility rate, total (live births per woman)[b,j]	1.8	1.8	1.8[c]
Life expectancy at birth (females/males, years)[b,j]	81.7 / 74.9	82.9 / 76.1	83.7 / 77.7[c]
Population age distribution (0-14 and 60+ years, %)[b]	17.3 / 21.5	16.5 / 24.8	16.4 / 27.8[a]
International migrant stock (000/% of total pop.)[b]	192.2 / 3.7	248.1 / 4.6	315.9 / 5.7[c]
Refugees and others of concern to UNHCR (000)	12.7[k]	14.0[k]	32.6[d]
Infant mortality rate (per 1 000 live births)[b,j]	3.2	2.7	2.3[c]
Health: Total expenditure (% of GDP)	8.4	9.0	9.7[h]
Health: Physicians (per 1 000 pop.)	3.2[l]	3.0	3.0[m]
Education: Government expenditure (% of GDP)	6.1	6.5	7.2[h]
Education: Primary gross enrol. ratio (f/m per 100 pop.)	98.2 / 98.9	98.8 / 99.5	101.4 / 101.7[c]
Education: Secondary gross enrol. ratio (f/m per 100 pop.)	114.5 / 109.5	109.8 / 104.9	156.3 / 142.8[c]
Education: Tertiary gross enrol. ratio (f/m per 100 pop.)	100.6 / 83.4	103.7 / 85.0	95.6 / 79.3[c]
Intentional homicide rate (per 100 000 pop.)	2.3	2.2	1.6[c]
Seats held by women in national parliaments (%)	37.5	40.0	42.0

Environment and infrastructure indicators	2005	2010	2017
Mobile-cellular subscriptions (per 100 inhabitants)	100.4	156.3[n]	135.5[o,c]
Individuals using the Internet (per 100 inhabitants)[p]	74.5	86.9	92.7[c]
Research & Development expenditure (% of GDP)	3.3	3.7	3.2[h]
Threatened species (number)	25[q]	18	36
Forested area (% of land area)	72.7	73.1	73.1[f,h]
CO2 emission estimates (million tons/tons per capita)	54.6 / 10.4	62.1 / 11.6	47.3 / 8.6[h]
Energy production, primary (Petajoules)	695	727	757[h]
Energy supply per capita (Gigajoules)	274	284	257[h]
Tourist/visitor arrivals at national borders (000)	2 080[i]	2 319	2 622[c]
Important sites for terrestrial biodiversity protected (%)	73.1	73.4	73.8
Pop. using improved drinking water (urban/rural, %)	100.0 / 100.0	100.0 / 100.0	100.0 / 100.0[c]
Pop. using improved sanitation facilities (urban/rural, %)	99.4 / 88.1	99.4 / 88.1	99.4 / 88.0[c]
Net Official Development Assist. disbursed (% of GNI)[r]	0.46	0.55	0.44[s,d]

a Projected estimate (medium fertility variant). **b** Including Åland Islands. **c** 2015. **d** 2016. **e** Data classified according to ISIC Rev. 4. **f** Estimate. **g** Series linked to former series. **h** 2014. **i** Break in the time series. **j** Data refers to a 5-year period preceding the reference year. **k** Data as at the end of December. **l** 2002. **m** 2013. **n** Includes data-only subscriptions. **o** Excludes data-only subscriptions. **p** Population aged 16 to 74 years. **q** 2004. **r** Development Assistance Committee member (OECD) **s** Provisional data.

France

Region	Western Europe	UN membership date	24 October 1945
Population (000, 2017)	64 980[a]	Surface area (km2)	551 500[b]
Pop. density (per km2, 2017)	118.7[a]	Sex ratio (m per 100 f, 2017)	96.7[a]
Capital city	Paris	National currency	Euro (EUR)
Capital city pop. (000)	10 843.3[b]	Exchange rate (per US$)	0.9[c]

Economic indicators	2005	2010	2017
GDP: Gross domestic product (million current US$)[d]	2 203 624	2 646 837	2 418 946[b]
GDP growth rate (annual %, const. 2005 prices)[d]	1.6	2.0	1.3[b]
GDP per capita (current US$)[d]	34 832.9	40 667.0	36 304.2[b]
Economy: Agriculture (% of GVA)[d,e]	1.9	1.8	1.7[b]
Economy: Industry (% of GVA)[d,e]	21.5	19.6	19.5[b]
Economy: Services and other activity (% of GVA)[d,e]	76.6	78.6	78.8[b]
Employment: Agriculture (% of employed)[f]	3.6	2.9	2.7
Employment: Industry (% of employed)[f]	23.8	22.2	20.5
Employment: Services (% of employed)[f]	72.6	74.9	76.8
Unemployment (% of labour force)	8.9	9.3	9.8[f]
Labour force participation (female/male pop. %)[f]	50.0 / 61.9	50.9 / 61.3	50.3 / 59.4
CPI: Consumer Price Index (2000=100)	110	119	125[g]
Agricultural production index (2004-2006=100)	100	97	103[g]
Food production index (2004-2006=100)	100	97	103[g]
Index of industrial production (2005=100)[h]	100	90	87[g]
International trade: Exports (million US$)[i]	434 354	511 651	488 885[c]
International trade: Imports (million US$)[i]	475 857	599 172	560 555[c]
International trade: Balance (million US$)[i]	- 41 503	- 87 520	- 71 670[c]
Balance of payments, current account (million US$)	- 137	- 22 034	- 4 861[b]

Major trading partners					2016
Export partners (% of exports)	Germany	16.1	Spain	7.5	United States	7.4
Import partners (% of imports)	Germany	16.9	China	9.1	Italy	7.5

Social indicators	2005	2010	2017
Population growth rate (average annual %)[j]	0.5	0.6	0.4[b]
Urban population (% of total population)	77.1	78.3	79.5[b]
Urban population growth rate (average annual %)[j]	1.1	0.9	0.8[b]
Fertility rate, total (live births per woman)[j]	1.9	2.0	2.0[b]
Life expectancy at birth (females/males, years)[j]	83.1 / 75.8	84.3 / 77.4	85.0 / 78.8[b]
Population age distribution (0-14 and 60+ years, %)	18.4 / 20.9	18.4 / 23.1	18.1 / 25.7[a]
International migrant stock (000/% of total pop.)	6 737.6 / 11.0	7 196.5 / 11.4	7 784.4 / 12.1[b]
Refugees and others of concern to UNHCR (000)	179.5[k]	250.4[k]	356.2[c]
Infant mortality rate (per 1 000 live births)[j]	4.3	3.7	3.4[b]
Health: Total expenditure (% of GDP)[l]	10.6	11.2	11.5[g]
Health: Physicians (per 1 000 pop.)	...	3.7[m]	3.2[b]
Education: Government expenditure (% of GDP)	5.5	5.7	5.5[n]
Education: Primary gross enrol. ratio (f/m per 100 pop.)	108.2 / 109.5	107.6 / 108.9	105.0 / 105.7[g]
Education: Secondary gross enrol. ratio (f/m per 100 pop.)	112.4 / 112.2	111.7 / 111.0	111.2 / 110.1[g]
Education: Tertiary gross enrol. ratio (f/m per 100 pop.)	62.0 / 49.1	63.9 / 50.6	71.0 / 57.9[g]
Intentional homicide rate (per 100 000 pop.)	1.6	1.3	1.6[b]
Seats held by women in national parliaments (%)	12.2	18.9	25.8

Environment and infrastructure indicators	2005	2010	2017
Mobile-cellular subscriptions (per 100 inhabitants)	78.3	91.4	102.6[b]
Individuals using the Internet (per 100 inhabitants)	42.9[o,p]	77.3[q]	84.7[q,b]
Research & Development expenditure (% of GDP)	2.0	2.2[r]	2.3[s,g]
Threatened species (number)	120[t]	168	278
Forested area (% of land area)[f]	29.0	30.0	30.8[g]
CO2 emission estimates (million tons/tons per capita)[u]	385.4 / 6.3	353.0 / 5.6	303.3 / 4.7[g]
Energy production, primary (Petajoules)[u]	5 692	5 623	5 694[g]
Energy supply per capita (Gigajoules)[u]	186	173	158[g]
Tourist/visitor arrivals at national borders (000)	74 988[r]	76 647	84 452[b]
Important sites for terrestrial biodiversity protected (%)	69.3	80.6	81.6
Pop. using improved drinking water (urban/rural, %)	100.0 / 100.0	100.0 / 100.0	100.0 / 100.0[b]
Pop. using improved sanitation facilities (urban/rural, %)	98.6 / 98.9	98.6 / 98.9	98.6 / 98.9[b]
Net Official Development Assist. disbursed (% of GNI)[v]	0.47	0.50	0.38[s,c]

a Projected estimate (medium fertility variant). b 2015. c 2016. d Including Guadeloupe, Martinique, Réunion and French Guiana. e Data classified according to ISIC Rev. 4. f Estimate. g 2014. h Excluding the Overseas Departments (French Guiana, Guadeloupe, Martinique, Mayotte and Réunion). i Beginning 1997, trade data for France include the import and export values of French Guiana, Guadeloupe, Martinique, and Réunion. j Data refers to a 5-year period preceding the reference year. k Data as at the end of December. l Estimates are based on different national accounting bases (2000, 2005 and 2010) with major breaks in the data for 2003 and 2011. m 2007. n 2013. o Users in the last month. p Population aged 11 years and over. q Population aged 16 to 74 years. r Break in the time series. s Provisional data. t 2004. u Including Monaco. v Development Assistance Committee member (OECD).

French Guiana

Region	South America	
Surface area (km2)	83 534[b]	
Sex ratio (m per 100 f, 2017)	100.0[a]	
National currency	Euro (EUR)	
Exchange rate (per US$)	0.9[d]	

Population (000, 2017)	283[a]	
Pop. density (per km2, 2017)	3.4[a]	
Capital city	Cayenne	
Capital city pop. (000)	58.1[c]	

Economic indicators	2005	2010	2017
Employment: Industry (% of employed)[e,f]	...	14.1	14.9[g]
Employment: Services (% of employed)[e,f]	...	51.5	58.3[g]
Unemployment (% of labour force)[f]	24.8	21.0	21.3[h,i]
Labour force participation (female/male pop. %)[f]	36.3 / 48.2	43.2 / 54.9	48.4 / 58.8[h,i]
CPI: Consumer Price Index (2000=100)	108	119	126[c]
Agricultural production index (2004-2006=100)	97	95	120[c]
Food production index (2004-2006=100)	97	95	120[c]

Social indicators	2005	2010	2017
Population growth rate (average annual %)[j]	4.5	2.8	2.8[b]
Urban population (% of total population)	81.1	82.9	84.4[b]
Urban population growth rate (average annual %)[j]	4.5	3.1	2.8[b]
Fertility rate, total (live births per woman)[j]	3.7	3.6	3.5[b]
Life expectancy at birth (females/males, years)[j]	80.1 / 72.8	81.4 / 75.0	82.6 / 76.1[b]
Population age distribution (0-14 and 60+ years, %)	36.1 / 5.7	35.3 / 6.5	33.2 / 8.4[a]
International migrant stock (000/% of total pop.)	86.5 / 42.5	96.3 / 41.2	106.1 / 39.5[b]
Infant mortality rate (per 1 000 live births)[j]	13.6	10.6	9.3[b]
Intentional homicide rate (per 100 000 pop.)	22.1	13.2[k]	...

Environment and infrastructure indicators	2005	2010	2017
Threatened species (number)	49[l]	56	73
Forested area (% of land area)[m]	99.4	99.0	98.9[c]
CO2 emission estimates (million tons/tons per capita)	0.6 / 2.8	0.6 / 2.8	0.7 / 2.8[c]
Energy production, primary (Petajoules)	2[m]	3	3[c]
Energy supply per capita (Gigajoules)	49	48[m]	50[m,c]
Tourist/visitor arrivals at national borders (000)	95	189	199[b]
Important sites for terrestrial biodiversity protected (%)	58.4	70.8	70.8
Pop. using improved drinking water (urban/rural, %)	91.8 / 73.4	94.5 / 75.1	94.5 / 75.1[c]
Pop. using improved sanitation facilities (urban/rural, %)	90.8 / 68.0	94.9 / 75.8	94.9 / 75.8[c]

a Projected estimate (medium fertility variant). **b** 2015. **c** 2014. **d** 2016. **e** Population aged 15 to 64 years. **f** Excluding the institutional population. **g** 2012. **h** Break in the time series. **i** 2013. **j** Data refers to a 5-year period preceding the reference year. **k** 2009. **l** 2004. **m** Estimate.

French Polynesia

Region	Polynesia	Population (000, 2017)	283[a]
Surface area (km2)	4 000[b]	Pop. density (per km2, 2017)	77.3[a]
Sex ratio (m per 100 f, 2017)	103.7[a]	Capital city	Papeete
National currency	CFP Franc (XPF)	Capital city pop. (000)	132.9[c,d]
Exchange rate (per US$)	113.2[e]		

Economic indicators

	2005	2010	2017
GDP: Gross domestic product (million current US$)	5 703	6 081	5 135[b]
GDP growth rate (annual %, const. 2005 prices)	1.4	- 2.5	1.6[b]
GDP per capita (current US$)	22 374.0	22 683.7	18 161.0[b]
Economy: Agriculture (% of GVA)	3.4	2.5	2.8[b]
Economy: Industry (% of GVA)	12.7	12.3	11.9[b]
Economy: Services and other activity (% of GVA)	83.9	85.2	85.2[b]
Employment: Agriculture (% of employed)[f]	9.1	9.6	8.9
Employment: Industry (% of employed)[f]	17.5	17.5	16.9
Employment: Services (% of employed)[f]	73.4	72.9	74.2
Unemployment (% of labour force)[f]	16.1	11.9	17.0
Labour force participation (female/male pop. %)[f]	47.2 / 65.8	47.0 / 64.1	46.4 / 63.0
CPI: Consumer Price Index (2000=100)	106	116	122[d]
Agricultural production index (2004-2006=100)	104	100	98[d]
Food production index (2004-2006=100)	104	100	98[d]
International trade: Exports (million US$)	210	153	173[e]
International trade: Imports (million US$)	1 702	1 726	1 491[e]
International trade: Balance (million US$)	- 1 491	- 1 573	- 1 319[e]
Balance of payments, current account (million US$)	9	- 18	208[d]

Major trading partners

					2016
Export partners (% of exports)	Japan	26.1	China, Hong Kong SAR	24.5	United States	18.0
Import partners (% of imports)	France	25.6	China	13.2	United States	10.4

Social indicators

	2005	2010	2017
Population growth rate (average annual %)[g]	1.4	1.0	0.7[b]
Urban population (% of total population)	56.4	56.5	55.9[b]
Urban population growth rate (average annual %)[g]	1.6	1.0	0.9[b]
Fertility rate, total (live births per woman)[g]	2.4	2.2	2.1[b]
Life expectancy at birth (females/males, years)[g]	76.0 / 70.6	77.4 / 72.8	78.6 / 74.0[b]
Population age distribution (0-14 and 60+ years, %)	27.7 / 8.0	25.2 / 9.3	23.3 / 11.9[a]
International migrant stock (000/% of total pop.)	32.3 / 12.7	31.6 / 11.8	30.1 / 10.6[b]
Infant mortality rate (per 1 000 live births)[g]	9.4	8.8	6.9[b]
Intentional homicide rate (per 100 000 pop.)	...	0.4[h]	...

Environment and infrastructure indicators

	2005	2010	2017
Mobile-cellular subscriptions (per 100 inhabitants)	47.1	80.5	94.9[b]
Individuals using the Internet (per 100 inhabitants)	21.5	49.0	64.6[f,b]
Threatened species (number)	122[i]	160	175
Forested area (% of land area)[f]	35.5	42.3	42.3[d]
CO2 emission estimates (million tons/tons per capita)	0.8 / 3.2	0.9 / 3.2	0.8 / 2.9[d]
Energy production, primary (Petajoules)	1	1	1[f,d]
Energy supply per capita (Gigajoules)	48	49	43[d]
Tourist/visitor arrivals at national borders (000)[j]	208	154	184[b]
Important sites for terrestrial biodiversity protected (%)	5.2	6.3	6.3
Pop. using improved drinking water (urban/rural, %)	100.0 / 100.0	100.0 / 100.0	100.0 / 100.0[b]
Pop. using improved sanitation facilities (urban/rural, %)	98.2 / 98.2	98.4 / 98.4	98.5 / 98.5[b]

a Projected estimate (medium fertility variant). **b** 2015. **c** Refers to the total population in the communes of Arue, Faaa, Mahina, Papara, Papeete, Pirae and Punaauia. **d** 2014. **e** 2016. **f** Estimate. **g** Data refers to a 5-year period preceding the reference year. **h** 2009. **i** 2004. **j** Excluding nationals residing abroad.

Gabon

Region	Middle Africa	UN membership date	20 September 1960
Population (000, 2017)	2 025[a]	Surface area (km2)	267 668[b]
Pop. density (per km2, 2017)	7.9[a]	Sex ratio (m per 100 f, 2017)	105.6[a]
Capital city	Libreville	National currency	CFA Franc (XAF)
Capital city pop. (000)	707.2[b]	Exchange rate (per US$)	622.3[c]

Economic indicators

	2005	2010	2017
GDP: Gross domestic product (million current US$)	9 579	12 882	13 735[b]
GDP growth rate (annual %, const. 2005 prices)	1.1	6.8	3.9[b]
GDP per capita (current US$)	6 952.5	8 354.4	7 960.7[b]
Economy: Agriculture (% of GVA)	5.2	4.6	3.8[b]
Economy: Industry (% of GVA)	62.6	55.6	54.5[b]
Economy: Services and other activity (% of GVA)	32.2	39.8	41.7[b]
Employment: Agriculture (% of employed)[d]	26.7	17.9	16.2
Employment: Industry (% of employed)[d]	14.1	17.5	19.1
Employment: Services (% of employed)[d]	59.2	64.6	64.8
Unemployment (% of labour force)	16.9	20.4	18.1[d]
Labour force participation (female/male pop. %)[d]	54.1 / 64.1	39.0 / 56.3	40.7 / 58.3
CPI: Consumer Price Index (2000=100)[e,f]	105	123	128[g]
Agricultural production index (2004-2006=100)	100	113	97[h]
Food production index (2004-2006=100)	100	111	92[h]
Index of industrial production (2005=100)[i,j]	100	117[k]	126[k,l]
International trade: Exports (million US$)	5 068	8 691	2 851[c]
International trade: Imports (million US$)	1 451	2 984	2 930[c]
International trade: Balance (million US$)	3 617	5 706	- 79[c]
Balance of payments, current account (million US$)	1 983	...	...

Major trading partners

							2016
Export partners (% of exports)	China	29.3	Trinidad and Tobago	12.6	Australia		9.2
Import partners (% of imports)	France	22.7	China	16.7	Congo		9.2

Social indicators

	2005	2010	2017
Population growth rate (average annual %)[m]	2.6	3.1	3.3[b]
Urban population (% of total population)	83.4	85.7	87.2[b]
Urban population growth rate (average annual %)[m]	3.2	2.9	2.7[b]
Fertility rate, total (live births per woman)[m]	4.4	4.2	4.0[b]
Life expectancy at birth (females/males, years)[m]	59.8 / 58.3	61.8 / 60.8	65.8 / 63.1[b]
Population age distribution (0-14 and 60+ years, %)	39.0 / 7.7	37.0 / 7.0	35.9 / 6.4[a]
International migrant stock (000/% of total pop.)[n]	214.1 / 15.5	244.0 / 15.6	268.4 / 15.6[b]
Refugees and others of concern to UNHCR (000)	13.7[o]	13.2[o]	2.9[c]
Infant mortality rate (per 1 000 live births)[m]	58.1	49.3	40.8[b]
Health: Total expenditure (% of GDP)	2.8	3.4	3.4[h]
Health: Physicians (per 1 000 pop.)	0.3[p]	...	...
Education: Government expenditure (% of GDP)	3.8[d,q]	3.1	2.7[h]
Education: Primary gross enrol. ratio (f/m per 100 pop.)	138.7 / 139.3[r]	... / ...	139.9 / 144.0[l]
Education: Tertiary gross enrol. ratio (f/m per 100 pop.)	6.2 / 10.6[r]	... / ...	... / ...
Intentional homicide rate (per 100 000 pop.)	11.2	9.3	9.0[b]
Seats held by women in national parliaments (%)	9.2	14.7	17.1

Environment and infrastructure indicators

	2005	2010	2017
Mobile-cellular subscriptions (per 100 inhabitants)	53.4[s]	103.5	168.9[b]
Individuals using the Internet (per 100 inhabitants)	4.9	7.2[d]	23.5[d,b]
Research & Development expenditure (% of GDP)	...	0.6[t]	...
Threatened species (number)	139[p]	204	270
Forested area (% of land area)	85.4	85.4	88.5[d,h]
CO2 emission estimates (million tons/tons per capita)	4.9 / 3.6	4.8 / 3.1	5.2 / 3.1[h]
Energy production, primary (Petajoules)	622	590	559[h]
Energy supply per capita (Gigajoules)	53	60	64[h]
Tourist/visitor arrivals at national borders (000)	269[u]	...	...
Important sites for terrestrial biodiversity protected (%)	61.2	61.2	61.2
Pop. using improved drinking water (urban/rural, %)	95.4 / 50.0	96.4 / 59.3	97.2 / 66.7[b]
Pop. using improved sanitation facilities (urban/rural, %)	41.0 / 33.7	42.3 / 32.5	43.4 / 31.5[b]
Net Official Development Assist. received (% of GNI)	0.59	0.85	0.73[b]

a Projected estimate (medium fertility variant). **b** 2015. **c** 2016. **d** Estimate. **e** Libreville **f** African population. **g** 2013. **h** 2014. **i** Data classified according to ISIC Rev. 3. **j** Country data supplemented with data from the Observatoire Economique et Statistique d'Afrique Subsaharienne (Afristat). **k** Data refers to manufacturing and utilities only. **l** 2011. **m** Data refers to a 5-year period preceding the reference year. **n** Refers to foreign citizens. **o** Data as at the end of December. **p** 2004. **q** 2000. **r** 2003. **s** Includes inactive subscriptions. **t** 2009. **u** Arrivals of non-resident tourists at Libreville airport.

Gambia

Region	Western Africa	UN membership date	21 September 1965
Population (000, 2017)	2 101 [a]	Surface area (km2)	11 295 [b]
Pop. density (per km2, 2017)	207.6 [a]	Sex ratio (m per 100 f, 2017)	98.0 [a]
Capital city	Banjul	National currency	Dalasi (GMD)
Capital city pop. (000)	503.6 [c,b]	Exchange rate (per US$)	45.3 [d]

Economic indicators	2005	2010	2017
GDP: Gross domestic product (million current US$)	624	952	942 [b]
GDP growth rate (annual %, const. 2005 prices)	- 0.9	6.5	4.7 [b]
GDP per capita (current US$)	433.3	562.6	473.2 [b]
Economy: Agriculture (% of GVA)	28.6	30.7	21.1 [b]
Economy: Industry (% of GVA)	14.9	13.1	14.9 [b]
Economy: Services and other activity (% of GVA)	56.5	56.3	64.0 [b]
Employment: Agriculture (% of employed) [e]	40.3	34.4	30.4
Employment: Industry (% of employed) [e]	9.5	11.7	14.4
Employment: Services (% of employed) [e]	50.2	53.8	55.2
Unemployment (% of labour force) [e]	29.7	29.8	29.7
Labour force participation (female/male pop. %) [e]	71.7 / 83.5	72.2 / 83.2	72.2 / 82.6
CPI: Consumer Price Index (2000=100) [f]	157	193	223 [g]
Agricultural production index (2004-2006=100)	94	137	82 [d]
Food production index (2004-2006=100)	94	137	82 [d]
International trade: Exports (million US$)	7	68	32 [h]
International trade: Imports (million US$)	260	284	471 [h]
International trade: Balance (million US$)	- 252	- 215	- 439 [h]
Balance of payments, current account (million US$)	- 50	21	...

Major trading partners						2016
Export partners (% of exports)	Mali	37.9	Guinea	24.7	Senegal	16.0
Import partners (% of imports)	Côte d'Ivoire	20.6	Brazil	11.0	China	8.3

Social indicators	2005	2010	2017
Population growth rate (average annual %) [i]	3.2	3.2	3.1 [b]
Urban population (% of total population)	52.3	56.3	59.6 [b]
Urban population growth rate (average annual %) [i]	4.9	4.6	4.3 [b]
Fertility rate, total (live births per woman) [i]	5.9	5.8	5.6 [b]
Life expectancy at birth (females/males, years) [i]	58.1 / 55.9	60.2 / 57.6	61.6 / 59.1 [b]
Population age distribution (0-14 and 60+ years, %)	46.3 / 4.0	46.3 / 3.7	45.3 / 3.8 [a]
International migrant stock (000/% of total pop.)	181.9 / 12.6	185.8 / 11.0	192.5 / 9.7 [b]
Refugees and others of concern to UNHCR (000)	8.0 [j]	8.5 [j]	7.9 [h]
Infant mortality rate (per 1 000 live births) [i]	59.4	52.4	49.8 [b]
Health: Total expenditure (% of GDP)	5.0	5.8	7.3 [d]
Health: Physicians (per 1 000 pop.)	0.1	0.1 [k]	...
Education: Government expenditure (% of GDP)	1.1	4.2	2.8 [g]
Education: Primary gross enrol. ratio (f/m per 100 pop.)	92.1 / 89.3	85.6 / 83.2	96.8 / 90.1 [h]
Education: Secondary gross enrol. ratio (f/m per 100 pop.)	... / ...	56.0 / 58.9 [e]	... / ...
Education: Tertiary gross enrol. ratio (f/m per 100 pop.)	0.4 / 1.9 [l]	1.8 / 2.6	2.5 / 3.7 [m]
Intentional homicide rate (per 100 000 pop.)	9.8	9.8	9.1 [b]
Seats held by women in national parliaments (%)	13.2	7.5	9.4

Environment and infrastructure indicators	2005	2010	2017
Mobile-cellular subscriptions (per 100 inhabitants)	17.2	88.0	131.3 [b]
Individuals using the Internet (per 100 inhabitants)	3.8 [e]	9.2	17.1 [e,b]
Research & Development expenditure (% of GDP)	...	-0.0 [n,o]	0.1 [p,q]
Threatened species (number)	21 [l]	43	67
Forested area (% of land area)	46.5	47.4	48.1 [e,d]
CO2 emission estimates (million tons/tons per capita)	0.3 / 0.2	0.4 / 0.3	0.5 / 0.3 [d]
Energy production, primary (Petajoules)	6	6	7 [d]
Energy supply per capita (Gigajoules)	7	7	7 [d]
Tourist/visitor arrivals at national borders (000) [r]	108	91	135 [b]
Important sites for terrestrial biodiversity protected (%)	34.6	34.6	34.6
Pop. using improved drinking water (urban/rural, %)	91.5 / 79.7	93.5 / 83.0	94.2 / 84.4 [b]
Pop. using improved sanitation facilities (urban/rural, %)	60.5 / 57.7	61.2 / 55.8	61.5 / 55.0 [b]
Net Official Development Assist. received (% of GNI)	10.26	12.83	12.35 [d]

a Projected estimate (medium fertility variant). b 2015. c Refers to the local government areas of Banjul and Kanifing. d 2014. e Estimate. f Banjul, Kombo St. Mary g 2013. h 2016. i Data refers to a 5-year period preceding the reference year. j Data as at the end of December. k 2008. l 2004. m 2012. n Partial data. o 2009. p Overestimated or based on overestimated data. q 2011. r Charter tourists only.

Georgia

Region	Western Asia	UN membership date	31 July 1992	
Population (000, 2017)	3 912[a,b]	Surface area (km2)	69 700[c]	
Pop. density (per km2, 2017)	56.3[a,b]	Sex ratio (m per 100 f, 2017)	91.4[a,b]	
Capital city	Tbilisi	National currency	Lari (GEL)	
Capital city pop. (000)	1 147.5[c]	Exchange rate (per US$)	2.6[d]	

Economic indicators	2005	2010	2017
GDP: Gross domestic product (million current US$)	6 411	11 638	13 965[c]
GDP growth rate (annual %, const. 2005 prices)	9.6	6.2	2.8[c]
GDP per capita (current US$)	1 432.5	2 738.3	3 491.4[c]
Economy: Agriculture (% of GVA)	16.5	8.3	9.0[c]
Economy: Industry (% of GVA)	26.5	22.0	24.1[c]
Economy: Services and other activity (% of GVA)	57.0	69.8	66.9[c]
Employment: Agriculture (% of employed)[e]	54.4	49.1	44.7
Employment: Industry (% of employed)[e]	9.2	10.4	11.2
Employment: Services (% of employed)[e]	36.4	40.5	44.1
Unemployment (% of labour force)	13.8	16.3	11.4[e]
Labour force participation (female/male pop. %)[e]	55.4 / 73.3	56.2 / 75.4	57.9 / 79.0
CPI: Consumer Price Index (2000=100)[f]	132	189	...
Agricultural production index (2004-2006=100)	121	67	85[g]
Food production index (2004-2006=100)	121	68	86[g]
Index of industrial production (2005=100)[h]	100	137	185[g]
International trade: Exports (million US$)	865	1 677	2 114[d]
International trade: Imports (million US$)	2 490	5 236	7 236[d]
International trade: Balance (million US$)	- 1 624	- 3 558	- 5 122[d]
Balance of payments, current account (million US$)	- 757	- 1 330	- 1 775[c]

Major trading partners						2016
Export partners (% of exports)	Russian Federation	9.8	Turkey	8.2	China	8.0
Import partners (% of imports)	Turkey	18.7	Russian Federation	9.3	China	7.6

Social indicators	2005	2010	2017
Population growth rate (average annual %)[b,i]	- 1.0	- 1.2	- 1.4[c]
Urban population (% of total population)[b]	52.5	52.9	53.6[c]
Urban population growth rate (average annual %)[b,i]	- 1.2	- 0.2	- 0.1[c]
Fertility rate, total (live births per woman)[b,i]	1.6	1.8	2.0[c]
Life expectancy at birth (females/males, years)[b,i]	76.1 / 68.9	76.5 / 68.6	77.0 / 68.5[c]
Population age distribution (0-14 and 60+ years, %)[b]	19.5 / 18.2	18.0 / 18.8	19.2 / 20.8[a]
International migrant stock (000/% of total pop.)[b]	199.8 / 4.5	182.2 / 4.3	168.8 / 4.2[c]
Refugees and others of concern to UNHCR (000)	238.6[j]	362.2[j]	274.1[d]
Infant mortality rate (per 1 000 live births)[b,i]	29.0	20.2	11.2[c]
Health: Total expenditure (% of GDP)[k]	8.6	10.1	7.4[g]
Health: Physicians (per 1 000 pop.)	...	4.3	4.8[g]
Education: Government expenditure (% of GDP)	2.5	3.2[e,l]	2.0[m]
Education: Primary gross enrol. ratio (f/m per 100 pop.)	93.6 / 96.5	110.7 / 109.3	118.2 / 115.5[c]
Education: Secondary gross enrol. ratio (f/m per 100 pop.)	80.3 / 83.0	88.5 / 92.8[n]	103.8 / 103.6[c]
Education: Tertiary gross enrol. ratio (f/m per 100 pop.)	47.2 / 45.9	32.3 / 25.6	47.8 / 39.2[c]
Intentional homicide rate (per 100 000 pop.)	9.0	4.4	2.7[g]
Seats held by women in national parliaments (%)	9.4	5.1	16.0

Environment and infrastructure indicators	2005	2010	2017
Mobile-cellular subscriptions (per 100 inhabitants)	26.2	90.6[o,p]	129.0[c]
Individuals using the Internet (per 100 inhabitants)	6.1[e]	26.9	45.2[q,r,c]
Research & Development expenditure (% of GDP)	0.2	...	0.1[s,t,g]
Threatened species (number)	43[u]	46	120
Forested area (% of land area)	39.9	40.6[e]	40.6[e,g]
CO2 emission estimates (million tons/tons per capita)	5.1 / 1.1	6.3 / 1.5	9.0 / 2.2[g]
Energy production, primary (Petajoules)	53	58	61[g]
Energy supply per capita (Gigajoules)	30	33	47[g]
Tourist/visitor arrivals at national borders (000)	...	1 067	2 282[c]
Important sites for terrestrial biodiversity protected (%)	19.8	22.0	29.3
Pop. using improved drinking water (urban/rural, %)	98.3 / 87.2	99.5 / 93.8	100.0 / 100.0[c]
Pop. using improved sanitation facilities (urban/rural, %)	96.0 / 88.6	95.6 / 82.2	95.2 / 75.9[c]
Net Official Development Assist. received (% of GNI)	4.53	5.56	3.30[c]

a Projected estimate (medium fertility variant). b Including Abkhazia and South Ossetia. c 2015. d 2016. e Estimate. f Five cities. g 2014. h Data classified according to ISIC Rev. 3. i Data refers to a 5-year period preceding the reference year. j Data as at the end of December. k As a result of recent health-care reforms in Georgia, public compulsory insurance has since 2008 been implemented by private insurance companies. The voucher cost of this insurance is treated as general government health expenditure. l 2009. m 2012. n 2008. o Data refers to subscriptions active in the last month (or 30 days). p Break in the time series. q Users in the last 3 months. r Population aged 6 years and over. s R&D budget instead of R&D expenditure or based on R&D budget. t Higher Education only. u 2004.

Germany

Region	Western Europe	UN membership date	18 September 1973
Population (000, 2017)	82 114 [a]	Surface area (km2)	357 376 [b]
Pop. density (per km2, 2017)	235.6 [a]	Sex ratio (m per 100 f, 2017)	97.0 [a]
Capital city	Berlin	National currency	Euro (EUR)
Capital city pop. (000)	3 563.2 [b]	Exchange rate (per US$)	0.9 [c]

Economic indicators	2005	2010	2017
GDP: Gross domestic product (million current US$)	2 861 339	3 417 095	3 363 600 [b]
GDP growth rate (annual %, const. 2005 prices)	0.7	4.1	1.7 [b]
GDP per capita (current US$)	35 217.9	42 482.5	41 686.2 [b]
Economy: Agriculture (% of GVA) [d]	0.8	0.7	0.6 [b]
Economy: Industry (% of GVA) [d]	29.4	30.2	30.5 [b]
Economy: Services and other activity (% of GVA) [d]	69.8	69.1	68.9 [b]
Employment: Agriculture (% of employed) [e]	2.4	1.6	1.4
Employment: Industry (% of employed) [e]	29.8	28.4	27.5
Employment: Services (% of employed) [e]	67.8	70.0	71.2
Unemployment (% of labour force)	11.2	7.0	4.2 [e]
Labour force participation (female/male pop. %) [e]	50.6 / 66.9	52.8 / 66.5	54.5 / 66.1
CPI: Consumer Price Index (2000=100)	108	117	125 [f]
Agricultural production index (2004-2006=100)	100	103	111 [f]
Food production index (2004-2006=100)	100	103	111 [f]
Index of industrial production (2005=100)	100	104 [g]	112 [g,f]
International trade: Exports (million US$)	977 132	1 271 096	1 340 752 [c]
International trade: Imports (million US$)	779 819	1 066 817	1 060 672 [c]
International trade: Balance (million US$)	197 313	204 280	280 080 [c]
Balance of payments, current account (million US$)	131 661	193 034	279 969 [b]

Major trading partners					2016
Export partners (% of exports)	United States	8.8	France	8.3	United Kingdom 7.0
Import partners (% of imports)	China	9.9	Netherlands	8.7	France 6.9

Social indicators	2005	2010	2017
Population growth rate (average annual %) [h]	~0.0	- 0.2	0.2 [b]
Urban population (% of total population)	73.4	74.3	75.3 [b]
Urban population growth rate (average annual %) [h]	0.2	0.1	0.2 [b]
Fertility rate, total (live births per woman) [h]	1.4	1.4	1.4 [b]
Life expectancy at birth (females/males, years) [h]	81.5 / 75.6	82.4 / 77.0	82.9 / 77.9 [b]
Population age distribution (0-14 and 60+ years, %)	14.4 / 24.9	13.6 / 26.1	13.1 / 28.0 [a]
International migrant stock (000/% of total pop.)	10 299.2 / 12.7	11 605.7 / 14.4	12 005.7 / 14.9 [b]
Refugees and others of concern to UNHCR (000)	784.0 [i]	670.6 [i]	1 052.1 [c]
Infant mortality rate (per 1 000 live births) [h]	4.2	3.7	3.4 [b]
Health: Total expenditure (% of GDP)	10.5	11.3	11.3 [f]
Health: Physicians (per 1 000 pop.)	...	3.8	4.1 [f]
Education: Government expenditure (% of GDP)	...	4.9	5.0 [f]
Education: Primary gross enrol. ratio (f/m per 100 pop.)	104.7 / 104.7	103.6 / 103.8	104.7 / 105.2 [b]
Education: Secondary gross enrol. ratio (f/m per 100 pop.)	101.1 / 103.8	101.2 / 106.6	99.6 / 105.6 [b]
Education: Tertiary gross enrol. ratio (f/m per 100 pop.)	... / ...	... / ...	66.8 / 69.7 [b]
Intentional homicide rate (per 100 000 pop.)	1.1	1.0	0.8 [b]
Seats held by women in national parliaments (%)	32.8	32.8	37.0

Environment and infrastructure indicators	2005	2010	2017
Mobile-cellular subscriptions (per 100 inhabitants)	94.6 [i]	106.5 [k,l,m]	116.7 [k,m,b]
Individuals using the Internet (per 100 inhabitants) [n]	68.7	82.0	87.6 [b]
Research & Development expenditure (% of GDP)	2.4	2.7 [e]	2.9 [e,f]
Threatened species (number)	78 [o]	79	116
Forested area (% of land area)	32.6	32.7	32.7 [e,f]
CO2 emission estimates (million tons/tons per capita)	797.2 / 9.6	758.9 / 9.4	719.9 / 8.9 [f]
Energy production, primary (Petajoules)	5 704	5 377	5 004 [f]
Energy supply per capita (Gigajoules)	170	170	158 [f]
Tourist/visitor arrivals at national borders (000)	21 500	26 875	34 970 [b]
Important sites for terrestrial biodiversity protected (%)	71.2	78.3	78.7
Pop. using improved drinking water (urban/rural, %)	100.0 / 100.0	100.0 / 100.0	100.0 / 100.0 [b]
Pop. using improved sanitation facilities (urban/rural, %)	99.3 / 99.0	99.3 / 99.0	99.3 / 99.0 [b]
Net Official Development Assist. disbursed (% of GNI) [p]	0.36	0.39	0.70 [q,c]

a Projected estimate (medium fertility variant). **b** 2015. **c** 2016. **d** Data classified according to ISIC Rev. 4. **e** Estimate. **f** 2014. **g** Excluding water and waste management. **h** Data refers to a 5-year period preceding the reference year. **i** Data as at the end of December. **j** Includes inactive subscriptions. **k** Excludes data-only subscriptions. **l** Break in the time series. **m** Data refers to active subscriptions only. **n** Population aged 16 to 74 years. **o** 2004. **p** Development Assistance Committee member (OECD) **q** Provisional data.

Ghana

Region	Western Africa	UN membership date	08 March 1957
Population (000, 2017)	28 834 [a]	Surface area (km2)	238 537 [b]
Pop. density (per km2, 2017)	126.7 [a]	Sex ratio (m per 100 f, 2017)	99.3 [a]
Capital city	Accra	National currency	Ghana Cedi (GHS)
Capital city pop. (000)	2 277.3 [b]	Exchange rate (per US$)	4.2 [c]

Economic indicators

	2005	2010	2017
GDP: Gross domestic product (million current US$)	17 199	32 174	37 156 [b]
GDP growth rate (annual %, const. 2005 prices)	6.2	7.9	3.9 [b]
GDP per capita (current US$)	804.1	1 323.1	1 355.6 [b]
Economy: Agriculture (% of GVA)	31.8	29.8 [d]	19.0 [d,b]
Economy: Industry (% of GVA)	20.3	19.1 [d]	26.9 [d,b]
Economy: Services and other activity (% of GVA)	47.9	51.1 [d]	54.1 [d,b]
Employment: Agriculture (% of employed) [e]	59.3	53.4	41.9
Employment: Industry (% of employed) [e]	13.2	13.1	14.2
Employment: Services (% of employed) [e]	27.5	33.5	43.8
Unemployment (% of labour force)	4.9 [e]	4.2	5.9 [e]
Labour force participation (female/male pop. %) [e]	67.6 / 71.7	71.6 / 75.2	75.7 / 78.8
CPI: Consumer Price Index (2000=100)	251	511	783 [f]
Agricultural production index (2004-2006=100)	100	124	144 [f]
Food production index (2004-2006=100)	100	124	144 [f]
International trade: Exports (million US$)	3 060	5 233	7 221 [c]
International trade: Imports (million US$)	4 878	8 057	11 939 [c]
International trade: Balance (million US$)	- 1 819	- 2 824	- 4 718 [c]
Balance of payments, current account (million US$)	- 1 105	- 2 747	- 2 809 [b]

Major trading partners

						2016
Export partners (% of exports)	Switzerland	23.0	India	13.9	China	12.5
Import partners (% of imports)	China	30.9	Nigeria	6.3	Netherlands	6.2

Social indicators

	2005	2010	2017
Population growth rate (average annual %) [g]	2.6	2.6	2.4 [b]
Urban population (% of total population)	47.3	50.7	54.0 [b]
Urban population growth rate (average annual %) [g]	4.0	3.9	3.4 [b]
Fertility rate, total (live births per woman) [g]	4.6	4.4	4.2 [b]
Life expectancy at birth (females/males, years) [g]	58.3 / 56.7	60.9 / 59.2	62.6 / 60.7 [b]
Population age distribution (0-14 and 60+ years, %)	40.6 / 5.2	39.6 / 5.4	38.5 / 5.3 [a]
International migrant stock (000/% of total pop.)	304.4 / 1.4	337.0 / 1.4	399.5 / 1.5 [b]
Refugees and others of concern to UNHCR (000)	60.2 [h]	14.8 [h]	27.3 [c]
Infant mortality rate (per 1 000 live births) [g]	60.9	55.4	46.5 [b]
Health: Total expenditure (% of GDP) [i]	4.5	5.3	3.6 [f]
Health: Physicians (per 1 000 pop.)	0.2 [j]	0.1	...
Education: Government expenditure (% of GDP)	7.4	5.5	6.2 [f]
Education: Primary gross enrol. ratio (f/m per 100 pop.)	88.6 / 92.1	104.5 / 106.5 [k]	108.7 / 107.3 [c]
Education: Secondary gross enrol. ratio (f/m per 100 pop.)	37.2 / 44.9 [e]	46.5 / 53.0 [k]	61.1 / 63.1 [c]
Education: Tertiary gross enrol. ratio (f/m per 100 pop.)	4.1 / 7.7	6.7 / 11.4 [k]	13.2 / 19.1 [b]
Intentional homicide rate (per 100 000 pop.)	1.8	1.7	1.7 [l]
Seats held by women in national parliaments (%)	10.9	8.3	12.7

Environment and infrastructure indicators

	2005	2010	2017
Mobile-cellular subscriptions (per 100 inhabitants)	13.4	71.9	129.7 [b]
Individuals using the Internet (per 100 inhabitants)	1.8	7.8 [m,n]	23.5 [e,b]
Research & Development expenditure (% of GDP)	...	0.4 [m]	...
Threatened species (number)	160 [j]	202	238
Forested area (% of land area)	39.8 [e]	40.4	40.9 [e,f]
CO2 emission estimates (million tons/tons per capita)	7.0 / 0.3	10.0 / 0.4	14.5 / 0.6 [f]
Energy production, primary (Petajoules)	164	148	410 [f]
Energy supply per capita (Gigajoules)	12	11	14 [f]
Tourist/visitor arrivals at national borders (000) [o]	429	931	897 [b]
Important sites for terrestrial biodiversity protected (%)	85.0	85.0	85.0
Pop. using improved drinking water (urban/rural, %)	89.3 / 66.1	90.9 / 75.1	92.6 / 84.0 [b]
Pop. using improved sanitation facilities (urban/rural, %)	17.6 / 6.9	19.2 / 8.0	20.2 / 8.6 [b]
Net Official Development Assist. received (% of GNI)	10.87	5.36	4.81 [b]

a Projected estimate (medium fertility variant). b 2015. c 2016. d Data classified according to ISIC Rev. 4. e Estimate. f 2014. g Data refers to a 5-year period preceding the reference year. h Data as at the end of December. i In 2010, Ghana revalued its economy from 1993 base to 2006, increasing its overall GDP by more than 60 per cent. Estimates have been updated taking into account 2010 GDP rebasing data series. j 2004. k 2009. l 2011. m Break in the time series. n Population aged 12 years and over. o Including nationals residing abroad.

Gibraltar

Region	Southern Europe	Population (000, 2017)	35 [a]
Surface area (km2)	6 [b]	Pop. density (per km2, 2017)	3 457.1 [a]
Sex ratio (m per 100 f, 2017)	101.8 [c,b]	Capital city	Gibraltar
National currency	Gibraltar Pound (GIP)	Capital city pop. (000)	29.3 [d]
Exchange rate (per US$)	0.8 [e]		

Economic indicators

	2005	2010	2017
Labour force participation (female/male pop. %)	57.5 / 78.8 [f]	... / ...	... / ...
CPI: Consumer Price Index (2000=100)	111	128	142 [d]
International trade: Exports (million US$)	195	259	234 [e]
International trade: Imports (million US$)	501	627	533 [e]
International trade: Balance (million US$)	- 306	- 368	- 299 [e]

Major trading partners

						2016
Export partners (% of exports)	Spain	28.6	Poland	24.9	Belgium	12.5
Import partners (% of imports)	United States	22.6	Russian Federation	14.5	United Kingdom	12.4

Social indicators

	2005	2010	2017
Population growth rate (average annual %) [g]	0.6	0.7	0.6 [b]
Urban population (% of total population)	100.0	100.0	100.0 [b]
Urban population growth rate (average annual %) [g]	1.2	0.1	0.1 [b]
Life expectancy at birth (females/males, years)	83.3 / 78.5 [f]	... / ...	... / ...
Population age distribution (0-14 and 60+ years, %)	18.4 / 20.5 [h,f]	... / ...	18.1 / 22.4 [c,i,j]
International migrant stock (000/% of total pop.)	9.2 / 31.7	10.4 / 33.7	11.1 / 34.3 [b]

Environment and infrastructure indicators

	2005	2010	2017
Mobile-cellular subscriptions (per 100 inhabitants)	68.8 [k]	102.6 [k]	129.5 [d]
Individuals using the Internet (per 100 inhabitants)	39.1 [k]	65.0	65.0 [k,j]
Threatened species (number)	18 [l]	22	31
Forested area (% of land area) [k]	0.0	0.0	0.0 [d]
CO2 emission estimates (million tons/tons per capita)	0.4 / 13.7	0.5 / 15.2	0.5 / 16.5 [d]
Energy supply per capita (Gigajoules)	219	238	259 [d]
Important sites for terrestrial biodiversity protected (%)	35.0	35.0	35.0

a Projected estimate (medium fertility variant). **b** 2015. **c** Excluding military personnel, visitors and transients. **d** 2014. **e** 2016. **f** 2001. **g** Data refers to a 5-year period preceding the reference year. **h** Excluding families of military personnel, visitors and transients. **i** De jure population. **j** 2012. **k** Estimate. **l** 2004.

Greece

Region	Southern Europe	UN membership date	25 October 1945
Population (000, 2017)	11 160[a]	Surface area (km2)	131 957[b]
Pop. density (per km2, 2017)	86.6[a]	Sex ratio (m per 100 f, 2017)	96.9[a]
Capital city	Athens	National currency	Euro (EUR)
Capital city pop. (000)	3 051.9[c,b]	Exchange rate (per US$)	0.9[d]

Economic indicators	2005	2010	2017
GDP: Gross domestic product (million current US$)	247 777	299 362	194 860[b]
GDP growth rate (annual %, const. 2005 prices)	0.6	- 5.5	- 0.2[b]
GDP per capita (current US$)	22 383.4	26 782.5	17 788.0[b]
Economy: Agriculture (% of GVA)[e]	4.8	3.3	4.1[b]
Economy: Industry (% of GVA)[e]	19.8	15.7	15.7[b]
Economy: Services and other activity (% of GVA)[e]	75.4	81.1	80.2[b]
Employment: Agriculture (% of employed)[f]	12.2	12.5	12.9
Employment: Industry (% of employed)[f]	22.4	19.6	15.0
Employment: Services (% of employed)[f]	65.4	67.9	72.1
Unemployment (% of labour force)	10.0	12.7	23.0[f]
Labour force participation (female/male pop. %)[f]	42.1 / 64.2	44.2 / 63.7	44.1 / 60.1
CPI: Consumer Price Index (2000=100)	118[g]	139	142[h]
Agricultural production index (2004-2006=100)	103	83	86[h]
Food production index (2004-2006=100)	103	86	87[h]
Index of industrial production (2005=100)	100	84	74[h]
International trade: Exports (million US$)	17 434	27 586	27 811[d]
International trade: Imports (million US$)	54 894	66 453	47 595[d]
International trade: Balance (million US$)	- 37 459	- 38 867	- 19 784[d]
Balance of payments, current account (million US$)	- 18 233	- 30 275	218[b]

Major trading partners						2016
Export partners (% of exports)	Italy	11.2	Germany	7.7	Cyprus	6.1
Import partners (% of imports)	Germany	10.9	Italy	8.3	China	6.7

Social indicators	2005	2010	2017
Population growth rate (average annual %)[i]	0.3	0.3	- 0.4[b]
Urban population (% of total population)	74.5	76.3	78.0[b]
Urban population growth rate (average annual %)[i]	0.6	0.6	0.5[b]
Fertility rate, total (live births per woman)[i]	1.3	1.5	1.3[b]
Life expectancy at birth (females/males, years)[i]	81.9 / 76.4	82.8 / 77.3	83.3 / 78.0[b]
Population age distribution (0-14 and 60+ years, %)	15.1 / 22.5	14.9 / 24.0	14.2 / 26.5[a]
International migrant stock (000/% of total pop.)	1 190.7 / 10.8	1 269.7 / 11.4	1 242.5 / 11.3[b]
Refugees and others of concern to UNHCR (000)	14.3[j]	57.4[j]	94.7[d]
Infant mortality rate (per 1 000 live births)	4.6	3.5	3.3[b]
Health: Total expenditure (% of GDP)	9.4	9.2	8.1[h]
Health: Physicians (per 1 000 pop.)	...	6.2	6.3[h]
Education: Government expenditure (% of GDP)	4.0	...	...
Education: Primary gross enrol. ratio (f/m per 100 pop.)	97.8 / 100.3	99.3 / 101.2	97.1 / 98.1[h]
Education: Secondary gross enrol. ratio (f/m per 100 pop.)	97.4 / 101.7	101.5 / 108.3	103.4 / 109.5[h]
Education: Tertiary gross enrol. ratio (f/m per 100 pop.)	92.7 / 81.9	104.9 / 100.6	113.7 / 114.0[h]
Intentional homicide rate (per 100 000 pop.)	1.2	1.6	0.8[b]
Seats held by women in national parliaments (%)	14.0	17.3	18.3

Environment and infrastructure indicators	2005	2010	2017
Mobile-cellular subscriptions (per 100 inhabitants)	92.9	110.6	114.0[k,b]
Individuals using the Internet (per 100 inhabitants)[l]	24.0	44.4	66.8[b]
Research & Development expenditure (% of GDP)	0.6	0.6[f]	0.8[h]
Threatened species (number)	75[m]	156	374
Forested area (% of land area)[f]	29.1	30.3	31.2[h]
CO2 emission estimates (million tons/tons per capita)	98.7 / 8.8	83.9 / 7.5	67.3 / 6.1[h]
Energy production, primary (Petajoules)	432	396	368[h]
Energy supply per capita (Gigajoules)	115	105	89[h]
Tourist/visitor arrivals at national borders (000)	14 765	15 007	23 599[b]
Important sites for terrestrial biodiversity protected (%)	65.7	72.5	72.5
Pop. using improved drinking water (urban/rural, %)	99.9 / 98.1	100.0 / 100.0	100.0 / 100.0[b]
Pop. using improved sanitation facilities (urban/rural, %)	98.3 / 93.6	98.9 / 97.2	99.2 / 98.1[b]
Net Official Development Assist. disbursed (% of GNI)[n]	0.17	0.17	0.14[o,d]

a Projected estimate (medium fertility variant). b 2015. c Refers to the localities of Calithèa, Peristérion and Piraeus, among others. d 2016. e Data classified according to ISIC Rev. 4. f Estimate. g Series linked to former series. h 2014. i Data refers to a 5-year period preceding the reference year. j Data as at the end of December. k Four companies compete on the local market. The latest company entered the market at the 4 quarter of 2014. Data on the new entrant concern the 9th month of 2015. l Population aged 16 to 74 years. m 2004. n Development Assistance Committee member (OECD) o Provisional data.

Greenland

Region	Northern America	Population (000, 2017)	56[a]
Surface area (km2)	2 166 086[b]	Pop. density (per km2, 2017)	0.1[a]
Sex ratio (m per 100 f, 2017)	112.1[c,d,e]	Capital city	Nuuk
National currency	Danish Krone (DKK)	Capital city pop. (000)	16.9[f]
Exchange rate (per US$)	7.1[e]		

Economic indicators

	2005	2010	2017
GDP: Gross domestic product (million current US$)	1 650	2 287	2 078[b]
GDP growth rate (annual %, const. 2005 prices)	3.7	2.5	0.3[b]
GDP per capita (current US$)	28 968.6	40 450.4	36 976.7[b]
Economy: Agriculture (% of GVA)	10.2	7.5	10.0[b]
Economy: Industry (% of GVA)	15.3	17.6	15.9[b]
Economy: Services and other activity (% of GVA)	74.5	74.9	74.1[b]
Employment: Agriculture (% of employed)	...	...	4.6[g,h,i]
Employment: Industry (% of employed)	...	...	12.6[g,h,i]
Employment: Services (% of employed)	...	...	82.5[g,h,i]
Unemployment (% of labour force)	9.3	8.4[j]	9.7[h,k,l,m]
CPI: Consumer Price Index (2000=100)	113	132	144[f]
Agricultural production index (2004-2006=100)	100	99	99[f]
Food production index (2004-2006=100)	99	99	99[f]
International trade: Exports (million US$)	402	391	553[e]
International trade: Imports (million US$)	700	854	623[e]
International trade: Balance (million US$)	- 297	- 463	- 71[e]

Major trading partners

						2016
Export partners (% of exports)	Denmark	81.3	Portugal	8.3	Areas nes[n]	6.0
Import partners (% of imports)	Denmark	72.2	Sweden	9.8	China	2.6

Social indicators

	2005	2010	2017
Population growth rate (average annual %)[o]	0.3	- 0.1	- 0.1[b]
Urban population (% of total population)	82.9	84.4	86.4[b]
Urban population growth rate (average annual %)[o]	0.6	0.2	0.7[b]
Fertility rate, total (live births per woman)	2.3	2.3	2.0[f]
Life expectancy at birth (females/males, years)[p]	... / ...	71.0 / 65.7	73.4 / 68.7[e]
Population age distribution (0-14 and 60+ years, %)[d,c]	25.0 / 9.6	22.6 / 10.9	21.0 / 13.2[e]
International migrant stock (000/% of total pop.)	6.7 / 11.7	6.2 / 11.0	6.0 / 10.7[b]
Intentional homicide rate (per 100 000 pop.)	17.6	31.8	12.5[b]

Environment and infrastructure indicators

	2005	2010	2017
Mobile-cellular subscriptions (per 100 inhabitants)	81.6	101.4	106.5[q,b]
Individuals using the Internet (per 100 inhabitants)	57.7	63.0	67.6[q,b]
Threatened species (number)	12[r]	14	23
Forested area (% of land area)[q]	~0.0	~0.0	~0.0[f]
CO2 emission estimates (million tons/tons per capita)	0.6 / 10.6	0.7 / 11.7	0.5 / 9.0[f]
Energy production, primary (Petajoules)	1	1	2[f]
Energy supply per capita (Gigajoules)	165	186	154[f]
Important sites for terrestrial biodiversity protected (%)	26.1	26.4	30.3
Pop. using improved drinking water (urban/rural, %)	100.0 / 100.0	100.0 / 100.0	100.0 / 100.0[b]
Pop. using improved sanitation facilities (urban/rural, %)	100.0 / 100.0	100.0 / 100.0	100.0 / 100.0[b]

a Projected estimate (medium fertility variant). **b** 2015. **c** Population statistics are compiled from registers. **d** De jure population. **e** 2016. **f** 2014. **g** Population aged 15 to 64 years. **h** Nationals, residents. **i** 2011. **j** 2006. **k** Population aged 18 to 64 years. **l** Break in the time series. **m** 2013. **n** Areas not elsewhere specified. **o** Data refers to a 5-year period preceding the reference year. **p** Data refers to a 5-year period up to and including the reference year. **q** Estimate. **r** 2004.

Grenada

Region	Caribbean	
Population (000, 2017)	108[a]	
Pop. density (per km2, 2017)	317.1[a]	
Capital city	Saint George's	
Capital city pop. (000)	37.8[d]	

UN membership date	17 September 1974
Surface area (km2)	345[b]
Sex ratio (m per 100 f, 2017)	100.9[a]
National currency	E. Caribbean Dollar (XCD)[c]
Exchange rate (per US$)	2.7[e]

Economic indicators	2005	2010	2017
GDP: Gross domestic product (million current US$)	701	777	954[b]
GDP growth rate (annual %, const. 2005 prices)	13.3	- 0.5	6.2[b]
GDP per capita (current US$)	6 804.3	7 418.1	8 933.8[b]
Economy: Agriculture (% of GVA)	3.4	5.2	8.3[b]
Economy: Industry (% of GVA)	26.1	16.8	13.9[b]
Economy: Services and other activity (% of GVA)	70.5	78.1	77.8[b]
Unemployment (% of labour force)	10.2[f]	...	...
CPI: Consumer Price Index (2000=100)	112	136[g]	142[h]
Agricultural production index (2004-2006=100)	79	97	103[d]
Food production index (2004-2006=100)	79	98	103[d]
International trade: Exports (million US$)	28	24	30[e]
International trade: Imports (million US$)	334	317	350[e]
International trade: Balance (million US$)	- 306	- 293	- 320[e]
Balance of payments, current account (million US$)	- 193	- 204	- 213[h]

Major trading partners						2016
Export partners (% of exports)	United States	32.5	Saint Lucia	12.3	Germany	6.1
Import partners (% of imports)	United States	39.1	Trinidad and Tobago	10.4	United Kingdom	5.0

Social indicators	2005	2010	2017
Population growth rate (average annual %)[i]	0.3	0.3	0.4[b]
Urban population (% of total population)	35.9	35.7	35.6[b]
Urban population growth rate (average annual %)[i]	0.3	0.2	0.3[b]
Fertility rate, total (live births per woman)[i]	2.4	2.3	2.2[b]
Life expectancy at birth (females/males, years)[i]	73.2 / 68.5	74.4 / 69.6	75.6 / 70.8[b]
Population age distribution (0-14 and 60+ years, %)	30.0 / 9.9	27.5 / 9.6	26.3 / 10.5[a]
International migrant stock (000/% of total pop.)	6.9 / 6.7	7.0 / 6.7	7.1 / 6.6[b]
Refugees and others of concern to UNHCR (000)	...	~0.0[i]	~0.0[e]
Infant mortality rate (per 1 000 live births)[i]	12.0	10.2	9.6[b]
Health: Total expenditure (% of GDP)	5.5	6.4	6.1[d]
Health: Physicians (per 1 000 pop.)	0.6[k]	0.7[l]	...
Education: Government expenditure (% of GDP)	3.9[k]	...	...
Education: Primary gross enrol. ratio (f/m per 100 pop.)	95.5 / 98.4	101.5 / 105.1	102.9 / 106.8[b]
Education: Secondary gross enrol. ratio (f/m per 100 pop.)	98.7 / 96.9[m]	109.4 / 106.2	99.0 / 99.4[b]
Education: Tertiary gross enrol. ratio (f/m per 100 pop.)	... / ...	60.9 / 44.8[n]	97.9 / 84.5[b]
Intentional homicide rate (per 100 000 pop.)	10.7	9.6	7.5[d]
Seats held by women in national parliaments (%)	26.7	13.3	33.3

Environment and infrastructure indicators	2005	2010	2017
Mobile-cellular subscriptions (per 100 inhabitants)	45.5	116.5	112.2[b]
Individuals using the Internet (per 100 inhabitants)[m]	20.5	27.0	53.8[b]
Threatened species (number)	23[o]	37	54
Forested area (% of land area)[m]	50.0	50.0	50.0[d]
CO2 emission estimates (million tons/tons per capita)	0.2 / 2.1	0.3 / 2.5	0.2 / 2.3[d]
Energy production, primary (Petajoules)	0	0	0[d]
Energy supply per capita (Gigajoules)	33	38	35[d]
Tourist/visitor arrivals at national borders (000)	99	110	141[b]
Important sites for terrestrial biodiversity protected (%)	30.2	30.2	42.7
Pop. using improved drinking water (urban/rural, %)	99.0 / 95.3	99.0 / 95.3	99.0 / 95.3[b]
Pop. using improved sanitation facilities (urban/rural, %)	97.5 / 98.3	97.5 / 98.3	97.5 / 98.3[b]
Net Official Development Assist. received (% of GNI)	7.89	4.63	2.55[b]

a Projected estimate (medium fertility variant). b 2015. c East Caribbean Dollar. d 2014. e 2016. f 2001. g Series linked to former series. h 2013. i Data refers to a 5-year period preceding the reference year. j Data as at the end of December. k 2003. l 2006. m Estimate. n 2009. o 2004.

Guadeloupe

Region	Caribbean
Surface area (km2)	1 705 [c]
Sex ratio (m per 100 f, 2017)	86.4 [a,b]
National currency	Euro (EUR)
Exchange rate (per US$)	0.9 [e]

Population (000, 2017)	450 [a,b]
Pop. density (per km2, 2017)	266.0 [a,b]
Capital city	Basse-Terre
Capital city pop. (000)	55.3 [d]

Economic indicators	2005	2010	2017
Employment: Agriculture (% of employed)	...	...	3.3 [f,g,h]
Employment: Industry (% of employed) [f,g]	...	13.8	13.5 [h]
Employment: Services (% of employed) [f,g]	...	64.4	65.5 [h]
Unemployment (% of labour force) [g]	25.9	23.8	26.1 [i,j]
Labour force participation (female/male pop. %) [g]	37.7 / 46.8	39.5 / 44.2	49.6 / 56.5 [i,j]
CPI: Consumer Price Index (2000=100)	112	122	129 [d]
Agricultural production index (2004-2006=100)	103	89	100 [d]
Food production index (2004-2006=100)	103	89	100 [d]

Social indicators	2005	2010	2017
Population growth rate (average annual %) [a,k]	0.7	0.5	--0.0 [c]
Urban population (% of total population) [a]	98.4	98.4	98.4 [c]
Urban population growth rate (average annual %) [a,k]	0.8	0.7	0.5 [c]
Fertility rate, total (live births per woman) [a,k]	2.1	2.1	2.0 [c]
Life expectancy at birth (females/males, years) [a,k]	81.4 / 74.2	82.9 / 75.7	84.0 / 76.8 [c]
Population age distribution (0-14 and 60+ years, %) [a]	23.8 / 15.6	22.0 / 19.3	18.6 / 23.6 [b]
International migrant stock (000/% of total pop.) [a]	89.1 / 19.8	94.9 / 20.8	98.5 / 21.0 [c]
Infant mortality rate (per 1 000 live births) [a,k]	8.7	7.0	5.8 [c]
Intentional homicide rate (per 100 000 pop.)	5.1	7.9 [l]	...

Environment and infrastructure indicators	2005	2010	2017
Threatened species (number) [m]	33 [n]	54	73
Forested area (% of land area) [o]	43.8	43.1	43.0 [d]
CO2 emission estimates (million tons/tons per capita)	2.2 / 5.0	2.3 / 5.0	2.6 / 5.5 [d]
Energy production, primary (Petajoules)	3 [o]	4 [o]	5 [d]
Energy supply per capita (Gigajoules)	71	72 [o]	80 [o,d]
Tourist/visitor arrivals at national borders (000) [m,p]	372	392	512 [c]
Important sites for terrestrial biodiversity protected (%)	54.2	80.6	80.7
Pop. using improved drinking water (urban/rural, %)	98.6 / 99.7	99.3 / 99.8	99.3 / 99.8 [c]
Pop. using improved sanitation facilities (urban/rural, %)	95.5 / 89.5	97.0 / 89.5	97.0 / 89.5 [c,d]

a Including Saint Barthélemy and Saint Martin (French part). **b** Projected estimate (medium fertility variant). **c** 2015. **d** 2014. **e** 2016. **f** Population aged 15 to 64 years. **g** Excluding the institutional population. **h** 2012. **i** Break in the time series. **j** 2013. **k** Data refers to a 5-year period preceding the reference year. **l** 2009. **m** Excluding the north islands, Saint Barthélemy and Saint Martin (French part). **n** 2004. **o** Estimate. **p** Arrivals by air.

Guam

Region	Micronesia	Population (000, 2017)	164[a]
Surface area (km2)	549[b]	Pop. density (per km2, 2017)	304.1[a]
Sex ratio (m per 100 f, 2017)	102.6[a]	Capital city	Hagåtña
National currency	US Dollar (USD)	Capital city pop. (000)	143.4[c]

Economic indicators	2005	2010	2017
Employment: Agriculture (% of employed)[d]	0.4	0.3	0.2
Employment: Industry (% of employed)[d]	12.6	13.8	14.0
Employment: Services (% of employed)[d]	87.1	85.9	85.7
Unemployment (% of labour force)	7.0	8.2	10.7[d]
Labour force participation (female/male pop. %)[d]	56.1 / 69.7	54.8 / 70.1	55.2 / 68.7
CPI: Consumer Price Index (2000=100)	116	154	165[c]
Agricultural production index (2004-2006=100)	99	96	88[c]
Food production index (2004-2006=100)	99	96	88[c]

Social indicators	2005	2010	2017
Population growth rate (average annual %)[e]	0.4	0.1	0.3[b]
Urban population (% of total population)	93.6	94.1	94.5[b]
Urban population growth rate (average annual %)[e]	0.5	0.2	1.4[b]
Fertility rate, total (live births per woman)[e]	2.7	2.5	2.4[b]
Life expectancy at birth (females/males, years)[e]	78.5 / 73.6	80.3 / 74.7	81.5 / 76.4[b]
Population age distribution (0-14 and 60+ years, %)	29.5 / 9.2	27.5 / 11.1	24.7 / 14.0[a]
International migrant stock (000/% of total pop.)	74.7 / 47.2	75.4 / 47.3	76.1 / 44.8[b]
Infant mortality rate (per 1 000 live births)[e]	13.5	11.4	9.6[b]
Intentional homicide rate (per 100 000 pop.)	4.4	1.9	2.5[f]

Environment and infrastructure indicators	2005	2010	2017
Mobile-cellular subscriptions (per 100 inhabitants)	17.5[g]	...	...
Individuals using the Internet (per 100 inhabitants)	38.6	54.0[d]	73.1[d,b]
Threatened species (number)	24[h]	34	99
Forested area (% of land area)[d]	46.3	46.3	46.3[c]
Tourist/visitor arrivals at national borders (000)	1 228	1 197	1 409[b]
Important sites for terrestrial biodiversity protected (%)	60.2	60.2	60.2
Pop. using improved drinking water (urban/rural, %)	99.6 / 99.6	99.5 / 99.5	99.5 / 99.5[b]
Pop. using improved sanitation facilities (urban/rural, %)	89.4 / 89.4	89.7 / 89.7	89.8 / 89.8[b]

a Projected estimate (medium fertility variant). b 2015. c 2014. d Estimate. e Data refers to a 5-year period preceding the reference year. f 2011. g 2000. h 2004.

Guatemala

Region	Central America	UN membership date	21 November 1945
Population (000, 2017)	16 914[a]	Surface area (km2)	108 889[b]
Pop. density (per km2, 2017)	157.8[a]	Sex ratio (m per 100 f, 2017)	96.9[a]
Capital city	Guatemala City	National currency	Quetzal (GTQ)
Capital city pop. (000)	2 918.3[b]	Exchange rate (per US$)	7.5[c]

Economic indicators	2005	2010	2017
GDP: Gross domestic product (million current US$)	27 211	41 338	63 794[b]
GDP growth rate (annual %, const. 2005 prices)	3.3	2.9	4.1[b]
GDP per capita (current US$)	2 064.0	2 806.0	3 903.5[b]
Economy: Agriculture (% of GVA)	13.1	11.4	10.8[b]
Economy: Industry (% of GVA)	28.6	28.0	27.2[b]
Economy: Services and other activity (% of GVA)	58.3	60.6	62.0[b]
Employment: Agriculture (% of employed)[d]	36.7	38.8	32.0
Employment: Industry (% of employed)[d]	21.2	19.5	18.5
Employment: Services (% of employed)[d]	42.2	41.7	49.4
Unemployment (% of labour force)	2.5[d]	3.7	2.4[d]
Labour force participation (female/male pop. %)[d]	45.1 / 87.6	41.8 / 85.7	41.7 / 84.0
CPI: Consumer Price Index (2000=100)	144	193	229[e]
Agricultural production index (2004-2006=100)	99	133	158[e]
Food production index (2004-2006=100)	97	132	158[e]
International trade: Exports (million US$)	5 381	8 460	10 572[c]
International trade: Imports (million US$)	10 500	13 830	16 987[c]
International trade: Balance (million US$)	- 5 119	- 5 370	- 6 415[c]
Balance of payments, current account (million US$)	- 1 301	- 563	- 96[b]

Major trading partners						2016
Export partners (% of exports)	United States	35.0	El Salvador	11.6	Honduras	8.5
Import partners (% of imports)	United States	37.1	Mexico	11.6	China	10.6

Social indicators	2005	2010	2017
Population growth rate (average annual %)[f]	2.3	2.2	2.1[b]
Urban population (% of total population)	47.2	49.3	51.6[b]
Urban population growth rate (average annual %)[f]	3.4	3.4	3.4[b]
Fertility rate, total (live births per woman)[f]	4.3	3.6	3.2[b]
Life expectancy at birth (females/males, years)[f]	72.1 / 65.7	73.7 / 67.2	75.6 / 69.2[b]
Population age distribution (0-14 and 60+ years, %)	42.3 / 5.9	39.4 / 6.1	35.1 / 6.9[a]
International migrant stock (000/% of total pop.)[g]	57.3 / 0.4	66.4 / 0.5	76.4 / 0.5[b]
Refugees and others of concern to UNHCR (000)	0.4[h]	0.1[h]	1.8[c]
Infant mortality rate (per 1 000 live births)[f]	37.3	31.3	26.9[b]
Health: Total expenditure (% of GDP)[i]	6.8	6.6	6.2[e]
Health: Physicians (per 1 000 pop.)	...	0.9[j]	...
Education: Government expenditure (% of GDP)	...	2.8	3.0[b]
Education: Primary gross enrol. ratio (f/m per 100 pop.)	107.5 / 115.4	115.2 / 118.7	99.8 / 103.8[b]
Education: Secondary gross enrol. ratio (f/m per 100 pop.)	47.6 / 51.9	61.0 / 65.2	63.3 / 67.9[b]
Education: Tertiary gross enrol. ratio (f/m per 100 pop.)	7.5 / 10.2[k]	17.1 / 16.7[l]	23.5 / 20.2[b]
Intentional homicide rate (per 100 000 pop.)	35.0[m]	40.5	31.2[e]
Seats held by women in national parliaments (%)	8.2	12.0	12.7

Environment and infrastructure indicators	2005	2010	2017
Mobile-cellular subscriptions (per 100 inhabitants)	35.6	126.0	111.5[b]
Individuals using the Internet (per 100 inhabitants)	5.7	10.5[d]	27.1[d,b]
Research & Development expenditure (% of GDP)[n]	~0.0	~0.0	~0.0[o]
Threatened species (number)	208[m]	230	290
Forested area (% of land area)	36.7	34.7[d]	33.4[d,e]
CO2 emission estimates (million tons/tons per capita)	12.6 / 1.0	11.7 / 0.8	18.3 / 1.1[e]
Energy production, primary (Petajoules)	255	279	327[e]
Energy supply per capita (Gigajoules)	29	27	32[e]
Tourist/visitor arrivals at national borders (000)	...	1 119	1 473[b]
Important sites for terrestrial biodiversity protected (%)	27.6	30.8	30.8
Pop. using improved drinking water (urban/rural, %)	95.4 / 80.1	97.3 / 84.3	98.4 / 86.8[b]
Pop. using improved sanitation facilities (urban/rural, %)	75.0 / 43.0	76.6 / 46.9	77.5 / 49.3[b]
Net Official Development Assist. received (% of GNI)	0.95	0.97	0.66[b]

a Projected estimate (medium fertility variant). b 2015. c 2016. d Estimate. e 2014. f Data refers to a 5-year period preceding the reference year. g Including refugees. h Data as at the end of December. i Data revision. j 2009. k 2002. l 2007. m 2004. n Partial data. o 2012.

Guinea

Region	Western Africa	UN membership date	12 December 1958
Population (000, 2017)	12 717[a]	Surface area (km2)	245 857[b]
Pop. density (per km2, 2017)	51.8[a]	Sex ratio (m per 100 f, 2017)	100.6[a]
Capital city	Conakry	National currency	Guinean Franc (GNF)
Capital city pop. (000)	1 936.0[b]	Exchange rate (per US$)	9 225.3[c]

Economic indicators

	2005	2010	2017
GDP: Gross domestic product (million current US$)	4 063	6 853	8 875[b]
GDP growth rate (annual %, const. 2005 prices)	3.0	4.2	0.1[b]
GDP per capita (current US$)	420.2	622.3	703.9[b]
Economy: Agriculture (% of GVA)	14.9	18.6	19.8[b]
Economy: Industry (% of GVA)	34.9	34.3	32.8[b]
Economy: Services and other activity (% of GVA)	50.3	47.1	47.4[b]
Employment: Agriculture (% of employed)[d]	74.5	74.3	69.7
Employment: Industry (% of employed)[d]	5.6	5.8	7.4
Employment: Services (% of employed)[d]	19.9	19.9	22.9
Unemployment (% of labour force)[d]	6.9	6.9	6.8
Labour force participation (female/male pop. %)[d]	62.7 / 80.9	66.1 / 80.9	79.4 / 85.1
CPI: Consumer Price Index (2000=100)[e]	185	439	753[f]
Agricultural production index (2004-2006=100)	100	120	130[f]
Food production index (2004-2006=100)	101	120	131[f]
International trade: Exports (million US$)	796	1 471	1 753[c]
International trade: Imports (million US$)	1 648	1 405	2 082[c]
International trade: Balance (million US$)	- 852	66	- 329[c]
Balance of payments, current account (million US$)	- 160	- 329	- 1 240[g]

Major trading partners

						2016
Export partners (% of exports)	Ghana	22.0	India	16.4	United Arab Emirates	9.9
Import partners (% of imports)	China	14.9	Netherlands	13.4	India	10.9

Social indicators

	2005	2010	2017
Population growth rate (average annual %)[h]	1.9	2.2	2.3[b]
Urban population (% of total population)	32.8	34.9	37.2[b]
Urban population growth rate (average annual %)[h]	2.9	3.8	3.8[b]
Fertility rate, total (live births per woman)[h]	5.9	5.5	5.1[b]
Life expectancy at birth (females/males, years)[h]	51.3 / 51.3	56.4 / 54.5	58.4 / 57.4[b]
Population age distribution (0-14 and 60+ years, %)	44.0 / 5.1	43.5 / 4.9	42.3 / 5.2[a]
International migrant stock (000/% of total pop.)[i,j]	229.6 / 2.4	205.1 / 1.9	228.4 / 1.8[b]
Refugees and others of concern to UNHCR (000)	97.0[k]	15.0[k]	9.2[c]
Infant mortality rate (per 1 000 live births)[h]	95.2	77.7	65.7[b]
Health: Total expenditure (% of GDP)	2.8	4.5	5.6[f]
Health: Physicians (per 1 000 pop.)	0.1	...	...
Education: Government expenditure (% of GDP)	1.8	3.7	3.2[f]
Education: Primary gross enrol. ratio (f/m per 100 pop.)	70.4 / 87.8	76.4 / 92.6	83.8 / 98.6[f]
Education: Secondary gross enrol. ratio (f/m per 100 pop.)	19.4 / 38.9[d]	24.9 / 43.1[l]	30.7 / 46.8[f]
Education: Tertiary gross enrol. ratio (f/m per 100 pop.)	1.1 / 4.7	5.1 / 15.4	6.7 / 14.9[f]
Intentional homicide rate (per 100 000 pop.)	10.1	9.3	8.5[b]
Seats held by women in national parliaments (%)	19.3	19.3[m,l]	21.9

Environment and infrastructure indicators

	2005	2010	2017
Mobile-cellular subscriptions (per 100 inhabitants)	2.0	36.8	87.2[b]
Individuals using the Internet (per 100 inhabitants)	0.5	1.0[d]	4.7[d,b]
Threatened species (number)	67[n]	134	185
Forested area (% of land area)[d]	27.4	26.6	26.0[f]
CO2 emission estimates (million tons/tons per capita)	1.8 / 0.2	2.6 / 0.2	2.4 / 0.2[f]
Energy production, primary (Petajoules)	109	111	113[f]
Energy supply per capita (Gigajoules)	15	13	12[f]
Tourist/visitor arrivals at national borders (000)[o]	45	12	35[b]
Important sites for terrestrial biodiversity protected (%)	67.2	67.2	67.2
Pop. using improved drinking water (urban/rural, %)	90.3 / 56.8	91.7 / 62.7	92.7 / 67.4[b]
Pop. using improved sanitation facilities (urban/rural, %)	27.9 / 9.2	31.3 / 10.6	34.1 / 11.8[b]
Net Official Development Assist. received (% of GNI)	7.26	5.14	8.65[b]

a Projected estimate (medium fertility variant). **b** 2015. **c** 2016. **d** Estimate. **e** Conakry **f** 2014. **g** 2013. **h** Data refers to a 5-year period preceding the reference year. **i** Refers to foreign citizens. **j** Including refugees. **k** Data as at the end of December. **l** 2008. **m** The parliament was dissolved following the December 2008 coup. **n** 2004. **o** Arrivals by air at Conakry airport.

Guinea-Bissau

Region	Western Africa	UN membership date	17 September 1974
Population (000, 2017)	1 861 a	Surface area (km2)	36 125 b
Pop. density (per km2, 2017)	66.2 a	Sex ratio (m per 100 f, 2017)	96.9 a
Capital city	Bissau	National currency	CFA Franc (XOF)
Capital city pop. (000)	492.1 b	Exchange rate (per US$)	622.3 c

Economic indicators

	2005	2010	2017
GDP: Gross domestic product (million current US$)	587	849	978 b
GDP growth rate (annual %, const. 2005 prices)	4.3	4.6	4.8 b
GDP per capita (current US$)	401.1	519.6	530.0 b
Economy: Agriculture (% of GVA)	45.4	46.2	45.0 b
Economy: Industry (% of GVA)	14.7	13.5	14.5 b
Economy: Services and other activity (% of GVA)	39.9	40.3	40.5 b
Employment: Agriculture (% of employed) d	63.6	62.4	60.1
Employment: Industry (% of employed) d	5.3	5.3	5.8
Employment: Services (% of employed) d	31.1	32.3	34.1
Unemployment (% of labour force) d	6.7	6.7	6.5
Labour force participation (female/male pop. %) d	65.9 / 78.8	66.6 / 78.4	67.4 / 78.5
CPI: Consumer Price Index (2000=100) e,f	104	122 g	...
Agricultural production index (2004-2006=100)	101	129	137 h
Food production index (2004-2006=100)	100	129	138 h
International trade: Exports (million US$)	23	120	885 c
International trade: Imports (million US$)	112	197	212 c
International trade: Balance (million US$)	- 88	- 77	673 c
Balance of payments, current account (million US$)	- 46	- 99	- 53 i

Major trading partners

					2016
Export partners (% of exports)	India	70.3	Viet Nam	11.0	Belarus 10.9
Import partners (% of imports)	Portugal	28.1	Senegal	17.2	India 7.1

Social indicators

	2005	2010	2017
Population growth rate (average annual %) j	2.1	2.4	2.6 b
Urban population (% of total population)	40.9	45.2	49.3 b
Urban population growth rate (average annual %) j	4.4	4.2	4.1 b
Fertility rate, total (live births per woman) j	5.6	5.2	4.9 b
Life expectancy at birth (females/males, years) j	53.3 / 52.0	55.6 / 52.8	57.7 / 54.3 b
Population age distribution (0-14 and 60+ years, %)	43.6 / 4.5	42.3 / 4.6	41.5 / 4.9 a
International migrant stock (000/% of total pop.) k	20.7 / 1.4	21.1 / 1.3	22.3 / 1.2 b
Refugees and others of concern to UNHCR (000)	7.8 l	8.0 l	8.8 c
Infant mortality rate (per 1 000 live births) j	101.0	91.1	80.4 b
Health: Total expenditure (% of GDP) m,n,o	5.7	6.7	5.6 h
Health: Physicians (per 1 000 pop.)	0.1 p	0.1 q	...
Education: Government expenditure (% of GDP)	...	1.9	2.2 i
Education: Primary gross enrol. ratio (f/m per 100 pop.)	57.6 / 86.1 r	109.8 / 117.5	... / ...
Education: Secondary gross enrol. ratio (f/m per 100 pop.)	12.1 / 22.3 r	... / ...	... / ...
Intentional homicide rate (per 100 000 pop.)	11.0	10.0	9.2 b
Seats held by women in national parliaments (%)	14.0	10.0	13.7

Environment and infrastructure indicators

	2005	2010	2017
Mobile-cellular subscriptions (per 100 inhabitants)	7.0	42.7	69.3 b
Individuals using the Internet (per 100 inhabitants)	1.9	2.4 d	3.5 d,b
Threatened species (number)	22 p	52	77
Forested area (% of land area) d	73.7	71.9	70.5 h
CO2 emission estimates (million tons/tons per capita)	0.2 / 0.1	0.2 / 0.1	0.3 / 0.1 h
Energy production, primary (Petajoules)	22	24	25 h
Energy supply per capita (Gigajoules)	19	17	17 h
Tourist/visitor arrivals at national borders (000) s	5	22	44 b
Important sites for terrestrial biodiversity protected (%)	52.2	52.2	52.6
Pop. using improved drinking water (urban/rural, %)	77.9 / 48.9	88.4 / 54.6	98.8 / 60.3 b
Pop. using improved sanitation facilities (urban/rural, %)	29.7 / 5.9	32.4 / 7.8	33.5 / 8.5 b
Net Official Development Assist. received (% of GNI)	11.61	15.13	9.03 b

a Projected estimate (medium fertility variant). b 2015. c 2016. d Estimate. e Index base: 2003=100. f Bissau g Series linked to former series. h 2014. i 2013. j Data refers to a 5-year period preceding the reference year. k Including refugees. l Data as at the end of December. m Estimates should be viewed with caution as these are derived from scarce data. n Data revision. o Government expenditures show fluctuations due to variations in capital investment. p 2004. q 2009. r 2000. s Arrivals by air.

Guyana

Region	South America	
Population (000, 2017)	778[a]	
Pop. density (per km2, 2017)	4.0[a]	
Capital city	Georgetown	
Capital city pop. (000)	123.9[c]	

UN membership date	20 September 1966
Surface area (km2)	214 969[b]
Sex ratio (m per 100 f, 2017)	101.9[a]
National currency	Guyana Dollar (GYD)
Exchange rate (per US$)	206.5[d]

Economic indicators	2005	2010	2017
GDP: Gross domestic product (million current US$)	1 315	2 259	3 282[b]
GDP growth rate (annual %, const. 2005 prices)	- 2.0	4.4	3.1[b]
GDP per capita (current US$)	1 771.6	2 998.9	4 278.8[b]
Economy: Agriculture (% of GVA)	25.7	17.6	17.6[b]
Economy: Industry (% of GVA)	28.7	34.5	31.7[b]
Economy: Services and other activity (% of GVA)	45.6	47.9	50.6[b]
Employment: Agriculture (% of employed)[e]	22.5	20.7	18.4
Employment: Industry (% of employed)[e]	23.3	25.9	25.4
Employment: Services (% of employed)[e]	54.1	53.3	56.2
Unemployment (% of labour force)[e]	10.2	10.9	11.3
Labour force participation (female/male pop. %)[e]	38.7 / 82.1	40.4 / 79.7	41.9 / 77.0
CPI: Consumer Price Index (2000=100)[f]	128	177[g]	186[h]
Agricultural production index (2004-2006=100)	94	108	142[c]
Food production index (2004-2006=100)	94	108	143[c]
International trade: Exports (million US$)	539	901	1 453[d]
International trade: Imports (million US$)	778	1 452	1 625[d]
International trade: Balance (million US$)	- 239	- 551	- 172[d]
Balance of payments, current account (million US$)	- 96	- 246	- 144[b]

Major trading partners						2016
Export partners (% of exports)	Canada	30.6	United States	20.6	Trinidad and Tobago	11.4
Import partners (% of imports)	Trinidad and Tobago	29.1	United States	27.6	China	7.3

Social indicators	2005	2010	2017
Population growth rate (average annual %)[i]	- 0.1	- 0.1	0.6[b]
Urban population (% of total population)	28.3	28.2	28.6[b]
Urban population growth rate (average annual %)[i]	0.2	0.6	0.8[b]
Fertility rate, total (live births per woman)[i]	2.9	2.7	2.6[b]
Life expectancy at birth (females/males, years)[i]	68.1 / 62.6	68.4 / 63.4	68.6 / 64.0[b]
Population age distribution (0-14 and 60+ years, %)	36.2 / 6.0	32.7 / 7.2	29.0 / 8.6[a]
International migrant stock (000/% of total pop.)	10.9 / 1.5	13.1 / 1.7	15.4 / 2.0[b]
Refugees and others of concern to UNHCR (000)	...	-0.0[j]	-0.0[d]
Infant mortality rate (per 1 000 live births)[i]	36.5	34.4	33.2[b]
Health: Total expenditure (% of GDP)	5.8	6.6	5.2[c]
Health: Physicians (per 1 000 pop.)	0.5[k]	0.2	...
Education: Government expenditure (% of GDP)	8.1	3.7	3.2[l]
Education: Primary gross enrol. ratio (f/m per 100 pop.)	96.1 / 102.6	83.7 / 87.0	83.9 / 86.9[l]
Education: Secondary gross enrol. ratio (f/m per 100 pop.)	94.5 / 99.3	88.6 / 88.7	89.0 / 89.7[l]
Education: Tertiary gross enrol. ratio (f/m per 100 pop.)	17.2 / 8.5	18.9 / 7.5	16.8 / 8.2[l]
Intentional homicide rate (per 100 000 pop.)	19.1	18.6	19.4[b]
Seats held by women in national parliaments (%)	30.8	30.0	31.9

Environment and infrastructure indicators	2005	2010	2017
Mobile-cellular subscriptions (per 100 inhabitants)	37.0	71.3	67.2[b]
Individuals using the Internet (per 100 inhabitants)	6.6[k]	29.9	38.2[e,b]
Threatened species (number)	65[m]	69	94
Forested area (% of land area)[e]	84.3	84.2	84.0[c]
CO2 emission estimates (million tons/tons per capita)	1.4 / 1.9	1.7 / 2.3	2.0 / 2.6[c]
Energy production, primary (Petajoules)	9	8	7[c]
Energy supply per capita (Gigajoules)	39	43	46[c]
Tourist/visitor arrivals at national borders (000)[n]	117	152	207[b]
Pop. using improved drinking water (urban/rural, %)	95.9 / 88.0	97.0 / 93.1	98.2 / 98.3[b]
Pop. using improved sanitation facilities (urban/rural, %)	87.0 / 79.0	87.7 / 81.5	87.9 / 82.0[b]
Net Official Development Assist. received (% of GNI)	19.28	7.37	0.97[b]

a Projected estimate (medium fertility variant). b 2015. c 2014. d 2016. e Estimate. f Georgetown g Series linked to former series. h 2011. i Data refers to a 5-year period preceding the reference year. j Data as at the end of December. k 2000. l 2012. m 2004. n Arrivals to Timehri airport only.

Haiti

Region	Caribbean	UN membership date	24 October 1945
Population (000, 2017)	10 981 [a]	Surface area (km2)	27 750 [b]
Pop. density (per km2, 2017)	398.4 [a]	Sex ratio (m per 100 f, 2017)	97.8 [a]
Capital city	Port-au-Prince	National currency	Gourde (HTG)
Capital city pop. (000)	2 439.8 [b]	Exchange rate (per US$)	67.4 [c]

Economic indicators	2005	2010	2017
GDP: Gross domestic product (million current US$)	4 154	6 708	8 501 [b]
GDP growth rate (annual %, const. 2005 prices)	1.8	- 5.5	1.7 [b]
GDP per capita (current US$)	448.5	670.8	793.7 [b]
Economy: Agriculture (% of GVA)	22.4	21.0	16.7 [b]
Economy: Industry (% of GVA)	32.9	33.7	38.2 [b]
Economy: Services and other activity (% of GVA)	44.8	45.4	45.1 [b]
Employment: Agriculture (% of employed) [d]	50.5	49.8	46.9
Employment: Industry (% of employed) [d]	10.6	10.6	12.6
Employment: Services (% of employed) [d]	39.0	39.6	40.6
Unemployment (% of labour force) [d]	14.2	14.5	12.9
Labour force participation (female/male pop. %) [d]	58.4 / 69.4	60.2 / 70.5	62.0 / 71.7
CPI: Consumer Price Index (2000=100)	252 [e,f]	375	478 [g]
Agricultural production index (2004-2006=100)	102	135	163 [g]
Food production index (2004-2006=100)	101	136	166 [g]
International trade: Exports (million US$)	470	579	984 [c]
International trade: Imports (million US$)	1 449	3 147	3 316 [c]
International trade: Balance (million US$)	- 979	- 2 568	- 2 332 [c]
Balance of payments, current account (million US$)	- 356	- 1 942	- 723 [b]

Major trading partners					2016
Export partners (% of exports)	United States	80.6	Dominican Republic	5.9	Mexico 2.6
Import partners (% of imports)	United States	36.8	China	15.2	Dominican Republic 15.1

Social indicators	2005	2010	2017
Population growth rate (average annual %) [h]	1.6	1.5	1.4 [b]
Urban population (% of total population)	44.1	52.0	58.6 [b]
Urban population growth rate (average annual %) [h]	5.8	4.6	3.8 [b]
Fertility rate, total (live births per woman) [h]	4.0	3.5	3.1 [b]
Life expectancy at birth (females/males, years) [h]	60.1 / 56.5	62.3 / 58.2	64.4 / 60.2 [b]
Population age distribution (0-14 and 60+ years, %)	38.0 / 6.4	35.9 / 6.5	33.0 / 7.3 [a]
International migrant stock (000/% of total pop.)	30.5 / 0.3	35.1 / 0.4	39.5 / 0.4 [b]
Refugees and others of concern to UNHCR (000)	...	~0.0 [i]	1.9 [c]
Infant mortality rate (per 1 000 live births) [h]	56.0	52.2	46.9 [b]
Health: Total expenditure (% of GDP) [j]	4.4	8.1	7.6 [g]
Intentional homicide rate (per 100 000 pop.)	...	6.8	10.0 [k]
Seats held by women in national parliaments (%)	3.6	4.1	2.6

Environment and infrastructure indicators	2005	2010	2017
Mobile-cellular subscriptions (per 100 inhabitants)	5.4 [d]	40.4	69.9 [b]
Individuals using the Internet (per 100 inhabitants) [d]	6.4	8.4	12.2 [b]
Threatened species (number)	116 [l]	137	205
Forested area (% of land area) [d]	3.8	3.7	3.5 [g]
CO2 emission estimates (million tons/tons per capita)	2.1 / 0.2	2.1 / 0.2	2.9 / 0.3 [g]
Energy production, primary (Petajoules)	115	131	136 [g]
Energy supply per capita (Gigajoules)	15	16	16 [g]
Tourist/visitor arrivals at national borders (000) [m]	112	255 [n]	516 [n,b]
Important sites for terrestrial biodiversity protected (%)	5.4	5.4	5.4
Pop. using improved drinking water (urban/rural, %)	75.6 / 48.7	69.7 / 48.1	64.9 / 47.6 [b]
Pop. using improved sanitation facilities (urban/rural, %)	33.4 / 16.0	33.5 / 17.7	33.6 / 19.2 [b]
Net Official Development Assist. received (% of GNI)	9.71	45.71	11.73 [b]

a Projected estimate (medium fertility variant). b 2015. c 2016. d Estimate. e Series linked to former series. f Break in the time series. g 2014. h Data refers to a 5-year period preceding the reference year. i Data as at the end of December. j Data revision. k 2012. l 2004. m Arrivals by air. n Including nationals residing abroad.

Holy See

Region	Southern Europe	Population (000, 2017)	1 [a]
Surface area (km2)	~0 [b,c]	Pop. density (per km2, 2017)	1 800.0 [a]
Sex ratio (m per 100 f, 2017)	219.2 [d]	Capital city	Vatican City
National currency	Euro (EUR)	Capital city pop. (000)	0.8 [e]
Exchange rate (per US$)	0.9 [f]		

Social indicators	2005	2010	2017
Population growth rate (average annual %) [g]	0.3	~0.0	~0.0 [c]
Urban population (% of total population)	100.0	100.0	100.0 [c]
Urban population growth rate (average annual %) [g]	0.3	~0.0	~0.0 [c]
International migrant stock (000/% of total pop.) [h]	0.8 / 99.4	0.8 / 100.0	0.8 / 100.0 [c]

Environment and infrastructure indicators	2005	2010	2017
Threatened species (number)	...	1	1

a Projected estimate (medium fertility variant). b Surface area is 0.44 Km2. c 2015. d 2009. e 2014. f 2016. g Data refers to a 5-year period preceding the reference year. h Estimate.

Honduras

Region	Central America	UN membership date	17 December 1945
Population (000, 2017)	9 265[a]	Surface area (km2)	112 492[b]
Pop. density (per km2, 2017)	82.8[a]	Sex ratio (m per 100 f, 2017)	99.4[a]
Capital city	Tegucigalpa	National currency	Lempira (HNL)
Capital city pop. (000)	1 122.5[b]	Exchange rate (per US$)	23.5[c]

Economic indicators	2005	2010	2017
GDP: Gross domestic product (million current US$)	9 757	15 839	20 365[b]
GDP growth rate (annual %, const. 2005 prices)	6.1	3.7	3.6[b]
GDP per capita (current US$)	1 418.1	2 110.8	2 521.9[b]
Economy: Agriculture (% of GVA)	13.1	11.9	13.0[b]
Economy: Industry (% of GVA)	27.6	26.2	25.1[b]
Economy: Services and other activity (% of GVA)	59.3	62.0	61.9[b]
Employment: Agriculture (% of employed)[d]	36.7	35.0	29.4
Employment: Industry (% of employed)[d]	19.5	18.9	21.6
Employment: Services (% of employed)[d]	43.8	46.1	49.0
Unemployment (% of labour force)	4.2	4.8	5.6[d]
Labour force participation (female/male pop. %)[d]	36.3 / 83.1	44.2 / 84.6	47.6 / 84.5
CPI: Consumer Price Index (2000=100)	150	208	260[e]
Agricultural production index (2004-2006=100)	103	111	122[e]
Food production index (2004-2006=100)	104	109	119[e]
Index of industrial production (2005=100)[f]	100	113	130[e]
International trade: Exports (million US$)	1 294	3 104	3 657[c]
International trade: Imports (million US$)	4 419	6 895	8 448[c]
International trade: Balance (million US$)	- 3 125	- 3 791	- 4 791[c]
Balance of payments, current account (million US$)	- 304	- 682	- 1 291[b]

Major trading partners						2016
Export partners (% of exports)	United States	44.2	Germany	8.0	El Salvador	6.5
Import partners (% of imports)	United States	35.0	China	15.4	Guatemala	8.0

Social indicators	2005	2010	2017
Population growth rate (average annual %)[g]	2.4	2.1	1.8[b]
Urban population (% of total population)	48.5	51.7	54.7[b]
Urban population growth rate (average annual %)[g]	3.3	3.3	3.1[b]
Fertility rate, total (live births per woman)[g]	3.8	3.2	2.6[b]
Life expectancy at birth (females/males, years)[g]	73.4 / 68.6	74.5 / 69.6	75.4 / 70.4[b]
Population age distribution (0-14 and 60+ years, %)	39.9 / 5.5	36.6 / 5.8	31.6 / 7.0[a]
International migrant stock (000/% of total pop.)[h]	27.9 / 0.4	27.3 / 0.4	28.1 / 0.3[b]
Refugees and others of concern to UNHCR (000)	0.1[i]	~0.0[i]	176.2[c]
Infant mortality rate (per 1 000 live births)[g]	31.2	29.4	27.8[b]
Health: Total expenditure (% of GDP)	7.8	8.5	8.7[e]
Health: Physicians (per 1 000 pop.)	0.4	...	...
Education: Government expenditure (% of GDP)	...	...	5.9[j]
Education: Primary gross enrol. ratio (f/m per 100 pop.)	111.4 / 111.8	116.3 / 116.8	110.1 / 111.3[b]
Education: Secondary gross enrol. ratio (f/m per 100 pop.)	... / ...	80.0 / 65.5	77.0 / 64.8[b]
Education: Tertiary gross enrol. ratio (f/m per 100 pop.)	20.0 / 14.1[d,k]	22.0 / 19.3	25.4 / 18.8[b]
Intentional homicide rate (per 100 000 pop.)	46.7	83.1	63.8[b]
Seats held by women in national parliaments (%)	5.5	18.0	25.8

Environment and infrastructure indicators	2005	2010	2017
Mobile-cellular subscriptions (per 100 inhabitants)	18.6	124.7	95.5[b]
Individuals using the Internet (per 100 inhabitants)	6.5[d,l]	11.1	20.4[d,b]
Research & Development expenditure (% of GDP)	~0.0[k]	...	...
Threatened species (number)	206[k]	240	301
Forested area (% of land area)[d]	51.8	46.4	42.1[e]
CO2 emission estimates (million tons/tons per capita)	7.6 / 1.1	8.0 / 1.1	9.5 / 1.2[e]
Energy production, primary (Petajoules)	77	93	105[e]
Energy supply per capita (Gigajoules)	25	25	28[e]
Tourist/visitor arrivals at national borders (000)	673	863	880[b]
Important sites for terrestrial biodiversity protected (%)	57.5	57.6	65.0
Pop. using improved drinking water (urban/rural, %)	95.4 / 74.2	96.4 / 79.0	97.4 / 83.8[b]
Pop. using improved sanitation facilities (urban/rural, %)	80.4 / 61.1	83.9 / 70.3	86.7 / 77.7[b]
Net Official Development Assist. received (% of GNI)	7.51	4.20	2.86[b]

a Projected estimate (medium fertility variant). **b** 2015. **c** 2016. **d** Estimate. **e** 2014. **f** Data classified according to ISIC Rev. 3. **g** Data refers to a 5-year period preceding the reference year. **h** Including refugees. **i** Data as at the end of December. **j** 2013. **k** 2004. **l** Population aged 5 years and over.

Hungary

Region	Eastern Europe	UN membership date	14 December 1955
Population (000, 2017)	9 722 [a]	Surface area (km2)	93 024 [b]
Pop. density (per km2, 2017)	107.4 [a]	Sex ratio (m per 100 f, 2017)	90.7 [a]
Capital city	Budapest	National currency	Forint (HUF)
Capital city pop. (000)	1 713.9 [b]	Exchange rate (per US$)	293.7 [c]

Economic indicators	2005	2010	2017
GDP: Gross domestic product (million current US$)	112 589	130 256	121 715 [b]
GDP growth rate (annual %, const. 2005 prices)	4.4	0.7	3.1 [b]
GDP per capita (current US$)	11 151.9	13 006.5	12 350.6 [b]
Economy: Agriculture (% of GVA) [d]	4.3	3.6	4.1 [b]
Economy: Industry (% of GVA) [d]	31.4	30.2	31.9 [b]
Economy: Services and other activity (% of GVA) [d]	64.3	66.3	64.0 [b]
Employment: Agriculture (% of employed) [e]	4.9	4.5	4.3
Employment: Industry (% of employed) [e]	32.5	30.7	29.8
Employment: Services (% of employed) [e]	62.7	64.8	65.9
Unemployment (% of labour force)	7.2	11.2	4.5 [e]
Labour force participation (female/male pop. %) [e]	42.9 / 58.3	43.7 / 58.3	46.6 / 62.4
CPI: Consumer Price Index (2000=100)	133	173	193 [f]
Agricultural production index (2004-2006=100)	97	80	99 [f]
Food production index (2004-2006=100)	96	80	99 [f]
Index of industrial production (2005=100)	100	108 [g]	122 [g,f]
International trade: Exports (million US$)	62 272	94 749	103 071 [c]
International trade: Imports (million US$)	65 920	87 432	92 044 [c]
International trade: Balance (million US$)	- 3 648	7 317	11 027 [c]
Balance of payments, current account (million US$)	- 7 883	346	3 946 [b]

Major trading partners						2016
Export partners (% of exports)	Germany	27.5	Romania	5.0	Slovakia	4.9
Import partners (% of imports)	Germany	26.4	Austria	6.4	Poland	5.6

Social indicators	2005	2010	2017
Population growth rate (average annual %) [h]	- 0.3	- 0.3	- 0.3 [b]
Urban population (% of total population)	66.4	68.9	71.2 [b]
Urban population growth rate (average annual %) [h]	0.3	0.6	0.5 [b]
Fertility rate, total (live births per woman) [h]	1.3	1.3	1.3 [b]
Life expectancy at birth (females/males, years) [h]	76.7 / 68.3	77.8 / 69.6	78.8 / 71.7 [b]
Population age distribution (0-14 and 60+ years, %)	15.5 / 21.4	14.9 / 22.1	14.3 / 26.0 [a]
International migrant stock (000/% of total pop.) [i]	366.8 / 3.6	436.6 / 4.4	449.6 / 4.6 [b]
Refugees and others of concern to UNHCR (000)	8.9 [j]	5.8 [j]	14.4 [c]
Infant mortality rate (per 1 000 live births) [h]	7.4	5.7	4.9 [b]
Health: Total expenditure (% of GDP)	8.3	7.9	7.4 [f]
Health: Physicians (per 1 000 pop.)	3.2	2.9	3.3 [f]
Education: Government expenditure (% of GDP)	5.3	4.8	4.7 [f]
Education: Primary gross enrol. ratio (f/m per 100 pop.)	97.1 / 99.1	101.6 / 102.6	101.3 / 101.9 [b]
Education: Secondary gross enrol. ratio (f/m per 100 pop.)	95.7 / 96.7	99.1 / 100.7	105.3 / 105.1 [b]
Education: Tertiary gross enrol. ratio (f/m per 100 pop.)	77.6 / 53.1	69.7 / 51.4	56.7 / 45.3 [b]
Intentional homicide rate (per 100 000 pop.)	1.6	1.4	1.5 [f]
Seats held by women in national parliaments (%)	9.1	11.1	10.1

Environment and infrastructure indicators	2005	2010	2017
Mobile-cellular subscriptions (per 100 inhabitants)	92.3	119.9	118.9 [b]
Individuals using the Internet (per 100 inhabitants) [k]	39.0	65.0	72.8 [b]
Research & Development expenditure (% of GDP)	0.9	1.1	1.4 [f]
Threatened species (number)	51 [l]	47	66
Forested area (% of land area)	22.1	22.6	22.8 [e,f]
CO2 emission estimates (million tons/tons per capita)	58.0 / 5.8	50.2 / 5.0	42.1 / 4.3 [f]
Energy production, primary (Petajoules)	434	461	423 [f]
Energy supply per capita (Gigajoules)	115	108	97 [f]
Tourist/visitor arrivals at national borders (000) [m]	9 979	9 510	14 316 [b]
Important sites for terrestrial biodiversity protected (%)	79.9	81.7	81.8
Pop. using improved drinking water (urban/rural, %)	99.7 / 98.4	100.0 / 100.0	100.0 / 100.0 [b]
Pop. using improved sanitation facilities (urban/rural, %)	97.8 / 98.6	97.8 / 98.6	97.8 / 98.6 [b]
Net Official Development Assist. disbursed (% of GNI) [n]	0.11	0.09	0.13 [o,c]

a Projected estimate (medium fertility variant). **b** 2015. **c** 2016. **d** Data classified according to ISIC Rev. 4. **e** Estimate. **f** 2014. **g** Excluding water and waste management. **h** Data refers to a 5-year period preceding the reference year. **i** Including refugees. **j** Data as at the end of December. **k** Population aged 16 to 74 years. **l** 2004. **m** New series. **n** Development Assistance Committee member (OECD) **o** Provisional data.

Iceland

Region	Northern Europe	UN membership date	19 November 1946
Population (000, 2017)	335 [a]	Surface area (km2)	103 000 [b]
Pop. density (per km2, 2017)	3.3 [a]	Sex ratio (m per 100 f, 2017)	100.7 [a]
Capital city	Reykjavik	National currency	Iceland Krona (ISK)
Capital city pop. (000)	184.2 [c]	Exchange rate (per US$)	112.8 [d]

Economic indicators	2005	2010	2017
GDP: Gross domestic product (million current US$)	16 691	13 255	16 780 [b]
GDP growth rate (annual %, const. 2005 prices)	6.7	- 3.6	4.2 [b]
GDP per capita (current US$)	56 247.7	41 676.3	50 936.0 [b]
Economy: Agriculture (% of GVA) [e]	5.7	7.4	6.4 [b]
Economy: Industry (% of GVA) [e]	24.9	24.8	24.0 [b]
Economy: Services and other activity (% of GVA) [e]	69.3	67.8	69.7 [b]
Employment: Agriculture (% of employed) [f]	6.5	5.5	4.0
Employment: Industry (% of employed) [f]	21.7	18.4	17.7
Employment: Services (% of employed) [f]	71.7	76.0	78.2
Unemployment (% of labour force)	2.5	7.6	3.6 [f]
Labour force participation (female/male pop. %) [f]	70.8 / 80.2	70.4 / 78.6	70.3 / 77.2
CPI: Consumer Price Index (2000=100) [g]	122	182	211 [c]
Agricultural production index (2004-2006=100)	99	110	117 [c]
Food production index (2004-2006=100)	99	110	117 [c]
International trade: Exports (million US$)	3 091	4 603	4 450 [d]
International trade: Imports (million US$)	4 979	3 914	5 703 [d]
International trade: Balance (million US$)	- 1 888	689	- 1 254 [d]
Balance of payments, current account (million US$)	- 2 339	- 308	854 [b]

Major trading partners						2016
Export partners (% of exports)	Netherlands	25.5	United Kingdom	11.3	Spain	10.4
Import partners (% of imports)	Germany	10.0	United States	10.0	Norway	9.0

Social indicators	2005	2010	2017
Population growth rate (average annual %) [h]	1.0	1.6	0.6 [b]
Urban population (% of total population)	93.0	93.6	94.1 [b]
Urban population growth rate (average annual %) [h]	1.2	1.5	1.3 [b]
Fertility rate, total (live births per woman) [h]	2.0	2.1	2.0 [b]
Life expectancy at birth (females/males, years) [h]	82.6 / 78.8	83.2 / 79.6	83.8 / 80.6 [b]
Population age distribution (0-14 and 60+ years, %)	22.2 / 15.8	20.8 / 16.9	20.1 / 20.1 [a]
International migrant stock (000/% of total pop.)	25.5 / 8.6	35.1 / 11.0	37.5 / 11.4 [b]
Refugees and others of concern to UNHCR (000)	0.4 [i]	0.2 [i]	0.5 [d]
Infant mortality rate (per 1 000 live births) [h]	2.5	2.0	1.6 [b]
Health: Total expenditure (% of GDP)	9.2	8.9	8.9 [c]
Health: Physicians (per 1 000 pop.)	3.6	3.6	3.8 [b]
Education: Government expenditure (% of GDP)	7.4	7.2	7.8 [i]
Education: Primary gross enrol. ratio (f/m per 100 pop.)	96.7 / 99.1	99.0 / 98.4	98.6 / 99.7 [i]
Education: Secondary gross enrol. ratio (f/m per 100 pop.)	110.3 / 108.0	110.4 / 108.3	121.0 / 116.3 [i]
Education: Tertiary gross enrol. ratio (f/m per 100 pop.)	92.9 / 48.6	101.3 / 56.2	103.1 / 60.2 [i]
Intentional homicide rate (per 100 000 pop.)	1.0	0.6	0.9 [b]
Seats held by women in national parliaments (%)	30.2	42.9	47.6

Environment and infrastructure indicators	2005	2010	2017
Mobile-cellular subscriptions (per 100 inhabitants)	95.4	107.2	114.0 [b]
Individuals using the Internet (per 100 inhabitants)	87.0 [k]	93.4 [k,l]	98.2 [f,b]
Research & Development expenditure (% of GDP)	2.7	2.7 [m]	1.9 [c]
Threatened species (number)	15 [n]	17	27
Forested area (% of land area)	0.4	0.4	0.5 [f,c]
CO2 emission estimates (million tons/tons per capita)	2.2 / 7.5	2.0 / 6.2	2.0 / 6.1 [c]
Energy production, primary (Petajoules)	127	252	284 [c]
Energy supply per capita (Gigajoules)	534	875	952 [c]
Tourist/visitor arrivals at national borders (000)	374	489	1 289 [b]
Important sites for terrestrial biodiversity protected (%)	15.0	15.7	18.0
Pop. using improved drinking water (urban/rural, %)	100.0 / 100.0	100.0 / 100.0	100.0 / 100.0 [b]
Pop. using improved sanitation facilities (urban/rural, %)	98.7 / 100.0	98.7 / 100.0	98.7 / 100.0 [b]
Net Official Development Assist. disbursed (% of GNI) [o]	0.18	0.26	0.25 [p,d]

a Projected estimate (medium fertility variant). **b** 2015. **c** 2014. **d** 2016. **e** Data classified according to ISIC Rev. 4. **f** Estimate. **g** Annual averages are based on the months February-December and January of the following year. **h** Data refers to a 5-year period preceding the reference year. **i** Data as at the end of December. **j** 2013. **k** Population aged 16 to 74 years. **l** Users in the last 3 months. **m** 2009. **n** 2004. **o** Development Assistance Committee member (OECD) **p** Provisional data.

India

Region	Southern Asia	
Population (000, 2017)	1 339 180 [a]	
Pop. density (per km2, 2017)	450.4 [a]	
Capital city	New Delhi	
Capital city pop. (000)	250.0 [c]	

UN membership date	30 October 1945	
Surface area (km2)	3 287 263 [b]	
Sex ratio (m per 100 f, 2017)	107.6 [a]	
National currency	Indian Rupee (INR)	
Exchange rate (per US$)	68.0 [d]	

Economic indicators	2005	2010	2017
GDP: Gross domestic product (million current US$)	812 059	1 650 635	2 116 239 [b]
GDP growth rate (annual %, const. 2005 prices)	9.3	10.3	7.6 [b]
GDP per capita (current US$)	709.6	1 340.9	1 614.2 [b]
Economy: Agriculture (% of GVA) [e]	19.5	18.9	17.0 [b]
Economy: Industry (% of GVA) [e]	33.6	32.5	29.7 [b]
Economy: Services and other activity (% of GVA) [e]	46.9	48.7	53.2 [b]
Employment: Agriculture (% of employed) [f]	55.8	51.0	44.3
Employment: Industry (% of employed) [f]	19.0	22.5	24.5
Employment: Services (% of employed) [f]	25.2	26.5	31.2
Unemployment (% of labour force)	4.4	3.6	3.4 [f]
Labour force participation (female/male pop. %) [f]	36.8 / 83.1	28.6 / 80.5	27.0 / 79.1
CPI: Consumer Price Index (2000=100) [g]	122	183	256 [h]
Agricultural production index (2004-2006=100)	100	124	143 [h]
Food production index (2004-2006=100)	100	123	142 [h]
Index of industrial production (2005=100) [i,j]	100	152	163 [h]
International trade: Exports (million US$) [k]	100 353	220 408	260 327 [d]
International trade: Imports (million US$) [k]	140 862	350 029	356 705 [d]
International trade: Balance (million US$) [k]	- 40 509	- 129 621	- 96 378 [d]
Balance of payments, current account (million US$)	- 10 284	- 54 516	- 22 457 [b]

Major trading partners					2016
Export partners (% of exports)	United States	16.1	United Arab Emirates	11.5	China, Hong Kong SAR 5.1
Import partners (% of imports)	China	16.7	United States	6.4	United Arab Emirates 5.4

Social indicators	2005	2010	2017
Population growth rate (average annual %) [l]	1.7	1.5	1.2 [b]
Urban population (% of total population)	29.2	30.9	32.7 [b]
Urban population growth rate (average annual %) [l]	2.7	2.5	2.4 [b]
Fertility rate, total (live births per woman) [l]	3.1	2.8	2.4 [b]
Life expectancy at birth (females/males, years) [l]	64.4 / 62.7	66.5 / 64.7	69.1 / 66.2 [b]
Population age distribution (0-14 and 60+ years, %)	32.8 / 7.3	30.9 / 7.8	27.8 / 9.4 [a]
International migrant stock (000/% of total pop.) [m]	5 923.6 / 0.5	5 436.0 / 0.4	5 241.0 / 0.4 [b]
Refugees and others of concern to UNHCR (000)	142.4 [n]	193.7 [n]	211.1 [d]
Infant mortality rate (per 1 000 live births) [l]	59.9	49.8	41.3 [b]
Health: Total expenditure (% of GDP) [o,p]	4.3	4.3	4.7 [q,h]
Health: Physicians (per 1 000 pop.)	0.6	0.7	0.7 [h]
Education: Government expenditure (% of GDP)	3.1	3.4	3.8 [r]
Education: Primary gross enrol. ratio (f/m per 100 pop.)	101.5 / 104.3 [s]	110.4 / 108.1 [f]	115.1 / 102.8 [b]
Education: Secondary gross enrol. ratio (f/m per 100 pop.)	48.7 / 59.2 [f]	60.9 / 65.5	74.5 / 73.5 [b]
Education: Tertiary gross enrol. ratio (f/m per 100 pop.)	8.8 / 12.5	15.0 / 20.6	26.7 / 27.0 [b]
Intentional homicide rate (per 100 000 pop.)	3.6	3.4	3.2 [h]
Seats held by women in national parliaments (%)	8.3	10.8	11.8

Environment and infrastructure indicators	2005	2010	2017
Mobile-cellular subscriptions (per 100 inhabitants)	8.0	62.4 [n]	78.8 [n,b]
Individuals using the Internet (per 100 inhabitants) [f]	2.4	7.5	26.0 [b]
Research & Development expenditure (% of GDP)	0.8	0.8	0.8 [c]
Threatened species (number)	552 [t]	758	1 052
Forested area (% of land area)	22.8	23.5 [f]	23.7 [f,h]
CO2 emission estimates (million tons/tons per capita)	1 222.6 / 1.1	1 719.7 / 1.4	2 238.4 / 1.7 [h]
Energy production, primary (Petajoules)	18 315	22 598	23 103 [h]
Energy supply per capita (Gigajoules)	20	23	27 [h]
Tourist/visitor arrivals at national borders (000) [u]	3 919	5 776	8 027 [b]
Important sites for terrestrial biodiversity protected (%)	22.9	22.9	26.5
Pop. using improved drinking water (urban/rural, %)	94.0 / 82.0	95.7 / 87.9	97.1 / 92.6 [b]
Pop. using improved sanitation facilities (urban/rural, %)	57.4 / 19.5	60.3 / 24.5	62.6 / 28.5 [b]
Net Official Development Assist. received (% of GNI)	0.23	0.17	0.16 [b]

a Projected estimate (medium fertility variant). **b** 2015. **c** 2011. **d** 2016. **e** Data classified according to ISIC Rev. 4. **f** Estimate. **g** Industrial workers. **h** 2014. **i** Data classified according to ISIC Rev. 3. **j** Twelve months beginning 1 April of the year stated. **k** Excluding military goods, fissionable materials, bunkers, ships and aircraft. **l** Data refers to a 5-year period preceding the reference year. **m** Including refugees. **n** Data as at the end of December. **o** General government expenditure series was fully revised. **p** Data revision. **q** Break in the time series. **r** 2013. **s** 2003. **t** 2004. **u** Excluding nationals residing abroad.

Indonesia

Region	South-eastern Asia		UN membership date		28 September 1950
Population (000, 2017)	263 991 [a]		Surface area (km2)		1 910 931 [b]
Pop. density (per km2, 2017)	145.7 [a]		Sex ratio (m per 100 f, 2017)		101.4 [a]
Capital city	Jakarta		National currency		Rupiah (IDR)
Capital city pop. (000)	10 323.1 [c,b]		Exchange rate (per US$)		13 436.0 [d]

Economic indicators

	2005	2010	2017
GDP: Gross domestic product (million current US$)	304 372	755 094	861 934 [b]
GDP growth rate (annual %, const. 2005 prices)	5.7	6.2	4.8 [b]
GDP per capita (current US$)	1 345.3	3 125.2	3 346.5 [b]
Economy: Agriculture (% of GVA) [e]	12.1	14.3	14.0 [b]
Economy: Industry (% of GVA) [e]	43.1	43.9	41.3 [b]
Economy: Services and other activity (% of GVA) [e]	44.8	41.8	44.7 [b]
Employment: Agriculture (% of employed) [f]	43.3	38.7	31.4
Employment: Industry (% of employed) [f]	17.9	18.4	22.4
Employment: Services (% of employed) [f]	38.8	42.9	46.2
Unemployment (% of labour force)	11.2	7.1	5.8 [f]
Labour force participation (female/male pop. %) [f]	50.0 / 85.3	51.9 / 84.3	51.0 / 83.7
CPI: Consumer Price Index (2000=100)	156	227	283 [g,h]
Agricultural production index (2004-2006=100)	98	123	139 [h]
Food production index (2004-2006=100)	98	124	140 [h]
International trade: Exports (million US$)	85 660	157 779	144 490 [d]
International trade: Imports (million US$)	57 701	135 663	135 653 [d]
International trade: Balance (million US$)	27 959	22 116	8 837 [d]
Balance of payments, current account (million US$)	278	5 144 [i]	- 17 697 [b]

Major trading partners

					2016
Export partners (% of exports)	China	11.6	United States	11.2	Japan	11.1
Import partners (% of imports)	China	22.7	Singapore	10.7	Japan	9.6

Social indicators

	2005	2010	2017
Population growth rate (average annual %) [j]	1.4	1.3	1.2 [b]
Urban population (% of total population)	45.9	49.9	53.7 [b]
Urban population growth rate (average annual %) [j]	3.2	3.1	2.7 [b]
Fertility rate, total (live births per woman) [j]	2.5	2.5	2.4 [b]
Life expectancy at birth (females/males, years) [j]	68.5 / 64.9	69.8 / 65.6	70.7 / 66.6 [b]
Population age distribution (0-14 and 60+ years, %)	30.0 / 7.4	29.0 / 7.4	27.4 / 8.6 [a]
International migrant stock (000/% of total pop.) [k]	289.6 / 0.1	305.4 / 0.1	328.8 / 0.1 [b]
Refugees and others of concern to UNHCR (000)	0.4 [l]	2.9 [l]	13.8 [d]
Infant mortality rate (per 1 000 live births) [j]	36.5	29.7	25.0 [b]
Health: Total expenditure (% of GDP)	2.8	2.7	2.8 [h]
Health: Physicians (per 1 000 pop.)	0.1 [m]	0.1	0.2 [n]
Education: Government expenditure (% of GDP)	2.9 [f]	2.8	3.6 [b]
Education: Primary gross enrol. ratio (f/m per 100 pop.)	106.1 / 109.4 [f]	110.5 / 106.9	104.4 / 107.2 [b]
Education: Secondary gross enrol. ratio (f/m per 100 pop.)	59.8 / 60.4 [f]	76.8 / 76.3	86.0 / 85.7 [b]
Education: Tertiary gross enrol. ratio (f/m per 100 pop.)	14.7 / 18.5 [o]	22.6 / 25.8	25.7 / 22.9 [b]
Intentional homicide rate (per 100 000 pop.)	0.6 [o]	0.4	0.5 [h]
Seats held by women in national parliaments (%)	11.3	18.0	19.8

Environment and infrastructure indicators

	2005	2010	2017
Mobile-cellular subscriptions (per 100 inhabitants)	20.9	87.8	132.4 [f,b]
Individuals using the Internet (per 100 inhabitants)	3.6	10.9	22.0 [p,b]
Research & Development expenditure (% of GDP)	~0.0 [q,r]	0.1 [i,q,s]	0.1 [t]
Threatened species (number)	833 [o]	1 142	1 281
Forested area (% of land area)	54.0	52.1 [f]	50.6 [f,h]
CO2 emission estimates (million tons/tons per capita)	342.0 / 1.5	428.8 / 1.8	464.2 / 1.8 [h]
Energy production, primary (Petajoules) [u]	11 351	16 854	19 481 [h]
Energy supply per capita (Gigajoules) [u]	31	34	35 [h]
Tourist/visitor arrivals at national borders (000)	5 002	7 003	10 407 [b]
Important sites for terrestrial biodiversity protected (%)	21.3	22.8	23.5
Pop. using improved drinking water (urban/rural, %)	92.3 / 72.0	93.2 / 75.7	94.2 / 79.5 [b]
Pop. using improved sanitation facilities (urban/rural, %)	68.1 / 38.6	70.4 / 43.5	72.3 / 47.5 [b]
Net Official Development Assist. received (% of GNI)	0.93	0.19	0.00 [b]

a Projected estimate (medium fertility variant). **b** 2015. **c** Refers to the functional urban area. **d** 2016. **e** Data classified according to ISIC Rev. 4. **f** Estimate. **g** Series linked to former series. **h** 2014. **i** Break in the time series. **j** Data refers to a 5-year period preceding the reference year. **k** Including refugees. **l** Data as at the end of December. **m** 2003. **n** 2012. **o** 2004. **p** Population aged 5 years and over. **q** Partial data. **r** 2001. **s** 2009. **t** 2013. **u** Data include Timor-Leste.

Iran (Islamic Republic of)

Region	Southern Asia	UN membership date	24 October 1945
Population (000, 2017)	81 163[a]	Surface area (km2)	1 628 750[b,c]
Pop. density (per km2, 2017)	49.8[a]	Sex ratio (m per 100 f, 2017)	101.2[a]
Capital city	Tehran	National currency	Iranian Rial (IRR)
Capital city pop. (000)	8 432.2[c]	Exchange rate (per US$)	32 376.0[d]

Economic indicators	2005	2010	2017
GDP: Gross domestic product (million current US$)	219 846	467 790	398 563[c]
GDP growth rate (annual %, const. 2005 prices)	4.2	6.6	0.4[c]
GDP per capita (current US$)	3 135.2	6 299.9	5 038.1[c]
Economy: Agriculture (% of GVA)	6.4	6.7	8.6[c]
Economy: Industry (% of GVA)	45.7	40.3	39.1[c]
Economy: Services and other activity (% of GVA)	47.9	53.1	52.3[c]
Employment: Agriculture (% of employed)[e]	24.7	19.2	16.6
Employment: Industry (% of employed)[e]	30.4	32.2	32.5
Employment: Services (% of employed)[e]	44.9	48.6	50.9
Unemployment (% of labour force)	12.1	13.5	11.3[e]
Labour force participation (female/male pop. %)[e]	19.4 / 74.2	16.0 / 69.9	16.3 / 73.2
CPI: Consumer Price Index (2000=100)	193	386	913[f]
Agricultural production index (2004-2006=100)	102	106	106[f]
Food production index (2004-2006=100)	102	106	107[f]
International trade: Exports (million US$)[g,h]	60 012	83 785	45 627[d]
International trade: Imports (million US$)[g,h]	38 869	54 697	35 333[d]
International trade: Balance (million US$)[g,h]	21 143	29 088	10 294[d]

Major trading partners					2016
Export partners (% of exports)	China	31.3	India	17.3	Turkey	9.7
Import partners (% of imports)	China	31.3	United Arab Emirates	12.0	Turkey	9.4

Social indicators	2005	2010	2017
Population growth rate (average annual %)[i]	1.3	1.1	1.2[c]
Urban population (% of total population)	67.6	70.6	73.4[c]
Urban population growth rate (average annual %)[i]	2.3	2.1	2.1[c]
Fertility rate, total (live births per woman)[i]	2.0	1.8	1.7[c]
Life expectancy at birth (females/males, years)[i]	72.3 / 70.0	74.6 / 71.0	76.2 / 74.0[c]
Population age distribution (0-14 and 60+ years, %)	26.1 / 6.8	23.5 / 7.1	23.7 / 8.8[a]
International migrant stock (000/% of total pop.)[i]	2 568.9 / 3.7	2 761.6 / 3.7	2 726.4 / 3.4[c]
Refugees and others of concern to UNHCR (000)	1 319.4[k]	1 085.3[k]	978.3[d]
Infant mortality rate (per 1 000 live births)[i]	25.0	18.9	14.8[c]
Health: Total expenditure (% of GDP)	5.7	7.2	7.5[f]
Health: Physicians (per 1 000 pop.)	0.9	...	1.5[f]
Education: Government expenditure (% of GDP)	4.2	3.9	2.9[c]
Education: Primary gross enrol. ratio (f/m per 100 pop.)	98.8 / 101.3	105.3 / 106.2	111.7 / 106.3[c]
Education: Secondary gross enrol. ratio (f/m per 100 pop.)	74.4 / 77.2	81.1 / 82.7	88.9 / 89.4[c]
Education: Tertiary gross enrol. ratio (f/m per 100 pop.)	23.5 / 22.2	42.3 / 42.9	67.7 / 75.9[c]
Intentional homicide rate (per 100 000 pop.)	5.4	5.2	4.1[c]
Seats held by women in national parliaments (%)	4.1	2.8	5.9

Environment and infrastructure indicators	2005	2010	2017
Mobile-cellular subscriptions (per 100 inhabitants)	12.1[m]	72.6	93.4[c]
Individuals using the Internet (per 100 inhabitants)	8.1[e]	15.9[n]	44.1[e,c]
Research & Development expenditure (% of GDP)	0.6	0.3[o,p]	0.3[q]
Threatened species (number)	69[r]	102	134
Forested area (% of land area)	6.6	6.6	6.6[e,f]
CO2 emission estimates (million tons/tons per capita)	468.8 / 6.7	573.0 / 7.7	649.5 / 8.3[f]
Energy production, primary (Petajoules)	13 006	14 283	13 291[f]
Energy supply per capita (Gigajoules)	104	116	127[f]
Tourist/visitor arrivals at national borders (000)	...	2 938	5 237[c]
Important sites for terrestrial biodiversity protected (%)	47.9	48.6	48.6
Pop. using improved drinking water (urban/rural, %)	98.0 / 88.8	97.8 / 90.9	97.7 / 92.1[c]
Pop. using improved sanitation facilities (urban/rural, %)	88.2 / 74.5	92.3 / 79.6	92.8 / 82.3[c]
Net Official Development Assist. received (% of GNI)	0.05	0.02	0.02[f]

a Projected estimate (medium fertility variant). **b** Land area only. **c** 2015. **d** 2016. **e** Estimate. **f** 2014. **g** Data include oil and gas. The value of oil exports and total exports are rough estimates based on information published in various petroleum industry journals. **h** Year ending 20 March of the year stated. **i** Data refers to a 5-year period preceding the reference year. **j** Including refugees. **k** Data as at the end of December. **l** Exchange rate changed in 2002 from multiple to a managed floating exchange rate. Inter-bank market rate used prior to 2002. **m** Data as at the end of October. **n** Population aged 6 years and over. **o** Excluding government. **p** Excluding private non-profit. **q** 2012. **r** 2004.

Iraq

Region	Western Asia	UN membership date	21 December 1945
Population (000, 2017)	38 275 [a]	Surface area (km2)	435 052 [b]
Pop. density (per km2, 2017)	88.1 [a]	Sex ratio (m per 100 f, 2017)	102.5 [a]
Capital city	Baghdad	National currency	Iraqi Dinar (IQD)
Capital city pop. (000)	6 642.8 [b]	Exchange rate (per US$)	1 182.0 [c]

Economic indicators	2005	2010	2017
GDP: Gross domestic product (million current US$)	36 268	117 138	164 234 [b]
GDP growth rate (annual %, const. 2005 prices)	4.4	5.5	- 2.4 [b]
GDP per capita (current US$)	1 342.4	3 794.8	4 509.0 [b]
Economy: Agriculture (% of GVA)	6.9	5.1	4.6 [b]
Economy: Industry (% of GVA)	63.3	55.4	58.0 [b]
Economy: Services and other activity (% of GVA)	29.9	39.4	37.4 [b]
Employment: Agriculture (% of employed) [d]	22.6	22.4	20.4
Employment: Industry (% of employed) [d]	18.3	18.8	21.0
Employment: Services (% of employed) [d]	59.1	58.9	58.6
Unemployment (% of labour force)	18.0	15.2 [d]	16.1 [d]
Labour force participation (female/male pop. %) [d]	13.7 / 68.9	14.5 / 69.3	15.3 / 69.9
CPI: Consumer Price Index (2000=100)	323 [e]	660 [f]	770 [g]
Agricultural production index (2004-2006=100)	104	104	123 [g]
Food production index (2004-2006=100)	104	104	123 [g]
International trade: Exports (million US$)	19 773	52 483	27 341 [c]
International trade: Imports (million US$)	12 861	31 764	45 831 [c]
International trade: Balance (million US$)	6 912	20 718	- 18 490 [c]
Balance of payments, current account (million US$)	- 7 513	6 488	4 121 [b]

Major trading partners						2016
Export partners (% of exports)	China	22.9	India	21.3	United States	13.5
Import partners (% of imports)	Areas nes [h]	70.4	China	9.0	United Arab Emirates	4.7

Social indicators	2005	2010	2017
Population growth rate (average annual %) [i]	2.7	2.6	3.2 [b]
Urban population (% of total population)	68.8	69.0	69.5 [b]
Urban population growth rate (average annual %) [i]	2.9	2.5	3.0 [b]
Fertility rate, total (live births per woman) [i]	4.7	4.6	4.6 [b]
Life expectancy at birth (females/males, years) [i]	71.0 / 66.9	71.2 / 65.1	71.4 / 67.0 [b]
Population age distribution (0-14 and 60+ years, %)	42.0 / 5.1	41.7 / 4.8	40.4 / 5.0 [a]
International migrant stock (000/% of total pop.) [j,k]	132.9 / 0.5	117.4 / 0.4	353.9 / 1.0 [b]
Refugees and others of concern to UNHCR (000)	1 578.2 [l]	1 796.3 [l]	4 736.2 [c]
Infant mortality rate (per 1 000 live births) [i]	34.7	33.3	32.1 [b]
Health: Total expenditure (% of GDP) [e,m,n]	4.1	3.8	5.5 [g]
Health: Physicians (per 1 000 pop.)	...	0.6	0.9 [g]
Education: Primary gross enrol. ratio (f/m per 100 pop.)	95.2 / 113.1 [o]	98.7 / 117.0 [p]	... / ...
Education: Secondary gross enrol. ratio (f/m per 100 pop.)	38.2 / 56.5 [o]	45.6 / 60.9 [p]	... / ...
Education: Tertiary gross enrol. ratio (f/m per 100 pop.)	11.9 / 20.0 [d]	... / ...	... / ...
Intentional homicide rate (per 100 000 pop.) [q]	...	9.7	10.1 [g]
Seats held by women in national parliaments (%)	6.4 [r]	25.5	25.3

Environment and infrastructure indicators	2005	2010	2017
Mobile-cellular subscriptions (per 100 inhabitants)	5.6	75.1	93.8 [d,b]
Individuals using the Internet (per 100 inhabitants)	0.9 [d]	2.5	17.2 [d,b]
Research & Development expenditure (% of GDP) [u]	...	~0.0 [s,t]	~0.0 [e,g]
Threatened species (number)	35 [o]	60	72
Forested area (% of land area) [d]	1.9	1.9	1.9 [g]
CO2 emission estimates (million tons/tons per capita)	113.5 / 4.1	112.2 / 3.6	168.4 / 4.8 [g]
Energy production, primary (Petajoules)	4 147	5 274	6 744 [g]
Energy supply per capita (Gigajoules)	54	47	58 [g]
Tourist/visitor arrivals at national borders (000)	...	1 518	892 [v]
Important sites for terrestrial biodiversity protected (%)	0.0	1.3	5.1
Pop. using improved drinking water (urban/rural, %)	94.4 / 57.1	90.0 / 65.2	93.8 / 70.1 [b]
Pop. using improved sanitation facilities (urban/rural, %)	84.6 / 67.6	85.7 / 77.8	86.4 / 83.8 [b]
Net Official Development Assist. received (% of GNI)	43.51	1.55	0.88 [b]

a Projected estimate (medium fertility variant). **b** 2015. **c** 2016. **d** Estimate. **e** Break in the time series. **f** Series linked to former series. **g** 2014. **h** Areas not elsewhere specified. **i** Data refers to a 5-year period preceding the reference year. **j** Including refugees. **k** Refers to foreign citizens. **l** Data as at the end of December. **m** Estimates should be viewed with caution as these are derived from scarce data. **n** The estimates do not include expenditures for Northern Iraq. **o** 2004. **p** 2007. **q** Data refer to Central Iraq. **r** 2000. **s** Excluding business enterprise. **t** R&D budget instead of R&D expenditure or based on R&D budget. **u** Excluding private non-profit. **v** 2013.

Ireland

Region	Northern Europe	UN membership date	14 December 1955
Population (000, 2017)	4 762 [a]	Surface area (km2)	69 797 [b]
Pop. density (per km2, 2017)	69.1 [a]	Sex ratio (m per 100 f, 2017)	98.4 [a]
Capital city	Dublin	National currency	Euro (EUR)
Capital city pop. (000)	1 169.4 [b]	Exchange rate (per US$)	0.9 [c]

Economic indicators	2005	2010	2017
GDP: Gross domestic product (million current US$)	211 680	221 343	283 716 [b]
GDP growth rate (annual %, const. 2005 prices)	5.8	2.0	26.3 [b]
GDP per capita (current US$)	50 355.5	47 937.5	60 513.6 [b]
Economy: Agriculture (% of GVA) [d]	1.2	1.1	1.0 [b]
Economy: Industry (% of GVA) [d]	34.3	26.1	41.7 [b]
Economy: Services and other activity (% of GVA) [d]	64.5	72.9	57.3 [b]
Employment: Agriculture (% of employed) [e]	5.9	4.5	4.8
Employment: Industry (% of employed) [e]	27.6	19.5	17.7
Employment: Services (% of employed) [e]	66.5	76.0	77.4
Unemployment (% of labour force)	4.3	13.9	7.6 [e]
Labour force participation (female/male pop. %) [e]	52.4 / 72.9	53.3 / 69.2	51.9 / 67.1
CPI: Consumer Price Index (2000=100)	119	128	134 [f]
Agricultural production index (2004-2006=100)	99	100	102 [f]
Food production index (2004-2006=100)	99	100	102 [f]
Index of industrial production (2005=100)	100	109 [g]	128 [g,f]
International trade: Exports (million US$)	110 003	118 338	129 315 [c]
International trade: Imports (million US$)	70 284	60 550	76 997 [c]
International trade: Balance (million US$)	39 719	57 788	52 318 [c]
Balance of payments, current account (million US$)	- 7 150	2 319	28 967 [b]

Major trading partners						2016
Export partners (% of exports)	United States	25.8	United Kingdom	12.8	Belgium	12.6
Import partners (% of imports)	United Kingdom	23.8	United States	16.5	France	12.5

Social indicators	2005	2010	2017
Population growth rate (average annual %) [h]	1.8	1.9	0.3 [b]
Urban population (% of total population)	60.5	61.8	63.2 [b]
Urban population growth rate (average annual %) [h]	2.2	1.9	1.6 [b]
Fertility rate, total (live births per woman) [h]	2.0	2.0	2.0 [b]
Life expectancy at birth (females/males, years) [h]	80.4 / 75.3	82.0 / 77.4	83.0 / 78.7 [b]
Population age distribution (0-14 and 60+ years, %)	20.2 / 14.8	20.7 / 16.1	21.6 / 19.1 [a]
International migrant stock (000/% of total pop.)	589.0 / 14.0	730.5 / 15.8	746.3 / 15.9 [b]
Refugees and others of concern to UNHCR (000)	9.5 [i]	14.2 [i]	10.5 [c]
Infant mortality rate (per 1 000 live births) [h]	5.2	3.7	3.4 [b]
Health: Total expenditure (% of GDP) [j]	7.3	8.8	7.8 [f]
Health: Physicians (per 1 000 pop.)	...	...	2.8 [b]
Education: Government expenditure (% of GDP)	4.5	6.1	5.3 [k]
Education: Primary gross enrol. ratio (f/m per 100 pop.)	106.3 / 107.0	107.0 / 106.6	102.0 / 100.9 [b]
Education: Secondary gross enrol. ratio (f/m per 100 pop.)	114.7 / 104.6	126.2 / 120.8	129.4 / 125.6 [b]
Education: Tertiary gross enrol. ratio (f/m per 100 pop.)	60.7 / 48.0	66.5 / 59.6	87.6 / 80.1 [b]
Intentional homicide rate (per 100 000 pop.)	1.2	1.2	0.6 [b]
Seats held by women in national parliaments (%)	13.3	13.9	22.2

Environment and infrastructure indicators	2005	2010	2017
Mobile-cellular subscriptions (per 100 inhabitants)	102.7	105.2	103.7 [b]
Individuals using the Internet (per 100 inhabitants) [l]	41.6	69.8	80.1 [b]
Research & Development expenditure (% of GDP)	1.2	1.6 [e]	1.5 [e,f]
Threatened species (number)	22 [m]	27	50
Forested area (% of land area)	10.1	10.5	10.9 [e,f]
CO2 emission estimates (million tons/tons per capita)	43.5 / 10.5	40.1 / 8.7	34.1 / 7.3 [f]
Energy production, primary (Petajoules)	69	77	84 [f]
Energy supply per capita (Gigajoules)	147	132	114 [f]
Tourist/visitor arrivals at national borders (000) [n]	7 333	7 134 [o]	9 528 [b]
Important sites for terrestrial biodiversity protected (%)	86.7	89.3	90.0
Pop. using improved drinking water (urban/rural, %)	96.6 / 97.2	97.3 / 97.6	97.9 / 97.8 [b]
Pop. using improved sanitation facilities (urban/rural, %)	88.2 / 92.0	88.7 / 92.5	89.1 / 92.9 [b]
Net Official Development Assist. disbursed (% of GNI) [p]	0.42	0.52	0.33 [q,c]

a Projected estimate (medium fertility variant). **b** 2015. **c** 2016. **d** Data classified according to ISIC Rev. 4. **e** Estimate. **f** 2014. **g** Excluding water and waste management. **h** Data refers to a 5-year period preceding the reference year. **i** Data as at the end of December. **j** Ireland has reviewed and improved its data collection as part of the transition to SHA 2011 leading to more complete SHA 2011 data than available under SHA 1.0 **k** 2013. **l** Population aged 16 to 74 years. **m** 2004. **n** Including tourists from Northern Ireland. **o** Break in the time series. **p** Development Assistance Committee member (OECD) **q** Provisional data.

Isle of Man

Region	Northern Europe	Population (000, 2017)	84[a]
Surface area (km2)	572[b]	Pop. density (per km2, 2017)	147.9[a]
Sex ratio (m per 100 f, 2017)	98.2[c,d]	Capital city	Douglas
National currency	Pound Sterling (GBP)	Capital city pop. (000)	28.7[e]
Exchange rate (per US$)	0.8[d]		

Economic indicators	2005	2010	2017
Employment: Agriculture (% of employed)[f]	1.4[g]	1.9[h]	...
Employment: Industry (% of employed)[f]	16.1[g]	14.8[h]	...
Employment: Services (% of employed)[f]	82.5[g]	83.3[h]	...
Unemployment (% of labour force)	1.6[g]	2.4[h]	2.6[i,j,k]
Labour force participation (female/male pop. %)	55.7 / 71.4[g]	56.3 / 69.9[h]	57.5 / 69.3[i,l,m]
CPI: Consumer Price Index (2000=100)	117	140	161[e]

Social indicators	2005	2010	2017
Population growth rate (average annual %)[n]	1.0	1.0	0.8[b]
Urban population (% of total population)	51.9	52.0	52.2[b]
Urban population growth rate (average annual %)[n]	0.9	0.9	0.8[b]
Population age distribution (0-14 and 60+ years, %)[c]	17.3 / 22.1	16.4 / 24.1[o]	16.0 / 26.9[d]
International migrant stock (000/% of total pop.)	41.5 / 51.6	43.4 / 51.5	45.2 / 51.5[b]

Environment and infrastructure indicators	2005	2010	2017
Threatened species (number)	...	2	3
Forested area (% of land area)[p]	6.1	6.1	6.1[e]
Energy production, primary (Petajoules)[p]	0	0	0[e]
Energy supply per capita (Gigajoules)	6[p]	2	3[p,e]

a Projected estimate (medium fertility variant). b 2015. c De jure population. d 2016. e 2014. f Data classified according to ISIC Rev. 3. g 2001. h 2006. i Break in the time series. j Population aged 15 to 64 years. k 2013. l Population aged 16 years and over. m 2011. n Data refers to a 5-year period preceding the reference year. o 2009. p Estimate.

Israel

Region	Western Asia	UN membership date	11 May 1949
Population (000, 2017)	8 322[a]	Surface area (km2)	22 072[b]
Pop. density (per km2, 2017)	384.5[a]	Sex ratio (m per 100 f, 2017)	98.7[a]
Capital city	Jerusalem[c]	National currency	New Israeli Sheqel (ILS)
Capital city pop. (000)	839.1[d,b]	Exchange rate (per US$)	3.8[e]

Economic indicators

	2005	2010	2017
GDP: Gross domestic product (million current US$)	142 462	233 756	299 413[b]
GDP growth rate (annual %, const. 2005 prices)	4.2	5.7	2.5[b]
GDP per capita (current US$)	21 573.2	31 502.0	37 129.4[b]
Economy: Agriculture (% of GVA)[f]	1.8	1.7	1.3[b]
Economy: Industry (% of GVA)[f]	23.0	22.8	21.2[b]
Economy: Services and other activity (% of GVA)[f]	75.2	75.5	77.5[b]
Employment: Agriculture (% of employed)[g]	2.0	1.6	1.0
Employment: Industry (% of employed)[g]	21.6	20.2	17.9
Employment: Services (% of employed)[g]	76.4	78.1	81.0
Unemployment (% of labour force)	11.3	8.5	5.9[g]
Labour force participation (female/male pop. %)[g]	55.4 / 69.3	57.1 / 69.7	58.5 / 69.0
CPI: Consumer Price Index (2000=100)	109	124	133[h]
Agricultural production index (2004-2006=100)	100	104	112[h]
Food production index (2004-2006=100)	100	105	112[h]
Index of industrial production (2005=100)[i]	...	126	136[h]
International trade: Exports (million US$)[j]	42 771	58 413	60 571[e]
International trade: Imports (million US$)[j]	45 032	59 194	65 803[e]
International trade: Balance (million US$)[j]	- 2 262	- 781	- 5 232[e]
Balance of payments, current account (million US$)	4 043	7 854	13 642[k,b]

Major trading partners

						2016
Export partners (% of exports)	United States	33.2	China, Hong Kong SAR	7.3	United Kingdom	6.6
Import partners (% of imports)	United States	12.3	China	9.0	Switzerland	6.5

Social indicators

	2005	2010	2017
Population growth rate (average annual %)[l]	1.9	2.3	1.6[b]
Urban population (% of total population)	91.5	91.8	92.1[b]
Urban population growth rate (average annual %)[l]	1.9	2.4	1.4[b]
Fertility rate, total (live births per woman)[l]	2.9	2.9	3.0[b]
Life expectancy at birth (females/males, years)[l]	81.6 / 77.4	82.8 / 79.0	83.7 / 80.0[b]
Population age distribution (0-14 and 60+ years, %)	27.9 / 13.2	27.3 / 14.9	27.9 / 16.1[a]
International migrant stock (000/% of total pop.)[m]	1 889.5 / 28.6	1 950.6 / 26.3	2 011.7 / 24.9[b]
Refugees and others of concern to UNHCR (000)	1.5[n]	31.1[n]	44.7[e]
Infant mortality rate (per 1 000 live births)[l]	5.0	4.0	3.4[b]
Health: Total expenditure (% of GDP)	7.4	7.4	7.8[h]
Health: Physicians (per 1 000 pop.)	...	3.4	3.6[h]
Education: Government expenditure (% of GDP)	5.7	5.5	5.8[h]
Education: Primary gross enrol. ratio (f/m per 100 pop.)	103.8 / 103.3	104.5 / 104.0	105.1 / 104.4[b]
Education: Secondary gross enrol. ratio (f/m per 100 pop.)	104.4 / 105.0	103.3 / 100.9	103.0 / 102.0[b]
Education: Tertiary gross enrol. ratio (f/m per 100 pop.)	66.4 / 50.1	70.7 / 54.5[o]	75.5 / 54.6[b]
Intentional homicide rate (per 100 000 pop.)	2.5	2.0	1.4[b]
Seats held by women in national parliaments (%)	15.0	19.2	27.5

Environment and infrastructure indicators

	2005	2010	2017
Mobile-cellular subscriptions (per 100 inhabitants)	117.5	122.8[g]	133.5[g,b]
Individuals using the Internet (per 100 inhabitants)	25.2	67.5[p]	78.9[g,b]
Research & Development expenditure (% of GDP)[q]	4.0	3.9	4.1[h]
Threatened species (number)	57[r]	131	174
Forested area (% of land area)	7.2	7.1	7.5[g,h]
CO2 emission estimates (million tons/tons per capita)	57.0 / 8.6	68.9 / 9.3	64.6 / 8.1[h]
Energy production, primary (Petajoules)	87	162	313[h]
Energy supply per capita (Gigajoules)	116	130	119[h]
Tourist/visitor arrivals at national borders (000)[s]	1 903	2 803	2 799[b]
Important sites for terrestrial biodiversity protected (%)	13.8	15.6	15.7
Pop. using improved drinking water (urban/rural, %)	100.0 / 100.0	100.0 / 100.0	100.0 / 100.0[b]
Pop. using improved sanitation facilities (urban/rural, %)	100.0 / 100.0	100.0 / 100.0	100.0 / 100.0[b]
Net Official Development Assist. disbursed (% of GNI)	0.07	0.07	0.07[t,e]

a Projected estimate (medium fertility variant). b 2015. c Designation and data provided by Israel. The position of the United Nations on Jerusalem is stated in A/RES/181 (II) and subsequent General Assembly and Security Council resolutions. d Including East Jerusalem. e 2016. f Data classified according to ISIC Rev. 4. g Estimate. h 2014. i Data refers to mining and manufacturing. j Imports and exports net of returned goods. The figures also exclude Judea and Samaria and the Gaza area. k Break in the time series. l Data refers to a 5-year period preceding the reference year. m Including refugees. n Data as at the end of December. o 2009. p Population aged 20 years and over. q Excluding Defence (all or mostly). r 2004. s Excluding nationals residing abroad. t Provisional data.

Italy

Region	Southern Europe	UN membership date	14 December 1955
Population (000, 2017)	59 360 a	Surface area (km2)	302 073 b
Pop. density (per km2, 2017)	201.8 a	Sex ratio (m per 100 f, 2017)	95.1 a
Capital city	Rome	National currency	Euro (EUR)
Capital city pop. (000)	3 718.0 b	Exchange rate (per US$)	0.9 c

Economic indicators

	2005	2010	2017
GDP: Gross domestic product (million current US$)	1 852 616	2 125 058	1 821 580 b
GDP growth rate (annual %, const. 2005 prices)	0.9	1.7	0.7 b
GDP per capita (current US$)	31 583.7	35 662.5	30 462.4 b
Economy: Agriculture (% of GVA) d	2.2	2.0	2.2 b
Economy: Industry (% of GVA) d	25.8	24.4	23.5 b
Economy: Services and other activity (% of GVA) d	71.9	73.7	74.2 b
Employment: Agriculture (% of employed) e	4.2	3.8	3.5
Employment: Industry (% of employed) e	30.7	28.7	27.1
Employment: Services (% of employed) e	65.1	67.5	69.4
Unemployment (% of labour force)	7.7	8.4	11.4 e
Labour force participation (female/male pop. %) e	37.8 / 61.0	37.8 / 59.0	39.2 / 57.8
CPI: Consumer Price Index (2000=100)	112 f	123 f	133 g
Agricultural production index (2004-2006=100)	100	97	89 g
Food production index (2004-2006=100)	100	97	89 g
Index of industrial production (2005=100)	100	89 h	80 h.g
International trade: Exports (million US$)	372 957	446 840	461 529 c
International trade: Imports (million US$)	384 836	486 984	404 578 c
International trade: Balance (million US$)	- 11 878	- 40 145	56 951 c
Balance of payments, current account (million US$)	- 29 744	- 73 118	29 348 b

Major trading partners

							2016
Export partners (% of exports)	Germany	12.6	France	10.5	United States	8.9
Import partners (% of imports)	Germany	16.3	France	8.9	China	7.5

Social indicators

	2005	2010	2017
Population growth rate (average annual %) i	0.5	0.3	- 0.1 b
Urban population (% of total population)	67.7	68.3	69.0 b
Urban population growth rate (average annual %) i	0.7	0.8	0.4 b
Fertility rate, total (live births per woman) i	1.3	1.4	1.4 b
Life expectancy at birth (females/males, years) i	83.1 / 77.3	84.1 / 78.8	84.7 / 79.9 b
Population age distribution (0-14 and 60+ years, %)	14.1 / 25.1	14.0 / 26.9	13.5 / 29.4 a
International migrant stock (000/% of total pop.)	3 954.8 / 6.7	5 787.9 / 9.7	5 788.9 / 9.7 b
Refugees and others of concern to UNHCR (000)	21.6 j	61.3 j	216.7 c
Infant mortality rate (per 1 000 live births) i	4.1	3.4	3.0 b
Health: Total expenditure (% of GDP)	8.7	9.4	9.2 g
Health: Physicians (per 1 000 pop.)	...	...	3.9 g
Education: Government expenditure (% of GDP)	4.2	4.4	4.1 g
Education: Primary gross enrol. ratio (f/m per 100 pop.)	100.9 / 102.0	101.6 / 102.7	100.6 / 101.4 b
Education: Secondary gross enrol. ratio (f/m per 100 pop.)	97.9 / 98.6	101.5 / 102.9	101.7 / 104.1 b
Education: Tertiary gross enrol. ratio (f/m per 100 pop.)	74.3 / 54.3	78.1 / 54.8	72.2 / 53.2 b
Intentional homicide rate (per 100 000 pop.)	1.0	0.9	0.8 b
Seats held by women in national parliaments (%)	11.5	21.3	31.0

Environment and infrastructure indicators

	2005	2010	2017
Mobile-cellular subscriptions (per 100 inhabitants)	121.9	154.8	151.3 b
Individuals using the Internet (per 100 inhabitants) k	35.0	53.7	65.6 b
Research & Development expenditure (% of GDP)	1.0	1.2	1.3 l.g
Threatened species (number)	114 m	174	359
Forested area (% of land area)	29.8	30.7 e	31.4 e.g
CO2 emission estimates (million tons/tons per capita) n	473.4 / 8.1	405.4 / 6.8	320.4 / 5.4 g
Energy production, primary (Petajoules) o	1 269	1 384	1 539 g
Energy supply per capita (Gigajoules) o	134	123	103 g
Tourist/visitor arrivals at national borders (000) p	36 513	43 626	50 732 b
Important sites for terrestrial biodiversity protected (%)	75.4	78.2	78.2
Pop. using improved drinking water (urban/rural, %)	100.0 / 100.0	100.0 / 100.0	100.0 / 100.0 b
Pop. using improved sanitation facilities (urban/rural, %)	99.5 / 99.6	99.5 / 99.6	99.5 / 99.6 b
Net Official Development Assist. disbursed (% of GNI) q	0.29	0.15	0.26 l.c

a Projected estimate (medium fertility variant). b 2015. c 2016. d Data classified according to ISIC Rev. 4. e Estimate. f Excluding tobacco. g 2014. h Excluding water and waste management. i Data refers to a 5-year period preceding the reference year. j Data as at the end of December. k Population aged 16 to 74 years. l Provisional data. m 2004. n Including San Marino. o Data include San Marino and the Holy See. p Excluding seasonal and border workers. q Development Assistance Committee member (OECD)

Jamaica

Region	Caribbean	UN membership date	18 September 1962
Population (000, 2017)	2 890[a]	Surface area (km2)	10 990[b]
Pop. density (per km2, 2017)	266.9[a]	Sex ratio (m per 100 f, 2017)	99.0[a]
Capital city	Kingston	National currency	Jamaican Dollar (JMD)
Capital city pop. (000)	587.7[b]	Exchange rate (per US$)	128.0[c]

Economic indicators	2005	2010	2017
GDP: Gross domestic product (million current US$)	11 244	13 220	14 262[b]
GDP growth rate (annual %, const. 2005 prices)	0.9	- 1.5	1.0[b]
GDP per capita (current US$)	4 198.8	4 822.6	5 105.8[b]
Economy: Agriculture (% of GVA)	5.7	5.9	7.1[b]
Economy: Industry (% of GVA)	23.9	20.0	22.3[b]
Economy: Services and other activity (% of GVA)	70.4	74.1	70.5[b]
Employment: Agriculture (% of employed)[d]	18.4	20.2	17.9
Employment: Industry (% of employed)[d]	18.0	15.9	15.3
Employment: Services (% of employed)[d]	63.6	63.8	66.8
Unemployment (% of labour force)	10.9	12.4	13.1[d]
Labour force participation (female/male pop. %)[d]	57.3 / 75.1	55.1 / 71.0	58.1 / 72.7
CPI: Consumer Price Index (2000=100)	166	296	403[e]
Agricultural production index (2004-2006=100)	97	98	102[e]
Food production index (2004-2006=100)	97	98	102[e]
International trade: Exports (million US$)	1 514	1 328	1 202[c]
International trade: Imports (million US$)	4 885	5 225	4 767[c]
International trade: Balance (million US$)	- 3 370	- 3 898	- 3 565[c]
Balance of payments, current account (million US$)	- 1 071	- 934	- 400[b]

Major trading partners						2016
Export partners (% of exports)	United States	41.5	Canada	12.1	Netherlands	10.4
Import partners (% of imports)	United States	39.5	Trinidad and Tobago	7.3	China	6.5

Social indicators	2005	2010	2017
Population growth rate (average annual %)[f]	0.6	0.5	0.4[b]
Urban population (% of total population)	52.8	53.7	54.8[b]
Urban population growth rate (average annual %)[f]	1.1	0.8	0.9[b]
Fertility rate, total (live births per woman)[f]	2.4	2.3	2.1[b]
Life expectancy at birth (females/males, years)[f]	75.6 / 70.0	76.8 / 71.6	77.9 / 73.1[b]
Population age distribution (0-14 and 60+ years, %)	30.1 / 10.8	27.0 / 11.6	22.7 / 13.6[a]
International migrant stock (000/% of total pop.)	24.3 / 0.9	23.7 / 0.9	23.2 / 0.8[b]
Refugees and others of concern to UNHCR (000)	...	~0.0[g]	~0.0[c]
Infant mortality rate (per 1 000 live births)[f]	20.0	17.9	15.0[b]
Health: Total expenditure (% of GDP)[h]	4.1	5.3	5.4[e]
Health: Physicians (per 1 000 pop.)	0.8[i]	0.4[i]	...
Education: Government expenditure (% of GDP)	4.6	6.3	5.5[b]
Education: Primary gross enrol. ratio (f/m per 100 pop.)	97.4 / 97.1[k]	... / ...	... / ...
Education: Secondary gross enrol. ratio (f/m per 100 pop.)	93.4 / 87.9	96.6 / 89.2	85.1 / 79.2[b]
Education: Tertiary gross enrol. ratio (f/m per 100 pop.)	26.0 / 12.0[l]	38.3 / 16.6	34.6 / 20.1[b]
Intentional homicide rate (per 100 000 pop.)	62.5	52.8	43.2[b]
Seats held by women in national parliaments (%)	11.7	13.3	17.5

Environment and infrastructure indicators	2005	2010	2017
Mobile-cellular subscriptions (per 100 inhabitants)	73.9	116.1	111.5[b]
Individuals using the Internet (per 100 inhabitants)	12.8[d]	27.7[m]	43.2[d,b]
Research & Development expenditure (% of GDP)	0.1[l]	...	...
Threatened species (number)	267[k]	282	311
Forested area (% of land area)[d]	31.3	31.1	31.0[e]
CO2 emission estimates (million tons/tons per capita)	10.5 / 3.9	7.3 / 2.7	7.4 / 2.7[e]
Energy production, primary (Petajoules)	15	6	8[e]
Energy supply per capita (Gigajoules)	56	38	37[e]
Tourist/visitor arrivals at national borders (000)[n]	1 479	1 922	2 123[b]
Important sites for terrestrial biodiversity protected (%)	22.0	22.0	22.0
Pop. using improved drinking water (urban/rural, %)	97.6 / 89.1	97.5 / 89.3	97.5 / 89.4[b]
Pop. using improved sanitation facilities (urban/rural, %)	79.5 / 82.9	79.7 / 83.7	79.9 / 84.1[b]
Net Official Development Assist. received (% of GNI)	0.38	1.10	0.42[b]

a Projected estimate (medium fertility variant). **b** 2015. **c** 2016. **d** Estimate. **e** 2014. **f** Data refers to a 5-year period preceding the reference year. **g** Data as at the end of December. **h** Data revision. **i** 2003. **j** 2008. **k** 2004. **l** 2002. **m** Population aged 14 years and over. **n** Arrivals of non-resident tourists by air. Including nationals residing abroad. E/D cards.

Japan

Region	Eastern Asia	UN membership date	18 December 1956
Population (000, 2017)	127 484[a]	Surface area (km2)	377 930[b,c]
Pop. density (per km2, 2017)	349.7[a]	Sex ratio (m per 100 f, 2017)	95.4[a]
Capital city	Tokyo	National currency	Yen (JPY)
Capital city pop. (000)	38 001.0[d,e]	Exchange rate (per US$)	116.8[f]

Economic indicators	2005	2010	2017
GDP: Gross domestic product (million current US$)	4 755 410	5 700 098	4 383 076[e]
GDP growth rate (annual %, const. 2005 prices)	1.7	4.2	1.2[e]
GDP per capita (current US$)	37 450.4	44 769.9	34 628.7[e]
Economy: Agriculture (% of GVA)[g]	1.2	1.2	1.2[e]
Economy: Industry (% of GVA)[g]	28.1	27.5	26.4[e]
Economy: Services and other activity (% of GVA)[g]	70.6	71.3	72.4[e]
Employment: Agriculture (% of employed)[h]	4.5	4.1	3.7
Employment: Industry (% of employed)[h]	28.3	26.1	26.5
Employment: Services (% of employed)[h]	67.2	69.8	69.8
Unemployment (% of labour force)	4.4	5.1	3.0[h]
Labour force participation (female/male pop. %)[h]	48.4 / 73.3	49.4 / 71.6	48.9 / 69.7
CPI: Consumer Price Index (2000=100)	98[i]	97	100[i]
Agricultural production index (2004-2006=100)	101	97	96[i]
Food production index (2004-2006=100)	101	97	97[i]
International trade: Exports (million US$)	594 941	769 774	644 932[f]
International trade: Imports (million US$)	515 866	694 059	606 924[f]
International trade: Balance (million US$)	79 074	75 715	38 008[f]
Balance of payments, current account (million US$)	170 123	220 888	135 608[e]

Major trading partners						2016
Export partners (% of exports)	United States	20.2	China	17.6	Republic of Korea	7.2
Import partners (% of imports)	China	25.8	United States	11.4	Australia	5.0

Social indicators	2005	2010	2017
Population growth rate (average annual %)[k]	0.1	~0.0	- 0.1[e]
Urban population (% of total population)	86.0	90.5	93.5[e]
Urban population growth rate (average annual %)[k]	2.0	1.1	0.6[e]
Fertility rate, total (live births per woman)[k]	1.3	1.3	1.4[e]
Life expectancy at birth (females/males, years)[k]	85.2 / 78.3	86.0 / 79.2	86.4 / 80.0[e]
Population age distribution (0-14 and 60+ years, %)	13.8 / 26.3	13.4 / 30.3	12.9 / 33.4[a]
International migrant stock (000/% of total pop.)[l]	2 012.9 / 1.6	2 134.2 / 1.7	2 043.9 / 1.6[e]
Refugees and others of concern to UNHCR (000)	4.2[m]	7.0[m]	19.4[h,f]
Infant mortality rate (per 1 000 live births)[k]	3.0	2.6	2.2[e]
Health: Total expenditure (% of GDP)	8.2	9.6	10.2[i]
Health: Physicians (per 1 000 pop.)	2.1[n]	2.2	2.3[o]
Education: Government expenditure (% of GDP)	3.4	3.6	3.6[i]
Education: Primary gross enrol. ratio (f/m per 100 pop.)	101.9 / 101.9	102.2 / 102.2	101.2 / 101.3[i]
Education: Secondary gross enrol. ratio (f/m per 100 pop.)	101.1 / 100.9	101.7 / 101.5	101.9 / 101.6[i]
Education: Tertiary gross enrol. ratio (f/m per 100 pop.)	51.7 / 58.1	54.7 / 61.3	60.9 / 65.7[i]
Intentional homicide rate (per 100 000 pop.)	0.5	0.4	0.3[i]
Seats held by women in national parliaments (%)	7.1	11.3	9.3

Environment and infrastructure indicators	2005	2010	2017
Mobile-cellular subscriptions (per 100 inhabitants)	76.0[p]	96.8[p]	125.6[m,q,e]
Individuals using the Internet (per 100 inhabitants)	66.9[r]	78.2[r]	93.3[h,e]
Research & Development expenditure (% of GDP)	3.3	3.3	3.6[i]
Threatened species (number)	205[n]	330	404
Forested area (% of land area)[h]	68.4	68.5	68.5[i]
CO2 emission estimates (million tons/tons per capita)	1 239.3 / 9.8	1 171.6 / 9.2	1 214.0 / 9.6[i]
Energy production, primary (Petajoules)	4 172	4 116	1 114[i]
Energy supply per capita (Gigajoules)	172	164	146[i]
Tourist/visitor arrivals at national borders (000)[s]	6 728	8 611	19 737[e]
Important sites for terrestrial biodiversity protected (%)	64.5	64.7	68.5
Pop. using improved drinking water (urban/rural, %)	100.0 / 100.0	100.0 / 100.0	100.0 / 100.0[e]
Pop. using improved sanitation facilities (urban/rural, %)	100.0 / 100.0	100.0 / 100.0	100.0 / 100.0[e]
Net Official Development Assist. disbursed (% of GNI)[t]	0.28	0.20	0.20[u,f]

a Projected estimate (medium fertility variant). **b** Data refer to 1 October. **c** 2007. **d** Major metropolitan areas. **e** 2015. **f** 2016. **g** Data classified according to ISIC Rev. 4. **h** Estimate. **i** Series linked to former series. **j** 2014. **k** Data refers to a 5-year period preceding the reference year. **l** Refers to foreign citizens. **m** Data as at the end of December. **n** 2004. **o** 2012. **p** Including Personal Handy-phone System (PHS) subscriptions. **q** Including Personal Handy-phone System (PHS) and data-only subscriptions. **r** Population aged 6 years and over. **s** Excluding nationals residing abroad. **t** Development Assistance Committee member (OECD) **u** Provisional data.

Jordan

Region	Western Asia	UN membership date	14 December 1955
Population (000, 2017)	9 702 [a]	Surface area (km2)	89 318 [b]
Pop. density (per km2, 2017)	109.3 [a]	Sex ratio (m per 100 f, 2017)	102.6 [a]
Capital city	Amman	National currency	Jordanian Dinar (JOD)
Capital city pop. (000)	1 154.7 [c,b]	Exchange rate (per US$)	0.7 [d]

Economic indicators

	2005	2010	2017
GDP: Gross domestic product (million current US$)	12 589	26 425	37 517 [b]
GDP growth rate (annual %, const. 2005 prices)	8.1	2.3	2.4 [b]
GDP per capita (current US$)	2 360.5	4 054.3	4 940.1 [b]
Economy: Agriculture (% of GVA)	3.0	3.2	4.0 [b]
Economy: Industry (% of GVA)	26.9	28.7	27.7 [b]
Economy: Services and other activity (% of GVA)	70.1	68.1	68.4 [b]
Employment: Agriculture (% of employed) [e]	3.4	2.0	2.0
Employment: Industry (% of employed) [e]	20.7	18.7	17.8
Employment: Services (% of employed) [e]	75.9	79.3	80.2
Unemployment (% of labour force)	14.8	12.5	13.4 [e]
Labour force participation (female/male pop. %) [e]	12.3 / 67.6	15.4 / 67.6	14.5 / 64.5
CPI: Consumer Price Index (2000=100)	113	149	177 [f]
Agricultural production index (2004-2006=100)	97	129	134 [f]
Food production index (2004-2006=100)	97	129	135 [f]
Index of industrial production (2005=100) [g]	100	105	109 [f]
International trade: Exports (million US$)	4 284	7 023	7 509 [d]
International trade: Imports (million US$)	10 455	15 262	19 207 [d]
International trade: Balance (million US$)	- 6 170	- 8 239	- 11 698 [d]
Balance of payments, current account (million US$)	- 2 271	- 1 882 [h]	- 3 332 [b]

Major trading partners

						2016
Export partners (% of exports)	United States	20.9	Saudi Arabia	13.2	India	7.6
Import partners (% of imports)	China	14.0	Saudi Arabia	12.1	United States	7.0

Social indicators

	2005	2010	2017
Population growth rate (average annual %) [i]	2.3	4.6	4.9 [b]
Urban population (% of total population)	81.2	82.5	83.7 [b]
Urban population growth rate (average annual %) [i]	2.2	4.5	3.8 [b]
Fertility rate, total (live births per woman) [i]	3.9	3.7	3.6 [b]
Life expectancy at birth (females/males, years) [i]	73.8 / 70.8	74.6 / 71.5	75.5 / 72.2 [b]
Population age distribution (0-14 and 60+ years, %)	37.8 / 5.3	37.0 / 5.4	35.5 / 5.7 [a]
International migrant stock (000/% of total pop.) [j,k]	2 325.4 / 43.6	2 723.0 / 41.8	3 112.0 / 41.0 [b]
Refugees and others of concern to UNHCR (000)	17.9 [l]	453.2 [l]	721.4 [d]
Infant mortality rate (per 1 000 live births) [i]	22.4	19.7	17.1 [b]
Health: Total expenditure (% of GDP) [m,n]	8.9	8.4	7.5 [f]
Health: Physicians (per 1 000 pop.)	2.4	2.5	2.6 [f]
Education: Primary gross enrol. ratio (f/m per 100 pop.)	106.3 / 104.8	90.9 / 91.1	97.6 / 97.1 [f]
Education: Secondary gross enrol. ratio (f/m per 100 pop.)	92.4 / 89.7	91.1 / 86.1	84.8 / 80.2 [f]
Education: Tertiary gross enrol. ratio (f/m per 100 pop.)	40.6 / 37.3	43.5 / 37.7	47.3 / 42.5 [b]
Intentional homicide rate (per 100 000 pop.)	1.3	1.8	2.0 [o]
Seats held by women in national parliaments (%)	5.5	6.4	15.4

Environment and infrastructure indicators

	2005	2010	2017
Mobile-cellular subscriptions (per 100 inhabitants)	59.9	102.6	179.4 [b]
Individuals using the Internet (per 100 inhabitants)	12.9	27.2 [p]	53.4 [e,b]
Research & Development expenditure (% of GDP)	0.3 [q]	0.4 [r]	...
Threatened species (number)	30 [s]	90	113
Forested area (% of land area) [e]	1.1	1.1	1.1 [f]
CO2 emission estimates (million tons/tons per capita)	21.1 / 4.0	21.2 / 3.3	26.5 / 3.6 [f]
Energy production, primary (Petajoules)	10	9	7 [f]
Energy supply per capita (Gigajoules)	54	46	47 [f]
Tourist/visitor arrivals at national borders (000) [t]	2 987	4 207	3 761 [b]
Important sites for terrestrial biodiversity protected (%)	6.2	6.2	7.7
Pop. using improved drinking water (urban/rural, %)	98.1 / 91.5	98.0 / 91.9	97.8 / 92.3 [b]
Pop. using improved sanitation facilities (urban/rural, %)	98.4 / 97.2	98.5 / 98.2	98.6 / 98.9 [b]
Net Official Development Assist. received (% of GNI)	5.49	3.64	5.80 [b]

a Projected estimate (medium fertility variant). b 2015. c Excluding Syrian refugees. d 2016. e Estimate. f 2014. g Data classified according to ISIC Rev. 3. h Break in the time series. i Data refers to a 5-year period preceding the reference year. j Refers to foreign citizens. k Including refugees. l Data as at the end of December. m Data revision. n The public expenditure on health includes contributions from the United Nations Relief and Works Agency for Palestine Refugees in the Near East (UNRWA) made to Palestinian refugees residing in Jordanian territories. o 2013. p Population aged 5 years and over. q 2002. r 2008. s 2004. t Including nationals residing abroad.

Kazakhstan

Region	Central Asia	UN membership date	02 March 1992
Population (000, 2017)	18 204 [a]	Surface area (km2)	2 724 902 [b]
Pop. density (per km2, 2017)	6.7 [a]	Sex ratio (m per 100 f, 2017)	93.9 [a]
Capital city	Astana	National currency	Tenge (KZT)
Capital city pop. (000)	759.0 [b]	Exchange rate (per US$)	333.3 [c]

Economic indicators	2005	2010	2017
GDP: Gross domestic product (million current US$)	57 124	148 047	181 754 [b]
GDP growth rate (annual %, const. 2005 prices)	9.7	7.3	1.2 [b]
GDP per capita (current US$)	3 696.9	9 076.7	10 312.1 [b]
Economy: Agriculture (% of GVA) [d]	6.6	4.6	5.0 [b]
Economy: Industry (% of GVA) [d]	39.2	41.8	32.5 [b]
Economy: Services and other activity (% of GVA) [d]	54.2	53.6	62.5 [b]
Employment: Agriculture (% of employed) [e]	32.4	28.3	18.1
Employment: Industry (% of employed) [e]	17.9	18.7	20.4
Employment: Services (% of employed) [e]	49.6	53.0	61.6
Unemployment (% of labour force)	8.1	5.8	5.6 [e]
Labour force participation (female/male pop. %) [e]	64.4 / 75.2	65.5 / 75.8	66.3 / 77.5
CPI: Consumer Price Index (2000=100)	140	198 [f]	...
Agricultural production index (2004-2006=100)	100	107	126 [g]
Food production index (2004-2006=100)	100	108	127 [g]
Index of industrial production (2005=100) [h]	100	115 [f]	...
International trade: Exports (million US$)	27 846	57 244	36 775 [c]
International trade: Imports (million US$)	17 333	24 024	25 175 [c]
International trade: Balance (million US$)	10 513	33 220	11 601 [c]
Balance of payments, current account (million US$)	- 1 036	1 386	- 5 464 [b]

Major trading partners						2016
Export partners (% of exports)	Italy	20.3	China	11.5	Russian Federation	9.5
Import partners (% of imports)	Russian Federation	36.3	China	14.6	Germany	5.7

Social indicators	2005	2010	2017
Population growth rate (average annual %) [i]	0.6	1.1	1.6 [b]
Urban population (% of total population)	54.7	53.7	53.2 [b]
Urban population growth rate (average annual %) [i]	0.3	0.7	0.9 [b]
Fertility rate, total (live births per woman) [i]	2.0	2.5	2.7 [b]
Life expectancy at birth (females/males, years) [i]	70.4 / 59.1	71.9 / 60.6	73.9 / 64.3 [b]
Population age distribution (0-14 and 60+ years, %)	24.5 / 10.1	24.0 / 9.9	27.9 / 11.1 [a]
International migrant stock (000/% of total pop.)	3 103.0 / 20.1	3 334.6 / 20.4	3 546.8 / 20.1 [b]
Refugees and others of concern to UNHCR (000)	57.9 [j]	12.7 [j]	9.2 [c]
Infant mortality rate (per 1 000 live births) [i]	32.0	23.9	14.1 [b]
Health: Total expenditure (% of GDP)	4.1	4.4	4.4 [g]
Health: Physicians (per 1 000 pop.)	...	3.5	3.3 [g]
Education: Government expenditure (% of GDP)	2.3	3.1 [k]	2.8 [b]
Education: Primary gross enrol. ratio (f/m per 100 pop.)	101.7 / 101.8	107.9 / 107.3	109.1 / 108.8 [c]
Education: Secondary gross enrol. ratio (f/m per 100 pop.)	95.4 / 91.5 [l]	98.0 / 97.5	113.5 / 110.6 [c]
Education: Tertiary gross enrol. ratio (f/m per 100 pop.)	34.1 / 29.4 [l]	51.5 / 40.5	51.3 / 41.4 [c]
Intentional homicide rate (per 100 000 pop.) [m]	11.7	8.6	4.8 [b]
Seats held by women in national parliaments (%)	10.4	17.8	27.1

Environment and infrastructure indicators	2005	2010	2017
Mobile-cellular subscriptions (per 100 inhabitants)	35.8	121.9	187.2 [b]
Individuals using the Internet (per 100 inhabitants)	3.0	31.6 [n]	72.9 [o,b]
Research & Development expenditure (% of GDP)	0.3	0.2	0.2 [p]
Threatened species (number)	53 [q]	73	82
Forested area (% of land area) [e]	1.2	1.2	1.2 [g]
CO2 emission estimates (million tons/tons per capita)	177.3 / 11.7	248.5 / 15.3	248.3 / 14.3 [g]
Energy production, primary (Petajoules)	5 131	6 770	7 091 [g]
Energy supply per capita (Gigajoules)	155	206	193 [g]
Tourist/visitor arrivals at national borders (000)	3 143	2 991	4 560 [g]
Important sites for terrestrial biodiversity protected (%)	10.3	14.8	16.3
Pop. using improved drinking water (urban/rural, %)	98.5 / 87.4	99.0 / 86.4	99.4 / 85.6 [b]
Pop. using improved sanitation facilities (urban/rural, %)	96.7 / 97.5	96.9 / 97.9	97.0 / 98.1 [b]
Net Official Development Assist. disbursed (% of GNI)	...	...	0.02 [b]
Net Official Development Assist. received (% of GNI)	0.43	0.17	0.05 [b]

a Projected estimate (medium fertility variant). b 2015. c 2016. d Data classified according to ISIC Rev. 4. e Estimate. f 2008. g 2014. h Data classified according to ISIC Rev. 3. i Data refers to a 5-year period preceding the reference year. j Data as at the end of December. k 2009. l 2000. m Break in the time series. n Population aged 16 to 74 years. o Population aged 6 to 74 years. p 2013. q 2004.

Kenya

Region	Eastern Africa	
Population (000, 2017)	49 700[a]	
Pop. density (per km2, 2017)	87.3[a]	
Capital city	Nairobi	
Capital city pop. (000)	3 914.8[b]	

UN membership date	16 December 1963	
Surface area (km2)	591 958[b]	
Sex ratio (m per 100 f, 2017)	98.8[a]	
National currency	Kenyan Shilling (KES)	
Exchange rate (per US$)	102.3[b]	

Economic indicators	2005	2010	2017
GDP: Gross domestic product (million current US$)	21 506	40 000	63 399[b]
GDP growth rate (annual %, const. 2005 prices)	5.9	8.4	5.6[b]
GDP per capita (current US$)	608.4	991.9	1 376.7[b]
Economy: Agriculture (% of GVA)[c]	23.2	27.1	32.0[b]
Economy: Industry (% of GVA)[c]	22.3	20.3	19.0[b]
Economy: Services and other activity (% of GVA)[c]	54.5	52.6	49.0[b]
Employment: Agriculture (% of employed)[d]	66.3	64.8	61.9
Employment: Industry (% of employed)[d]	7.4	8.0	8.6
Employment: Services (% of employed)[d]	26.3	27.2	29.5
Unemployment (% of labour force)[d]	10.7	12.2	10.8
Labour force participation (female/male pop. %)[d]	59.9 / 69.8	61.0 / 71.4	62.4 / 72.4
CPI: Consumer Price Index (2000=100)	149[e,f]	134[g,h,i]	188[g,i]
Agricultural production index (2004-2006=100)	103	123	126[j]
Food production index (2004-2006=100)	103	124	126[j]
International trade: Exports (million US$)	3 420	5 169	5 688[k]
International trade: Imports (million US$)	5 846	12 093	14 109[k]
International trade: Balance (million US$)	- 2 426	- 6 924	- 8 420[k]
Balance of payments, current account (million US$)	- 252	- 2 369	- 6 339[j]

Major trading partners						2016
Export partners (% of exports)	United States	10.8	Netherlands	8.2	Pakistan	7.7
Import partners (% of imports)	China	34.7	India	15.0	Japan	4.5

Social indicators	2005	2010	2017
Population growth rate (average annual %)[l]	2.7	2.7	2.7[b]
Urban population (% of total population)	21.7	23.6	25.6[b]
Urban population growth rate (average annual %)[l]	4.4	4.4	4.3[b]
Fertility rate, total (live births per woman)[l]	5.0	4.6	4.1[b]
Life expectancy at birth (females/males, years)[l]	54.5 / 51.0	61.3 / 58.1	67.8 / 63.0[b]
Population age distribution (0-14 and 60+ years, %)	43.8 / 3.7	43.2 / 3.8	40.5 / 4.3[a]
International migrant stock (000/% of total pop.)[m]	756.9 / 2.1	927.0 / 2.3	1 084.4 / 2.4[b]
Refugees and others of concern to UNHCR (000)	268.2[n]	751.0[n]	582.4[k]
Infant mortality rate (per 1 000 live births)[l]	62.2	49.4	39.4[b]
Health: Total expenditure (% of GDP)[o]	4.4	4.0	5.7[j]
Health: Physicians (per 1 000 pop.)	0.1[p]	0.2	0.2[q]
Education: Government expenditure (% of GDP)	7.4	5.5	5.3[b]
Education: Primary gross enrol. ratio (f/m per 100 pop.)	105.5 / 109.8	112.0 / 114.5[r]	108.7 / 109.3[b]
Education: Secondary gross enrol. ratio (f/m per 100 pop.)	46.8 / 49.0[d]	57.4 / 63.5[r]	... / ...
Education: Tertiary gross enrol. ratio (f/m per 100 pop.)	2.2 / 3.7[d]	3.3 / 4.8[r]	... / ...
Intentional homicide rate (per 100 000 pop.)	3.6	5.6	5.8[b]
Seats held by women in national parliaments (%)	7.1	9.8	19.4

Environment and infrastructure indicators	2005	2010	2017
Mobile-cellular subscriptions (per 100 inhabitants)	12.9	61.0	80.7[b]
Individuals using the Internet (per 100 inhabitants)	3.1	14.0	45.6[d,b]
Research & Development expenditure (% of GDP)	...	0.8[i]	...
Threatened species (number)	229[s]	338	480
Forested area (% of land area)[d]	7.1	7.4	7.7[j]
CO2 emission estimates (million tons/tons per capita)	8.6 / 0.3	12.2 / 0.3	14.3 / 0.3[j]
Energy production, primary (Petajoules)	338	650[d]	750[j]
Energy supply per capita (Gigajoules)	12	20[d]	20[j]
Tourist/visitor arrivals at national borders (000)	1 399	1 470	1 114[b]
Important sites for terrestrial biodiversity protected (%)	35.5	36.8	37.5
Pop. using improved drinking water (urban/rural, %)	85.4 / 47.3	83.3 / 52.9	81.6 / 56.8[b]
Pop. using improved sanitation facilities (urban/rural, %)	29.5 / 27.6	30.5 / 28.8	31.2 / 29.7[b]
Net Official Development Assist. received (% of GNI)	4.04	4.09	3.93[b]

a Projected estimate (medium fertility variant). b 2015. c Data classified according to ISIC Rev. 4. d Estimate. e Low income group. f Nairobi g Index base: 2007=100. h Series linked to former series. i Break in the time series. j 2014. k 2016. l Data refers to a 5-year period preceding the reference year. m Including refugees. n Data as at the end of December. o In 2014, Kenya revalued its base year from 2002 to 2009, which increased its GDP by 25 per cent in 2013. p 2002. q 2013. r 2009. s 2004.

Kiribati

Region	Micronesia	UN membership date	14 September 1999
Population (000, 2017)	116[a]	Surface area (km2)	726[b,c]
Pop. density (per km2, 2017)	143.7[a]	Sex ratio (m per 100 f, 2017)	97.3[a]
Capital city	Bairiki	National currency	Australian Dollar (AUD)
Capital city pop. (000)	3.5[d]	Exchange rate (per US$)	1.4[e]

Economic indicators	2005	2010	2017
GDP: Gross domestic product (million current US$)	112	153	162[c]
GDP growth rate (annual %, const. 2005 prices)	5.0	- 1.6	3.7[c]
GDP per capita (current US$)	1 214.5	1 493.3	1 442.9[c]
Economy: Agriculture (% of GVA)[f]	21.8	24.6	24.1[c]
Economy: Industry (% of GVA)[f]	9.3	10.3	13.6[c]
Economy: Services and other activity (% of GVA)[f]	68.9	65.0	62.2[c]
Employment: Agriculture (% of employed)	7.1[g]	22.1	...
Employment: Industry (% of employed)	8.4[g]	16.1	...
Employment: Services (% of employed)	81.1[g]	61.8	...
Unemployment (% of labour force)[h]	14.7	30.6	...
Labour force participation (female/male pop. %)	20.4 / 32.8[i,j]	52.3 / 66.8[j]	... / ...
CPI: Consumer Price Index (2000=100)	110[k]	125[l]	...
Agricultural production index (2004-2006=100)	95	60	61[m]
Food production index (2004-2006=100)	95	60	61[m]
International trade: Exports (million US$)	4	4	3[e]
International trade: Imports (million US$)	74	73	116[e]
International trade: Balance (million US$)	- 70	- 69	- 113[e]
Balance of payments, current account (million US$)	...	- 3	45[m]

Major trading partners						2016
Export partners (% of exports)	Thailand	63.7	Viet Nam	9.2	China	7.4
Import partners (% of imports)	Fiji	27.0	China	18.8	Japan	13.5

Social indicators	2005	2010	2017
Population growth rate (average annual %)[n]	1.8	2.1	1.8[c]
Urban population (% of total population)	43.6	43.8	44.3[c]
Urban population growth rate (average annual %)[n]	2.0	1.6	1.8[c]
Fertility rate, total (live births per woman)[n]	4.0	3.9	3.8[c]
Life expectancy at birth (females/males, years)[n]	67.5 / 61.6	68.1 / 62.0	68.9 / 62.4[c]
Population age distribution (0-14 and 60+ years, %)	36.9 / 5.4	36.1 / 5.4	35.0 / 6.4[a]
International migrant stock (000/% of total pop.)[n]	2.5 / 2.7	2.9 / 2.8	3.2 / 2.8[c]
Infant mortality rate (per 1 000 live births)[n]	51.6	49.3	46.9[c]
Health: Total expenditure (% of GDP)	10.1	10.5	10.2[m]
Health: Physicians (per 1 000 pop.)	...	0.3[l]	0.2[o]
Education: Government expenditure (% of GDP)	12.0[p]	...	...
Education: Primary gross enrol. ratio (f/m per 100 pop.)	112.8 / 111.2	113.8 / 108.0[q]	106.1 / 102.9[c]
Education: Secondary gross enrol. ratio (f/m per 100 pop.)	95.3 / 83.1	91.6 / 82.9[l]	... / ...
Intentional homicide rate (per 100 000 pop.)	...	3.9	7.5[r]
Seats held by women in national parliaments (%)	4.8	4.3	6.5

Environment and infrastructure indicators	2005	2010	2017
Mobile-cellular subscriptions (per 100 inhabitants)	0.7	10.8	38.8[c]
Individuals using the Internet (per 100 inhabitants)	4.0[s]	9.1	13.0[s,c]
Threatened species (number)	11[t]	90	104
Forested area (% of land area)[s]	15.0	15.0	15.0[m]
CO2 emission estimates (million tons/tons per capita)	0.1 / 0.7	0.1 / 0.6	0.1 / 0.6[m]
Energy production, primary (Petajoules)	0	0	0[m]
Energy supply per capita (Gigajoules)	10[s]	9[s]	8[m]
Tourist/visitor arrivals at national borders (000)[u]	4	5	4[c]
Important sites for terrestrial biodiversity protected (%)	27.7	65.7	65.7
Pop. using improved drinking water (urban/rural, %)	83.3 / 46.0	86.2 / 49.3	87.3 / 50.6[c]
Pop. using improved sanitation facilities (urban/rural, %)	48.7 / 27.2	50.5 / 29.6	51.2 / 30.6[c]
Net Official Development Assist. received (% of GNI)	17.46	10.50	20.05[c]

a Projected estimate (medium fertility variant). **b** Land area only. Excluding 84 square km of uninhabited islands. **c** 2015. **d** 2010. **e** 2016. **f** At factor cost. **g** Data classified according to ISIC Rev. 2. **h** De facto population. **i** Break in the time series. **j** Persons present (de facto). **k** Tarawa **l** 2008. **m** 2014. **n** Data refers to a 5-year period preceding the reference year. **o** 2013. **p** 2001. **q** 2009. **r** 2012. **s** Estimate. **t** 2004. **u** Air arrivals. Tarawa and Christmas Island.

Kuwait

Region	Western Asia	UN membership date	14 May 1963
Population (000, 2017)	4 136[a]	Surface area (km2)	17 818[b]
Pop. density (per km2, 2017)	232.1[a]	Sex ratio (m per 100 f, 2017)	134.9[a]
Capital city	Kuwait City	National currency	Kuwaiti Dinar (KWD)
Capital city pop. (000)	2 778.7[b]	Exchange rate (per US$)	0.3[c]

Economic indicators	2005	2010	2017
GDP: Gross domestic product (million current US$)	80 798	115 416	114 054[b]
GDP growth rate (annual %, const. 2005 prices)	10.6	- 2.4	1.8[b]
GDP per capita (current US$)	35 694.4	37 724.2	29 303.9[b]
Economy: Agriculture (% of GVA)	0.3	0.4	0.6[b]
Economy: Industry (% of GVA)	60.2	58.2	48.7[b]
Economy: Services and other activity (% of GVA)	39.5	41.4	50.7[b]
Employment: Agriculture (% of employed)[d]	2.7	2.5	2.6
Employment: Industry (% of employed)[d]	21.2	25.9	27.3
Employment: Services (% of employed)[d]	76.1	71.6	70.1
Unemployment (% of labour force)	2.0	1.8	2.2[d]
Labour force participation (female/male pop. %)[d]	45.0 / 81.9	46.9 / 83.8	47.7 / 83.6
CPI: Consumer Price Index (2000=100)	109	141	157[e]
Agricultural production index (2004-2006=100)	95	136	199[e]
Food production index (2004-2006=100)	95	136	199[e]
Index of industrial production (2005=100)[f]	100	89	114[g]
International trade: Exports (million US$)	44 869	62 698	46 238[c]
International trade: Imports (million US$)	15 801	22 691	30 825[c]
International trade: Balance (million US$)	29 068	40 007	15 413[c]
Balance of payments, current account (million US$)	30 071	36 989	8 584[b]

Major trading partners						2016
Export partners (% of exports)	Republic of Korea	15.2	China	12.4	Japan	9.0
Import partners (% of imports)	China	16.0	United States	9.4	United Arab Emirates	9.3

Social indicators	2005	2010	2017
Population growth rate (average annual %)[h]	2.1	5.5	5.4[b]
Urban population (% of total population)	98.2	98.3	98.3[b]
Urban population growth rate (average annual %)[h]	3.7	5.3	3.6[b]
Fertility rate, total (live births per woman)[h]	2.6	2.4	2.0[b]
Life expectancy at birth (females/males, years)[h]	74.4 / 72.6	74.8 / 73.0	75.5 / 73.5[b]
Population age distribution (0-14 and 60+ years, %)	26.0 / 3.6	23.2 / 3.4	21.1 / 4.9[a]
International migrant stock (000/% of total pop.)[i,j]	1 333.3 / 58.9	1 871.5 / 61.2	2 866.1 / 73.6[b]
Refugees and others of concern to UNHCR (000)	102.7[k]	96.5[k]	94.7[c]
Infant mortality rate (per 1 000 live births)[h]	10.2	9.6	8.4[b]
Health: Total expenditure (% of GDP)	2.4	2.8	3.0[e]
Health: Physicians (per 1 000 pop.)	...	1.9[l]	1.9[e]
Education: Government expenditure (% of GDP)	4.7	3.8[d,m]	...
Education: Primary gross enrol. ratio (f/m per 100 pop.)	107.6 / 109.8	104.9 / 100.9	103.0 / 102.4[e]
Education: Secondary gross enrol. ratio (f/m per 100 pop.)	118.3 / 103.4[d]	90.6 / 96.5	102.7 / 88.2[b]
Education: Tertiary gross enrol. ratio (f/m per 100 pop.)	28.1 / 13.6[d,n]	... / ...	33.1 / 20.4[g]
Intentional homicide rate (per 100 000 pop.)	...	2.0	1.8[o]
Seats held by women in national parliaments (%)	0.0	7.7	3.1

Environment and infrastructure indicators	2005	2010	2017
Mobile-cellular subscriptions (per 100 inhabitants)	60.2[p]	133.0	231.8[d,b]
Individuals using the Internet (per 100 inhabitants)	25.9	61.4[d]	82.1[d,b]
Research & Development expenditure (% of GDP)	0.1[q,r]	0.1[q,r]	0.3[s,t,u,g]
Threatened species (number)	20[n]	41	49
Forested area (% of land area)[d]	0.3	0.4	0.4[e]
CO2 emission estimates (million tons/tons per capita)	71.5 / 31.6	89.6 / 29.3	95.4 / 25.4[e]
Energy production, primary (Petajoules)[v]	6 080	5 557	6 941[e]
Energy supply per capita (Gigajoules)[v]	500	441	380[e]
Tourist/visitor arrivals at national borders (000)	3 474	5 208	6 941[e]
Important sites for terrestrial biodiversity protected (%)	35.4	35.4	59.0
Pop. using improved drinking water (urban/rural, %)	99.0 / 99.0	99.0 / 99.0	99.0 / 99.0[b]
Pop. using improved sanitation facilities (urban/rural, %)	100.0 / 100.0	100.0 / 100.0	100.0 / 100.0[b]

a Projected estimate (medium fertility variant). b 2015. c 2016. d Estimate. e 2014. f Data classified according to ISIC Rev. 3. g 2013. h Data refers to a 5-year period preceding the reference year. i Including refugees. j Refers to foreign citizens. k Data as at the end of December. l 2009. m 2006. n 2004. o 2012. p Does not include data from all operators. q Partial data. r Government only. s Excluding business enterprise. t Break in the time series. u Excluding private non-profit. v The data for crude oil production include 50 per cent of the output of the Neutral Zone.

Kyrgyzstan

Region	Central Asia	UN membership date	02 March 1992
Population (000, 2017)	6 045 [a]	Surface area (km2)	199 949 [b]
Pop. density (per km2, 2017)	31.5 [a]	Sex ratio (m per 100 f, 2017)	98.4 [a]
Capital city	Bishkek	National currency	Som (KGS)
Capital city pop. (000)	865.2 [b]	Exchange rate (per US$)	69.2 [c]

Economic indicators	2005	2010	2017
GDP: Gross domestic product (million current US$)	2 460	4 794	6 572 [b]
GDP growth rate (annual %, const. 2005 prices)	- 0.2	- 0.5	3.5 [b]
GDP per capita (current US$)	480.9	877.4	1 106.4 [b]
Economy: Agriculture (% of GVA) [d]	31.3	18.8	15.4 [b]
Economy: Industry (% of GVA) [d]	22.1	28.2	25.9 [b]
Economy: Services and other activity (% of GVA) [d]	46.6	53.0	58.7 [b]
Employment: Agriculture (% of employed) [e]	38.5	29.1	29.2
Employment: Industry (% of employed) [e]	17.6	23.5	21.0
Employment: Services (% of employed) [e]	43.9	47.3	49.8
Unemployment (% of labour force)	8.1	8.6	7.7 [e]
Labour force participation (female/male pop. %) [e]	54.1 / 76.1	52.2 / 76.6	49.7 / 77.5
CPI: Consumer Price Index (2000=100)	122	...	...
Agricultural production index (2004-2006=100)	98	105	108 [f]
Food production index (2004-2006=100)	98	106	110 [f]
Index of industrial production (2005=100) [g]	100	69	78 [h]
International trade: Exports (million US$)	672	1 488	1 423 [c]
International trade: Imports (million US$)	1 108	3 223	3 844 [c]
International trade: Balance (million US$)	- 436	- 1 734	- 2 421 [c]
Balance of payments, current account (million US$)	- 62	- 448 [i]	- 721 [b]

Major trading partners						2016
Export partners (% of exports)	Switzerland	45.5	Kazakhstan	10.6	Russian Federation	10.2
Import partners (% of imports)	China	38.1	Russian Federation	20.8	Kazakhstan	16.5

Social indicators	2005	2010	2017
Population growth rate (average annual %) [j]	0.6	1.3	1.6 [b]
Urban population (% of total population)	35.3	35.3	35.7 [b]
Urban population growth rate (average annual %) [j]	0.3	1.1	1.6 [b]
Fertility rate, total (live births per woman) [j]	2.5	2.8	3.1 [b]
Life expectancy at birth (females/males, years) [j]	71.0 / 63.0	71.7 / 63.5	74.3 / 66.4 [b]
Population age distribution (0-14 and 60+ years, %)	31.0 / 7.1	29.9 / 6.4	31.8 / 7.6 [a]
International migrant stock (000/% of total pop.)	312.9 / 6.1	231.5 / 4.2	204.4 / 3.4 [b]
Refugees and others of concern to UNHCR (000)	103.1 [k]	304.2 [k]	8.2 [c]
Infant mortality rate (per 1 000 live births) [j]	37.8	30.3	19.6 [b]
Health: Total expenditure (% of GDP)	5.8	6.7	6.5 [f]
Health: Physicians (per 1 000 pop.)	...	1.9	1.9 [f]
Education: Government expenditure (% of GDP)	4.9	5.8	5.5 [f]
Education: Primary gross enrol. ratio (f/m per 100 pop.)	97.0 / 98.4	97.5 / 98.4	106.8 / 107.9 [b]
Education: Secondary gross enrol. ratio (f/m per 100 pop.)	86.3 / 86.2	86.5 / 86.7	92.8 / 91.4 [b]
Education: Tertiary gross enrol. ratio (f/m per 100 pop.)	47.1 / 37.7	47.5 / 36.6	53.3 / 40.8 [b]
Intentional homicide rate (per 100 000 pop.)	8.2	19.6	5.1 [b]
Seats held by women in national parliaments (%)	10.0	25.6	19.2

Environment and infrastructure indicators	2005	2010	2017
Mobile-cellular subscriptions (per 100 inhabitants)	10.7	98.9	132.8 [b]
Individuals using the Internet (per 100 inhabitants)	10.5	16.3 [e]	30.2 [e,b]
Research & Development expenditure (% of GDP)	0.2	0.2	0.1 [f]
Threatened species (number)	16 [l]	40	44
Forested area (% of land area) [e]	4.5	3.5	3.4 [f]
CO2 emission estimates (million tons/tons per capita)	5.6 / 1.1	6.4 / 1.2	9.6 / 1.7 [f]
Energy production, primary (Petajoules)	61	53	80 [f]
Energy supply per capita (Gigajoules)	23	21	27 [f]
Tourist/visitor arrivals at national borders (000)	...	855	3 051 [b]
Important sites for terrestrial biodiversity protected (%)	22.4	22.4	22.6
Pop. using improved drinking water (urban/rural, %)	96.3 / 74.6	96.5 / 80.4	96.7 / 86.2 [b]
Pop. using improved sanitation facilities (urban/rural, %)	90.9 / 93.1	90.0 / 94.3	89.1 / 95.6 [b]
Net Official Development Assist. received (% of GNI)	11.28	8.55	12.16 [b]

a Projected estimate (medium fertility variant). b 2015. c 2016. d Data classified according to ISIC Rev. 4. e Estimate. f 2014. g Data classified according to ISIC Rev. 3. h 2011. i Break in the time series. j Data refers to a 5-year period preceding the reference year. k Data as at the end of December. l 2004.

Lao People's Democratic Republic

Region	South-eastern Asia	UN membership date	14 December 1955	
Population (000, 2017)	6 858[a]	Surface area (km2)	236 800[b]	
Pop. density (per km2, 2017)	29.7[a]	Sex ratio (m per 100 f, 2017)	99.5[a]	
Capital city	Vientiane	National currency	Lao Kip (LAK)	
Capital city pop. (000)	996.6[b]	Exchange rate (per US$)	8 204.0[c]	

Economic indicators

	2005	2010	2017
GDP: Gross domestic product (million current US$)	2 717	6 744	12 585[b]
GDP growth rate (annual %, const. 2005 prices)	6.8	8.1	7.6[b]
GDP per capita (current US$)	472.9	1 077.2	1 850.2[b]
Economy: Agriculture (% of GVA)	36.3	29.7	23.6[b]
Economy: Industry (% of GVA)	23.2	28.9	32.8[b]
Economy: Services and other activity (% of GVA)	40.5	41.4	43.6[b]
Employment: Agriculture (% of employed)[d]	83.4	81.9	78.3
Employment: Industry (% of employed)[d]	3.5	3.5	4.0
Employment: Services (% of employed)[d]	13.1	14.6	17.7
Unemployment (% of labour force)	1.4	1.4[d]	1.5[d]
Labour force participation (female/male pop. %)[d]	78.9 / 78.8	77.9 / 77.0	77.9 / 77.8
CPI: Consumer Price Index (2000=100)	163[e,f]	208	258[g]
Agricultural production index (2004-2006=100)	100	132	193[g]
Food production index (2004-2006=100)	100	130	186[g]
International trade: Exports (million US$)	552	1 746	2 066[c]
International trade: Imports (million US$)	874	2 059	4 513[c]
International trade: Balance (million US$)	- 322	- 312	- 2 447[c]
Balance of payments, current account (million US$)	- 174	29	- 2 264[b]

Major trading partners

						2016
Export partners (% of exports)	Thailand	33.4	China	31.7	Viet Nam	14.5
Import partners (% of imports)	Thailand	66.1	China	15.7	Viet Nam	8.9

Social indicators

	2005	2010	2017
Population growth rate (average annual %)[h]	1.5	1.6	1.3[b]
Urban population (% of total population)	27.4	33.1	38.6[b]
Urban population growth rate (average annual %)[h]	5.8	5.8	4.9[b]
Fertility rate, total (live births per woman)[h]	3.9	3.4	2.9[b]
Life expectancy at birth (females/males, years)[h]	61.7 / 59.0	64.5 / 61.8	66.8 / 63.9[b]
Population age distribution (0-14 and 60+ years, %)	40.3 / 5.5	36.3 / 5.6	32.9 / 6.3[a]
International migrant stock (000/% of total pop.)[i,j]	20.4 / 0.4	21.2 / 0.3	22.2 / 0.3[b]
Infant mortality rate (per 1 000 live births)[h]	69.2	56.7	47.3[b]
Health: Total expenditure (% of GDP)	4.3	2.7	1.9[f,g]
Health: Physicians (per 1 000 pop.)	0.3	0.2[k]	0.2[l]
Education: Government expenditure (% of GDP)	2.4	1.7	3.3[g]
Education: Primary gross enrol. ratio (f/m per 100 pop.)	104.1 / 119.1	117.9 / 127.8	109.1 / 113.5[b]
Education: Secondary gross enrol. ratio (f/m per 100 pop.)	37.4 / 49.6	41.7 / 50.4	59.3 / 64.1[b]
Education: Tertiary gross enrol. ratio (f/m per 100 pop.)	6.5 / 9.2	14.2 / 18.5	16.5 / 17.3[b]
Intentional homicide rate (per 100 000 pop.)	9.6	8.0	6.9[b]
Seats held by women in national parliaments (%)	22.9	25.2	27.5

Environment and infrastructure indicators

	2005	2010	2017
Mobile-cellular subscriptions (per 100 inhabitants)	11.4	62.6	53.1[b]
Individuals using the Internet (per 100 inhabitants)	0.9	7.0	18.2[d,b]
Research & Development expenditure (% of GDP)	~0.0[m,n]	...	...
Threatened species (number)	91[o]	132	209
Forested area (% of land area)	73.1	77.2[d]	80.5[d,g]
CO2 emission estimates (million tons/tons per capita)	1.4 / 0.3	1.6 / 0.3	2.0 / 0.3[g]
Energy production, primary (Petajoules)	80	79	72[g]
Energy supply per capita (Gigajoules)	13	12	12[g]
Tourist/visitor arrivals at national borders (000)	672	1 670	3 543[b]
Important sites for terrestrial biodiversity protected (%)	44.0	45.5	45.5
Pop. using improved drinking water (urban/rural, %)	77.0 / 49.2	81.8 / 60.4	85.6 / 69.4[b]
Pop. using improved sanitation facilities (urban/rural, %)	76.3 / 31.1	86.4 / 44.9	94.5 / 56.0[b]
Net Official Development Assist. received (% of GNI)	11.14	6.16	4.03[b]

a Projected estimate (medium fertility variant). **b** 2015. **c** 2016. **d** Estimate. **e** Series linked to former series. **f** Break in the time series. **g** 2014. **h** Data refers to a 5-year period preceding the reference year. **i** Including refugees. **j** Refers to foreign citizens. **k** 2009. **l** 2012. **m** Partial data. **n** 2002. **o** 2004.

Latvia

Region	Northern Europe	UN membership date	17 September 1991
Population (000, 2017)	1 950[a]	Surface area (km2)	64 573[b]
Pop. density (per km2, 2017)	31.3[a]	Sex ratio (m per 100 f, 2017)	84.9[a]
Capital city	Riga	National currency	Euro (EUR)
Capital city pop. (000)	620.8[b]	Exchange rate (per US$)	0.9[c]

Economic indicators

	2005	2010	2017
GDP: Gross domestic product (million current US$)	16 922	23 765	27 004[b]
GDP growth rate (annual %, const. 2005 prices)	10.7	- 3.8	2.7[b]
GDP per capita (current US$)	7 596.7	11 368.1	13 704.1[b]
Economy: Agriculture (% of GVA)[d]	4.3	4.4	3.2[b]
Economy: Industry (% of GVA)[d]	22.9	23.9	23.3[b]
Economy: Services and other activity (% of GVA)[d]	72.8	71.7	73.5[b]
Employment: Agriculture (% of employed)[e]	12.1	8.8	7.3
Employment: Industry (% of employed)[e]	26.5	24.0	23.0
Employment: Services (% of employed)[e]	61.5	67.1	69.7
Unemployment (% of labour force)	10.0	19.5	9.6[e]
Labour force participation (female/male pop. %)[e]	50.9 / 66.3	53.8 / 65.4	54.5 / 67.7
CPI: Consumer Price Index (2000=100)	122	169	181[f]
Agricultural production index (2004-2006=100)	105	110	130[f]
Food production index (2004-2006=100)	105	110	130[f]
Index of industrial production (2005=100)	100	98[g]	111[g,f]
International trade: Exports (million US$)	5 303	8 851	11 433[c]
International trade: Imports (million US$)	8 770	11 143	13 596[c]
International trade: Balance (million US$)	- 3 468	- 2 292	- 2 163[c]
Balance of payments, current account (million US$)	- 1 988	492	- 210[b]

Major trading partners

						2016
Export partners (% of exports)	Lithuania	18.3	Estonia	12.1	Russian Federation	7.6
Import partners (% of imports)	Lithuania	17.5	Germany	11.9	Poland	10.8

Social indicators

	2005	2010	2017
Population growth rate (average annual %)[h]	- 1.1	- 1.2	- 1.2[b]
Urban population (% of total population)	68.0	67.7	67.4[b]
Urban population growth rate (average annual %)[h]	- 1.3	- 1.4	- 0.7[b]
Fertility rate, total (live births per woman)[h]	1.3	1.5	1.5[b]
Life expectancy at birth (females/males, years)[h]	76.2 / 65.2	77.0 / 66.0	78.7 / 68.8[b]
Population age distribution (0-14 and 60+ years, %)	14.7 / 22.5	14.1 / 23.6	15.4 / 26.2[a]
International migrant stock (000/% of total pop.)	376.7 / 16.9	313.8 / 15.0	263.1 / 13.4[b]
Refugees and others of concern to UNHCR (000)	418.7[i]	327.0[i]	252.6[c]
Infant mortality rate (per 1 000 live births)[h]	9.9	7.8	6.5[b]
Health: Total expenditure (% of GDP)	6.4	6.6	5.9[f]
Health: Physicians (per 1 000 pop.)	3.7	3.1	3.2[f]
Education: Government expenditure (% of GDP)	4.9[j]	5.1	5.3[f]
Education: Primary gross enrol. ratio (f/m per 100 pop.)	91.7 / 95.5	105.4 / 106.2	99.2 / 100.1[b]
Education: Secondary gross enrol. ratio (f/m per 100 pop.)	104.2 / 103.9	97.5 / 99.2	119.1 / 119.9[b]
Education: Tertiary gross enrol. ratio (f/m per 100 pop.)	101.7 / 56.9	90.3 / 51.4	79.2 / 55.5[f]
Intentional homicide rate (per 100 000 pop.)	5.7	3.4	4.1[b]
Seats held by women in national parliaments (%)	21.0	22.0	16.0

Environment and infrastructure indicators

	2005	2010	2017
Mobile-cellular subscriptions (per 100 inhabitants)	84.0	110.3[e]	127.0[k,b]
Individuals using the Internet (per 100 inhabitants)[l]	46.0	68.4	79.2[b]
Research & Development expenditure (% of GDP)	0.5	0.6	0.7[m,f]
Threatened species (number)	23[j]	18	30
Forested area (% of land area)	53.0	53.9	54.0[e,f]
CO2 emission estimates (million tons/tons per capita)	7.5 / 3.3	8.1 / 3.9	7.0 / 3.5[f]
Energy production, primary (Petajoules)	78	95	108[f]
Energy supply per capita (Gigajoules)	82	97	99[f]
Tourist/visitor arrivals at national borders (000)[n]	1 116	1 373	2 024[b]
Important sites for terrestrial biodiversity protected (%)	97.2	97.3	97.3
Pop. using improved drinking water (urban/rural, %)	99.7 / 96.2	99.7 / 97.3	99.8 / 98.3[b]
Pop. using improved sanitation facilities (urban/rural, %)	88.0 / 73.9	89.4 / 77.7	90.8 / 81.5[b]
Net Official Development Assist. disbursed (% of GNI)	0.07	0.06	0.10[m,c]

a Projected estimate (medium fertility variant). **b** 2015. **c** 2016. **d** Data classified according to ISIC Rev. 4. **e** Estimate. **f** 2014. **g** Excluding water and waste management. **h** Data refers to a 5-year period preceding the reference year. **i** Data as at the end of December. **j** 2004. **k** Data as at the end of July. **l** Population aged 16 to 74 years. **m** Provisional data. **n** Non-resident departures. Survey of persons crossing the state border.

Lebanon

Region	Western Asia	UN membership date	24 October 1945
Population (000, 2017)	6 082 [a]	Surface area (km2)	10 452 [b]
Pop. density (per km2, 2017)	594.6 [a]	Sex ratio (m per 100 f, 2017)	100.6 [a]
Capital city	Beirut	National currency	Lebanese Pound (LBP)
Capital city pop. (000)	2 226.5 [c,b]	Exchange rate (per US$)	1 507.5 [d]

Economic indicators

	2005	2010	2017
GDP: Gross domestic product (million current US$)	21 490	38 420	50 149 [b]
GDP growth rate (annual %, const. 2005 prices)	2.7	8.0	1.5 [b]
GDP per capita (current US$)	5 390.2	8 858.3	8 571.4 [b]
Economy: Agriculture (% of GVA) [e]	4.0	4.3	3.2 [b]
Economy: Industry (% of GVA) [e]	16.7	15.7	19.6 [b]
Economy: Services and other activity (% of GVA) [e]	79.3	80.1	77.2 [b]
Employment: Agriculture (% of employed) [f]	8.5	8.0	8.2
Employment: Industry (% of employed) [f]	16.6	17.3	22.4
Employment: Services (% of employed) [f]	74.9	74.7	69.4
Unemployment (% of labour force) [f]	8.1	6.2	7.0
Labour force participation (female/male pop. %) [f]	20.3 / 70.6	22.0 / 70.0	23.8 / 70.6
CPI: Consumer Price Index (2000=100)	105 [g]	105 [h,i]	126 [h,j,k]
Agricultural production index (2004-2006=100)	97	94	95 [k]
Food production index (2004-2006=100)	97	94	95 [k]
International trade: Exports (million US$)	1 879	4 254	3 402 [d]
International trade: Imports (million US$)	9 327	17 970	20 409 [d]
International trade: Balance (million US$)	- 7 448	- 13 716	- 17 007 [d]
Balance of payments, current account (million US$)	- 2 748	- 7 552	- 8 146 [b]

Major trading partners

						2016
Export partners (% of exports)	Saudi Arabia	11.4	United Arab Emirates	9.7	South Africa	9.0
Import partners (% of imports)	China	12.1	Italy	8.0	France	6.2

Social indicators

	2005	2010	2017
Population growth rate (average annual %) [l]	4.2	1.7	6.0 [b]
Urban population (% of total population)	86.6	87.2	87.8 [b]
Urban population growth rate (average annual %) [l]	4.3	1.8	3.2 [b]
Fertility rate, total (live births per woman) [l]	2.0	1.6	1.7 [b]
Life expectancy at birth (females/males, years) [l]	77.4 / 73.9	79.7 / 76.0	80.9 / 77.3 [b]
Population age distribution (0-14 and 60+ years, %)	27.9 / 10.7	23.7 / 11.9	23.1 / 12.0 [a]
International migrant stock (000/% of total pop.) [m]	756.8 / 19.0	820.7 / 18.9	1 997.8 / 34.1 [b]
Refugees and others of concern to UNHCR (000)	3.0 [n]	9.5 [n]	1 054.2 [d]
Infant mortality rate (per 1 000 live births) [l]	13.8	10.6	9.2 [b]
Health: Total expenditure (% of GDP)	8.4	7.2	6.4 [k]
Health: Physicians (per 1 000 pop.)	3.4 [o]	2.7	2.4 [k]
Education: Government expenditure (% of GDP)	2.7	1.6	2.6 [p]
Education: Primary gross enrol. ratio (f/m per 100 pop.)	99.0 / 107.8 [f]	100.0 / 109.6	88.3 / 96.6 [b]
Education: Secondary gross enrol. ratio (f/m per 100 pop.)	80.8 / 80.2 [f]	76.1 / 74.5	61.0 / 61.5 [b]
Education: Tertiary gross enrol. ratio (f/m per 100 pop.)	45.2 / 43.0	49.3 / 47.4	45.7 / 39.5 [k]
Intentional homicide rate (per 100 000 pop.)	...	3.8	4.0 [b]
Seats held by women in national parliaments (%)	2.3	3.1	3.1

Environment and infrastructure indicators

	2005	2010	2017
Mobile-cellular subscriptions (per 100 inhabitants)	24.9 [f]	66.0	87.1 [f,b]
Individuals using the Internet (per 100 inhabitants)	10.1 [q]	43.7 [f,r]	74.0 [f,b]
Threatened species (number)	26 [s]	50	87
Forested area (% of land area) [f]	13.3	13.4	13.4 [k]
CO2 emission estimates (million tons/tons per capita)	16.2 / 4.0	20.0 / 4.6	24.1 / 4.3 [k]
Energy production, primary (Petajoules)	10	9	7 [k]
Energy supply per capita (Gigajoules)	51	60	55 [k]
Tourist/visitor arrivals at national borders (000) [t]	1 140	2 168	1 518 [b]
Important sites for terrestrial biodiversity protected (%)	11.6	11.6	13.1
Pop. using improved drinking water (urban/rural, %)	91.7 / 91.7	97.7 / 97.7	99.0 / 99.0 [b]
Pop. using improved sanitation facilities (urban/rural, %)	82.0 / 82.0	80.9 / 80.9	80.7 / 80.7 [b]
Net Official Development Assist. received (% of GNI)	1.09	1.19	2.04 [b]

a Projected estimate (medium fertility variant). **b** 2015. **c** Excluding Syrian refugees. **d** 2016. **e** Data classified according to ISIC Rev. 4. **f** Estimate. **g** Beirut **h** Index base: 2008=100. **i** Break in the time series. **j** Series linked to former series. **k** 2014. **l** Data refers to a 5-year period preceding the reference year. **m** Including refugees. **n** Data as at the end of December. **o** 2001. **p** 2013. **q** Population aged 6 years and over. **r** Population aged 15 years and over. **s** 2004. **t** Excluding nationals residing abroad, Syrian nationals and Palestinians.

Lesotho

Region	Southern Africa	UN membership date	17 October 1966
Population (000, 2017)	2 233[a]	Surface area (km2)	30 355[b]
Pop. density (per km2, 2017)	73.6[a]	Sex ratio (m per 100 f, 2017)	94.4[a]
Capital city	Maseru	National currency	Loti (LSL)
Capital city pop. (000)	266.6[c]	Exchange rate (per US$)	13.7[d]

Economic indicators

	2005	2010	2017
GDP: Gross domestic product (million current US$)	1 368	2 187	2 008[b]
GDP growth rate (annual %, const. 2005 prices)	2.7	7.9	2.8[b]
GDP per capita (current US$)	710.5	1 087.9	940.6[b]
Economy: Agriculture (% of GVA)	8.9	8.3	7.7[b]
Economy: Industry (% of GVA)	32.8	31.2	31.3[b]
Economy: Services and other activity (% of GVA)	58.2	60.5	61.0[b]
Employment: Agriculture (% of employed)[e]	53.2	42.0	39.7
Employment: Industry (% of employed)[e]	14.1	20.2	20.0
Employment: Services (% of employed)[e]	32.7	37.9	40.3
Unemployment (% of labour force)[e]	36.0	25.6	27.5
Labour force participation (female/male pop. %)[e]	61.8 / 75.5	58.6 / 73.2	59.7 / 74.6
CPI: Consumer Price Index (2000=100)	140	198[f]	244[c]
Agricultural production index (2004-2006=100)	103	112	101[c]
Food production index (2004-2006=100)	102	113	100[c]
International trade: Exports (million US$)	650	503	648[d]
International trade: Imports (million US$)	1 410	1 277	1 727[d]
International trade: Balance (million US$)	- 760	- 773	- 1 079[d]
Balance of payments, current account (million US$)	166[g]	- 158	- 168[b]

Major trading partners

						2016
Export partners (% of exports)	United States	35.1	South Africa	32.0	Belgium	24.8
Import partners (% of imports)	South Africa	84.6	China	4.1	Asia nes[h]	4.0

Social indicators

	2005	2010	2017
Population growth rate (average annual %)[i]	0.8	0.9	1.3[b]
Urban population (% of total population)	22.2	24.8	27.3[b]
Urban population growth rate (average annual %)[i]	3.3	3.0	3.0[b]
Fertility rate, total (live births per woman)[i]	3.8	3.4	3.3[b]
Life expectancy at birth (females/males, years)[i]	46.4 / 44.6	50.2 / 47.6	54.7 / 50.1[b]
Population age distribution (0-14 and 60+ years, %)	39.4 / 6.3	37.3 / 6.6	35.4 / 6.7[a]
International migrant stock (000/% of total pop.)[j,k]	6.3 / 0.3	6.4 / 0.3	6.6 / 0.3[b]
Refugees and others of concern to UNHCR (000)	...	...	~0.0[d]
Infant mortality rate (per 1 000 live births)[i]	86.8	74.1	59.8[b]
Health: Total expenditure (% of GDP)	6.3	10.9	10.6[c]
Health: Physicians (per 1 000 pop.)	~0.0[l]	...	...
Education: Government expenditure (% of GDP)	12.1	11.4[m]	...
Education: Primary gross enrol. ratio (f/m per 100 pop.)	117.5 / 116.8	109.4 / 111.5	104.0 / 107.0[b]
Education: Secondary gross enrol. ratio (f/m per 100 pop.)	44.9 / 34.5	59.3 / 41.7	62.0 / 45.7[b]
Education: Tertiary gross enrol. ratio (f/m per 100 pop.)	4.3 / 3.1	4.4 / 3.4[n]	11.7 / 8.0[c]
Intentional homicide rate (per 100 000 pop.)	...	38.0	...
Seats held by women in national parliaments (%)	11.7	24.2	25.0

Environment and infrastructure indicators

	2005	2010	2017
Mobile-cellular subscriptions (per 100 inhabitants)	13.0	49.2	105.5[b]
Individuals using the Internet (per 100 inhabitants)[e]	2.6	3.9	16.1[b]
Research & Development expenditure (% of GDP)[o]	0.1[p]	~0.0[q]	~0.0[r,s]
Threatened species (number)	13[p]	16	18
Forested area (% of land area)	1.4	1.4	1.6[e,c]
CO2 emission estimates (million tons/tons per capita)	2.0 / 1.0	2.3 / 1.1	2.5 / 1.2[c]
Energy production, primary (Petajoules)	25	27	31[c]
Energy supply per capita (Gigajoules)	23	26	28[c]
Tourist/visitor arrivals at national borders (000)	304	426	1 082[b]
Important sites for terrestrial biodiversity protected (%)	15.3	15.3	15.3
Pop. using improved drinking water (urban/rural, %)	93.6 / 76.0	94.1 / 76.5	94.6 / 77.0[b]
Pop. using improved sanitation facilities (urban/rural, %)	35.9 / 23.4	36.7 / 25.8	37.3 / 27.6[b]
Net Official Development Assist. received (% of GNI)	3.66	9.87	4.11[c]

a Projected estimate (medium fertility variant). **b** 2015. **c** 2014. **d** 2016. **e** Estimate. **f** Series linked to former series. **g** Break in the time series. **h** Asia not elsewhere specified. **i** Data refers to a 5-year period preceding the reference year. **j** Including refugees. **k** Refers to foreign citizens. **l** 2003. **m** 2008. **n** 2006. **o** Partial data. **p** 2004. **q** 2009. **r** Higher Education only. **s** 2011.

Liberia

Region	Western Africa	UN membership date	02 November 1945
Population (000, 2017)	4 732 [a]	Surface area (km2)	111 369 [b]
Pop. density (per km2, 2017)	49.1 [a]	Sex ratio (m per 100 f, 2017)	101.8 [a]
Capital city	Monrovia	National currency	Liberian Dollar (LRD)
Capital city pop. (000)	1 263.8 [b]	Exchange rate (per US$)	102.5 [c]

Economic indicators	2005	2010	2017
GDP: Gross domestic product (million current US$)	608	1 074	2 053 [b]
GDP growth rate (annual %, const. 2005 prices)	9.5	10.8	0.3 [b]
GDP per capita (current US$)	185.9	271.3	455.9 [b]
Economy: Agriculture (% of GVA)	68.8	70.0	70.8 [d,b]
Economy: Industry (% of GVA)	9.8	11.3	11.4 [d,b]
Economy: Services and other activity (% of GVA)	21.5	18.7	17.9 [d,b]
Employment: Agriculture (% of employed) [e]	52.5	47.3	45.3
Employment: Industry (% of employed) [e]	6.8	10.6	11.7
Employment: Services (% of employed) [e]	40.7	42.0	43.0
Unemployment (% of labour force)	4.9 [e]	3.7	4.1 [e]
Labour force participation (female/male pop. %) [e]	58.5 / 62.9	58.1 / 64.3	57.9 / 64.1
Agricultural production index (2004-2006=100)	103	104	104 [f]
Food production index (2004-2006=100)	102	127	121 [f]
International trade: Exports (million US$)	130	222	641 [c]
International trade: Imports (million US$)	309	710	727 [c]
International trade: Balance (million US$)	- 179	- 488	- 86 [c]
Balance of payments, current account (million US$)	- 208	- 737	- 860 [b]

Major trading partners						2016
Export partners (% of exports)	Areas nes [g]	21.1	Switzerland	13.2	United Arab Emirates	9.5
Import partners (% of imports)	China	32.2	Singapore	12.3	Republic of Korea	8.2

Social indicators	2005	2010	2017
Population growth rate (average annual %) [h]	2.5	3.8	2.6 [b]
Urban population (% of total population)	46.1	47.8	49.7 [b]
Urban population growth rate (average annual %) [h]	3.2	4.6	3.4 [b]
Fertility rate, total (live births per woman) [h]	5.7	5.2	4.8 [b]
Life expectancy at birth (females/males, years) [h]	53.2 / 51.6	59.0 / 57.2	61.6 / 59.8 [b]
Population age distribution (0-14 and 60+ years, %)	43.3 / 4.9	43.3 / 4.8	41.8 / 4.9 [a]
International migrant stock (000/% of total pop.)	87.2 / 2.7	99.1 / 2.5	113.8 / 2.5 [b]
Refugees and others of concern to UNHCR (000)	508.8 [i]	26.6 [i]	22.1 [c]
Infant mortality rate (per 1 000 live births) [h]	96.9	71.8	59.0 [b]
Health: Total expenditure (% of GDP)	8.0	11.9	10.0 [f]
Health: Physicians (per 1 000 pop.)	~0.0 [j]	~0.0 [k]	...
Education: Government expenditure (% of GDP)	...	3.2 [k]	2.8 [l]
Education: Primary gross enrol. ratio (f/m per 100 pop.)	95.4 / 129.6 [m]	94.1 / 105.0 [n]	89.1 / 98.5 [b]
Education: Secondary gross enrol. ratio (f/m per 100 pop.)	29.6 / 40.7 [m]	... / ...	32.5 / 41.9 [b]
Education: Tertiary gross enrol. ratio (f/m per 100 pop.)	13.8 / 24.9 [m]	6.4 / 12.1	9.0 / 14.2 [l]
Intentional homicide rate (per 100 000 pop.)	...	3.3	3.2 [l]
Seats held by women in national parliaments (%)	5.3	12.5	12.3

Environment and infrastructure indicators	2005	2010	2017
Mobile-cellular subscriptions (per 100 inhabitants)	4.9	39.7	81.1 [e,b]
Individuals using the Internet (per 100 inhabitants)	~0.0 [m]	2.3	5.9 [e,b]
Threatened species (number)	94 [i]	147	172
Forested area (% of land area)	46.5	44.9	43.7 [e,f]
CO2 emission estimates (million tons/tons per capita)	0.7 / 0.2	0.8 / 0.2	0.9 / 0.2 [f]
Energy production, primary (Petajoules)	53	64	73 [f]
Energy supply per capita (Gigajoules)	20	19	19 [f]
Important sites for terrestrial biodiversity protected (%)	14.8	14.8	14.8
Pop. using improved drinking water (urban/rural, %)	80.4 / 55.2	84.5 / 58.9	88.6 / 62.6 [b]
Pop. using improved sanitation facilities (urban/rural, %)	25.8 / 4.5	26.9 / 5.2	28.0 / 5.9 [b]
Net Official Development Assist. received (% of GNI)	56.37	127.09	61.73 [b]

a Projected estimate (medium fertility variant). b 2015. c 2016. d Includes taxes less subsidies on production and imports. e Estimate. f 2014. g Areas not elsewhere specified. h Data refers to a 5-year period preceding the reference year. i Data as at the end of December. j 2004. k 2008. l 2012. m 2000. n 2009.

Libya

Region	Northern Africa	UN membership date	14 December 1955
Population (000, 2017)	6 375 [a]	Surface area (km2)	1 676 198 [b]
Pop. density (per km2, 2017)	3.6 [a]	Sex ratio (m per 100 f, 2017)	101.7 [a]
Capital city	Tripoli	National currency	Libyan Dinar (LYD)
Capital city pop. (000)	1 126.1 [b]	Exchange rate (per US$)	1.4 [c]

Economic indicators	2005	2010	2017
GDP: Gross domestic product (million current US$)	45 451	80 942	34 457 [b]
GDP growth rate (annual %, const. 2005 prices)	10.3	4.3	- 10.2 [b]
GDP per capita (current US$)	7 834.4	12 918.3	5 488.2 [b]
Economy: Agriculture (% of GVA)	2.2	2.5	0.9 [b]
Economy: Industry (% of GVA)	75.7	74.0	67.1 [b]
Economy: Services and other activity (% of GVA)	22.2	23.5	32.0 [b]
Employment: Agriculture (% of employed) [d]	14.9	14.2	19.1
Employment: Industry (% of employed) [d]	25.6	28.5	25.1
Employment: Services (% of employed) [d]	59.5	57.3	55.8
Unemployment (% of labour force) [d]	19.2	18.4	19.2
Labour force participation (female/male pop. %) [d]	28.6 / 75.9	29.8 / 77.7	27.8 / 78.4
Agricultural production index (2004-2006=100)	101	110	113 [e]
Food production index (2004-2006=100)	101	110	114 [e]
International trade: Exports (million US$)	31 272	36 440	4 615 [c]
International trade: Imports (million US$)	6 058	17 674	8 876 [c]
International trade: Balance (million US$)	25 215	18 766	- 4 261 [c]
Balance of payments, current account (million US$)	14 945	16 801	- 108 [f]

Major trading partners						2016
Export partners (% of exports)	Italy	26.0	United Arab Emirates	12.4	Spain	12.2
Import partners (% of imports)	China	11.7	Italy	11.5	Turkey	8.7

Social indicators	2005	2010	2017
Population growth rate (average annual %) [g]	1.6	1.3	0.2 [b]
Urban population (% of total population)	76.9	77.6	78.6 [b]
Urban population growth rate (average annual %) [g]	1.7	1.7	1.1 [b]
Fertility rate, total (live births per woman) [g]	2.6	2.4	2.4 [b]
Life expectancy at birth (females/males, years) [g]	72.8 / 69.1	74.4 / 69.5	74.4 / 68.8 [b]
Population age distribution (0-14 and 60+ years, %)	30.1 / 5.9	28.4 / 6.0	28.2 / 6.6 [a]
International migrant stock (000/% of total pop.) [h]	625.2 / 10.8	684.0 / 10.9	771.1 / 12.3 [b]
Refugees and others of concern to UNHCR (000)	12.4 [i]	11.2 [i]	472.5 [c]
Infant mortality rate (per 1 000 live births) [g]	27.2	24.3	24.3 [b]
Health: Total expenditure (% of GDP) [j]	2.7	3.1	5.0 [e]
Health: Physicians (per 1 000 pop.)	1.2 [k]	1.9 [l]	2.1 [e]
Education: Primary gross enrol. ratio (f/m per 100 pop.)	107.6 / 108.7	112.1 / 116.8 [m]	... / ...
Education: Secondary gross enrol. ratio (f/m per 100 pop.)	103.3 / 86.7 [d]	109.9 / 93.6 [m]	... / ...
Education: Tertiary gross enrol. ratio (f/m per 100 pop.)	64.3 / 58.1 [d,n]	... / ...	... / ...
Intentional homicide rate (per 100 000 pop.)	3.7	3.1	2.5 [b]
Seats held by women in national parliaments (%)	...	7.7	16.0

Environment and infrastructure indicators	2005	2010	2017
Mobile-cellular subscriptions (per 100 inhabitants)	35.8	180.4 [d]	157.0 [d,b]
Individuals using the Internet (per 100 inhabitants) [d]	3.9	14.0	19.0 [b]
Threatened species (number)	25 [k]	44	63
Forested area (% of land area) [d]	0.1	0.1	0.1 [e]
CO2 emission estimates (million tons/tons per capita)	52.1 / 9.0	62.0 / 9.9	57.0 / 9.1 [e]
Energy production, primary (Petajoules)	4 062	4 294	1 505 [e]
Energy supply per capita (Gigajoules)	126	137	119 [e]
Tourist/visitor arrivals at national borders (000)	81	...	...
Important sites for terrestrial biodiversity protected (%)	4.6	4.6	4.6
Pop. using improved drinking water (urban/rural, %)	72.1 / 68.4 [o]	... / ...	... / ...
Pop. using improved sanitation facilities (urban/rural, %)	96.8 / 95.7	96.8 / 95.7	96.8 / 95.7 [b]
Net Official Development Assist. received (% of GNI)	0.05	0.01	0.51 [b]

a Projected estimate (medium fertility variant). **b** 2015. **c** 2016. **d** Estimate. **e** 2014. **f** 2013. **g** Data refers to a 5-year period preceding the reference year. **h** Refers to foreign citizens. **i** Data as at the end of December. **j** Estimates should be viewed with caution as these are derived from scarce data. **k** 2004. **l** 2009. **m** 2006. **n** 2003. **o** 2000.

Liechtenstein

Region	Western Europe	UN membership date	18 September 1990
Population (000, 2017)	38[a]	Surface area (km2)	160[b]
Pop. density (per km2, 2017)	237.0[a]	Sex ratio (m per 100 f, 2017)	98.4[c,d]
Capital city	Vaduz	National currency	Swiss Franc (CHF)
Capital city pop. (000)	5.3[e]	Exchange rate (per US$)	1.0[d]

Economic indicators	2005	2010	2017
GDP: Gross domestic product (million current US$)	4 087	5 678	6 361[b]
GDP growth rate (annual %, const. 2005 prices)	4.8	7.4	1.4[b]
GDP per capita (current US$)	117 279.2	156 533.4	169 491.8[b]
Economy: Agriculture (% of GVA)[f]	0.9	0.8	0.7[b]
Economy: Industry (% of GVA)[f]	38.6	39.0	40.1[b]
Economy: Services and other activity (% of GVA)[f]	60.5	60.2	59.2[b]
Unemployment (% of labour force)[g]	...	2.6	2.6[h]
Labour force participation (female/male pop. %)	52.8 / 73.7	52.6 / 70.9	53.5 / 70.6[h]
Agricultural production index (2004-2006=100)	100	100	102[e]
Food production index (2004-2006=100)	100	100	102[e]

Social indicators	2005	2010	2017
Population growth rate (average annual %)[i]	0.9	0.7	0.8[b]
Urban population (% of total population)	14.7	14.5	14.3[b]
Urban population growth rate (average annual %)[i]	0.4	0.4	0.5[b]
Fertility rate, total (live births per woman)	1.5	1.4	1.5[j]
Population age distribution (0-14 and 60+ years, %)	17.5 / 16.8[c]	16.0 / 20.1	14.9 / 22.7[c,d]
International migrant stock (000/% of total pop.)	18.9 / 54.2	22.3 / 61.6	23.5 / 62.6[b]
Refugees and others of concern to UNHCR (000)	0.2[k]	0.1[k]	0.3[d]
Education: Government expenditure (% of GDP)	2.4[l]	2.0[m]	2.6[n]
Education: Primary gross enrol. ratio (f/m per 100 pop.)[o]	108.5 / 109.9[l]	102.3 / 108.6	104.8 / 106.5[b]
Education: Secondary gross enrol. ratio (f/m per 100 pop.)[o]	103.9 / 117.2[l]	100.0 / 117.6	101.7 / 130.7[b]
Education: Tertiary gross enrol. ratio (f/m per 100 pop.)[o]	13.3 / 35.7[l]	27.4 / 44.3	21.9 / 44.8[b]
Intentional homicide rate (per 100 000 pop.)	2.9[l]	2.8	2.7[e]
Seats held by women in national parliaments (%)	12.0	24.0	12.0

Environment and infrastructure indicators	2005	2010	2017
Mobile-cellular subscriptions (per 100 inhabitants)	79.2[o]	98.3[o]	108.8[b]
Individuals using the Internet (per 100 inhabitants)	63.4	80.0[o]	96.6[o,b]
Threatened species (number)	8[l]	2	6
Forested area (% of land area)[o]	43.1	43.1	43.1[e]
CO2 emission estimates (million tons/tons per capita)	... / ...	0.1 / 1.5	~0.0 / 1.1[e]
Energy production, primary (Petajoules)	...	1	1[e]
Energy supply per capita (Gigajoules)	...	81	74[e]
Tourist/visitor arrivals at national borders (000)	...	64	57[p,b]
Important sites for terrestrial biodiversity protected (%)	80.8	80.8	80.8
Net Official Development Assist. disbursed (% of GNI)	...	0.62	0.50[e]

a Projected estimate (medium fertility variant). **b** 2015. **c** De jure population. **d** 2016. **e** 2014. **f** Data classified according to ISIC Rev. 4. **g** Population aged 15 to 64 years. **h** 2013. **i** Data refers to a 5-year period preceding the reference year. **j** 2012. **k** Data as at the end of December. **l** 2004. **m** 2008. **n** 2011. **o** Estimate. **p** Excluding long term tourists on campgrounds and in holiday flats.

Lithuania

Region	Northern Europe		UN membership date	17 September 1991	
Population (000, 2017)	2 890[a]		Surface area (km2)	65 286[b]	
Pop. density (per km2, 2017)	46.1[a]		Sex ratio (m per 100 f, 2017)	85.4[a]	
Capital city	Vilnius		National currency	Euro (EUR)	
Capital city pop. (000)	516.8[b]		Exchange rate (per US$)	0.9[c]	

Economic indicators	2005	2010	2017
GDP: Gross domestic product (million current US$)	26 141	37 130	41 402[b]
GDP growth rate (annual %, const. 2005 prices)	7.7	1.6	1.8[b]
GDP per capita (current US$)	7 819.1	11 889.9	14 383.7[b]
Economy: Agriculture (% of GVA)[d]	4.8	3.3	3.6[b]
Economy: Industry (% of GVA)[d]	32.7	29.1	29.8[b]
Economy: Services and other activity (% of GVA)[d]	62.5	67.6	66.5[b]
Employment: Agriculture (% of employed)[e]	14.3	9.0	8.7
Employment: Industry (% of employed)[e]	29.1	24.6	24.5
Employment: Services (% of employed)[e]	56.7	66.4	66.8
Unemployment (% of labour force)	8.3	17.8	9.2[e]
Labour force participation (female/male pop. %)[e]	50.5 / 62.7	52.6 / 62.1	54.1 / 66.1
CPI: Consumer Price Index (2000=100)	104[f]	134	146[g]
Agricultural production index (2004-2006=100)	106	99	125[g]
Food production index (2004-2006=100)	106	99	125[g]
Index of industrial production (2005=100)	100	103	117[g]
International trade: Exports (million US$)	12 070	20 814	25 025[c]
International trade: Imports (million US$)	15 704	23 378	27 501[c]
International trade: Balance (million US$)	- 3 634	- 2 564	- 2 476[c]
Balance of payments, current account (million US$)	- 1 891	- 119	- 977[b]

Major trading partners					2016
Export partners (% of exports)	Russian Federation	13.5	Latvia	9.9	Poland	9.1
Import partners (% of imports)	Russian Federation	14.4	Germany	12.1	Poland	10.8

Social indicators	2005	2010	2017
Population growth rate (average annual %)[h]	- 0.9	- 1.4	- 1.3[b]
Urban population (% of total population)	66.6	66.8	66.5[b]
Urban population growth rate (average annual %)[h]	- 1.4	- 1.3	- 0.5[b]
Fertility rate, total (live births per woman)[h]	1.3	1.4	1.6[b]
Life expectancy at birth (females/males, years)[h]	77.5 / 65.7	77.8 / 66.0	79.3 / 68.5[b]
Population age distribution (0-14 and 60+ years, %)	16.8 / 21.1	14.8 / 22.4	14.8 / 25.3[a]
International migrant stock (000/% of total pop.)	201.2 / 6.0	160.8 / 5.1	136.0 / 4.7[b]
Refugees and others of concern to UNHCR (000)	9.3[i]	4.6[i]	4.7[c]
Infant mortality rate (per 1 000 live births)[h]	7.7	6.0	4.4[b]
Health: Total expenditure (% of GDP)[j]	5.8	7.1	6.6[g]
Health: Physicians (per 1 000 pop.)	...	3.9	4.3[g]
Education: Government expenditure (% of GDP)	4.9	5.3	4.6[k]
Education: Primary gross enrol. ratio (f/m per 100 pop.)	94.4 / 94.9	99.5 / 100.6	103.7 / 103.2[b]
Education: Secondary gross enrol. ratio (f/m per 100 pop.)	103.7 / 104.6	100.0 / 101.9	106.1 / 110.3[b]
Education: Tertiary gross enrol. ratio (f/m per 100 pop.)	98.5 / 62.9	103.1 / 68.7	82.0 / 55.8[g]
Intentional homicide rate (per 100 000 pop.)	11.1	7.0	6.0[b]
Seats held by women in national parliaments (%)	22.0	19.1	21.3

Environment and infrastructure indicators	2005	2010	2017
Mobile-cellular subscriptions (per 100 inhabitants)	132.4[l]	159.4	139.5[b]
Individuals using the Internet (per 100 inhabitants)[n]	36.2[m]	62.1[m]	71.4[b]
Research & Development expenditure (% of GDP)	0.7	0.8	1.0[o.g]
Threatened species (number)	17[p]	17	26
Forested area (% of land area)	33.8	34.6	34.8[e.g]
CO2 emission estimates (million tons/tons per capita)	13.9 / 4.1	13.5 / 4.3	12.8 / 4.4[g]
Energy production, primary (Petajoules)	170	64	74[g]
Energy supply per capita (Gigajoules)	106	92	98[g]
Tourist/visitor arrivals at national borders (000)	2 000	1 507	2 071[b]
Important sites for terrestrial biodiversity protected (%)	89.6	91.6	91.6
Pop. using improved drinking water (urban/rural, %)	97.7 / 83.6	98.8 / 87.4	99.7 / 90.4[b]
Pop. using improved sanitation facilities (urban/rural, %)	94.7 / 76.1	95.9 / 79.4	97.2 / 82.8[b]
Net Official Development Assist. disbursed (% of GNI)	0.06	0.10	0.14[o.c]

a Projected estimate (medium fertility variant). **b** 2015. **c** 2016. **d** Data classified according to ISIC Rev. 4. **e** Estimate. **f** Series linked to former series. **g** 2014. **h** Data refers to a 5-year period preceding the reference year. **i** Data as at the end of December. **j** For years 2010 to 2012, total health expenditure (THE) is greater than the sum of government (HF.1) and private expenditure (HF.2) due to rest-of-the-world (external) payments for health goods and services consumed by residents (HF.3). **k** 2013. **l** Data refers to active subscriptions only. **m** Users in the last 12 months. **n** Population aged 16 to 74 years. **o** Provisional data. **p** 2004.

Luxembourg

Region	Western Europe	UN membership date	24 October 1945
Population (000, 2017)	584[a]	Surface area (km2)	2 586[b]
Pop. density (per km2, 2017)	225.3[a]	Sex ratio (m per 100 f, 2017)	101.0[a]
Capital city	Luxembourg	National currency	Euro (EUR)
Capital city pop. (000)	106.7[c]	Exchange rate (per US$)	0.9[d]

Economic indicators	2005	2010	2017
GDP: Gross domestic product (million current US$)	36 976	52 906	56 802[b]
GDP growth rate (annual %, const. 2005 prices)	3.2	5.8	3.5[b]
GDP per capita (current US$)	80 761.6	104 168.9	100 160.8[b]
Economy: Agriculture (% of GVA)[e]	0.4	0.3	0.2[b]
Economy: Industry (% of GVA)[e]	16.6	12.7	12.1[b]
Economy: Services and other activity (% of GVA)[e]	83.0	87.0	87.7[b]
Employment: Agriculture (% of employed)[f]	1.7	1.1	1.3
Employment: Industry (% of employed)[f]	17.3	13.3	10.2
Employment: Services (% of employed)[f]	81.0	85.6	88.5
Unemployment (% of labour force)	4.5	4.4	5.6[f]
Labour force participation (female/male pop. %)[f]	45.4 / 64.7	48.8 / 65.4	52.0 / 65.5
CPI: Consumer Price Index (2000=100)	112[g]	125	136[c]
Agricultural production index (2004-2006=100)	99	94	98[c]
Food production index (2004-2006=100)	99	94	98[c]
Index of industrial production (2005=100)	100	89[h]	86[h,c]
International trade: Exports (million US$)	12 715[i]	13 911	12 838[d]
International trade: Imports (million US$)	17 586[i]	20 400	19 124[d]
International trade: Balance (million US$)	- 4 871[i]	- 6 489	- 6 285[d]
Balance of payments, current account (million US$)	4 107	3 585	2 962[b]

Major trading partners						2016
Export partners (% of exports)	Germany	26.9	France	14.8	Belgium	11.7
Import partners (% of imports)	Germany	24.4	Belgium	22.9	France	11.5

Social indicators	2005	2010	2017
Population growth rate (average annual %)[j]	1.0	2.1	2.2[b]
Urban population (% of total population)	86.6	88.5	90.2[b]
Urban population growth rate (average annual %)[j]	1.5	2.5	1.7[b]
Fertility rate, total (live births per woman)[j]	1.7	1.6	1.5[b]
Life expectancy at birth (females/males, years)[j]	81.4 / 75.1	82.2 / 76.7	83.4 / 78.8[b]
Population age distribution (0-14 and 60+ years, %)	18.6 / 19.0	17.6 / 19.0	16.4 / 19.6[a]
International migrant stock (000/% of total pop.)	150.6 / 32.9	163.1 / 32.1	249.3 / 44.0[b]
Refugees and others of concern to UNHCR (000)	1.9[k]	4.1[k]	4.2[d]
Infant mortality rate (per 1 000 live births)[j]	5.0	2.3	3.4[b]
Health: Total expenditure (% of GDP)	7.9	7.7	6.9[c]
Health: Physicians (per 1 000 pop.)	...	2.8	2.9[b]
Education: Government expenditure (% of GDP)	3.6[l]	...	4.1[c]
Education: Primary gross enrol. ratio (f/m per 100 pop.)	100.9 / 100.7	98.1 / 97.1	97.3 / 96.9[c]
Education: Secondary gross enrol. ratio (f/m per 100 pop.)	97.9 / 92.9	102.9 / 99.9	103.5 / 101.1[c]
Education: Tertiary gross enrol. ratio (f/m per 100 pop.)	13.3 / 11.1[m]	19.2 / 17.3	20.7 / 18.2[n]
Intentional homicide rate (per 100 000 pop.)	...	2.0	0.7[c]
Seats held by women in national parliaments (%)	23.3	20.0	28.3

Environment and infrastructure indicators	2005	2010	2017
Mobile-cellular subscriptions (per 100 inhabitants)	111.4	143.1	148.5[b]
Individuals using the Internet (per 100 inhabitants)[o]	70.0	90.6	97.3[b]
Research & Development expenditure (% of GDP)	1.6	1.5	1.3[f,c]
Threatened species (number)	10[p]	5	11
Forested area (% of land area)[f]	33.5	33.5	33.5[c]
CO2 emission estimates (million tons/tons per capita)	11.5 / 25.3	11.0 / 21.6	9.7 / 17.3[c]
Energy production, primary (Petajoules)	4	5	6[c]
Energy supply per capita (Gigajoules)	405	351	290[c]
Tourist/visitor arrivals at national borders (000)	913	805	1 090[b]
Important sites for terrestrial biodiversity protected (%)	56.9	56.9	71.8
Pop. using improved drinking water (urban/rural, %)	100.0 / 100.0	100.0 / 100.0	100.0 / 100.0[b]
Pop. using improved sanitation facilities (urban/rural, %)	97.5 / 98.7	97.5 / 98.6	97.5 / 98.5[b]
Net Official Development Assist. disbursed (% of GNI)[q]	0.79	1.05	1.00[r,d]

a Projected estimate (medium fertility variant). b 2015. c 2014. d 2016. e Data classified according to ISIC Rev. 4. f Estimate. g Series linked to former series. h Excluding water and waste management. i Prior to 1997, included under Belgium. See also footnote for Belgium. j Data refers to a 5-year period preceding the reference year. k Data as at the end of December. l 2001. m 2003. n 2012. o Population aged 16 to 74 years. p 2004. q Development Assistance Committee member (OECD) r Provisional data.

Madagascar

Region	Eastern Africa	UN membership date	20 September 1960
Population (000, 2017)	25 571 [a]	Surface area (km2)	587 295 [b]
Pop. density (per km2, 2017)	44.0 [a]	Sex ratio (m per 100 f, 2017)	99.5 [a]
Capital city	Antananarivo	National currency	Malagasy Ariary (MGA)
Capital city pop. (000)	2 609.7 [b]	Exchange rate (per US$)	3 347.9 [c]

Economic indicators	2005	2010	2017
GDP: Gross domestic product (million current US$)	5 039	8 730	9 739 [b]
GDP growth rate (annual %, const. 2005 prices)	4.6	0.4	3.1 [b]
GDP per capita (current US$)	275.5	414.1	401.8 [b]
Economy: Agriculture (% of GVA)	28.1	27.6	24.9 [b]
Economy: Industry (% of GVA)	18.6	19.5	18.4 [b]
Economy: Services and other activity (% of GVA)	53.3	52.9	56.7 [b]
Employment: Agriculture (% of employed) [d]	81.5	79.6	74.2
Employment: Industry (% of employed) [d]	3.4	5.2	9.4
Employment: Services (% of employed) [d]	15.1	15.2	16.5
Unemployment (% of labour force)	2.6	3.8	2.3 [d]
Labour force participation (female/male pop. %) [d]	84.1 / 89.1	87.2 / 91.0	83.8 / 89.0
CPI: Consumer Price Index (2000=100)	153 [e]	263	344 [f]
Agricultural production index (2004-2006=100)	103	122	119 [f]
Food production index (2004-2006=100)	103	123	120 [f]
Index of industrial production (2005=100) [g]	100	124 [h]	...
International trade: Exports (million US$)	836	1 082	2 256 [c]
International trade: Imports (million US$)	1 686	2 546	2 965 [c]
International trade: Balance (million US$)	- 850	- 1 464	- 709 [c]
Balance of payments, current account (million US$)	- 767	- 896	- 622 [i]

Major trading partners						2016
Export partners (% of exports)	France	23.8	United States	13.0	Germany	8.4
Import partners (% of imports)	China	21.3	France	6.9	India	6.5

Social indicators	2005	2010	2017
Population growth rate (average annual %) [j]	3.0	2.9	2.7 [b]
Urban population (% of total population)	28.8	31.9	35.1 [b]
Urban population growth rate (average annual %) [j]	4.2	4.9	4.7 [b]
Fertility rate, total (live births per woman) [j]	5.3	4.8	4.4 [b]
Life expectancy at birth (females/males, years) [j]	61.3 / 58.8	63.7 / 60.8	66.0 / 63.0 [b]
Population age distribution (0-14 and 60+ years, %)	44.7 / 4.4	43.5 / 4.3	41.0 / 4.8 [a]
International migrant stock (000/% of total pop.) [k]	26.1 / 0.1	28.9 / 0.1	32.1 / 0.1 [b]
Refugees and others of concern to UNHCR (000)	...	~0.0 [l]	0.1 [c]
Infant mortality rate (per 1 000 live births) [j]	58.0	45.5	36.8 [b]
Health: Total expenditure (% of GDP) [m]	5.0	4.9	3.0 [f]
Health: Physicians (per 1 000 pop.)	0.2	0.2	0.1 [n]
Education: Government expenditure (% of GDP)	3.8	3.2 [o]	2.1 [i]
Education: Primary gross enrol. ratio (f/m per 100 pop.)	135.3 / 141.4	143.3 / 145.9	148.9 / 148.9 [b]
Education: Secondary gross enrol. ratio (f/m per 100 pop.)	20.7 / 21.6 [d]	29.4 / 31.3 [o,d]	38.1 / 38.8 [f]
Education: Tertiary gross enrol. ratio (f/m per 100 pop.)	2.7 / 3.0	3.4 / 3.8	4.6 / 5.0 [f]
Intentional homicide rate (per 100 000 pop.)	1.8	0.6	...
Seats held by women in national parliaments (%)	6.9	7.9 [o]	19.2

Environment and infrastructure indicators	2005	2010	2017
Mobile-cellular subscriptions (per 100 inhabitants)	2.8	36.6	46.0 [d,b]
Individuals using the Internet (per 100 inhabitants) [d]	0.6	1.7	4.2 [b]
Research & Development expenditure (% of GDP) [p]	0.2	0.1	~0.0 [e,q,f]
Threatened species (number)	530 [r]	663	1 324
Forested area (% of land area) [d]	22.1	21.6	21.5 [f]
CO2 emission estimates (million tons/tons per capita)	1.7 / 0.1	2.0 / 0.1	3.1 / 0.1 [f]
Energy production, primary (Petajoules)	104	124	129 [f]
Energy supply per capita (Gigajoules)	7	7	7 [f]
Tourist/visitor arrivals at national borders (000) [s]	277	196	244 [b]
Important sites for terrestrial biodiversity protected (%)	39.3	40.1	40.8
Pop. using improved drinking water (urban/rural, %)	77.5 / 27.8	79.6 / 31.5	81.6 / 35.3 [b]
Pop. using improved sanitation facilities (urban/rural, %)	16.9 / 8.3	17.5 / 8.5	18.0 / 8.7 [b]
Net Official Development Assist. received (% of GNI)	18.47	5.53	7.05 [b]

a Projected estimate (medium fertility variant). b 2015. c 2016. d Estimate. e Break in the time series. f 2014. g Data classified according to ISIC Rev. 3. h 2008. i 2013. j Data refers to a 5-year period preceding the reference year. k Refers to foreign citizens. l Data as at the end of December. m Data revision. n 2012. o 2009. p Partial data. q Government only. r 2004. s Arrivals of non-resident tourists by air.

Malawi

Region	Eastern Africa	UN membership date	01 December 1964
Population (000, 2017)	18 622[a]	Surface area (km2)	118 484[b]
Pop. density (per km2, 2017)	197.5[a]	Sex ratio (m per 100 f, 2017)	98.2[a]
Capital city	Lilongwe	National currency	Malawi Kwacha (MWK)
Capital city pop. (000)	905.4[b]	Exchange rate (per US$)	725.0[c]

Economic indicators	2005	2010	2017
GDP: Gross domestic product (million current US$)	3 656	6 960	6 420[b]
GDP growth rate (annual %, const. 2005 prices)	3.3	6.9	3.0[b]
GDP per capita (current US$)	286.8	471.2	372.9[b]
Economy: Agriculture (% of GVA)[d]	37.1	31.9	26.1[b]
Economy: Industry (% of GVA)[d]	16.8	16.4	16.6[b]
Economy: Services and other activity (% of GVA)[d]	46.1	51.7	57.3[b]
Employment: Agriculture (% of employed)[e]	72.4	70.5	69.9
Employment: Industry (% of employed)[e]	4.3	4.8	4.8
Employment: Services (% of employed)[e]	23.2	24.7	25.4
Unemployment (% of labour force)	7.8	6.5[e]	6.8[e]
Labour force participation (female/male pop. %)[e]	78.7 / 85.8	83.6 / 80.6	81.3 / 81.0
CPI: Consumer Price Index (2000=100)	198	309	636[f,g]
Agricultural production index (2004-2006=100)	86	156	149[g]
Food production index (2004-2006=100)	85	157	150[g]
Index of industrial production (2005=100)	100[h]	...	...
International trade: Exports (million US$)	495	1 066	875[c]
International trade: Imports (million US$)	1 165	2 173	1 649[c]
International trade: Balance (million US$)	- 670	- 1 107	- 774[c]
Balance of payments, current account (million US$)	- 507	- 969	- 710[b]

Major trading partners						2016
Export partners (% of exports)	Belgium	10.6	Zimbabwe	9.3	Mozambique	9.2
Import partners (% of imports)	South Africa	18.1	China	13.1	United Arab Emirates	11.0

Social indicators	2005	2010	2017
Population growth rate (average annual %)[i]	2.7	3.0	2.9[b]
Urban population (% of total population)	15.1	15.5	16.3[b]
Urban population growth rate (average annual %)[i]	3.2	3.6	3.8[b]
Fertility rate, total (live births per woman)[i]	6.0	5.7	4.9[b]
Life expectancy at birth (females/males, years)[i]	48.9 / 45.7	55.2 / 51.5	63.1 / 58.2[b]
Population age distribution (0-14 and 60+ years, %)	46.7 / 4.4	46.2 / 4.5	44.0 / 4.3[a]
International migrant stock (000/% of total pop.)[j]	221.7 / 1.7	217.7 / 1.5	215.2 / 1.2[b]
Refugees and others of concern to UNHCR (000)	9.6[k]	15.2[k]	25.7[c]
Infant mortality rate (per 1 000 live births)[i]	99.1	79.7	66.5[b]
Health: Total expenditure (% of GDP)	8.2	10.0	11.4[g]
Health: Physicians (per 1 000 pop.)	~0.0[l]	~0.0[m]	...
Education: Government expenditure (% of GDP)	3.2[n]	3.5	5.6[b]
Education: Primary gross enrol. ratio (f/m per 100 pop.)	128.0 / 126.3	138.4 / 135.1	147.0 / 144.0[b]
Education: Secondary gross enrol. ratio (f/m per 100 pop.)	24.3 / 30.3	31.2 / 34.9	41.0 / 45.8[b]
Education: Tertiary gross enrol. ratio (f/m per 100 pop.)	0.3 / 0.6[e]	0.5 / 0.9	0.6 / 1.0[o]
Intentional homicide rate (per 100 000 pop.)	1.6	3.5	1.8[p]
Seats held by women in national parliaments (%)	14.0	20.8	16.7

Environment and infrastructure indicators	2005	2010	2017
Mobile-cellular subscriptions (per 100 inhabitants)	3.3	20.8	35.3[b]
Individuals using the Internet (per 100 inhabitants)	0.4	2.3	9.3[e,b]
Threatened species (number)	50[l]	158	176
Forested area (% of land area)	36.1	34.3	33.6[e,g]
CO2 emission estimates (million tons/tons per capita)	0.9 / 0.1	1.1 / 0.1	1.3 / 0.1[g]
Energy production, primary (Petajoules)	80	86	89[g]
Energy supply per capita (Gigajoules)	7	7	6[g]
Tourist/visitor arrivals at national borders (000)[q]	438	746	805[b]
Important sites for terrestrial biodiversity protected (%)	81.6	81.6	81.6
Pop. using improved drinking water (urban/rural, %)	93.8 / 67.9	94.8 / 78.5	95.7 / 89.1[b]
Pop. using improved sanitation facilities (urban/rural, %)	46.6 / 34.8	47.0 / 37.3	47.3 / 39.8[b]
Net Official Development Assist. received (% of GNI)	15.86	14.85	16.53[b]

a Projected estimate (medium fertility variant). **b** 2015. **c** 2016. **d** Data classified according to ISIC Rev. 4. **e** Estimate. **f** Series linked to former series. **g** 2014. **h** Data classified according to ISIC Rev. 3. **i** Data refers to a 5-year period preceding the reference year. **j** Including refugees. **k** Data as at the end of December. **l** 2004. **m** 2009. **n** 2003. **o** 2011. **p** 2012. **q** Departures.

Malaysia

Region	South-eastern Asia	
Population (000, 2017)	31 624[a,b]	
Pop. density (per km2, 2017)	96.3[a,b]	
Capital city	Kuala Lumpur[d]	
Capital city pop. (000)	6 836.9[e,c]	

UN membership date	17 September 1957
Surface area (km2)	330 323[c]
Sex ratio (m per 100 f, 2017)	106.7[a,b]
National currency	Malaysian Ringgit (MYR)
Exchange rate (per US$)	4.5[f]

Economic indicators	2005	2010	2017
GDP: Gross domestic product (million current US$)	143 534	255 018	296 284[c]
GDP growth rate (annual %, const. 2005 prices)	5.3	7.4	5.0[c]
GDP per capita (current US$)	5 564.2	9 069.1	9 768.4[c]
Economy: Agriculture (% of GVA)[g,h]	8.4	10.2	8.6[c]
Economy: Industry (% of GVA)[g,h]	46.9	40.9	39.6[c]
Economy: Services and other activity (% of GVA)[g,h]	44.7	48.9	51.8[c]
Employment: Agriculture (% of employed)[i]	14.6	14.2	11.8
Employment: Industry (% of employed)[i]	29.8	27.7	27.3
Employment: Services (% of employed)[i]	55.6	58.0	60.9
Unemployment (% of labour force)	3.5	3.4	3.3[i]
Labour force participation (female/male pop. %)[i]	44.2 / 77.8	43.8 / 75.9	49.3 / 77.8
CPI: Consumer Price Index (2000=100)	109[j]	124	137[k]
Agricultural production index (2004-2006=100)	100	111	122[k]
Food production index (2004-2006=100)	100	115	130[k]
Index of industrial production (2005=100)[l]	100	107	116[m]
International trade: Exports (million US$)	141 624	198 791	189 414[f]
International trade: Imports (million US$)	114 290	164 586	168 375[f]
International trade: Balance (million US$)	27 334	34 204	21 039[f]
Balance of payments, current account (million US$)	19 980	25 644[n]	8 960[c]

Major trading partners						2016
Export partners (% of exports)	Singapore	14.6	China	12.5	United States	10.2
Import partners (% of imports)	China	20.4	Singapore	10.4	Japan	8.2

Social indicators	2005	2010	2017
Population growth rate (average annual %)[b,o]	2.0	1.8	1.8[c]
Urban population (% of total population)[b]	66.6	70.9	74.7[c]
Urban population growth rate (average annual %)[b,o]	3.4	3.1	2.7[c]
Fertility rate, total (live births per woman)[b,o]	2.5	2.2	2.1[c]
Life expectancy at birth (females/males, years)[b,o]	75.4 / 71.2	76.1 / 71.6	77.1 / 72.6[c]
Population age distribution (0-14 and 60+ years, %)[b]	30.5 / 7.1	27.9 / 7.9	24.3 / 9.7[a]
International migrant stock (000/% of total pop.)[b,p,q]	1 722.3 / 6.7	2 406.0 / 8.6	2 514.2 / 8.3[c]
Refugees and others of concern to UNHCR (000)	106.1[r]	212.9[r]	238.6[f]
Infant mortality rate (per 1 000 live births)[b,o]	6.8	6.8	6.5[c]
Health: Total expenditure (% of GDP)	3.3	4.0	4.2[k]
Health: Physicians (per 1 000 pop.)	0.7[s]	1.2	1.3[t]
Education: Government expenditure (% of GDP)	5.9[u]	5.0	5.0[c]
Education: Primary gross enrol. ratio (f/m per 100 pop.)	101.4 / 101.4	100.6 / 99.7	101.9 / 101.7[c]
Education: Secondary gross enrol. ratio (f/m per 100 pop.)	72.1 / 65.5	69.3 / 64.5	80.7 / 74.6[c]
Education: Tertiary gross enrol. ratio (f/m per 100 pop.)	31.9 / 24.1	43.2 / 31.4	31.8 / 20.8[c]
Intentional homicide rate (per 100 000 pop.)	2.3	1.9	...
Seats held by women in national parliaments (%)	9.1	9.9	10.4

Environment and infrastructure indicators	2005	2010	2017
Mobile-cellular subscriptions (per 100 inhabitants)	75.6	119.7	143.9[c]
Individuals using the Internet (per 100 inhabitants)	48.6	56.3	71.1[v,c]
Research & Development expenditure (% of GDP)	0.6[u]	1.0	1.3[k]
Threatened species (number)	892[u]	1 180	1 272
Forested area (% of land area)[i]	63.6	67.3	67.5[k]
CO2 emission estimates (million tons/tons per capita)	174.5 / 6.7	218.5 / 7.8	242.8 / 8.1[k]
Energy production, primary (Petajoules)	3 770	3 450	3 738[k]
Energy supply per capita (Gigajoules)	101	105	118[k]
Tourist/visitor arrivals at national borders (000)[w]	16 431	24 577	25 721[c]
Important sites for terrestrial biodiversity protected (%)	38.8	39.3	39.3
Pop. using improved drinking water (urban/rural, %)	98.5 / 90.2	99.6 / 91.7	100.0 / 93.0[c]
Pop. using improved sanitation facilities (urban/rural, %)	94.4 / 91.3	95.9 / 94.2	96.1 / 95.9[c]
Net Official Development Assist. received (% of GNI)	0.02	0.00	0.00[c]

a Projected estimate (medium fertility variant). **b** Including Sabah and Sarawak. **c** 2015. **d** Kuala Lumpur is the capital and Putrajaya is the administrative capital. **e** Refers to the Greater Kuala Lumpur. **f** 2016. **g** Data classified according to ISIC Rev. 4. **h** At producers' prices. **i** Estimate. **j** Series linked to former series. **k** 2014. **l** Data classified according to ISIC Rev. 3. **m** 2013. **n** Break in the time series. **o** Data refers to a 5-year period preceding the reference year. **p** Including refugees. **q** Refers to foreign citizens. **r** Data as at the end of December. **s** 2002. **t** 2011. **u** 2004. **v** Population aged 15 years and over. **w** Including Singapore residents crossing the frontier by road through Johore Causeway.

Maldives

Region	Southern Asia	UN membership date	21 September 1965
Population (000, 2017)	436[a]	Surface area (km2)	300[b]
Pop. density (per km2, 2017)	1 454.4[a]	Sex ratio (m per 100 f, 2017)	131.8[a]
Capital city	Male	National currency	Rufiyaa (MVR)
Capital city pop. (000)	156.4[c]	Exchange rate (per US$)	15.4[d]

Economic indicators	2005	2010	2017
GDP: Gross domestic product (million current US$)	1 120	2 323	3 435[b]
GDP growth rate (annual %, const. 2005 prices)	- 8.1	7.2	2.8[b]
GDP per capita (current US$)	3 671.9	6 986.2	9 446.5[b]
Economy: Agriculture (% of GVA)[e]	7.5[f]	4.1[f]	3.1[b]
Economy: Industry (% of GVA)	14.8[f]	14.9[f]	22.0[b]
Economy: Services and other activity (% of GVA)	77.7[f]	81.0[f]	74.9[b]
Employment: Agriculture (% of employed)[g]	13.3	15.0	7.7
Employment: Industry (% of employed)[g]	27.4	16.1	22.8
Employment: Services (% of employed)[g]	59.3	68.8	69.5
Unemployment (% of labour force)	7.0[g]	11.7	2.9[g]
Labour force participation (female/male pop. %)[g]	50.4 / 74.5	55.2 / 76.3	57.8 / 79.6
CPI: Consumer Price Index (2000=100)[h]	107[i]	146	196[c]
Agricultural production index (2004-2006=100)	89	75	65[c]
Food production index (2004-2006=100)	89	75	65[c]
International trade: Exports (million US$)	154	74	140[d]
International trade: Imports (million US$)	745	1 095	2 128[d]
International trade: Balance (million US$)	- 591	- 1 021	- 1 988[d]
Balance of payments, current account (million US$)	- 273	- 196	- 326[b]

Major trading partners						2016
Export partners (% of exports)	Thailand	34.4	Sri Lanka	10.2	United States	8.9
Import partners (% of imports)	United Arab Emirates	15.7	Singapore	14.3	China	13.4

Social indicators	2005	2010	2017
Population growth rate (average annual %)[j]	2.6	2.7	2.8[b]
Urban population (% of total population)	33.8	40.0	45.5[b]
Urban population growth rate (average annual %)[j]	5.7	5.2	4.5[b]
Fertility rate, total (live births per woman)[j]	2.6	2.3	2.2[b]
Life expectancy at birth (females/males, years)[j]	73.9 / 71.1	76.8 / 74.6	77.4 / 75.4[b]
Population age distribution (0-14 and 60+ years, %)	31.6 / 6.3	25.5 / 6.0	23.4 / 6.3[a]
International migrant stock (000/% of total pop.)[k,l]	45.0 / 14.8	73.6 / 22.1	94.1 / 25.9[b]
Infant mortality rate (per 1 000 live births)[j]	26.7	14.8	9.0[b]
Health: Total expenditure (% of GDP)	9.5	7.9	13.7[c]
Health: Physicians (per 1 000 pop.)	1.0[m]	1.6	...
Education: Government expenditure (% of GDP)	5.2	4.6	5.2[b]
Education: Primary gross enrol. ratio (f/m per 100 pop.)	114.5 / 117.6	100.8 / 104.0[n]	98.6 / 97.3[d]
Education: Secondary gross enrol. ratio (f/m per 100 pop.)	74.0 / 65.8[g,m]	... / ...	... / ...
Education: Tertiary gross enrol. ratio (f/m per 100 pop.)	0.3 / 0.1[o]	13.5 / 12.0[p]	20.3 / 12.4[c]
Intentional homicide rate (per 100 000 pop.)	...	1.8	0.8[q]
Seats held by women in national parliaments (%)	12.0	6.5	5.9

Environment and infrastructure indicators	2005	2010	2017
Mobile-cellular subscriptions (per 100 inhabitants)	68.4	151.8	206.7[b]
Individuals using the Internet (per 100 inhabitants)	6.9[g,r]	26.5[s]	54.5[g,b]
Threatened species (number)	12[m]	59	75
Forested area (% of land area)[g]	3.3	3.3	3.3[c]
CO2 emission estimates (million tons/tons per capita)	0.6 / 2.1	0.9 / 2.8	1.3 / 3.7[c]
Energy production, primary (Petajoules)	0	0	0[c]
Energy supply per capita (Gigajoules)	30	40	54[c]
Tourist/visitor arrivals at national borders (000)[t]	395	792	1 234[b]
Important sites for terrestrial biodiversity protected (%)	0.0	0.0	0.0
Pop. using improved drinking water (urban/rural, %)	99.7 / 95.4	99.6 / 97.5	99.5 / 97.9[b]
Pop. using improved sanitation facilities (urban/rural, %)	97.6 / 84.8	97.5 / 97.2	97.5 / 98.3[b]
Net Official Development Assist. received (% of GNI)	7.03	5.55	0.95[b]

a Projected estimate (medium fertility variant). **b** 2015. **c** 2014. **d** 2016. **e** Includes mining and quarrying. **f** At producers' prices. **g** Estimate. **h** Male **i** Series linked to former series. **j** Data refers to a 5-year period preceding the reference year. **k** Refers to foreign citizens. **l** Including refugees. **m** 2004. **n** 2009. **o** 2003. **p** 2008. **q** 2013. **r** Excluding mobile internet users. **s** Population aged 15 years and over. **t** Arrivals by air.

Mali

Region	Western Africa	UN membership date		28 September 1960
Population (000, 2017)	18 542[a]	Surface area (km2)		1 240 192[b]
Pop. density (per km2, 2017)	15.2[a]	Sex ratio (m per 100 f, 2017)		100.2[a]
Capital city	Bamako	National currency		CFA Franc (XOF)
Capital city pop. (000)	2 515.0[b]	Exchange rate (per US$)		622.3[c]

Economic indicators	2005	2010	2017
GDP: Gross domestic product (million current US$)	6 245	10 679	13 100[b]
GDP growth rate (annual %, const. 2005 prices)	10.4	10.9	7.6[b]
GDP per capita (current US$)	484.8	704.1	744.3[b]
Economy: Agriculture (% of GVA)	34.4	34.9	39.9[b]
Economy: Industry (% of GVA)	25.9	25.3	19.6[b]
Economy: Services and other activity (% of GVA)	39.6	39.7	40.5[b]
Employment: Agriculture (% of employed)[d]	51.2	58.9	56.7
Employment: Industry (% of employed)[d]	14.8	13.8	14.7
Employment: Services (% of employed)[d]	34.0	27.3	28.6
Unemployment (% of labour force)	9.6[d]	7.3	8.1[d]
Labour force participation (female/male pop. %)[d]	38.3 / 70.1	50.3 / 81.4	50.5 / 82.3
CPI: Consumer Price Index (2000=100)[e]	112	131[f]	142[g]
Agricultural production index (2004-2006=100)	102	141	154[g]
Food production index (2004-2006=100)	102	152	157[g]
Index of industrial production (2005=100)[h,i]	100	74	91[g]
International trade: Exports (million US$)	1 075	1 996	3 030[c]
International trade: Imports (million US$)	1 544	4 704	2 510[c]
International trade: Balance (million US$)	- 468	- 2 707	520[c]
Balance of payments, current account (million US$)	- 438[j]	- 1 190	- 676[g]

Major trading partners					2016
Export partners (% of exports)	United Arab Emirates	59.6	Switzerland	18.8	India	6.0
Import partners (% of imports)	Senegal	13.8	Côte d'Ivoire	13.1	France	12.2

Social indicators	2005	2010	2017
Population growth rate (average annual %)[k]	3.1	3.3	2.9[b]
Urban population (% of total population)	32.1	36.0	39.9[b]
Urban population growth rate (average annual %)[k]	5.5	5.5	5.1[b]
Fertility rate, total (live births per woman)[k]	6.8	6.7	6.4[b]
Life expectancy at birth (females/males, years)[k]	50.6 / 49.3	54.6 / 53.4	56.9 / 55.6[b]
Population age distribution (0-14 and 60+ years, %)	46.9 / 4.6	47.5 / 4.2	47.7 / 4.0[a]
International migrant stock (000/% of total pop.)[l]	256.8 / 2.0	336.6 / 2.2	363.1 / 2.1[b]
Refugees and others of concern to UNHCR (000)	13.1[m]	15.3[m]	90.8[c]
Infant mortality rate (per 1 000 live births)[k]	106.6	89.1	78.5[b]
Health: Total expenditure (% of GDP)	6.3	5.3	7.0[g]
Health: Physicians (per 1 000 pop.)	0.1[n]	0.1	...
Education: Government expenditure (% of GDP)	3.5	3.3	3.7[g]
Education: Primary gross enrol. ratio (f/m per 100 pop.)	64.8 / 81.3	77.1 / 88.7	72.1 / 79.3[b]
Education: Secondary gross enrol. ratio (f/m per 100 pop.)	19.6 / 31.2[d]	31.9 / 45.4	36.8 / 45.6[b]
Education: Tertiary gross enrol. ratio (f/m per 100 pop.)	1.4 / 2.7[o]	3.6 / 8.4	4.1 / 9.6[p]
Intentional homicide rate (per 100 000 pop.)	12.6	12.1	10.8[b]
Seats held by women in national parliaments (%)	10.2	10.2	8.8

Environment and infrastructure indicators	2005	2010	2017
Mobile-cellular subscriptions (per 100 inhabitants)	6.4	53.2	139.6[q,b]
Individuals using the Internet (per 100 inhabitants)	0.5	2.0[d]	10.3[d,b]
Research & Development expenditure (% of GDP)	...	0.7[r]	...
Threatened species (number)	25[n]	29	42
Forested area (% of land area)	4.5	4.2[d]	3.9[d,g]
CO2 emission estimates (million tons/tons per capita)	0.9 / 0.1	1.0 / 0.1	1.4 / 0.1[g]
Energy production, primary (Petajoules)	49	52	55[g]
Energy supply per capita (Gigajoules)	5	4	4[g]
Tourist/visitor arrivals at national borders (000)	...	169	159[b]
Important sites for terrestrial biodiversity protected (%)	33.8	33.8	33.8
Pop. using improved drinking water (urban/rural, %)	79.1 / 46.1	87.8 / 55.1	96.5 / 64.1[b]
Pop. using improved sanitation facilities (urban/rural, %)	34.8 / 13.3	36.2 / 14.7	37.5 / 16.1[b]
Net Official Development Assist. received (% of GNI)	12.00	10.64	9.45[b]

a Projected estimate (medium fertility variant). **b** 2015. **c** 2016. **d** Estimate. **e** Bamako **f** Series linked to former series. **g** 2014. **h** Data classified according to ISIC Rev. 3. **i** Country data supplemented with data from the Observatoire Économique et Statistique d'Afrique Subsaharienne (Afristat). **j** Break in the time series. **k** Data refers to a 5-year period preceding the reference year. **l** Including refugees. **m** Data as at the end of December. **n** 2004. **o** 2002. **p** 2012. **q** Decrease due to implementation of subscriber registration. **r** Excluding business enterprise.

Malta

Region	Southern Europe	UN membership date	01 December 1964
Population (000, 2017)	431[a]	Surface area (km2)	315[b]
Pop. density (per km2, 2017)	1 346.4[a]	Sex ratio (m per 100 f, 2017)	100.9[a]
Capital city	Valletta	National currency	Euro (EUR)
Capital city pop. (000)	197.4[c]	Exchange rate (per US$)	0.9[d]

Economic indicators

	2005	2010	2017
GDP: Gross domestic product (million current US$)	6 393	8 741	9 747[b]
GDP growth rate (annual %, const. 2005 prices)	3.8	3.5	6.2[b]
GDP per capita (current US$)	16 099.8	21 211.6	23 280.7[b]
Economy: Agriculture (% of GVA)[e]	2.2	1.7	1.4[b]
Economy: Industry (% of GVA)[e]	23.3	19.1	15.0[b]
Economy: Services and other activity (% of GVA)[e]	74.5	79.3	83.6[b]
Employment: Agriculture (% of employed)[f]	2.1	1.3	1.2
Employment: Industry (% of employed)[f]	29.8	25.2	20.9
Employment: Services (% of employed)[f]	68.1	73.5	77.9
Unemployment (% of labour force)	6.9	6.8	5.4[f]
Labour force participation (female/male pop. %)[f]	29.1 / 68.8	32.6 / 66.0	39.4 / 65.7
CPI: Consumer Price Index (2000=100)	113	127[g]	136[c]
Agricultural production index (2004-2006=100)	97	98	96[c]
Food production index (2004-2006=100)	97	98	96[c]
Index of industrial production (2005=100)	100	102	97[c]
International trade: Exports (million US$)	2 431	3 717	4 039[d]
International trade: Imports (million US$)	3 865	5 732	7 182[d]
International trade: Balance (million US$)	- 1 435	- 2 015	- 3 143[d]
Balance of payments, current account (million US$)	- 418	- 420	539[b]

Major trading partners

						2016
Export partners (% of exports)	United States	20.5	Germany	11.1	Bunkers[h]	9.4
Import partners (% of imports)	Italy	19.2	Cayman Islands	10.2	Canada	9.0

Social indicators

	2005	2010	2017
Population growth rate (average annual %)[i]	0.5	0.5	0.5[b]
Urban population (% of total population)	93.6	94.7	95.4[b]
Urban population growth rate (average annual %)[i]	0.6	0.7	0.5[b]
Fertility rate, total (live births per woman)[i]	1.5	1.4	1.4[b]
Life expectancy at birth (females/males, years)[i]	80.2 / 76.8	81.1 / 77.7	82.0 / 78.6[b]
Population age distribution (0-14 and 60+ years, %)	17.7 / 18.8	15.2 / 22.9	14.4 / 26.1[a]
International migrant stock (000/% of total pop.)	24.6 / 6.2	33.1 / 8.0	41.4 / 9.9[b]
Refugees and others of concern to UNHCR (000)	2.1[j]	7.4[j]	8.1[d]
Infant mortality rate (per 1 000 live births)[i]	6.9	5.8	4.8[b]
Health: Total expenditure (% of GDP)	8.8	8.3	9.7[c]
Health: Physicians (per 1 000 pop.)	...	3.1	3.9[b]
Education: Government expenditure (% of GDP)	4.5[k]	6.5	7.8[l]
Education: Primary gross enrol. ratio (f/m per 100 pop.)	95.7 / 98.0	99.3 / 98.7	104.7 / 102.2[b]
Education: Secondary gross enrol. ratio (f/m per 100 pop.)	100.3 / 104.5	98.0 / 109.7	98.1 / 91.7[b]
Education: Tertiary gross enrol. ratio (f/m per 100 pop.)	37.3 / 27.5	42.7 / 31.6	55.2 / 40.3[b]
Intentional homicide rate (per 100 000 pop.)	1.0	1.0	1.0[b]
Seats held by women in national parliaments (%)	9.2	8.7	12.5

Environment and infrastructure indicators

	2005	2010	2017
Mobile-cellular subscriptions (per 100 inhabitants)	78.1	107.3	129.3[b]
Individuals using the Internet (per 100 inhabitants)[m]	41.2	63.0	76.2[b]
Research & Development expenditure (% of GDP)	0.6	0.7	0.8[n,c]
Threatened species (number)	25[k]	26	39
Forested area (% of land area)[f]	1.1	1.1	1.1[c]
CO2 emission estimates (million tons/tons per capita)	2.7 / 6.6	2.6 / 6.2	2.3 / 5.6[c]
Energy production, primary (Petajoules)	0	0	1[c]
Energy supply per capita (Gigajoules)	91	86	78[c]
Tourist/visitor arrivals at national borders (000)[o]	1 171	1 339	1 791[b]
Important sites for terrestrial biodiversity protected (%)	83.1	84.3	90.4
Pop. using improved drinking water (urban/rural, %)	100.0 / 100.0	100.0 / 100.0	100.0 / 100.0[b]
Pop. using improved sanitation facilities (urban/rural, %)	100.0 / 100.0	100.0 / 100.0	100.0 / 100.0[b]
Net Official Development Assist. disbursed (% of GNI)	...	0.18	0.20[n,d]

a Projected estimate (medium fertility variant). **b** 2015. **c** 2014. **d** 2016. **e** Data classified according to ISIC Rev. 4. **f** Estimate. **g** Series linked to former series. **h** Bunkers, ship stores. **i** Data refers to a 5-year period preceding the reference year. **j** Data as at the end of December. **k** 2004. **l** 2013. **m** Population aged 16 to 74 years. **n** Provisional data. **o** Departures by air and by sea.

Marshall Islands

Region	Micronesia
Population (000, 2017)	53 [a]
Pop. density (per km2, 2017)	295.2 [a]
Capital city	Majuro
Capital city pop. (000)	30.9 [e]

UN membership date	17 September 1991
Surface area (km2)	181 [b]
Sex ratio (m per 100 f, 2017)	104.5 [c,d]
National currency	US Dollar (USD)

Economic indicators	2005	2010	2017
GDP: Gross domestic product (million current US$)	138	164	183 [b]
GDP growth rate (annual %, const. 2005 prices)	2.6	6.2	0.6 [b]
GDP per capita (current US$)	2 647.0	3 124.3	3 452.6 [b]
Economy: Agriculture (% of GVA)	9.1	15.4	16.4 [b]
Economy: Industry (% of GVA)	9.2	11.6	10.2 [b]
Economy: Services and other activity (% of GVA)	81.6	72.9	73.3 [b]
Employment: Agriculture (% of employed)	...	11.0 [c,f]	...
Employment: Industry (% of employed)		9.4 [c,f]	
Employment: Services (% of employed)		79.6 [c,f]	
Unemployment (% of labour force)	...	...	4.7 [c,g]
Labour force participation (female/male pop. %)	... / ...	... / ...	29.0 / 53.3 [g]
CPI: Consumer Price Index (2000=100) [h]	107	135 [i]	...
Agricultural production index (2004-2006=100)	97	112	115 [e]
Food production index (2004-2006=100)	97	112	115 [e]
International trade: Exports (million US$)	11	17	27 [d]
International trade: Imports (million US$)	68	76	86 [d]
International trade: Balance (million US$)	- 57	- 60	- 58 [d]
Balance of payments, current account (million US$)	- 3 [c]	- 14	- 5 [e]

Major trading partners						2016
Export partners (% of exports)	United States	23.4	Spain	11.5	Thailand	10.9
Import partners (% of imports)	Singapore	29.0	China	23.5	Republic of Korea	16.1

Social indicators	2005	2010	2017
Population growth rate (average annual %) [j]	-0.0	0.1	0.2 [b]
Urban population (% of total population)	69.9	71.3	72.7 [b]
Urban population growth rate (average annual %) [j]	0.4	0.6	0.6 [b]
Fertility rate, total (live births per woman)	...	...	4.1 [g]
Life expectancy at birth (females/males, years)	70.6 / 67.0 [k]	... / ...	72.5 / 71.3 [c,g]
Population age distribution (0-14 and 60+ years, %)	40.6 / 3.6 [l,m,k]	40.9 / 4.5 [l,m]	39.0 / 5.5 [c,d]
International migrant stock (000/% of total pop.)	2.4 / 4.6	3.1 / 5.9	3.3 / 6.2 [b]
Infant mortality rate (per 1 000 live births)	...	...	25.4 [n,g]
Health: Total expenditure (% of GDP) [o]	17.4	17.3	17.1 [e]
Health: Physicians (per 1 000 pop.)	...	0.6 [p]	0.5 [q]
Education: Government expenditure (% of GDP)	12.2 [r]	...	...
Education: Primary gross enrol. ratio (f/m per 100 pop.)	129.9 / 103.0	107.9 / 107.4 [s]	93.3 / 93.5 [b]
Education: Secondary gross enrol. ratio (f/m per 100 pop.)	75.7 / 75.6	104.4 / 101.4 [s]	80.4 / 73.1 [b]
Education: Tertiary gross enrol. ratio (f/m per 100 pop.)	18.3 / 14.2 [t]	... / ...	41.2 / 44.6 [q]
Intentional homicide rate (per 100 000 pop.)	...	...	4.7 [q]
Seats held by women in national parliaments (%)	3.0	3.0	9.1

Environment and infrastructure indicators	2005	2010	2017
Mobile-cellular subscriptions (per 100 inhabitants)	1.3	...	29.2 [u,b]
Individuals using the Internet (per 100 inhabitants)	3.9	7.0 [u]	19.3 [u,b]
Threatened species (number)	13 [k]	84	101
Forested area (% of land area) [u]	70.2	70.2	70.2 [e]
CO2 emission estimates (million tons/tons per capita)	0.1 / 1.7	0.1 / 2.0	0.1 / 1.9 [e]
Energy production, primary (Petajoules)	...	...	0 [u,e]
Energy supply per capita (Gigajoules) [u]	23	28	27 [e]
Tourist/visitor arrivals at national borders (000) [v]	9 [w]	5	6 [b]
Important sites for terrestrial biodiversity protected (%)	32.1	32.1	32.1
Pop. using improved drinking water (urban/rural, %)	92.5 / 96.5	93.1 / 97.2	93.5 / 97.6 [b]
Pop. using improved sanitation facilities (urban/rural, %)	82.0 / 50.9	83.5 / 54.2	84.5 / 56.2 [b]
Net Official Development Assist. received (% of GNI)	31.71	16.48	24.11 [e]

a Projected estimate (medium fertility variant). **b** 2015. **c** Break in the time series. **d** 2016. **e** 2014. **f** Data classified according to ISIC Rev. 3. **g** 2011. **h** Majuro **i** 2008. **j** Data refers to a 5-year period preceding the reference year. **k** 2004. **l** Projections are prepared by the Secretariat of the Pacific Community based on 1999 census of population and housing. **m** Estimates should be viewed with caution as these are derived from scarce data. **n** Data refers to a 3-year period up to and including the reference year. **o** Data revision. **p** 2007. **q** 2012. **r** 2003. **s** 2009. **t** 2002. **u** Estimate. **v** Arrivals by air. **w** Air and sea arrivals.

Martinique

Region	Caribbean	Population (000, 2017)	385[a]	
Surface area (km2)	1 128[b]	Pop. density (per km2, 2017)	363.1[a]	
Sex ratio (m per 100 f, 2017)	83.5[a]	Capital city	Fort-de-France	
National currency	Euro (EUR)	Capital city pop. (000)	85.8[c]	
Exchange rate (per US$)	0.9[d]			

Economic indicators

	2005	2010	2017
Employment: Agriculture (% of employed)[e,f]	...	4.1	3.9[g]
Employment: Industry (% of employed)[e,f]	...	11.9	11.8[g]
Employment: Services (% of employed)[e,f]	...	65.3	69.0[g]
Unemployment (% of labour force)[f]	18.7	21.0	22.8[h,i]
Labour force participation (female/male pop. %)[f]	39.6 / 48.5	43.3 / 49.1	52.6 / 53.8[h,i]
CPI: Consumer Price Index (2000=100)	111	121	129[c]
Agricultural production index (2004-2006=100)	99	82	78[c]
Food production index (2004-2006=100)	99	82	78[c]

Social indicators

	2005	2010	2017
Population growth rate (average annual %)[j]	0.5	- 0.1	- 0.5[b]
Urban population (% of total population)	89.3	89.0	88.9[b]
Urban population growth rate (average annual %)[j]	0.5	0.2	0.2[b]
Fertility rate, total (live births per woman)[j]	1.9	2.1	2.0[b]
Life expectancy at birth (females/males, years)[j]	82.2 / 75.5	83.2 / 76.7	84.4 / 77.8[b]
Population age distribution (0-14 and 60+ years, %)	21.1 / 18.0	19.6 / 20.6	17.7 / 25.7[a]
International migrant stock (000/% of total pop.)	57.0 / 14.4	59.6 / 15.1	61.7 / 15.6[b]
Infant mortality rate (per 1 000 live births)[j]	8.5	7.6	6.4[b]
Intentional homicide rate (per 100 000 pop.)	4.8	2.8[k]	...

Environment and infrastructure indicators

	2005	2010	2017
Threatened species (number)	29[l]	31	48
Forested area (% of land area)[m]	45.8	45.8	45.8[c]
CO2 emission estimates (million tons/tons per capita)	2.2 / 5.5	2.0 / 5.1	2.3 / 5.8[c]
Energy production, primary (Petajoules)[m]	0	1	1[c]
Energy supply per capita (Gigajoules)	73	69	79[m,c]
Tourist/visitor arrivals at national borders (000)	484	478	487[b]
Important sites for terrestrial biodiversity protected (%)	75.1	99.1	99.1
Pop. using improved drinking water (urban/rural, %)	95.5 / 99.8	100.0 / 99.8	100.0 / 99.8[b]
Pop. using improved sanitation facilities (urban/rural, %)	93.9 / 72.7	94.0 / 72.7	94.0 / 72.7[c]

a Projected estimate (medium fertility variant). b 2015. c 2014. d 2016. e Population aged 15 to 64 years. f Excluding the institutional population. g 2012. h Break in the time series. i 2013. j Data refers to a 5-year period preceding the reference year. k 2009. l 2004. m Estimate.

Mauritania

Region	Western Africa	UN membership date	27 October 1961
Population (000, 2017)	4 420[a]	Surface area (km2)	1 030 700[b]
Pop. density (per km2, 2017)	4.3[a]	Sex ratio (m per 100 f, 2017)	101.6[a]
Capital city	Nouakchott	National currency	Ouguiya (MRO)
Capital city pop. (000)	967.5[b]	Exchange rate (per US$)	339.0[b]

Economic indicators	2005	2010	2017
GDP: Gross domestic product (million current US$)	2 184	4 338	5 023[b]
GDP growth rate (annual %, const. 2005 prices)	9.0	4.8	1.2[b]
GDP per capita (current US$)	692.6	1 207.8	1 235.0[b]
Economy: Agriculture (% of GVA)	29.8	21.3	20.9[b]
Economy: Industry (% of GVA)	32.4	40.9	41.7[b]
Economy: Services and other activity (% of GVA)	37.9	37.8	37.4[b]
Employment: Agriculture (% of employed)[c]	48.4	44.1	40.3
Employment: Industry (% of employed)[c]	9.0	9.2	9.5
Employment: Services (% of employed)[c]	42.5	46.7	50.2
Unemployment (% of labour force)[c]	10.9	10.8	12.0
Labour force participation (female/male pop. %)[c]	27.8 / 65.9	28.8 / 65.5	29.3 / 65.5
CPI: Consumer Price Index (2000=100)	139	185	214[d]
Agricultural production index (2004-2006=100)	100	111	125[e]
Food production index (2004-2006=100)	100	111	125[e]
International trade: Exports (million US$)	556	1 819	1 623[f]
International trade: Imports (million US$)	1 342	1 708	2 174[f]
International trade: Balance (million US$)	- 786	111	- 551[f]
Balance of payments, current account (million US$)	...	...	- 1 066[b]

Major trading partners						2016
Export partners (% of exports)	China	36.9	Switzerland	13.5	Spain	8.9
Import partners (% of imports)	United States	13.4	United Arab Emirates	11.9	Belgium	9.2

Social indicators	2005	2010	2017
Population growth rate (average annual %)[g]	2.9	2.8	2.9[b]
Urban population (% of total population)	53.1	56.7	59.9[b]
Urban population growth rate (average annual %)[g]	4.5	4.0	3.5[b]
Fertility rate, total (live births per woman)[g]	5.3	5.1	4.9[b]
Life expectancy at birth (females/males, years)[g]	61.9 / 58.6	62.8 / 59.8	64.1 / 61.2[b]
Population age distribution (0-14 and 60+ years, %)	42.1 / 4.8	41.2 / 4.8	39.9 / 5.0[a]
International migrant stock (000/% of total pop.)[h,i]	58.1 / 1.8	84.7 / 2.4	138.2 / 3.4[b]
Refugees and others of concern to UNHCR (000)	30.2[j]	27.0[j]	69.0[f]
Infant mortality rate (per 1 000 live births)[g]	75.6	72.4	68.0[b]
Health: Total expenditure (% of GDP)	4.2	3.3	3.8[e]
Health: Physicians (per 1 000 pop.)	0.1[k]	0.1[l]	...
Education: Government expenditure (% of GDP)	2.5[c,k]	3.6	2.9[d]
Education: Primary gross enrol. ratio (f/m per 100 pop.)	92.2 / 89.3	98.4 / 94.3	105.0 / 100.0[b]
Education: Secondary gross enrol. ratio (f/m per 100 pop.)	20.8 / 23.7	18.7 / 21.9[c]	29.5 / 31.7[b]
Education: Tertiary gross enrol. ratio (f/m per 100 pop.)	1.5 / 4.3	2.5 / 6.3	3.6 / 7.1[f]
Intentional homicide rate (per 100 000 pop.)	12.3	10.9	10.2[b]
Seats held by women in national parliaments (%)	3.7	22.1	25.2

Environment and infrastructure indicators	2005	2010	2017
Mobile-cellular subscriptions (per 100 inhabitants)	23.7[m]	76.9[m]	89.3[n,b]
Individuals using the Internet (per 100 inhabitants)	0.7	4.0[c]	15.2[c,b]
Threatened species (number)	26[k]	58	86
Forested area (% of land area)	0.3	0.2	0.2[c,e]
CO2 emission estimates (million tons/tons per capita)	1.6 / 0.5	2.2 / 0.6	2.7 / 0.7[e]
Energy production, primary (Petajoules)	15	34	31[e]
Energy supply per capita (Gigajoules)	12	12	13[c,e]
Important sites for terrestrial biodiversity protected (%)	14.6	14.6	14.6
Pop. using improved drinking water (urban/rural, %)	50.4 / 45.9	55.4 / 52.9	58.4 / 57.1[b]
Pop. using improved sanitation facilities (urban/rural, %)	46.0 / 10.9	53.2 / 12.7	57.5 / 13.8[b]
Net Official Development Assist. received (% of GNI)	8.39	8.75	5.02[e]

a Projected estimate (medium fertility variant). **b** 2015. **c** Estimate. **d** 2013. **e** 2014. **f** 2016. **g** Data refers to a 5-year period preceding the reference year. **h** Including refugees. **i** Refers to foreign citizens. **j** Data as at the end of December. **k** 2004. **l** 2009. **m** Includes inactive subscriptions. **n** Data refers to active subscriptions only.

Mauritius

Region	Eastern Africa	UN membership date	24 April 1968
Population (000, 2017)	1 265[a,b]	Surface area (km2)	1 969[c,d]
Pop. density (per km2, 2017)	623.2[a,b]	Sex ratio (m per 100 f, 2017)	97.9[a,b]
Capital city	Port Louis	National currency	Mauritius Rupee (MUR)
Capital city pop. (000)	135.5[e]	Exchange rate (per US$)	36.0[f]

Economic indicators	2005	2010	2017
GDP: Gross domestic product (million current US$)	6 489	9 718	11 511[d]
GDP growth rate (annual %, const. 2005 prices)	1.8	4.1	3.5[d]
GDP per capita (current US$)	5 309.9	7 787.4	9 040.9[d]
Economy: Agriculture (% of GVA)	5.7	3.6[g]	2.9[g,d]
Economy: Industry (% of GVA)	26.6	26.6[g]	22.7[g,d]
Economy: Services and other activity (% of GVA)	67.8	69.8[g]	74.4[g,d]
Employment: Agriculture (% of employed)[h]	10.0	8.5	7.3
Employment: Industry (% of employed)[h]	32.5	28.8	25.2
Employment: Services (% of employed)[h]	57.5	62.7	67.5
Unemployment (% of labour force)	9.6	7.7	7.6[h]
Labour force participation (female/male pop. %)[h]	41.1 / 76.8	43.2 / 74.4	46.9 / 74.3
CPI: Consumer Price Index (2000=100)	128	176	208[e]
Agricultural production index (2004-2006=100)	98	99	96[e]
Food production index (2004-2006=100)	98	99	96[e]
Index of industrial production (2005=100)[i]	100	112	117[j]
International trade: Exports (million US$)	2 144	1 850	2 194[f]
International trade: Imports (million US$)	3 160	4 402	4 655[f]
International trade: Balance (million US$)	- 1 016	- 2 553	- 2 461[f]
Balance of payments, current account (million US$)	- 324	- 1 006	- 566[d]

Major trading partners						2016
Export partners (% of exports)	France	14.8	United Kingdom	12.0	United States	11.4
Import partners (% of imports)	China	17.7	India	16.5	France	7.8

Social indicators	2005	2010	2017
Population growth rate (average annual %)[b,k]	0.6	0.4	0.2[d]
Urban population (% of total population)[b]	41.6	40.6	39.7[d]
Urban population growth rate (average annual %)[b,k]	—0.0	- 0.2	- 0.1[d]
Fertility rate, total (live births per woman)[b,k]	1.9	1.7	1.5[d]
Life expectancy at birth (females/males, years)[b,k]	75.4 / 68.8	76.2 / 69.4	77.7 / 70.7[d]
Population age distribution (0-14 and 60+ years, %)[b]	24.7 / 9.6	21.9 / 12.1	18.4 / 16.6[a]
International migrant stock (000/% of total pop.)[b,l]	19.6 / 1.6	24.8 / 2.0	28.6 / 2.2[d]
Infant mortality rate (per 1 000 live births)[b,k]	13.4	13.2	12.0[d]
Health: Total expenditure (% of GDP)	4.5	5.3	4.8[e]
Health: Physicians (per 1 000 pop.)	1.1[m]	...	...
Education: Government expenditure (% of GDP)	4.2	3.6	4.9[d]
Education: Primary gross enrol. ratio (f/m per 100 pop.)	103.1 / 103.3	103.1 / 102.5	103.9 / 102.2[d]
Education: Secondary gross enrol. ratio (f/m per 100 pop.)	87.6 / 89.7[h]	91.3 / 87.2[h]	97.9 / 93.6[d]
Education: Tertiary gross enrol. ratio (f/m per 100 pop.)	21.7 / 21.0[h]	36.9 / 30.5	41.7 / 31.7[d]
Intentional homicide rate (per 100 000 pop.)	...	2.6	2.7[j]
Seats held by women in national parliaments (%)	5.7	17.1	11.6

Environment and infrastructure indicators	2005	2010	2017
Mobile-cellular subscriptions (per 100 inhabitants)	54.2	96.8	140.6[d]
Individuals using the Internet (per 100 inhabitants)	15.2[h]	28.3[n]	50.1[n,d]
Research & Development expenditure (% of GDP)	0.4[o,p]	...	0.2[q,r,s]
Threatened species (number)	147[m]	222	257
Forested area (% of land area)	18.8	18.9	19.0[h,e]
CO2 emission estimates (million tons/tons per capita)	3.3 / 2.6	3.9 / 3.2	4.2 / 3.3[e]
Energy production, primary (Petajoules)	12	11	10[e]
Energy supply per capita (Gigajoules)	45	50	51[e]
Tourist/visitor arrivals at national borders (000)	761	935	1 152[d]
Important sites for terrestrial biodiversity protected (%)	24.5	24.6	25.7
Pop. using improved drinking water (urban/rural, %)	99.8 / 99.2	99.9 / 99.6	99.9 / 99.8[d]
Pop. using improved sanitation facilities (urban/rural, %)	93.6 / 90.9	93.8 / 92.0	93.9 / 92.6[d]
Net Official Development Assist. received (% of GNI)	0.55	1.27	0.67[d]

a Projected estimate (medium fertility variant). **b** Including Agalega, Rodrigues and Saint Brandon. **c** Excludes the islands of Saint Brandon and Agalega. **d** 2015. **e** 2014. **f** 2016. **g** Data classified according to ISIC Rev. 4. **h** Estimate. **i** Data classified according to ISIC Rev. 3. **j** 2011. **k** Data refers to a 5-year period preceding the reference year. **l** Refers to foreign citizens. **m** 2004. **n** Population aged 5 years and over. **o** Overestimated or based on overestimated data. **p** R&D budget instead of R&D expenditure or based on R&D budget. **q** Excluding business enterprise. **r** Break in the time series. **s** 2012.

Mayotte

Region	Eastern Africa	Population (000, 2017)	253[a]	
Pop. density (per km2, 2017)	674.8[a]	Sex ratio (m per 100 f, 2017)	96.7[a]	
Capital city	Mamoudzou	National currency	Euro (EUR)	
Capital city pop. (000)	5.7[b]	Exchange rate (per US$)	0.9[c]	

Economic indicators	2005	2010	2017
International trade: Exports (million US$)	6	...	...
International trade: Imports (million US$)	309	...	...
International trade: Balance (million US$)	- 303	...	...

Social indicators	2005	2010	2017
Population growth rate (average annual %)[d]	3.4	3.2	2.8[e]
Urban population (% of total population)	50.2	49.0	47.0[e]
Urban population growth rate (average annual %)[d]	4.3	2.6	1.9[e]
Fertility rate, total (live births per woman)[d]	4.8	4.6	4.1[e]
Life expectancy at birth (females/males, years)[d]	80.6 / 73.0	81.9 / 74.5	82.9 / 76.0[e]
Population age distribution (0-14 and 60+ years, %)	42.4 / 4.8	42.9 / 5.1	40.6 / 5.8[a]
International migrant stock (000/% of total pop.)	63.2 / 35.5	72.8 / 34.9	77.0 / 32.1[e]
Infant mortality rate (per 1 000 live births)[d]	7.6	5.6	4.2[e]
Intentional homicide rate (per 100 000 pop.)	...	5.9[f]	...

Environment and infrastructure indicators	2005	2010	2017
Mobile-cellular subscriptions (per 100 inhabitants)	0.0[g,h]	...	...
Individuals using the Internet (per 100 inhabitants)	1.2[h]	...	...
Threatened species (number)	7[i]	69	88
Forested area (% of land area)[j]	20.7	18.2	16.1[b]
Energy production, primary (Petajoules)	0	0	0[j,b]
Energy supply per capita (Gigajoules)	17[i]	20	19[j,b]
Important sites for terrestrial biodiversity protected (%)	2.7	14.5	14.5

a Projected estimate (medium fertility variant). **b** 2014. **c** 2016. **d** Data refers to a 5-year period preceding the reference year. **e** 2015. **f** 2009. **g** Data refers to active subscriptions only. **h** 2000. **i** 2004. **j** Estimate.

Mexico

Region	Central America	UN membership date	07 November 1945
Population (000, 2017)	129 163[a]	Surface area (km2)	1 964 375[b]
Pop. density (per km2, 2017)	66.4[a]	Sex ratio (m per 100 f, 2017)	99.2[a]
Capital city	Mexico City	National currency	Mexican Peso (MXN)
Capital city pop. (000)	20 998.5[c,b]	Exchange rate (per US$)	20.7[d]

Economic indicators	2005	2010	2017
GDP: Gross domestic product (million current US$)	864 810	1 049 925	1 140 724[b]
GDP growth rate (annual %, const. 2005 prices)	3.1	5.2	2.5[b]
GDP per capita (current US$)	7 880.0	8 851.3	8 980.9[b]
Economy: Agriculture (% of GVA)[e]	3.2	3.3	3.6[b]
Economy: Industry (% of GVA)[e]	38.8	38.3	36.0[b]
Economy: Services and other activity (% of GVA)[e]	58.1	58.3	60.4[b]
Employment: Agriculture (% of employed)[f]	15.0	13.1	13.4
Employment: Industry (% of employed)[f]	25.8	25.5	25.2
Employment: Services (% of employed)[f]	59.2	61.5	61.3
Unemployment (% of labour force)	3.6	5.3	4.1[f]
Labour force participation (female/male pop. %)[f]	41.0 / 80.9	43.8 / 80.7	45.5 / 79.5
CPI: Consumer Price Index (2000=100)	127	158	184[g]
Agricultural production index (2004-2006=100)	98	108	120[g]
Food production index (2004-2006=100)	98	108	120[g]
Index of industrial production (2005=100)	100[h]	101	110[g]
International trade: Exports (million US$)[i,j]	214 207	298 305	373 883[d]
International trade: Imports (million US$)[i,j]	221 819	301 482	387 064[d]
International trade: Balance (million US$)[i,j]	- 7 612	- 3 177	- 13 181[d]
Balance of payments, current account (million US$)	- 9 069	- 5 270	- 33 216[b]

Major trading partners						2016
Export partners (% of exports)	United States	81.0	Canada	2.8	China	1.4
Import partners (% of imports)	United States	46.5	China	18.0	Japan	4.6

Social indicators	2005	2010	2017
Population growth rate (average annual %)[k]	1.3	1.6	1.4[b]
Urban population (% of total population)	76.3	77.8	79.2[b]
Urban population growth rate (average annual %)[k]	1.7	1.6	1.6[b]
Fertility rate, total (live births per woman)[k]	2.6	2.4	2.3[b]
Life expectancy at birth (females/males, years)[k]	77.4 / 72.4	78.1 / 73.3	78.9 / 74.0[b]
Population age distribution (0-14 and 60+ years, %)	32.3 / 7.7	29.8 / 8.4	26.7 / 10.1[a]
International migrant stock (000/% of total pop.)[l]	712.5 / 0.6	969.5 / 0.8	1 193.2 / 0.9[b]
Refugees and others of concern to UNHCR (000)	3.4[m]	1.6[m]	5.9[d]
Infant mortality rate (per 1 000 live births)[k]	20.5	19.9	18.8[b]
Health: Total expenditure (% of GDP)	6.0	6.4	6.3[g]
Health: Physicians (per 1 000 pop.)	1.9[n]	1.9	2.1[o]
Education: Government expenditure (% of GDP)	4.9	5.2	5.3[g]
Education: Primary gross enrol. ratio (f/m per 100 pop.)	102.2 / 103.8	102.8 / 104.0	103.2 / 103.6[g]
Education: Secondary gross enrol. ratio (f/m per 100 pop.)	82.6 / 76.0	86.8 / 79.7	93.5 / 87.7[g]
Education: Tertiary gross enrol. ratio (f/m per 100 pop.)	23.3 / 22.9	26.6 / 25.7	30.0 / 29.9[g]
Intentional homicide rate (per 100 000 pop.)	9.0	21.7	16.4[b]
Seats held by women in national parliaments (%)	22.6	27.6	42.6

Environment and infrastructure indicators	2005	2010	2017
Mobile-cellular subscriptions (per 100 inhabitants)	42.6	77.5	85.3[p,b]
Individuals using the Internet (per 100 inhabitants)	17.2[f,q]	31.0[f,q]	57.4[r,s,b]
Research & Development expenditure (% of GDP)	0.4	0.5	0.5[f,g]
Threatened species (number)	748[t]	943	1 162
Forested area (% of land area)	34.5	34.2	34.0[f,g]
CO2 emission estimates (million tons/tons per capita)	466.4 / 4.4	464.3 / 3.9	480.3 / 3.8[g]
Energy production, primary (Petajoules)	10 716	9 040	8 514[g]
Energy supply per capita (Gigajoules)	70	62	62[g]
Tourist/visitor arrivals at national borders (000)[u]	21 915	23 290	32 093[b]
Important sites for terrestrial biodiversity protected (%)	24.1	29.0	31.0
Pop. using improved drinking water (urban/rural, %)	95.0 / 79.8	96.2 / 86.7	97.2 / 92.1[b]
Pop. using improved sanitation facilities (urban/rural, %)	84.6 / 59.5	86.4 / 67.8	88.0 / 74.5[b]
Net Official Development Assist. received (% of GNI)	0.02	0.04	0.03[b]

a Projected estimate (medium fertility variant). b 2015. c Refers to the total population in seventy-six municipalities of the Metropolitan Area of Mexico City. d 2016. e Data classified according to ISIC Rev. 4. f Estimate. g 2014. h Including construction. i Trade data include maquiladoras and exclude goods from customs-bonded warehouses. Total exports include revaluation and exports of silver. j Imports FOB. k Data refers to a 5-year period preceding the reference year. l Including refugees. m Data as at the end of December. n 2000. o 2013. p Provisional data. q December. r Break in the time series. s Population aged 6 years and over. t 2004. u Including nationals residing abroad.

Micronesia (Federated States of)

Region	Micronesia	UN membership date	17 September 1991
Population (000, 2017)	106 [a]	Surface area (km2)	702 [b]
Pop. density (per km2, 2017)	150.8 [a]	Sex ratio (m per 100 f, 2017)	105.1 [a]
Capital city	Palikir	National currency	US Dollar (USD)
Capital city pop. (000)	6.8 [c]		

Economic indicators	2005	2010	2017
GDP: Gross domestic product (million current US$)	251	297	315 [b]
GDP growth rate (annual %, const. 2005 prices)	2.1	3.3	3.7 [b]
GDP per capita (current US$)	2 360.2	2 866.5	3 015.2 [b]
Economy: Agriculture (% of GVA)	24.2	26.7	27.8 [b]
Economy: Industry (% of GVA)	5.7	7.8	6.5 [b]
Economy: Services and other activity (% of GVA)	70.2	65.5	65.8 [b]
Agricultural production index (2004-2006=100)	99	85	99 [c]
Food production index (2004-2006=100)	99	85	99 [c]
International trade: Exports (million US$) [d]	13	23	6 [e]
International trade: Imports (million US$) [d]	128	168	40 [e]
International trade: Balance (million US$) [d]	- 115	- 145	- 34 [e]
Balance of payments, current account (million US$)	...	- 25	22 [c]

Major trading partners						2016
Export partners (% of exports)	Thailand	30.1	Indonesia	25.3	China	17.9
Import partners (% of imports)	Republic of Korea	29.6	United States	24.0	Asia nes [f]	13.6

Social indicators	2005	2010	2017
Population growth rate (average annual %) [g]	- 0.2	- 0.5	0.2 [b]
Urban population (% of total population)	22.3	22.3	22.4 [b]
Urban population growth rate (average annual %) [g]	- 0.2	- 0.5	0.3 [b]
Fertility rate, total (live births per woman) [g]	4.0	3.6	3.3 [b]
Life expectancy at birth (females/males, years) [g]	68.2 / 66.9	69.1 / 67.6	69.8 / 67.7 [b]
Population age distribution (0-14 and 60+ years, %)	38.8 / 5.5	36.9 / 6.2	33.1 / 8.0 [a]
International migrant stock (000/% of total pop.)	2.9 / 2.7	2.8 / 2.7	2.8 / 2.6 [b]
Refugees and others of concern to UNHCR (000)	...	...	~0.0 [e]
Infant mortality rate (per 1 000 live births) [g]	37.9	34.9	33.2 [b]
Health: Total expenditure (% of GDP)	12.1	13.8	13.7 [c]
Health: Physicians (per 1 000 pop.)	0.6	0.2 [h]	...
Education: Government expenditure (% of GDP)	6.7 [i,j]	...	12.5 [b]
Education: Primary gross enrol. ratio (f/m per 100 pop.)	109.8 / 112.8	112.4 / 110.9 [k]	95.7 / 95.4 [b]
Education: Secondary gross enrol. ratio (f/m per 100 pop.)	86.7 / 80.1	... / ...	... / ...
Intentional homicide rate (per 100 000 pop.)	4.6	4.5	4.7 [b]
Seats held by women in national parliaments (%)	0.0	0.0	0.0

Environment and infrastructure indicators	2005	2010	2017
Mobile-cellular subscriptions (per 100 inhabitants)	13.3	26.6	30.3 [i]
Individuals using the Internet (per 100 inhabitants)	11.9	20.0 [i]	31.5 [i,b]
Threatened species (number)	30 [m]	148	167
Forested area (% of land area) [i]	91.4	91.6	91.8 [c]
CO2 emission estimates (million tons/tons per capita)	0.1 / 1.1	0.1 / 1.1	0.2 / 1.4 [c]
Energy production, primary (Petajoules)	0	0	0 [c]
Energy supply per capita (Gigajoules)	16	17	22 [i,c]
Tourist/visitor arrivals at national borders (000) [n]	19	45	30 [b]
Important sites for terrestrial biodiversity protected (%)	0.0	0.0	0.0
Pop. using improved drinking water (urban/rural, %)	94.4 / 88.3	94.7 / 87.6	94.8 / 87.4 [b]
Pop. using improved sanitation facilities (urban/rural, %)	72.6 / 35.0	81.6 / 45.0	85.1 / 49.0 [b]
Net Official Development Assist. received (% of GNI)	41.10	20.79	34.11 [c]

a Projected estimate (medium fertility variant). **b** 2015. **c** 2014. **d** Imports FOB. **e** 2016. **f** Asia not elsewhere specified. **g** Data refers to a 5-year period preceding the reference year. **h** 2009. **i** Estimate. **j** 2000. **k** 2007. **l** 2013. **m** 2004. **n** Arrivals in the States of Kosrae, Chuuk, Pohnpei and Yap; excluding FSM citizens.

Monaco

Region	Western Europe	UN membership date	28 May 1993
Population (000, 2017)	39[a]	Surface area (km2)	2[b]
Pop. density (per km2, 2017)	25 969.8[a]	Sex ratio (m per 100 f, 2017)	94.7[c,d]
Capital city	Monaco	National currency	Euro (EUR)
Capital city pop. (000)	38.1[e]	Exchange rate (per US$)	0.9[f]

Economic indicators	2005	2010	2017
GDP: Gross domestic product (million current US$)	4 203	5 362	6 258[b]
GDP growth rate (annual %, const. 2005 prices)	1.6	2.2	5.4[b]
GDP per capita (current US$)	124 319.0	145 538.1	165 870.6[b]
Economy: Industry (% of GVA)[g,h]	12.2	12.9	13.4[b]
Economy: Services and other activity (% of GVA)[g,h]	87.8	87.1	86.6[b]
Unemployment (% of labour force)	3.6[i,j]	...	...
Labour force participation (female/male pop. %)	35.1 / 57.3[i,j]	... / ...	... / ...

Social indicators	2005	2010	2017
Population growth rate (average annual %)[k]	1.0	1.9	0.6[b]
Urban population (% of total population)	100.0	100.0	100.0[b]
Urban population growth rate (average annual %)[k]	1.0	1.7	0.8[b]
Population age distribution (0-14 and 60+ years, %)	13.2 / 28.9[c,j]	12.7 / 31.2[c,d]	... / ...
International migrant stock (000/% of total pop.)	21.3 / 63.0	21.1 / 57.4	21.0 / 55.8[b]
Refugees and others of concern to UNHCR (000)	...	~0.0[l]	~0.0[f]
Health: Total expenditure (% of GDP)[m]	4.0	4.4	4.3[e]
Health: Physicians (per 1 000 pop.)	...	...	6.6[e]
Education: Government expenditure (% of GDP)	1.2[n]	1.3	1.0[e]
Intentional homicide rate (per 100 000 pop.)	3.0	2.9[o]	...
Seats held by women in national parliaments (%)	20.8	26.1	20.8

Environment and infrastructure indicators	2005	2010	2017
Mobile-cellular subscriptions (per 100 inhabitants)	50.8	63.6	88.8[b]
Individuals using the Internet (per 100 inhabitants)	55.5	75.0	93.4[p,b]
Research & Development expenditure (% of GDP)	~0.0[q]	...	...
Threatened species (number)	9[n]	11	21
Tourist/visitor arrivals at national borders (000)	286	279	331[b]
Pop. using improved drinking water (urban/rural, %)	100.0 / ...	100.0 / ...	100.0 / ...[b]
Pop. using improved sanitation facilities (urban/rural, %)	100.0 / ...	100.0 / ...	100.0 / ...[b]

a Projected estimate (medium fertility variant). **b** 2015. **c** De jure population. **d** 2008. **e** 2014. **f** 2016. **g** Data classified according to ISIC Rev. 4. **h** At producers' prices. **i** Population aged 17 years and over. **j** 2000. **k** Data refers to a 5-year period preceding the reference year. **l** Data as at the end of December. **m** Estimates should be viewed with caution as these are derived from scarce data. **n** 2004. **o** 2006. **p** Estimate. **q** Partial data.

Mongolia

Region	Eastern Asia	UN membership date	27 October 1961
Population (000, 2017)	3 076 [a]	Surface area (km2)	1 564 116 [b]
Pop. density (per km2, 2017)	2.0 [a]	Sex ratio (m per 100 f, 2017)	97.9 [a]
Capital city	Ulaanbaatar	National currency	Tugrik (MNT)
Capital city pop. (000)	1 377.3 [b]	Exchange rate (per US$)	2 489.5 [c]

Economic indicators	2005	2010	2017
GDP: Gross domestic product (million current US$)	2 926	7 189	11 758 [b]
GDP growth rate (annual %, const. 2005 prices)	7.3	6.4	2.3 [b]
GDP per capita (current US$)	1 158.1	2 650.3	3 973.4 [b]
Economy: Agriculture (% of GVA) [d]	17.8	13.1	14.8 [b]
Economy: Industry (% of GVA) [d]	37.4	37.0	34.1 [b]
Economy: Services and other activity (% of GVA) [d]	44.8	50.0	51.1 [b]
Employment: Agriculture (% of employed) [e]	47.9	33.5	28.4
Employment: Industry (% of employed) [e]	11.3	16.2	20.7
Employment: Services (% of employed) [e]	40.8	50.2	51.0
Unemployment (% of labour force)	3.3	6.5	6.3 [e]
Labour force participation (female/male pop. %) [e]	55.4 / 65.2	55.1 / 67.6	56.8 / 69.3
CPI: Consumer Price Index (2000=100)	138 [f]	166 [g,h]	181 [g,i]
Agricultural production index (2004-2006=100)	97	114	147 [j]
Food production index (2004-2006=100)	97	115	149 [j]
Index of industrial production (2005=100) [k]	100	155	183 [j]
International trade: Exports (million US$)	1 064	2 899	4 917 [c]
International trade: Imports (million US$)	1 183	3 278	3 358 [c]
International trade: Balance (million US$)	- 118	- 378	1 559 [c]
Balance of payments, current account (million US$)	88	- 885	- 948 [b]

Major trading partners					2016
Export partners (% of exports)	China	83.5	United Kingdom	7.2	Switzerland	2.3
Import partners (% of imports)	China	35.8	Russian Federation	26.9	Japan	7.2

Social indicators	2005	2010	2017
Population growth rate (average annual %) [l]	1.0	1.4	1.9 [b]
Urban population (% of total population)	62.5	67.6	72.0 [b]
Urban population growth rate (average annual %) [l]	2.8	3.0	2.8 [b]
Fertility rate, total (live births per woman) [l]	2.1	2.4	2.8 [b]
Life expectancy at birth (females/males, years) [l]	67.7 / 60.8	70.3 / 62.4	72.7 / 64.5 [b]
Population age distribution (0-14 and 60+ years, %)	28.9 / 5.6	27.0 / 5.7	29.7 / 6.6 [a]
International migrant stock (000/% of total pop.) [m]	11.5 / 0.5	16.1 / 0.6	17.6 / 0.6 [b]
Refugees and others of concern to UNHCR (000)	0.6 [n]	0.3 [n]	~0.0 [c]
Infant mortality rate (per 1 000 live births) [l]	40.8	30.5	22.8 [b]
Health: Total expenditure (% of GDP)	5.1	4.7	4.7 [j]
Health: Physicians (per 1 000 pop.)	2.8 [o]	2.8	2.9 [j]
Education: Government expenditure (% of GDP)	4.3 [p]	4.6	4.6 [j]
Education: Primary gross enrol. ratio (f/m per 100 pop.)	98.0 / 98.0	124.2 / 127.1	100.0 / 101.8 [b]
Education: Secondary gross enrol. ratio (f/m per 100 pop.)	95.0 / 85.6	94.8 / 88.4	92.4 / 90.5 [b]
Education: Tertiary gross enrol. ratio (f/m per 100 pop.)	55.9 / 33.8	65.3 / 42.5	79.7 / 57.7 [b]
Intentional homicide rate (per 100 000 pop.)	15.8	8.8	7.2 [b]
Seats held by women in national parliaments (%)	6.8	3.9	17.1

Environment and infrastructure indicators	2005	2010	2017
Mobile-cellular subscriptions (per 100 inhabitants)	22.0	92.5	105.0 [b]
Individuals using the Internet (per 100 inhabitants)	1.3 [q]	10.2	21.4 [b]
Research & Development expenditure (% of GDP) [r]	0.2	0.2	0.2 [j]
Threatened species (number)	39 [p]	36	41
Forested area (% of land area) [e]	7.3	8.4	8.1 [j]
CO2 emission estimates (million tons/tons per capita)	8.6 / 3.4	13.8 / 5.1	20.8 / 7.2 [j]
Energy production, primary (Petajoules)	138	655	677 [j]
Energy supply per capita (Gigajoules)	41	62	84 [j]
Tourist/visitor arrivals at national borders (000) [s]	338	456	386 [b]
Important sites for terrestrial biodiversity protected (%)	36.5	39.1	42.0
Pop. using improved drinking water (urban/rural, %)	71.6 / 41.3	69.0 / 50.3	66.4 / 59.2 [b]
Pop. using improved sanitation facilities (urban/rural, %)	65.5 / 31.4	65.9 / 37.0	66.4 / 42.6 [b]
Net Official Development Assist. received (% of GNI)	8.94	4.60	2.21 [b]

a Projected estimate (medium fertility variant). **b** 2015. **c** 2016. **d** Data classified according to ISIC Rev. 4. **e** Estimate. **f** Ulan Bator **g** Index base: 2006=100. **h** Break in the time series. **i** 2011. **j** 2014. **k** Data classified according to ISIC Rev. 3. **l** Data refers to a 5-year period preceding the reference year. **m** Refers to foreign citizens. **n** Data as at the end of December. **o** 2002. **p** 2004. **q** 2000. **r** Partial data. **s** Excluding diplomats and foreign residents in Mongolia.

Montenegro

Region	Southern Europe	UN membership date	28 June 2006
Population (000, 2017)	629[a]	Surface area (km2)	13 812[b]
Pop. density (per km2, 2017)	46.8[a]	Sex ratio (m per 100 f, 2017)	97.4[a]
Capital city	Podgorica	National currency	Euro (EUR)
Capital city pop. (000)	165.0[c]	Exchange rate (per US$)	0.9[d]

Economic indicators

	2005	2010	2017
GDP: Gross domestic product (million current US$)	2 272	4 139	4 020[b]
GDP growth rate (annual %, const. 2005 prices)	4.2	2.5	4.5[b]
GDP per capita (current US$)	3 686.0	6 654.8	6 424.1[b]
Economy: Agriculture (% of GVA)[e]	10.4	9.2	9.8[b]
Economy: Industry (% of GVA)[e]	21.6	20.5	17.5[b]
Economy: Services and other activity (% of GVA)[e]	68.0	70.3	72.6[b]
Employment: Agriculture (% of employed)[f]	8.6	6.8	7.5
Employment: Industry (% of employed)[f]	19.2	18.6	17.3
Employment: Services (% of employed)[f]	72.1	74.7	75.2
Unemployment (% of labour force)	19.6[f]	19.7	17.4[f]
Labour force participation (female/male pop. %)[f]	42.6 / 59.0	42.9 / 58.9	41.8 / 55.9
CPI: Consumer Price Index (2000=100)[g]	100	122	...
Agricultural production index (2004-2006=100)	...	91	66[c]
Food production index (2004-2006=100)	...	91	66[c]
Index of industrial production (2005=100)	100	79[h]	64[h,c]
International trade: Exports (million US$)	...	437	354[d]
International trade: Imports (million US$)	...	2 182	2 263[d]
International trade: Balance (million US$)	...	- 1 745	- 1 908[d]
Balance of payments, current account (million US$)	...	- 952	- 533[b]

Major trading partners

							2016
Export partners (% of exports)	Serbia	25.7	Hungary	10.9	Areas nes[i]	8.7
Import partners (% of imports)	Serbia	22.3	Germany	10.5	China	9.0

Social indicators

	2005	2010	2017
Population growth rate (average annual %)[j]	0.1	0.3	0.1[b]
Urban population (% of total population)	62.2	63.1	64.0[b]
Urban population growth rate (average annual %)[j]	1.4	0.4	0.3[b]
Fertility rate, total (live births per woman)[j]	1.9	1.8	1.7[b]
Life expectancy at birth (females/males, years)[j]	76.2 / 70.6	76.5 / 71.9	78.8 / 74.0[b]
Population age distribution (0-14 and 60+ years, %)	20.2 / 17.0	19.2 / 17.9	18.1 / 21.3[a]
International migrant stock (000/% of total pop.)	... / ...	78.5 / 12.6	82.5 / 13.2[b]
Refugees and others of concern to UNHCR (000)	...	18.3[k]	16.0[d]
Infant mortality rate (per 1 000 live births)[j]	11.6	10.9	4.1[b]
Health: Total expenditure (% of GDP)	8.5	6.9	6.4[c]
Health: Physicians (per 1 000 pop.)	...	2.0	2.3[b]
Education: Primary gross enrol. ratio (f/m per 100 pop.)	112.6 / 112.7	105.8 / 107.7	93.3 / 95.2[b]
Education: Secondary gross enrol. ratio (f/m per 100 pop.)	95.8 / 93.2	101.4 / 100.1	90.3 / 90.4[b]
Education: Tertiary gross enrol. ratio (f/m per 100 pop.)	27.2 / 17.2	61.8 / 49.2	... / ...
Intentional homicide rate (per 100 000 pop.)	...	2.4	2.7[b]
Seats held by women in national parliaments (%)	...	11.1	23.5

Environment and infrastructure indicators

	2005	2010	2017
Mobile-cellular subscriptions (per 100 inhabitants)	88.2	188.7[f]	162.2[b]
Individuals using the Internet (per 100 inhabitants)[f]	27.1	37.5	64.6[b]
Research & Development expenditure (% of GDP)	0.9	1.1[l]	0.4[c]
Threatened species (number)	...	72	98
Forested area (% of land area)[f]	...	61.5	61.5[c]
CO2 emission estimates (million tons/tons per capita)	... / ...	2.6 / 4.1	2.2 / 3.5[c]
Energy production, primary (Petajoules)	25	35	29[c]
Energy supply per capita (Gigajoules)	67	77	64[c]
Tourist/visitor arrivals at national borders (000)	272	1 088	1 560[b]
Important sites for terrestrial biodiversity protected (%)	2.1	2.1	2.1
Pop. using improved drinking water (urban/rural, %)	99.3 / 95.6	99.8 / 97.4	100.0 / 99.2[b]
Pop. using improved sanitation facilities (urban/rural, %)	92.5 / 88.2	95.4 / 90.2	98.0 / 92.2[b]
Net Official Development Assist. received (% of GNI)	0.17	1.95	2.44[b]

a Projected estimate (medium fertility variant). **b** 2015. **c** 2014. **d** 2016. **e** Data classified according to ISIC Rev. 4. **f** Estimate. **g** Index base: 2005=100. **h** Excluding water and waste management. **i** Areas not elsewhere specified. **j** Data refers to a 5-year period preceding the reference year. **k** Data as at the end of December. **l** 2007.

Montserrat

Region	Caribbean	Population (000, 2017)	5[a]
Surface area (km2)	103[b]	Pop. density (per km2, 2017)	51.8[a]
Sex ratio (m per 100 f, 2017)	106.0[c]	Capital city	Brades Estate
National currency	E. Caribbean Dollar (XCD)[d]	Capital city pop. (000)	0.5[e]
Exchange rate (per US$)	2.7[c]		

Economic indicators	2005	2010	2017
GDP: Gross domestic product (million current US$)	49	56	59[b]
GDP growth rate (annual %, const. 2005 prices)	3.1	- 2.8	0.4[b]
GDP per capita (current US$)	10 231.1	11 207.6	11 553.4[b]
Economy: Agriculture (% of GVA)	0.9	1.1	1.4[b]
Economy: Industry (% of GVA)	16.7	13.3	12.7[b]
Economy: Services and other activity (% of GVA)	82.5	85.7	85.9[b]
Unemployment (% of labour force)	9.5[f,g]	...	5.6[h]
Labour force participation (female/male pop. %)	80.6 / 89.2[f,g]	... / ...	... / ...
Agricultural production index (2004-2006=100)	99	102	103[e]
Food production index (2004-2006=100)	99	103	103[e]
International trade: Exports (million US$)	1	1	4[c]
International trade: Imports (million US$)	30	29	36[c]
International trade: Balance (million US$)	- 28	- 28	- 32[c]
Balance of payments, current account (million US$)	- 16	- 19	- 27[i]

Major trading partners						2016
Export partners (% of exports)	United States	29.0	France	23.0	Saint Kitts and Nevis	22.2
Import partners (% of imports)	United States	72.8	Trinidad and Tobago	6.0	United Kingdom	4.1

Social indicators	2005	2010	2017
Population growth rate (average annual %)[j]	- 0.7	0.7	0.7[b]
Urban population (% of total population)	9.3	9.2	9.0[b]
Urban population growth rate (average annual %)[j]	29.3	0.3	0.7[b]
Fertility rate, total (live births per woman)	1.7[k]	...	...
Population age distribution (0-14 and 60+ years, %)	19.3 / 19.9[g]	19.6 / 19.0[l,m]	19.7 / 19.6[n,h]
International migrant stock (000/% of total pop.)	1.2 / 26.0	1.3 / 25.8	1.4 / 26.4[b]
Refugees and others of concern to UNHCR (000)	...	~0.0[o]	...
Education: Government expenditure (% of GDP)	...	5.1[p]	...
Education: Primary gross enrol. ratio (f/m per 100 pop.)	118.7 / 114.6[q]	112.9 / 101.2[q,r]	... / ...
Education: Secondary gross enrol. ratio (f/m per 100 pop.)	122.5 / 111.0[q]	103.2 / 101.1[q,r]	... / ...
Intentional homicide rate (per 100 000 pop.)	20.9	20.4[s]	...

Environment and infrastructure indicators	2005	2010	2017
Mobile-cellular subscriptions (per 100 inhabitants)	9.9[t]	84.8	96.6[q,b]
Individuals using the Internet (per 100 inhabitants)	...	35.0	54.6[h]
Threatened species (number)	21[k]	35	55
Forested area (% of land area)[q]	25.0	25.0	25.0[e]
CO2 emission estimates (million tons/tons per capita)	~0.0 / 6.6	0.1 / 13.0	~0.0 / 9.6[e]
Energy supply per capita (Gigajoules)	93[q]	175	133[e]
Tourist/visitor arrivals at national borders (000)	10	6	9[b]
Important sites for terrestrial biodiversity protected (%)	0.0	0.0	30.6
Pop. using improved drinking water (urban/rural, %)	98.9 / 99.0	98.9 / 99.0	99.0 / 99.0[b]
Pop. using improved sanitation facilities (urban/rural, %)	82.9 / 82.9	... / ...	... / ...

a Projected estimate (medium fertility variant). b 2015. c 2016. d East Caribbean Dollar. e 2014. f Break in the time series. g 2001. h 2011. i 2013. j Data refers to a 5-year period preceding the reference year. k 2004. l Intercensus data. m 2006. n De jure population. o Data as at the end of December. p 2009. q Estimate. r 2007. s 2008. t 2000.

Morocco

Region	Northern Africa	
Population (000, 2017)	35 740 [a]	
Pop. density (per km2, 2017)	80.1 [a]	
Capital city	Rabat	
Capital city pop. (000)	1 966.8 [c,b]	

UN membership date	12 November 1956
Surface area (km2)	446 550 [b]
Sex ratio (m per 100 f, 2017)	98.1 [a]
National currency	Moroccan Dirham (MAD)
Exchange rate (per US$)	10.1 [d]

Economic indicators

	2005	2010	2017
GDP: Gross domestic product (million current US$) [e]	62 545	93 217	100 359 [b]
GDP growth rate (annual %, const. 2005 prices) [e]	3.0	3.8	4.4 [b]
GDP per capita (current US$) [e]	2 058.4	2 903.3	2 919.3 [b]
Economy: Agriculture (% of GVA) [e]	13.1	14.4	13.7 [b]
Economy: Industry (% of GVA) [e]	28.9	28.6	28.9 [b]
Economy: Services and other activity (% of GVA) [e]	58.0	56.9	57.4 [b]
Employment: Agriculture (% of employed) [f]	40.3	36.3	32.6
Employment: Industry (% of employed) [f]	18.4	20.0	20.7
Employment: Services (% of employed) [f]	41.3	43.7	46.8
Unemployment (% of labour force)	11.0	9.1	10.4 [f]
Labour force participation (female/male pop. %) [f]	27.6 / 77.2	25.7 / 75.2	25.6 / 74.5
CPI: Consumer Price Index (2000=100)	107	108 [g,h]	113 [h,i]
Agricultural production index (2004-2006=100)	93	126	130 [i]
Food production index (2004-2006=100)	93	126	130 [i]
International trade: Exports (million US$)	11 185	17 765	22 858 [d]
International trade: Imports (million US$)	20 803	35 379	41 696 [d]
International trade: Balance (million US$)	- 9 618	- 17 614	- 18 838 [d]
Balance of payments, current account (million US$)	949	- 4 209	- 2 161 [b]

Major trading partners

							2016
Export partners (% of exports)	Spain	23.8	France	21.1	Italy	4.6
Import partners (% of imports)	Spain	15.7	France	13.2	China	9.1

Social indicators

	2005	2010	2017
Population growth rate (average annual %) [j]	1.1	1.2	1.4 [b]
Urban population (% of total population)	55.1	57.7	60.2 [b]
Urban population growth rate (average annual %) [j]	1.6	1.9	2.3 [b]
Fertility rate, total (live births per woman) [j]	2.7	2.6	2.6 [b]
Life expectancy at birth (females/males, years) [j]	71.4 / 68.5	74.4 / 71.3	76.0 / 73.7 [b]
Population age distribution (0-14 and 60+ years, %)	30.8 / 8.2	28.5 / 8.6	27.4 / 10.7 [a]
International migrant stock (000/% of total pop.) [k]	54.4 / 0.2	70.9 / 0.2	88.5 / 0.3 [b]
Refugees and others of concern to UNHCR (000)	2.1 [l]	1.1 [l]	6.4 [d]
Infant mortality rate (per 1 000 live births) [j]	36.6	33.2	28.1 [b]
Health: Total expenditure (% of GDP)	5.1	5.9	5.9 [i]
Health: Physicians (per 1 000 pop.)	0.5 [m]	0.7 [n]	0.6 [i]
Education: Government expenditure (% of GDP)	...	5.3 [n]	...
Education: Primary gross enrol. ratio (f/m per 100 pop.)	99.8 / 110.0	108.8 / 115.6	111.6 / 117.7 [b]
Education: Secondary gross enrol. ratio (f/m per 100 pop.)	45.8 / 53.7	58.3 / 66.9	63.5 / 74.4 [o]
Education: Tertiary gross enrol. ratio (f/m per 100 pop.)	10.5 / 13.0	13.7 / 15.2	27.5 / 28.7 [b]
Intentional homicide rate (per 100 000 pop.)	1.5	1.4	1.0 [i]
Seats held by women in national parliaments (%)	10.8	10.5	20.5

Environment and infrastructure indicators

	2005	2010	2017
Mobile-cellular subscriptions (per 100 inhabitants)	41.1	101.1	126.9 [b]
Individuals using the Internet (per 100 inhabitants)	15.1 [p,q]	52.0 [f,r,s]	57.1 [t,u,b]
Research & Development expenditure (% of GDP)	0.7 [v]	0.7	...
Threatened species (number)	50 [m]	157	207
Forested area (% of land area) [f]	12.1	12.7	12.6 [i]
CO2 emission estimates (million tons/tons per capita)	45.8 / 1.5	56.0 / 1.7	59.9 / 1.7 [i]
Energy production, primary (Petajoules)	72	81	78 [i]
Energy supply per capita (Gigajoules)	20	23	23 [i]
Tourist/visitor arrivals at national borders (000) [w]	5 843	9 288	10 177 [b]
Important sites for terrestrial biodiversity protected (%)	13.8	15.2	43.5
Pop. using improved drinking water (urban/rural, %)	96.9 / 61.0	98.1 / 63.7	98.7 / 65.3 [b]
Pop. using improved sanitation facilities (urban/rural, %)	82.9 / 51.7	83.7 / 60.3	84.1 / 65.5 [b]
Net Official Development Assist. received (% of GNI)	1.18	1.07	1.51 [b]

a Projected estimate (medium fertility variant). **b** 2015. **c** Including Salé and Temara. **d** 2016. **e** Including Western Sahara. **f** Estimate. **g** Break in the time series. **h** Index base: 2006=100. **i** 2014. **j** Data refers to a 5-year period preceding the reference year. **k** Refers to foreign citizens. **l** Data as at the end of December. **m** 2004. **n** 2009. **o** 2012. **p** Population aged 12 to 65 years. **q** Users in the last month. **r** Living in electrified areas. **s** Population aged 6 to 74 years. **t** Users in the last 3 months. **u** Population aged 5 years and over. **v** 2003. **w** Including nationals residing abroad.

Mozambique

Region	Eastern Africa	UN membership date	16 September 1975	
Population (000, 2017)	29 669 [a]	Surface area (km2)	799 380 [b]	
Pop. density (per km2, 2017)	37.7 [a]	Sex ratio (m per 100 f, 2017)	95.5 [a]	
Capital city	Maputo	National currency	Mozambique Metical (MZN)	
Capital city pop. (000)	1 187.2 [b]	Exchange rate (per US$)	71.4 [c]	

Economic indicators	2005	2010	2017
GDP: Gross domestic product (million current US$)	7 724	10 154	14 806 [b]
GDP growth rate (annual %, const. 2005 prices)	8.7	6.7	6.6 [b]
GDP per capita (current US$)	365.6	417.5	529.2 [b]
Economy: Agriculture (% of GVA) [d]	25.4	28.9	24.6 [b]
Economy: Industry (% of GVA) [d]	20.7	18.6	21.0 [b]
Economy: Services and other activity (% of GVA) [d]	53.8	52.5	54.4 [b]
Employment: Agriculture (% of employed) [e]	76.4	75.5	75.0
Employment: Industry (% of employed) [e]	3.7	3.8	4.1
Employment: Services (% of employed) [e]	20.0	20.7	21.0
Unemployment (% of labour force) [e]	23.2	23.5	24.1
Labour force participation (female/male pop. %) [e]	87.0 / 82.8	84.3 / 78.7	82.2 / 75.6
CPI: Consumer Price Index (2000=100)	173 [f]	287	350 [g]
Agricultural production index (2004-2006=100)	96	151	137 [g]
Food production index (2004-2006=100)	95	157	137 [g]
International trade: Exports (million US$)	1 745	2 243	3 352 [c]
International trade: Imports (million US$)	2 408	3 564	5 295 [c]
International trade: Balance (million US$)	- 663	- 1 321	- 1 943 [c]
Balance of payments, current account (million US$)	- 761	- 1 679	- 5 833 [b]

Major trading partners					2016
Export partners (% of exports)	South Africa	21.0	Netherlands	20.9	India	20.2
Import partners (% of imports)	South Africa	30.0	Singapore	8.1	China	7.9

Social indicators	2005	2010	2017
Population growth rate (average annual %) [h]	2.9	2.9	2.9 [b]
Urban population (% of total population)	30.0	31.0	32.2 [b]
Urban population growth rate (average annual %) [h]	3.4	3.3	3.3 [b]
Fertility rate, total (live births per woman) [h]	5.8	5.6	5.4 [b]
Life expectancy at birth (females/males, years) [h]	51.2 / 47.9	55.0 / 51.4	58.1 / 54.0 [b]
Population age distribution (0-14 and 60+ years, %)	45.6 / 4.8	45.7 / 4.8	44.8 / 4.8 [a]
International migrant stock (000/% of total pop.) [i]	204.8 / 1.0	214.6 / 0.9	222.9 / 0.8 [b]
Refugees and others of concern to UNHCR (000)	6.0 [j]	10.0 [j]	24.0 [c]
Infant mortality rate (per 1 000 live births) [h]	94.3	78.1	67.3 [b]
Health: Total expenditure (% of GDP) [k]	6.9	5.4	7.0 [g]
Health: Physicians (per 1 000 pop.)	~0.0 [l]	~0.0	0.1 [m]
Education: Government expenditure (% of GDP)	4.4	4.3 [n]	6.5 [m]
Education: Primary gross enrol. ratio (f/m per 100 pop.)	87.8 / 104.4	103.0 / 114.7	101.2 / 110.4 [e,b]
Education: Secondary gross enrol. ratio (f/m per 100 pop.)	10.7 / 15.5	21.7 / 26.6	31.1 / 33.8 [e,b]
Education: Tertiary gross enrol. ratio (f/m per 100 pop.)	0.9 / 1.9	3.6 / 5.5	5.4 / 7.4 [b]
Intentional homicide rate (per 100 000 pop.)	5.2	3.6	3.4 [o]
Seats held by women in national parliaments (%)	34.8	39.2	39.6

Environment and infrastructure indicators	2005	2010	2017
Mobile-cellular subscriptions (per 100 inhabitants)	7.2	30.1	74.2 [b]
Individuals using the Internet (per 100 inhabitants)	0.9 [e]	4.2	9.0 [e,b]
Research & Development expenditure (% of GDP)	0.4 [p,q,r]	0.4 [f,s]	...
Threatened species (number)	115 [l]	209	309
Forested area (% of land area)	51.0	49.6	48.5 [e,g]
CO2 emission estimates (million tons/tons per capita)	1.8 / 0.1	2.7 / 0.1	8.4 / 0.3 [g]
Energy production, primary (Petajoules)	430	516	779 [g]
Energy supply per capita (Gigajoules)	18	17	20 [g]
Tourist/visitor arrivals at national borders (000)	578	1 718 [f,t]	1 552 [t,b]
Important sites for terrestrial biodiversity protected (%)	22.2	22.2	36.5
Pop. using improved drinking water (urban/rural, %)	77.0 / 31.0	79.2 / 34.8	80.6 / 37.0 [b]
Pop. using improved sanitation facilities (urban/rural, %)	39.0 / 6.8	41.1 / 8.9	42.4 / 10.1 [b]
Net Official Development Assist. received (% of GNI)	17.52	19.80	12.54 [b]

a Projected estimate (medium fertility variant). **b** 2015. **c** 2016. **d** Data classified according to ISIC Rev. 4. **e** Estimate. **f** Break in the time series. **g** 2014. **h** Data refers to a 5-year period preceding the reference year. **i** Including refugees. **j** Data as at the end of December. **k** Data revision. **l** 2004. **m** 2013. **n** 2006. **o** 2011. **p** Overestimated or based on overestimated data. **q** S&T budget instead of R&D expenditure. **r** 2002. **s** Excluding business enterprise. **t** The data of all the border posts of the country are used.

Myanmar

Region	South-eastern Asia	
Population (000, 2017)	53 371 [a]	
Pop. density (per km2, 2017)	81.7 [a]	
Capital city	Nay Pyi Taw	
Capital city pop. (000)	1 029.7 [b]	

UN membership date	19 April 1948
Surface area (km2)	676 577 [b]
Sex ratio (m per 100 f, 2017)	95.5 [a]
National currency	Kyat (MMK)
Exchange rate (per US$)	1 357.5 [c]

Economic indicators	2005	2010	2017
GDP: Gross domestic product (million current US$)	11 931	41 445	62 601 [b]
GDP growth rate (annual %, const. 2005 prices)	13.6	10.2	7.3 [b]
GDP per capita (current US$)	238.7	801.1	1 161.5 [b]
Economy: Agriculture (% of GVA) [d]	46.7	36.9	26.7 [b]
Economy: Industry (% of GVA) [d]	17.5	26.5	34.5 [b]
Economy: Services and other activity (% of GVA) [d,e]	35.8	36.7	38.7 [b]
Employment: Agriculture (% of employed) [f]	44.0	38.3	23.6
Employment: Industry (% of employed) [f]	11.7	13.8	14.6
Employment: Services (% of employed) [f]	44.3	48.0	61.7
Unemployment (% of labour force) [f]	0.9	0.8	0.8
Labour force participation (female/male pop. %) [f]	75.4 / 80.8	75.8 / 81.5	74.7 / 80.8
CPI: Consumer Price Index (2000=100)	297 [g]	156 [g,h]	166 [h,i]
Agricultural production index (2004-2006=100)	99	135	130 [j]
Food production index (2004-2006=100)	99	135	128 [j]
International trade: Exports (million US$)	3 776	7 625	11 673 [c]
International trade: Imports (million US$)	1 907	4 164	15 696 [c]
International trade: Balance (million US$)	1 869	3 461	- 4 023 [c]
Balance of payments, current account (million US$)	582	1 574	- 3 921 [b]

Major trading partners						2016
Export partners (% of exports)	China	40.8	Thailand	19.2	India	8.9
Import partners (% of imports)	China	34.4	Singapore	14.5	Thailand	12.7

Social indicators	2005	2010	2017
Population growth rate (average annual %) [k]	1.0	0.7	0.9 [b]
Urban population (% of total population)	28.9	31.4	34.1 [b]
Urban population growth rate (average annual %) [k]	2.1	2.3	2.5 [b]
Fertility rate, total (live births per woman) [k]	2.9	2.6	2.3 [b]
Life expectancy at birth (females/males, years) [k]	65.0 / 60.9	66.3 / 62.2	68.3 / 63.7 [b]
Population age distribution (0-14 and 60+ years, %)	30.9 / 7.0	30.0 / 7.5	26.8 / 9.4 [a]
International migrant stock (000/% of total pop.) [l]	83.0 / 0.2	76.4 / 0.1	73.3 / 0.1 [b]
Refugees and others of concern to UNHCR (000)	236.5 [m]	859.4 [m]	1 392.1 [c]
Infant mortality rate (per 1 000 live births) [k]	57.9	52.2	45.0 [b]
Health: Total expenditure (% of GDP) [n]	1.8	1.9	2.3 [j]
Health: Physicians (per 1 000 pop.)	0.4	0.5	0.6 [i]
Education: Primary gross enrol. ratio (f/m per 100 pop.)	98.4 / 98.2	96.3 / 97.1	98.3 / 101.0 [j]
Education: Secondary gross enrol. ratio (f/m per 100 pop.)	43.6 / 45.0	49.3 / 47.0	52.0 / 50.6 [i]
Education: Tertiary gross enrol. ratio (f/m per 100 pop.)	... / ...	12.2 / 8.9 [o]	14.9 / 12.1 [i]
Intentional homicide rate (per 100 000 pop.)	1.5	1.6	2.4 [b]
Seats held by women in national parliaments (%)	...	...	10.2

Environment and infrastructure indicators	2005	2010	2017
Mobile-cellular subscriptions (per 100 inhabitants)	0.3	1.1 [f]	76.7 [b]
Individuals using the Internet (per 100 inhabitants)	0.1	0.2	21.8 [f,b]
Research & Development expenditure (% of GDP)	0.2 [p,q]	...	...
Threatened species (number)	147 [r]	249	321
Forested area (% of land area)	51.0	48.6	45.3 [f,j]
CO2 emission estimates (million tons/tons per capita)	11.6 / 0.3	12.5 / 0.3	21.6 / 0.4 [j]
Energy production, primary (Petajoules)	927	962	1 078 [j]
Energy supply per capita (Gigajoules)	13	13	15 [j]
Tourist/visitor arrivals at national borders (000)	660	792	4 681 [b]
Important sites for terrestrial biodiversity protected (%)	22.6	22.6	22.6
Pop. using improved drinking water (urban/rural, %)	88.0 / 66.0	91.4 / 72.0	92.7 / 74.4 [b]
Pop. using improved sanitation facilities (urban/rural, %)	81.0 / 64.6	83.4 / 73.5	84.3 / 77.1 [b]
Net Official Development Assist. received (% of GNI)	...	...	2.23 [j]

a Projected estimate (medium fertility variant). **b** 2015. **c** 2016. **d** At producers' prices. **e** Includes gas and water. **f** Estimate. **g** Break in the time series. **h** Index base: 2006=100. **i** 2012. **j** 2014. **k** Data refers to a 5-year period preceding the reference year. **l** Refers to foreign citizens. **m** Data as at the end of December. **n** Newly found data for government expenditures for years 2012-2014 (UNICEP) has made some ratios have kinks for these years. The market exchange rate is used to estimate the per capita figures. Revision of PPPs has increased per capita (PPP) values for all years. **o** 2007. **p** Partial data. **q** 2002. **r** 2004.

Namibia

Region	Southern Africa	UN membership date	23 April 1990
Population (000, 2017)	2 534[a]	Surface area (km2)	824 116[b]
Pop. density (per km2, 2017)	3.1[a]	Sex ratio (m per 100 f, 2017)	94.7[a]
Capital city	Windhoek	National currency	Namibia Dollar (NAD)
Capital city pop. (000)	368.0[b]	Exchange rate (per US$)	13.7[c]

Economic indicators	2005	2010	2017
GDP: Gross domestic product (million current US$)	7 121	11 282	11 491[b]
GDP growth rate (annual %, const. 2005 prices)	2.5	6.0	5.3[b]
GDP per capita (current US$)	3 513.2	5 143.1	4 673.6[b]
Economy: Agriculture (% of GVA)	11.4	9.2	6.6[b]
Economy: Industry (% of GVA)	27.3	29.8	30.6[b]
Economy: Services and other activity (% of GVA)	61.3	61.1	62.8[b]
Employment: Agriculture (% of employed)[d]	35.6	31.7	29.1
Employment: Industry (% of employed)[d]	13.4	12.7	14.6
Employment: Services (% of employed)[d]	51.0	55.5	56.3
Unemployment (% of labour force)	23.1[d]	22.1	24.9[d]
Labour force participation (female/male pop. %)[d]	55.5 / 67.7	56.5 / 66.3	56.4 / 64.3
CPI: Consumer Price Index (2000=100)[e]	114[f]	160	200[g]
Agricultural production index (2004-2006=100)	104	90	88[g]
Food production index (2004-2006=100)	104	90	89[g]
Index of industrial production (2005=100)[h]	100	116	127[i]
International trade: Exports (million US$)	2 726	5 848	4 816[c]
International trade: Imports (million US$)	2 525	5 980	6 721[c]
International trade: Balance (million US$)	201	- 131	- 1 905[c]
Balance of payments, current account (million US$)	267	- 717	- 1 700[b]

Major trading partners						2016
Export partners (% of exports)	Switzerland	18.8	South Africa	16.0	Botswana	14.1
Import partners (% of imports)	South Africa	57.2	Botswana	6.8	Zambia	4.1

Social indicators	2005	2010	2017
Population growth rate (average annual %)[j]	1.4	1.3	2.2[b]
Urban population (% of total population)	36.6	41.6	46.7[b]
Urban population growth rate (average annual %)[j]	3.8	4.0	4.2[b]
Fertility rate, total (live births per woman)[j]	3.8	3.6	3.6[b]
Life expectancy at birth (females/males, years)[j]	55.9 / 51.7	56.6 / 53.3	64.3 / 59.1[b]
Population age distribution (0-14 and 60+ years, %)	39.8 / 5.0	38.4 / 5.2	36.7 / 5.5[a]
International migrant stock (000/% of total pop.)	106.3 / 5.2	102.4 / 4.7	93.9 / 3.8[b]
Refugees and others of concern to UNHCR (000)	9.1[k]	8.8[k]	4.8[c]
Infant mortality rate (per 1 000 live births)[j]	59.4	46.6	36.4[b]
Health: Physicians (per 1 000 pop.)	0.3[l]	0.4[m]	...
Education: Government expenditure (% of GDP)	6.1[n]	8.3	...
Education: Primary gross enrol. ratio (f/m per 100 pop.)	108.9 / 109.2	106.3 / 109.0	109.5 / 113.3[i]
Education: Secondary gross enrol. ratio (f/m per 100 pop.)	67.2 / 59.8	69.6 / 60.1[m]	... / ...
Education: Tertiary gross enrol. ratio (f/m per 100 pop.)	6.3 / 7.4	10.4 / 8.2[o]	... / ...
Intentional homicide rate (per 100 000 pop.)	17.6[l]	14.3	16.9[p]
Seats held by women in national parliaments (%)	25.0	26.9[q]	41.3

Environment and infrastructure indicators	2005	2010	2017
Mobile-cellular subscriptions (per 100 inhabitants)	22.1	89.5	102.1[b]
Individuals using the Internet (per 100 inhabitants)	4.0[d]	11.6	22.3[d,b]
Research & Development expenditure (% of GDP)	...	0.1[r,s]	...
Threatened species (number)	69[l]	92	115
Forested area (% of land area)[d]	9.3	8.9	8.5[g]
CO2 emission estimates (million tons/tons per capita)	2.3 / 1.1	3.1 / 1.4	3.8 / 1.6[g]
Energy production, primary (Petajoules)	17	17	19[g]
Energy supply per capita (Gigajoules)	26	30	31[g]
Tourist/visitor arrivals at national borders (000)	778	984	1 388[b]
Important sites for terrestrial biodiversity protected (%)	44.6	82.4	85.4
Pop. using improved drinking water (urban/rural, %)	98.4 / 74.2	98.3 / 79.4	98.2 / 84.6[b]
Pop. using improved sanitation facilities (urban/rural, %)	57.1 / 14.0	55.8 / 15.4	54.5 / 16.8[b]
Net Official Development Assist. received (% of GNI)	1.59	2.41	1.24[b]

a Projected estimate (medium fertility variant). b 2015. c 2016. d Estimate. e Index base: 2002=100. f Break in the time series. g 2014. h Data classified according to ISIC Rev. 3. i 2013. j Data refers to a 5-year period preceding the reference year. k Data as at the end of December. l 2004. m 2007. n 2003. o 2008. p 2012. q Figure excludes 11 members yet to be sworn in. r Partial data. s Excluding government.

Nauru

Region	Micronesia	UN membership date	14 September 1999
Population (000, 2017)	11 [a]	Surface area (km2)	21 [b]
Pop. density (per km2, 2017)	568.0 [a]	Sex ratio (m per 100 f, 2017)	101.9 [c,d]
Capital city	Yaren	National currency	Australian Dollar (AUD)
Capital city pop. (000)	10.1 [e,f]	Exchange rate (per US$)	1.4 [d]

Economic indicators	2005	2010	2017
GDP: Gross domestic product (million current US$)	26	62	189 [b]
GDP growth rate (annual %, const. 2005 prices)	- 12.1	20.1	18.7 [b]
GDP per capita (current US$)	2 599.4	6 233.9	18 469.2 [b]
Economy: Agriculture (% of GVA) [g]	7.8	4.2	3.0 [b]
Economy: Industry (% of GVA) [g]	- 6.5	47.4	59.9 [b]
Economy: Services and other activity (% of GVA) [g]	98.7	48.4	37.1 [b]
Unemployment (% of labour force)	22.7 [h,i]	...	23.0 [c,j]
Labour force participation (female/male pop. %)	69.6 / 86.8 [h,i]	... / ...	49.3 / 78.9 [j]
Agricultural production index (2004-2006=100)	100	106	112 [f]
Food production index (2004-2006=100)	100	106	112 [f]

Social indicators	2005	2010	2017
Population growth rate (average annual %) [k]	0.1	- 0.2	2.3 [b]
Urban population (% of total population)	100.0	100.0	100.0 [b]
Urban population growth rate (average annual %) [k]	0.1	- 0.2	0.2 [b]
Fertility rate, total (live births per woman)	...	...	3.9 [l,m]
Life expectancy at birth (females/males, years)	64.0 / 57.0 [n]	58.2 / 52.5 [o,p]	64.8 / 57.8 [c,l,m]
Population age distribution (0-14 and 60+ years, %)	38.1 / 2.5 [i]	... / ...	39.5 / 4.0 [c,d]
International migrant stock (000/% of total pop.) [q]	2.3 / 22.3	2.1 / 21.1	3.2 / 31.1 [b]
Refugees and others of concern to UNHCR (000)	...	...	0.8 [d]
Infant mortality rate (per 1 000 live births)	...	...	18.0 [l,m]
Health: Total expenditure (% of GDP) [r]	12.6	9.1	3.3 [f]
Health: Physicians (per 1 000 pop.)	1.0 [s]	1.0	...
Education: Primary gross enrol. ratio (f/m per 100 pop.) [t]	128.5 / 122.3	96.0 / 90.1 [u]	100.4 / 109.5 [f]
Education: Secondary gross enrol. ratio (f/m per 100 pop.) [t]	50.3 / 44.4	68.9 / 57.6 [u]	83.4 / 81.9 [f]
Intentional homicide rate (per 100 000 pop.)	...	...	1.3 [v]
Seats held by women in national parliaments (%)	0.0	0.0	10.5

Environment and infrastructure indicators	2005	2010	2017
Mobile-cellular subscriptions (per 100 inhabitants)	12.0 [t,n]	61.8	67.8 [v]
Individuals using the Internet (per 100 inhabitants)	...	...	54.0 [j]
Threatened species (number)	5 [s]	74	82
Forested area (% of land area) [t]	0.0	0.0	0.0 [f]
CO2 emission estimates (million tons/tons per capita)	0.1 / 6.1	~0.0 / 4.3	~0.0 / 4.8 [f]
Energy production, primary (Petajoules)	...	0 [t]	0 [f]
Energy supply per capita (Gigajoules)	84 [t]	58	63 [t,f]
Pop. using improved drinking water (urban/rural, %)	94.4 / ...	95.7 / ...	96.5 / ... [b]
Pop. using improved sanitation facilities (urban/rural, %)	65.7 / ...	65.6 / ...	65.6 / ... [b]

a Projected estimate (medium fertility variant). b 2015. c Break in the time series. d 2016. e Refers to Nauru. f 2014. g At producers' prices. h Population aged 16 years and over. i 2002. j 2011. k Data refers to a 5-year period preceding the reference year. l Data refers to a 3-year period up to and including the reference year. m 2013. n 2000. o Data refers to a 6-year period up to and including the reference year. p 2007. q Refers to foreign citizens. r Data revision. s 2004. t Estimate. u 2008. v 2012.

Nepal

Region	Southern Asia	UN membership date	14 December 1955
Population (000, 2017)	29 305[a]	Surface area (km2)	147 181[b]
Pop. density (per km2, 2017)	204.4[a]	Sex ratio (m per 100 f, 2017)	94.3[a]
Capital city	Kathmandu	National currency	Nepalese Rupee (NPR)
Capital city pop. (000)	1 182.6[c,b]	Exchange rate (per US$)	109.0[d]

Economic indicators

	2005	2010	2017
GDP: Gross domestic product (million current US$)	8 259	16 281	20 658[b]
GDP growth rate (annual %, const. 2005 prices)	3.1	4.8	2.7[b]
GDP per capita (current US$)	323.8	605.8	724.5[b]
Economy: Agriculture (% of GVA)	35.2	35.4	31.8[b]
Economy: Industry (% of GVA)	17.1	15.1	14.9[b]
Economy: Services and other activity (% of GVA)	47.7	49.5	53.3[b]
Employment: Agriculture (% of employed)[e]	71.6	74.3	72.6
Employment: Industry (% of employed)[e]	11.9	10.5	10.9
Employment: Services (% of employed)[e]	16.6	15.2	16.5
Unemployment (% of labour force)[e]	3.2	2.5	3.0
Labour force participation (female/male pop. %)[e]	80.4 / 89.0	79.8 / 87.5	79.7 / 86.7
CPI: Consumer Price Index (2000=100)	123[f]	193[g]	271[h]
Agricultural production index (2004-2006=100)	100	114	139[h]
Food production index (2004-2006=100)	100	114	139[h]
International trade: Exports (million US$)	863	874	703[d]
International trade: Imports (million US$)	2 282	5 116	5 249[d]
International trade: Balance (million US$)	- 1 419	- 4 242	- 4 547[d]
Balance of payments, current account (million US$)	153	- 128	2 447[b]

Major trading partners

						2016
Export partners (% of exports)	India	63.5	United States	10.7	Germany	4.1
Import partners (% of imports)	India	60.6	China	13.9	United Arab Emirates	4.0

Social indicators

	2005	2010	2017
Population growth rate (average annual %)[i]	1.5	1.1	1.2[b]
Urban population (% of total population)	15.2	16.8	18.6[b]
Urban population growth rate (average annual %)[i]	4.2	3.2	3.2[b]
Fertility rate, total (live births per woman)[i]	3.6	3.0	2.3[b]
Life expectancy at birth (females/males, years)[i]	65.2 / 62.9	68.1 / 65.5	70.4 / 67.4[b]
Population age distribution (0-14 and 60+ years, %)	39.7 / 6.7	37.0 / 7.4	30.9 / 8.8[a]
International migrant stock (000/% of total pop.)[j]	679.5 / 2.7	578.7 / 2.2	518.3 / 1.8[b]
Refugees and others of concern to UNHCR (000)	538.6[k]	891.3[k]	30.7[d]
Infant mortality rate (per 1 000 live births)[i]	52.9	41.3	32.8[b]
Health: Total expenditure (% of GDP)	5.7	6.4	5.8[h]
Health: Physicians (per 1 000 pop.)	0.2[l]	...	...
Education: Government expenditure (% of GDP)	3.4	3.6	3.7[b]
Education: Primary gross enrol. ratio (f/m per 100 pop.)	110.1 / 120.3	147.1 / 137.8	141.2 / 130.7[d]
Education: Secondary gross enrol. ratio (f/m per 100 pop.)[e]	43.6 / 53.9	57.3 / 60.3	72.2 / 67.1[d]
Education: Tertiary gross enrol. ratio (f/m per 100 pop.)	5.6 / 10.6	11.1 / 18.2	15.1 / 14.8[b]
Intentional homicide rate (per 100 000 pop.)	3.6	3.0	2.3[h]
Seats held by women in national parliaments (%)	5.9[m]	33.2	29.6

Environment and infrastructure indicators

	2005	2010	2017
Mobile-cellular subscriptions (per 100 inhabitants)	0.9	34.2	96.8[k,b]
Individuals using the Internet (per 100 inhabitants)	0.8	7.9[n]	17.6[e,b]
Research & Development expenditure (% of GDP)	...	0.3[o,p]	...
Threatened species (number)	77[l]	93	104
Forested area (% of land area)	25.4	25.4	25.4[e,h]
CO2 emission estimates (million tons/tons per capita)	3.1 / 0.1	5.1 / 0.2	8.0 / 0.3[h]
Energy production, primary (Petajoules)	349	384	451[h]
Energy supply per capita (Gigajoules)	14	17	19[h]
Tourist/visitor arrivals at national borders (000)[q]	375	603	539[b]
Important sites for terrestrial biodiversity protected (%)	50.3	54.6	54.6
Pop. using improved drinking water (urban/rural, %)	93.1 / 80.2	92.0 / 86.0	90.9 / 91.8[b]
Pop. using improved sanitation facilities (urban/rural, %)	47.8 / 26.7	51.9 / 35.1	56.0 / 43.5[b]
Net Official Development Assist. received (% of GNI)	5.19	5.05	5.73[b]

a Projected estimate (medium fertility variant). **b** 2015. **c** Refers to the municipality. **d** 2016. **e** Estimate. **f** Break in the time series. **g** Series linked to former series. **h** 2014. **i** Data refers to a 5-year period preceding the reference year. **j** Including refugees. **k** Data as at the end of December. **l** 2004. **m** 2000. **n** December. **o** R&D budget instead of R&D expenditure or based on R&D budget. **p** Partial data. **q** Including arrivals from India.

Netherlands

Region	Western Europe	UN membership date	10 December 1945
Population (000, 2017)	17 036 [a]	Surface area (km2)	41 542 [b]
Pop. density (per km2, 2017)	505.2 [a]	Sex ratio (m per 100 f, 2017)	99.0 [a]
Capital city	Amsterdam [c]	National currency	Euro (EUR)
Capital city pop. (000)	1 090.8 [b]	Exchange rate (per US$)	0.9 [d]

Economic indicators

	2005	2010	2017
GDP: Gross domestic product (million current US$)	678 517	836 390	750 318 [b]
GDP growth rate (annual %, const. 2005 prices)	2.2	1.4	2.0 [b]
GDP per capita (current US$)	41 546.1	50 289.3	44 332.1 [b]
Economy: Agriculture (% of GVA) [e]	2.0	1.9	1.8 [b]
Economy: Industry (% of GVA) [e]	24.0	22.1	20.0 [b]
Economy: Services and other activity (% of GVA) [e]	74.0	76.0	78.2 [b]
Employment: Agriculture (% of employed) [f]	3.3	3.1	2.2
Employment: Industry (% of employed) [f]	20.5	17.6	15.9
Employment: Services (% of employed) [f]	76.1	79.3	81.9
Unemployment (% of labour force)	4.7	4.5	5.6 [f]
Labour force participation (female/male pop. %) [f]	56.7 / 72.5	58.1 / 71.2	57.3 / 69.7
CPI: Consumer Price Index (2000=100)	113	122	133 [g]
Agricultural production index (2004-2006=100)	100	112	115 [g]
Food production index (2004-2006=100)	100	112	115 [g]
Index of industrial production (2005=100)	100	107	103 [g]
International trade: Exports (million US$)	349 813	492 646	511 714 [d]
International trade: Imports (million US$)	310 591	439 987	420 969 [d]
International trade: Balance (million US$)	39 222	52 659	90 745 [d]
Balance of payments, current account (million US$)	41 599	61 820	65 129 [b]

Major trading partners

							2016
Export partners (% of exports)	Germany	23.9	Belgium	10.4	United Kingdom	8.9
Import partners (% of imports)	Germany	18.0	Belgium	10.1	China	9.0

Social indicators

	2005	2010	2017
Population growth rate (average annual %) [h]	0.5	0.4	0.3 [b]
Urban population (% of total population)	82.6	87.1	90.5 [b]
Urban population growth rate (average annual %) [h]	2.0	1.4	1.0 [b]
Fertility rate, total (live births per woman) [h]	1.7	1.7	1.7 [b]
Life expectancy at birth (females/males, years) [h]	81.0 / 76.2	82.2 / 78.0	83.1 / 79.4 [b]
Population age distribution (0-14 and 60+ years, %)	18.3 / 19.3	17.5 / 22.0	16.4 / 25.0 [a]
International migrant stock (000/% of total pop.)	1 736.1 / 10.6	1 832.5 / 11.0	1 979.5 / 11.7 [b]
Refugees and others of concern to UNHCR (000)	139.7 [i]	90.1 [i]	116.3 [d]
Infant mortality rate (per 1 000 live births) [h]	4.9	4.1	3.5 [b]
Health: Total expenditure (% of GDP) [j]	9.6	10.5	10.9 [g]
Health: Physicians (per 1 000 pop.)	...	3.0	3.4 [g]
Education: Government expenditure (% of GDP)	5.2	5.6	5.5 [g]
Education: Primary gross enrol. ratio (f/m per 100 pop.)	105.5 / 108.2	108.5 / 109.8	104.4 / 105.0 [b]
Education: Secondary gross enrol. ratio (f/m per 100 pop.)	118.2 / 120.5	122.2 / 124.0	136.3 / 134.7 [b]
Education: Tertiary gross enrol. ratio (f/m per 100 pop.)	62.1 / 57.5	68.9 / 61.6	82.5 / 74.7 [k]
Intentional homicide rate (per 100 000 pop.)	1.1	0.9	0.6 [b]
Seats held by women in national parliaments (%)	36.7	42.0	38.0

Environment and infrastructure indicators

	2005	2010	2017
Mobile-cellular subscriptions (per 100 inhabitants)	97.1	115.4 [l,m]	123.5 [b]
Individuals using the Internet (per 100 inhabitants) [o]	81.0 [n]	90.7 [n]	93.1 [b]
Research & Development expenditure (% of GDP)	1.8	1.7	2.0 [p,g]
Threatened species (number)	34 [q]	24	40
Forested area (% of land area)	10.8	11.1	11.1 [f,g]
CO2 emission estimates (million tons/tons per capita)	181.5 / 11.1	183.1 / 11.0	167.3 / 9.9 [g]
Energy production, primary (Petajoules)	2 610	2 917	2 447 [g]
Energy supply per capita (Gigajoules)	206	207	178 [g]
Tourist/visitor arrivals at national borders (000)	10 012	10 883	15 007 [b]
Important sites for terrestrial biodiversity protected (%)	90.7	90.8	90.8
Pop. using improved drinking water (urban/rural, %)	100.0 / 100.0	100.0 / 100.0	100.0 / 100.0 [b]
Pop. using improved sanitation facilities (urban/rural, %)	97.5 / 99.9	97.5 / 99.9	97.5 / 99.9 [b]
Net Official Development Assist. disbursed (% of GNI) [r]	0.82	0.81	0.65 [p,d]

a Projected estimate (medium fertility variant). b 2015. c Amsterdam is the capital and The Hague is the seat of government. d 2016. e Data classified according to ISIC Rev. 4. f Estimate. g 2014. h Data refers to a 5-year period preceding the reference year. i Data as at the end of December. j Total health expenditure does not include capital. k 2012. l Decrease due to operator updating their records to exclude inactive subscriptions. m Data as at the end of July. n Users in the last 12 months. o Population aged 16 to 74 years. p Provisional data. q 2004. r Development Assistance Committee member (OECD)

New Caledonia

Region	Melanesia	Population (000, 2017)	276[a]	
Surface area (km2)	18 575[b]	Pop. density (per km2, 2017)	15.1[a]	
Sex ratio (m per 100 f, 2017)	101.5[a]	Capital city	Nouméa	
National currency	CFP Franc (XPF)	Capital city pop. (000)	181.0[c]	
Exchange rate (per US$)	113.2[d]			

Economic indicators	2005	2010	2017
GDP: Gross domestic product (million current US$)	6 236	9 355	8 937[b]
GDP growth rate (annual %, const. 2005 prices)	3.6	6.9	3.2[b]
GDP per capita (current US$)	27 269.8	37 976.1	33 965.7[b]
Economy: Agriculture (% of GVA)	1.7	1.4	1.4[b]
Economy: Industry (% of GVA)	26.6	25.5	26.0[b]
Economy: Services and other activity (% of GVA)	71.7	73.1	72.6[b]
Employment: Agriculture (% of employed)[e]	3.8	3.4	3.0
Employment: Industry (% of employed)[e]	26.1	27.4	26.9
Employment: Services (% of employed)[e]	70.1	69.2	70.1
Unemployment (% of labour force)[e]	16.7	13.9	15.1
Labour force participation (female/male pop. %)[e]	47.8 / 69.9	45.8 / 67.3	45.5 / 66.9
CPI: Consumer Price Index (2000=100)[f]	108	119	126[c]
Agricultural production index (2004-2006=100)	100	100	102[c]
Food production index (2004-2006=100)	100	100	103[c]
International trade: Exports (million US$)	1 114	1 268	1 344[d]
International trade: Imports (million US$)	1 774	3 303	2 422[d]
International trade: Balance (million US$)	- 660	- 2 036	- 1 079[d]
Balance of payments, current account (million US$)	- 112	- 1 360	- 1 469[c]

Major trading partners						2016
Export partners (% of exports)	China	35.7	Japan	15.9	Republic of Korea	15.1
Import partners (% of imports)	France	25.7	China	10.2	Singapore	8.2

Social indicators	2005	2010	2017
Population growth rate (average annual %)[g]	1.8	1.5	1.4[b]
Urban population (% of total population)	64.0	67.3	70.2[b]
Urban population growth rate (average annual %)[g]	2.4	2.5	2.2[b]
Fertility rate, total (live births per woman)[g]	2.3	2.3	2.2[b]
Life expectancy at birth (females/males, years)[g]	77.2 / 71.3	78.3 / 72.4	79.3 / 73.7[b]
Population age distribution (0-14 and 60+ years, %)	27.5 / 10.3	24.1 / 13.1	22.5 / 14.2[a]
International migrant stock (000/% of total pop.)	55.4 / 24.2	61.2 / 24.8	64.3 / 24.4[b]
Infant mortality rate (per 1 000 live births)[g]	17.4	15.1	13.0[b]
Intentional homicide rate (per 100 000 pop.)	...	3.3[h]	...

Environment and infrastructure indicators	2005	2010	2017
Mobile-cellular subscriptions (per 100 inhabitants)	58.7	89.6	93.5[e,b]
Individuals using the Internet (per 100 inhabitants)	32.4	42.0[e]	74.0[e,b]
Threatened species (number)	262[i]	415	526
Forested area (% of land area)[e]	45.9	45.9	45.9[c]
CO2 emission estimates (million tons/tons per capita)	2.8 / 12.2	3.5 / 14.4	4.3 / 16.5[c]
Energy production, primary (Petajoules)	1	1	1[c]
Energy supply per capita (Gigajoules)	161	186	215[c]
Tourist/visitor arrivals at national borders (000)[j]	101	99	114[b]
Important sites for terrestrial biodiversity protected (%)	15.5	67.8	68.0
Pop. using improved drinking water (urban/rural, %)	95.5 / 95.5	98.0 / 98.0	98.5 / 98.5[b]
Pop. using improved sanitation facilities (urban/rural, %)	100.0 / 100.0	100.0 / 100.0	100.0 / 100.0[b]

a Projected estimate (medium fertility variant). **b** 2015. **c** 2014. **d** 2016. **e** Estimate. **f** Nouméa **g** Data refers to a 5-year period preceding the reference year. **h** 2009. **i** 2004. **j** Including nationals residing abroad.

New Zealand

Region	Oceania	UN membership date	24 October 1945	
Population (000, 2017)	4 706[a]	Surface area (km2)	268 107[b]	
Pop. density (per km2, 2017)	17.9[a]	Sex ratio (m per 100 f, 2017)	96.7[a]	
Capital city	Wellington	National currency	New Zealand Dollar (NZD)	
Capital city pop. (000)	382.9[b]	Exchange rate (per US$)	1.4[c]	

Economic indicators

	2005	2010	2017
GDP: Gross domestic product (million current US$)	114 721	146 584	173 417[b]
GDP growth rate (annual %, const. 2005 prices)	3.3	1.0	3.1[b]
GDP per capita (current US$)	27 745.9	33 550.7	38 294.3[b]
Economy: Agriculture (% of GVA)[d]	4.9	7.1	6.5[b]
Economy: Industry (% of GVA)[d]	25.8	23.0	23.0[b]
Economy: Services and other activity (% of GVA)[d]	69.3	69.9	70.6[b]
Employment: Agriculture (% of employed)[e]	7.1	6.9	5.9
Employment: Industry (% of employed)[e]	22.2	21.0	21.4
Employment: Services (% of employed)[e]	70.7	72.2	72.6
Unemployment (% of labour force)	3.8	6.1	5.5[e]
Labour force participation (female/male pop. %)[e]	60.3 / 74.8	61.5 / 74.2	62.1 / 72.8
CPI: Consumer Price Index (2000=100)	113	130	140[f]
Agricultural production index (2004-2006=100)	99	104	116[f]
Food production index (2004-2006=100)	99	105	118[f]
Index of industrial production (2005=100)[g]	100	96	97[f]
International trade: Exports (million US$)	21 729	30 932	33 833[c]
International trade: Imports (million US$)	26 232	30 158	36 423[c]
International trade: Balance (million US$)	- 4 504	774	- 2 589[c]
Balance of payments, current account (million US$)	- 8 025	- 3 430	- 5 501[b]

Major trading partners

						2016
Export partners (% of exports)	China	19.4	Australia	17.0	United States	10.9
Import partners (% of imports)	China	19.9	Australia	12.5	United States	11.4

Social indicators

	2005	2010	2017
Population growth rate (average annual %)[h]	1.4	1.1	1.1[b]
Urban population (% of total population)	86.1	86.2	86.3[b]
Urban population growth rate (average annual %)[h]	1.5	1.1	1.0[b]
Fertility rate, total (live births per woman)[h]	1.9	2.1	2.0[b]
Life expectancy at birth (females/males, years)[h]	81.3 / 76.8	82.3 / 78.3	83.1 / 79.5[b]
Population age distribution (0-14 and 60+ years, %)	21.5 / 16.4	20.5 / 18.4	19.8 / 20.8[a]
International migrant stock (000/% of total pop.)	840.0 / 20.3	947.4 / 21.7	1 039.1 / 23.0[b]
Refugees and others of concern to UNHCR (000)	5.7[i]	2.5[i]	1.7[c]
Infant mortality rate (per 1 000 live births)[h]	5.4	5.0	4.4[b]
Health: Total expenditure (% of GDP)	8.2	11.2	11.0[f]
Health: Physicians (per 1 000 pop.)	2.1[j]	2.6	2.9[f]
Education: Government expenditure (% of GDP)	6.3	7.0	6.4[b]
Education: Primary gross enrol. ratio (f/m per 100 pop.)	99.2 / 100.0	101.3 / 100.9	99.1 / 99.6[b]
Education: Secondary gross enrol. ratio (f/m per 100 pop.)	123.4 / 116.9	121.7 / 116.3	119.9 / 113.4[b]
Education: Tertiary gross enrol. ratio (f/m per 100 pop.)	95.8 / 65.8	98.6 / 67.3	96.7 / 71.6[b]
Intentional homicide rate (per 100 000 pop.)[k]	1.5	1.0	0.9[f]
Seats held by women in national parliaments (%)	28.3	33.6	34.2

Environment and infrastructure indicators

	2005	2010	2017
Mobile-cellular subscriptions (per 100 inhabitants)	85.4	107.8[l]	121.8[b]
Individuals using the Internet (per 100 inhabitants)[e]	62.7	80.5	88.2[b]
Research & Development expenditure (% of GDP)	1.1	1.3[m]	1.2[n]
Threatened species (number)	149[o]	153	199
Forested area (% of land area)	38.7	38.6	38.6[e,f]
CO2 emission estimates (million tons/tons per capita)	34.1 / 8.3	31.8 / 7.3	34.7 / 7.7[f]
Energy production, primary (Petajoules)	572	770	783[f]
Energy supply per capita (Gigajoules)	181	191	207[f]
Tourist/visitor arrivals at national borders (000)	2 353	2 435	3 039[b]
Important sites for terrestrial biodiversity protected (%)	45.8	47.0	47.1
Pop. using improved drinking water (urban/rural, %)	100.0 / 100.0	100.0 / 100.0	100.0 / 100.0[b]
Net Official Development Assist. disbursed (% of GNI)[p]	0.27	0.26	0.25[q,c]

a Projected estimate (medium fertility variant). **b** 2015. **c** 2016. **d** Data classified according to ISIC Rev. 4. **e** Estimate. **f** 2014. **g** Twelve months ending 31 March of the year stated. **h** Data refers to a 5-year period preceding the reference year. **i** Data as at the end of December. **j** 2002. **k** Data for 2000-2006 refer to offences, data for 2007 onwards refer to victims of intentional homicide. **l** Data refers to subscriptions active in the last 3 months (or 90 days). **m** 2009. **n** 2013. **o** 2004. **p** Development Assistance Committee member (OECD) **q** Provisional data.

Nicaragua

Region	Central America	UN membership date	24 October 1945
Population (000, 2017)	6 218[a]	Surface area (km2)	130 373[b]
Pop. density (per km2, 2017)	51.7[a]	Sex ratio (m per 100 f, 2017)	97.2[a]
Capital city	Managua	National currency	Cordoba Oro (NIO)
Capital city pop. (000)	956.2[b]	Exchange rate (per US$)	29.3[c]

Economic indicators	2005	2010	2017
GDP: Gross domestic product (million current US$)	6 321	8 741	12 693[b]
GDP growth rate (annual %, const. 2005 prices)	4.3	3.2	4.9[b]
GDP per capita (current US$)	1 175.1	1 523.5	2 086.9[b]
Economy: Agriculture (% of GVA)	17.7	18.8	18.8[b]
Economy: Industry (% of GVA)	23.0	24.3	26.8[b]
Economy: Services and other activity (% of GVA)	59.3	56.9	54.4[b]
Employment: Agriculture (% of employed)[d]	29.0	27.4	24.1
Employment: Industry (% of employed)[d]	19.6	14.0	14.5
Employment: Services (% of employed)[d]	51.4	58.7	61.4
Unemployment (% of labour force)	5.6	8.0	6.1[d]
Labour force participation (female/male pop. %)[d]	43.7 / 80.4	46.8 / 80.5	49.6 / 80.6
CPI: Consumer Price Index (2000=100)[e]	147[f]	234[g]	308[h]
Agricultural production index (2004-2006=100)	104	118	130[h]
Food production index (2004-2006=100)	102	119	130[h]
International trade: Exports (million US$)	866	1 848	2 225[c]
International trade: Imports (million US$)	2 536	4 191	5 927[c]
International trade: Balance (million US$)	- 1 670	- 2 343	- 3 701[c]
Balance of payments, current account (million US$)	- 784[f]	- 790	- 1 045[b]

Major trading partners					2016
Export partners (% of exports)	United States	53.7	Mexico	11.1	Venezuela (Bol. Rep.) 6.2
Import partners (% of imports)	United States	18.0	China	14.4	Mexico 10.4

Social indicators	2005	2010	2017
Population growth rate (average annual %)[i]	1.4	1.3	1.2[b]
Urban population (% of total population)	55.9	57.3	58.8[b]
Urban population growth rate (average annual %)[i]	1.8	1.8	2.0[b]
Fertility rate, total (live births per woman)[i]	2.8	2.6	2.3[b]
Life expectancy at birth (females/males, years)[i]	73.8 / 68.0	75.8 / 69.8	77.5 / 71.4[b]
Population age distribution (0-14 and 60+ years, %)	36.0 / 6.1	32.8 / 6.5	29.0 / 8.4[a]
International migrant stock (000/% of total pop.)[j]	34.9 / 0.6	37.3 / 0.7	40.3 / 0.7[b]
Refugees and others of concern to UNHCR (000)	0.2[k]	0.1[k]	0.6[c]
Infant mortality rate (per 1 000 live births)[i]	26.4	24.0	20.0[b]
Health: Total expenditure (% of GDP)	6.1	6.6	9.0[h]
Health: Physicians (per 1 000 pop.)	0.5	0.7	0.9[h]
Education: Government expenditure (% of GDP)	2.4[d,l]	4.5	...
Education: Primary gross enrol. ratio (f/m per 100 pop.)	120.2 / 121.9	122.7 / 123.8	... / ...
Education: Secondary gross enrol. ratio (f/m per 100 pop.)	74.1 / 63.7	78.8 / 69.8	... / ...
Education: Tertiary gross enrol. ratio (f/m per 100 pop.)	18.7 / 16.8[m]	... / ...	... / ...
Intentional homicide rate (per 100 000 pop.)	13.6	13.7	11.5[n]
Seats held by women in national parliaments (%)	20.7	20.7	45.7

Environment and infrastructure indicators	2005	2010	2017
Mobile-cellular subscriptions (per 100 inhabitants)	20.5	68.0[o]	116.1[o,b]
Individuals using the Internet (per 100 inhabitants)	2.6	10.0[d]	19.7[d,b]
Research & Development expenditure (% of GDP)	-0.0[m]	...	...
Threatened species (number)	90[p]	121	144
Forested area (% of land area)	28.8	25.9	25.9[d,h]
CO2 emission estimates (million tons/tons per capita)	4.3 / 0.8	4.5 / 0.8	4.9 / 0.8[h]
Energy production, primary (Petajoules)	62	66	91[h]
Energy supply per capita (Gigajoules)	22	22	26[h]
Tourist/visitor arrivals at national borders (000)[q]	712	1 011	1 386[b]
Important sites for terrestrial biodiversity protected (%)	73.7	73.7	73.7
Pop. using improved drinking water (urban/rural, %)	96.3 / 63.7	98.2 / 67.3	99.3 / 69.4[b]
Pop. using improved sanitation facilities (urban/rural, %)	70.8 / 45.4	74.3 / 51.8	76.5 / 55.7[b]
Net Official Development Assist. received (% of GNI)	12.39	7.77	3.68[b]

a Projected estimate (medium fertility variant). b 2015. c 2016. d Estimate. e Index base: 1999=100. f Break in the time series. g Series linked to former series. h 2014. i Data refers to a 5-year period preceding the reference year. j Including refugees. k Data as at the end of December. l 2003. m 2002. n 2012. o Includes inactive subscriptions. p 2004. q Including nationals residing abroad.

Niger

Region	Western Africa	UN membership date	20 September 1960
Population (000, 2017)	21 477[a]	Surface area (km2)	1 267 000[b]
Pop. density (per km2, 2017)	17.0[a]	Sex ratio (m per 100 f, 2017)	100.6[a]
Capital city	Niamey	National currency	CFA Franc (XOF)
Capital city pop. (000)	1 089.6[b]	Exchange rate (per US$)	622.3[c]

Economic indicators	2005	2010	2017
GDP: Gross domestic product (million current US$)	3 369	5 719	7 143[b]
GDP growth rate (annual %, const. 2005 prices)	7.4	8.4	3.6[b]
GDP per capita (current US$)	249.8	351.0	359.0[b]
Economy: Agriculture (% of GVA)[d]	45.5	43.8	39.6[b]
Economy: Industry (% of GVA)[d]	11.8	16.7	19.1[b]
Economy: Services and other activity (% of GVA)[d]	42.7	39.4	41.3[b]
Employment: Agriculture (% of employed)[e]	64.2	64.0	62.3
Employment: Industry (% of employed)[e]	13.0	13.8	14.4
Employment: Services (% of employed)[e]	22.8	22.3	23.3
Unemployment (% of labour force)	3.1	2.4[e]	2.7[e]
Labour force participation (female/male pop. %)[e]	39.2 / 90.7	39.8 / 90.1	40.4 / 89.2
CPI: Consumer Price Index (2000=100)[f,g]	114	128[h]	134[i]
Agricultural production index (2004-2006=100)	102	146	148[i]
Food production index (2004-2006=100)	102	146	148[i]
International trade: Exports (million US$)	486	479	927[c]
International trade: Imports (million US$)	736	2 273	1 861[c]
International trade: Balance (million US$)	- 250	- 1 794	- 933[c]
Balance of payments, current account (million US$)	- 312	- 1 136	- 1 150[j]

Major trading partners						2016
Export partners (% of exports)	France	31.3	Thailand	11.6	Malaysia	11.1
Import partners (% of imports)	France	28.3	China	16.2	United States	7.8

Social indicators	2005	2010	2017
Population growth rate (average annual %)[k]	3.6	3.7	3.8[b]
Urban population (% of total population)	16.7	17.6	18.7[b]
Urban population growth rate (average annual %)[k]	4.3	4.7	5.1[b]
Fertility rate, total (live births per woman)[k]	7.6	7.6	7.4[b]
Life expectancy at birth (females/males, years)[k]	52.0 / 50.8	55.6 / 54.2	59.5 / 57.6[b]
Population age distribution (0-14 and 60+ years, %)	49.2 / 4.1	50.0 / 4.1	50.2 / 4.2[a]
International migrant stock (000/% of total pop.)[l]	124.5 / 0.9	126.5 / 0.8	189.3 / 1.0[b]
Refugees and others of concern to UNHCR (000)	0.4[m]	0.3[m]	312.5[c]
Infant mortality rate (per 1 000 live births)[k]	88.1	74.8	65.8[b]
Health: Total expenditure (% of GDP)	7.1	6.4	6.0[i]
Health: Physicians (per 1 000 pop.)	~0.0[p]	~0.0[o]	...
Education: Government expenditure (% of GDP)	2.4[p]	3.7	6.7[i]
Education: Primary gross enrol. ratio (f/m per 100 pop.)	40.8 / 56.7	56.8 / 69.6	66.8 / 77.9[b]
Education: Secondary gross enrol. ratio (f/m per 100 pop.)	7.7 / 12.2	10.9 / 16.2	17.2 / 24.2[b]
Education: Tertiary gross enrol. ratio (f/m per 100 pop.)	0.6 / 1.8	0.8 / 2.2	0.9 / 2.6[q]
Intentional homicide rate (per 100 000 pop.)	...	...	4.5[q]
Seats held by women in national parliaments (%)	12.4	9.7	17.0

Environment and infrastructure indicators	2005	2010	2017
Mobile-cellular subscriptions (per 100 inhabitants)	2.5	23.1	46.5[e,b]
Individuals using the Internet (per 100 inhabitants)[e]	0.2	0.8	2.2[b]
Threatened species (number)	15[n]	26	34
Forested area (% of land area)[e]	1.0	1.0	0.9[i]
CO2 emission estimates (million tons/tons per capita)	0.7 / 0.1	1.2 / 0.1	2.1 / 0.1[i]
Energy production, primary (Petajoules)	70[e]	56	101[e,i]
Energy supply per capita (Gigajoules)	6[e]	4	5[e,i]
Tourist/visitor arrivals at national borders (000)	58	74	135[b]
Important sites for terrestrial biodiversity protected (%)	40.7	40.7	42.7
Pop. using improved drinking water (urban/rural, %)	86.4 / 41.2	94.8 / 45.3	100.0 / 48.6[b]
Pop. using improved sanitation facilities (urban/rural, %)	30.8 / 3.4	34.8 / 4.1	37.9 / 4.6[b]
Net Official Development Assist. received (% of GNI)	15.40	13.07	12.26[b]

a Projected estimate (medium fertility variant). **b** 2015. **c** 2016. **d** Data classified according to ISIC Rev. 4. **e** Estimate. **f** Niamey **g** African population. **h** Series linked to former series. **i** 2014. **j** 2013. **k** Data refers to a 5-year period preceding the reference year. **l** Including refugees. **m** Data as at the end of December. **n** 2004. **o** 2008. **p** 2003. **q** 2012.

Nigeria

Region	Western Africa	UN membership date	07 October 1960
Population (000, 2017)	190 886[a]	Surface area (km2)	923 768[b]
Pop. density (per km2, 2017)	209.6[a]	Sex ratio (m per 100 f, 2017)	102.7[a]
Capital city	Abuja	National currency	Naira (NGN)
Capital city pop. (000)	2 440.2[b]	Exchange rate (per US$)	305.0[c]

Economic indicators

	2005	2010	2017
GDP: Gross domestic product (million current US$)	180 502	369 062	494 583[b]
GDP growth rate (annual %, const. 2005 prices)	6.5	7.8	2.7[b]
GDP per capita (current US$)	1 292.9	2 315.0	2 714.5[b]
Economy: Agriculture (% of GVA)[d]	25.6	23.9	20.9[b]
Economy: Industry (% of GVA)[d]	23.7	25.3	20.4[b]
Economy: Services and other activity (% of GVA)[d]	50.7	50.8	58.8[b]
Employment: Agriculture (% of employed)[e]	47.0	30.6	27.9
Employment: Industry (% of employed)[e]	10.2	14.1	14.7
Employment: Services (% of employed)[e]	42.8	55.3	57.4
Unemployment (% of labour force)[e]	7.1	7.3	5.4
Labour force participation (female/male pop. %)[e]	47.6 / 62.1	47.9 / 63.2	48.5 / 64.3
CPI: Consumer Price Index (2000=100)[f]	207	338[g]	493[h]
Agricultural production index (2004-2006=100)	100	105	116[h]
Food production index (2004-2006=100)	100	105	117[h]
International trade: Exports (million US$)	55 144	86 568	104 084[c]
International trade: Imports (million US$)	21 314	44 235	36 533[c]
International trade: Balance (million US$)	33 831	42 333	67 551[c]
Balance of payments, current account (million US$)	36 529	13 111	- 15 763[b]

Major trading partners

						2016
Export partners (% of exports)	India	14.6	Netherlands	10.2	Spain	9.3
Import partners (% of imports)	China	21.9	United States	10.4	Belgium	7.2

Social indicators

	2005	2010	2017
Population growth rate (average annual %)[i]	2.5	2.6	2.7[b]
Urban population (% of total population)	39.1	43.5	47.8[b]
Urban population growth rate (average annual %)[i]	4.8	4.8	4.7[b]
Fertility rate, total (live births per woman)[i]	6.1	5.9	5.7[b]
Life expectancy at birth (females/males, years)[i]	47.8 / 46.1	50.5 / 49.0	52.6 / 51.2[b]
Population age distribution (0-14 and 60+ years, %)	43.7 / 4.6	44.0 / 4.5	44.0 / 4.5[a]
International migrant stock (000/% of total pop.)[j,k]	648.0 / 0.5	920.1 / 0.6	1 199.1 / 0.7[b]
Refugees and others of concern to UNHCR (000)	12.7[l]	10.6[l]	2 437.5[c]
Infant mortality rate (per 1 000 live births)[i]	104.0	89.9	76.3[b]
Health: Total expenditure (% of GDP)[m]	4.1	3.5	3.7[h]
Health: Physicians (per 1 000 pop.)	0.3	0.4[n]	...
Education: Primary gross enrol. ratio (f/m per 100 pop.)	92.6 / 109.0	80.9 / 88.3[e]	92.8 / 94.5[o]
Education: Secondary gross enrol. ratio (f/m per 100 pop.)	31.7 / 37.6	41.2 / 46.4	53.5 / 57.8[b]
Education: Tertiary gross enrol. ratio (f/m per 100 pop.)	8.7 / 12.1	8.1 / 10.8	8.3 / 11.8[p]
Intentional homicide rate (per 100 000 pop.)	11.8	10.7	9.8[b]
Seats held by women in national parliaments (%)	4.7	7.0	5.6

Environment and infrastructure indicators

	2005	2010	2017
Mobile-cellular subscriptions (per 100 inhabitants)	13.3	54.7	82.2[b]
Individuals using the Internet (per 100 inhabitants)[e]	3.5	24.0	47.4[b]
Research & Development expenditure (% of GDP)	...	0.2[q,r]	...
Threatened species (number)	232[s]	297	361
Forested area (% of land area)[e]	12.2	9.9	8.1[h]
CO2 emission estimates (million tons/tons per capita)	106.1 / 0.8	91.5 / 0.6	96.3 / 0.6[h]
Energy production, primary (Petajoules)	9 734	10 595	10 851[h]
Energy supply per capita (Gigajoules)	31	31	32[h]
Tourist/visitor arrivals at national borders (000)	1 010	1 555	1 255[b]
Important sites for terrestrial biodiversity protected (%)	76.0	79.6	79.6
Pop. using improved drinking water (urban/rural, %)	79.0 / 44.2	79.9 / 50.7	80.8 / 57.3[b]
Pop. using improved sanitation facilities (urban/rural, %)	34.8 / 30.6	33.8 / 28.0	32.8 / 25.4[b]
Net Official Development Assist. received (% of GNI)	6.47	0.59	0.52[b]

a Projected estimate (medium fertility variant). **b** 2015. **c** 2016. **d** Data classified according to ISIC Rev. 4. **e** Estimate. **f** Rural and urban areas. **g** Series linked to former series. **h** 2014. **i** Data refers to a 5-year period preceding the reference year. **j** Refers to foreign citizens. **k** Including refugees. **l** Data as at the end of December. **m** In 2014, a revised GDP series was published following a statistical rebasing exercise (the base year changed from 1990 to 2010). Nigeria has emerged as Africa's largest economy, with a GDP increase of 89% for year 2013. **n** 2009. **o** 2013. **p** 2011. **q** Excluding business enterprise. **r** 2007. **s** 2004.

Niue

Region	Polynesia	Population (000, 2017)	2 [a]
Surface area (km2)	260 [b]	Pop. density (per km2, 2017)	6.2 [a]
Sex ratio (m per 100 f, 2017)	100.0 [c,d]	Capital city	Alofi
National currency	New Zealand Dollar (NZD)	Capital city pop. (000)	0.5 [e]
Exchange rate (per US$)	1.4 [d]		

Economic indicators	2005	2010	2017
Employment: Agriculture (% of employed)	4.8 [c,f,g]	...	...
Employment: Industry (% of employed)	9.3 [c,f,g]	...	...
Employment: Services (% of employed)	85.9 [c,f,g]	...	...
Unemployment (% of labour force)	9.7 [c,g]	...	...
Labour force participation (female/male pop. %)	74.8 / 76.7 [h]	... / ...	... / ...
CPI: Consumer Price Index (2000=100)	119	158 [i]	...
Agricultural production index (2004-2006=100)	100	98	101 [e]
Food production index (2004-2006=100)	100	98	101 [e]

Social indicators	2005	2010	2017
Population growth rate (average annual %) [j]	- 2.4	- 0.7	- 0.1 [b]
Urban population (% of total population)	35.2	38.7	42.5 [b]
Urban population growth rate (average annual %) [j]	- 1.1	- 0.9	- 0.9 [b]
Fertility rate, total (live births per woman)	...	...	2.6 [k,l]
Life expectancy at birth (females/males, years)	... / ...	76.0 / 67.0 [m]	76.3 / 70.1 [c,n,l]
Population age distribution (0-14 and 60+ years, %)	26.1 / 15.1 [o]	25.7 / 16.8 [o]	22.8 / 20.1 [c,d]
International migrant stock (000/% of total pop.)	0.5 / 31.0	0.5 / 33.6	0.6 / 34.6 [b]
Infant mortality rate (per 1 000 live births)	...	...	8.1 [n,l]
Health: Total expenditure (% of GDP)	8.2	8.3	7.4 [e]
Health: Physicians (per 1 000 pop.)	2.3 [p]	1.8 [q]	...
Education: Primary gross enrol. ratio (f/m per 100 pop.)	105.9 / 118.9 [r]	... / ...	120.2 / 147.2 [r,b]
Education: Secondary gross enrol. ratio (f/m per 100 pop.)	116.5 / 71.3 [r]	... / ...	114.1 / 104.1 [r,b]
Intentional homicide rate (per 100 000 pop.)	...	...	3.1 [s]

Environment and infrastructure indicators	2005	2010	2017
Mobile-cellular subscriptions (per 100 inhabitants)	21.6 [t]	...	...
Individuals using the Internet (per 100 inhabitants)	51.7	77.0 [r]	79.6 [r,l]
Threatened species (number)	12 [p]	43	52
Forested area (% of land area) [r]	73.5	71.5	70.0 [e]
CO2 emission estimates (million tons/tons per capita)	~0.0 / 1.8	~0.0 / 1.9	~0.0 / 5.7 [e]
Energy production, primary (Petajoules)	0	0	0 [e]
Energy supply per capita (Gigajoules)	42	53	62 [e]
Tourist/visitor arrivals at national borders (000) [u]	3	6	8 [b]
Pop. using improved drinking water (urban/rural, %)	98.8 / 98.8	98.5 / 98.6	98.4 / 98.6 [b]
Pop. using improved sanitation facilities (urban/rural, %)	89.9 / 89.9	100.0 / 100.0	100.0 / 100.0 [b]

a Projected estimate (medium fertility variant). b 2015. c Break in the time series. d 2016. e 2014. f Data classified according to ISIC Rev. 3. g 2002. h 2001. i 2009. j Data refers to a 5-year period preceding the reference year. k Data refers to a 3-year period up to and including the reference year. l 2011. m 2006. n Data refers to a 5-year period up to and including the reference year. o De jure population. p 2004. q 2008. r Estimate. s 2012. t 2000. u Including Niueans residing usually in New Zealand.

Northern Mariana Islands

Region	Micronesia	Population (000, 2017)	55[a]
Surface area (km2)	457[b]	Pop. density (per km2, 2017)	119.9[a]
Sex ratio (m per 100 f, 2017)	107.1[c,d]	Capital city	Garapan
National currency	US Dollar (USD)	Capital city pop. (000)	4.0[e]

Economic indicators	2005	2010	2017
Employment: Agriculture (% of employed)	1.5[c,f,g,h]	...	...
Employment: Industry (% of employed)	47.2[c,f,g,h]	...	...
Employment: Services (% of employed)	45.8[c,f,g,h]	...	...
Unemployment (% of labour force)[f]	6.5	11.2[c]	
Labour force participation (female/male pop. %)	81.3 / 82.5[f,j]	66.6 / 77.6[c,f]	... / ...
CPI: Consumer Price Index (2000=100)	100[j]	122[k]	...
International trade: Exports (million US$)	1 254	1 453	1 735[d]
International trade: Imports (million US$)	1 952	2 867	4 553[d]
International trade: Balance (million US$)	- 699	- 1 414	- 2 818[d]

Major trading partners						2016
Export partners (% of exports)	Areas nes[l]	91.1	Singapore	3.2	Republic of Korea	1.8
Import partners (% of imports)	Areas nes[l]	66.1	China, Hong Kong SAR	8.5	Viet Nam	8.3

Social indicators	2005	2010	2017
Population growth rate (average annual %)[m]	- 1.6	- 3.2	0.1[b]
Urban population (% of total population)	89.8	89.5	89.2[b]
Urban population growth rate (average annual %)[m]	- 1.3	- 3.6	0.4[b]
Fertility rate, total (live births per woman)	1.5	2.2	1.6[n]
Life expectancy at birth (females/males, years)	77.8 / 72.5[h]	79.9 / 74.4[k]	77.9 / 74.9[c,o]
Population age distribution (0-14 and 60+ years, %)	22.9 / 3.7[p,q]	26.7 / 5.8	23.5 / 10.0[c,d]
International migrant stock (000/% of total pop.)	37.5 / 58.3	24.2 / 44.9	21.6 / 39.3[b]
Infant mortality rate (per 1 000 live births)	...	...	6.4[o]

Environment and infrastructure indicators	2005	2010	2017
Mobile-cellular subscriptions (per 100 inhabitants)	4.4[h]	...	...
Threatened species (number)	28[r]	85	102
Forested area (% of land area)[s]	67.7	65.9	64.5[t]
Tourist/visitor arrivals at national borders (000)	507[u]	379[u]	479[b]
Important sites for terrestrial biodiversity protected (%)	15.5	40.6	40.6
Pop. using improved drinking water (urban/rural, %)	96.4 / 96.4	97.2 / 97.2	97.5 / 97.5[b]
Pop. using improved sanitation facilities (urban/rural, %)	76.2 / 76.2	78.7 / 78.7	79.7 / 79.7[b]

a Projected estimate (medium fertility variant). **b** 2015. **c** Break in the time series. **d** 2016. **e** 2010. **f** Population aged 16 years and over. **g** Data classified according to ISIC Rev. 2. **h** 2000. **i** 2003. **j** Saipan **k** 2009. **l** Areas not elsewhere specified. **m** Data refers to a 5-year period preceding the reference year. **n** 2013. **o** 2012. **p** Refers to the island of Saipan. **q** Estimates should be viewed with caution as these are derived from scarce data. **r** 2004. **s** Estimate. **t** 2014. **u** Arrivals by air.

Norway

Region	Northern Europe	UN membership date	27 November 1945
Population (000, 2017)	5 305[a,b]	Surface area (km2)	386 194[a,c]
Pop. density (per km2, 2017)	14.5[a,b]	Sex ratio (m per 100 f, 2017)	101.8[a,b]
Capital city	Oslo	National currency	Norwegian Krone (NOK)
Capital city pop. (000)	986.1[c]	Exchange rate (per US$)	8.6[d]

Economic indicators	2005	2010	2017
GDP: Gross domestic product (million current US$)	308 722	428 527	386 578[c]
GDP growth rate (annual %, const. 2005 prices)	2.6	0.6	1.6[c]
GDP per capita (current US$)	66 759.6	87 610.9	74 185.5[c]
Economy: Agriculture (% of GVA)[e]	1.6	1.8	1.8[c]
Economy: Industry (% of GVA)[e]	42.5	39.0	34.6[c]
Economy: Services and other activity (% of GVA)[e]	55.9	59.2	63.5[c]
Employment: Agriculture (% of employed)[f]	3.3	2.5	2.2
Employment: Industry (% of employed)[f]	20.9	19.7	20.2
Employment: Services (% of employed)[f]	75.8	77.8	77.6
Unemployment (% of labour force)	4.4	3.5	5.1[f]
Labour force participation (female/male pop. %)[f]	60.3 / 70.5	61.4 / 70.0	61.1 / 68.3
CPI: Consumer Price Index (2000=100)	109	122	130[g]
Agricultural production index (2004-2006=100)	99	102	103[g]
Food production index (2004-2006=100)	99	102	104[g]
Index of industrial production (2005=100)	100	88[h]	85[h,g]
International trade: Exports (million US$)	103 759	130 657	89 120[d]
International trade: Imports (million US$)	55 488	77 330	72 473[d]
International trade: Balance (million US$)	48 271	53 327	16 647[d]
Balance of payments, current account (million US$)	49 967	50 258	33 746[c]

Major trading partners						2016
Export partners (% of exports)	United Kingdom	20.7	Germany	14.3	Netherlands	10.6
Import partners (% of imports)	Germany	12.0	Sweden	12.0	China	11.1

Social indicators	2005	2010	2017
Population growth rate (average annual %)[a,i]	0.6	1.1	1.2[c]
Urban population (% of total population)[a]	77.5	79.1	80.5[c]
Urban population growth rate (average annual %)[a,i]	0.9	1.5	1.3[c]
Fertility rate, total (live births per woman)[a,i]	1.8	1.9	1.8[c]
Life expectancy at birth (females/males, years)[a,i]	81.8 / 76.8	82.8 / 78.3	83.6 / 79.5[c]
Population age distribution (0-14 and 60+ years, %)[a]	19.6 / 19.8	18.8 / 21.0	17.8 / 22.3[b]
International migrant stock (000/% of total pop.)	361.1 / 7.8	526.8 / 10.8	741.8 / 14.2[c]
Refugees and others of concern to UNHCR (000)	44.2[j]	55.9[i]	73.2[d]
Infant mortality rate (per 1 000 live births)[a,i]	3.5	3.0	2.4[c]
Health: Total expenditure (% of GDP)	8.9	9.3	9.7[g]
Health: Physicians (per 1 000 pop.)	...	4.1	4.4[g]
Education: Government expenditure (% of GDP)	6.9	6.8	7.4[k]
Education: Primary gross enrol. ratio (f/m per 100 pop.)	98.7 / 98.4	99.1 / 98.9	100.3 / 100.5[c]
Education: Secondary gross enrol. ratio (f/m per 100 pop.)	114.4 / 113.4	112.4 / 114.0	111.1 / 114.7[c]
Education: Tertiary gross enrol. ratio (f/m per 100 pop.)	95.2 / 62.5	90.4 / 56.1	91.5 / 62.8[c]
Intentional homicide rate (per 100 000 pop.)	0.7	0.6	0.6[g]
Seats held by women in national parliaments (%)	38.2	39.6	39.6

Environment and infrastructure indicators	2005	2010	2017
Mobile-cellular subscriptions (per 100 inhabitants)	102.8	114.5	113.6[l,c]
Individuals using the Internet (per 100 inhabitants)[m]	82.0	93.4	96.8[c]
Research & Development expenditure (% of GDP)	1.5	1.7	1.7[g]
Threatened species (number)	33[n]	36	64
Forested area (% of land area)	33.1	33.1	33.2[f,g]
CO2 emission estimates (million tons/tons per capita)	42.4 / 9.2	60.1 / 12.3	47.6 / 9.2[g]
Energy production, primary (Petajoules)[a]	9 372	8 759	8 204[g]
Energy supply per capita (Gigajoules)[a]	242	291	233[g]
Tourist/visitor arrivals at national borders (000)	3 824	4 767[o]	5 361[p,c]
Important sites for terrestrial biodiversity protected (%)	52.2	54.3	54.7
Pop. using improved drinking water (urban/rural, %)	100.0 / 100.0	100.0 / 100.0	100.0 / 100.0[c]
Pop. using improved sanitation facilities (urban/rural, %)	98.0 / 98.3	98.0 / 98.3	98.0 / 98.3[c]
Net Official Development Assist. disbursed (% of GNI)[q]	0.94	1.05	1.11[r,d]

a Including Svalbard and Jan Mayen Islands. b Projected estimate (medium fertility variant). c 2015. d 2016. e Data classified according to ISIC Rev. 4. f Estimate. g 2014. h Excluding water and waste management. i Data refers to a 5-year period preceding the reference year. j Data as at the end of December. k 2013. l Data as at the end of June. m Population aged 16 to 74 years. n 2004. o Arrivals of non-resident tourists at national borders. p Non-resident tourists staying in all types of accommodation establishments. q Development Assistance Committee member (OECD). r Provisional data.

Oman

			UN membership date	07 October 1971
Region	Western Asia			
Population (000, 2017)	4 636[a]		Surface area (km2)	309 500[b]
Pop. density (per km2, 2017)	15.0[a]		Sex ratio (m per 100 f, 2017)	192.8[a]
Capital city	Muscat		National currency	Rial Omani (OMR)
Capital city pop. (000)	838.0[c,b]		Exchange rate (per US$)	0.4[d]

Economic indicators	2005	2010	2017
GDP: Gross domestic product (million current US$)	31 082	58 641	69 832[b]
GDP growth rate (annual %, const. 2005 prices)	2.5	4.8	5.7[b]
GDP per capita (current US$)	12 398.6	19 920.6	15 550.8[b]
Economy: Agriculture (% of GVA)	1.6	1.4	1.5[b]
Economy: Industry (% of GVA)	62.1	62.8	51.1[b]
Economy: Services and other activity (% of GVA)	36.3	35.9	47.3[b]
Employment: Agriculture (% of employed)[e]	9.5	5.1	5.0
Employment: Industry (% of employed)[e]	24.6	36.8	39.6
Employment: Services (% of employed)[e]	66.0	58.1	55.4
Unemployment (% of labour force)[e]	19.2	18.3	17.8
Labour force participation (female/male pop. %)[e]	25.4 / 77.1	27.6 / 80.7	30.1 / 85.4
CPI: Consumer Price Index (2000=100)	102[f]	134	146[g,h]
Agricultural production index (2004-2006=100)	112	120	134[h]
Food production index (2004-2006=100)	112	120	134[h]
Index of industrial production (2005=100)[i]	100	165	181[h]
International trade: Exports (million US$)	18 692	36 600	24 455[d]
International trade: Imports (million US$)	8 970	19 775	23 260[d]
International trade: Balance (million US$)	9 722	16 825	1 195[d]
Balance of payments, current account (million US$)	5 178	4 884	- 10 807[b]

Major trading partners						2016
Export partners (% of exports)	China	43.6	Areas nes[j]	10.3	United Arab Emirates	7.5
Import partners (% of imports)	United Arab Emirates	45.1	Areas nes[j]	11.2	China	4.8

Social indicators	2005	2010	2017
Population growth rate (average annual %)[k]	2.0	3.8	6.5[b]
Urban population (% of total population)	72.4	75.2	77.6[b]
Urban population growth rate (average annual %)[k]	3.0	2.9	8.5[b]
Fertility rate, total (live births per woman)[k]	3.2	2.9	2.9[b]
Life expectancy at birth (females/males, years)[k]	75.5 / 71.4	77.5 / 73.2	78.7 / 74.5[b]
Population age distribution (0-14 and 60+ years, %)	32.5 / 4.1	25.7 / 3.9	21.8 / 4.0[a]
International migrant stock (000/% of total pop.)[l]	666.2 / 26.6	816.2 / 27.7	1 845.0 / 41.1[b]
Refugees and others of concern to UNHCR (000)	~0.0[m]	0.1[m]	0.6[d]
Infant mortality rate (per 1 000 live births)[k]	14.6	9.8	9.6[b]
Health: Total expenditure (% of GDP)	2.6	2.7	3.6[h]
Health: Physicians (per 1 000 pop.)	1.7	2.0	1.5[h]
Education: Government expenditure (% of GDP)	3.5	4.2[n]	5.0[o]
Education: Primary gross enrol. ratio (f/m per 100 pop.)	87.7 / 89.7	100.0 / 106.7[n]	111.2 / 107.4[b]
Education: Secondary gross enrol. ratio (f/m per 100 pop.)	86.0 / 91.0	95.3 / 107.1[n]	107.9 / 101.0[b]
Intentional homicide rate (per 100 000 pop.)	...	0.7[p]	1.1[q]
Seats held by women in national parliaments (%)	2.4	0.0	1.2

Environment and infrastructure indicators	2005	2010	2017
Mobile-cellular subscriptions (per 100 inhabitants)	52.9	164.3	159.9[b]
Individuals using the Internet (per 100 inhabitants)	6.7	35.8[r]	74.2[e,b]
Research & Development expenditure (% of GDP)	...	...	0.2[o]
Threatened species (number)	55[s]	79	99
Forested area (% of land area)	~0.0	~0.0	~0.0[e,h]
CO2 emission estimates (million tons/tons per capita)	29.9 / 12.3	47.4 / 16.1	61.2 / 14.4[h]
Energy production, primary (Petajoules)	2 351	2 793	3 101[h]
Energy supply per capita (Gigajoules)	183	264	239[h]
Tourist/visitor arrivals at national borders (000)	891	1 441	1 897[b]
Important sites for terrestrial biodiversity protected (%)	7.8	7.8	11.5
Pop. using improved drinking water (urban/rural, %)	90.8 / 79.9	94.1 / 84.3	95.5 / 86.1[b]
Pop. using improved sanitation facilities (urban/rural, %)	96.8 / 84.2	97.3 / 94.7	97.3 / 94.7[b]
Net Official Development Assist. received (% of GNI)	0.06	- 0.04	...

a Projected estimate (medium fertility variant). **b** 2015. **c** Refers to Muscat governorate. **d** 2016. **e** Estimate. **f** Break in the time series. **g** Series linked to former series. **h** 2014. **i** Data classified according to ISIC Rev. 3. **j** Areas not elsewhere specified. **k** Data refers to a 5-year period preceding the reference year. **l** Refers to foreign citizens. **m** Data as at the end of December. **n** 2009. **o** 2013. **p** 2008. **q** 2011. **r** Population aged 5 years and over. **s** 2004.

Pakistan

Region	Southern Asia	
Population (000, 2017)	197 016[a]	
Pop. density (per km2, 2017)	255.6[a]	
Capital city	Islamabad	
Capital city pop. (000)	1 364.5[b]	

UN membership date	30 September 1947
Surface area (km2)	796 095[b]
Sex ratio (m per 100 f, 2017)	105.6[a]
National currency	Pakistan Rupee (PKR)
Exchange rate (per US$)	104.8[c]

Economic indicators	2005	2010	2017
GDP: Gross domestic product (million current US$)	117 708	174 508	266 458[b]
GDP growth rate (annual %, const. 2005 prices)	7.7	1.6	5.5[b]
GDP per capita (current US$)	767.5	1 026.3	1 410.4[b]
Economy: Agriculture (% of GVA)[d]	24.5	24.3	25.5[b]
Economy: Industry (% of GVA)[d]	21.3	20.6	19.0[b]
Economy: Services and other activity (% of GVA)[d]	54.2	55.1	55.5[b]
Employment: Agriculture (% of employed)[e]	43.4	45.0	42.1
Employment: Industry (% of employed)[e]	20.5	19.1	19.8
Employment: Services (% of employed)[e]	36.1	35.9	38.1
Unemployment (% of labour force)	7.7	5.6	5.9[e]
Labour force participation (female/male pop. %)[e]	19.3 / 84.1	23.9 / 82.8	24.8 / 82.5
CPI: Consumer Price Index (2000=100)	129	234	316[f]
Agricultural production index (2004-2006=100)	100	110	135[f]
Food production index (2004-2006=100)	101	113	138[f]
International trade: Exports (million US$)	16 050	21 413	20 534[c]
International trade: Imports (million US$)	25 097	37 537	46 998[c]
International trade: Balance (million US$)	- 9 046	- 16 124	- 26 464[c]
Balance of payments, current account (million US$)	- 3 606[g]	- 1 354	- 1 603[b]

Major trading partners						2016
Export partners (% of exports)	United States	16.7	China	7.7	United Kingdom	7.6
Import partners (% of imports)	China	29.1	United Arab Emirates	13.2	Indonesia	4.4

Social indicators	2005	2010	2017
Population growth rate (average annual %)[h]	2.1	2.1	2.1[b]
Urban population (% of total population)	34.7	36.6	38.8[b]
Urban population growth rate (average annual %)[h]	2.8	2.9	2.8[b]
Fertility rate, total (live births per woman)[h]	4.2	4.0	3.7[b]
Life expectancy at birth (females/males, years)[h]	64.2 / 62.5	65.3 / 63.5	66.8 / 65.0[b]
Population age distribution (0-14 and 60+ years, %)	38.2 / 6.5	36.2 / 6.6	34.8 / 6.7[a]
International migrant stock (000/% of total pop.)[i]	3 171.1 / 2.1	3 941.6 / 2.3	3 629.0 / 1.9[b]
Refugees and others of concern to UNHCR (000)	1 549.2[j]	4 151.0[j]	2 739.4[c]
Infant mortality rate (per 1 000 live births)[h]	84.0	76.9	69.8[b]
Health: Total expenditure (% of GDP)[k,l]	2.9	3.0	2.6[f]
Health: Physicians (per 1 000 pop.)	0.8	0.9	0.8[f]
Education: Government expenditure (% of GDP)	2.3	2.3	2.6[b]
Education: Primary gross enrol. ratio (f/m per 100 pop.)	76.3 / 99.2	87.8 / 103.1	85.2 / 99.7[b]
Education: Secondary gross enrol. ratio (f/m per 100 pop.)	... / ...	31.1 / 40.3	39.2 / 49.5[b]
Education: Tertiary gross enrol. ratio (f/m per 100 pop.)	4.6 / 5.3	6.3 / 7.5[e,m]	9.2 / 10.6[b]
Intentional homicide rate (per 100 000 pop.)	6.3	7.8	7.8[n]
Seats held by women in national parliaments (%)	21.3	22.2	20.6

Environment and infrastructure indicators	2005	2010	2017
Mobile-cellular subscriptions (per 100 inhabitants)	8.1	57.3	66.9[o,b]
Individuals using the Internet (per 100 inhabitants)	6.3	8.0[e]	18.0[e,p,b]
Research & Development expenditure (% of GDP)[q,r]	0.4	0.4[m]	0.3[s]
Threatened species (number)	72[t]	109	140
Forested area (% of land area)[e]	2.5	2.2	2.0[f]
CO2 emission estimates (million tons/tons per capita)	136.6 / 0.8	161.4 / 1.0	166.3 / 0.9[f]
Energy production, primary (Petajoules)	2 020	2 105	2 202[e,f]
Energy supply per capita (Gigajoules)	17	17	17[f]
Tourist/visitor arrivals at national borders (000)	798	907	...
Important sites for terrestrial biodiversity protected (%)	40.3	40.3	40.3
Pop. using improved drinking water (urban/rural, %)	94.9 / 86.7	94.4 / 88.3	93.9 / 89.9[b]
Pop. using improved sanitation facilities (urban/rural, %)	75.4 / 30.1	79.3 / 40.6	83.1 / 51.1[b]
Net Official Development Assist. received (% of GNI)	1.45	1.64	1.32[b]

a Projected estimate (medium fertility variant). b 2015. c 2016. d Data classified according to ISIC Rev. 4. e Estimate. f 2014. g Break in the time series. h Data refers to a 5-year period preceding the reference year. i Including refugees. j Data as at the end of December. k Data revision. l Total level of government expenditure on health increased due to the inclusion of local government expenditure, as well as a more-comprehensive estimation of regional expenditure on health. m 2009. n 2012. o Figure is reported after a biometric re-verification of SIMs by all Cellular Mobile Operators. p Population aged 10 years and over. q Excluding private non-profit. r Excluding business enterprise. s 2013. t 2004.

Palau

Region	Micronesia	UN membership date	15 December 1994
Population (000, 2017)	22[a]	Surface area (km2)	459[b]
Pop. density (per km2, 2017)	47.2[a]	Sex ratio (m per 100 f, 2017)	113.3[c,d]
Capital city	Melekeok	National currency	US Dollar (USD)
Capital city pop. (000)	11.6[e,f]		

Economic indicators	2005	2010	2017
GDP: Gross domestic product (million current US$)	180	186	258[b]
GDP growth rate (annual %, const. 2005 prices)	5.5	- 6.4	5.7[b]
GDP per capita (current US$)	9 037.0	9 084.0	12 122.5[b]
Economy: Agriculture (% of GVA)[g]	4.2	4.6	3.8[b]
Economy: Industry (% of GVA)[g]	17.5	9.9	8.0[b]
Economy: Services and other activity (% of GVA)[g]	78.2	85.5	88.2[b]
Employment: Agriculture (% of employed)[i]	7.1[h,j]	2.4[k,l]	...
Employment: Industry (% of employed)[i]	13.8[h,j]	11.8[k,l]	...
Employment: Services (% of employed)[i]	79.1[h,j]	85.9[k,l]	...
Unemployment (% of labour force)	4.2[i]	...	...
Labour force participation (female/male pop. %)	58.1 / 75.4[i]	... / ...	... / ...
International trade: Exports (million US$)	14	12	7[d]
International trade: Imports (million US$)	156	107	154[d]
International trade: Balance (million US$)	- 143	- 96	- 147[d]
Balance of payments, current account (million US$)	- 40[c]	- 19	- 24[b]

Major trading partners						2016
Export partners (% of exports)	Areas nes[m]	73.9	United States	8.4	Japan	5.7
Import partners (% of imports)	United States	42.0	Japan	13.0	Singapore	11.4

Social indicators	2005	2010	2017
Population growth rate (average annual %)[n]	0.8	0.6	0.8[b]
Urban population (% of total population)	77.7	83.4	87.1[b]
Urban population growth rate (average annual %)[n]	2.8	2.0	1.7[b]
Fertility rate, total (live births per woman)	1.5[j]	...	2.2[c,o,b]
Life expectancy at birth (females/males, years)	72.1 / 66.3	... / ...	77.8 / 68.1[c,b]
Population age distribution (0-14 and 60+ years, %)	24.1 / 8.2[p]	... / ...	20.3 / 13.1[c,d]
International migrant stock (000/% of total pop.)	6.0 / 30.4	5.8 / 28.3	5.7 / 26.6[b]
Refugees and others of concern to UNHCR (000)	...	...	~0.0[d]
Infant mortality rate (per 1 000 live births)	...	...	13.3[b]
Health: Total expenditure (% of GDP)[q]	8.2	10.6	9.0[f]
Health: Physicians (per 1 000 pop.)	...	1.4	...
Education: Government expenditure (% of GDP)	7.5[r,s]	...	...
Education: Primary gross enrol. ratio (f/m per 100 pop.)	101.1 / 104.6[r,t]	... / ...	99.0 / 100.3[r,d]
Education: Secondary gross enrol. ratio (f/m per 100 pop.)	99.9 / 97.7[r,t]	... / ...	95.2 / 96.2[r,d]
Education: Tertiary gross enrol. ratio (f/m per 100 pop.)	52.3 / 25.6[r,s]	... / ...	76.1 / 49.1[r,u]
Intentional homicide rate (per 100 000 pop.)	...	...	3.1[v]
Seats held by women in national parliaments (%)	0.0	0.0	12.5

Environment and infrastructure indicators	2005	2010	2017
Mobile-cellular subscriptions (per 100 inhabitants)	30.4	70.9	111.5[b]
Threatened species (number)	21[t]	128	182
Forested area (% of land area)[r]	87.6	87.6	87.6[f]
CO2 emission estimates (million tons/tons per capita)	0.3 / 13.1	0.3 / 12.3	0.3 / 12.4[f]
Energy supply per capita (Gigajoules)[r]	184	172	172[f]
Tourist/visitor arrivals at national borders (000)[w]	81	85	162[b]
Important sites for terrestrial biodiversity protected (%)	17.3	17.3	50.7
Pop. using improved drinking water (urban/rural, %)	97.1 / 84.4	97.0 / 86.0	97.0 / 86.0[b,x]
Pop. using improved sanitation facilities (urban/rural, %)	100.0 / 91.2	100.0 / 100.0	100.0 / 100.0[b]
Net Official Development Assist. received (% of GNI)	12.86	16.25	5.05[b]

a Projected estimate (medium fertility variant). **b** 2015. **c** Break in the time series. **d** 2016. **e** Refers to Koror. **f** 2014. **g** Data classified according to ISIC Rev. 4. **h** Data classified according to ISIC Rev. 2. **i** Population aged 16 years and over. **j** 2000. **k** Data classified according to ISIC Rev. 3. **l** 2008. **m** Areas not elsewhere specified. **n** Data refers to a 5-year period preceding the reference year. **o** Preliminary census results. **p** De jure population. **q** Data revision. **r** Estimate. **s** 2002. **t** 2004. **u** 2013. **v** 2012. **w** Air arrivals (Palau International Airport). **x** 2011.

Panama

Region	Central America	UN membership date	13 November 1945
Population (000, 2017)	4 099[a]	Surface area (km2)	75 320[b]
Pop. density (per km2, 2017)	55.1[a]	Sex ratio (m per 100 f, 2017)	100.4[a]
Capital city	Panama City	National currency	Balboa (PAB)
Capital city pop. (000)	1 672.8[c,b]	Exchange rate (per US$)	1.0[d]

Economic indicators

	2005	2010	2017
GDP: Gross domestic product (million current US$)	15 465	28 917	52 132[b]
GDP growth rate (annual %, const. 2005 prices)	7.2	5.8	5.8[b]
GDP per capita (current US$)	4 659.0	7 987.1	13 268.1[b]
Economy: Agriculture (% of GVA)	6.8	3.9	2.8[b]
Economy: Industry (% of GVA)	16.3	20.3	27.1[b]
Economy: Services and other activity (% of GVA)	76.9	75.8	70.0[b]
Employment: Agriculture (% of employed)[e]	15.7	17.4	14.5
Employment: Industry (% of employed)[e]	17.3	18.7	19.6
Employment: Services (% of employed)[e]	67.0	63.9	65.9
Unemployment (% of labour force)	9.8	6.5	6.2[e]
Labour force participation (female/male pop. %)[e]	47.9 / 81.1	49.0 / 82.0	50.5 / 80.4
CPI: Consumer Price Index (2000=100)[f,g]	103[h]	127	148[i]
Agricultural production index (2004-2006=100)	99	107	117[i]
Food production index (2004-2006=100)	99	108	118[i]
International trade: Exports (million US$)	963	10 987	636[d]
International trade: Imports (million US$)	4 152	16 737	11 697[d]
International trade: Balance (million US$)	- 3 189	- 5 751	- 11 061[d]
Balance of payments, current account (million US$)	- 1 064	- 3 113	- 3 377[h,b]

Major trading partners

						2016
Export partners (% of exports)	United States	19.9	Germany	13.2	Costa Rica	7.9
Import partners (% of imports)	United States	28.7	China	15.9	Mexico	5.3

Social indicators

	2005	2010	2017
Population growth rate (average annual %)[k]	1.9	1.8	1.7[b]
Urban population (% of total population)	63.7	65.1	66.6[b]
Urban population growth rate (average annual %)[k]	2.4	2.2	2.1[b]
Fertility rate, total (live births per woman)[k]	2.7	2.6	2.6[b]
Life expectancy at birth (females/males, years)[k]	78.2 / 73.0	79.4 / 73.5	80.5 / 74.3[b]
Population age distribution (0-14 and 60+ years, %)	30.4 / 8.8	29.1 / 9.7	27.4 / 11.4[a]
International migrant stock (000/% of total pop.)	117.6 / 3.5	157.3 / 4.3	184.7 / 4.7[b]
Refugees and others of concern to UNHCR (000)	12.4[l]	17.6[l]	21.5[l]
Infant mortality rate (per 1 000 live births)[k]	19.8	16.8	15.2[b]
Health: Total expenditure (% of GDP)	7.5	8.0	8.0[i]
Health: Physicians (per 1 000 pop.)	1.4	1.4	1.6[i]
Education: Government expenditure (% of GDP)	3.6[e,m]	3.6[n]	3.2[o]
Education: Primary gross enrol. ratio (f/m per 100 pop.)	105.4 / 109.1	104.9 / 109.0	100.9 / 103.5[i]
Education: Secondary gross enrol. ratio (f/m per 100 pop.)	70.6 / 65.9	73.5 / 69.2	78.3 / 72.9[i]
Education: Tertiary gross enrol. ratio (f/m per 100 pop.)	52.5 / 32.1	53.8 / 35.2	46.5 / 31.2[i]
Intentional homicide rate (per 100 000 pop.)	11.0	21.0	11.4[b]
Seats held by women in national parliaments (%)	16.7	8.5	18.3

Environment and infrastructure indicators

	2005	2010	2017
Mobile-cellular subscriptions (per 100 inhabitants)	52.0	180.7	174.2[e,b]
Individuals using the Internet (per 100 inhabitants)	11.5	40.1[e]	51.2[p,b]
Research & Development expenditure (% of GDP)	0.2	0.1	0.1[i]
Threatened species (number)	310[m]	347	383
Forested area (% of land area)	64.3	63.2[e]	62.3[e,i]
CO2 emission estimates (million tons/tons per capita)	6.8 / 2.1	9.2 / 2.5	8.8 / 2.3[i]
Energy production, primary (Petajoules)	32	26	31[i]
Energy supply per capita (Gigajoules)	37	40	35[i]
Tourist/visitor arrivals at national borders (000)	702	1 324	2 110[b]
Important sites for terrestrial biodiversity protected (%)	37.8	38.8	38.8
Pop. using improved drinking water (urban/rural, %)	97.8 / 80.2	97.7 / 84.4	97.7 / 88.6[b]
Pop. using improved sanitation facilities (urban/rural, %)	80.5 / 50.5	82.0 / 54.2	83.5 / 58.0[b]
Net Official Development Assist. received (% of GNI)	0.13	0.49	0.02[b]

a Projected estimate (medium fertility variant). **b** 2015. **c** Refers to the metropolitan area of Panama City. **d** 2016. **e** Estimate. **f** Urban areas. **g** Index base: 2003=100. **h** Break in the time series. **i** 2013. **j** 2014. **k** Data refers to a 5-year period preceding the reference year. **l** Data as at the end of December. **m** 2004. **n** 2008. **o** 2011. **p** Population aged 10 years and over.

Papua New Guinea

Region	Melanesia	UN membership date	10 October 1975
Population (000, 2017)	8 251 [a]	Surface area (km2)	462 840 [b]
Pop. density (per km2, 2017)	18.2 [a]	Sex ratio (m per 100 f, 2017)	103.5 [a]
Capital city	Port Moresby	National currency	Kina (PGK)
Capital city pop. (000)	345.2 [b]	Exchange rate (per US$)	3.2 [c]

Economic indicators	2005	2010	2017
GDP: Gross domestic product (million current US$)	7 312	14 205	21 315 [b]
GDP growth rate (annual %, const. 2005 prices)	3.9	11.2	6.6 [b]
GDP per capita (current US$)	1 201.3	2 074.4	2 797.6 [b]
Economy: Agriculture (% of GVA)	22.7	20.3	20.1 [b]
Economy: Industry (% of GVA)	34.0	33.6	28.2 [b]
Economy: Services and other activity (% of GVA)	43.3	46.0	51.8 [b]
Employment: Agriculture (% of employed) [d]	73.5	72.8	68.3
Employment: Industry (% of employed) [d]	3.8	4.5	5.7
Employment: Services (% of employed) [d]	22.7	22.7	26.0
Unemployment (% of labour force) [d]	2.6	2.4	2.5
Labour force participation (female/male pop. %) [d]	71.3 / 74.4	70.5 / 72.9	69.6 / 71.2
CPI: Consumer Price Index (2000=100)	146	189	217 [e]
Agricultural production index (2004-2006=100)	99	112	84 [f]
Food production index (2004-2006=100)	99	113	83 [f]
International trade: Exports (million US$)	3 276	5 742	8 760 [c]
International trade: Imports (million US$)	1 728	3 950	8 874 [c]
International trade: Balance (million US$)	1 548	1 792	- 114 [c]
Balance of payments, current account (million US$)	539	- 914	5 326 [b]

Major trading partners						2016
Export partners (% of exports)	Australia	30.4	Japan	23.0	China	18.6
Import partners (% of imports)	Australia	30.7	China	15.8	Singapore	9.2

Social indicators	2005	2010	2017
Population growth rate (average annual %) [g]	2.5	2.4	2.2 [b]
Urban population (% of total population)	13.1	13.0	13.0 [b]
Urban population growth rate (average annual %) [g]	2.4	2.2	2.1 [b]
Fertility rate, total (live births per woman) [g]	4.4	4.1	3.8 [b]
Life expectancy at birth (females/males, years) [g]	65.1 / 60.3	66.7 / 61.8	67.4 / 62.6 [b]
Population age distribution (0-14 and 60+ years, %)	39.1 / 5.1	38.3 / 5.4	35.9 / 6.1 [a]
International migrant stock (000/% of total pop.) [h,i]	30.0 / 0.5	25.4 / 0.4	25.8 / 0.3 [b]
Refugees and others of concern to UNHCR (000)	10.1 [j]	9.7 [i]	9.7 [c]
Infant mortality rate (per 1 000 live births) [g]	55.5	51.9	49.0 [b]
Health: Total expenditure (% of GDP)	6.4	4.2	4.3 [f]
Health: Physicians (per 1 000 pop.)	0.1 [k]	0.1	...
Education: Primary gross enrol. ratio (f/m per 100 pop.)	53.3 / 62.7	56.9 / 63.8 [l]	109.3 / 119.8 [m]
Education: Secondary gross enrol. ratio (f/m per 100 pop.)	... / ...	... / ...	34.6 / 45.8 [m]
Intentional homicide rate (per 100 000 pop.)	9.9	10.4	...
Seats held by women in national parliaments (%)	0.9	0.9	2.7

Environment and infrastructure indicators	2005	2010	2017
Mobile-cellular subscriptions (per 100 inhabitants)	1.2	27.8 [n]	46.6 [d,b]
Individuals using the Internet (per 100 inhabitants)	1.7	1.3 [o]	7.9 [d,b]
Threatened species (number)	295 [p]	453	493
Forested area (% of land area) [d]	74.2	74.1	74.1 [f]
CO2 emission estimates (million tons/tons per capita)	4.4 / 0.7	4.8 / 0.7	6.3 / 0.8 [f]
Energy production, primary (Petajoules)	174	95	114 [d,f]
Energy supply per capita (Gigajoules)	21	21	22 [d,f]
Tourist/visitor arrivals at national borders (000)	69	140	184 [b]
Important sites for terrestrial biodiversity protected (%)	7.3	7.3	7.3
Pop. using improved drinking water (urban/rural, %)	87.7 / 29.5	87.9 / 31.8	88.0 / 32.8 [b]
Pop. using improved sanitation facilities (urban/rural, %)	58.4 / 13.1	57.0 / 13.3	56.4 / 13.3 [b]
Net Official Development Assist. received (% of GNI)	5.89	5.62	3.51 [f]

a Projected estimate (medium fertility variant). **b** 2015. **c** 2016. **d** Estimate. **e** 2013. **f** 2014. **g** Data refers to a 5-year period preceding the reference year. **h** Refers to foreign citizens. **i** Including refugees. **j** Data as at the end of December. **k** 2000. **l** 2008. **m** 2012. **n** Global System for Mobile Communications (GSM). **o** Population aged 10 years and over. **p** 2004.

Paraguay

Region	South America	UN membership date	24 October 1945	
Population (000, 2017)	6 811[a]	Surface area (km2)	406 752[b]	
Pop. density (per km2, 2017)	17.1[a]	Sex ratio (m per 100 f, 2017)	102.9[a]	
Capital city	Asunción	National currency	Guaraní (PYG)	
Capital city pop. (000)	2 356.2[c,b]	Exchange rate (per US$)	5 766.9[d]	

Economic indicators

	2005	2010	2017
GDP: Gross domestic product (million current US$)	8 735	20 048	27 714[b]
GDP growth rate (annual %, const. 2005 prices)	2.1	13.1	3.1[b]
GDP per capita (current US$)	1 507.1	3 228.3	4 174.4[b]
Economy: Agriculture (% of GVA)	19.6	22.5	19.0[b]
Economy: Industry (% of GVA)	34.8	30.1	29.5[b]
Economy: Services and other activity (% of GVA)	45.7	47.4	51.6[b]
Employment: Agriculture (% of employed)[e]	31.9	26.8	19.6
Employment: Industry (% of employed)[e]	15.6	18.8	19.5
Employment: Services (% of employed)[e]	52.5	54.3	61.0
Unemployment (% of labour force)	5.8	5.7	5.5[e]
Labour force participation (female/male pop. %)[e]	54.3 / 85.7	54.6 / 84.6	58.3 / 84.7
CPI: Consumer Price Index (2000=100)[f]	150	212	256[g]
Agricultural production index (2004-2006=100)	97	137	160[g]
Food production index (2004-2006=100)	98	141	166[g]
Index of industrial production (2005=100)[h]	100	110	124[g]
International trade: Exports (million US$)	3 153	6 517	8 494[d]
International trade: Imports (million US$)	3 274	10 033	9 753[d]
International trade: Balance (million US$)	- 121	- 3 517	- 1 259[d]
Balance of payments, current account (million US$)	- 68	- 57	- 462[b]

Major trading partners   2016

Export partners (% of exports)	Brazil	35.4	Argentina	10.7	Russian Federation	7.6
Import partners (% of imports)	China	27.1	Brazil	24.2	Argentina	14.7

Social indicators

	2005	2010	2017
Population growth rate (average annual %)[i]	1.8	1.4	1.3[b]
Urban population (% of total population)	57.4	58.5	59.7[b]
Urban population growth rate (average annual %)[i]	2.7	2.2	2.1[b]
Fertility rate, total (live births per woman)[i]	3.2	2.9	2.6[b]
Life expectancy at birth (females/males, years)[i]	72.9 / 68.7	73.9 / 69.7	74.9 / 70.7[b]
Population age distribution (0-14 and 60+ years, %)	35.3 / 7.1	32.7 / 7.9	29.4 / 9.4[a]
International migrant stock (000/% of total pop.)	168.2 / 2.9	160.3 / 2.6	156.5 / 2.4[b]
Refugees and others of concern to UNHCR (000)	0.1[j]	0.1[j]	0.2[d]
Infant mortality rate (per 1 000 live births)[i]	35.5	32.0	28.8[b]
Health: Total expenditure (% of GDP)	6.1	9.1	9.8[g]
Health: Physicians (per 1 000 pop.)	1.2[k]	...	1.3[l]
Education: Government expenditure (% of GDP)	3.4[m]	3.8	5.0[l]
Education: Primary gross enrol. ratio (f/m per 100 pop.)	110.3 / 113.5	101.8 / 105.9	104.3 / 107.6[l]
Education: Secondary gross enrol. ratio (f/m per 100 pop.)	67.8 / 66.0	70.2 / 66.5	79.1 / 74.2[l]
Education: Tertiary gross enrol. ratio (f/m per 100 pop.)	27.5 / 24.3	41.2 / 29.1	... / ...
Intentional homicide rate (per 100 000 pop.)	18.6	11.9	9.3[b]
Seats held by women in national parliaments (%)	10.0	12.5	13.8

Environment and infrastructure indicators

	2005	2010	2017
Mobile-cellular subscriptions (per 100 inhabitants)	32.0	91.7	105.4[b]
Individuals using the Internet (per 100 inhabitants)	7.9[n,o]	19.8[n,o]	44.4[e,b]
Research & Development expenditure (% of GDP)	0.1	0.1[p]	0.1[l]
Threatened species (number)	50[m]	48	59
Forested area (% of land area)[e]	46.5	42.7	39.4[g]
CO2 emission estimates (million tons/tons per capita)	3.8 / 0.7	5.1 / 0.8	5.7 / 0.9[g]
Energy production, primary (Petajoules)	288	327	325[g]
Energy supply per capita (Gigajoules)	31	38	38[g]
Tourist/visitor arrivals at national borders (000)[q,r]	341	465	1 214[b]
Important sites for terrestrial biodiversity protected (%)	23.3	23.3	23.3
Pop. using improved drinking water (urban/rural, %)	94.1 / 66.0	97.2 / 80.5	100.0 / 94.9[b]
Pop. using improved sanitation facilities (urban/rural, %)	87.6 / 59.9	92.3 / 69.2	95.5 / 78.4[b]
Net Official Development Assist. received (% of GNI)	0.70	0.65	0.22[b]

a Projected estimate (medium fertility variant). **b** 2015. **c** Refers to the metropolitan area of Asunción. **d** 2016. **e** Estimate. **f** Asunción **g** 2014. **h** Data classified according to ISIC Rev. 3. **i** Data refers to a 5-year period preceding the reference year. **j** Data as at the end of December. **k** 2002. **l** 2012. **m** 2004. **n** Population aged 10 years and over. **o** Users in the last 3 months. **p** 2008. **q** Excluding nationals residing abroad and crew members. **r** E/D cards in the "Silvio Petirossi" airport and passenger counts at the national border crossings - National Police and SENATUR.

Peru

Region	South America	UN membership date	31 October 1945
Population (000, 2017)	32 166[a]	Surface area (km2)	1 285 216[b]
Pop. density (per km2, 2017)	25.1[a]	Sex ratio (m per 100 f, 2017)	99.8[a]
Capital city	Lima	National currency	Sol (PEN)
Capital city pop. (000)	9 897.0[c,b]	Exchange rate (per US$)	3.4[d]

Economic indicators	2005	2010	2017
GDP: Gross domestic product (million current US$)	76 080	147 528	190 428[b]
GDP growth rate (annual %, const. 2005 prices)	6.3	8.3	3.3[b]
GDP per capita (current US$)	2 755.5	5 022.4	6 069.1[b]
Economy: Agriculture (% of GVA)[e]	7.5	7.5	7.6[b]
Economy: Industry (% of GVA)[e]	37.7	39.1	33.3[b]
Economy: Services and other activity (% of GVA)[e]	54.7	53.5	59.2[b]
Employment: Agriculture (% of employed)[f]	1.6	25.7	24.4
Employment: Industry (% of employed)[f]	24.4	17.7	17.3
Employment: Services (% of employed)[f]	74.0	56.6	58.3
Unemployment (% of labour force)	8.3	4.0	5.3[f]
Labour force participation (female/male pop. %)[f]	57.5 / 78.9	65.6 / 84.3	66.1 / 82.8
CPI: Consumer Price Index (2000=100)[g,h]	110	126[i]	144[i]
Agricultural production index (2004-2006=100)	99	128	145[j]
Food production index (2004-2006=100)	100	130	148[j]
Index of industrial production (2005=100)[k]	100	130	142[l]
International trade: Exports (million US$)[m]	17 114	35 807	36 040[d]
International trade: Imports (million US$)[m]	12 502	29 966	36 185[d]
International trade: Balance (million US$)[m]	4 612	5 842	- 145[d]
Balance of payments, current account (million US$)	1 148	- 3 782	- 9 210[b]

Major trading partners						2016
Export partners (% of exports)	China	23.5	United States	17.3	Switzerland	7.1
Import partners (% of imports)	China	22.8	United States	19.6	Brazil	5.9

Social indicators	2005	2010	2017
Population growth rate (average annual %)[n]	1.3	1.2	1.3[b]
Urban population (% of total population)	75.0	76.9	78.6[b]
Urban population growth rate (average annual %)[n]	1.8	1.6	1.7[b]
Fertility rate, total (live births per woman)[n]	2.8	2.6	2.5[b]
Life expectancy at birth (females/males, years)[n]	74.3 / 69.0	75.9 / 70.5	76.8 / 71.5[b]
Population age distribution (0-14 and 60+ years, %)	31.7 / 8.1	29.4 / 8.9	27.4 / 10.4[a]
International migrant stock (000/% of total pop.)	77.5 / 0.3	84.1 / 0.3	90.9 / 0.3[b]
Refugees and others of concern to UNHCR (000)	1.2[o]	1.4[o]	2.5[d]
Infant mortality rate (per 1 000 live births)[n]	27.4	21.0	18.6[b]
Health: Total expenditure (% of GDP)[p]	4.7	5.0	5.5[i]
Health: Physicians (per 1 000 pop.)	...	0.9[q]	1.1[r]
Education: Government expenditure (% of GDP)	2.8	2.9	4.0[b]
Education: Primary gross enrol. ratio (f/m per 100 pop.)	118.0 / 117.0	111.0 / 108.9	101.7 / 101.7[b]
Education: Secondary gross enrol. ratio (f/m per 100 pop.)	84.6 / 86.3	94.9 / 94.5	95.8 / 95.7[b]
Education: Tertiary gross enrol. ratio (f/m per 100 pop.)	33.6 / 32.8	42.5 / 38.6	... / ...
Intentional homicide rate (per 100 000 pop.)	11.1	9.2	7.2[b]
Seats held by women in national parliaments (%)	18.3	27.5	27.7

Environment and infrastructure indicators	2005	2010	2017
Mobile-cellular subscriptions (per 100 inhabitants)	20.1	99.5	109.9[b]
Individuals using the Internet (per 100 inhabitants)	17.1[f]	34.8[s]	40.9[s,b]
Research & Development expenditure (% of GDP)	0.2[t]	...	...
Threatened species (number)	508[t]	551	685
Forested area (% of land area)[f]	59.0	58.4	57.9[i]
CO2 emission estimates (million tons/tons per capita)	37.1 / 1.4	57.6 / 1.9	61.7 / 2.0[i]
Energy production, primary (Petajoules)	455	783	1 020[i]
Energy supply per capita (Gigajoules)	20	26	30[i]
Tourist/visitor arrivals at national borders (000)[v,w]	1 571[u]	2 299	3 456[f,b]
Important sites for terrestrial biodiversity protected (%)	23.1	28.9	30.7
Pop. using improved drinking water (urban/rural, %)	90.0 / 59.1	90.7 / 64.2	91.4 / 69.2[b]
Pop. using improved sanitation facilities (urban/rural, %)	77.7 / 37.4	80.1 / 45.3	82.5 / 53.2[b]
Net Official Development Assist. received (% of GNI)	0.65	- 0.22	0.18[b]

a Projected estimate (medium fertility variant). b 2015. c Refers to Gran Lima. d 2016. e Data classified according to ISIC Rev. 4. f Estimate. g Lima h Metropolitan areas. i Series linked to former series. j 2014. k Data classified according to ISIC Rev. 3. l 2013. m Imports FOB. n Data refers to a 5-year period preceding the reference year. o Data as at the end of December. p Data revision. q 2009. r 2012. s Population aged 6 years and over. t 2004. u Break in the time series. v Including nationals residing abroad. w Including tourists with identity document other than a passport.

Philippines

Region	South-eastern Asia
Population (000, 2017)	104 918[a]
Pop. density (per km2, 2017)	351.9[a]
Capital city	Manila
Capital city pop. (000)	12 946.3[c,b]

UN membership date	24 October 1945
Surface area (km2)	300 000[b]
Sex ratio (m per 100 f, 2017)	101.3[a]
National currency	Philippine Peso (PHP)
Exchange rate (per US$)	49.8[d]

Economic indicators

	2005	2010	2017
GDP: Gross domestic product (million current US$)	103 072	199 591	292 449[b]
GDP growth rate (annual %, const. 2005 prices)	4.8	7.6	5.9[b]
GDP per capita (current US$)	1 196.5	2 145.2	2 904.2[b]
Economy: Agriculture (% of GVA)[e,f]	12.7	12.3	10.5[b]
Economy: Industry (% of GVA)[e,f]	33.8	32.6	31.3[b]
Economy: Services and other activity (% of GVA)[e,f]	53.5	55.1	58.2[b]
Employment: Agriculture (% of employed)[g]	35.9	33.2	27.7
Employment: Industry (% of employed)[g]	15.6	15.0	16.3
Employment: Services (% of employed)[g]	48.5	51.8	56.1
Unemployment (% of labour force)	7.7	7.4	5.9[g]
Labour force participation (female/male pop. %)[g]	49.8 / 80.0	50.2 / 79.6	50.8 / 78.9
CPI: Consumer Price Index (2000=100)	130	166	192[h]
Agricultural production index (2004-2006=100)	100	113	122[h]
Food production index (2004-2006=100)	100	113	120[h]
International trade: Exports (million US$)	41 255	51 498	56 313[d]
International trade: Imports (million US$)	49 487	58 468	85 909[d]
International trade: Balance (million US$)	- 8 233	- 6 970	- 29 596[d]
Balance of payments, current account (million US$)	1 990[i]	7 179	7 694[b]

Major trading partners

						2016
Export partners (% of exports)	Japan	20.7	United States	15.4	China, Hong Kong SAR	11.7
Import partners (% of imports)	China	18.5	Japan	11.9	United States	8.9

Social indicators

	2005	2010	2017
Population growth rate (average annual %)[j]	2.0	1.7	1.6[b]
Urban population (% of total population)	46.6	45.3	44.4[b]
Urban population growth rate (average annual %)[j]	1.4	1.1	1.3[b]
Fertility rate, total (live births per woman)[j]	3.7	3.3	3.0[b]
Life expectancy at birth (females/males, years)[j]	70.8 / 64.4	71.5 / 64.8	72.1 / 65.4[b]
Population age distribution (0-14 and 60+ years, %)	37.1 / 5.4	33.9 / 6.5	31.7 / 7.6[a]
International migrant stock (000/% of total pop.)[k,l]	257.5 / 0.3	208.6 / 0.2	211.9 / 0.2[b]
Refugees and others of concern to UNHCR (000)	0.9[m]	139.9[m]	240.2[d]
Infant mortality rate (per 1 000 live births)[j]	28.1	25.0	22.2[b]
Health: Total expenditure (% of GDP)[n]	3.9	4.4	4.7[h]
Health: Physicians (per 1 000 pop.)	1.1[o]	...	...
Education: Government expenditure (% of GDP)	2.4	2.7[p]	...
Education: Primary gross enrol. ratio (f/m per 100 pop.)	105.4 / 106.6	108.6 / 109.1[p]	116.9 / 116.8[q]
Education: Secondary gross enrol. ratio (f/m per 100 pop.)	87.6 / 78.3	87.6 / 81.0[p]	92.7 / 84.4[q]
Education: Tertiary gross enrol. ratio (f/m per 100 pop.)	30.4 / 24.7	33.1 / 26.5	40.3 / 31.4[h]
Intentional homicide rate (per 100 000 pop.)[j]	7.5	9.6	9.8[h]
Seats held by women in national parliaments (%)	15.3	21.0	29.5

Environment and infrastructure indicators

	2005	2010	2017
Mobile-cellular subscriptions (per 100 inhabitants)	40.5	89.0	118.1[g,b]
Individuals using the Internet (per 100 inhabitants)	5.4[g]	25.0	40.7[g,b]
Research & Development expenditure (% of GDP)	0.1	0.1[p]	0.1[q]
Threatened species (number)	456[o]	697	783
Forested area (% of land area)	23.7	22.9	26.2[h]
CO2 emission estimates (million tons/tons per capita)	74.8 / 0.9	84.9 / 0.9	105.7 / 1.1[h]
Energy production, primary (Petajoules)	762	865	991[h]
Energy supply per capita (Gigajoules)	17	17	19[h]
Tourist/visitor arrivals at national borders (000)[r]	2 623	3 520	5 361[b]
Important sites for terrestrial biodiversity protected (%)	38.7	41.4	41.7
Pop. using improved drinking water (urban/rural, %)	92.6 / 85.1	93.1 / 87.7	93.7 / 90.3[b]
Pop. using improved sanitation facilities (urban/rural, %)	74.3 / 60.8	76.1 / 65.8	77.9 / 70.8[b]
Net Official Development Assist. received (% of GNI)	0.44	0.20	0.15[b]

a Projected estimate (medium fertility variant). **b** 2015. **c** Refers to the National Capital Region. **d** 2016. **e** Data classified according to ISIC Rev. 4. **f** Includes taxes less subsidies on production and imports. **g** Estimate. **h** 2014. **i** Break in the time series. **j** Data refers to a 5-year period preceding the reference year. **k** Including refugees. **l** Refers to foreign citizens. **m** Data as at the end of December. **n** The Philippine Statistics Authority implemented a revision in the estimation methodology for local government units (LGU) health expenditures between 2010 and 2011 resulting to a significant decrease in estimated LGU expenditures between the two years. **o** 2004. **p** 2009. **q** 2013. **r** Including nationals residing abroad.

Poland

Region	Eastern Europe	UN membership date	24 October 1945
Population (000, 2017)	38 171[a]	Surface area (km2)	312 679[b]
Pop. density (per km2, 2017)	124.6[a]	Sex ratio (m per 100 f, 2017)	93.4[a]
Capital city	Warsaw	National currency	Zloty (PLN)
Capital city pop. (000)	1 722.3[b]	Exchange rate (per US$)	4.2[c]

Economic indicators

	2005	2010	2017
GDP: Gross domestic product (million current US$)	306 127	479 321	477 066[b]
GDP growth rate (annual %, const. 2005 prices)	3.5	3.6	3.9[b]
GDP per capita (current US$)	7 958.9	12 425.8	12 355.5[b]
Economy: Agriculture (% of GVA)[d]	3.3	2.9	2.6[b]
Economy: Industry (% of GVA)[d]	32.2	33.2	34.1[b]
Economy: Services and other activity (% of GVA)[d]	64.5	63.9	63.3[b]
Employment: Agriculture (% of employed)[e]	17.4	12.8	10.9
Employment: Industry (% of employed)[e]	29.2	30.1	29.6
Employment: Services (% of employed)[e]	53.4	57.1	59.5
Unemployment (% of labour force)	17.7	9.6	5.3[e]
Labour force participation (female/male pop. %)[e]	47.5 / 62.5	48.3 / 64.3	49.1 / 64.9
CPI: Consumer Price Index (2000=100)	115[f]	131	143[g]
Agricultural production index (2004-2006=100)	98	101	113[g]
Food production index (2004-2006=100)	98	101	113[g]
Index of industrial production (2005=100)	100	134	154[g]
International trade: Exports (million US$)	89 378	157 065	196 455[c]
International trade: Imports (million US$)	101 539	174 128	188 518[c]
International trade: Balance (million US$)	- 12 161	- 17 063	7 937[c]
Balance of payments, current account (million US$)	- 7 981	- 25 875	- 2 932[b]

Major trading partners

						2016
Export partners (% of exports)	Germany	27.0	United Kingdom	6.6	Czechia	6.5
Import partners (% of imports)	Germany	22.9	China	12.4	Russian Federation	6.1

Social indicators

	2005	2010	2017
Population growth rate (average annual %)[h]	- 0.1	~-0.0	~0.0[b]
Urban population (% of total population)	61.5	60.9	60.5[b]
Urban population growth rate (average annual %)[h]	- 0.2	- 0.2	- 0.1[b]
Fertility rate, total (live births per woman)[h]	1.3	1.4	1.3[b]
Life expectancy at birth (females/males, years)[h]	78.8 / 70.4	79.8 / 71.3	81.0 / 72.9[b]
Population age distribution (0-14 and 60+ years, %)	16.6 / 17.0	15.2 / 17.4	14.8 / 24.0[a]
International migrant stock (000/% of total pop.)	722.5 / 1.9	642.4 / 1.7	619.4 / 1.6[b]
Refugees and others of concern to UNHCR (000)	6.3[i]	18.4[i]	23.7[c]
Infant mortality rate (per 1 000 live births)[h]	7.1	5.7	4.5[b]
Health: Total expenditure (% of GDP)	6.2	6.9	6.4[g]
Health: Physicians (per 1 000 pop.)	...	2.2	2.3[g]
Education: Government expenditure (% of GDP)	5.4	5.1	4.9[g]
Education: Primary gross enrol. ratio (f/m per 100 pop.)	96.0 / 96.5	98.3 / 98.9	100.7 / 100.5[g]
Education: Secondary gross enrol. ratio (f/m per 100 pop.)	98.1 / 98.9	96.2 / 97.2	106.1 / 110.0[g]
Education: Tertiary gross enrol. ratio (f/m per 100 pop.)	74.1 / 52.4	88.3 / 58.6	82.6 / 54.2[g]
Intentional homicide rate (per 100 000 pop.)	1.4	1.1	0.7[b]
Seats held by women in national parliaments (%)	20.2	20.0	28.0

Environment and infrastructure indicators

	2005	2010	2017
Mobile-cellular subscriptions (per 100 inhabitants)	76.3	122.9[j]	148.7[e,b]
Individuals using the Internet (per 100 inhabitants)[k]	38.8	62.3	68.0[b]
Research & Development expenditure (% of GDP)	0.6	0.7	0.9[g]
Threatened species (number)	46[l]	37	58
Forested area (% of land area)	30.0	30.5	30.7[e,g]
CO2 emission estimates (million tons/tons per capita)	302.5 / 7.9	316.3 / 8.2	285.7 / 7.4[g]
Energy production, primary (Petajoules)	3 280	2 808	2 819[g]
Energy supply per capita (Gigajoules)	102	110	102[g]
Tourist/visitor arrivals at national borders (000)	15 200	12 470	16 722[b]
Important sites for terrestrial biodiversity protected (%)	73.4	87.9	88.1
Pop. using improved drinking water (urban/rural, %)	99.1 / 93.1	99.2 / 95.2	99.3 / 96.9[b]
Pop. using improved sanitation facilities (urban/rural, %)	95.2 / 83.3	96.5 / 90.8	97.5 / 96.7[b]
Net Official Development Assist. disbursed (% of GNI)[m]	0.07	0.08	0.13[n,c]

a Projected estimate (medium fertility variant). **b** 2015. **c** 2016. **d** Data classified according to ISIC Rev. 4. **e** Estimate. **f** Break in the time series. **g** 2014. **h** Data refers to a 5-year period preceding the reference year. **i** Data as at the end of December. **j** Includes data-only subscriptions. **k** Population aged 16 to 74 years. **l** 2004. **m** Development Assistance Committee member (OECD) **n** Provisional data.

Portugal

Region	Southern Europe	UN membership date	14 December 1955
Population (000, 2017)	10 330[a]	Surface area (km2)	92 226[b]
Pop. density (per km2, 2017)	112.8[a]	Sex ratio (m per 100 f, 2017)	89.8[a]
Capital city	Lisbon	National currency	Euro (EUR)
Capital city pop. (000)	2 884.3[c,b]	Exchange rate (per US$)	0.9[d]

Economic indicators	2005	2010	2017
GDP: Gross domestic product (million current US$)	197 300	238 303	199 122[b]
GDP growth rate (annual %, const. 2005 prices)	0.8	1.9	1.6[b]
GDP per capita (current US$)	18 826.1	22 513.7	19 239.2[b]
Economy: Agriculture (% of GVA)[e]	2.6	2.2	2.3[b]
Economy: Industry (% of GVA)[e]	24.6	22.6	22.3[b]
Economy: Services and other activity (% of GVA)[e]	72.7	75.2	75.4[b]
Employment: Agriculture (% of employed)[f]	12.1	10.9	8.0
Employment: Industry (% of employed)[f]	30.4	27.7	23.8
Employment: Services (% of employed)[f]	57.6	61.4	68.2
Unemployment (% of labour force)	7.6	10.8	10.5[f]
Labour force participation (female/male pop. %)[f]	55.4 / 69.3	55.8 / 66.8	53.3 / 63.7
CPI: Consumer Price Index (2000=100)[g]	117	127	135[h]
Agricultural production index (2004-2006=100)	97	105	104[h]
Food production index (2004-2006=100)	97	105	104[h]
Index of industrial production (2005=100)	100	92	88[h]
International trade: Exports (million US$)	38 672	49 414	55 658[d]
International trade: Imports (million US$)	63 904	77 682	67 580[d]
International trade: Balance (million US$)	- 25 232	- 28 268	- 11 922[d]
Balance of payments, current account (million US$)	- 19 537	- 24 199	842[b]

Major trading partners						2016
Export partners (% of exports)	Spain	26.2	France	12.6	Germany	11.7
Import partners (% of imports)	Spain	32.8	Germany	13.5	France	7.8

Social indicators	2005	2010	2017
Population growth rate (average annual %)[i]	0.4	0.2	- 0.4[b]
Urban population (% of total population)	57.5	60.6	63.5[b]
Urban population growth rate (average annual %)[i]	1.5	1.2	1.2[b]
Fertility rate, total (live births per woman)[i]	1.5	1.4	1.3[b]
Life expectancy at birth (females/males, years)[i]	81.0 / 74.1	82.5 / 76.0	83.5 / 77.3[b]
Population age distribution (0-14 and 60+ years, %)	15.4 / 22.5	15.0 / 24.7	13.6 / 27.9[a]
International migrant stock (000/% of total pop.)	771.2 / 7.4	762.8 / 7.2	837.3 / 8.1[b]
Refugees and others of concern to UNHCR (000)	0.4[j]	0.5[j]	1.8[d]
Infant mortality rate (per 1 000 live births)[i]	4.5	3.3	2.9[b]
Health: Total expenditure (% of GDP)[k]	10.0	10.4	9.5[h]
Health: Physicians (per 1 000 pop.)	3.4	3.8	4.4[h]
Education: Government expenditure (% of GDP)	5.1	5.4	5.1[h]
Education: Primary gross enrol. ratio (f/m per 100 pop.)	115.4 / 121.2	110.2 / 113.6	105.3 / 109.4[b]
Education: Secondary gross enrol. ratio (f/m per 100 pop.)	102.8 / 93.5	108.4 / 105.5	117.3 / 121.0[b]
Education: Tertiary gross enrol. ratio (f/m per 100 pop.)	63.0 / 48.2	71.2 / 60.3	65.7 / 58.0[b]
Intentional homicide rate (per 100 000 pop.)	1.3	1.2	1.0[b]
Seats held by women in national parliaments (%)	19.1	27.4	34.8

Environment and infrastructure indicators	2005	2010	2017
Mobile-cellular subscriptions (per 100 inhabitants)	108.9	115.3[l]	110.4[m,b]
Individuals using the Internet (per 100 inhabitants)[n]	35.0	53.3	68.6[b]
Research & Development expenditure (% of GDP)	0.8	1.5	1.3[o,h]
Threatened species (number)	148[p]	171	281
Forested area (% of land area)[f]	36.0	35.4	34.9[h]
CO2 emission estimates (million tons/tons per capita)	65.3 / 6.2	48.1 / 4.5	45.1 / 4.3[h]
Energy production, primary (Petajoules)[q]	151	242	250[h]
Energy supply per capita (Gigajoules)[q]	105	92	84[h]
Tourist/visitor arrivals at national borders (000)	5 769	6 756	9 957[b]
Important sites for terrestrial biodiversity protected (%)	60.5	71.0	73.8
Pop. using improved drinking water (urban/rural, %)	99.2 / 98.3	99.7 / 99.5	100.0 / 100.0[b]
Pop. using improved sanitation facilities (urban/rural, %)	98.7 / 96.2	99.2 / 98.7	99.6 / 99.8[b]
Net Official Development Assist. disbursed (% of GNI)[r]	0.21	0.29	0.17[o,d]

a Projected estimate (medium fertility variant). **b** 2015. **c** Refers to Grande Lisboa, the Peninsula of Setúbal, and the municipality Azambuja. **d** 2016. **e** Data classified according to ISIC Rev. 4. **f** Estimate. **g** Excluding "Rent". **h** 2014. **i** Data refers to a 5-year period preceding the reference year. **j** Data as at the end of December. **k** Portugal is currently reviewing its health expenditure series and new figures will be published consistent with the System of Health Accounts (SHA 2011) methodology. **l** Includes data-only subscriptions. **m** Excludes data-only subscriptions. **n** Population aged 16 to 74 years. **o** Provisional data. **p** 2004. **q** Data includes the Azores and Madeira. **r** Development Assistance Committee member (OECD)